(Continued on back endsheets)

Dictionary of Literary Biography® • Volume One Hundred Thirty-Three

Nineteenth-Century German Writers to 1840

Dictionary of Literary Biography® • Volume One Hundred Thirty-Three

Nineteenth-Century German Writers to 1840

Edited by
James Hardin
University of South Carolina
and
Siegfried Mews
University of North Carolina at Chapel Hill

A Bruccoli Clark Layman Book
Gale Research Inc.
Detroit, Washington, D.C., London

Matthew J. Bruccoli and Richard Layman, Editorial Directors
C. E. Frazer Clark, Jr., Managing Editor
Karen L. Rood, Senior Editor

Printed in the United States of America

Published simultaneously in the United Kingdom
by Gale Research International Limited
(An affiliated company of Gale Research Inc.)

The paper used in this publication meets the minimum requirements of American National Standard for Information Sciences–Permanence Paper for Printed Library Materials, ANSI Z39.48-1984. ∞™

Library of Congress Catalog Card Number 93-8481
ISBN 0-8103-5392-X

I(T)P

The trademark **ITP** is used under license.

10 9 8 7 6 5 4 3 2 1

For Christoph E. Schweitzer

Contents

Plan of the Series

. . . Almost the most prodigious asset of a country, and perhaps its most precious possession, is its native literary product – when that product is fine and noble and enduring.

Mark Twain*

The advisory board, the editors, and the publisher of the *Dictionary of Literary Biography* are joined in endorsing Mark Twain's declaration. The literature of a nation provides an inexhaustible resource of permanent worth. We intend to make literature and its creators better understood and more accessible to students and the reading public, while satisfying the standards of teachers and scholars.

To meet these requirements, *literary biography* has been construed in terms of the author's achievement. The most important thing about a writer is his writing. Accordingly, the entries in *DLB* are career biographies, tracing the development of the author's canon and the evolution of his reputation.

The purpose of *DLB* is not only to provide reliable information in a convenient format but also to place the figures in the larger perspective of literary history and to offer appraisals of their accomplishments by qualified scholars.

The publication plan for *DLB* resulted from two years of preparation. The project was proposed to Bruccoli Clark by Frederick C. Ruffner, president of the Gale Research Company, in November 1975. After specimen entries were prepared and typeset, an advisory board was formed to refine the entry format and develop the series rationale. In meetings held during 1976, the publisher, series editors, and advisory board approved the scheme for a comprehensive biographical dictionary of persons who contributed to North American literature. Editorial work on the first volume began in January 1977, and it was published in 1978. In order to make *DLB* more than a reference tool and to compile volumes that individually have claim to status as literary history, it was decided to organize volumes by topic, period, or genre. Each of these freestanding volumes provides a biographical-bibliographical guide and overview for a particular area of literature. We are convinced that this organization – as opposed to a single alphabet method – constitutes a valuable innovation in the presentation of reference material. The volume plan necessarily requires many decisions for the placement and treatment of authors who might properly be included in two or three volumes. In some instances a major figure will be included in separate volumes, but with different entries emphasizing the aspect of his career appropriate to each volume. Ernest Hemingway, for example, is represented in *American Writers in Paris, 1920–1939* by an entry focusing on his expatriate apprenticeship; he is also in *American Novelists, 1910–1945* with an entry surveying his entire career. Each volume includes a cumulative index of the subject authors and articles. Comprehensive indexes to the entire series are planned.

With volume ten in 1982 it was decided to enlarge the scope of *DLB*. By the end of 1986 twenty-one volumes treating British literature had been published, and volumes for Commonwealth and Modern European literature were in progress. The series has been further augmented by the *DLB Yearbooks* (since 1981) which update published entries and add new entries to keep the *DLB* current with contemporary activity. There have also been *DLB Documentary Series* volumes which provide biographical and critical source materials for figures whose work is judged to have particular interest for students. One of these companion volumes is entirely devoted to Tennessee Williams.

We define literature as the *intellectual commerce of a nation:* not merely as belles lettres but as that ample and complex process by which ideas are generated, shaped, and transmitted. *DLB* entries are not limited to "creative writers" but extend to other figures who in their time and in their way influenced the mind of a people. Thus the series encompasses historians, journalists, publishers, and screenwriters. By this means readers of *DLB* may be aided to perceive literature not as cult scripture in the keeping of intellectual high priests but firmly po-

**From an unpublished section of Mark Twain's autobiography, copyright by the Mark Twain Company*

sitioned at the center of a nation's life.

DLB includes the major writers appropriate to each volume and those standing in the ranks immediately behind them. Scholarly and critical counsel has been sought in deciding which minor figures to include and how full their entries should be. Wherever possible, useful references are made to figures who do not warrant separate entries.

Each *DLB* volume has a volume editor responsible for planning the volume, selecting the figures for inclusion, and assigning the entries. Volume editors are also responsible for preparing, where appropriate, appendices surveying the major periodicals and literary and intellectual movements for their volumes, as well as lists of further readings. Work on the series as a whole is coordinated at the Bruccoli Clark Layman editorial center in Columbia, South Carolina, where the editorial staff is responsible for accuracy of the published volumes.

One feature that distinguishes *DLB* is the illustration policy – its concern with the iconography of literature. Just as an author is influenced by his surroundings, so is the reader's understanding of the author enhanced by a knowledge of his environment. Therefore *DLB* volumes include not only drawings, paintings, and photographs of authors, often depicting them at various stages in their careers, but also illustrations of their families and places where they lived. Title pages are regularly reproduced in facsimile along with dust jackets for modern authors. The dust jackets are a special feature of *DLB* because they often document better than anything else the way in which an author's work was perceived in its own time. Specimens of the writers' manuscripts are included when feasible.

Samuel Johnson rightly decreed that "The chief glory of every people arises from its authors." The purpose of the *Dictionary of Literary Biography* is to compile literary history in the surest way available to us – by accurate and comprehensive treatment of the lives and work of those who contributed to it.

The *DLB* Advisory Board

Introduction

The first half of the nineteenth century offers two convenient demarcation points: the years 1815 and 1848 witnessed major political events of European rather than purely German significance. At the Congress of Vienna in 1815 delegates from all the European powers sought to restore the sociopolitical order that had prevailed before the French Revolution of 1789, thereby initiating the repressive Restauration period; the March Revolutions of 1848 endeavored – largely unsuccessfully – to reform or abolish the order established by the Restauration.

These dates draw attention to the significance of political events for the literary history of a period that lacked a towering figure such as Johann Wolfgang von Goethe. The death in 1832 of Goethe, whose dominance over his era is expressed in the title of the influential study *Geist der Goethezeit* (Spirit of the Age of Goethe, 1923–1957), by Hermann August Korff, was widely viewed as the end of the classical-idealistic period in German literary and intellectual history and the beginning of a new phase of uncertain direction. As the fiction writer, dramatist, and theater director Karl Immermann said in his *Memorabilien* (Memoirs, 1840–1843), a widespread feeling of inadequacy, Hamletian self-doubt, and uncertainty arose among those who were born around 1800 and began establishing their literary careers around the time of Goethe's death. They keenly felt that their literary efforts suffered from the comparison with the greatness of the Age of Goethe. The title of Immermann's bildungsroman *Die Epigonen* (The Epigones, 1836) provided the label for the generation of post-Goethean writers who were keenly aware of living in an age of transition.

This feeling of insufficiency was, no doubt, in part attributable to the political conditions that came into being after the defeat of Napoléon and the collapse of his domination over the German-speaking countries as a result of the Befreiungskriege (wars of liberation) from 1813 to 1815. The Restauration entailed only a partial restoration of the conditions that had obtained before the French Revolution: although the Bourbons returned to the French throne, no attempt was made to restore the German Holy Roman Empire, which had been dissolved in 1806. Rather, some thirty-five sovereign principalities and four free cities formed the Deutscher Bund (German Confederation) at the Congress of Vienna. The Deutscher Bund sought to preserve and maintain both the internal and external security of its member states; it was dominated by its two most powerful members, Prussia and Austria. In 1815 these two states also joined Russia in the Holy Alliance, an international apparatus for the preservation of the political status quo that sought to suppress liberal ideas and democratic movements that were perceived to be a threat to the hereditary rights of princes and monarchs. The reactionary policies of the Restauration period are especially associated with Prince Klemens von Metternich, the leading figure of the Congress of Vienna, Austrian chancellor from 1821 to 1848 and architect of the repressive order that became known as the Metternichsches System (Metternich System).

Liberal ideas were particularly prevalent among bourgeois intellectuals and students, many of whom had participated in the Befreiungskriege. The defeat of Napoléon left unresolved the two important issues of constitutional government and German unification. Although most smaller German states had adopted constitutions by 1820, the two most populous states, Prussia and Austria, did not do so. Their intransigence caused continuing demands for democratic reforms. Students began to form Burschenschaften (fraternities), and in October 1817 members of many of these Burschenschaften gathered at the Wartburg, a castle near Eisenach in Thuringia where Martin Luther had been given asylum in 1522. They celebrated both the beginning of the Reformation in October 1517, when Luther posted his Ninety-Five Theses condemning papal letters of indulgence, and the Battle of Leipzig in October 1813, when Napoleon suffered a decisive defeat by the combined Prussian, Austrian, and Russian armies. The Wartburg celebration turned into a demonstration for democratic freedoms and German unification.

The murder in 1819 of the writer of comedies August von Kotzebue – despised by the Burschenschaften as an opponent of their national and democratic ideals and as the czar's informant on German university life – by the radical theology student Karl Ludwig Sand set in motion the repressive machinery of the Deutscher Bund, resulting in the infamous

Karlsbader Beschlüsse (Karlsbad Decrees). These reactionary measures entailed strict supervision of the political activities of students and professors, the suppression of the Burschenschaften, and censorship of all publications of fewer than twenty sheets or 320 printed pages (to preclude the printing and distribution of poems or pamphlets containing political messages). The so-called Demagogenverfolgungen (persecution of demagogues) continued with varying degrees of intensity until the outbreak of the 1848 Revolutions.

The Metternichsches System did not completely suppress the progressive ideas that had taken hold in Europe in the wake of the French Revolution. As a result of the July 1830 Revolution in Paris, which deposed the Bourbons and installed the "bourgeois" king Louis Philippe on the throne, social unrest broke out in Germany, leading to the adoption of constitutions in several German states.

In May 1832 the thirty thousand participants in the Hambacher Fest (Hambach Festival), a radical assembly that included members of the banned Burschenschaften, called for a united German republic and proclaimed the sovereignty of the people instead of the legitimating principle of the Metternichsches System, the sovereignty of princes. As a consequence of the Hambacher Fest a new wave of repression set in, and freedom of the press and the right of assembly were abolished.

In 1835 the past, present, and future writings of the so-called Junges Deutschland (Young Germany) were prohibited. The decree specifically named Heinrich Heine, Karl Gutzkow, Heinrich Laube, Ludolf Wienbarg, and Theodor Mundt, although other writers, such as Hermann von Pückler-Muskau, may also be counted among the Jungdeutschen (Young Germans). Although these writers had not conceived of themselves as a group, the authorities, who derived the name *Junges Deutschland* from Wienbarg's *Ästhetische Feldzüge* (Aesthetic Campaigns, 1834), created a feeling of solidarity among them. The immediate cause of the decree banning the writings of Junges Deutschland was the publication of Gutzkow's *Wally, die Zweiflerin* (1835; translated as *Wally the Skeptic,* 1974). Charges of obscenity and blasphemy were leveled against the novel on account of the heroine's appearing naked in one scene and later renouncing religion; but because she considers her life empty and meaningless without the solace of religion, she commits suicide in the end. Gutzkow was sentenced to a brief prison term, and *Wally, die Zweiflerin* soon attained the status of the most controversial German work of fiction of the nineteenth century, as a result of a scathing review by the critic Wolfgang Menzel. Menzel not only condemned the novel as immoral but chastised all the Jungdeutschen as "Auswurf der Nation" (excrement of the nation) who were inspired by French licentiousness.

Despite considerable differences among the Jungdeutschen, they had certain beliefs in common. The desire of the Jungdeutschen to deal with topical issues such as women's rights and the emancipation of Jews was pronounced; they opposed the absolutist state, the established church, and restrictive moral and social conventions such as marriage. Because the Jungdeutschen strove to address problems that were of immediate concern to their contemporaries, they adopted a concise, journalistic mode of expression that also tended to be playful, witty, and polemical. Reiseliteratur (travel literature) became a favorite subgenre of the Jungdeutschen; it afforded the writer the opportunity to engage, under the guise of a travelogue, in reflections on social, artistic, and moral conditions. The adoption of Reiseliteratur, a subgenre that lacked strict generic requirements, also constituted a deliberate departure on the part of the Jungdeutschen from the Goethean model. The "Olympian" Goethe cast a long shadow, and younger writers endeavored to establish their independence from his influence in both aesthetic and political matters.

Yet, despite their political engagement and their enthusiasm for the democratic ideas emanating from France, the Jungdeutschen were not revolutionaries in the later Marxist sense. Their goal was to effect a change in the intellectual culture and social conventions rather than to change the economic underpinnings of society; hence, their reading public was the bourgeois intelligentsia rather than the untutored masses. Georg Büchner, wanted in his native Hesse for his revolutionary activities and forced to flee to Strasbourg in 1835, pointed out in an 1836 letter to Gutzkow the basic flaw in the political ideas of the Jungdeutschen: "Die Gesellschaft mittels der Idee, von der gebildeten Klasse aus reformieren? Unmöglich!" (To reform society through ideas, on the basis of the educated class? Impossible!). Büchner drew attention to the explosive potential inherent in the disenfranchised and impoverished masses – the true instrument of revolutionary changes. (The seminal writings of Büchner, who died in Swiss exile in 1837 at the age of twenty-four, were not discovered until the end of the nineteenth century.)

The year 1840 is cited by some literary historians as denoting the beginning of the Vormärz (Pre-March) proper – in distinction to the Vormärz era in a general sense, which may be said to encompass the entire period from the Congress of Vienna to the outbreak of the March 1848 Revolutions. Since the term *Vormärz* seems to place undue emphasis on the politics of the period, some literary scholars prefer *Biedermeierzeit* (Biedermeier period), a name that Friedrich Sengle uses in his monumental, authoritative literary history, *Biedermeierzeit: Deutsche Literatur im Spannungsfeld zwischen Restauration und Revolution 1815–1848* (The Period of the Biedermeier: German Literature between the Opposing Forces of Restoration and Revolution, 1971–1980). As the subtitle of Sengle's study indicates, the tension between the two opposite poles of restoration and revolution is the chief characteristic of the time from 1815 to 1848. This tension is reflected in literature; hence, it is possible to distinguish between writers of a progressive and those of a conservative bent. Although the term *Biedermeier* was initially used to parody the philistinism of the lower middle class during the first half of the nineteenth century, in the early twentieth century it was appropriated by literary historians to designate those writers and poets during the Restauration who shunned political engagement and accepted the political status quo as an imperfect but stable order that was preferable to revolutionary upheaval.

Progressive writers pinned their hopes on Friedrich Wilhelm IV, erroneously believed to be sympathetic to the liberal cause, who in 1840 ascended the Prussian throne. The new king lessened the restrictions of censorship and the severity of Demagogenverfolgungen, but he did not institute a parliament of elected representatives. The limits of the king's tolerance of liberalism became apparent in 1842. The first part of Georg Herwegh's *Gedichte eines Lebendigen* (Poems by One Who Is Alive) had been published in Swiss exile in 1841. This collection, which captured with great pathos the yearning for freedom among the younger generation, made Herwegh instantly famous. In 1842 he undertook a triumphal tour through Germany, but his journey ended ignominiously when a private letter Herwegh wrote to the king was made public. The king took offense at Herwegh's presumed indiscretion, and Herwegh was deported from Prussia.

The Vormärz writers used the poem as one of their favorite means of expression because it was suitable for the quick dissemination of topical issues via broadsides, posters, or oral delivery. These poems were designed to speak directly to the masses by appealing to their emotions. In contrast to the indirectness of the Jungdeutschen, the Vormärz poets openly used poetry as the vehicle for direct political messages. Ferdinand Freiligrath's poem "Aus Spanien" (From Spain, 1841), about the death of a reactionary Spanish general, included the lines: "Der Dichter steht auf einer höheren Warte, / Als auf den Zinnen der Partei" (The poet assumes a vantage point higher / Than that of a [political] party). Faced with what he perceived as a call to fellow poets to acquiesce in the intolerance and persecution of the Restauration period, Herwegh replied with the poem "An Ferdinand Freiligrath" (To Ferdinand Freiligrath, 1841), which was later renamed "Die Partei" (The Party), in which he postulated that the poet must opt for unambiguous political commitment in the fight against reactionary forces and for the democratic cause. Herwegh proclaimed his partisan stance: "*Ich* hab gewählt, ich habe mich entschieden, / Und *meinen* Lorbeer flechte die *Partei!*" (*I* have chosen, *I* have made my decision, / And the [political] *party* may wind *my* laurel wreath). Herwegh envisioned an activist role for the poet – "Die Fürsten träumen, laßt die Dichter handeln!" (The princes are dreaming, let the poets act!) – that would be exercised through the power of the poetic word: "Ein Schwert in eurer Hand ist das Gedicht" (The poem turns into a sword in your [the poets'] hands). The controversy between Herwegh and Freiligrath went beyond a purely literary feud in that it pitted conservatives and liberals against each other. Whereas the conservative press praised Freiligrath for not tampering with the political and social status quo, progressives such as Karl Marx, who was then editor of the Cologne newspaper *Rheinische Zeitung* (Rhenish Newspaper), Arnold Ruge, then editor of the *Deutsche Jahrbücher* (German Yearbooks), and Robert Prutz, in his essay "Die politische Poesie der Deutschen," (The Political Poetry of the Germans, 1845) criticized Freiligrath's stance and supported Herwegh's positing of the validity of political poetry.

In 1842 Freiligrath accepted an annual stipend from Friedrich Wilhelm IV and thereby seemed to confirm his subservience to the prevailing order. But with the further intensification of political repression he revised his position, rejected the king's stipend, became a friend of Marx's, and in his collection of poems *Ein Glaubensbekenntnis* (A Profession of Faith, 1844) swore allegiance to the opposition.

In contrast to the conspicuous presence in the public sphere of Freiligrath and Herwegh, the Protestant parson Eduard Mörike led a self-sufficient, unheroic, and apolitical life in the provincial confines of his native Swabia. The tendency toward the idyllic and the love for a small, circumscribed sphere of activities whose harmony is not disrupted by outside interference are also hallmarks of Mörike's poetry – qualities that earned him the epithet of quintessential Biedermeier poet. Yet, as Mörike's novella *Mozart auf der Reise nach Prag* (1865; translated as "Mozart's Journey from Vienna to Prague," 1913) reveals, the spirit of the Biedermeier cannot be reduced to naive complacency. In Mörike's novella, impending death casts a dark shadow over Wolfgang Amadeus Mozart, a supreme artist who does not conform to the restrictions of bourgeois life.

The tensions between conservative and progressive tendencies of the period are evident in the life and work of the Austrian dramatist Franz Grillparzer. As a liberal, he hailed the revolution that did away with the Metternichsches System, but he did not actively participate in it. Grillparzer, who had achieved recognition with his early plays, subsequently was hampered by censorship – especially of his plays about Austrian history. Both his character traits and the constraints that circumscribed literary activities in Metternich's Vienna contributed to Grillparzer's mood of resignation and sense of failure. Although today Grillparzer is acknowledged as an Austrian classic, he is also often cited as a prime example of the dominance of the Biedermeier in Austria.

During the first half of the nineteenth century the German-speaking countries lacked a political and cultural capital comparable to Paris or London, but Vienna had a thriving theater that contributed to the formation of a distinct Austrian identity. Whereas Grillparzer represented the historical-classical drama in the manner of Goethe and Friedrich Schiller and appealed to an audience of the upper bourgeoisie and aristocracy in the inner-city Burgtheater (court theater), the Volksstücke (popular plays) of Johann Nestroy were staged at theaters in Vienna's outlying districts and attracted the lower middle classes, artisans, and workers. The enormously prolific Nestroy, who directed and acted in his own plays, aggressively and satirically exposed the human weaknesses of his fellow citizens and castigated the sociopolitical conditions of the Viennese Vormärz. Inevitably, his activities attracted the attention of the censors. They were unable, however, to bar the immensely popular Nestroy from the stage. Nestroy's success in the face of inhospitable political conditions stands in stark contrast to the fates of the dramatists Büchner and Christian Dietrich Grabbe. Büchner was a victim of political circumstances; Grabbe, who is occasionally compared to Büchner as a proponent of realist drama, never succeeded in becoming established because of his volatile temperament and lack of social graces, which were exacerbated by his increasing alcoholism.

Although Vienna and, to a lesser extent, Berlin were focal points of cultural activities, regional literary and cultural production during the Restauration was quite pronounced. The Swabian Mörike, the Austrian Adalbert Stifter, the Westphalian Annette von Droste-Hülshoff, and the Swiss Jeremias Gotthelf (pen name of Albert Bitzius) are prominent examples of Biedermeier writers whose literary reputations far surpass the regions with which they are identified. Stifter's aesthetics are encompassed by the "sanftes Gesetz" (gentle law), a divinely inspired law that is supposedly at work in society and in nature. Stifter posits that loving immersion into the seemingly small and insignificant will lead to the ultimate revelation of true greatness and nobility. Hence, Stifter's novellas, particularly those that take place in the Bohemian forests of his youth, tend to depict a simple, rustic world in which life goes on in unspectacular fashion and in which human beings and nature live in harmony.

Stifter's narratives dwell on the unexceptional and are marked by a deliberately simple style; Droste-Hülshoff's novella "Die Judenbuche" (1842; translated as "The Jew's Beech-Tree," 1913), in contrast, is a tale of crime and punishment, of transgression and divine retribution. Both Stifter and Droste-Hülshoff, who is today recognized as one of the greatest German woman poets of the nineteenth century, belong to the conservative camp. They shared the belief in a divinely ordained universe, distrusted attempts to violently change the social order of the Restauration, and hewed to the Biedermeier ethic of Entsagung (resignation, renunciation) that considers the reckless pursuit of personal happiness as a manifestation of egotism. "Die Judenbuche" is infused with the author's intimate knowledge of the rural milieu of her native region. The realistic depiction of the landscape and its inhabitants relates "Die Judenbuche" to the Dorfgeschichte (village tale), a subgenre that began to thrive during the 1840s and that typically dealt with the everyday problems of ordinary people in a specific locality. Unlike "Die Judenbuche," which betrays the distanced, even condescending, viewpoint of its aristocratic author, the Dorfgeschichte tended to feature sympathetically drawn protagonists who often spoke in dialect and with whom readers could easily identify.

The Swiss Protestant clergyman Gotthelf inveighed against the liberal ideas that spread from the cities and praised the harmonious life of God-fearing farmers who upheld traditional values against the encroachment of modern perceptions. Gotthelf's depiction of a dualistic pattern of good and evil reflects a staunchly conservative stance in the face of the threat posed by the Jungdeutschen, the Vormärz writers, and their adherents and imitators. The didactic bent is less pronounced in Berthold Auerbach's *Schwarzwälder Dorfgeschichten* (1843–1854; first two volumes translated as *Black Forest Village Stories,*

1869). Auerbach, a former member of the persecuted Burschenschaften and of Jewish descent, advanced progressive notions such as the emancipation of the Jews, but he also used the contrast – a familiar feature of the Dorfgeschichte – between the naturalness of the simple folk life in the country and the debilitating influences of life in the city.

The popularity of the Dorfgeschichte, with its tendentious idealization of rural conditions in a specific region and its inherent propensity for condemning the city as the source of destructive progressive ideas, may be viewed as a reflection of the sociopolitical backwardness of Germany. The regionalism and provincialism evident in the Dorfgeschichte stood in marked contrast to the contemporary social novel in France and England; the protagonists' narrowly circumscribed sphere of activity also distinguishes the Dorfgeschichte from the adventure novels by Charles Sealsfield (pen name of Karl Postl) that take place in North America. In comparison to the democratic United States, the Metternichsches System appeared grossly deficient and inadequate. The Dorfgeschichte, with its essentially conservative bias, rarely served as a vehicle for promoting emancipation; for example, the role of women in society remained outside its purview. The traditional view of women in Dorfgeschichten and the conventional roles assigned to them in such tales differ drastically from such radical demands as the "Wiedereinsetzung des Fleisches" (restitution of the rights of the flesh), proclaimed in Mundt's novel *Madonna: Unterhaltungen mit einer Heiligen* (Madonna: Conversations with a Saint, 1835) and supported by many Jungdeutschen. Along with the Jungdeutschen, women writers such as Countess Ida Gräfin von Hahn-Hahn and Louise von Gall began to devote their attention to women and to write novels featuring female protagonists.

As the name implies, the Vormärz came to an end with the outbreak of the March 1848 Revolutions. The revolutions failed to resolve the two paramount issues that the Congress of Vienna had ignored: German unification and constitutional government. Writers responded by adopting directions and emphases that lacked the antiestablishment fervor of the Jungdeutschen and the revolutionary élan of the Vormärz poets and constituted an accommodation to the postrevolutionary state of affairs.

One of the results of the failed March Revolutions was the growing awareness among the middle class that it was difficult, if not impossible, to achieve liberal reforms and German political unity in opposition to the prevailing order. As a consequence, a withdrawal from politics and a concentration on economic issues ensued. This change in the intellectual climate is reflected in literature: in the postrevolutionary era both the engaged prose writings of Junges Deutschland and the political poetry of the Vormärz were replaced by the literature of realism. The dominant style of the second half of the nineteenth century, realism generally shunned the treatment of social conflicts and politically inopportune views.

The erstwhile Vormärz poet Freiligrath, who extolled the German republic, exemplifies the accommodation to the political status quo. In 1868 Freiligrath returned from English exile; during the Franco-Prussian War of 1870–1871, which resulted in German unification, he wrote patriotic, nationalist poems endorsing the Bismarckian solution of the German question and thereby distancing himself from his former ideals.

– *Siegfried Mews*

ACKNOWLEDGMENTS

This book was produced by Bruccoli Clark Layman, Inc. Karen L. Rood is senior editor for the *Dictionary of Literary Biography* series. Philip B. Dematteis was the in-house editor.

Photography editors are Edward Scott and Timothy C. Lundy. Layout and graphics supervisor is Penney L. Haughton. Copyediting supervisor is Bill Adams. Typesetting supervisor is Kathleen M. Flanagan. Samuel Bruce, Darren Harris-Fain, and Julie E. Frick are editorial associates. Systems manager is George F. Dodge. The production staff includes Rowena Betts, Steve Borsanyi, Barbara Brannon, Patricia Coate, Rebecca Crawford, Margaret McGinty Cureton, Denise Edwards, Sarah A. Estes, Joyce Fowler, Robert Fowler, Laurel M. Gladden, Jolyon M. Helterman, Tanya D. Locklair, Ellen McCracken, Kathy Lawler Merlette, John Morrison Myrick, Pamela D. Norton, Thomas J. Pickett, Patricia Salisbury, Maxine K. Smalls, Deborah P. Stokes, William L. Thomas, Jr., Jennifer Carroll Jenkins Turley, and Wilma Weant.

Walter W. Ross and Brenda Gross did library research. They were assisted by the following librarians at the Thomas Cooper Library of the University of South Carolina: Linda Holderfield and the interlibrary-loan staff; reference librarians Gwen Baxter, Daniel Boice, Faye Chadwell, Cathy Eckman, Gary Geer, Qun "Gerry" Jiao, Jean Rhyne, Carol Tobin, Carolyn Tyler, Virginia Weathers, Elizabeth Whiznant, and Connie Widney; circulation-department head Thomas Marcil; and acquisitions-searching supervisor David Haggard.

Dictionary of Literary Biography® • Volume One Hundred Thirty-Three

Nineteenth-Century German Writers to 1840

Dictionary of Literary Biography

Willibald Alexis (Georg Wilhelm Heinrich Häring)

(29 June 1798 - 16 December 1871)

Wulf Koepke
Texas A&M University

BOOKS: *Die Treibjagd: Ein scherzhaft idyllisches Epos in vier Gesängen* (Berlin: Dümmler, 1820);

Die Schlacht bei Torgau; Der Schatz der Tempelherren: Zwei Novellen (Berlin: Herbig, 1823);

Walladmor: Frei nach dem Englischen des Walter Scott, anonymous, 3 volumes (Berlin: Herbig, 1824); translated anonymously by Thomas de Quincey as *Walladmor,* 2 volumes (London: Taylor & Hessey, 1825);

Die Geächteten: Novelle (Berlin: Duncker & Humblot, 1825);

Schloß Avalon: Frei nach dem Englischen des Walter Scott vom Uebersetzer des Walladmor, anonymous, 2 volumes (Leipzig: Brockhaus, 1827);

Herbstreise durch Scandinavien, 2 volumes (Berlin: Schlesinger, 1828);

Wanderungen im Süden (Berlin: Schlesinger, 1828);

Gesammelte Novellen, 4 volumes (Berlin: Duncker & Humblot, 1830-1831);

Cabanis: Roman in sechs Büchern, 6 volumes (Berlin: Fincke, 1832);

Wiener Bilder (Leipzig: Brockhaus, 1833);

Schattenrisse aus Süddeutschland (Berlin: Schlesinger, 1834);

Das Haus Düsterweg: Eine Geschichte aus der Gegenwart, 2 volumes (Leipzig: Brockhaus, 1835);

Balladen (Berlin: Dümmler, 1836);

Neue Novellen, 2 volumes (Berlin: Duncker & Humblot, 1836);

Babiolen: Novellen und Novelletten. Nebst polemischen Papierstreifen, by Alexis, E. Ferrand, and A. Mueller, 2 volumes (Leipzig: Focke, 1837);

Zwölf Nächte: Ein Roman in sechs Büchern, 3 volumes (Berlin: Duncker & Humblot, 1838);

Willibald Alexis

Der Roland von Berlin: Roman, 3 volumes (Leipzig: Brockhaus, 1840); translated by W. A. G. as *The Burgomaster of Berlin,* 3 volumes (London: Saunders & Otley, 1843);

Der falsche Woldemar: Roman, 3 volumes (Berlin: Buchhandlung des Berliner Lesekabinetts, 1842);

Urban Grandier oder die Besessenen von Loudun, 2 volumes (Berlin: Buchhandlung des Berliner Lesekabinetts, 1843);

Warren Hastings: Ein Vortrag, gehalten am 9. März im wissenschaftlichen Vereine in Berlin (Berlin: Buchhandlung des Berliner Lesekabinetts, 1844);

Die Hosen des Herrn von Bredow: Vaterländischer Roman, 2 volumes (Berlin: Adolf, 1846–1848);

Der Wärwolf: Vaterländischer Roman in drei Büchern, 3 volumes (Berlin: Adolf, 1848);

Arnstadt: Ein Bild aus Thüringen (Arnstadt: Meinhardt, 1851);

Der Zauberer Virgilius: Ein Märchen aus der Gegenwart (Berlin: Adolf, 1851);

Ruhe ist die erste Bürgerpflicht, oder Vor fünfzig Jahren: Vaterländischer Roman, 5 volumes (Berlin: Barthol, 1852);

Isegrimm: Vaterländischer Roman, 3 volumes (Berlin: Barthol, 1854);

Friedrich Perthes (Berlin: Barthol, 1855);

Reise-Pitaval (Leipzig: Brockhaus, 1855);

Dorothe: Ein Roman aus der Brandenburgischen Geschichte, 3 volumes (Berlin: Barthol, 1856);

Nettelbeck (Berlin: Barthol, 1856);

Oberpräsident Vincke (Berlin: Barthol, 1856);

Ja in Neapel: Novelle (Berlin: Janke, 1860);

Gesammelte Werke, 18 volumes (Berlin: Janke, 1861–1866);

Erinnerungen von Willibald Alexis, edited by Max Ewert (Berlin: Concordia Deutsche Verlags-Anstalt, 1900).

OTHER: "Zur Beurtheilung Hoffmann's als Dichter," in E. T. A. Hoffmann, *Aus Hoffmann's Leben und Nachlaß,* edited by Julius Eduard Hitzig, volume 2 (Berlin: Dümmler, 1823), pp. 325–357;

Berliner Konversationsblatt für Poesie, Literatur und Kritik, edited by Alexis and Friedrich Förster (1827–1829);

Der Freimüthige oder: Berliner Conversations-Blatt, edited by Alexis (1830–1835);

"Hans Preller von Lauffen: Eine schweizer Sage," in *Jahreszeiten,* edited by Oswald Marbach (Leipzig: Frühling, 1839), pp. 105–140; translated by Carl L. Lewes as "Hans Preller: A Legend," in *Tales from Blackwood,* series 1, volume 3 (Edinburgh & London: Blackwood, 1905);

Andalusien: Spiegelbilder aus dem südspanischen Leben. Aus den Briefen eines jungen Deutschen, edited by Alexis (Berlin: Buchhandlung des Berliner Lesekabinetts, 1842);

Der neue Pitaval: Eine Sammlung der interessantesten Criminalgeschichten, 30 volumes, edited by Alexis and Hitzig (Leipzig: Brockhaus, 1842–1862);

Harriet Martineau, *Die Ansiedler im eigenen Hause,* edited by Alexis (Berlin: Buchhandlung des Berliner Lesekabinetts, 1846);

Martineau, *Rolf und Erika, oder Der Aberglaube des Nordens,* edited by Alexis (Berlin: Adolf, 1847);

Vossische Zeitung, political section edited by Alexis (1849);

Katharina Diez, *Frühlings-Märchen,* introduction by Alexis (Berlin: Krüger, 1851);

Volks-Kalender für 1854, edited by Alexis (Berlin: Barthol, 1854);

Volks-Kalender für 1855, edited by Alexis (Berlin: Barthol, 1855);

Volks-Kalender für 1856, edited by Alexis (Berlin: Barthol, 1856);

Volks-Kalender für 1857, edited by Alexis (Berlin: Barthol, 1857);

Clara Ernst, *Feldblumen,* introduction by Alexis (Berlin: Grieben, 1860).

TRANSLATIONS: Sir Walter Scott, *Die Jungfrau vom See: Ein Gedicht in sechs Gesängen,* 2 volumes (Zwickau: Schumann, 1822);

Scott, *Das Lied des letzten Minstrels: Ein Gedicht in sechs Gesängen* (Zwickau: Schumann, 1824);

James K. Paulding, *Königsmark, der lange Finne: Ein Roman aus der neuen Welt,* 2 volumes (Berlin: Herbig, 1824);

Thomas Colley Gratton, *Heer- und Querstraßen oder Erzählungen, gesammelt auf einer Wanderung durch Frankreich, von einem fußreisenden Gentleman,* 5 volumes (Berlin: Duncker & Humblot, 1824–1828);

Scott, *Historische und romantische Balladen der schottischen Gränzlande,* 3 volumes (Zwickau: Schumann, 1826);

Robert Folkestone Williams, *Shakespeare und seine Freunde oder Das goldene Zeitalter des lustigen Englands,* 3 volumes (Berlin: Duncker & Humblot, 1839);

Miss Pardoe, *Der Roman des Herzens: Ein Cyclus orientalischer Erzählungen,* translated by Alexis and J. Neumark (Berlin: Liebmann, 1840).

SELECTED PERIODICAL PUBLICATIONS – UNCOLLECTED: "Drei Tage im Riesen-Gebirge," *Der Gesellschafter,* nos. 87–94 (1–13 June 1821);

"The Romances of Walter Scott – Romane von Scott," *Jahrbücher der Literatur,* 22 (1823): 1-75;

"Heinrich Heine: Tragödien," *Jahrbücher der Literatur,* 31 (1825): 157-185;

"Die ehrlichen Leute: Novelle nach dem Spanischen," *Frauentaschenbuch,* 11 (1825): 43-116;

"Das Goethe-Fest in Berlin," *Der Gesellschafter,* nos. 144-146 (1826);

"Der Collaborator Liborius: Novelle," *Urania,* 2 (1827): 313-466;

Die Sonette: Lustspiel in einem Akt, in *Jahrbuch deutscher Bühnenspiele,* 7 (1828): 317-362;

Aennchen von Tharau: Drama in drei Akten, in *Jahrbuch deutscher Bühnenspiele,* 8 (1829): 129-206;

"Rosamunde: Novelle," *Vesta: Taschenbuch für 1836* (1836): 19-104;

"Herr von Sacken: Novelle," *Deutsches Taschenbuch,* 6 (1837): 211-314;

"Der Fluch des Mauren: Erzählung," *Penelope,* 17 (1838): 286-351;

"Der rechte Erbe: Novelle," *Berliner Kalender auf 1840* (1840): 169-304;

Der verwunschene Schneidergesell: Fastnachtsschwank, in *Jahrbuch deutscher Bühnenspiele,* 20 (1841): 149-220;

"Die unsichtbare Geliebte: Novelle," *Blätter und Blüthen* (1841): 31-102;

Der Prinz von Pisa: Lustspiel, in *Jahrbuch deutscher Bühnenspiele,* 22 (1843): 113-208;

"Der Wilddieb: Erzählung von ihm selbst erzählt," *Urania,* new series 6 (1844): 229-308;

"Anton Reiser," *Prutzens literar-historisches Taschenbuch,* 5 (1847): 1-71;

"Die Flucht nach Amerika: Novelle," *Urania,* new series 10 (1848): 129-222.

Sir Walter Scott had many admirers – Johann Wolfgang von Goethe among them – and imitators in Germany, as he had elsewhere. Foremost among the German imitators was Willibald Alexis, who is chiefly remembered for his eight Vaterländische Romane (Patriotic Novels) on the history of the Mark Brandenburg since the Middle Ages. He was also a remarkable literary critic, but his own work was generally ignored by other critics and has also been neglected by literary historians. The best assessments of his writing can be seen in the efforts of his two major rivals, Gustav Freytag and Theodor Fontane who tried to surpass and replace him in the field of the historical novel.

Like Heinrich Heine, Alexis belonged to the literary generation between romanticism and realism that has been characterized as the age of Zerrissenheit (inner strife). He was an astute observer of and participant in the struggles of German society toward industrialism and democracy. A lawyer, historian, and man of letters, he produced novels and novellas, documentary fiction, legal and historical accounts, poetry, literary criticism, political journalism, travel books, and autobiographical accounts. He clearly embodied the spirit of his period of transition, tension, and hope for progress, but he also reflected the undertone of deep melancholy that was never absent from German writing between 1830 and 1860.

Alexis was born Georg Wilhelm Heinrich Häring on 29 June 1798 in Breslau (today Wroclaw, Poland), the capital of the Prussian province of Silesia. He typifies the new Prussian urban middle class in his family background, his education, his career choices, and his political views. A significant aspect of this Prussian heritage was his insistence that he had French Huguenot ancestors: he was convinced that his family came from Normandy and had originally been called Harenc. Silesia was an area of much economic activity, textile manufacturing in particular, and as a border region it had an ethnically mixed population. Häring's father, Georg Wilhelm Häring, was a Prussian official; his mother, Henriette Häring, née Rellstab, was his father's second wife and was seventeen years her husband's junior. Häring's half sister Florentine ("Florchen"), from his father's first marriage, was not much younger than her stepmother.

Alexis's father died in 1802. In 1806, because of the siege and bombardment of Breslau during the Napoleonic Wars, Henriette Häring moved back to her native city, Berlin, where her family owned a music store and bookstore. Alexis grew up there in close company with his cousin Ludwig Rellstab, who would become a prominent music critic but would also write poems, librettos, stories, and historical novels. In 1810 the two boys began attending the Friedrichwerder Gymnasium.

At the age of thirteen Alexis wrote his first play, the tragedy "Herzog Othelrich von Böhmen" (Duke Othelrich of Bohemia), which was never published; his first stories were written in 1814. He volunteered for military service in 1815 when Napoleon returned from Elba and threatened the peace of Europe. His unit started marching west in the summer, too late to take part in the decisive Battle of Waterloo. The war dragged on, and Alexis spent the fall and winter in boring marches and sieges of small Belgian fortresses. This experience cured his enthusiasm for the military; while he remained an ardent Prussian patriot, his many depictions of battles and military life are characterized by realism rather than heroic exploits.

After the war Alexis returned to the gymnasium, from which he graduated in 1817. He began his university studies in Berlin, spent a year in Breslau, and returned to Berlin for his third year. Among his professors he was most impressed by Karl von Savigny, founder of the Historical School of Law, which emphasized empirical research over philosophical speculation and advocated basing new laws on tradition. Alexis also studied with Friedrich von Raumer, a historian, author of historical plays, and liberal politician. During his student days in Berlin and Breslau, he was active as a journalist.

In 1820 Alexis joined the Prussian civil service. He advanced from Auskultator (research assistant) to Referendar (junior barrister); in the latter position he reported and prepared cases for the judges of the criminal division of the Prussian central court. Also in 1820 his long epic poem *Die Treibjagd* (The Battue) was published. He also translated *The Lady of the Lake* (1810) as *Die Jungfrau vom See* (1822) and *The Lay of the Last Minstrel* (1805) as *Das Lied des letzten Minstrels* (1824) as part of a projected German edition of Scott's works. In 1824 he resigned from the civil service to try his luck as a free-lance writer. He found mentors among the Romantic writers E. T. A. Hoffmann, Ludwig Tieck, and especially Friedrich Baron de la Motte Fouqué. Among the well-known Berlin authors with whom he became acquainted were Joseph von Eichendorff, Adelbert von Chamisso, and Karl Varnhagen von Ense. He felt the closest affinity with writers of his own generation who are classified as late romantics or transitional figures: Wilhelm Müller, Wilhelm Hauff, and Karl Immermann. He respected Heine, but they never developed a personal relationship. In his many book and theater reviews Alexis showed an open mind and a desire for nonpartisan evaluations at a time of fierce literary feuds and a time when, chiefly through the writers of "Young Germany," politics had entered into literary judgments. Alexis was critical of the Young Germans but had cordial relations with some of them, especially Karl Gutzkow. Alexis's only real enemy, Ludwig Börne, came from the far Left. Among Alexis's more significant reviews were positive evaluations of Hoffmann, of Heine's early works, and of Eichendorff's "Aus dem Leben eines Taugenichts" (1826; translated as *Memoirs of a Good-for-Nothing,* 1866); he also reviewed English and American literature.

One of Alexis's major critical achievements was a long review of Scott's works, published in 1823 in the *Jahrbücher der Literatur* (Yearbooks of Literature). Alexis, who had immersed himself in Scott's literary world and novelistic techniques, went on to create a hoax that became his greatest popular success but also the curse of his career. His novel *Walladmor* (1824) purported to be a translation of a novel by Scott; in fact, it was both an imitation and a parody of Scott. Any attentive critic should have been suspicious; but the parody aspects were overlooked, the book became an instant success, and it was translated into English by Thomas de Quincey in 1825 as a retranslation of a free translation of a work by Scott. Alexis's game proved to be too clever; he never lost his image as an imitator.

Walladmor is set in contemporary Wales. A young man named Bertram turns out to be the long-lost son of the Walladmor family and wins his bride, Ginievra, when he becomes the heir of Walladmor Castle. The story line, in the manner of romances, is the sort of chain of exciting episodes, both serious and funny, known to today's audiences through the later classic of the genre, *Les Trois Mousquetaires* (The Three Musketeers, 1844), by Alexandre Dumas. The book illustrates British customs and institutions that were generally unknown to Germans. There are constant allusions to medieval traditions and supernatural elements that are attributed to the backwardness of the country.

A best-seller demands a sequel, and Alexis obliged: in 1827 his *Schloß Avalon* (The Avalon Castle), another novel patterned after the work of Scott, was published. A lengthy introduction tries to lay to rest the *Walladmor* hoax; on the other hand, the novel is declared on the title page to be "frei nach dem Englischen des Walter Scott vom Uebersetzer des Walladmor" (freely adapted from the English of Walter Scott by the translator of *Walladmor*). *Schloß Avalon* is a historical novel dealing with the reigns of Charles II and James II, the rebellion of the duke of Monmouth, and the Glorious Revolution of William and Mary in 1688. Much attention is given to the religious feuds among the Anglican establishment, the Catholics, and the Presbyterians. The political action is intertwined with the adventure and love stories of Sir Robert Fletcher of Salton and his friend Raleigh Loscelyne of Avalon. Fletcher's father, a Whig, had been exiled, and his son takes up his cause. He supports the duke of Monmouth and narrowly escapes death at the disastrous battle at Sedgemoor. His childhood sweetheart, Anna Tennison, is his match in courage and determination. They overcome all obstacles and marry after the ascent to the throne of William and Mary, under whose rule Fletcher obtains high military honors.

The transition of power from the Stuarts to William and Mary is the advent of a new age. William is pragmatic, sober, and bourgeois, in contrast to the flamboyant gallantry of the other characters, such as Monmouth. The gallant knight par excellence is Raleigh Loscelyne, who remains loyal to James II although he criticizes the corruption at court and is mostly out of favor with the Stuarts. His great love is Harriet Wentworth, the mistress of the duke of Monmouth. Only when Raleigh is on his deathbed does Harriet consent to marry him. She then retires to a convent in Belgium. With the death of Raleigh and the departure of James II, the age of chivalry will be replaced by that of rationalism and utilitarianism. Later in life, Alexis compared *Walladmor* to a hot-air balloon or a soap bubble, but he maintained that *Schloß Avalon* was a serious work.

One of Alexis's early activities as a free-lance writer was the writing of travel accounts, a genre that was quite popular at the time. His *Herbstreise durch Scandinavien* (Journey through Scandinavia in the Fall, 1828) describes the stormy passage from Denmark to Sweden, the conflicts between the Swedish administration and the Norwegian Storting (parliament) – the king of Sweden at that time was also the king of Norway – and the development of democracy in the small settlement of Christiania, later renamed Oslo. Most of the book is devoted to an account of the awesome natural landscape and the brave inhabitants of the northern regions. The journey ends in Stockholm. His *Wiener Bilder* (Pictures of Vienna, 1833) starts with a journey from Berlin to Vienna through Bohemia and includes a boat trip on the Danube. Alexis's sympathetic depiction of the Viennese, who were generally despised in Germany, and his calls for cooperation among the social classes and for freedom of the press were controversial. The work presents a vivid and realistic picture of life in Vienna in the 1830s.

Alexis's trip to Vienna was partly for personal reasons: he was engaged to the actress Julie Gley, who had moved from Berlin to Vienna. Alexis subsequently broke off the engagement. She later became famous under her married name, Julie Rettich.

When Alexis wrote his first novel on the history of Brandenburg, he had no grand design in mind; but later he incorporated *Cabanis* (1832) into his Vaterländische Romane. In the opinion of Alexis's contemporaries and of posterity these eight novels constitute his claim to be the German Walter Scott. Republished well into the twentieth century, the Vaterländische Romane were, paradoxically, attacked as lacking in patriotism by chauvinistic proponents of the German Empire that was founded in 1871 and later by the Nazis; conversely, post–World War II critics deemed the novels too Prussian in view of the consequences of nationalistic excesses in Prussian and German history. Alexis did not write about history for history's sake: the references to his own times are unmistakable. But he studied and made extensive use of old chronicles and documents. He had a keen sense for identifying typical traits and historical developments and translating them into concrete situations. He also shows a distinct tendency in his novels to bring to light the unknown side of history, both the criminal aspects and the daily life of the common people. In all of his books Alexis aims at a depiction of the entire society; all social classes are represented and given their due.

While *Cabanis,* the first novel in the series, deals with the eighteenth century, and the last, *Dorothe* (1856), is set in the late seventeenth century, the entire cycle takes the reader from the early fourteenth century to the nineteenth century. *Der falsche Woldemar* (The False Woldemar, 1842) recalls a curious episode at a low point of the history of Brandenburg. After the death of Margrave Woldemar on the way to the Holy Land in 1319, the emperor Ludwig the Bavarian gave Brandenburg to his son, one of whose successors ceded the country to the emperor Charles IV of the House of Luxemburg. Before the Hohenzollerns restored stability in 1415, Brandenburg was the object of dynastic quarrels among the Bavarians and Luxemburgers, the rulers of Anhalt and Saxony, the archbishop of Magdeburg, and the dukes of Mecklenburg and Pomerania. At the beginning of the rule of Charles IV an old man appeared who claimed to be the late Margrave Woldemar. He attracted a large following from 1348 to 1350 and was favored by Charles IV for his own purposes. Alexis chronicles the dark intrigues surrounding this episode; he describes small-town burghers, robber bands in the woods forming a true counterculture, peasants, and the Brandenburg nobility. There are happy and tragic love stories and a memorable femme fatale, the countess of Nordheim, who goes to any length to acquire more power. Alexis pits chivalrous knights such as Ludwig the Bavarian against the pragmatists and politicians typified by Charles IV. While Alexis's sympathies lie with chivalry, the knights are the losers. Above all, Alexis deplores lawlessness and bemoans the fact that Brandenburg is a pawn in the hands of foreigners instead of a politically active, thriving entity.

Der Roland von Berlin (The Roland [Statue] of Berlin, 1840; translated as *The Burgomaster of Berlin,*

1843) takes place in the fifteenth century as the Hohenzollern elector Friedrich II, nicknamed "der Eiserne" (the Iron Man), fights to impose his authority on the cities. Cities not subject to a ruler were entitled to erect "Roland" statues as symbols of their freedom from territorial laws. The elector was ultimately successful because of divisions within the cities. The dissension in Berlin cut several ways: the old rivalry between Berlin and its sister city, Cölln, remained, and there were conflicts between the social classes as the merchants defended their privileges against the craft guilds. Alexis personalizes these conflicts in his main characters. Johannes von Rathenow, the mayor of Berlin, is one of the many crusty conservatives in Alexis's works. He defends not only the independence of the city but also outworn class differences. His foster son, Henning Mollner, exhibits the enterprising spirit of the rising lower classes. He and the elector see in each other the spirit of the new age and become allies. Rathenow refuses to consent to a marriage between his daughter, Elsbeth, and Henning as long as the Roland statue stands. After many military and legal confrontations, the elector wins, and the Roland statue is dismantled and thrown into the Spree River. Rathenow prefers exile to submission and leaves for Saxony but is murdered at the border by robbers; Henning marries Elsbeth and raises a successful family. Friedrich's victory, in Alexis's eyes, is tragic: with the independence of the cities destroyed, society will be ruled from above instead of by the free interplay of social forces.

Die Hosen des Herrn von Bredow (Herr von Bredow's Leather Pants, 1846–1848) has remained Alexis's most popular novel due to its quick succession of exciting, often funny, episodes. Whereas *Der Roland von Berlin* documents the demise of the cities, *Die Hosen des Herrn von Bredow* describes the self-destruction of the aristocratic opposition to the ruler.

The action takes place at the beginning of the rule of Elector Joachim I in 1499. Götz von Bredow, the lord of Castle Hohenziatz in the Havel River region, returns from the diet of the nobles. As usual, the session ended with a drinking bout, and Bredow retires to sleep off the effects; he sleeps for six days and six nights. Brigitte, his wife, takes this opportunity to do the laundry, which includes the washing of the ancient leather pants with which Götz ordinarily refuses to part. The washing party is entertained by the antics of the dishonest peddler Hedderich, who has little success in selling his fake goods. A thunderstorm drives the party back to the castle; the leather pants are left behind and eagerly appropriated by Hedderich. A relative of the Bredows, the councillor Wilkin von Lindenburg, who is the elector's right-hand man, also seeks refuge in the castle. He tempts the other men into a gambling and drinking party, but he loses more money than he has. To recoup his losses he persuades Hans Jochen, Götz von Bredow's favorite foster son, to help him rob Hedderich. Götz's other foster son, Hans Jürgen, who had been sent out to look for the leather pants finds Hedderich tied to a tree where the robbers left him. He releases the peddler and takes the pants back to the castle. To protect the image of the aristocracy, Lindenberg persuades Götz to take the blame for the crime; but the elector stages a scene which results in Lindenberg being identified as the culprit, and Lindenberg is hanged. The Brandenburg nobles, furious about the execution of Lindenberg, prepare an ambush for the elector; but he is warned by Hans Jürgen. Brigitte has prevented Götz von Bredow from participating in the conspiracy by hiding his leather pants. Seventy of the conspirators are hanged, and the power of the aristocracy is broken. Hans Jürgen is knighted and wins the hand of Evchen, Götz's daughter, as well as a position at the court.

Der Wärwolf (The Werewolf, 1848) is a sequel to *Die Hosen des Herrn von Bredow*. In the last years of his reign, Joachim I stubbornly refuses to allow the Lutheran church to gain legitimacy even though the vast majority of the population wants it. The religious strife leads to renewed conflicts with the cities and the aristocracy and produces a schism in the elector's family: his wife, Elisabeth, converts to Protestantism, and is exiled to Saxony. The elector's son Joachim, who distinguishes himself in the war against the Turks, sides with his mother against his father. The widowed Brigitte von Bredow is appalled by the sale of indulgences, especially by the notorious Tetzel, and fights against it. Hans Jürgen, by now the Marschall, the highest official at court, tries to avoid religious strife and fanaticism, but he, too, is banished. A symptom of the elector's wrongheadedness is his belief in superstition: according to astrological predictions in which he believes, the world will soon be submerged by a new Flood, and he takes refuge on the Tempelhof hill. In Alexis's view, Lutheranism will enlighten the minds of the people and chase superstitions away. Joachim I dies in 1535; four years later, Joachim II establishes the Lutheran church as the official church of Brandenburg.

Dorothe (1856), Alexis's last completed novel, takes place in the late seventeenth century during the final years of the reign of Friedrich Wilhelm, the Great Elector, which were overshadowed by political defeats and intrigues. In 1679 Brandenburg had to accept the peace of Saint-Germain, which robbed it of most of its gains in the war against Sweden. Belief in ghosts and alchemy are symptoms of a crisis in the society. The elector's second wife, Dorothe, wants to gain part of Brandenburg for her children, who would normally have no right of succession. She persuades the elector to write a will to that effect and fights openly against the crown prince, future King Friedrich I. There is another Dorothe, an orphan who is rising in favor at court. When she becomes the object of political intrigues she finds a friend in Benedict Skytte, a Dutch teacher who has come to Brandenburg to realize his utopian dream of a Latin-speaking city dedicated to the free pursuit of knowledge, to peace, and to tolerance for all religions. Skytte fights for the orphan Dorothe as her legal counsel and also rescues her when she is kidnapped. Other characters include the false count Balsamo, an Italian alchemist who meddles in politics; the upstart Marschall Derfflinger; and the crown prince's confidant, Dankelmann. The entire action seems to take place in darkness, and the mood remains gloomy in spite of the happy ending for the orphan Dorothe and Skytte. Dorothe the elector's wife, however, sees her plans thwarted: after the elector's death, his will is invalidated because it is in conflict with old laws of succession in Brandenburg. The dark atmosphere reflects Alexis's mood after the failure of the Revolutions of 1848; there is little of the comedy that is found in the previous Vaterländische Romane.

Cabanis, still written with a degree of youthful exuberance, takes place during the Seven Years' War of 1756 to 1763. The son of the Marquis Cabanis, Stefan, grows up among Huguenots in Berlin ignorant of his true identity. He enlists in the Hungarian army, rises to the rank of lieutenant, then defects to the Prussians. He fights bravely but never achieves his goal of being recognized by King Friedrich II (Frederick the Great); the only time he is decorated is after a battle in which he had actually made serious military errors. Gottlieb, Stefan's half brother, had also joined the military. He is often disciplined for his rebellious attitude, which stems from a sense of honor that is deemed inappropriate in a commoner. Gottlieb becomes a criminal because of his violated pride. After many encounters, the brothers finally recognize each other at the time of Gottlieb's death.

Friederich II is not shown in his best light; his military genius, especially, does not shine in the novel. The disastrous defeat at Hochkirch, which could easily have been avoided, is described in detail; and Friedrich hardly ever recognizes true merit.

Alexis in 1841; engraving by A. Korneck after a drawing by G. Alboth

The remaining two Vaterländische Romane are the longest and most complex works in the series. This description is particularly true of *Ruhe ist die erste Bürgerpflicht* (Quiet is the Citizen's First Duty, 1852). The novel ends with the catastrophic defeat of the Prussian army by Napoleon's troops at Jena in 1806, upon which the governor of Berlin issued the proclamation from which the title is derived. The novel is designed to present the causes of this calamitous event, which was regarded in Prussia and the rest of Germany as the symptom of a deep moral crisis. It is significant that Alexis wrote this novel after what he regarded as the disastrous outcome of the Revolution of 1848, another crisis point in Prussian history.

In his portrayal of prewar society Alexis shows that moral corruption is widespread in the upper classes, whereas "das Volk" (the common people) still preserve their values. Kriegsrat (War Councillor) Alltag, an honest civil servant, has a daughter, Adelheid, of exceptional beauty. This beauty attracts members of the upper classes to her. The Legationsrat (legation councillor) von Wandel secures Adelheid a position in the household of the Geheimrätin (wife of the privy councillor) Lupinus. There she is tutored by Walter von Asten, the son of a rich merchant. His friend Louis Bovillard, the profligate son of a high-ranking diplomat, falls in love with Adelheid and eventually finds his way to an honest patriotism. Adelheid initially falls in love with Walter but comes to understand that he is totally devoted to rebuilding his fatherland. He becomes an assistant to Karl, Reichsfreiherr vom und zum Stein, the Prussian minister who, in his short tenure in 1807–1808, initiated the reforms that started the country on its way to recovery. Adelheid escapes from the corrupt milieu of Lupinus and Wandel, finally entering the entourage of Queen Luise of Prussia. During her rise to the top Adelheid sees both the bright and the dark sides of high society. Bovillard dies after warning Queen Luise of impending danger after the battle of Jena. On his deathbed he is united in marriage with Adelheid. Not only is there no happy ending to the love story, but the political outcome also is left open. Compared to the previous Vaterländische Romane, the number of lengthy political debates in this novel is conspicuous. Alexis wanted the work to generate discussion of current issues.

Isegrimm (1854) is chronologically the last novel in the series. The bulk of the action takes place between 1807 and 1810, but it extends into the 1830s. The novel is set in the Havel region of the Mark Brandenburg, where the resistance to the French occupation and the movement for a moral and political renewal are centered. Paradoxically, Alexis chooses as his protagonist Herr von der Quarbitz, who is modeled on Friedrich August Ludwig von der Marwitz, the leader of the conservative opposition to the planned reforms of the governments of Stein and his successor, Karl August von Hardenberg. Stein and Hardenberg considered eliminating most of the privileges of the nobility; opening all careers, including that of military officer, to all classes; self-government for the cities; instituting free trade; abolishing serfdom; emancipating the Jews; and making sweeping reforms in education and the army. Quarbitz is forced to witness the breakdown of the old social order after the French Revolution. Fortunes and titles of nobility are now acquired instantaneously. Quarbitz's daughter Karoline marries the French colonel d'Espinac, an adventurer of uncertain origin. Another daughter, Wilhelmine, who has bourgeois tastes and attitudes, marries Reichsgraf (Count) von Waltron, a true aristocrat. Amalie, her father's favorite, almost breaks his heart when she insists on marrying the liberal clergyman Mauritz. Around this family drama a larger picture unfolds. The guerrilla warfare against the French in the town of Nauwalk and the village of Querbelitz brings together characters from all classes and walks of life. In the triumphant rise to arms in 1813 both Quarbitz and Mauritz demonstrate their courage. The deaths of Quarbitz and Mauritz in the 1830s close the novel and a chapter of Prussian history. Both the old conservatism and humanistic liberalism are now things of the past; the future is uncertain.

This series of historical novels reveals that Alexis believed in a healthy counterbalance of all social classes, not an egalitarian system. He was opposed to absolutism but also to a written constitution. He saw history as a natural alternation of birth and decay. He considered it futile to go against the tide of history, although his sympathy lay with tragic figures who try to oppose new trends that they consider harmful. He portrayed men and women of all social classes and never gave in to the temptation to glorify legendary figures such as King Friedrich II or the Great Elector, Friedrich Wilhelm. While Alexis believed that social classes were natural phenomena, he pleaded for an open system in which a person of merit could rise to the top.

The period of Alexis's major activities saw the rise not only of the historical novel but also of the Zeitroman (novel providing social commentary on contemporary events). Alexis tried his hand at the genre, without much success, in *Das Haus Düsterweg* (The House of Düsterweg, 1835), an epistolary novel that focuses on the literary scene but also has political aspects. Epistolary novels were no longer popular in the 1830s, but the form gave Alexis the opportunity to express a variety of viewpoints and allowed for unlimited digressions. The convoluted plot involves the familiar love-hate relationship of two brothers who were separated as infants and do not know that they are brothers. Eberhard, a revolutionary and writer brought up by a government official and then by a cynical doctor, meets another writer, Baron Landschaden von Düsterweg. Eberhard despairs of the world, goes insane, and perishes during a revolution while Landschaden attempts in vain to rescue him. Landschaden is a moderate who is rejected by the reactionaries as well as by ultraliberals such as the writer Ludwig Börne, who makes a brief appearance in the novel. Eberhard and Landschaden are illegitimate sons of the late Baron von Düsterweg, a misanthrope who

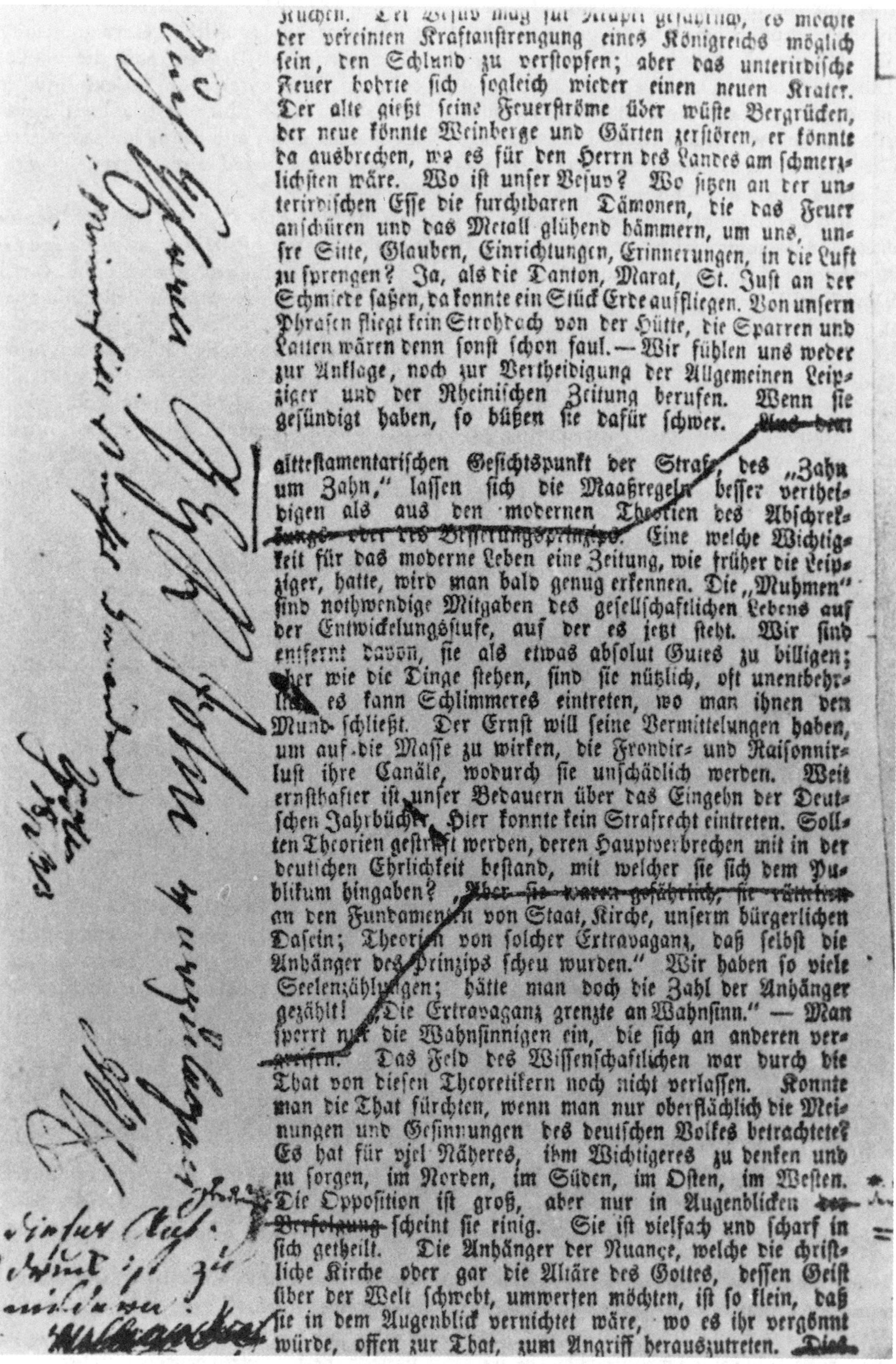

[illegible] es möchte der vereinten Kraftanstrengung eines Königreichs möglich sein, den Schlund zu verstopfen; aber das unterirdische Feuer bohrte sich sogleich wieder einen neuen Krater. Der alte gießt seine Feuerströme über wüste Bergrücken, der neue könnte Weinberge und Gärten zerstören, er könnte da ausbrechen, wo es für den Herrn des Landes am schmerzlichsten wäre. Wo ist unser Vesuv? Wo sitzen an der unterirdischen Esse die furchtbaren Dämonen, die das Feuer anschüren und das Metall glühend hämmern, um uns, unsre Sitte, Glauben, Einrichtungen, Erinnerungen, in die Luft zu sprengen? Ja, als die Danton, Marat, St. Just an der Schmiede saßen, da konnte ein Stück Erde auffliegen. Von unsern Phrasen fliegt kein Strohdach von der Hütte, die Sparren und Latten wären denn sonst schon faul.—Wir fühlen uns weder zur Anklage, noch zur Vertheidigung der Allgemeinen Leipziger und der Rheinischen Zeitung berufen. Wenn sie gesündigt haben, so büßen sie dafür schwer. Aus dem alttestamentarischen Gesichtspunkt der Strafe, des „Zahn um Zahn," lassen sich die Maaßregeln besser vertheidigen als aus den modernen Theorien des Abschreckungs- oder des Besserungsprinzips. Eine welche Wichtigkeit für das moderne Leben eine Zeitung, wie früher die Leipziger, hatte, wird man bald genug erkennen. Die „Muhmen" sind nothwendige Mitgaben des gesellschaftlichen Lebens auf der Entwickelungsstufe, auf der es jetzt steht. Wir sind entfernt davon, sie als etwas absolut Gutes zu billigen; aber wie die Dinge stehen, sind sie nützlich, oft unentbehrlich, es kann Schlimmeres eintreten, wo man ihnen den Mund schließt. Der Ernst will seine Vermittelungen haben, um auf die Masse zu wirken, die Frondir- und Raisonnirlust ihre Canäle, wodurch sie unschädlich werden. Weit ernsthafter ist unser Bedauern über das Eingehn der Deutschen Jahrbücher. Hier konnte kein Strafrecht eintreten. Sollten Theorien gestraft werden, deren Hauptverbrechen mit in der deutschen Ehrlichkeit bestand, mit welcher sie sich dem Publikum hingaben? „Aber sie waren gefährlich, sie rüttelten an den Fundamenten von Staat, Kirche, unserm bürgerlichen Dasein; Theorien von solcher Extravaganz, daß selbst die Anhänger des Prinzips scheu wurden." Wir haben so viele Seelenzählungen; hätte man doch die Zahl der Anhänger gezählt! „Die Extravaganz grenzte an Wahnsinn." — Man sperrt nur die Wahnsinnigen ein, die sich an anderen vergreifen. Das Feld des Wissenschaftlichen war durch die That von diesen Theoretikern noch nicht verlassen. Konnte man die That fürchten, wenn man nur oberflächlich die Meinungen und Gesinnungen des deutschen Volkes betrachtete? Es hat für viel Näheres, ihm Wichtigeres zu denken und zu sorgen, im Norden, im Süden, im Osten, im Westen. Die Opposition ist groß, aber nur in Augenblicken der Verfolgung scheint sie einig. Sie ist vielfach und scharf in sich getheilt. Die Anhänger der Nuance, welche die christliche Kirche oder gar die Altäre des Gottes, dessen Geist über der Welt schwebt, umwerfen möchten, ist so klein, daß sie in dem Augenblick vernichtet wäre, wo es ihr vergönnt würde, offen zur That, zum Angriff herauszutreten. Dies

Part of a galley proof for an article Alexis wrote for the Vossische Zeitung *in 1843, showing emendations by the censors (from H. H. Houben,* Der ewige Zensor, *1978)*

left a grotesque will that puts a succession of roadblocks in the way of his heir. Landschaden finally claims the inheritance, marries, and retires to the ruined Düsterweg castle. The novel attempts to provide a panorama of the contemporary scene, but most of its allusions will be lost on modern readers; even in its own time it had a negative reception.

Although Alexis made his name in narrative fiction, he also wrote ballads. His small volume titled *Balladen* (1836) contains romantic ballads, ballads with elements of the supernatural, ballads with Spanish and English settings, and Volkslieder (folk ballads), including his popular song "Friedericus Rex."

Alexis wrote a considerable number of novellas; while they should not be compared to later nineteenth century masterworks by writers such as Gottfried Keller and Theodor Storm, there are interesting and well-told stories among them. "Eine Parlamentswahl" (A Parliamentary Election), in the collection *Neue Novellen* (New Novellas, 1836), humorously describes a small-town election campaign contested by the Whigs, the Tories, and the radicals in contemporary England. The narrator is clearly fascinated by the commotion but sees little to recommend a transfer of such practices to Germany. Political parties did not exist in Germany at that time, and public life was subdued under the watchful eyes of the police. Thus, the contrast with England and its boisterous campaigns is all the more telling.

One of Alexis's better-known novellas, "Herr von Sacken," was published in the *Deutsches Taschenbuch* (German Pocketbook) in 1837. It is set in Russia in the early eighteenth century. The action centers around Sacken, a member of the old aristocracy, and Biron, an opportunist who rises to become duke of Kurland and the most powerful man in Russia. There is no hero: Sacken deserves his failures, but Biron does not deserve his victories. Alexis offers colorful descriptions of student life in Königsberg (today Kaliningrad), of the German aristocracy in the Baltic states, and of the nationalist conflicts in the region. The arbitrary nature of the Russian regime seems to be demonstrated when Sacken is banished to Siberia; but the banishment is only a cruel joke played by Biron, and all ends well. The message is that it does not pay to challenge political power. The story is told with a good dose of humor, and Sacken is reminiscent of some of E. T. A. Hoffmann's characters. The narrator bemoans the loss of political independence by the Baltic states, and he is anything but sympathetic with Biron and his opportunistic tactics.

In 1837 Alexis met Laetitia Perceval, an Englishwoman living with a German family. They were married on 21 May 1838; the couple had no children. The enterprising Alexis invested in a bookstore, the Berliner Lesekabinett (Berlin Reading Room), and a publishing house connected with it. He also speculated in real estate, but with limited success.

In 1841 Alexis entered into collaboration with his old friend Julius Hitzig, a writer and expert on crime, to edit *Der neue Pitaval* (The New Pitaval, 1842–1862), a thirty-volume collection of accounts of noteworthy criminal cases patterned after François Gayot de Pitaval's *Causes célèbres et interessantes avec les jugemens qui les ont decidées* (1735–1745). Alexis did most of the writing, and he carried on after Hitzig's death in 1849. The editors plead for an enlightened system of justice, tolerance, and humane treatment of prisoners. The collection includes both recent and historical cases from various countries, especially England and France.

Der neue Pitaval is a ready-made sourcebook for literature, and Alexis used some of the material for his documentary novel *Urban Grandier* (1843). In Loudun, France, in the seventeenth century the priest Urban Grandier was accused of having a compact with the devil and was burned at the stake. The novel includes political intrigues, outbreaks of female hysteria, illicit love, hatred and revenge, corruption in the administration, factions in the Catholic church, and the use of superstition for political purposes. The narrator remains objective, although his point of view is clearly discernible.

In 1842 Alexis became a columnist for the *Vossische Zeitung* (Voss's Newspaper) in Berlin, but he soon fell afoul of the censors and gave up the position. An extended trip to Italy with his wife in 1847–1848 was cut short by the news of the revolutions in Germany. Alexis felt it his duty to become involved, and in 1849 he served as political editor of the *Vossische Zeitung;* again, he was thwarted by censorship.

Dejected by the failure of the revolution and feeling the strain of overexertion, Alexis began to retire from the Berlin literary and political scenes. He spent the summer of 1851 in Arnstadt in Thüringen, and he liked it so much that he made it his permanent home in 1857. Early in 1856 he had suffered a stroke that partially incapacitated him; a more severe stroke in 1860 left him unable to write. In 1867 he was honored by King Wilhelm I of Prussia with the Hohenzollernscher Hausorden (Hohenzollern Royal Order). He died on 16 December 1871.

Bibliographies:

Karl Goedeke, *Grundriß zur Geschichte der deutschen Dichtung,* volume 9 (1910), pp. 448-483, volume 15 (1955), pp. 107-118, 984-985;

Paul K. Richter, *Willibald Alexis als Literatur- und Theaterkritiker* (Berlin: Ebering, 1931).

Biography:

Lionel Thomas, *Willibald Alexis, A German Writer of the Nineteenth Century* (Oxford: Blackwell, 1964).

References:

Wolfgang Beutin, *Königtum und Adel in den historischen Romanen von Willibald Alexis* (Berlin: Schmidt, 1966);

Hildegard Emmel, *Geschichte des deutschen Romans,* volume 2 (Bern: Francke, 1975);

Theodor Fontane, "Willibald Alexis," in his *Sämtliche Werke,* part 1, volume 21 (Munich: Nymphenburger Verlagsanstalt, 1963), pp. 154-213;

Gerhard Friesen, *The German Panoramic Novel of the 19th Century* (Bern & Frankfurt am Main: Lang, 1972);

Wolfgang Gast, *Der deutsche Geschichtsroman im 19. Jahrhundert: Willibald Alexis. Untersuchungen zur Technik seiner "Vaterländischen Romane"* (Freiburg im Breisgau: Universitätsverlag Becksmann, 1972);

Hermann August Korff, *Scott und Alexis: Eine Studie zur Technik des historischen Romans* (Heidelberg: Hörning & Berkenbusch, 1907);

Paul K. Richter, *Willibald Alexis als Literatur- und Theaterkritiker* (Berlin: Ebering, 1931);

Julian Schmidt, "Willibald Alexis: Eine Studie," *Westermanns Monatshefte* (February 1872): 417-432, 514-531;

Friedrich Sengle, *Biedermeier: Deutsche Literatur im Spannungsfeld zwischen Restauration und Revolution 1815-1848,* volumes 1 and 2 (Stuttgart: Metzler, 1971-1972);

Hartmut Steinecke, *Romantheorie und Romankritik in Deutschland,* volume 1: *Die Entwicklung des Gattungsverständnisses von der Scott-Rezeption bis zum programmatischen Realismus* (Stuttgart: Metzler, 1975);

Lynne Tatlock, *Willibald Alexis' Zeitroman* Das Haus Düsterweg *and the Vormärz* (Frankfurt am Main, Bern & New York: Lang, 1984);

Lionel Thomas, "Willibald Alexis: Tagebuchauszug und Briefwechsel der Jahre 1829-1835," *Zeitschrift für deutsche Philologie,* 95 (1976): 213-235;

Thomas, "Willibald Alexis und seine Zeitgenossen," *Zeitschrift für deutsche Philologie,* 75 (1956): 162-171.

Berthold Auerbach

(28 February 1812 – 8 February 1882)

Nancy Kaiser
University of Wisconsin – Madison

BOOKS: *Friedrich der Große, König von Preußen: Sein Leben und Wirken; nebst einer gedrängten Geschichte des siebenjährigen Krieges. Für Leser aller Stände nach den besten Quellen historisch-biographisch bearbeitet,* as Theobald Chauber (Stuttgart: Scheible, 1834);

Das Judenthum und die neueste Literatur: Kritischer Versuch (Stuttgart: Brodhag, 1836);

Spinoza: Ein historischer Roman, 2 volumes (Stuttgart: Scheible, 1837); revised as *Spinoza: Ein Denkerleben* (Mannheim: Bassermann & Mathy, 1854); translated by E. Nicholson as *Spinoza: A Novel,* 2 volumes (Leipzig: Tauchnitz / London: Low, Marston, Searle & Rivington, 1882);

Dichter und Kaufmann: Ein Lebensgemälde, 2 volumes (Stuttgart: Krabbe, 1840); revised as *Dichter und Kaufmann: Ein Lebensgemälde aus der Zeit Moses Mendelssohns* (Mannheim: Bassermann, 1855); translated by Charles T. Brooks as *Poet and Merchant: A Picture of Life from the Time of Moses Mendelssohn* (New York: Holt, 1877);

Der gebildete Bürger: Buch für den denkenden Mittelstand (Karlsruhe: Bielefeld, 1843);

Schwarzwälder Dorfgeschichten, 2 volumes (Mannheim: Bassermann, 1843); excerpts translated by Meta Taylor as *Village Tales from the Black Forest,* 2 volumes (London: Bogue, 1846–1847); first complete edition in English translated by Charles Goepp as *Black Forest Village Stories* (New York: Leypolt & Holt, 1869);

Schrift und Volk: Grundzüge der volksthümlichen Literatur, angeschlossen an eine Charakteristik J. P. Hebels (Leipzig: Brockhaus, 1846);

Schwarzwälder Dorfgeschichten: Neue Folge (Mannheim: Bassermann, 1849) – includes "Die Frau Professorin," translated by Maria Howitt as *The Professor's Lady* (New York: Harper, 1850);

Tagebuch aus Wien: Von Latour bis auf Windischgrätz (September bis November 1848) (Breslau: Schletter, 1849); translated by John Edward Taylor as *Narrative of Events in Vienna, from Latour to Windischgrätz* (London: Bogue, 1849);

Berthold Auerbach

Andree Hofer: Geschichtliches Trauerspiel in fünf Aufzügen (Leipzig: Wigand, 1850);

Epilog zur Lessing-Feier: Nach der Aufführung von "Emilia Galotti" im Königlichen Hoftheater zu Dresden gesprochen von Emil Devrient (Dresden: Arnold, 1850);

Deutsche Abende (Mannheim: Bassermann, 1851);

Neues Leben: Eine Erzählung, 3 volumes (Mannheim: Bassermann, 1852);

Schwarzwälder Dorfgeschichten, volume 3 (Mannheim: Bassermann, 1853);
Schwarzwälder Dorfgeschichten, volume 4 (Mannheim: Bassermann & Mathy, 1854);
Der Wahlbruder: Trauerspiel in fünf Aufzügen (Dresden: Teuber, 1855);
Barfüßele (Stuttgart: Cotta, 1856); translated by Edward H. Wehnert as *The Barefooted Maiden* (London: Low, 1857);
Gesammelte Schriften (20 volumes, Stuttgart: Cotta, 1857–1858; republished, 22 volumes, Stuttgart: Cotta, 1863–1864);
Der Wahrspruch: Schauspiel in fünf Akten (Leipzig: Weber, 1859);
Joseph im Schnee: Eine Erzählung (Stuttgart: Cotta, 1860); translated anonymously as *Joseph in the Snow* (New York & London: Lovell, 1867);
Edelweiß: Eine Erzählung (Stuttgart: Cotta, 1861); translated by Ellen Frothingham as *Edelweiss* (Boston: Roberts, 1869);
Goethe und die Erzählungskunst: Vortrag, zum Besten des Goethe-Denkmals gehalten in der Sing-Akademie zu Berlin (Stuttgart: Cotta, 1861);
Auf der Höhe: Roman in acht Büchern, 3 volumes (Stuttgart: Cotta, 1865); translated by Fanny E. Bunnett as *On the Heights,* 3 volumes (Leipzig: Tauchnitz / New York: Leypoldt & Holt, 1867);
Der Kuß des Kaisers: Mit einem kleinen Vorwort als Spende zum Passa-Fest der Israeliten 1866. Allen wohlwollenden Gönnern und wahren Freunden gewidmet hochachtungsvoll von Ferdinand Maria Friedmann (Munich: Deschler, 1866);
Deutsche Abende: Neue Folge (Stuttgart: Cotta, 1867); translated by Joseph L. Lowdell as *German Evenings* (London: Chapman & Hall, 1869; Boston: Roberts, 1869) – includes selections by other authors;
Das Landhaus am Rhein: Roman, 5 volumes (Stuttgart: Cotta, 1869); translated by James Davis as *The Villa on the Rhine* (New York: Leypoldt & Holt, 1869);
Wieder Unser!: Gedenkblätter zur Geschichte dieser Tage (Stuttgart: Cotta, 1871);
Zur guten Stunde: Gesammelte Volkserzählungen, 2 volumes (Stuttgart: Hoffmann, 1872); translated by Henry William Dulcken as *The Good Hour; or, Evening Holiday* (London & New York: Routledge, 1875);
Waldfried, 3 volumes (Stuttgart: Cotta, 1874); translated by Simon A. Stern as *Waldfried: A Novel* (New York: Holt, 1874); translated anonymously as *Waldfried,* 3 volumes (London: Low, 1874);
Tausend Gedanken des Collaborators (Berlin: Hofmann, 1875);
Drei einzige Töchter: Novellen (Stuttgart: Cotta, 1875);
Nicolaus Lenau: Erinnerung und Betrachtung. Vortrag (Vienna: Gerold, 1876);
Nach dreißig Jahren: Neue Dorfgeschichten, 3 volumes (Stuttgart: Cotta, 1876) – includes "Des Lorles Reinhard," translated by Charles Brooks as *Loreley and Reinhard* (New York: Holt, 1877);
Das erlösende Wort: Lustspiel in einem Aufzug (Leipzig: Mutze, 1877);
Riegel vor!: Stimmungsbild (Berlin: Mosse, 1877);
Landolin von Reutershöfen: Erzählung (Berlin: Paetel, 1878); translated by Annie B. Irish as *Landolin* (New York: Holt, 1880);
Unterwegs: Kleine Geschichten und Lustspiele (Berlin: Paetel, 1879);
Der Forstmeister: Roman, 2 volumes (Berlin: Paetel, 1879); translated anonymously as *The Foresters* (New York: Appleton, 1880);
Eine seltene Frau: Lustspiel in einem Aufzug (Berlin: Mosse, 1880);
Brigitta: Erzählung (Stuttgart: Cotta, 1880); translated by Clara Bell as *Brigitta* (Leipzig: Tauchnitz / London: Low, 1880);
Die Genesis des Nathan: Gedenkworte zu Lessing's 100jährigem Todestag (Berlin: Auerbach, 1881);
Dramatische Eindrücke: Aus dem Nachlasse, edited by Otto Neumann-Hofer (Stuttgart: Cotta, 1893).

OTHER: *Friedrich der Große, König von Preußen: Seine Sämmtlichen werke in einer Auswahl des Geistvollsten für Leser aller stände bearbeitet,* edited by Auerbach as Theobald Chauber (Stuttgart: Scheible, 1835);
Galerie der ausgezeichnetsten Israeliten aller Jahrhunderte, ihre Porträts und Biographien, volume 4, with contributions by Auerbach, edited by Auerbach and N. Frankfurter (Stuttgart: Brodhag, 1836);
Galerie der ausgezeichnetsten Israeliten aller Jahrhunderte, ihre Porträts und Biographien, volume 5, edited with contributions by Auerbach (Stuttgart: Brodhag, 1838);
Baruch von Spinozas sämtliche Werke: Aus dem Lateinischen mit dem Leben Spinozas, 5 volumes, edited and translated by Auerbach (Stuttgart: Scheible, Rieger & Sattler, 1841);
Der Gevattersmann: Neuer Kalender für den Stadt- und Landbürger, 5 volumes (volumes 1–3, Karlsruhe: Gutsch & Rupp, 1844–1846; volumes 4 and 5, Brunswick: Westermann, 1847, 1848);
Schatzkästlein des Gevattersmanns, edited by Auerbach (Stuttgart: Cotta, 1856);

Deutscher Familienkalender auf das Jahr 1858, edited by Auerbach (Stuttgart: Cotta, 1858);

Deutscher Familienkalender auf das Jahr 1859, edited by Auerbach (Stuttgart: Cotta, 1859);

Deutscher Volks-Kalender, 10 volumes, edited by Auerbach (Leipzig: Keil, 1860–1869);

Eduard Lasker, *Erlebnisse einer Mannes-Seele,* edited by Auerbach (Stuttgart: Cotta, 1873);

Benjamin Franklin: Sein Leben, von ihm selbst beschrieben, translated and edited by Auerbach (Stuttgart: Auerbach, 1876);

Deutsche illustrierte Volksbücher, 3 volumes, edited by Auerbach (Stuttgart: Cotta, 1880–1881).

The writer and cultural critic Berthold Auerbach witnessed and recorded the turbulence of his century. His life began in the Napoleonic period, a time of fragmentation and unrest for German lands, and ended in the consolidated German Empire. As a Jew who insistently sought to assert the compatibility of his Jewish heritage with German culture, he experienced keenly the tensions between Germans and Jews in the nineteenth century. A celebrated author during his lifetime, Auerbach traveled widely and played an active role in literary and cultural circles in various German cities. Throughout his career he wrote Dorfgeschichten (village tales) about his native region, the Black Forest, and the stories formed a central focus of debates concerning literary realism in journals in the 1840s. His works were widely read and translated; between 1847 and 1882 only the writings of Johann Wolfgang von Goethe and Friedrich Schiller were more often reprinted or reviewed in the United States. The Russian writers Leo Tolstoy and Ivan Turgenev were impressed by Auerbach's novels, and his essays and reviews appeared in major newspapers and journals. In his writings and life Auerbach consistently attempted to integrate the liberal humanist tradition of the Enlightenment, his German identity, and his Jewish heritage.

The grandson of a rabbi, Moses Baruch Auerbacher – the name Berthold Auerbach dates from his schooldays – was born on 28 February 1812 in Nordstetten in the Black Forest, the ninth of twelve children of Jacob and Edel Frank Auerbacher. The Jewish community comprised 40 percent of the population of Nordstetten. Although there was little tension between Jews and Christians in Nordstetten, Auerbach was once the victim of anti-Semitic cruelty at the hands of a band of young boys from the neighboring village of Horb. He was educated in Hebrew and in German at the first German school founded by a Jewish congregation in Württemberg; Bernhard Frankfurter, one of his teachers, was to remain a mentor and friend. Following his Bar Mitzvah, Auerbach attended a school in Hechingen devoted to the study of the Talmud. In 1827 he was sent to school in Karlsruhe. There he met a distant relative, Jakob Auerbach, who became another lifelong friend. Auerbach's letters to Jakob, beginning in 1830, offer insights into the stages of his life and career.

In 1830, after passing a special entrance examination on the second attempt, Auerbach enrolled at the gymnasium in Stuttgart. Two years later he entered the University of Tübingen, where he initially studied law but then returned to his original plan to follow in his grandfather's footsteps and become a rabbi. A student and follower of Gabriel Riesser, a forceful proponent of political equality for German Jews, Auerbach was intellectually shaped also by his contacts with the liberal Protestant theologian David Friedrich Strauß, the writer Ludwig Uhland, and the Jewish reformer Abraham Geiger. Accused of participation in revolutionary acts allegedly carried out by the fraternity Germania, he was arrested in June 1833. Although Auerbach was opposed to the reactionary regimes in German lands, his participation in Germania had been limited to social interaction. At the time of his arrest Auerbach was studying at the University of Munich, where he had moved partly to avoid the police and partly to elude his creditors in Tübingen. He was expelled from the university; he moved on to Heidelberg University, but his professional plans had undergone a radical change: due to the arrest a career as a rabbi was closed to him.

During his Heidelberg years he partially financed his studies by writing a biography of the Prussian king Friedrich II and editing a selection of the king's writings. Readily apparent in the biography, *Friedrich der Große, König von Preußen* (Frederick the Great, King of Prussia, 1834), published under the pseudonym Theobald Chauber, is Auerbach's talent for anecdotal narrative. As a historical work the volume has little merit; Auerbach never included it in editions of his collected works. But the project did immerse him in the intellectual tradition of the German Enlightenment, a heritage that was to prove formative for his career.

Auerbach wrote several of the biographical essays in the two volumes he edited of *Galerie der ausgezeichnetsten Israeliten aller Jahrhunderte, ihre Porträts und Biographien* (Gallery of the Most Outstanding Israelis of all Centuries, Their Portraits and Biographies, 1836, 1838), including the entry on Riesser. The pamphlet *Das Judenthum und die neueste Literatur* (Jewry and Recent Literature, 1836) is a defense of Jewish culture and a demonstration of its inherent bond with German culture. Auerbach's goal was integration without renunciation of the Jewish heritage. Auerbach also sought in the pamphlet to discredit Heinrich Heine and to distance himself from the group of writers known as the Young Germans. In 1837 he was sentenced to two months in the Hohenasperg prison for his association with Germania.

The philosopher Baruch Spinoza had long been an important figure for Auerbach, both intellectually and emotionally, and in 1837 Auerbach's novel *Spinoza* (translated, 1882) was published. Auerbach was fascinated by the Amsterdam sage's valiant struggle against narrow-minded orthodoxy, his insistence on spiritual values, his faith in rationality, his humanistic pantheism, and his underlying Jewish identity. The novel illustrates Auerbach's conviction that the Jewish heritage could be combined with the principles of the German Enlightenment. The novel sold fairly well, but mostly after Auerbach's reputation had been established in the 1840s with his village tales.

In early 1838 Auerbach moved to Frankfurt am Main to become the drama critic and later the literary critic for the journal *Europa*. The main accomplishment of his time in Frankfurt am Main was *Dichter und Kaufmann* (1840; translated as *Poet and Merchant,* 1877), a biography of the little-known eighteenth-century German-Jewish writer Ephraim Kuh. It provides an opposing portrait to that of the strong figure of Spinoza: Kuh does not achieve a synthesis of German culture and his Jewish heritage. His failure, and the miserable personal life that accompanied it, indicate the necessity of such a synthesis. In 1840 Auerbach moved to Bonn; the following year he became the editor of an almanac in Karlsruhe.

In the 1840s Auerbach found the genre most suited to him, the one that was to bring him popularity and a place in literary history. *Schwarzwälder Dorfgeschichten* (1843; translated as *Black Forest Village Stories,* 1869) established his reputation and played an important role in discussions of literary realism. The stories allowed Auerbach to indulge his talents for short narrative forms, vivid characterization and description, anecdotal stories, generally clear-cut moral lessons, and local color. Several of the tales had appeared in journals, and it took several attempts to find a publisher for the book. But in 1843 Friedrich Bassermann, a newly established publisher in Mannheim, printed a collection of seven short tales and two longer stories. The venture came at a critical moment for Auerbach; he had tried his hand at drama with marked lack of success and was in financial difficulty. The Black Forest tales brought him money and fame, and in 1845 he resigned his editorship to live as a freelance author. The stories were praised for their simplicity and their positive portrayal of the German Volk (people). Further collections were published in 1849, 1853, and 1854.

Auerbach in 1846; painting by J. Hübner (Archiv für Kunst und Geschichte, Berlin)

In the treatise *Schrift und Volk* (Writing and the People, 1846) Auerbach depicts the task of literature as the inculcation of "thatige Humanität" (active humanity) and defines the concept of the "Volk" as including a common soul and shared traditions at all levels of a nation. In the 1840s such a perspective placed Auerbach in the moderate liberal tradition; in his political beliefs he was a constitutional monarchist.

In 1847 Auerbach married Auguste Schreiber, whom he had met in Breslau; they settled in Heidelberg. During the upheavals that took place across Europe in 1848, Auerbach was in Vienna. His diary from this period, *Tagebuch aus Wien* (1849; translated as *Narrative of Events in Vienna,* 1849), is testimony to his liberal stance. In the spring of 1848, a month after the birth of their son, Konrad Berthold August, Auguste Auerbach died of lacteal fever. Grief-stricken, Auerbach moved with his son to Breslau to be near

Pencil sketch of Auerbach, made on 7 August 1855 by Carl Spitzweg (Schiller-Nationalmuseum, Marbach am Neckar)

his in-laws. He remained close to his first father-in-law even after his marriage to Nina Landesmann on 1 July 1849. He had made the acquaintance of the Landesmann family in Vienna in 1848; Nina's brother Heinrich was a writer known under the pseudonym Hieronymous Lorm. The second marriage was a stormy one, but it produced three children: Ottilie Agnes Philippine, born in 1850; Eugen Rudolf Berthold, born in 1852; and Rudolf Hermann Berthold, born in 1855.

In 1849, while living in Dresden and participating in the weekly meetings of the literary circle Montagsgesellschaft (Monday Society), Auerbach once again attempted a dramatic work. The result was *Andree Hofer* (1850); even his closest friends advised him to revise, cut the manuscript by half, or abandon the project. The drama centers around Andreas Hofer, an eighteenth-century Tirolean freedom fighter against the French. It reflects Auerbach's liberal sentiments and desire for political reform, but it does not do justice to the historical complexities nor is it dramatically well constructed. Living in the same house in Dresden as the sculptor Ernst Rietschel, Auerbach worked with the writer Karl Gutzkow and the theater director Eduard Devrient to raise money for Rietschel's statue of Gotthold Ephraim Lessing. In similar fashion he would later be involved in promoting the statue of Goethe and Schiller in Weimar. A close friend of the writer Nikolaus Lenau, who had gone insane in 1844, Auerbach composed a tribute to his colleague in the story "Erinnerung und Betrachtung: Lenaus letzter Sommer" (Remembrance and Observation: Lenau's Final Summer, 1849) in the journal *Deutsches Museum* (German Museum). A collection of his philosophical novellas appeared in 1851 under the title *Deutsche Abende* (German Evenings).

The hero of Auerbach's novel *Neues Leben* (New Life, 1852), Count Eugen Falkenberg, takes part in the revolutionary uprisings of 1848 and then trades places with a village schoolteacher, enabling the latter to immigrate to the United States. In his new identity as the schoolteacher Eugen Baumann the count works for reform through education. The novel was not particularly successful, but it had at least one ardent admirer. Years later a stranger entered Auerbach's study and announced that he was Eugen Baumann. The visitor praised *Neues Leben* effusively, described a similar village school that he had established on his own estate, and then revealed that he was Leo Tolstoy.

The novel was not really Auerbach's strong suit; the author Gustav Freytag, a close friend and editor of the influential journal *Die Grenzboten* (The Border Messengers), addressed a public letter to Auerbach in 1852 urging him to return to the village tale, the genre in which he was master. The third volume of *Schwarzwälder Dorfgeschichten*, published in 1853, included "Die Geschichte des Diethelm von Buchenberg" (The Story of Diethelm von Buchenberg), a psychological tale of an ambitious peasant led astray by financial speculation and insurance fraud. The story criticizes aspects of contemporary capitalism and emphasizes the values of modesty and simplicity.

In 1855 Auerbach was considering a trip to the United States to gain fresh ideas, but his publisher Bassermann suggested that he visit the Black Forest instead. A few months later Bassermann committed suicide. Auerbach signed a contract with the Cotta firm, the major publisher of German literature in this period. Cotta published Auerbach's *Barfüßele* (1856; translated as *The Barefooted Maiden,* 1857); originally titled "Das neue Aschenputtel" (The New Cinderella), it is the tale of an orphaned country girl who marries and moves to the city. The plot is realistic rather than of a fairy-tale nature, but it is also extremely sentimental. The work became a best-seller.

Auerbach's other Dresden activities included editing yearly almanacs containing anecdotes, stories, essays, and illustrations. Such projects were in keeping with his conviction that popular literature should have a didactic emphasis. Having worked diligently for the establishment of the Deutsche Schillerstiftung (Schiller Foundation) in 1855, Auerbach was deeply wounded when he was not chosen for a seat on its board; anti-Semitism may have been a factor. When the writer Hermann Hettner was chosen to fill the first vacancy on the board, Auerbach requested an explanation. Hettner submitted a letter of resignation, but it insulted Auerbach by calling him childish. Auerbach never forgave Hettner.

In late 1859 Auerbach left Dresden for Berlin. In the Prussian capital he found respect and friendship and received financial assistance from the court, but the Black Forest author never felt at home there. Trips to his homeland were always necessary for renewed artistic productivity. Much in demand as a keynote speaker at cultural events, he also edited the cultural section of the popular magazine *Die Gartenlaube* (The Arbor).

Auerbach's novel *Auf der Höhe* (1865; translated as *On the Heights,* 1867) traces the paths of two women, juxtaposing the spheres of the court and rural life. Walpurga is a peasant woman who comes to court as a wet nurse for the queen; her innocence is contrasted with the corrupt royal life-style. Countess Irma Wildenort, the strong-willed daughter of a reform-minded count, becomes the mistress of the king; later she does penance in the simplicity of a rural existence.

Between 1866 and 1869 Auerbach spent a considerable amount of time in the Rheingau area, and his next novel, *Das Landhaus am Rhein* (1869; translated as *The Villa on the Rhine,* 1869), reflected his surroundings. Having recently become wealthy, the Sonnenkamp family settles in a villa on the Rhine River and hires a tutor for their pampered son Roland. The tutor, Dournay, educates Roland with precepts borrowed from Benjamin Franklin and marries the Sonnenkamps' daughter. The dreadful secret behind the sudden accumulation of wealth is eventually exposed: it was gleaned through the slave trade in the New World. The father returns to America to fight for the Confederacy in the Civil War and is killed. Roland undertakes the same journey but fights for the North, at times with a regiment of freed slaves.

One of Auerbach's long-cherished dreams came true with the unification of German lands under Prussian leadership in 1871. His immediate reaction to the Franco-Prussian War and the founding of the German Empire in 1870–1871 was jubilation. A collection of his writings from this period was published under the triumphant title *Wieder Unser!* (Ours Again!, 1871), referring to Strasbourg. Nevertheless, he felt pity for the besieged inhabitants of Strasbourg and left the camp of the Grand Duke of Baden where he was serving as a military correspondent for the *Augsburger Allgemeine Zeitung* (Augsburg General Newspaper), after only three weeks. His 1874 novel, *Waldfried* (translated as *Waldfried: A Novel,* 1874), gives his reading of the historical developments of his lifetime in the story of a southern German family from 1817 to 1870. The patriarch of the family, Heinrich Waldfried, is a sturdy German citizen who plays an active role in the National Assembly in Frankfurt am Main in 1848 and later serves in Parliament. The novel again reveals Auerbach's lack of aptitude for the longer narrative form.

The volume *Nach dreißig Jahren* (After Thirty Years, 1876) is a collection of stories revisiting characters and places familiar from his earlier village tales. Auerbach wrote a few more tales and plays before his death, but the rising tide of anti-Semitism in the German Empire came to occupy most of his time and energies. He was active in the disputes concerning the plight of the Jews in Romania, where civil rights were still being denied. He addressed a personal letter to Imperial Chancellor Otto von Bismarck concerning the circulation of the *Judenpetition* (Petition against the Jews). This petition, which Auerbach characterized as an attack on both constitutional law and the unwritten law of humanity, collected a quarter of a million signatures in 1880. It demanded the revocation of many of the legal and social rights that Jews had been granted in German lands in 1869. The *Judenpetition* precipitated two days of debate in the Imperial Diet on the status of Jews in the empire. After watching some of the parliamentary proceedings, Auerbach exclaimed: "Vergebens gelebt und gearbeitet" (I have lived and worked in vain). He says in a letter that the anti-Semitic activities of 1880–1881 caused "der Sturz von meinem Idealturm" (the precipitous fall from my tower of ideals). The emotional and intellectual turmoil added to the strain of a lung infection he contracted in 1881, and Auerbach died in Cannes, France, on 8 February 1882. In accordance with his wishes, he was buried in the Jewish cemetery in Nordstetten.

Letters:

Briefe an seinen Freund Jakob Auerbach: Ein biographisches Denkmal. Mit Vorbemerkungen von Friedrich Spielhagen und dem Herausgeber, edited by Jakob Auerbach (Frankfurt am Main: Literarische Anstalt Rütten & Loening, 1884);

Bräutigamsbriefe, edited by Anton Bettelheim (Berlin: Mosse, 1910);

Aus Ferdinand Hillers Briefwechsel: Beiträge zu einer Biographie Ferdinand Hillers, volume 6, edited by Reinhold Sietz (Cologne: Volk, 1968).

Bibliography:

Georg Minde-Pouet and Eva Rothe, eds., *Goedekes Grundriß zur Geschichte der deutschen Dichtung. Neue Folge,* volume 1 (Berlin: Akademie, 1962), pp. 475–554.

Biographies:

Anton Bettelheim, *Berthold Auerbach: Der Mann – Sein Werk – Sein Nachlaß* (Stuttgart & Berlin: Cotta, 1907);

Thomas Scheuffelen, *Berthold Auerbach 1812–1882* (Marbach: Deutsches Literaturarchiv, 1985).

References:

Uwe Baur, *Dorfgeschichte: Zur Entstehung und gesellschaftlichen Funktion einer literarischen Gattung im Vormärz* (Munich: Fink, 1978);

Werner Hahl, "Gesellschaftlicher Konservatismus und literarischer Realismus. Das Modell einer deutschen Sozialverfassung in den Dorfgeschichten," in *Realismus und Gründerzeit,* volume 1, edited by Hahl, M. Bucher, G. Jäger, and R. Wittmann (Stuttgart: Metzler, 1976), pp. 48–95;

Jürgen Hein, *Dorfgeschichte* (Stuttgart: Metzler, 1976);

Hans Otto Horch, "Gustav Freytag und Berthold Auerbach: Eine repräsentative deutsch-jüdische Schriftstellerfreundschaft im 19. Jahrhundert. Mit unveröffentlichten Briefen beider Autoren," *Jahrbuch der Raabe-Gesellschaft* (1985): 154–174;

Edna Huttenmaier-Spitz, "Studien zu den Schwarzwälder Dorfgeschichten Berthold Auerbachs," Ph.D. dissertation, University of Vienna, 1957;

Nancy Kaiser, "Berthold Auerbach: The Dilemma of the Jewish Humanist from *Vormärz* to Empire," *German Studies Review,* 6 (October 1983): 399–413;

Kaiser, " 'Die Stellung der Juden ist allezeit der Barometerstand der Humanität': Berthold Auerbachs Traum einer deutsch-jüdischen Symbiose," in *Jüdische Intelligenz in Deutschland,* edited by Jost Hermand and Gert Mattenklott (Hamburg: Argument, 1988), pp. 34–46;

Jacob Katz, "Berthold Auerbach's Anticipation of the German-Jewish Tragedy," *Hebrew Union College Annual,* 53 (1982): 215–240;

Hermann Kinder, *Poesie als Synthese: Ausbreitung eines deutschen Realismusverständnisses in der Mitte des 19. Jahrhunderts* (Frankfurt am Main: Athenäum, 1973);

Peter Mettenleitner, *Destruktion der Heimatdichtung: Typologische Untersuchungen zu Gotthelf-Auerbach-Ganghofer* (Tübingen: Tübingener Vereinigung für Volkskunde E. V. Tübinger Schloß, 1974);

Margarita Pazi, "Berthold Auerbach and Moritz Hartmann: Two Jewish Writers of the Nineteenth Century," in *Leo Baeck Institute Year Book 1973* (London: Leo Baeck Institute, 1973), pp. 201–218;

Pazi, "Berthold Auerbach – dem jüdischen Autor der deutschen Dorfgeschichte zum 100. Todestag," *Neue deutsche Hefte,* 173 (1982): 95–109;

Pazi, "Revolution und Demokratie im Leben und Werk von Berthold Auerbach," *Revolution und Demokratie in Geschichte und Literatur. Festschrift für Walter Grab zum 60. Geburtstag,* edited by J. H. Schoeps and I. Geiss (Duisburg: Walter Braun, 1979), pp. 355–374;

Jeffrey Sammons, "Observations on Berthold Auerbach's Jewish Novels," *Orim: A Jewish Journal at Yale,* 1 (Spring 1986): 61–74;

David Sorkin, "The Invisible Community: Emancipation, Secular Culture and Jewish Identity in the Writings of Berthold Auerbach," in *The Jewish Response to German Culture from the Enlightenment to the Second World War,* edited by Jehuda Reinharz and Walter Schatzberg (Hanover, N.H.: University Press of New England, 1985), pp. 100–119;

Moses Isaac Zwick, *Berthold Auerbachs sozialpolitischer und ethischer Liberalismus* (Stuttgart: Kohlhammer, 1933).

Papers:

Berthold Auerbach's papers are at the Deutsches Literaturarchiv, Marbach, Germany.

Bruno Bauer

(6 September 1809 - 13 April 1882)

Lawrence S. Stepelevich
Villanova University

BOOKS: *Kritik der Geschichte der Offenbarung, Theil 1, Band 2: Die Religion des Alten Testaments in der geschichtlichen Entwickelung ihrer Prinzipien dargestellt,* 2 volumes (Berlin: Dümmler, 1838-1839; reprinted, Aalen: Scientia, 1983);

Herr Dr. Hengstenberg: Kritische Briefe über den Gegensatz des Gesetzes und des Evangeliums (Berlin: Dümmler, 1839);

Kritik der evangelischen Geschichte des Johannes (Bremen: Schünemann, 1840);

Die evangelische Landeskirche Preußens und die Wissenschaft (Leipzig: Wigand, 1840; reprinted, Aalen: Scientia, 1972);

Kritik der evangelischen Geschichte der Synoptiker, 3 volumes (Leipzig: Wigand, 1841-1842; reprinted, Hildesheim: Olms, 1974);

Die Posaune des jüngsten Gerichts über Hegel den Atheisten und Antichristen: Ein Ultimatum, anonymous (Leipzig: Wigand, 1841; reprinted, Aalen: Scientia, 1969); translated by Lawrence S. Stepelevich as *The Trumpet of the Last Judgment against Hegel the Atheist and Antichrist: An Ultimatum* (Lewiston, N.Y.: Mellen, 1989);

Hegel's Lehre von der Religion und Kunst von dem Standpuncte des Glaubens aus beurtheilt (Leipzig: Wigand, 1842; reprinted, Aalen: Scientia, 1967);

Die gute Sache der Freiheit und meine eigene Angelegenheit (Zurich & Winterthur: Literarisches Comptoir, 1842; reprinted, Aalen: Scientia, 1972);

Die Judenfrage (Brunswick: Otto, 1843); translated by Helen Lederer as *The Jewish Problem* (Cincinnati: Hebrew Union College-Jewish Institute of Religion, 1958);

Das entdeckte Christenthum: Eine Erinnerung an das achtzehnte Jahrhundert und ein Beitrag zur Krisis des neunzehnten (Zurich: Literarisches Comptoir, 1843; reprinted, Aalen: Scientia, 1989);

Bouillé und die Flucht Ludwig XVI. (Charlottenburg: Bauer, 1843);

Bruno Bauer

Der 20. Juni und der 10. August 1792 oder Der letzte Kampf des Königthums in Frankreich mit der Volksparthei (Charlottenburg: Bauer, 1843);

Geschichte der Politik, Cultur und Aufklärung des achtzehnten Jahrhunderts, 2 volumes (Charlottenburg: Bauer, 1843-1845; reprinted, Aalen: Scientia, 1965);

Die Septembertage 1792 und die ersten Kämpfe der Partheien der Republik in Frankreich, 2 volumes (Charlottenburg: Bauer, 1844);

Der Process Ludwig XVI und der 21. Januar 1793 (Charlottenburg: Bauer, 1844);

Briefwechsel zwischen Bruno Bauer und Edgar Bauer während der Jahre 1839–1842 aus Bonn und Berlin (Charlottenburg: Bauer, 1844; reprinted, Aalen: Scientia, 1969);

Actenstücke zu den Verhandlungen über die Beschlagnahme der Geschichte der Politik, Cultur und Aufklärung des achtzehnten Jahrhunderts (Christiania: Werner, 1844);

Geschichte Deutschlands und der französischen Revolution unter der Herrschaft Napoleons, 2 volumes (Charlottenburg: Bauer, 1846; reprinted, 3 volumes, Aalen: Scientia, 1979);

Geschichte der französischen Revolution bis zur Stiftung der Republik, by Bauer, Edgar Bauer, and Ernst Jungnitz, 3 volumes (Leipzig: Voigt & Fernau, 1847);

Vollständige Geschichte der Partheikämpfe in Deutschland während der Jahre 1842–1846, 3 volumes (Charlottenburg: Bauer, 1847; reprinted, 1 volume, Aalen: Scientia, 1964);

Die bürgerliche Revolution in Deutschland seit dem Anfang der deutsch-katholischen Bewegung bis zur Gegenwart (Berlin: Hempel, 1849; reprinted, Aalen: Scientia, 1979);

Der Untergang des Frankfurter Parlaments: Geschichte der deutschen constituirenden Nationalversammlung (Berlin: Gerhard, 1849);

Die Apostelgeschichte: Eine Ausgleichung des Paulinismus und des Judenthums innerhalb der christlichen Kirche (Berlin: Hempel, 1850);

Der Fall und der Untergang der neuesten Revolutionen, 5 volumes (Berlin: Hempel, 1850);

Kritik der Evangelien und Geschichte ihres Ursprungs (4 volumes, Berlin: Hempel, 1851–1852; reprinted, 2 volumes, Aalen: Scientia, 1983);

Kritik der Paulinischen Briefe, 3 volumes (Berlin: Hempel, 1852);

Rußland und das Germanenthum (Charlottenburg: Bauer, 1853; reprinted, Aalen: Scientia, 1972);

Die jetzige Stellung Rußlands (Charlottenburg: Bauer, 1854);

Aberdeen (Charlottenburg: Bauer, 1854);

Russland und England (Charlottenburg: Bauer, 1854; reprinted, Aalen: Scientia, 1972);

De la dictature occidentale (Charlottenburg: Bauer, 1854);

Deutschland und das Rußenthum, 2 volumes (Charlottenburg: Bauer, 1854–1855);

Das Judenthum in der Fremde (Berlin: Heinicke, 1863);

Philo, Strauss und Renan und das Urchristenthum (Berlin: Hempel, 1874; reprinted, Aalen: Scientia, 1972);

Christus und die Cäsaren: Der Ursprung des Christenthums aus dem römischen Griechenthum (Berlin: Grosser, 1877);

Einfluß des englischen Quäkerthums auf die deutsche Cultur und auf das englisch-russische Project einer Weltkirche (Berlin: Grosser, 1878; reprinted, Aalen: Scientia, 1972);

Zur Orientirung über die Bismarck'sche Ära (Chemnitz: Schmeitzer / New York: Steiger, 1880);

Das Urevangelium und die Gegner der Schrift: "Christus und die Cäsaren" (Berlin: Grosser, 1880);

Disraeli's romantischer und Bismarck's sozialistischer Imperialismus (Chemnitz: Schmeitzner / New York: Steiger, 1882; reprinted, Aalen: Scientia, 1979);

Feldzüge der Reinen Kritik, edited by Hans-Martin Sass (Frankfurt am Main: Suhrkamp, 1968).

The career of the Hegelian theologian Bruno Bauer is marked by his radical and sudden turn from a defender of Christianity into one of its most extreme critics, from a champion of orthodox Christianity into what one of his admirers called a "Robespierre of Theology." Although his many theological and historical writings are largely unread today, his ideas influenced his own age and have found reflection in the works of such twentieth-century thinkers as the theologian Hans Küng and the philosopher Jürgen Habermas.

Bauer was born on 6 September 1809 in Eisenberg, Martin Luther's birthplace, to Friedrich Wilhelm Bauer, a porcelain painter, and Caroline Wilhelmine Bauer, née Reichardt. He was the oldest of four brothers; the others were Egbert, born in 1811; Egino, born in 1813; and Edgar, born in 1820. In 1815, Friedrich moved his family to Berlin, where he entered into secure employment at the royal porcelain factory.

Bauer's parents were pious Lutherans who wanted Bruno, their favorite son, to become a minister. They managed, at no small financial sacrifice, to enroll both Bruno and Edgar in the prestigious Friedrich Wilhelm Gymnasium of Berlin to begin the study of theology. From the outset of his academic career, Bruno proved himself to be committed to the life of the mind; as the historian of philosophy Johann E. Erdmann later remarked, he was "einen Grübler aus sich zu machen, dessem seelische Empfindlichkeit durch eine schwächliche körperliche Gesundheit noch gesteigert werden mochte" (devoted to making himself into a brooding intellectual, whose mental capacity was made to rise above a weak and unhealthy body).

Bauer as a young man; crayon drawing by an unknown artist (from Ernst Barnikol, Bruno Bauer: Studien und Materialien, *1972)*

In the spring of 1828 Bauer entered the University of Berlin to continue his theological studies. He quickly acquired a reputation as a brilliant student. In July 1829 he received the faculty prize offered for the best student essay on Immanuel Kant's theory of the beautiful, a subject proposed by the philosopher Georg Wilhelm Friedrich Hegel. Bauer's essay was further honored by Hegel's comment that Bauer had "schlagend aufgezeigt" (strikingly presented) his thesis.

Although he attended the lectures of the theologian Friedrich Schleiermacher and the biblical scholar August Neander, he found that he could not follow them. It was an entirely different matter with Hegel. From the beginning, Bauer gave himself completely over to Hegelianism. In his curriculum vitae, written in 1839, Bauer vividly recalled what Harold Mah described as "a kind of conversion experience": "Hegel allein, dessen Vorlesungen, als ich sie in der ersten Stunde hörte, mich sofort gefesselt hielten . . . hat meinem schwankenden Geist Ruhe und Gewißheit zurückgegeben. Wie groß war jenes Mannes Einfachheit und Uneigennützigkeit im Erforschen der Wahrheit . . ." (Only Hegel, whose lectures enthralled me from the first, . . . restored peace and certainty to my unstable spirit. How great was that man's simplicity and unselfishness in the search for truth . . .).

Shortly after Hegel's death in 1831 his former colleagues at the university began to prepare an edition of his collected work. Bauer's detailed notes of Hegel's lectures proved invaluable to the editors. The aesthetician Heinrich Gustav Hotho used Bauer's notes to compile his edition of Hegel's lectures on fine art, and the theologian Philipp Marheineke not only based much of his edition of Hegel's lectures on the philosophy of religion on Bauer's notes but also engaged Bauer as his assistant. Bauer's reputation as an exact – and, one suspects, pedantic – Hegelian was established. Since Hegel's philosophy was then dominant in most German universities, Bauer's academic future seemed assured.

At this stage Bauer was concerned with the reconciliation of Hegelianism and orthodox religion – the theme of his doctoral dissertation. The issue was, and remains, difficult to resolve. On one hand, Hegel asserted that his philosophy was a Christian one, and he himself was a devout Lutheran. On the other hand, his historical conception of truth implies that traditional Christianity is only a stage in the development of knowledge. For Hegelianism, there are no "eternal truths."

Having passed his doctoral examination, on 15 March 1834 Bauer received his *licentia docendi* (license to teach) and became a Privatdozent. In this position he was officially associated with the university but not salaried; it was his responsibility to attract students to his lectures and to receive fees directly from them.

During his five years in Berlin Bauer wrote forty-three articles and reviews; twenty-four of them appeared in the *Jahrbücher für wissenschaftliche Kritik* (Yearbook for Scientific Criticism), a publication sometimes humorously referred to as the "Hegel-Gazette."

In the spring of 1836 Bauer was given permission by the state censors to publish his own journal, the *Zeitschrift für spekulative Theologie* (Journal for Speculative Theology). Six issues were published from the summer of 1836 until the spring of 1838. Bauer contributed eight articles and six reviews.

It was Bauer's intention, as a follower of Hegel, to elevate theological consciousness to a speculative level; the religious mind, which expressed itself in the contrary forms of traditional faith and modern critical reason, could only find peace in the higher synthesis of speculative thought. Theological consciousness expressed itself in concrete feelings and rich historical images; but it was inexorably driven, as a rational consciousness, to destroy its own creations. Just as only speculative philosophy could reconcile the opposition between sensory images and pure logic, for Bauer only speculative theology could reconcile traditional Christian belief, based on feeling and imagery, with the critical logic of modern rationalism.

Unhappily for Bauer, David Friedrich Strauss's *Leben Jesu, kritisch bearbeitet* (1835–1836; translated as the *Life of Jesus; or a Critical Examination of His History,* 1842–1844) destroyed the hope of the Hegelian theologians. For Strauss, the Gospel records were less an account of the historic Jesus than a literary creation generated out of the Messianic expectations of the Jews. As Strauss had declared his work to be inspired by his reading of Hegel, the Hegelians found themselves immediately and embarrassingly on the defensive. The editorial board of the *Jahrbücher für wissenschaftliche Kritik,* impressed by the conservative temper of Bauer's articles and reviews, chose him to respond to Strauss. Bauer attempted to reconcile his vision of Hegelianism with the orthodox view of the Gospels and strove to demonstrate that miracles such as the Virgin Birth were necessary consequences of the historical development of human self-consciousness. If Strauss had engaged in radical criticism rather than the half-finished criticism that marked his work, Bauer maintained, he would have exhausted the fullest possibilities of criticism – and so have exhausted criticism itself. In that case every objection, such as the tradition that supposedly had generated the miraculous Christ, would have dissolved into mere facets of the self-reflecting consciousness. Strauss and his opponents would have seen that objections, whether generated by faith or human reason, were merely creatures of their own incomplete thought. In short, Bauer proposed the self-transcending of criticism into a higher acceptance or faith. His pure or "critical" criticism would then terminate the course of theological reflection. "Criticism," for Bauer, meant that any thought one might have was subject to the dictates of the thinker. Uncritical thinking and the acceptance of tradition or custom to determine what was to be taken as true indicated a lack of self-consciousness, and self-consciousness was the mark of being human. By allowing his self-consciousness to dissolve critically all that had previously been taken as sacred or presupposed, the unquestioned certitudes of both supernaturalists and naturalists would become moot. In a dense and obscure two-volume work, *Die Religion des Alten Testaments in der geschichtlichen Entwickelung ihrer Prinzipien dargestellt* (The Religion of the Old Testament Presented in the Historical Development if its Principles, 1838–1839), Bauer tried to render the Gospel stories into the language of dialectical reason; the book was modeled after Hegel's great *Die Phänomenologie des Geistes* (1807; translated as *The Phenomenology of the Mind,* 1910).

In 1839 Bauer revealed the first open sign of unorthodoxy with a short polemical monograph setting forth his recognition of the incompatibility between his conception of Hegelianism and orthodox religion, *Herr Dr. Hengstenberg: Kritische Briefe über den Gegensatz des Gesetzes und des Evangeliums* (Dr.

Ew. Wohlgeboren

werden von Unterzeichnetem ganz ergebenst ersucht für die Herausgabe des **„gelehrten Berlins"** auf das Jahr 1845 nachstehende Rubriken gefälligst auszufüllen und der Buchhandlung Athenäum von Ch. Scherk, Französische Straße 41, zuzusenden.

I. Vor- und Zuname:

Bruno Bauer.

II. Tag, Jahr und Ort der Geburt:

Eisenberg im Herzogthum Altenburg, den 6ten September 1809.

III. Kurze Notiz über die frühere und jetzige Stellung.

Privatdocent der Theologie an der Universität zu Berlin seit Ostern 1834 – Michaelis 1839, Privatdocent in Bonn seit Michaelis 1839 – Ostern 1842.

IV. Chronologisch geordnetes Verzeichniß der literarischen Erzeugnisse.

Recensionen in den berliner Jahrbüchern für wissenschaftliche Kritik seit 1833–1841.
Zeitschrift für speculative Theologie. 3 Bände. 1836–1838 Berlin. bei Dümmler.
Die Religion des alten Testaments in der geschichtlichen Entwicklung ihrer Principien. 2 Bände. Berlin bei Dümmler. 1838.
Herr Dr. Hengstenberg. 1839. Berlin bei Dümmler.
Kritik der evangelischen Geschichte des Johannes. 1840. Bremen bei Schünemann.
Die evangelische Landeskirche Preussens und die Wissenschaft. Leipzig bei Otto Wigand. 1840.

Dr. W: Koner.

Form filled out by Bauer in 1845 giving information about his career and publications for inclusion in a directory of Berlin scholars (Staatsbibliothek Preußischer Kulturbesitz, Berlin)

Hengstenberg: Critical Letters concerning the Opposition of the Laws and the Gospels). He also became a leader of the Doktorklub (Doctor's Club), one of the many radical discussion groups that prepared Berlin for the Revolution of 1848. In late 1839 he received an appointment to the theological faculty of the University of Bonn, at a safe distance from the growing circle of orthodox hostility in Berlin. At Bonn he completed another complex theological work, *Kritik der evangelischen Geschichte des Johannes* (Critique of the Gospel of John, 1840).

Bauer's three-volume *Kritik der evangelischen Geschichte der Synoptiker* (Critique of the Synoptic Gospels, 1841–1842) reduces sacred history to an expression of an uncritical self-consciousness and solves the persistent problem of whether Jesus was a historical figure: "Die Frage, mit der sich unsere Zeit so viel beschäftigt hat, ob nämlich Dieser, ob Jesus der historische Christus sey, haben wir damit beantwortet, daß wir zeigen, daß Alles, was der historische Christus ist, was von ihm gesagt wird, was wir von ihm wissen, der Welt der Vorstellung und zwar der christlichen Vorstellung angehört, also auch mit einem Menschen, der derwirklichen Welt angehört, Nichts zu thun hat. Die Frage ist damit beantwortet, daß die für alle Zukunft gestrichen ist" (The question – which has so occupied our age – of whether Jesus was an authentic historical figure we answered that everything relating to the historical Jesus, all that we know of him, relates to the world of imagination – to be more exact, to the Christian imagination. This has no connection with any man who lived in the real world. The question is thus eliminated for the future).

Bauer's *Die Posaune des jüngsten Gerichts über Hegel den Atheisten und Antichristen: Ein Ultimatum* (1841; translated as *The Trumpet of the Last Judgment against Hegel the Atheist and Antichrist: An Ultimatum,* 1989) was published anonymously and appeared to be the work of a learned Pietist minister. Its temper is polemical; it is laced with citations from the Bible and mimics the pietistic objections to liberal theology and philosophy that surfaced during the reaction of church and state against the liberal movement in Germany in the wake of the 1830 French revolution. It makes clear the incompatibility of Hegelian philosophy with traditional Christian belief and conservative political order that Bauer thought had been concealed by the prudent "Old Hegelians." Bauer intended the work to rally the various interpreters of Hegel into one camp from which they could enter into what he termed the "Feldzüge der reinen Kritik" (campaigns of pure criticism). By clarifying the opposition between reason and faith, which he took to be expressed in Hegelian philosophy, Bauer hoped to draw a clear line of battle between the two. Among the radical Hegelians *Die Posaune des jüngsten Gerichts* was greeted enthusiastically for openly presenting their own feelings regarding the direction of Hegelianism after Hegel. *Die Posaune des jüngsten Gerichts* appeared at the high watermark of the Young Hegelian movement; shortly after it appeared, the loose unity of the school was sundered by disputes among its members.

On 29 March 1842 Bauer received official notice that his *licentia docendi* had been rescinded. It came as a surprise, although he ironically observed that his lecture hall had never been so filled with attentive students. He remained in Bonn only long enough to finish his lecture series on the New Testament. He then left for Berlin, arriving on 5 May.

In Berlin Bauer again took up his role as a leader of the Doktorklub, which, during his absence, had been transformed into the notorious Die Freien (The Free Ones). For the revolutionary Young Hegelians the group, which met at Hippel's Wine Room, provided a forum for drinking and debate. Bauer, as the martyred atheist theologian who had gone even beyond Strauss, was welcomed as a returning hero. Among those who welcomed him were his brother Edgar; Friedrich Engels, who prepared a suitable epic poem for the occasion; and Max Stirner (pseudonym of Johann Caspar Schmidt). But the time of pure theory was coming to an end, and an era of practical revolution was beginning; radical Hegelians were becoming less inclined to see the theological issue as fundamental. The new political revolutionaries could neither appreciate Bauer's arcane theoretical principles nor share his belief in the "Terrorismus der reinen Theorie" (terrorism of pure theory).

Bauer and his brothers launched a small newspaper, the *Allgemeine Literatur-Zeitung* (General Literature Newspaper). It lasted from December 1843 until December 1844.

Bauer's *Das entdeckte Christenthum: Eine Erinnerung an das achtzehnte Jahrhundert und ein Beitrag zur Krisis des neunzehnten* (Christianity Exposed: A Recollection of the Eighteenth Century and a Contribution to the Crisis of the Nineteenth, 1843) was intended to defend atheism through a dissection of Christian attitudes. Part of it is a reprint of a brief anti-Christian treatise by Johann C. Edelmann. Bauer's respect for this early Enlightenment atheist reflected his view that the progress made in the Enlightenment had been frustrated by the resurgent pietism of his own age. His belief that the "Age of

Reason" embodied the Hegelian trust in the rationality of the real was reflected in the four-volume *Geschichte der Politik, Cultur und Aufklärung des achtzehnten Jahrhunderts* (History of the Politics, Culture, and Enlightenment of the Eighteenth Century, 1843–1845). But Bauer's reputation suffered irreparable damage when three central figures rejected his "critical criticism": Stirner in *Der Einzige und sein Eigenthum* (1844; translated as *The Ego and His Own,* 1907) and Engels and Karl Marx in *Die heilige Familie oder Kritik der kritischen Kritik* (1845; translated as *The Holy Family; or, Critique of Critical Critique,* 1946).

Bauer's *Geschichte Deutschlands und der französischen Revolution* (History of Germany and the French Revolution, 1846) sets forth the history of Europe from the beginning of the eighteenth century until Napoleon's rise to power. The work is a cultural and political history of the Enlightenment, the period he considered of supreme importance for humanity.

Faced with mounting debts incurred from trying to support the small publishing house of his brother Egbert, Bauer finally turned to Stirner's wife, Marie Dähnhardt, who had inherited some money from her father. He borrowed a relatively large sum, which he honorably repaid out of his own slim income over several decades.

Adding to what must have been the most unhappy period of his life was the imprisonment of his brother Edgar: in 1844 Egbert's press published Edgar's *Der Streit der Kritik mit Kirche und Staat* (The Struggle of Criticism with Church and State), a work critical of the official treatment of Bruno; the work was immediately confiscated, but Edgar had it published in Switzerland. This imprudent action resulted in Edgar's incarceration for six years.

After these setbacks Bruno Bauer was more and more inclined to doubt that reason would prevail; his pessimism and increasing scorn of popular movements hardened him into a solitary cynic.

Contrary to its title, Bauer's three-volume *Vollständige Geschichte der Partheikämpfe in Deutschland während der Jahre 1842–1846* (Complete History of Party Struggles in Germany 1842–1846), published in 1847, covered only events through 1844; a fourth volume was to extend the time frame to 1847. But the Revolution of 1848 intervened, and the final volume was never completed. The completed volumes form a chronicle of disappointing political events, from the deceptively liberal appearance of King Friedrich Wilhelm IV to the increasingly oppressive measures taken by both state and church to stifle the democratic opposition. It is a bitter work that displays anger at democratic passivity.

In 1851–1852 Bauer returned to theological subjects with *Kritik der Evangelien und Geschichte ihres Ursprungs* (Critique of the Gospels and History of Their Origin). This work develops his theory of the "Urevangelist" (original evangelist) writer who first composed the fictional life of Jesus.

The looming Crimean War provided a backdrop for a series of studies on the relationship of Russia to the rest of Europe. The first result was *Rußland und das Germanenthum* (Russia and the Germanic World, 1853). It warned its German readers of the growing power of Russia and praised Catherine the Great for her autocratic, yet positive, direction of its people. It was followed by three more studies of the emergence of Russia as a world power. The final work in the series, *Deutschland und das Russenthum* (Germany and the Russian World, 1854–1855), served as a model for later German nationalistic philosophies of history in which Germany was seen as the destined, yet scorned, leader of the West. These Russian studies mark a turning point in Bauer's intellectual career from philosophical and theological speculation to empirical investigation of historical events, a stance supported by his reading of the French philosopher and social reformer Auguste Comte.

In the mid 1850s Bauer's energies slackened, and the volume of his writings diminished. His work was rejected both by his peers and by the public. Only a few of his old friends from Die Freien remained; their ranks were thinned particularly by the death in 1856 of his old comrade Stirner, with whom he had remained close friends despite their philosophical differences. In the later 1850s Bauer turned more and more to journeyman editorial work. It helped him to earn a living – something his own writing could not accomplish – and it allowed him to forget the bitter failure of his "Feldzüge der reinen Kritik." In 1859, after a few years in various insignificant editorial posts, Bauer became the associate of Hermann Wagener, the editor of such ultraconservative papers as the *Staats-und-Gesellschafts-lexikon* (State and Society Lexicon), *Kreuzzeitung* (Cross Newspaper), and *Berliner Revue.* For the next seven years Bauer enjoyed, for the first time in his life, a small but assured income. The work he produced at this time was not only scornful of the weak democratic forces in Prussia but also virulently anti-Semitic. As his early essay on *Die Judenfrage* (1843; translated as *The Jewish Problem,* 1958) indicates, Bauer's anti-Semitism was not a matter of his compromising with a Prussia dominated by the anti-

Semitic nationalists gathering around Minister-President Otto von Bismarck; rather, it was a matter of philosophic principle. For Bauer the Jewish religion was a particularly irrational survival from the past that should have vanished long ago and, in the interest of the progress of reason, should have transformed itself into humanistic philosophy. Bauer's anti-Semitism was not grounded in racial theories, since he favored racial mixing. He condemned Judaism because it was a source and support of Christianity, which Bauer regarded as the prime obstacle to human progress.

After he ceased editing for Wagener in 1866, Bauer took up farming in the Berlin suburb of Rixdorf. Alone, without family or friends, he faced the dreary end of a career that had begun with so much promise.

In a stable that he converted into a crude study Bauer wrote several works on the influence of history on religious doctrine. In *Christus und die Cäsaren: Der Ursprung des Christenthums aus dem römischen Griechenthum* (Christ and the Caesars: The Rise of Christianity out of the Roman Greek World, 1877) and *Jesus und die Cäsaren* (Jesus and the Caesars, 1880) Bauer fully developed the theory he had first proposed in the early 1840s: that it was not Jesus or Saint Paul but Seneca and Philo who were the spiritual creators of the Gospel story. His planned comprehensive study of the Roman Empire and the effect of its decline on the origins of Christianity never materialized.

In 1881 the publisher Ernst Schmeitzner appointed Bauer editor of his new anti-Semitic journal, *Schmeitzners Internationale Monatsschrift: Zeitschrift für allgemeine und nationale Kultur und deren Literatur* (Schmeitzner's International Monthly: Journal for Universal and National Culture and Its Literature). But Bauer died on 13 April 1882. To those who still took note of him, Bauer had become known as "Der Einsiedler von Rixdorf" (The Hermit of Rixdorf).

References:

Ernst Barnikol, *Bruno Bauer: Studien und Materialien,* edited by Peter Reimer and Hans-Martin Sass (Assen: Van Gorcum, 1972);

William J. Brazill, "Bauer, Stirner, and the Terrorism of Pure Theory," in his *The Young Hegelians* (New Haven: Yale University Press, 1970), pp. 175–225;

Johann E. Erdmann, *Grundriß der Geschichte der Philosophie* (Berlin: Hertz, 1866);

Harold Mah, "Bruno Bauer and the Crisis in Religious Theory," in his *The End of Philosophy, the Origin of "Ideology"* (Berkeley: University of California Press, 1987), pp. 45–86;

Zvi Rosen, *Bruno Bauer and Karl Marx* (The Hague: Martinus Nijhoff, 1977);

Lawrence S. Stepelevich, "Bruno Bauer," in his *The Young Hegelians: An Anthology* (New York,: Cambridge University Press, 1983), pp. 173–205;

John Edward Towes, "Bruno Bauer and the Reduction of Absolute Spirit to Human Self-consciousness," in his *Hegelianism: The Path toward Dialectical Humanism, 1805–1841* (New York: Cambridge University Press, 1980), pp. 288–326.

Georg Büchner

(17 October 1813 - 19 February 1837)

Rodney Taylor
Northeast Missouri State University

BOOKS: *Der Hessische Landbote: Erste Botschaft,* anonymous, by Büchner and Friedrich Ludwig Weidig (Offenbach: Preller, 1834); enlarged edition, anonymous, by Büchner, Weidig, and L. Eichelberg (Marburg, 1834); translated by Henry J. Schmidt as *The Hessian Courier* (New York: Continuum, 1986);

Danton's Tod: Dramatische Bilder aus Frankreichs Schreckensherrschaft (Frankfurt am Main: Sauerländer, 1835); translated by Geoffrey Dunlop as *Danton's Death,* in *The Plays of Georg Büchner* (London: Howe, 1927; New York: Viking, 1927);

Mémoire sur le système nerveux du barbeau (Cyprinus barbus L.) (Paris & Strasbourg: Levrault, 1835);

Nachgelassene Schriften, edited by Ludwig Büchner (Frankfurt am Main: Sauerländer, 1850) – includes "Lenz," translated by Stephen Spender in *Great European Short Stories,* edited by Spender (New York: Dell, 1960); *Leonce und Lena,* translated by Walter N. Green as *Leonce and Lena: A Comedy in Three Acts,* in *New Europe,* 13 (1919): 246–254, 275–283;

Sämmtliche Werke und handschriftlicher Nachlaß: Erste kritische Gesammt-Ausgabe, edited by Karl Emil Franzos (Frankfurt am Main: Sauerländer, 1879) – includes *Woyzeck,* translated by Dunlop as *Wozzeck* in *The Plays of Georg Büchner* (1927);

Georg Büchners Werke und Briefe, edited by Fritz Bergemann (Leipzig: Insel, 1926);

Sämtliche Werke, edited by Paul Stapf (Berlin: Tempel, 1959);

Werke, edited by Henri Poschmann (Berlin & Weimar: Aufbau, 1967);

Sämtliche Werke und Briefe: Historisch-kritische Ausgabe mit Kommentar, 2 volumes, edited by Werner R. Lehmann (Hamburg: Wegner, 1967, 1971);

Sämtliche Werke, edited by Gerhard P. Knapp (Munich: Goldmann, 1978);

Georg Büchner (engraving by Auerbach)

Werke und Briefe, edited by Karl Pörnbacher, Gerhard Schraub, Hans-Joachim Simm, and Edda Ziegler (Munich & Vienna: Hanser, 1988).

Editions in English: *Leonce and Lena,* translated by E. R. Bentley, in *From the Modern Repertoire,* edited by Bentley (Bloomington: Indiana University Press, 1956), pp. 1–37;

Danton's Death, translated by Bentley, in *The Modern Theatre,* volume 5, edited by Bentley (New York: Doubleday, 1957), pp. 69–160;

Danton's Death, translated by James Maxwell (San Francisco: Chandler, 1961; London: Methuen, 1968);

Woyzeck, and Leonce and Lena, translated by Carl Richard Mueller (San Francisco: Chandler, 1962);

Complete Plays and Prose, translated by Mueller (New York: Hill & Wang, 1963);

Lenz, translated by Michael Hamburger (Buffalo, N.Y.: Frontier Press, 1969);

Danton's Death, translated by Henry J. Schmidt (New York: Avon, 1971);

Leonce and Lena; Lenz; Woyzeck, translated by Hamburger (Chicago & London: University of Chicago Press, 1972);

Danton's Death, translated by Howard Brenton (London: Methuen, 1982);

Leonce and Lena, translated by Hedwig Rappolt (New York: Time and Space Limited, 1983);

Lenz, translated by Rappolt (New York: Time and Space Limited, 1983);

Complete Works and Letters, translated by Schmidt (New York: Continuum, 1986);

Danton's Death; Leonce and Lena; Woyzeck, translated by Victor Price (London & New York: Oxford University Press, 1988);

Woyzeck and Lenz, translated by Rappolt (New York: Time and Space Limited, 1988);

Woyzeck, translated by John Mackendrick (London: Heinemann, 1988);

Georg Büchner's Woyzeck, translated by Michael Ewans (New York: Lang, 1989).

TRANSLATIONS: Victor Hugo, *Lucretia Borgia; Maria Tudor,* volume 6 of Hugo's *Sämtliche Werke* (Frankfurt am Main: Sauerländer, 1835).

Although his work is profoundly rooted in the crises, conflicts, and ideals of his time, Georg Büchner's writings have far transcended the intellectual and historical framework of his turbulent age. Büchner, who died at twenty-three, was one of the most significant literary figures in the dark epoch between the Restoration and the Revolution of 1848. His work thus exhibits the deep existential melancholy and Weltschmerz that Friedrich Sengle suggests is an integral characteristic of this age of German realism. On the other hand, Büchner's writings reveal an exalted philosophical vision of human dignity and freedom. His depictions of monumental collisions between Freiheitsideale (ideals of freedom) and historical circumstance disclose his deep, often tormented concern for the fate of humanity. They also manifest his intense involvement with the meaning of history. Büchner's writings contain, moreover, highly perceptive critiques of the sociopolitical realities of his time. These critiques anticipate some of the social and political evils of the twentieth century, and Büchner's treatment of the interconnected problems of individual alienation and societal oppression influenced the work of Bertolt Brecht, Friedrich Dürrenmatt, Ingmar Bergman, Werner Herzog, as well as many other important twentieth-century artists. Subsequent literary movements exhibiting his influence include nineteenth-century German realism, German expressionism, epic theater, theater of the absurd, and documentary theater.

Karl Georg Büchner was born on 17 October 1813 in the village of Goddelau in Hesse; he was the eldest of six children. His father, Ernst Karl Büchner, a successful physician, was an enthusiastic student of the French Revolution, an admirer of French democracy, and a fervent supporter of the social reforms instituted by Napoleon in Germany. Büchner's mother, Caroline Luise Büchner, née Reuß, an impassioned patriot, longed for a unified German state and, unlike her husband, applauded the expulsion of Napoleon. While his father encouraged the young Büchner's interests in natural science and history, his mother fostered his reverence for nature and love of literature. Two of Büchner's siblings were to become leading cultural figures in Germany during the latter half of the nineteenth century, Luise as a writer and intellectual in the women's movement and Ludwig as a philosopher.

When Büchner was three his family moved to Darmstadt, the capital of the Grand Duchy of Hesse. In 1825 he matriculated at the Darmstädter Großherzogliches Gymnasium. This school, known as the "altes Pädagog" (Old Pedagogue), was one of the foremost educational institutions in the German-speaking countries. During his stay Büchner demonstrated outstanding intellectual potential, a tendency toward independent thinking, rebelliousness against authority, and an inchoate political awareness. A recurrent theme in his student essays and school speeches concerns the incontrovertible rights and dignity of the individual. In two of these pieces Büchner describes how heroic persons in history reacted when their moral autonomy was threatened by political oppression. His essays clearly exhibit an ethical as well as an implicitly political critique of the suppression of civil rights in Germany that had resulted from the mandates of the Deutscher Bund (German confederation), the loose confederation of thirty-nine German states set up by the Congress of Vienna in 1815.

Büchner's writings at the gymnasium also disclose a fundamental repugnance toward Christian

Der Hessische Landbote.

Erste Botschaft.

Darmstadt, im Juli 1834.

Vorbericht.

Dieses Blatt soll dem hessischen Lande die Wahrheit melden, aber wer die Wahrheit sagt, wird gehenkt, ja sogar der, welcher die Wahrheit liest, wird durch meineidige Richter vielleicht gestraft. Darum haben die, welchen dies Blatt zukommt, folgendes zu beobachten:

1) Sie müssen das Blatt sorgfältig außerhalb ihres Hauses vorder Polizei verwahren;
2) sie dürfen es nur an treue Freunde mittheilen;
3) denen, welchen sie nicht trauen, wie sich selbst, dürfen sie es nur heimlich hinlegen;
4) würde das Blatt dennoch bei Einem gefunden, der es gelesen hat, so muß er g.stehen, daß er es eben dem Kreisrath habe bringen wollen;
5) wer das Blatt nicht gelesen hat, wenn man es bei ihm fin- det, der ist natürlich ohne Schuld.

Friede den Hütten! Krieg den Pallästen!

Im Jahr 1834 siehet es aus, als würde die Bibel Lügen gestraft. Es sieht aus, als hätte Gott die Bauern und Handwerker am 5ten Tage, und die Fürsten und Vornehmen am 6ten gemacht, und als hätte der Herr zu diesen gesagt: Herrschet über alles Gethier, das auf Erden kriecht, und hätte die Bauern und Bürger zum Gewürm gezählt. Das Leben der Vornehmen ist ein langer Sonntag, sie wohnen in schönen Häusern, sie tragen zierliche Kleider, sie haben feiste Gesichter und reden eine eigne Sprache; das Volk aber liegt vor ihnen wie Dünger auf dem Acker. Der Bauer geht hinter dem Pflug, der Vornehme aber geht hinter ihm und dem Pflug und treibt ihn mit den Ochsen am Pflug, er nimmt das Korn und läßt ihm die Stoppeln. Das Leben des Bauern ist ein langer Werktag; Fremde verzehren seine Aecker vor seinen Augen, sein Leib ist eine Schwiele, sein Schweiß ist das Salz auf dem Tische des Vornehmen.

First page of Büchner's revolutionary political pamphlet

dogma. In opposition to the traditional Christian strictures against suicide, for example, Büchner argues in "Rede zur Vertheidigung des Kato von Utika" (In Defense of Cato of Utica) that suicide for the sake of preserving one's moral dignity is praiseworthy. In "Über den Selbstmord" (On Suicide) an evolutionary conception of nature is developed: life, says Büchner, signifies dynamic development; the great theologian Friedrich Schleiermacher's postulation that earthly existence is little more than an ethical testing ground is a vapid denial of the self-subsisting totality of universal Life. Büchner asserts that a human being who suffers from physical or psychological maladies so severe as to cause his developmental powers to disintegrate has a moral duty to end his own life. Büchner thus touches on a theme that will occupy him for the rest of his life: his vision of nature and humanity as inherently beautiful, noble, and good.

Upon completing his education at the gymnasium in 1831 Büchner embarked on the study of medicine and the natural sciences at the University of Strasbourg. Strasbourg was a hotbed of revolutionary sentiment and activity directed against the conservative government in Paris. The city was also a gathering place for German intellectuals seeking freedom from the increasingly repressive political measures being adopted across the border. As a re-

Büchner in 1834; sketch by Jean-Baptiste Alexis Muston (Volk und Wissen Archiv, Berlin)

sult of his association with revolutionary student groups in Strasbourg, Büchner became committed to radical democratic reform in Germany. He also participated in protests against the increasingly brutal methods of suppressing political opposition to which the French government was resorting. Nevertheless, Büchner and his fellow expatriates enjoyed considerable freedom of thought and expression, and his stay in Strasbourg was perhaps the happiest period of his life. During this time he met Wilhelmine (Minna) Jaeglé, the daughter of a liberal Protestant pastor, and they were soon engaged.

In Strasbourg, Büchner attended lectures by some of the leading scientists of the age. Constantly expanding his knowledge of the French Revolution, Büchner also read widely in the Greek and Roman classics as well as in French and German literature. His developing capacity for inquiring into the causes of political and economic injustice is exemplified by a letter to his parents dated 5 April 1883: "Man wirft den jungen Leuten den Gebrauch der Gewalt vor. Sind wir denn aber nicht in einem ewigen Gewaltzustand? . . . Was nennt Ihr denn *gesetzlichen Zustand?* Ein *Gesetz,* das die große Masse der Staatsbürger zum fronenden Vieh macht, um die unnatürlichen Bedürfnisse einer . . . verdorbenen Minderzahl zu befriedigen? Und dies Gesetz, unterstützt durch eine rohe Militärgewalt . . . ist eine *ewige, rohe Gewalt,* angetan dem Recht und der gesunden Vernunft, und ich werde mit *Mund und Hand* dagegen kämpfen" (Young people are accused of using violence. But aren't we in an eternal state of violence? . . . What do you call a *lawful state?* A law that transforms the great masses of citizens into toiling cattle in order to satisfy the unnatural needs of a . . . decadent minority? Supported by raw military might . . . this law is *eternal, brute force,* insulting justice and good sense, and I will fight *tooth and nail* against it). Büchner's evaluation of contemporary society here anticipates Karl Marx's view that the modern capitalist state is founded not on the principles of justice, equality, and human dignity but exists to promote the interests of the ruling elite. Like Marx, Büchner maintains that political power is used by the privileged few to subjugate and exploit the many. Consequently, violence and barbarity come to be institutionalized throughout the entire social hierarchy.

In 1833 Büchner left Strasbourg; following a brief stay with his parents in Darmstadt, he began the study of medicine and philosophy at the provincial University of Gießen in Upper Hesse. In contrast to his life in Strasbourg, Büchner's stay in Gießen was darkened by feelings of despair that were exacerbated by an attack of meningitis. The deep melancholy that permeated this period of Büchner's life became a leitmotif of his literary production.

Through a pastor from Butzbach, Dr. Friedrich Ludwig Weidig, Büchner became a member of one of the covert, loosely organized revolutionary circles then forming throughout the region. Early in 1834 he founded the Gesellschaft der Menschenrechte (Society for Human Rights), a group of students and laborers dedicated to radical social change. Together with Weidig he composed a political leaflet, *Der Hessische Landbote* (1834; translated as *The Hessian Courier,* 1986). While Weidig was convinced that social reform in Germany could only be effected by a wealthy bourgeoisie composed of enlightened industrialists, politicians, and intellectuals, for Büchner reform had to be accomplished through revolutionary activities by the impoverished German peasantry.

Der Hessische Landbote combines an ethical appeal having strong biblical overtones with an exposition of the economic and historical factors involved in the current state of affairs. The disparity between rich and poor in Hesse is for Büchner destructive of the spiritual potential of the people. The government of the Grand Duchy of Hesse exists solely for the benefit of the rich; its purpose is to extort taxes from those who labor and starve to maintain and enhance the luxurious way of life and traditional privileges enjoyed by a decadent, pampered few. The aristocrats justify high taxation as a means of preserving the state, but Büchner asserts that the state should exist only to promote the well-being of its citizens. Büchner's critique includes a striking attempt to demythologize the person of the Grand Duke and thereby to combat the notion that a prince's power is ultimately founded on divine election. This ostensibly superhuman figure, from whom an aura of divine authority seems to radiate, is nothing more than a mortal man: "[Er] ißt, wenn [er] hungert, und schläft wenn sein Auge dunkel wird. Sehet, [er] kroch so nackt und weich in die Welt, wie ihr und wird so hart und steif hinausgetragen, wie ihr, und doch hat [er] seinen Fuß auf eurem Nacken" ([He] eats when [he] is hungry and sleeps when his eyes grow heavy. Behold, like you [he] crept naked and soft into the world and like you [he] will be carried from it hard and stiff, and yet his foot is on your neck).

Because the French king abused his power and betrayed the people, he and many of his decadent aristocratic cohorts were justly executed; because the current governmental system in Germany was set up only to enrich and empower the elite while grinding down the laboring poor, it will inevitably become necessary for the people to overthrow it by force – just as the French did during the revolution.

Distribution of *Der Hessische Landbote* was undertaken by two of Büchner's fellow members in the Gesellschaft der Menschenrechte. One of them, Karl Minnigerode, was soon arrested, and copies of the tract were found sewn into his clothing. On hearing of the arrest, Büchner set out for Butzbach to warn Weidig and the other members. While he was gone his lodging in Gießen was searched by the police. For the time being, however, the authorities were uncertain as to the extent of his involvement in the affair; the authorship of the leaflet had, of course, been left anonymous. Becoming aware of his son's difficulties, Büchner's father forced him to return to Darmstadt in August 1834. The stay with his family was a time of extreme psychological distress for Büchner because of the continuing arrests of the members of his revolutionary group and the constant fear that his own incarceration was imminent. Eventually, Weidig was arrested; he would take his own life in prison in 1837.

Between October 1834 and January 1835 Büchner composed one of the greatest masterpieces of German literature. He submitted the work, a drama titled *Danton's Tod* (1835; translated as *Danton's Death,* 1927), to the prominent literary critic and editor Karl Gutzkow. The latter quickly resolved to publish Büchner's drama in installments in his journal, *Phönix: Frühlingszeitung für Deutschland* (Phoenix: Spring Paper for Germany). In late February, before receiving the news of his literary success, Büchner was summoned to appear in court. He decided to flee the country, returning to Strasbourg.

Danton's Tod is a highly complex historical drama encompassing many levels of meaning, extending from problems relating to the significance and purpose of history to the notion of theodicy: the metaphysical attempt to justify the significance and purpose of history to the attempt to justify human suffering in a presumably divinely ordered universe. Approximately one-sixth of the drama consists of quotations from documents written during the French Revolution; the play also contains many excerpts from historical studies. The work exhibits a dynamic convergence of supraindividual historical forces and human subjectivity that is particularly evident in the persona of Georges Danton himself. Danton decides to put an end to his life because of the impossibly heavy burden history has laid upon him. The sins he has committed for the sake of the revolution are incessantly reproduced in his memory; one incident in particular, the September Massacres of 1792, tortures him. Danton holds himself responsible for ordering the massacres, in which thousands of persons all over France were slaughtered by angry mobs: "Man hat mir von einer Krankheit erzählt, die einem das Gedächtnis verlieren mache. Der Tod soll etwas davon haben. Dann kommt mir manchmal die Hoffnung, daß er vielleicht noch kräftiger wirke und einen *Alles* verlieren mache. Wenn das wäre!" (I've heard of a sickness that makes one lose one's memory. Death, they say, is like that. Then I hope sometimes that death would be even stronger and make one lose *everything.* If only that were so!).

Büchner's portrayal of Danton as possessing sole responsibility for the September Massacres has the purpose of dramatizing the descent of an overwhelming historical necessity upon a solitary human being. History is not depicted as a blind neces-

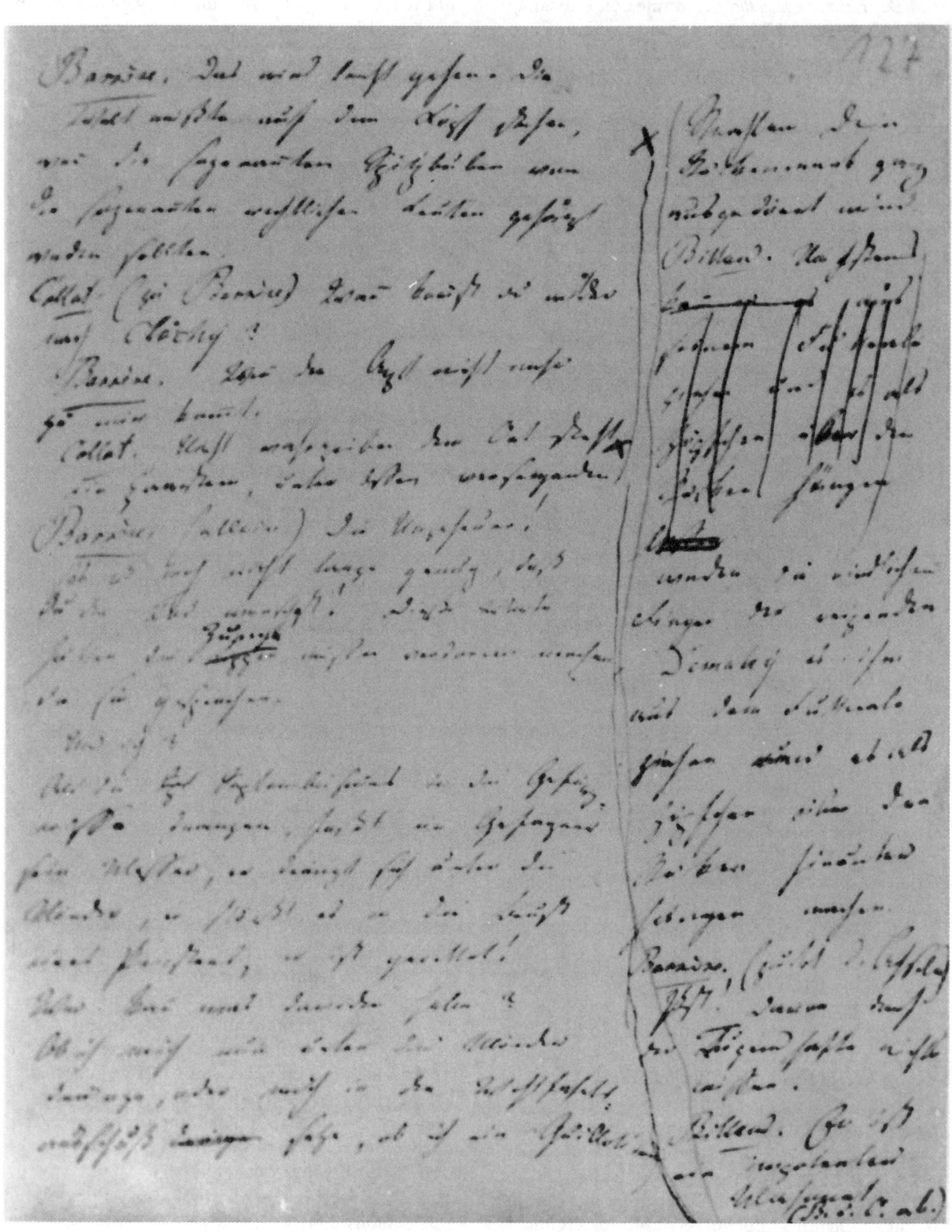

Page from the manuscript for Büchner's play Danton's Tod *(from Büchner's* Sämtliche Werke und Briefe, *volume 1, edited by Werner R. Lehmann, 1967)*

sity that acts independently of the subjects of history; Danton's actions originated in a vision of freedom based on the optimistic assumption that the course of history can be altered. But Danton's revolutionary will to freedom engenders a horrifying, irrational necessity that coerces him into mandating the shedding of blood. Danton's wife, Julie, attempts to console him by maintaining that his actions during September 1792 saved the country. But he responds: "Ja, das hab ich; das war Notwehr, wir mußten. Der Mann am Kreuze hat sich's bequem gemacht: es muß ja Ärgernis kommen. . . . Es muß; das war dies Muß. Wer will der Hand fluchen, auf die der Fluch des Muß gefallen? Wer hat das Muß gesprochen, wer? . . . Puppen sind wir, von unbekannten Gewalten am Draht gezogen; nichts, nichts wir selbst!" (Yes, I did. It was self-defense, we had to. The Man on the Cross made it easy for himself: it must needs be that offenses come. . . . It must; it was this 'must.' Who would curse the hand on which the curse of 'must' has fallen? Who has spoken this 'must,' who? . . . We are puppets, our strings are pulled by unknown forces, we ourselves are nothing!). By indicating that Christ "made it easy for himself " by abandoning history instead of remaining in this domain to assume the historical burden of his ethical vision, Danton equates his own importance with that of the Savior. Just as the temporal appearance of Christ effected radical historical changes, Danton asserts, his own revolutionary decisions have forever transformed the course of human history. In contrast to Christ's eschatological otherworldliness, however, Danton's actions were undertaken to save the downtrodden in this world. Christ was powerless to alter the lot of the common people; the kind of freedom he offered was, in the end, not of this world. It consequently remained impervious to the dark necessity that had precipitated Danton's political failure and personal destruction. Danton's subjective torment coincides with the historical result of the September Massacres: the Reign of Terror. Thus, his internal agony is mirrored by and, in turn, mirrors tragic contemporary events that he helped bring into being.

Büchner's return to Strasbourg marked the beginning of a period of relative happiness. He was reunited with his fiancée and resumed his academic studies. He wrote a scientific dissertation, *Mémoire sur le système nerveux du barbeau* (1835); after lecturing on the work in the spring of 1835 he became a member of the professional society of scholars in natural history in Strasbourg. Later he submitted the treatise to the philosophical faculty of the newly founded University of Zurich, which awarded him

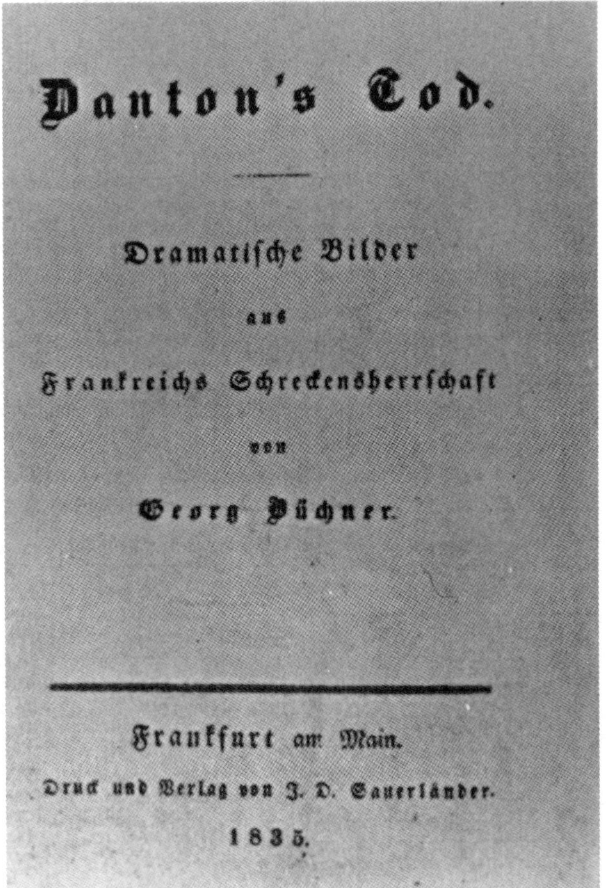
Danton's Tod.

Dramatische Bilder

aus

Frankreichs Schreckensherrschaft

von

Georg Büchner.

Frankfurt am Main.

Druck und Verlag von J. D. Sauerländer.

1835.

Title page for the first book publication of Büchner's play about the French Revolution

the doctorate of philosophy in September 1836. During his stay in Strasbourg, Büchner's political activities were minimal. He began once again to study philosophy, particularly Rationalist metaphysics and Georg Wilhelm Friedrich Hegel's *Encyklopädie der philosophischen Wissenschaften* (Encyclopedia of the Philosophical Sciences, 1817; translated as *The Logic of Hegel,* 1874).

During the summer of 1835 Büchner composed another masterpiece, a novella about the incipient stages of acute schizophrenia suffered by the eighteenth-century poet Jakob Michael Reinhold Lenz. "Lenz" (1850; translated, 1960) is the most unpolitical work in Büchner's small oeuvre; in its description of the states of consciousness experienced by the title character, the story is also the most subjective of Büchner's works. The narration of events in the story, both mental and external, is from a third-person standpoint; its recounting of Lenz's psychic turmoil – his suffering as well as his moments of exalted mystical intuition – is dispassionate and objective. The story contains a detailed phenomenological description of the drastic mental isolation symptomatic of schizophrenia: Lenz's illness includes a tormented sense of erosion of subjective identity. This loss of selfhood, however, is complemented by a passionate mystical longing to embrace what Lenz sees as the munificent oneness of life and nature.

Lenz's painful, often desperate yearning to attain union with the infinite life of nature reflects Büchner's affinity for the Rationalist philosopher Benedict de Spinoza's ontology, as delineated in the *Ethica* (Ethics, 1677). For Büchner and Spinoza, existence is infinite, perfect, and complete. It cannot, therefore, be made to conform to such presumptuous human notions as those postulating that it is designed by a divine creator. In his inaugural doctoral lecture, "Über Schädelnerven der Fische" (On the Cranial Nerves of Fish, 1850), given in 1836, Büchner asserts that nature exists in supreme indifference to human needs and desires. Moreover, nature in its totality is inexplicable by human cognition; it exists for its own sake alone.

While Büchner's perspective on existence manifests the influence of Spinoza, his philosophical notebooks on Spinoza and on Spinoza's Rationalist predecessor René Descartes – written during his second stay in Strasbourg – contain his objections to one of the overriding assumptions of Rationalist metaphysics: that being is ultimately identical with thought. Büchner insists that Spinoza's attempt to deduce existence from an abstract human thought-construction such as the *causa sui* (cause of itself) rests on the mistaken assumption that thought is more perfect than corporeal nature. Büchner's critique of Rationalism anticipates Ludwig Feuerbach's devastating attack on Spinoza and Hegel in his *Grundsätze der Philosophie der Zukunft* (1843; translated as *Principles of the Philosophy of the Future,* 1966).

Büchner's repudiation of purely intellectual attempts to arrive at an adequate comprehension of nature is evident in a passage in his novella where Lenz affirms that "Die einfachste, reinste Natur hinge am nächsten mit der elementarischen zusammen; je feiner der Mensch geistig fühlt und lebt, um so abgestumpfter würde dieser elementarische Sinn; er halte ihn nicht für einen hohen Zustand, er sei nicht selbstständig genug, aber er meine, es müsse ein unendliches Wonnegefühl sein, so von dem eigentümlichen Leben jeder Form berührt zu werden, für Gesteine, Metalle, Wasser und Pflanzen eine Seele zu haben" (The simplest, purest character was closest to elemental nature; the more sophisticated a person's intellectual feelings and life, the duller is this elemental sense; he did not consider it to be an elevated state of being, it was not independent enough, but he believed it must be boundless ecstasy to be touched in this way by the unique life of every form, to commune with rocks, metals, water, and plants). In this passage Büchner attributes his own deep adoration of material nature to his character, who communes in a kind of mystical ecstasy with the manifestations of being in its totality. This vision does not see in nature the dialectical workings of a transcendental Mind, as in the idealism of Hegel or Friedrich Wilhelm Joseph von Schelling. Its source is an awe-filled perception of the immense, majestic totality of organic and inorganic nature. Thus, his unique nature-mysticism is not based on a conception of the universe that seeks to transmute its autonomous existence into a "higher" spiritual reality.

The highly affirmative perception of nature Büchner attributes to Lenz is complemented by the latter's sensitive and loving behavior toward his fellow human beings. Lenz sees in humankind a dignity and beauty that originates in nature itself. Because human beings are manifestations of the universal beauty of nature, one must comport oneself to them with love and respect: "Nur eins bleibt: eine unendliche Schönheit, die aus einer Form in die andre tritt, ewig aufgeblättert, verändert. . . . Man muß die Menschheit lieben, um in das eigentümliche Wesen jedes einzudringen; es darf einem keiner zu gering, keiner zu häßlich sein, erst dann kann man sie verstehen" (Only one thing remains, an endless beauty moving from one form to another, eternally unfolding, changing. . . . One must love humanity in order to penetrate into the unique essence of each individual; no one can be too low or too ugly, only then can one understand them). Lenz also expresses his creator's views on aesthetics: he maintains that only works that are truly realistic, that reveal exacting concentration on the manifold richness of natural and human reality, can be viewed as genuine art.

Lenz's moments of mystical communion with the majestic totality of existence are followed, however, by a horrifying alienation from reality. This alienation brings him progressively nearer the "Abgrund" (abyss), the profound "Leere" (void) that inhabits his thinking and feeling self. Throughout Büchner's narrative, Lenz is harrowed by his sense of a terrifying internal emptiness that he perceives as gradually extinguishing his consciousness. Lenz's horror in experiencing this relentless darkening and disintegration of his self is intensified by his perception that the void will soon isolate him forever from his beloved nature and the human beings he wishes to serve. In his state of sickness and internal desolation Lenz is aware that the mystical plenitude and beauty flowing from nature is inexorably slipping away, dissolving into the nothingness of his advancing insanity and impending death: "Alles, was er an Ruhe aus der . . . Stille des Tals geschöpft hatte, war weg; die Welt, die er hatte nutzen wollen, hatte einen ungeheuern Riß, er hatte keinen Haß, keine Liebe, keine Hoffnung – eine schreckliche Leere und doch eine folternde Unruhe, sie auszufüllen. Er hatte *Nichts*" (All the peace he had derived from . . . the valley's stillness was gone; the world he had wished to serve had a gigantic crack, he felt no hate, no love, no hope, a terrible void and yet a tormenting anxiety to fill it. He had *nothing*).

Commentators such as Hans Mayer and Gerhard P. Knapp have pointed out that "Lenz" and *Danton's Tod* exhibit the extreme intellectual and spiritual dichotomies that tortured Büchner. During his second stay in Strasbourg, however, his surroundings offered a stable setting for his academic and literary labors. Gutzkow encouraged him to translate two plays by Victor Hugo; published in 1835, both were of mediocre quality. He also began work on an original play, "Pietro Aretino"; the manuscript for the drama, like much of Büchner's correspondence and his diary, has been lost. During the summer of 1836 Büchner received a visit from his mother and older sister; years later, Ludwig Büchner reported that during this visit his older brother told their mother of his foreboding that he would die young. That summer Büchner feverishly completed work on a play for the Cotta publishing house, which had advertised a literary competition with a prize for the best comedy submitted in prose or verse. Büchner's manuscript for *Leonce und Lena* (1850; translated as *Leonce and Lena,* 1927) did not meet the deadline set by the firm and was returned unopened.

A direct literary influence evident in *Leonce und Lena* is William Shakespeare's *As You Like It.* Büchner, however, does not emulate the structural complexity of Shakespeare's comedy; the plot of his play can be delineated in a few sentences. Leonce, a bored and pampered prince, is the victim of a melancholy so profound that it thwarts his every effort to involve himself in the affairs of life. Refusing the arranged marriage – to a princess he has never met – that his father, King Peter, wishes to force on him, he leaves the country with his friend Valerio. Similar events have been occurring in the life of the princess Lena. They meet, neither of them realizing that the other is the preselected mate, and fall in love. Leonce decides not to go through with his plan to commit suicide, and they marry and live happily ever after.

Büchner's comedy satirizes German classical and Romantic literature; it also presents social criticism in the guise of irony and satire. Any more direct critique of the societal status quo would not, Büchner was aware, have escaped the censor. In *Leonce und Lena* he uses a major characteristic of German classical drama: the focus on aristocratic characters. By portraying members of the upper classes, including the king, as boorish, spoiled, and empty-headed, Büchner succeeds both in attacking the absolutism of contemporary German society and in exposing the drama of Classicism as a dead form.

To satirize the totalitarian nature of the aristocratic police states existing under the aegis of the Deutscher Bund, Büchner has his bumbling philosopher-king compare the authority he incarnates with the "substance" that Spinoza describes as the self-subsistent ground upon which all other, lesser entities are contingent. As he is being dressed by his valets, King Peter says: "Der Mensch muß denken und ich muß für meine Untertanen denken; denn sie denken nicht. . . . Die Substanz ist das an sich, das bin ich. (*Er läuft fast nackt im Zimmer herum.*) . . . An sich ist an sich, versteht ihr? Jetzt kommen meine Attribute, Modifikationen, Affektionen und Akzidenzien, wo ist mein Hemd, meine Hose?" (Man must think, and I must think for my subjects, for they do not think. . . . The substance is the "thing-in-itself," that is I. (*He runs around the room almost naked.*) . . . In-itself is in-itself, you understand? Now for my attributes, modifications, affections, and accessories: where is my shirt, my pants?). King Peter perceives his supreme position as exalting him entirely above the subjects over whom he rules; just as Spinozan substance or being is absolutely uncontingent in nature, King Peter views political authority as dwelling within his person alone and as having no relation to the people on whom it is imposed. The indifferent, oafish philosopher-ruler thus embodies the diametrical opposite of Büchner's conviction, expressed in *Der Hessische Landbote,* that a ruler exists only for the benefit of the people.

Another theme in *Leonce und Lena* that resembles ideas developed in *Der Hessische Landbote* is the supercilious attitude adopted by Leonce and Valerio to labor and to those who, unlike themselves, must work to survive. Valerio insists that there are only four ways in which one can earn money – find it, win it, inherit it, or steal it – and that anyone who earns money in any other way is a "Verbrecher" (scoundrel). Leonce adds: "Denn wer arbeitet ist ein subtiler Selbstmörder, und ein

Page from the manuscript for Büchner's unfinished play Woyzeck *(from Georg Eckert, ed.,* Hundert Jahr deutsche Sozialdemokratie: Bilder und Dokumente, *1963)*

Selbstmörder ist ein Verbrecher und ein Verbrecher ist ein Schuft, also, wer arbeitet ist ein Schuft" (Because one who works is subtly committing suicide, and a suicide is a criminal, and a criminal is a scoundrel: therefore whoever works is a scoundrel). The two aristocrats assume that money is a vehicle for securing and multiplying the distractions of luxury; it is a means of survival only for the uncultivated, brutish masses, whose existence is, in any case, superfluous. In *Der Hessische Landbote* Büchner had expressed outrage at how the rich aristocrats of Hesse view those who labor as scarcely better than beasts of burden. Another concept developed in the political leaflet that is touched on in the aristocrats' conversation is Büchner's assertion that the laboring masses in Germany are, in effect, committing suicide by subjecting themselves to the demands put on them by the ruling elite. *Leonce und Lena* was published posthumously and was first performed in Munich in May 1895.

During the autumn and winter of 1836–1837 Büchner composed what is perhaps the greatest social drama in German literature; the work remained unfinished at his death. In spite of its fragmentary condition, *Woyzeck* (1879; translated as *Wozzeck,* 1927) contains the fullest literary realization of the sophisticated sociocritical analyses found in *Der Hessische Landbote.* In this play, which is based on actual events that took place in the 1820s, Büchner combines analysis of contemporary social conditions with an exposition of the psychological and metaphysical factors that universalize the significance of these conditions.

The title figure of Büchner's play, Franz Woyzeck, ekes out a meager existence as an army barber; his wife, Marie, has recently given birth to a child. The entire meaning of Woyzeck's life is bound up in his relationship with Marie, but he is driven to destroy the person he loves as a result of the intolerable conditions in which he, as the personification of the wretched lower classes, is forced to exist. Degraded to the point of near insanity by an inhuman social environment, Woyzeck is unable to endure Marie's unfaithfulness with a petty army officer, the Tambourmajor (drum major). His murder of Marie mirrors the cruelty and irrationality of a social order that has incessantly exploited him and negated his personhood. His society's denial of human dignity transmogrifies Woyzeck's innate affirmation of life, embodied in his love of Marie, into a hideous act of destruction.

Marie is also a victim of the indifference and cruelty of society. Some commentators have attributed her infidelity to her supposed overwhelming sexual desire for the mindless and brutish Tambourmajor; but as it is for Woyzeck, existence for Marie is a harsh and endless struggle to survive. Although stricken by conscience at her desire, she perceives the higher social status of the Tambourmajor as a way out of her otherwise hopeless poverty. Woyzeck, on the other hand, embodies a future for her and her child that signifies little more than perpetual suffering and want.

In addition to the dehumanization that is inseparable from her poverty, Marie is viewed by the Tambourmajor as a sexual object. Similarly, Woyzeck is treated as a soulless means to an end by his social superiors: the Hauptmann (captain), the Doktor, and the Professor. These figures, who represent the bourgeoisie, are no less callously exploitative than the aristocrats whose indifference and corruption Büchner censures in *Der Hessische Landbote* and *Leonce und Lena.* Their ruthless exploitation of Woyzeck follows from their inhuman ethical, metaphysical, and scientific worldviews. Woyzeck's dialogue with the Doktor, who is examining him, exemplifies this aspect of the play: "DOKTOR. Ich habs gesehn, Woyzeck: Er hat auf die Straß gepißt, an die Wand gepißt wie ein Hund. WOYZECK. Aber Herr Doktor, wenn einem die Natur kommt.... DOKTOR. Die Natur kommt! ... Hab ich nicht nachgewiesen, daß der musculus constrictor vesicae dem Willen unterworfen ist? Die Natur!" (DOCTOR. I saw it, Woyzeck: you pissed on the street, you pissed on the wall like a dog. WOYZECK. But Doctor, the call of nature.... DOCTOR. The call of nature! Haven't I proved that the *musculus constrictor vesicae* is subject to the will? Nature!). His condescending advice to Woyzeck reveals Büchner's sadistic Doktor as a Cartesian for whom the human mind is a "ghost in the machine" of the body. In its conception of the human body as a clocklike mechanical apparatus, Cartesian philosophical anthropology is synonymous, for Büchner, with the reduction of the human being to an automaton. The philosophical anthropology he espouses allows the Doktor to exploit Woyzeck as a guinea pig; thus, while the Doktor kicks Woyzeck repeatedly, he assures the latter that he is doing so only in the service of scientific analysis: "Nein Woyzeck, ich ärger mich nicht, Ärger ist ungesund, ist unwissenschaftlich.... Mein Puls hat seine gewöhnlichen 60 und ich sag's Ihm mit der größten Kaltblütigkeit" (No, Woyzeck, I'm not getting angry; anger is unhealthy, it is unscientific.... My pulse is beating at its usual sixty, and I'm telling you this in all cold-bloodedness). *Woyzeck* was first performed in November 1913 in Munich;

it was the basis for Alban Berg's opera *Wozzeck* (1921).

In October 1836 Büchner assumed a post as Privatdozent (unpaid lecturer) in comparative anatomy at the University of Zurich. His lectures were greeted with enthusiasm by one of the foremost scientists of the age, Lorenz Oken, who was rector of the university. In mid January 1837 a severe cold forced Büchner to interrupt his teaching activities; at the beginning of February symptoms of typhus became apparent. Büchner's condition deteriorated rapidly. Friends who were caring for him informed Minna Jaeglé of the situation; she arrived in Zurich as Büchner was entering into a coma, but he recognized his fiancée and was able to speak with her. Büchner died on 19 February. In 1923 the city of Darmstadt instituted the Georg Büchner Prize for literature, which has become one of the most prestigious literary awards in Germany.

Bibliographies:

Werner Schlick, *Das Georg-Büchner-Schrifttum bis 1965: Eine internationale Bibliographie* (Hildesheim: Olms, 1968);

Monika Rössing-Hager, *Wortindex zu Georg Büchner, Dichtungen und Übersetzungen* (Berlin & New York: De Gruyter, 1970);

Gerhard P. Knapp, *Georg Büchner: Eine kritische Einführung in die Forschung* (Frankfurt am Main: Athenaion, 1975).

Biography:

Gerhard P. Knapp, *Georg Büchner,* second edition (Stuttgart: Metzler, 1984).

References:

Winnifred R. Adolph, *Disintegrating Myths: A Study of Georg Büchner* (New York: Lang, 1989);

Heinz Ludwig Arnold, ed., *Text + Kritik: Georg Büchner I/II* (Munich: Edition text + kritik, 1979);

Alfred Behrmann and Joachim Wohlleben, *Büchner: Danton's Tod. Eine Dramenanalyse* (Stuttgart: Klett-Cotta, 1980);

Maurice B. Benn, *The Drama of Revolt: A Critical Study of Georg Büchner* (Cambridge & New York: Cambridge University Press, 1976);

Fausto Cercignani, ed., *Studia Büchneriana: Georg Büchner 1988* (Milan: Cisalpino, 1990);

Burghard Dedner, ed., *Der widerständige Klassiker: Einleitungen zu Büchner vom Nachmärz bis zur Weimarer Republik* (Frankfurt am Main: Athenäum, 1990);

Dedner, Alfons Glück, Walter Hinderer, and Michael Voges, *Georg Büchner: Dantons Tod, Lenz, Leonce und Lena, Woyzeck. Interpretationen* (Stuttgart: Reclam, 1990);

Heinz Fischer, *Georg Büchner und Alexis Muston: Untersuchungen zu einem Büchner-Fund* (Munich: Fink, 1987);

Reinhold Grimm, *Love, Lust and Rebellion: New Approaches to Georg Büchner* (Madison: University of Wisconsin Press, 1985);

Karlheinz Hasselbach, *Georg Büchner: Lenz. Interpretationen* (Munich: Oldenbourg, 1986);

Jan-Christoph Hauschild, *Georg Büchner: Studien und neue Quellen zu Leben, Werk und Wirkung* (Königstein: Athenäum, 1985);

Ronald Hauser, *Georg Büchner* (New York: Twayne, 1974);

Louis Ferdinand Helbig, *Das Geschichtsdrama Georg Büchners* (Bern: Lang, 1973);

Julian Hilton, *Georg Büchner* (New York: Grove, 1982);

Walter Hinderer, *Büchner Kommentar zum dichterischen Werk* (Munich: Winkler, 1977);

Dorothy James, *Georg Büchner's Dantons Tod: A Reappraisal* (London: Modern Humanities Research Association, 1982);

Gerhard Jancke, *Georg Büchner: Genese und Aktualität seines Werkes* (Kronberg: Skriptor, 1975);

Gerhard P. Knapp, *Georg Büchner: Dantons Tod* (Frankfurt am Main: Diesterweg, 1983);

Knapp, "Der Mythos des Schreckens: Maximilien Robespierre als Motiv in der deutschen Literatur des neunzehnten Jahrhunderts," in *Schreckensmythen-Hoffnungsbilder: Die Französische Revolution in der deutschen Literatur. Essays,* edited by Harro Zimmermann (Frankfurt am Main: Athenäum, 1989);

Erwin Kobel, *Georg Büchner* (Berlin: De Gruyter, 1972);

Helmut Krapp, *Der Dialog bei Georg Büchner* (Darmstadt: Gentner, 1958);

Herbert Lindenberger, *Georg Büchner* (Carbondale: Southern Illinois University Press, 1964);

Gyorgi Lukács, *Deutsche Literatur in zwei Jahrhunderten* (Neuwied: Luchterhand, 1964);

Wolfgang Martens, ed., *Georg Büchner* (Darmstadt: Wissenschaftliche Buchgesellschaft, 1965);

Hans Mayer, *Georg Büchner und seine Zeit* (Frankfurt am Main: Suhrkamp, 1972);

Albert Meier, *Georg Büchners Ästhetik* (Munich: Fink, 1983);

Henri Poschmann, *Georg Büchner: Dichtung der Revolution und Revolution der Dichtung* (Berlin & Weimar: Aufbau, 1983);

John Reddick, "Georg Büchner and the Agony of Authenticity," *Forum for Modern Language Studies,* 23 (October 1987): 289–324;

William C. Reeve, *Georg Büchner* (New York: Ungar, 1979);

William H. Rey, *Georg Büchners Dantons Tod* (Bern & Las Vegas: Lang, 1982);

David G. Richards, *Georg Büchner and the Birth of the Modern Drama* (Albany: State University of New York Press, 1977);

Henry J. Schmidt, *Satire, Caricature, and Perspectivism in the Works of Georg Büchner* (The Hague: Mouton, 1970);

Friedrich Sengle, *Biedermeierzeit, volume 3: Die Dichter* (Stuttgart: Metzler, 1980);

Rodney Taylor, *History and the Paradoxes of Metaphysics in Dantons Tod* (New York: Lang, 1990);

Taylor, "History and the Transcendence of Subjectivity in Büchner's Robespierre," *Neophilologus,* 72 (January 1988): 82–96;

Jan Thorn-Prikker, *Revolutionär ohne Revolution: Interpretationen der Werke Georg Büchners* (Stuttgart: Klett-Cotta, 1978);

Cornelie Ueding, *Denken, Sprechen, Handeln: Aufklärung und Aufklärungskritik im Werk Georg Büchners* (Frankfurt am Main: Lang, 1976);

Karl Vietor, *Georg Büchner: Politik, Dichtung, Wissenschaft* (Bern: Franke, 1949);

Leonard P. Wessell, "Eighteenth-Century Theodicy and the Death of God in Büchner's *Dantons Tod,*" *Seminar,* 8 (October 1972): 198–218;

Raleigh Whitinger, "Echoes of Novalis and Tieck in Büchner's *Lenz,*" *Seminar,* 25 (1989): 324–338;

Benno von Wiese, *Die deutsche Tragödie von Lessing bis Hebbel* (Hamburg: Hoffmann & Campe, 1961);

Wolfgang Wittkowski, *Georg Büchner: Persönlichkeit, Weltbild, Werk* (Heidelberg: Winter, 1978);

U-Tag Yang, *Reflexion und Desintegration: Zur Identitätskrise der Protagonisten im Werk Georg Büchners* (Bern & New York: Lang, 1989).

Papers:

Georg Büchner's papers are at the Goethe-und-Schiller-Archiv, Weimar.

Franz von Dingelstedt

(30 June 1814 - 15 May 1881)

Simon Williams
University of California, Santa Barbara

BOOKS: *Frauenspiegel* (Nuremberg: Schrag, 1838);

Gedichte (Kassel & Leipzig: Fischer, 1838);

Licht und Schatten in der Liebe: Novellen (Kassel & Leipzig: Fischer, 1838);

Die neuen Argonauten: Ein komischer Roman (Fulda: Müller, 1839);

Wanderbuch, 2 volumes (Leipzig: Einhorn, 1839-1843);

Das Weserthal von Münden bis Minden (Kassel: Fischer, 1839);

Das Gespenst der Ehre (Fulda: Published by the author, 1840);

Ein Osterwort aus Kurhessen (Marburg: Garthe, 1840);

Sechs Jahrhunderte aus Gutenbergs Leben: Kleine Gabe zum großen Feste (Kassel: Hotop, 1840); translated by Caroline O. Wintour as *John Gutenberg, First Master Printer, His Acts, and Most Remarkable Discourses, and His Death* (London: Philobiblon Society, 1860);

Unter der Erde: Ein Denkmal für die Lebendigen. Roman, 2 volumes (Leipzig: Einhorn, 1840);

Heptameron: Gesammelte Novellen, 2 volumes (Magdeburg: Baensch, 1841);

Eine stille Novelle (Kassel: Hotop, 1841);

Lieder eines kosmopolitischen Nachtwächters, anonymous (Hamburg: Hoffmann & Campe, 1842);

Sieben friedliche Erzählungen, 2 volumes (Stuttgart: Krabbe, 1844);

Gedichte (Stuttgart & Tübingen: Cotta, 1845);

Lichtenstein: Oper in fünf Aufzügen, music by Peter v. Lindpaintner (Stuttgart: Fein, 1846);

Jusqu'à la mer: Erinnerungen an Holland (Leipzig: Weber, 1847);

Zeitstimmungen aus Hessen: 1840-1848. Gedichte, by Dingelstedt and S. Jordan (Kassel: Hotop, 1848);

Gedenkblatt zur Feier von Goethe's hundertstem Geburtstag, den 28. August 1849: Geister der Paulskirche. Gedichtet zu Goethe's neun und neunzigstem Geburtstag (28. August 1848) (Frankfurt am Main: Baer, 1849);

Das Haus der Barneveldt (Dresden, 1850);

Franz von Dingelstedt, circa 1853; photograph by Alois Löcherer

Prolog bei der ersten Aufführung des Lohengrin . . . (Weimar: Urf-Druckerei, 1850);

Nacht und Morgen: Neue Zeit-Gedichte (Stuttgart & Tübingen: Cotta, 1851);

Novellen-Buch (Leipzig & Vienna: Hartleben, 1856);

Der Aerntekranz: Vorspiel für die Weimarische Jubelfeier (Weimar: Böhlau, 1857);

Studien und Copien nach Shakespeare (Vienna: Hartleben, 1858);

Frühlings-Anfang: Prolog (Berlin, 1861);

Die Amazone, 2 volumes (Stuttgart: Hallberger, 1868); translated by James Morgan Hart as *The Amazon* (New York: Putnam's, 1868; Edinburgh: Edmonston & Douglas, 1869);

Zu Molières Gedächtnisfeier am zweiten Säculartage seines Ablebens, 17. 2. 1873: Theaterrede gesprochen durch Herrn Lewinsky (Vienna: Hof- und Staatsdruckerei, 1873);

Eine Faust-Trilogie: Dramaturgische Studie (Berlin: Paetel, 1876);

Sämtliche Werke: Erste Gesammt-Ausgabe, 12 volumes (Berlin: Paetel, 1877);

Literarisches Bilderbuch, 2 volumes (Berlin: Hofmann, 1878);

Münchener Bilderbogen (Berlin: Paetel, 1879);

Ein Osterwort aus Hessen (Marburg: Ziwert, 1881);

Die Schule der Welt (Munich: Oldenbourg, 1884);

Blätter aus seinem Nachlaß, 2 volumes, edited by Julius Rodenberg (Berlin: Paetel, 1891);

Lieder eines kosmopolitischen Nachtwächters, edited by Heinrich Hubert Houben (Leipzig: Klinkhardt & Biermann, 1923);

Lieder eines kosmopolitischen Nachtwächters, edited by Hans-Peter Bayerdorfer (Tübingen: Niemeyer, 1978).

OTHER: *Die Wage: Belletristisches Beiblatt zur Kurhessischen Allgemeinen Landeszeitung,* nos. 1–63, edited by Dingelstedt (1837);

Hessisches Album für Literatur und Kunst, edited by Dingelstedt (Cassel: Bohné, 1838);

Der Salon: Wochenschrift für Heimat und Fremde, nos. 1–39, edited by Dingelstedt (1841);

Molière, *Der Geizige,* translated by Dingelstedt (Weimar: Hofdruckerei, 1858);

William Shakespeare, *Ein Wintermärchen,* translated by Dingelstedt (Berlin: Heinrich & Michaelson, 1859);

Pierre-Augustin Caron de Beaumarchais, *Ein toller Tag oder Figaros Hochzeit: Lustspiel in fünf Aufzügen,* translated by Dingelstedt (Weimar: Tartz, 1862);

Johann Valentin Teichmanns, weiland königl. preußischen Hofrathes, literarischer Nachlaß, edited by Dingelstedt (Stuttgart: Cotta, 1863);

Shakespeare, *Sturm,* translated by Dingelstedt (Hildburgshausen: Bibliographisches Institut, 1866);

Shakespeare, *Historien,* 3 volumes, adapted by Dingelstedt (Berlin: Reimer, 1867);

Shakespeare, *Komödie der Irrungen,* translated by Dingelstedt (Hildburgshausen: Bibliographisches Institut, 1868);

Shakespeare, *Was ihr wollt,* translated by Dingelstedt (Hildburgshausen: Bibliographisches Institut, 1869);

Shakespeare, *Wie es euch gefällt,* translated by Dingelstedt (Hildburgshausen: Bibliographisches Institut, 1869);

Heinrich von Kleist, *Der zerbrochene Krug,* edited by Dingelstedt (Berlin: Hoffmann, 1877);

Shakespeare, *Antonius und Cleopatra,* translated by Dingelstedt (Vienna: Gerold, 1879).

SELECTED PERIODICAL PUBLICATION – UNCOLLECTED: "Franz Dingelstedt: Die Produktion des Jahres 1840," *Heine Jahrbuch,* 24 (1985): 179–214.

Franz von Dingelstedt's varied career should have brought him great satisfaction. He made a striking start as a lyric poet, whose ironical, elegiac, and yet incipiently sentimental verse suggested that he might become a major figure among the writers of the Junges Deutschland (Young Germany) movement. His early journalistic writings and short stories offered similar promise. Though he never abandoned writing, as he approached middle age he turned his energies more exclusively toward the theater, where he had a brilliantly successful career as producer, stage director, theater manager, and ultimately Intendant (director) of both the Vienna Burgtheater and the Hofoperntheater (Court Opera). Few of his contemporaries in the worlds of letters or the theater achieved such prestige or wealth; yet Dingelstedt seems to have died a disappointed man. As Paul Lindau's sad epitaph puts it: "Wenn ihr mich (möglichst spät) begrabt, / Sei dies auf meinem Stein zu lesen: / Er hat zeitlebens Glück gehabt, / Doch glücklich ist er nie gewesen" (When you bury me [as late as possible], / Let this be read upon my stone: / Throughout his life he was lucky, / Yet he was never happy).

Dingelstedt was born on 30 June 1814 in the village of Halsdorf in Hesse. His father was a monastery steward who had been a sergeant in the Hessian army. In 1816 the family moved to Rinteln, a small town on the river Weser some forty miles southwest of Hannover. The divided loyalty between literature and the theater that was to mark his whole life became apparent in his early teens. His first visit to the theater took place when he was twelve; subsequent contacts with backstage workers fascinated him and encouraged him to build his own puppet theater. At the same time, poems he wrote for occasions such as his father's birthday indicated a talent for versification. As he grew older he displayed a bias toward radical thinking that is apparent from the speech "Über die Sehnsucht des Menschen nach einer besseren Zukunft" (On the

Longing of Mankind for a Better Future), which he delivered to his schoolmates at the Rinteln Gymnasium on the occasion of the French revolution of July 1830. The following year Dingelstedt enrolled as a theology student at the University of Marburg; but his involvement there with a theatrical troupe, which included a love affair with the leading actress, led him to conclude that the church was not his vocation.

On leaving Marburg in 1835 Dingelstedt was appointed teacher of German at the English school in Ricklingen, near Hannover. There followed eight years of creative activity on which his reputation as a lyric poet of some significance mainly rests. He mastered English and began a lifelong devotion to the works of William Shakespeare; he read widely in contemporary German and European literature; and he had theater and art criticism published in local journals. In April 1836 he was appointed teacher of modern languages and literature at the Lyceum Friedericianum in Kassel. In addition to his pedagogical duties he edited a literary periodical, *Die Wage* (The Scales) and wrote satirical short stories. In 1838 he left Kassel due to controversy caused by his writings and took up a teaching post in Fulda. He continued to write, notably the satirical novel *Die neuen Argonauten* (The New Argonauts, 1839) and a novel of political and social protest, *Unter der Erde* (Beneath the Earth, 1840), which contains some strikingly realistic descriptions of mining. The controversy aroused by these works led to Dingelstedt's dismissal from his position at Fulda. He immediately assumed the post of Paris correspondent for the Augsburg *Allgemeine Zeitung* (Universal Newspaper). As he departed for Paris, his most distinctive collection of poems, *Lieder eines kosmopolitischen Nachtwächters* (Songs of a Cosmopolitan Night Watchman, 1842), was published anonymously in Hamburg. With this publication Dingelstedt's work achieved national recognition.

Dingelstedt's early writing shows no signs of great originality. As a poet he took Friedrich Schiller as his first model, but later and more consistent influences were Heinrich Heine and Ferdinand Freiligrath. While Dingelstedt displayed a ready wit that could too easily border on malicious sarcasm, his satire is generally less pointed and certainly less penetrating than Heine's. Furthermore, he is often concerned to express his own moods, and the subjective note invests his work with a sentimental tone that softens the irony. As a prose writer Dingelstedt wrote with pleasing facility. He had an accurate though essentially shallow grasp of character and considerable skill at describing both social and natu-

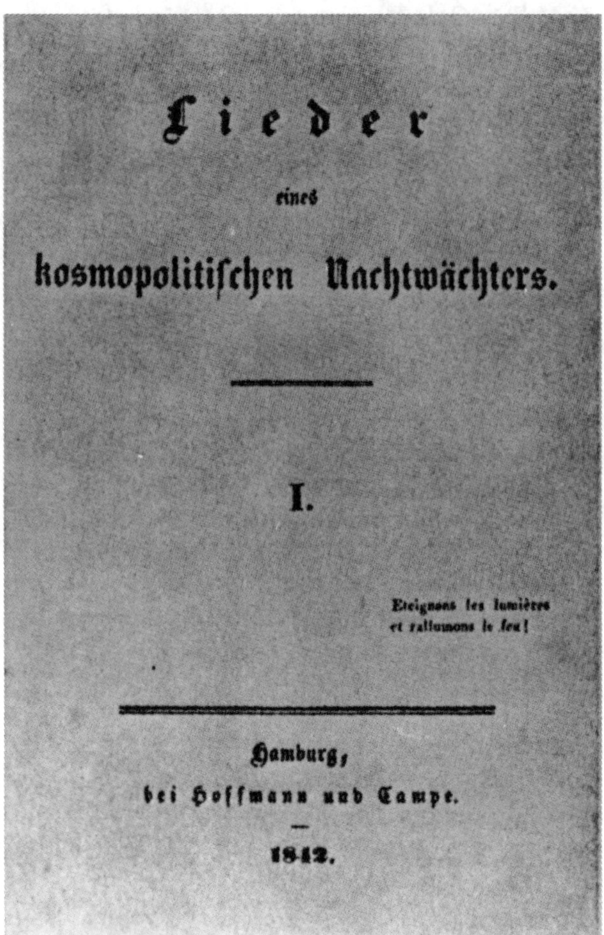

Lieder

eines

kosmopolitischen Nachtwächters.

I.

Eteignons les lumières
et rallumons le feu!

Hamburg,

bei Hoffmann und Campe.

1842.

Title page for the book of poems that brought Dingelstedt national recognition

ral environments. Indeed, his travel books – such as the description of his homeland, *Das Weserthal von Münden bis Minden* (The Weser Valley from Münden to Minden, 1839) – have considerable documentary value. But while his stories, most of which are set in the bourgeois and aristocratic circles of contemporary Germany, contain much criticism of the provinciality, materialism, philistinism, and general vacuousness of social life, his desire to entertain the reader and his tendency to express affection for the objects of his satire deprive much of his criticism of its potentially scathing edge.

Lieder eines kosmopolitischen Nachtwächters is the most successful and significant work in Dingelstedt's early literary output. The four cycles of poems that compose this collection are modeled on the then-popular genre of "Reisebilder" (travel pictures) cultivated by writers such as Heine, Anastasius Grün, Hoffmann von Fallersleben, and the writers of Junges Deutschland – a series of brief poems or prose pieces that highlighted, usually in a satirical mode, examples of social injustice observed by the narrator on his travels. In Dingelstedt's *Lieder eines kosmopolitischen Nachtwächters* the satire is both sustained and witty, while the tone of outrage and pity for the deprived and socially alienated is strong. In its time, the collection was regarded as a major work in the literary output of the Junges Deutschland movement, and recent critical reassessments have restored this reputation. In the first cycle, "Nachtwächters Stilleben" (Night Watchman's Still Life), the watchman walks through the sleeping small town he guards, meditating on the lives of those whose houses he passes. Here, more than anywhere else in Dingelstedt's writing, his subjectivity amplifies the satire so that it achieves a force and poignancy that is often surprising. Metaphors are spare, without the elaboration and mystical resonance characteristic of some romantic poetry of the previous generation. Whether the watchman speaks of the agony of death in a poor hovel, the inhumanity of burying suicides outside consecrated ground, or the incarceration in lunatic asylums of those whose ideas cannot be accommodated within the narrow scope of "reason," sympathy for the dispossessed is uppermost in his meditations. Accompanying this sympathy is harsh condemnation of indifferent authority as represented by the wealthy, the church, and local government. Dingelstedt's wit is at times concise yet trenchant – as in the brief poem where he imagines the red nose of the drunken Burgermeister as a spark in a bundle of straw, implying thereby the outbreak of revolution.

In the second cycle, "Nachtwächters Weltgang" (Night Watchman's Journey through the World), the watchman visits various cities and provinces of Germany. Here Dingelstedt protests in more overtly polemical terms gross inequities in wealth; the vulgarity, triviality, and intrigue of the ruling classes; and the cruel indifference of the privileged in German society to those with neither power nor wealth. The motto for this cycle might be found in Dingelstedt's description of the huge statue to Bavaria erected in Munich by Ludwig Schwanthaler: "ein Monument für das Jahrhundert / Von aussen glänzend' Erz, von innen hohl" (a monument for the century / On the outside gleaming bronze, on the inside hollow). The style and meter of the poems in this cycle are more varied than in the first, suggesting that Dingelstedt had the capacity to become a poet of considerable versatility. The strength and depth of his despair and the immensity of his anger at the ostentation and corruption of his time also offer a distinct promise that he might have matured to become a socially committed poet of major status.

The promise is belied by the final two brief cycles, "Empfindsame Reisen" (Sentimental Journies) and "Letzte Liebe" (Last Love), where Dingelstedt allows his sentimentality to get the better of him. Abandoning the unifying figure of the admonitory night watchman, he presents a series of touching though unremarkable poems on such topics as personal unfulfillment, nostalgia for the fatherland, and – ubiquitously – disappointed love.

In 1842 Dingelstedt visited London, where he fell in love with the Austrian opera singer Jenny Lutzer. He followed her when she returned to Vienna in the fall of that year; eighteen months later he married her. By this time he had, to the chagrin of Heine and other writers who had greatly admired *Lieder eines kosmopolitischen Nachtwächters,* accepted a position in Stuttgart as librarian to the king of Württemberg. He was accepted into court circles, and his writing talents were devoted mainly to providing materials for the crown prince's private theater. In effect, Dingelstedt had joined those whom, only a few years before, he had been violently attacking. In the course of this conversion his theatrical interests came to acquire greater importance than the literary ones. He served as producer at the royal theater; wrote the libretto for Peter von Lindpaintner's opera *Lichtenstein* (1846); and worked with the regisseurs Heinrich Moritz, Karl Grunert, and August Lewald, who were pioneers in the use of masses of actors on the stage. The one substantial product of this period was his play *Das Haus von Barneveldt* (The House of Barneveldt, 1850), which was completed in July 1850, performed in Dresden two months later, and then staged widely throughout Germany.

Initially, *Das Haus von Barneveldt,* which is based on historical events associated with the opposition of the Barneveldt family to the rule of William of Orange in the Netherlands, appears to be a political drama in which the cause of individual freedom and integrity will be pitted against absolutist repression. In the magnificently tense and carefully structured opening act, Dingelstedt's obvious debt to Schiller encourages this expectation. As in *Lieder eines kosmopolitischen Nachtwächters,* however, political themes are gradually abandoned for personal ones; and the dramatic action, which loses both momentum and coherence as the play proceeds, centers around the emotional consequences of the rivalry between the two sons of the heroic renegade Olden Barneveldt. While Wilhelm Bernhard Dewald, the single modern critic who has analyzed the play, claims that it was a revolutionary work because it disputed the prerogative of princes, the success of the play in several court theaters during the early 1850s suggests that these political implications were not apparent to Dingelstedt's contemporaries.

As a result of a successful performance of *Das Haus von Barneveldt* in Munich, Dingelstedt was appointed Intendant of the Hof- und Nationaltheater (Court and National Theater) there on 1 January 1851. During the six years of his tenure in Munich, Dingelstedt transformed the formerly undemanding repertoire. His primary ambition was to stage the classics, so Shakespeare, Schiller, Johann Wolfgang von Goethe, Sophocles, and Pedro Calderón de la Barca were central in his selection of plays. Works by Shakespeare included the first production in Germany of *The Tempest* and an adaptation of *Macbeth* that was widely produced. Dingelstedt did not, however, confine himself to the drama of the past; the works of modern playwrights such as Karl Gutzkow, Heinrich Laube, Otto Ludwig, and Franz Grillparzer were performed in his theater, while the dramas of Friedrich Hebbel, who was a close friend, received particular attention. Dingelstedt was responsible, too, for one of the most effective early productions of Richard Wagner's technically demanding opera *Tannhäuser* (1845).

Dingelstedt had a significant impact on the development of stagecraft in the German theater. Spectacular productions, especially in the presentation of grand opera and history plays, were not unknown in Germany during the first half of the nineteenth century; but the coordinated exploitation of such nonverbal elements as scenic painting, gesture, mass choric movement, and musical accompaniment as a means of complementing the text was underdeveloped. Wagner, in his theoretical essays written between 1849 and 1851, devised the theory of the Gesamtkunstwerk (total work of art) partly in protest against the lack of coordination he perceived in contemporary theatrical production. But while Wagner never achieved the total work of art in actuality, Dingelstedt balanced the constituents of theatrical production and performance in a way of which Wagner had only conceived. In 1854 he organized a Gesamtgastspiel (total ensemble), a summer festival in which the classics were performed by eminent actors from throughout Germany in both leading and subsidiary roles. The undertaking was cut short by an outbreak of cholera.

In 1857 Dingelstedt was dismissed from his post for several reasons: his extravagant productions had run up an immense deficit; Catholic conservatives objected to a Protestant from northern Germany having such an influential position in the cultural life of the city; the productions of *Tannhäuser* and Hebbel's *Agnes Bernauer* (1855) had offended audiences; and he became involved in a controversy over the authorship of a popular play, *Der Fechter von Ravenna* (The Gladiator of Ravenna, 1856), that was in fact written by Friedrich Halm. Immediately after his departure from Munich, Dingelstedt was appointed to the directorship of the Weimar court theater, where Franz Liszt was director of music. In Weimar he continued to explore both the classic and modern repertoire, his most significant achievements being the first performance in Germany of *The Winter's Tale* and the first complete production anywhere of Shakespeare's two history tetralogies, which were staged in 1864 in celebration of the three hundredth anniversary of Shakespeare's birth. In partnership with Wilhelm Oechelhäuser, Dingelstedt used the occasion of the gathering of scholars at the performance of the history cycles to found the Deutsche Shakespeare-Gesellschaft (German Shakespeare Society), which has subsequently sponsored much of the greatest modern scholarship on the playwright.

Dingelstedt's adaptations of Shakespeare's plays represent an important phase in the process through which the playwright was naturalized into the German theater. From the late eighteenth century, when Shakespeare's work first appeared on the German stage, the plays were rarely done in unadapted versions. Dingelstedt subscribed fully to the principle of adaptation, rewriting and re-forming the plays to suit mid-nineteenth-century tastes and to ensure the widest possible audience for them. Hence, his performing versions were quite different from the standard reading version of Shakespeare in German, the translations in the August Wilhelm Schlegel / Dorothea Tieck edition (1825–1833). Scenes are conflated and rearranged; acts are restructured; Shakespeare's imagery, which had been translated with fair accuracy by Schlegel and Tieck, is more generalized and is recast in the idiom of the day; and the characters in Dingelstedt's versions do not have the vivid personalities of the originals. Furthermore, there is no sense of inner conflict; instead, conflict of a rudimentary kind remains mainly between characters and is frequently lost in the spectacle that was Dingelstedt's primary interest. Innumerable cuts are made to speed up the action and increase tension, while dramatic climaxes are built with far greater deliberation than in Shakespeare's original plays. For these reasons, it is unlikely that his versions of *Macbeth* (included in his *Studien und Copien nach Shakespeare* [Studies and Copies after Shakespeare,

1858]), *The Tempest* (*Sturm,* 1866), *The Winter's Tale* (*Ein Wintermärchen,* 1859) and of the history cycles (*Historien,* 1867) would find sympathetic audiences today. Nevertheless, the seamlessness of his productions and the skill with which he combined acting, staging, and design were much to the taste of contemporary audiences and introduced some of Shakespeare's most challenging and enigmatic plays to the German repertoire, even though in simplified form.

Dingelstedt, an indefatigable worker who could judge with unerring accuracy what would appeal to public taste, did much to restore the reputation of Weimar as a vital center of German theatrical life. But the limited budgets and circumscribed audiences in Weimar frustrated his ambitions. The high point of his career came on 1 October 1867 when he was appointed director of the Vienna court opera. There he did much to improve production standards; and in May 1869 he presided over the opening of the new Opera House on the Ringstraße, which is still in operation today. That year he was responsible for notable new productions of Wagner's *Tannhaüser* and *Die Meistersinger von Nürnberg* (The Mastersingers of Nuremberg, 1868). In 1870 he was appointed director of the Burgtheater, a post he held concurrently with his position at the opera. Although he did not develop artistically in Vienna, his contribution to the growth of the theater was invaluable. His predecessor at the Burgtheater, Heinrich Laube, had created an ensemble of actors that was unequaled in the German-language theater; Dingelstedt retained this ensemble and extended its range. While Laube's repertoire had depended heavily on contemporary French drama, Dingelstedt restored a more catholic repertoire. Though he was known primarily for his work with the classics, he introduced to the Burgtheater stage the work of such characteristically modern dramatists as Ludwig Anzengruber and Henrik Ibsen. At the same time, he revived several of his successes from Munich and Weimar – in particular the complete history cycles, which were given a magnificently acted and opulently staged production in 1875. In contrast, Dingelstedt's predecessor Laube had stripped the scenery used on the Burgtheater stage to the barest minimum.

Soon after his arrival in Vienna, Dingelstedt's novel *Die Amazone* (1868; translated as *The Amazon,* 1868) was published; it was quite highly regarded in its day but has not stood the test of time. Intended to refute Goethe's theory of elective affinities as expounded in *Die Wahlverwandtschaften* (1809; translated as "Elective Affinities," 1854), its plot is of the

Engraving of Dingelstedt by A. Wegner

slightest. Centered on the world of the visual and performing arts in a south German or Austrian city, the action also touches on the spheres of business and diplomacy. Occasional passages are reminiscent of the writing of Charles Dickens, but the novel lacks the energy and passion of the English novelist's work. More successful literary efforts from this period are Dingelstedt's essays in criticism and theater history, collected in *Literarisches Bilderbuch* (Literary Picture-Book, 1878). Here he demonstrates a knowledge of the Elizabethan theater and the theater of Louis XIV that reflects the most current research of his time. In 1876

Dingelstedt was granted the title Freiherr (baron), which allowed him to add *von* to his name.

Given the remarkable success of Dingelstedt's career, one might wonder why Lindau commemorated it with such a melancholy epitaph. Probably it was because Dingelstedt never fulfilled the promise he seemed constantly to offer. Were it not for his celebrity as a theater director, his collected works would not have been published in 1877, and he would have remained a footnote in literary history. He was, with the exception of the *Lieder eines kosmopolitischen Nachtwächters,* a minor writer. His career in the theater was certainly more consequential, but even here Dingelstedt was disappointed. After he had seen performances by the renowned company of George II, Duke of Saxe-Meiningen during its first tour to Vienna, he complained: "Sehen Sie, so gehts. Das hab *ich* gemacht. Vielleicht hab ich schon zu viel gemacht. Und nun heißt es: die Meininger!" (Look at that, that's how it is. That is what *I* did. Perhaps I did too much. And now they call it the Meininger!). This contention was not entirely accurate: Dingelstedt was far more concerned with atmosphere and less with historical accuracy than the duke was. Accordingly, the true heir to Dingelstedt's work was the early twentieth-century director Max Reinhardt. In any case, Dingelstedt sensed a lack of completion in what he did.

In 1880 he relinquished the direction of the court opera but remained at the Burgtheater. When he died on 15 May 1881 he was one of the most celebrated and influential figures in the cultural life of Vienna.

Letters:

"Ungedruckte Briefe von Franz von Dingelstedt," edited by Otto Francke, in *Beiträge zur Literatur- und Theatergeschichte: Ludwig Geiger zum 70. Geburtstage. 5. Juni 1918* (Berlin, 1918), pp. 407–419;

Franz von Dingelstedt und Julius Hartmann: Eine Jugendfreundschaft in Briefen, edited by Werner Deetjen (Leipzig: Insel, 1922);

Aus der Briefmappe eines Burgtheaterdirectors, edited by Karl Glossy (Vienna: Schroll, 1925).

Biographies:

Julius Rodenberg, *Heimaterinnerungen an Franz Dingelstedt und Friedrich Oetker* (Berlin: Paetel, 1882);

Karl Glossy, "Franz von Dingelstedt: Eine biographische Skizze," in *Aus der Briefmappe eines Burgtheaterdirectors,* edited by Glossy (Vienna: Schroll, 1925), pp. 1–176;

H. Knudsen, "Franz Dingelstedt," in his *Lebensbilder aus Kurhessen und Waldeck,* volume 2 (Marburg: Elvert, 1940), pp. 90–103;

Karl von Stockmayer, "Franz Dingelstedt," *Schwäbische Lebensbilder,* 2 (1941): 92–109.

References:

Gosta Bergmann, "Der Eintritt des Berufsregisseurs in die deutschsprachige Bühne," *Maske und Kothurn,* 12 (1966);

Wilhelm Bernhard Dewald, *Dingelstedts Haus der Barneveldt auf seine Entstehung untersucht und gewürdigt* (Bremen: Schönemann, 1920);

Woldemar Jürgens, "Dingelstedt, Shakespeare und Weimar," *Shakespeare-Jahrbuch,* 55 (1919): 75–85;

Paul Lindau, "Laube und Dingelstedt als Regisseure," *Nord und Süd,* 98 (1901): 160–182;

Otto Liebscher, *Franz Dingelstedt: Seine dramaturgische Entwicklung und Tätigkeit bis 1857 und seine Bühnenleitung in München* (Halle: Paalzow, 1909);

Friedrich Rosenthal, *Unsterblichkeit des Theaters* (Bonn: Klopp, 1924);

Robert K. Sarlos, "Dingelstedt's Celebration of the Tercentenary: Shakespeare's Histories as a Cycle," *Theatre Survey,* 5 (November 1964): 117–131;

Simon Williams, *Shakespeare on the German Stage, 1586–1914* (Cambridge: Cambridge University Press, 1990).

Annette von Droste-Hülshoff

(10 January 1797 - 24 May 1848)

Monika Shafi
University of Delaware

Annette von Droste-Hülshoff

BOOKS: *Gedichte,* anonymous (Münster: Aschendorff, 1838);

Gedichte (Stuttgart: Tübingen: Cotta, 1844);

Das geistliche Jahr: Nebst einem Anhang religiöser Gedichte, edited by Christoph Bernhard Schlüter and Wilhelm Junkmann (Stuttgart & Tübingen: Cotta, 1851);

Letzte Gaben: Nachgelassene Blätter, edited by Levin Schücking (Hannover: Rümpler, 1860);

Gesammelte Schriften, 3 volumes, edited by Schücking (Stuttgart: Cotta, 1878–1879);

Gesammelte Werke, 4 volumes, edited by Elisabeth Freiin von Droste-Hülshoff and Wilhelm Kreiten (Münster & Paderborn: Schöningh, 1884–1887);

Der Familienschild, by Droste-Hülshoff and Schücking (N.p., 1898; reprinted, Münster: Aschendorff, 1960);

Sämtliche Werke, 6 volumes, edited by Eduard Arens (Leipzig: Hesse, 1904);

Sämtliche Werke, 6 volumes, edited by Julius Schwering (Berlin, Leipzig, Vienna & Stuttgart: Bong, 1912);

Sämtliche Werke, 4 volumes, edited by Karl Schulte Kemminghausen (Munich: Müller, 1925–1930);

Sämtliche Werke, in zeitlicher Folge geordnet, edited by Clemens Heselhaus (Munich: Hanser, 1952);

Sämtliche Werke, 2 volumes, edited by Günter Weydt and Winfried Woesler (Munich: Winkler, 1973, 1978);

Werke und Briefe, 2 volumes, edited by Manfred Häckel (Leipzig: Insel, 1976);

Historisch-kritische Ausgabe: Werke, Briefwechsel, 14 volumes, edited by Woesler (Tübingen: Niemeyer, 1978–1985).

Editions in English: "Pentecost," "The House in the Heath," The Boy on the Moor," "On the Tower," "The Desolate House," "The Jew's Beech-Tree," translated by Charles Wharton Stork and Lillie Winter, in *The German Classics of the Nineteenth and Twentieth Centuries,* volume 7, edited by Kuno Francke and William Guild Howard (New York: German Publication Society, 1913), pp. 437–496;

The Jew's Beech, translated by Lionel and Doris Thomas (London: Calder, 1958).

OTHER: Ferdinand Freiligrath and Levin Schücking, *Das malerische und romantische Westphalen,* contributions by Droste-Hülshoff (Leipzig: Volckmar, 1841).

Annette von Droste-Hülshoff is regarded as the greatest woman poet of nineteenth-century German literature, and her work has received more critical acclaim and attention than that of any other German woman writer. Her novella "Die Judenbuche" (published in her *Letzte Gaben* [Final Offerings], 1860; translated as "The Jew's Beech-Tree," 1913) is a highly intriguing crime story whose enigmatic plot and complex narrative structure bewildered generations of scholars and readers. Her many ballads and poems cover a wide range of topics and forms and feature a detailed, almost microscopic depiction of nature as well as a fascination with the uncanny, supernatural, and mysterious side of human nature. The depth of psychological insight displayed in these works goes far beyond the scope of the Biedermeier period and connects her writing to modern literature and consciousness.

Droste-Hülshoff's reputation as a leading figure of German literature was established several decades after her death; the public began to notice her only during the last years of her life. This relative anonymity, although to some extent sought by the author, reflects for the most part the many obstacles imposed on Droste-Hülshoff's creative development by her class, her sex, her religion, and her region. Besides struggling with a family that barely tolerated her literary efforts, she was troubled throughout her life by her poetic vocation. Although she never left the narrowly defined boundaries of her existence, she did question and challenge them in her writings.

Anna Elisabeth Franziska Adolfine Wilhelmina Luisa Maria, Freiin Droste-Hülshoff, nicknamed Annette, was born on 10 January 1797 in the castle of Hülshoff in Westphalia; her family could trace its aristocratic lineage as far back as the thirteenth century. She was born several weeks premature and survived thanks to the help of a wet nurse, Maria Katharina Plettendorf. Droste-Hülshoff would always feel a close emotional bond to this simple peasant woman and would take care of her until Plettendorf's death in 1845. Droste-Hülshoff had to cope throughout her life with poor health and frequent illnesses, suffering in particular from weak eyesight.

She was an extraordinarily gifted child, writing her first verses around the age of seven. Her mother, Therese Luise, née Haxthausen, an energetic and dominant woman, took great pride in her daughter's talents. She provided Droste-Hülshoff and the other three children with a thorough and extensive education. After the mother taught the children the elementary subjects, tutors were hired for the boys; Droste-Hülshoff and her older sister, Jenny, were allowed to follow their lessons in classical languages, French, mathematics, and natural history. Moreover, Droste-Hülshoff was introduced to a close observation and study of nature by her father, Clemens August von Droste-Hülshoff, an avid ornithologist and botanist. Visits to the theater in nearby Münster, family readings, and musical activities completed Droste-Hülshoff's education, which was far superior to that which most girls of her class received. Droste-Hülshoff also had an extensive social life. She seems, however, to have been at odds with her role and the behavior expected of her. In a revealing letter written in 1819 to her friend and literary mentor Matthias Sprickmann, she confesses the "wunderliches, verrücktes Unglück" (strange, crazy misery) caused by her desire to travel to exotic, faraway places; at the same time she scolds herself for wanting to be away from her family. This ambivalence between resisting and accepting her gender role, characteristic of much of her early writing, can be seen as a dominant theme connecting a diverse body of texts.

The play *Bertha oder Die Alpen* (Bertha; or, The Alps), written in 1813, of which she completed only one and a half acts; "Walther: Ein Gedicht in sechs Gesängen" (Walther: A Poem in Six Cantos), written in 1818; the prose fragment "Ledwina," written in 1819; some poems and letters; and part 1 of *Das geistliche Jahr* (The Spiritual Year, 1851), a cycle of poems linked to the ecclesiastical year, comprise Droste-Hülshoff's early works (all except *Das geistliche Jahr* were published in volume four [1886] of her *Gesammelte Werke* [1884–1887]). With the exception of *Das geistliche Jahr,* these texts have frequently been dismissed as lacking in originality and substance and as offering only glimpses of her future genius. Droste-Hülshoff seemed to be too incoherent in her choice of genre, plot, and theme. They reveal, however, an amazing awareness and insight into the limitations imposed on females, and in particular into the problems of the woman writer. This awareness is especially apparent in "Ledwina," the most innovative and best-written piece of the early period. Sickness and an intense awareness of the restrictions of her female role have turned Ledwina, a young woman of aristocratic background, into an outsider within her family and class. Droste-Hülshoff juxtaposes the portrayal of aristocratic social life with Ledwina's tormented inner world of wild, intense dreams and fantasies, thus combining romantic themes and motives with a realistically depicted social setting that foreshadows the Gesellschaftsroman (social novel) of late nineteenth-century realism. The many images of death and disease in "Ledwina" indicate the heroine's inability to resolve the conflicts between social expectations of her as a woman and her desire for a self-determined development. Droste-Hülshoff is clearly referring to her own experiences: she struggled to appease her own inner turmoil by seeking refuge in the safety of her family, her Catholic faith, and her native Westphalia. "Ledwina" is not, however, only a thinly veiled autobiographical account; the literary treatment of these conflicts allowed the author to explore alternatives to norms she had to comply with in real life.

While outwardly leading the aristocratic existence expected of her, Droste-Hülshoff tried to fulfill her own artistic needs. This precarious balance between inner and outer existence was severely affected during the summer of 1820, which she spent at Bökendorf, the estate of her maternal step-grandmother, as part of a large circle of young people. Droste-Hülshoff was attracted to two young men: Heinrich Straube, a student of modest means and background, and the aristocrat August von Arnswald. Insecure about her feelings and naive in handling relationships, Droste-Hülshoff fell victim to an intrigue in which she was portrayed as an arrogant and superficial person who deliberately played with the sincere feelings of the two men. Although the episode was rather trivial, it had a deep and lasting effect on Droste-Hülshoff, profoundly affecting her self-image and resulting in an overwhelming sense of guilt. The experience heightened her awareness of being an outsider who had failed not only in the social but also in the divine order. This sentiment is most acutely expressed in the poems of *Das geistliche Jahr,* although they never mention the incident. By the fall of 1820 she had finished the first part, the poems from the first day of the New Year until Easter Monday. But under the influence of the summer's experiences the focus and the purpose of the cycle had changed: it could no longer serve as a prayer book for her grandmother, as was originally intended. As Droste-Hülshoff wrote in a letter to her mother, the book was meant for "jene unglücklichen aber thörichten Menschen, die in einer Stunde mehr fragen, als sieben Weise in sieben Jahren beantworten können" (those unhappy but foolish people who ask more questions in one hour than seven wise men can answer in seven years). A strong confessional tone dominates the poems, which show a human being with an ardent desire to believe and feel worthy of God's love but at the same time overcome by doubt and fear. The mood of the poems is dark and somber. The

Caricature by Ludwig Emil Grimm depicting Droste-Hülshoff as the central figure in a romantic triangle. She is flanked by Heinrich Straube and August von Arnswald. The incident, which occurred in the summer of 1820, had a profound effect on Droste-Hülshoff (from Peter Berglar, Annette von Droste-Hülshoff in Selbstzeugnissen und Bilddokumenten, *1967)*

speaker voices guilt, despair, and anxiety in a way that neither leaves room for hope nor explains the reason for this incredible guilt. *Das geistliche Jahr* shows Droste-Hülshoff's familiarity with baroque liturgical cycles as well as with the religious poetry of the seventeenth and eighteenth centuries. She brings, however, a strikingly new and original tone to these conventional forms, re-creating the tradition to express an individual religious experience. *Das geistliche Jahr,* which Droste-Hülshoff considered to be her most useful work, contributed in the latter part of the nineteenth century to her reputation as a religious and conservative author firmly rooted in the Catholic faith. While this faith as well as her close ties to her family and class certainly shaped her work, Droste-Hülshoff also struggled with these forces because they hindered her personal and artistic development.

From 1820 until 1825 Droste-Hülshoff withdrew almost completely from the outside world and ceased her literary activities in an attempt to come to terms with the Straube-Arnswald affair. In the fall of 1825 she emerged from her solitude, travel-

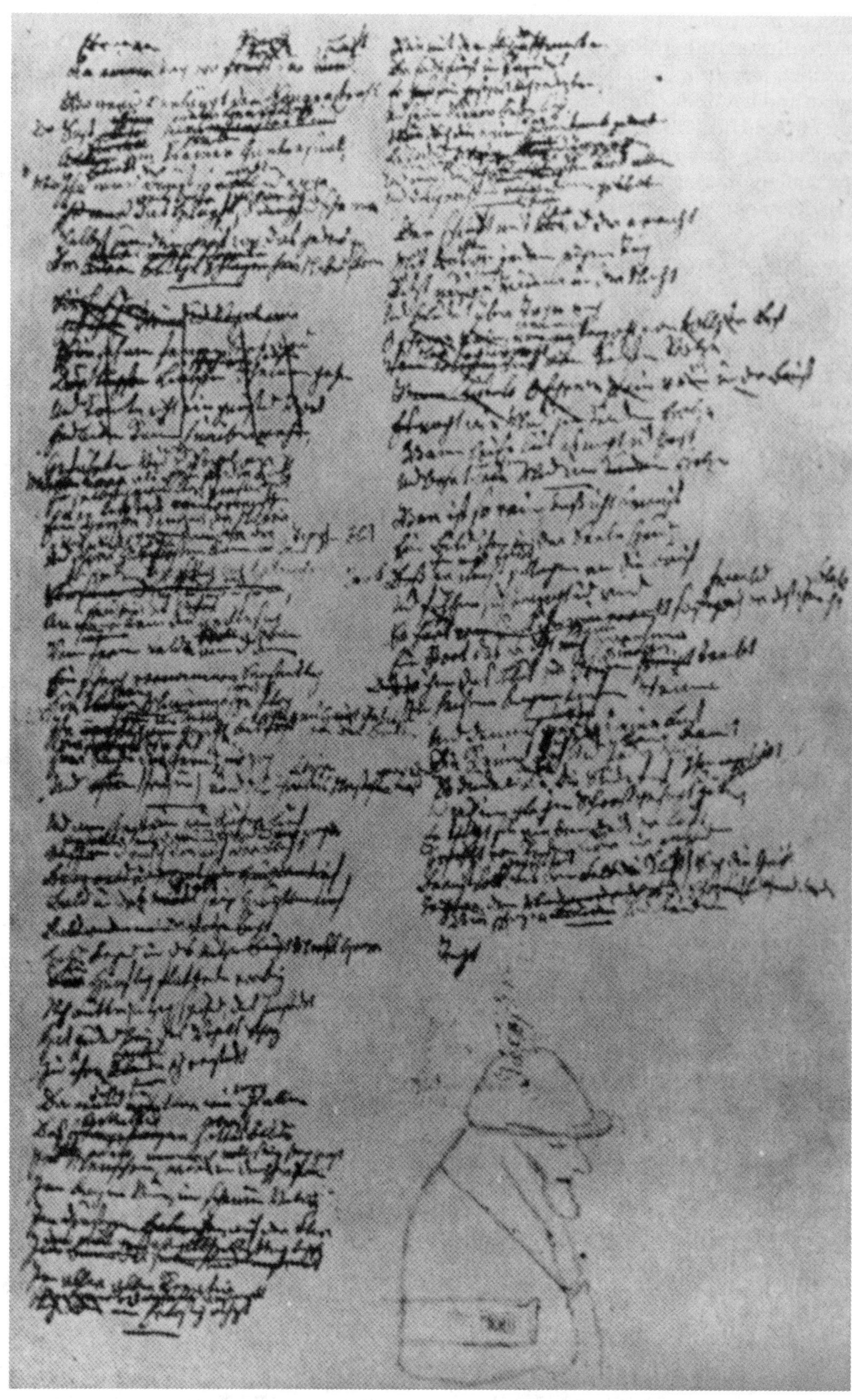

Manuscript for a poem by Droste-Hülshoff (Universitätsbibliothek Bonn)

ing to the Rhine region to visit relatives and friends in Cologne, Bonn, and Koblenz. The trip provided her with new social and intellectual stimuli; she also made new friends, the most important of whom was Sibylle Mertens-Schaafhausen, the wife of a rich merchant. She resumed her writing during her Rhine journey, making an attempt to finish "Ledwina"; but she finally gave up on the work.

Her father died in 1826, and she moved with her mother and sister to Rüschhaus, a small country manor not far from Hülshoff that was managed by her older brother and his wife. Life in Rüschhaus was uneventful and often lonely. Two years after her father's death Droste-Hülshoff's younger brother Ferdinand died, and Droste-Hülshoff fell seriously ill. Her frail health often left her unable to write for weeks and months, and the relatively small size of her oeuvre has to be understood in the light of these frequent bouts with illness. In addition, she dutifully took care of sick relatives – as expected from an unmarried woman – leaving her with little time for her own work.

Droste-Hülshoff traveled back to the Rhine region in 1828; that year she began to work on a verse epic, "Das Hospiz auf dem großen Sankt Bernhard" (The Hostel on the Great Mountain Saint Bernhard), the story of a rescue in the Swiss mountains. During a last Rhine visit from the fall of 1830 until the spring of 1831 she came to know Johanna and Adele Schopenhauer, the mother and sister of the philosopher Arthur Schopenhauer. Friendships, particularly with women, played an important role throughout Droste-Hülshoff's life, and many of her poems are dedicated to friends. In contrast to her family, these contacts provided her with encouragement and exchanges of ideas that proved beneficial for her writing.

In 1834 Droste-Hülshoff's sister Jenny married Josef von Laßberg, an avid collector of medieval manuscripts; he was also well connected in the literary and publishing world. The couple later moved to Meersburg, near Lake Constance, where Laßberg purchased an old castle that was to become an important retreat for Droste-Hülshoff; she traveled there three times.

In Rüschhaus, Droste-Hülshoff completed "Das Hospiz auf dem großen Sankt Bernhard" and two other verse epics, "Des Arztes Vermächtnis" (The Legacy of the Physician) in 1834 and "Die Schlacht im Loener Bruch" (The Battle in the Loener Marsh) – dealing with a historic event from the Thirty Years' War – in 1838. (Droste-Hülshoff finished all her verse epics, while many of her prose works remained fragments.) Of the three epics "Des Arztes Vermächtnis" is the most innovative and modern. It is a fascinating document of a mental disturbance caused by the mysterious events of a single night. The first-person narrative is a confession that is the "Vermächtnis" (legacy) a physician leaves to his son, who reads it after his father's death. The father describes how, on the night of 12 May, he was taken blindfolded to a robbers' hideout deep in the Bohemian forest to assist a gravely sick man who died in the course of the night. The physician thought that he recognized the dying man, as well as a beautiful woman in his company, as former members of Viennese aristocratic society. He was able to obtain his release from a young man, to whom he refers as "der Dunkle" (the dark one). The narrator is not absolutely sure whether these events really happened or whether they were the imaginations of his troubled mind. Did he, for example, witness the murder of the beautiful woman on his way back home? A hot spot where the dark one touched him has remained on his head after this night, reminding him of the occurrence that has left him a disturbed and guilt-ridden man. The blurring of dream and reality, the element of suspense, and the detailed descriptions of nature and of mental processes make this text a turning point in Droste-Hülshoff's work. Not only had she found themes that were to become hallmarks of her writing but she had also integrated them into a complex narrative that did not allow the reader to clarify the maze of visions, uncertainties, and doubts.

The three epics, together with some poems, a ballad, and a few pieces from *Das geistliche Jahr,* were published in 1838 as *Gedichte* (Poems). The forty-three-year-old author had to ask her mother for permission to have the work published, and it did not appear under her name. This edition turned out, however, to be an ill-fated first attempt. Droste-Hülshoff had no experience with publishing companies and left the negotiations to others, who did not fare much better in the task than she would have. The book did not sell well and received only a limited, albeit positive, reception. But despite its commercial failure, which Droste-Hülshoff found embarrassing, she had finally become a published author.

In her letters during these years Droste-Hülshoff frequently discusses possible new literary projects, revealing herself to be unsure which direction her writing should take. Her friend Christoph Bernhard Schlüter, a blind professor of philosophy whom she had met in 1834, unrelentingly reminded and encouraged her to finish *Das geistliche Jahr.* Even though she was reluctant to return to it, by the

Droste-Hülshoff in 1840; oil painting on wood by Johannes Sprick (Westfälisches Landesmuseum, Münster)

beginning of 1840 she had completed the second half (the poems from the first Sunday after Easter until New Year's Eve); but the cycle was not published during her lifetime. Considering the twenty-year interval, the two parts are remarkably coherent. Droste-Hülshoff did not change the tone or mood of the work but enlarged its focus by addressing indirectly matters such as the contemporary decline of religion and morality. The cycle is considered the most important work of religious poetry in the nineteenth century.

For many years members of her family had tried to persuade Droste-Hülshoff to display her sense of humor and comical talents in a literary work. Although she was hesitant to venture in this direction, Droste-Hülshoff succumbed to the pressure and decided "einen Versuch im Komischen zu unternehmen" (to try something in the comic genre). By the end of 1840 she had finished a one-act comedy, *Perdu! oder Dichter, Verleger und Blaustrümpfe* (Lost! or, Poets, Publishers and Bluestockings). A satire, it barely camouflages the personalities and activities of a small literary circle that had formed in the late 1830s in Münster whose gatherings Droste-Hülshoff attended from time to time. The play has not received much critical attention, but it reveals Droste-Hülshoff's perception of the contemporary literary world, particularly of women authors. While reiterating many clichés about women's inferior production, she portrays Frau von Thielen, her fictional alter ego, as a serious, uncompromising artist who feels uneasy about the publishing world. *Perdu!* is thus another example of Droste-Hülshoff's ambivalent attitude about writing and female creativity. According to the critic Gertrud Bauer-Pickar, Droste-Hülshoff viewed authorship as an essentially male prerogative yet tried to establish herself as a writer, thereby implicitly challenging her own beliefs as well as the dominant social norms. Droste-Hülshoff never had the play published, partly because the manuscript received – as was to be expected – a negative response from the members of the literary circle.

During the late 1830s Droste also worked on "Die Judenbuche," the only prose work she ever completed. It was originally part of an ethnographic description of Westphalia to be written in the style of Washington Irving's *Bracebridge Hall* (1822). She never finished the project, out of which only two pieces other than "Die Judenbuche" developed: "Westfälische Schilderungen aus einer westfälischen Feder" (Westphalian Portrayals from a Westphalian Pen), published anonymously in 1845 in the *Historisch-politische Blätter für das katholische Deutschland* (Historic-Political Papers for Catholic Germany), and a short narrative, "Bei uns zu Lande auf dem Lande" (With Us at Home in the Country). Droste-Hülshoff's original title for "Die Judenbuche," "Ein Sittengemälde aus dem gebirgichten Westfalen" (A Picture of Customs and Morals from the Wesphalian Mountains), reflects her intention to portray the people, customs, and values of the region she knew so well. The editor of Cotta's *Morgenblatt für gebildete Leser* (Morning Paper for Cultured Readers), where the novella was published in April and May 1842, chose, however, the more eye-catching "Die Judenbuche," using Droste-Hülshoff's phrase as a subtitle. The source of the novella is a document written by Droste-Hülshoff's uncle August von Haxthausen and published in 1818 under the title "Geschichte eines Algierer Sklaven" (Story of an Algerian Slave). It is the true story of a man from the Paderborn region who killed a Jew, fled, spent years in slavery, returned home, and committed suicide under the tree where the murder had happened. Droste-Hülshoff kept the basic plot but reinvented the main character as well as the narrative and thematic framework. Her story opens with a short poem admonishing the reader that a poor man's wrongdoings cannot be judged by people born into more fortunate circumstances. The poem's underlying notion of environmental influences on a person's development is a striking anticipation of modern thinking. The life of the protagonist, Friedrich Mergel, is described by carefully listing all the factors that contribute to his ill-fated destiny. To depict his entire life within the limited framework of a novella, Droste-Hülshoff uses a narrative strategy that has been referred to as "scene-sequencing," that is, showing decisive moments or turning points – a device that is also used in the modern cinema.

Born in 1738 in a remote region where law and order have been undermined by continuous infringement of the forest laws, and growing up in an unhappy family, Friedrich misses from the beginning moral guidance and positive role models. At nine he loses his father, a heavy drinker and social outcast. Three years later his maternal uncle, Simon, offers to take the boy. This uncle is a devious character, and under his influence Friedrich, who works as the village's shepherd, becomes arrogant and sly. Simon seems to be involved in the theft of timber and may have murdered the forester, Brandis, who tried to catch the thieves. But it was Friedrich who, after a heated argument with Brandis, sent him in the direction where he was to encounter the wood thieves. Shocked by the brutal murder, which he by no means anticipated, Friedrich is briefly plagued by a bad conscience; but he never confesses, and he forgets the incident rather quickly. Brandis's murderer is never identified. Four years later a second murder takes place. A Jew named Aaron is found dead under a beech tree three days after a big wedding at which he publicly accused Friedrich of not having paid for a silver watch. Because of this incident Friedrich is suspected of having committed the crime, but he and his companion Johannes Niemand, who is probably Simon's illegitimate son, have left the village. In this case, too, the murderer is never found. Twenty-eight years later a sick old man returns from Turkish slavery; he says that he is Johannes Niemand. After living for some time in the village the man suddenly disappears; he is discovered two weeks later, hanging from the tree under which Aaron was found dead. On careful examination of the corpse the old squire declares the dead man to be Friedrich Mergel. The last line of the novella reads: "Wenn du dich diesem Orte nahest, so wird es dir ergehen, wie du mir getan hast" (When you near this place, what happens to you will be the same as what you did to me). It is a translation of the Hebrew inscription the leaders of the Jewish community had engraved in the beech tree after Aaron's death.

Owing to the ingenious way in which Droste-Hülshoff simultaneously gives and conceals information, the reader never knows who really committed the murder; it is never explicitly said that Friedrich is Aaron's murderer, and a criminal named Lumpenmoises confesses having murdered a Jew named Aaron. A shift in narrative perspective from documentary description with careful chronicling of dates to the viewpoints of various characters who give subjective accounts of the occurrences further contributes to the enigmatic character of the story. While "Die Judenbuche" unfolds on one level as a suspenseful detective story, it is also a study in crime, guilt, and punishment with a religious or metaphysical dimension. Despite the strong environmental influences on his development, Friedrich is shown as having a choice between good and evil; but he opts for the latter. At the same time, the village experiences a continuous failure of its judicial system, which is unable to render justice in the two murder cases or in the wood theft. Finally, because the corpse is found hanging in the beech tree in September 1789 – the eve of the French Revolution – a wider sociopolitical context is established. The continuing fascination of the work results from the multitude of themes integrated into the framework of a detective story and from the tension between appearance and reality that Droste-Hülshoff so masterfully maintains. Despite all its realism there remains a mysterious, opaque atmosphere that challenges every reader anew.

Levin Schücking, one of the members of the Münster literary circle, asked Droste-Hülshoff to contribute to the collection *Das malerische und romantische Westfalen* (Picturesque and Romantic Westphalia, 1841), which he and Ferdinand Freiligrath were editing. As a result, Droste-Hülshoff produced almost a dozen ballads dealing with Westphalian history or legend. The genre of the ballad, with its combination of lyric, epic, and dramatic elements and its climactic structure, lent itself to Droste-Hülshoff's affinity for the uncanny and mysterious, and its focus on destiny allowed her to explorefurther the themes of crime, punishment, and guilt. In the ballad "Vorgeschichte" (Second Sight) a nobleman belonging to the "gequälte[s] Geschlecht" (tormented dynasty) of people who can foretell their futures wakes up from a nightmare but is unable to free his mind from the swirl of images, hallucinations, and visions that are beautifully described through moon and water symbols. He then "sees" the preparations for a funeral taking place in

Droste-Hülshoff at her brother-in-law's estate at Meersburg in 1846; drawing by her sister, Jenny von Laßberg (Archiv für Kunst und Geschichte, Berlin)

the courtyard of his castle and, relieved to recognize the coat of arms as his own and not his wife's, calms down and prepares his will. What is most striking about this poem is Droste-Hülshoff's vivid description of mental processes in which reason no longer prevails, a tormented mind on the brink of insanity. "Das Fräulein von Rodenschild" (Miss von Rodenschild), in which a young countess is confronted with her double, gives another brilliant example of a troubled consciousness. "Die Schwestern" (The Sisters) portrays a woman searching for her sister, who, in pursuing her erotic desires, became a social outcast. The ballad reveals the dual perspective that is a dominant feature in most of Droste-Hülshoff's work and that indicates her ambivalent perception of herself as a woman author in a time of great social and political change.

Droste-Hülshoff arrived in Meersburg for a visit in September 1841. She was joined a month later by Schücking, the person who most decisively influenced her artistic development. Droste-Hülshoff had known his mother, Katharina Busch Schücking, and after the mother's death in 1831 she felt an obligation to take care of Schücking. When Droste-Hülshoff had met him again in 1837, Schücking was an impecunious young poet and journalist. Although initially repelled by Schücking's vanity and dandyish behavior, Droste-Hülshoff soon grew fond of him, and she tried hard to find suitable employment for him. She finally convinced her brother-in-law to invite Schücking to Meersburg to work as a librarian. In Meersburg, Droste-Hülshoff could, for the first time, escape maternal control and satisfy her creative as well as her emotional needs. Much has been speculated about the extent of Droste-Hülshoff's amorous involvement with Schücking, who seemed an unlikely match for the conservative aristocrat. Not only was Schücking of bourgeois background and seventeen years her junior but he also held decidedly liberal views. Droste-Hülshoff's letters and poems dealing with the relationship and the devastation she felt after Schücking's sudden departure for new employment in February 1842 show a strong attachment and deep affection. Although he was only a modestly gifted writer, Schücking recognized Droste-Hülshoff's genius and was a perceptive critic of her work. He directed her away from the verse epic toward prose and lyric poetry, and he helped to unleash a tremendous creative outburst: during the months they spent together at Meersburg, Droste-Hülshoff prepared the final draft of "Die Judenbuche" and wrote more than fifty poems. Schücking later said that he used a trick to stimulate her creativity: provoked by his claim that the lyric inspiration occurs only rarely, Droste-Hülshoff promised to produce an entire volume of poetry within a few months. Some of these poems were published in journals, but the majority appeared in her *Gedichte* (1844). Published by the prestigious Cotta firm – Schücking had acted as an intermediary between Droste-Hülshoff and the publisher – the edition was a literary as well as a commercial success. It contributed to Droste-Hülshoff's growing reputation as an author, and the honorarium enabled her to buy Fürstenhausle (Prince's Cottage), a small retreat at Meersburg. Droste-Hülshoff's final breakthrough as an author was accompanied by a growing estrangement from the man who had contributed to it. It was difficult for Droste-Hülshoff to overcome the disappointment and loneliness caused by his sudden departure, but Schücking's marriage in 1843 hurt her even more. As the poem "Lebt wohl" (Farewell) shows, Droste-Hülshoff countered the desolation by affirming her poetic vocation. This affirmation, albeit often ambivalent, is manifest in the poems of the 1844 edition. The volume is divided into five sections: political and social issues dominate in "Zeitbilder" (Pictures of the Times); "Heidebilder" (Pictures of the Heath) and "Fels, Wald und See" (Rock, Forest, and Sea) contain nature poetry (the latter section includes some of Droste-Hülshoff's idyllic, genre-painting poetry, such as the small cycles "Die Elemente" [The Elements] and "Der Säntis"); under the heading "Gedichte vermischten Inhalts" (Miscellaneous Poems) verses dealing with personal experiences and occasional poems are grouped together; finally, in "Scherz und Ernst" (Fun and Seriousness) Droste-Hülshoff displays her humorous talent on political, artistic, and general topics.

The poems of "Zeitbilder" show Droste-Hülshoff as a staunch defender of a conservative social and religious order. As titles such as "Alte und neue Kinderzucht" (Old and New Upbringing) and "Vor vierzig Jahren" (Forty Years Ago) indicate, she contrasts a harmonious past with the present disintegration caused by liberal tendencies and admonishes the reader to follow a conservative, Christian ideology. While the poems in this group never became popular, those in "Heidebilder" as well as poems such as "Am Thurme" (On the Tower), "Im Moose" (On the Moss), and "Das Spiegelbild" (The Reflection in the Mirror) from the following two sections represent some of her best-known work. The striking originality of these poems lies in their observation of nature. Droste-Hülshoff not only chooses new and unusual locales, such as the moor and the marl pit, but she also perceives nature in its most detailed and intricate movements, observing the sound of a berry dropping to the ground or the fearful cry of a fly. Many of these poems feature such an abundance of images and sounds that they have been compared to impressionistic paintings. But despite the intensity of the visual and auditory descriptions these lyrics do not clarify the perception of nature; instead, they render it rather ambiguous and vague. The narrator of "Die Mergelgrube" (The Marl Pit) in "Heidebilder" is caught, for example, between dream and reality while exploring the pit and is unable to distinguish his inner vision from outer appearances. The nightly wanderer in "Der Hünenstein" (The Giant Stone), another poem in "Heidebilder," is at once attracted and repelled by a prehistoric cave, with its atmosphere of death and decay. Giving free play to his fantasies, he is drawn further and further into the past and is almost overcome with horror. "Der Knabe im Moor" (The Boy on the Moor), the concluding poem of "Heidebilder," is a striking example of the combination of detailed description of nature with supernatural figures such as ghosts. The ghosts frighten the child crossing the moor almost to death and cause him to lose his direction and footing. Fear and anxiety reign even in seemingly idyllic places, reflecting the troubled inner world of the poem's narrator. In the many poems dealing explicitly or implicitly with the poet's vocation, Droste-Hülshoff explores her painful struggle with her identity as a woman author. Their double structures and double figures, often presented as mirror images or hallucinations, echo similar constellations in her early works. They attest to the extent to which Droste-Hülshoff perceived her life and work as torn between opposite forces that spring not only from gender-specific constraints but also from Droste-Hülshoff's deep-seated feelings of inexpiable sin and guilt.

Droste-Hülshoff was unable to repeat the creative eruption that occurred during her first stay in Meersburg. She finished another verse epic, "Der Spiritus Familiaris des Roßtäuschers" (The Familiar Spirit of the Horse Dealer), which recounts an old folk legend. In the fall of 1844 she began another crime story, "Josef," but never completed it. Of the other poems she wrote, eighteen appeared during her lifetime; but most of this work was published posthumously by Schücking. By 1846, however, Droste-Hülshoff had broken off all relations with him. She strongly disapproved of Schücking's liberal-minded poems, in which he advocated freedom of the press and a more democratic form of government. What upset her most was the publication of his novel *Die Ritterbürtigen* (Of Noble Birth, 1846), an attack on the outmoded aristocratic class that drew much of its material from Droste-Hülshoff's intimate knowledge of the Westphalian aristocracy. She felt that Schücking had violated her trust and misused their friendship.

The final two years of her life were overshadowed by growing isolation and severe illness. Droste-Hülshoff suffered from overagitated nerves and sleeplessness; she was so overcome by weakness that she was unable to walk. Hoping for an improvement in the more favorable southern climate, in the fall of 1847 she traveled once again to Meersburg. Her health remained poor, and she died on 24 May 1848 at Meersburg. She is buried in the cemetery there.

Letters:

Briefe der Freiin Annette von Droste-Hülshoff, edited by Christoph Bernhard Schlüter (Münster: Russel, 1877);

Memorial bust of Droste-Hülshoff by Anton Rüller in Münster

Briefe von Annette von Droste-Hülshoff und Levin Schücking, edited by Theo Schücking (Leipzig: Grunow, 1893); enlarged edition, edited by Reinhold Conrad Muschler (Leipzig: Grunow, 1928);

Die Briefe der Dichterin Annette v. Droste-Hülshoff, edited by Hermann Cardauns (Münster: Aschendorff, 1909);

Die Briefe der Annette von Droste-Hülshoff: Gesamtausgabe, 2 volumes, edited by Karl Schulte-Kemminghausen (Jena: Diederich, 1944).

Bibliographies:

Eduard Arens and Karl Schulte Kemminghausen, *Droste-Bibliographie* (Münster: Aschendorff, 1932);

Clemens Heselhaus, "Droste-Bibliographie 1932–1948," *Droste Jahrbuch,* 2 (1948–1950): 334–352;

Hans Thiekötter, *Annette von Droste-Hülshoff: Eine Auswahlbibliographie* (Münster: Aschendorff, 1963);

Helmut Dees, *Annette von Droste-Hülshoffs Dichtungen in England und Amerika* (Tübingen: Fotodruck Präzis, 1966);

Winfried Theiss, "Droste-Bibliographie 1949–1969," *Droste-Jahrbuch,* 5 (1972): 147–244;

Walter Huge, "Annette von Droste-Hülshoff: Die Judenbuche. Ein Sittengemälde aus dem gebirgigten Westphalen," Ph.D. dissertation, University of Münster, 1977;

Aloys Haverbusch, "Droste-Bibliographie 1838–1900," in *Modellfall der Rezeptionsforschung: Droste-Rezeption im 19. Jahrhundert. Dokumentation, Analysen, Bibliographie,* edited by Winfried Woesler, 1 volume (Frankfurt am Main: Lang, 1980), pp. 1331–1582.

Biographies:

Levin Schücking, *Annette von Droste: Ein Lebensbild* (Hannover: Rümpler, 1862);

Hermann Hüffer, *Annette v. Droste-Hülshoff und ihre Werke* (Gotha: Perthes, 1887);

Hermann Hüffer, *Annette v. Droste-Hülshoff und ihre Werke* (Gotha: Perthes, 1887);

Mary Lavater-Sloman, *Einsamkeit: Das Leben der Annette von Droste-Hülshoff* (Zurich: Artemis, 1950);

Margaret Mare, *Annette von Droste-Hülshoff* (London: Methuen, 1965);

Peter Berglar, *Annette von Droste-Hülshoff in Selbstzeugnissen und Bilddokumenten* (Reinbek: Rowohlt, 1967);

Clemens Heselhaus, *Annette von Droste-Hülshoff: Werk und Leben* (Düsseldorf: Bagel, 1971);

Doris Maurer, *Annette von Droste-Hülshoff: Ein Leben zwischen Auflehnung und Gehorsam* (Bonn: Keil, 1982);

Mary E. Morgan, *Annette von Droste-Hülshoff: A Biography* (Bern, Frankfurt am Main & New York: Lang, 1984);

John Guthrie, *Annette von Droste-Hülshoff: A German Poet between Romanticism and Realism* (Oxford: Berg, 1989).

References:

Gertrud Bauer-Pickar, "*Perdu* Reclaimed: A Reappraisal of Droste's Comedy," *Monatshefte für den deutschen Unterricht,* 76 (Winter 1984): 409–421;

Bauer-Pickar, " 'Too manly is your spirit': Annette von Droste-Hülshoff," *Rice University Studies,* 64 (Winter 1978): 51–68;

Clifford Albrecht Bernd, "Clarity and Obscurity in Annette von Droste-Hülshoff's 'Judenbuche,' " *Studies in German Literature of the Nineteenth and Twentieth Centuries: Festschrift for Frederic E. Coenen,* edited by Siegfried Mews (Chapel Hill: University of North Carolina Press, 1970), pp. 64–77;

Stephan Berning, *Sinnbildsprache: Zur Bildstruktur des Geistlichen Jahres der Annette von Droste-Hülshoff* (Tübingen: Niemeyer, 1975);

Sylvia Bonati-Richner, *Der Feuermensch: Studien über das Verhältnis von Mensch und Landschaft in den erzählenden Werken der Annette von Droste-Hülshoff* (Bern: Francke, 1972);

Renate Böschenstein-Schäfer, "Die Struktur des Idyllischen im Werk der Annette von Droste-Hülshoff," *Kleinere Beiträge zur Drosteforschung,* 3 (1974–1975): 25–49;Artur Brall, *Vergangenheit und Vergänglichkeit: Zur Zeiterfahrung und Zeitdeutung im Werk Annette von Droste-Hülshoffs* (Marburg: Elwert, 1975);

Edson Chick, "Voices in Discord: Some Observations of 'Die Judenbuche,' " *German Quarterly,* 42 (March 1969): 147–157;

Elke Frederiksen and Monika Shafi, "Annette von Droste-Hülshoff (1797–1848): Konfliktstrukturen im Frühwerk," in *Out of Line/Ausgefallen: The Paradox of Marginality in the Writings of Nineteenth-Century German Women,* edited by Ruth-Ellen Boetcher Joeres and Marianne Burkhard (Amsterdam: Rodopi, 1989), pp. 115–136;

Wilhelm Gössmann, *Annette von Droste-Hülshoff: Ich und Spiegelbild. Zum Verständnis der Dichterin und ihres Werkes* (Düsseldorf: Droste, 1985);

Gössmann, "Trunkenheit und Desillusion: Das poetische Ich der Droste," *Zeitschrift für deutsche Philologie,* 101, no. 4 (1982): 506–525;

Gotthard Guder, "Annette von Droste-Hülshoff's Conception of Herself as Poet," *German Life and Letters,* 11 (1957): 13–24;

Günter Häntzschel, "Annette von Droste-Hülshoff," in *Zur Literatur der Restaurationsepoche 1815–1848: Forschungsreferate und Aufsätze,* edited by Jost Hermand and Manfred Windfuhr (Stuttgart: Metzler, 1970), pp. 151–199;

Häntzschel, *Tradition und Originalität: Allegorische Darstellung im Werk Annette von Droste-Hülshoffs* (Stuttgart: Kohlhammer, 1968);

Wolfgang Kayser, "Sprachform und Redeform in den 'Heidebildern' der Annette von Droste-Hülshoff," *Interpretationen I: Deutsche Lyrik von Weckherlin bis Benn,* edited by Jost Schillemeit (Frankfurt am Main: Fischer, 1965), pp. 212–244;

Janet K. King, "Conscience and Conviction in *Die Judenbuche,*" *Monatshefte für den deutschen Unterricht,* 64 (1972): 349–355;

Bernd Kortländer, *Annette von Droste-Hülshoff und die deutsche Literatur: Kenntnis, Beurteilung, Beeinflussung* (Münster: Aschendorff, 1979);

Herbert Kraft, *Mein Indien liegt in Rüschhaus* (Münster: Regensberg, 1987);

Mary Morgan, *Annette von Droste-Hülshoff: A Woman of Letters in a Period of Transition* (Bern: Lang, 1981);

Brigitte Peucker, "Droste-Hülshoff's Ophelia and the Recovery of Voice," *Journal of English and Germanic Philology,* 82 (July 1983): 374–391;

Peucker, "The Poetry of Regeneration: Droste-Hülshoff's Ophelia as Muse," in her *Lyric Descent in the German Romantic Tradition* (New Haven: Yale University Press, 1987), pp. 71–118;

Wolfgang Preisendanz, " '. . . und jede Lust, so Schauer nur gewähren mag': Die Poesie der Wahrnehmung in der Dichtung Annette von

Droste-Hülshoffs," *Droste-Forschung*, 4 (1976–1977): 9–21;

Irmgard Roebling, "Weibliches Schreiben im 19. Jahrhundert: Untersuchungen zur Naturmetaphorik der Droste," *Der Deutschunterricht*, 18 (1986): 36–56;

Heinz Rölleke, "Erzähltes Mysterium: Studien zur 'Judenbuche' der Annette von Droste-Hülshoff," *Deutsche Vierteljahrsschrift für Literaturwissenschaft und Geistesgeschichte*, 42 (August 1968): 399–426;

Ronald Schneider, *Annette von Droste-Hülshoff* (Stuttgart: Metzler, 1977);

Schneider, *Realismus und Restauration: Untersuchungen zu Poetik und epischem Werk der Annette von Droste-Hülshoff* (Kronberg: Scriptor, 1976);

Walter Silz, "Annette von Droste-Hülshoff, 'Die Judenbuche,' " in his *Realism and Reality: Studies in the German Novelle of Poetic Realism* (Chapel Hill: University of North Carolina Press, 1954), pp. 36–51;

Emil Staiger, *Annette von Droste-Hülshoff* (Frauenfeld: Huber, 1967);

Larry D. Wells, "Indeterminacy as Provocation: The Reader's Role in Annette von Droste-Hülshoff's 'Die Judenbuche,' " *Modern Language Notes*, 94 (April 1979): 475–492;

Zeitschrift für deutsche Philologie, special issue on Droste-Hülshoff, edited by Walter Huge and Winfried Woesler (1980).

Papers:

Eighty percent of Annette von Droste-Hülshoff's papers are in public libraries and museums. The most important are the Universitätsbibliothek (University Library), Bonn; the Stadt- und Landesbibliothek (City and State Library), Dortmund; the Deutsches Literaturarchiv/Schiller-Nationalmuseum (German Literature Archives/ Schiller National Museum), Marbach; the Fürstenhäusle, Meersburg; and the Annette von Droste-Gesellschaft (Annette von Droste Society), the Franziskanerkloster (Franciscan Cloister), the Universitätsbibliothek, and the Westfälisches Landesmuseum für Kunst und Kulturgeschichte (Westphalian State Museum for Art and Culture History), all in Münster.

Ernst Freiherr von Feuchtersleben

(29 April 1806 - 3 September 1849)

Wulf Koepke
Texas A&M University

BOOKS: *Über das erste hippokratische Buch von der Diät* (Vienna: Gerold, 1835);

Gedichte (Stuttgart & Tübingen: Cotta, 1836);

Beiträge zur Literatur-, Kunst- und Lebens-Theorie (Vienna: Braumüller, 1837);

Zur Diätetik der Seele (Vienna: Armbruster, 1838; enlarged edition, Vienna: Gerold, 1841; enlarged, 1842; enlarged, 1846; enlarged, 1848); translated by Henry A. Ouvry as *The Dietetics of the Soul* (London: Churchill, 1852); translated by Ludwig Lewisohn as *Health and Suggestion: The Dietetics of the Mind* (New York: Huebsch, 1910);

Die Gewißheit und Würde der Heilkunst: Für das nichtärztliche Publikum dargestellt (Vienna: Gerold, 1839);

Lebensblätter (Vienna: Hirschfeld, 1841);

Neuer Plutarch oder Bildnisse und Biographien der berühmtesten Männer und Frauen aller Nationen und Stände: Von den alten bis auf unsere Zeiten, 5 volumes, by Feuchtersleben and others (Pesth: Hartleben, 1842–1853);

Almanach von Radirungen, engravings by Moritz von Schwind (Zurich: Veith, 1843);

Lehrbuch der ärztlichen Seelenkunde: Als Skizze zu Vorträgen bearbeitet (Vienna: Gerold, 1845); translated by H. Evans Lloyd, revised by B. G. Babington as *The Principles of Medical Psychology* (London: Sydenham Society, 1847);

Sämtliche Werke: Mit Ausschluß der rein medizinischen, 7 volumes, edited by Friedrich Hebbel (Vienna: Gerold, 1851–1853);

Ausgewählte Werke, edited by Richard Guttmann (Leipzig: Hesse, 1907);

Pädagogische Schriften, edited by Kurt Gerhard Fischer (Paderborn: Schöningh, 1963);

Sämtliche Werke und Briefe: Kritische Ausgabe, 1 volume to date, edited by Herbert Seidler and Hedwig Heger (Vienna: Österreichische Akademie der Wissenschaften, 1987–).

OTHER: B. Eble, *Die Geschichte der practischen Arzneikunde (Systeme, Epidemien, Heilmittel, Bäder) vom Jahre 1800 bis 1825*, revised and edited by Feuchtersleben (Vienna: Gerold, 1840);

Wilhelm Friedrich von Meyern, *Hinterlassene kleine Schriften,* 3 volumes, edited by Feuchtersleben (Vienna: Klang, 1842);

Verhandlungen der k. k. Gesellschaft der Ärzte zu Wien, 4 volumes, edited by Feuchtersleben (volumes 1, 2, 4, Vienna: Braumüller & Seidel; volume 3, Vienna: Kaulfuss, Prandel, 1842–1844);

Johann Mayrhofer, *Gedichte: Neue Sammlung. Aus dessen Nachlasse mit Biographie und Vorwort,* edited by Feuchtersleben (Vienna: Klang, 1843);

Philipp Carl Hartmann, *Festrede vom Leben des Geistes,* translated from Latin and edited by Feuchtersleben (Vienna: Gerold, 1846);

Geist deutscher Klassiker: Eine Blumenlese ihrer geistreichsten und gemüthvollsten Gedanken, Maximen und Aussprüche, 10 volumes, edited by Feuchtersleben (Leipzig: Hartleben, 1851).

Ernst Freiherr (Baron) von Feuchtersleben is anything but a household name in literature, yet he was an important figure in Austrian intellectual life before 1848. He was a talented poet, a respected literary critic, a major force for progress in education, a political figure of stature in the revolutionary year 1848, and above all a great physician and a writer of both scientific and popular publications in the field of psychosomatic medicine, or what today would be termed psychiatry. His most successful book, with many editions throughout the nineteenth century and translations into several languages, was *Zur Diätetik der Seele* (1838; translated as *The Dietetics of the Soul,* 1852). Feuchtersleben has been called a "Populärphilosoph" (popular philosopher); the term was used in the eighteenth century for writers who tried to spread the ideas of the Enlightenment, but it assumed a pejorative meaning in the nineteenth century during the controversies between the Kantians and their adversaries. Feuchtersleben saw himself as a mediator and a popularizer. Influenced by Carl Gustav Carus, a great physician and gifted painter who also exerted a decisive influence on the psychologist Carl Gustav Jung, Feuchtersleben propagated the holistic approach in medicine. He also fought for the preservation of the aesthetic and moral principles of Johann Wolfgang von Goethe and Goethe's contemporaries and promoted the Goethean ideal of "Bildung" (education, development, cultivation), which in the Austrian context meant a liberalization of the educational system and the application of the principles of Immanuel Kant and Johann Gottfried Herder. While his own activities as an educational administrator lasted only a few months, many of his ideas were adopted in Austrian schools and universities. His impact on medicine, education, and the literary scene was greater and more durable than his personal fame.

Feuchtersleben, who lived in a Viennese society characterized by a laissez-faire attitude to morality, by opportunism, by fear of the police, by hedonism, and by resigned pessimism, went to extreme lengths to live by strong moral principles. Even as a young man he was considered a model of ethical behavior. His principles of veracity and integrity inform his writings, both in content and in style. He valued clarity and constantly strove for perfection. This self-critical attitude limited the amount of his production, although he was a tireless worker. The writings of this true *homme de lettres* are both personal and objective, filled with philosophical reflection and motivated by the urge to propagate an ethical life-style.

Feuchtersleben was descended from a noble family of Hildburghausen in Thuringia, one member of which had migrated to Vienna early in the eighteenth century. His father, also Ernst Freiherr von Feuchtersleben, was Hofrat (privy councillor) in the Austrian civil service. The elder Feuchtersleben's first marriage, to Josefine Soliman, produced a son, Eduard, born in 1798; he would also become a writer. After the death of his wife in 1801 the baron married again; his second wife was from the ancient noble Clusolis family. Their only son, Ernst, born on 29 April 1806, was weak and sickly; his mother was also of delicate health, and she died soon after his birth. The child was sent to the country so that the healthier air would strengthen his constitution. In these early years Feuchtersleben acquired a love for nature, a penchant for lonely meditation, and a stoic attitude toward adversity and suffering. His stoicism was even more necessary after Feuchtersleben, following his father's wishes, entered the Theresianische Akademie, or Theresianum, founded in 1746 by Empress Maria Theresa to prepare the offspring of the high nobility for key offices in the military and the civil service. Feuchtersleben spent twelve years in this institution, which gave him, as the Karlsschule had given Friedrich Schiller, an insatiable thirst for freedom and an aversion to discipline imposed from the outside. He did, however, acquire at the academy interests in classical antiquity and in the natural sciences.

On leaving the Theresianum in 1825 Feuchtersleben, rather than preparing for a career in the civil service, decided to study medicine, a field considered quite inappropriate for a person of his social class. For the next nine years he studied medicine, science, philology, and philosophy at the University of Vienna. During this period he had poems, aphorisms, essays, and reviews published in various magazines; he later collected these texts in books. Among his circle of close friends in Vienna were the composer Franz Schubert; the author of successful comedies Eduard von Bauernfeld; Johann Mayrhofer, a poet who would commit suicide in 1836 and whose works Feuchtersleben would edit in 1843; and the painter Moritz von Schwind.

In 1828 Feuchtersleben met Helene Kalcher, a woman five years older than he who was well below his social rank; a long relationship ensued that would culminate in a happy marriage. The most important of his professors was Philipp Carl Hartmann, who directed Feuchtersleben toward his field of specialization, medical psychology. Feuchtersleben received his M.D. on 9 June 1834 on the basis of a Latin dissertation on the doctrine of indications.

Also in 1834 Feuchtersleben's father drowned himself in the Danube, and it was revealed that he was bankrupt. Feuchtersleben had to fight to save his personal belongings from the creditors, but in spite of his precarious financial situation he opened his medical practice and married Kalcher.

A problem Feuchtersleben encountered when he started his medical practice was that some patients, ashamed to offer money as compensation for the services of a Freiherr from an eminent family, sent presents instead of payment – often presents of little practical value. Hardly able to make a living in spite of his rapidly growing reputation as a physician, he continued writing for journals. He also began to have scientific articles published in medical journals. In 1836 the Stuttgart firm Cotta, the major publisher of German literature, brought out Feuchtersleben's *Gedichte* (Poems); the work found little immediate response.

Feuchtersleben's philosophical and ethical positions are expressed in his poems, which are, except for some early nature poems, generally reflective and epigrammatic:

Klagt ihr über Druck von außen?
Druck von innen klaget an!
Dem dankt, der von Selbstbeschränkung
Toren! euch befreien kann.

(Do you complain about pressure from outside?
Rather blame pressure from inside!
Give thanks to that one who can, fools,
Liberate you from self-limitation.)

Those lines were written in the Austrian police state created by Prince Wenzel von Metternich. The following four-line poem comes close to expressing the central insight of the Diätetik:

Zwei Kräfte sind es, die mich halten,
Wenn Blatt auf Blatt vom Zweige fällt:
Natur! dein schöpferisches Walten,
Und deines, freie Geisterwelt!

(There are two forces that hold me
When leaf after leaf falls from the branch:
Nature! your creative life,
And yours, free world of the spirits!)

Immersion in nature sustains the human being as much as moving in the intellectual sphere strengthens the mind.

Feuchtersleben's holistic credo is proclaimed in this terse epigram: "Ich kann mein Heil nicht in Stücken finden: / Es muß sich alles zum Ganzen ründen" (I cannot find my fulfilment in pieces, / For me, everything has to become a whole).
Some of Feuchtersleben's poetry is highly personal:

Ich hab' – mit Dank muß ich's gewahren –
Drei Seligkeiten rein erfahren:
Des Geistes schaffendes Bewegen,
Der Schöpfung lebenquellend Regen,
Und wahrer Ehe stillen Segen.

(I have – I have to realize this with gratitude –
Experienced three blessings in a pure form:
The creative movement of the spirit,
Creation's life-emanating stirrings,
And true marriage's quiet blessings.)

One poem, in which Feuchtersleben imitates a folk song, has been set to music and is sometimes anthologized. The first stanza reads:

Es ist bestimmt in Gottes Rat,
Daß man, was man am liebsten hat,
Muß meiden.
Wiewohl nichts in dem Lauf der Welt
Dem Herzen, ach, so sauer fällt
Als Scheiden, ja Scheiden!

(It is determined in God's counsel,
That what we love most
We must leave.
Although in the course of the world
Nothing is harder for the heart
Than separating, yes, separating.)

The poem, which uses one of the most frequent rhymes of German folk poetry (*meiden–scheiden*), conveys Feuchtersleben's stoic attitude: accept fate to make it bearable. Occasionally Feuchtersleben gets closer to his age's witty style and its liking for literary feuds. Even here he is different, as in this "defense" of Heinrich Heine:

Schimpft mir nur ihr Guten nicht
Gar zu sehr den armen Heine!
Freilich bleibt der lose Wicht
Problematisch – doch ich meine:
Nicht was er – was *durch* ihn spricht,
Überhört der Kenner nicht.

(Don't scold, you good people,
Poor Heine too much!
It is true the loose bird
Remains a problem – but I would say:
Not what he says – but what speaks *through* him
Will not be missed by the knowledgeable person.)

He is trying to achieve two goals here: first, to decry personal attacks; second, to draw attention to Heine's genius. It was a noble defense of a banned and exiled poet by one of his nonadmirers. It would not win friends for Feuchtersleben in the Austrian government.

The next year a first collection of Feuchtersleben's essays, reviews, and aphorisms appeared under the title *Beiträge zur Literatur-, Kunst- und Lebens-Theorie* (Contributions to the Theory of Literature, Art, and Life, 1837). In the first essay, "Kritik" (Criticism), Feuchtersleben develops his concept of a true critic of literature and art. His main complaint is that most critics do not like what they review; they do not take the time to study and understand the work to find the creative aspect of it. Critics usually give their first impressions, telling more about themselves than about the subject of their review. Feuchtersleben advocates constructive criticism and positive appreciation. His criticism of contemporary Austrian art includes encouraging commentaries designed to give self-confidence to struggling artists. In his lengthy survey of contemporary literature most of the expected names of then-prominent writers are missing: in an age of vehement literary feuds, Feuchtersleben simply omitted discussing writers of whose work he disapproved. It is clear, however, that in terms of the labels of his time, his position was a conservative one. He gives guarded praise to the Austrian poet Nikolaus Lenau, tries hard to gain recognition for his friend Mayrhofer, and devotes the drama section primarily to Bauernfeld and Franz Grillparzer. In the section on narrative literature Walter Scott, the great favorite of the decade, is established as the leading novelist; attention is also given to Scott's English and American followers, including Washington Irving and James Fenimore Cooper.

If this idiosyncratic view of literature in the 1830s is conditioned by personal friendships, by the Viennese perspective, and by Feuchtersleben's rigorous ethical and aesthetic standards, he is typical in his admiration of Goethe. Feuchtersleben was part of a movement that enthroned Goethe as the German national classic. Feuchtersleben takes up a spirited defense of Goethe as a scientist in a long essay, "Goethe's naturwissenschaftliche Ansichten" (Goethe's Scientific Views) – a controversial subject at that time and since. Rather than specific doctrines, Feuchtersleben supports Goethe's general approach, his holistic attitude, and his respect for nature. Both Goethe and Feuchtersleben reject a purely mechanistic and materialistic view and are aware that machines and experiments may not reveal nature's secrets but distort its laws.

In a commentary on Goethe's notes to the *West-östlicher Divan* (Divan of West and East, 1819) Feuchtersleben adds more information on the Persian poets; he was no doubt aided in his research by his friend Joseph von Hammer-Purgstall, whose translation of Háfez's *Divan* Goethe had used in his work. Feuchtersleben also comments on the first wave of information about Goethe in the works of Rahel Varnhagen, Bettina Brentano, and Goethe's secretary Johann Peter Eckermann. From these works, and from Feuchtersleben's essays, emerged the image of the elderly Goethe in Weimar, towering over Germany. Feuchtersleben wanted to present Goethe as a model to be emulated. He dismissed the often-raised question whether Goethe or Schiller should be considered the greater writer; for Feuchtersleben, it was the heritage of the entire Goethean age that mattered. Feuchtersleben considered an emphasis on moral principles, empathy with nature, and a true understanding of Greek antiquity essential for a healthy culture and society.

Zur Diätetik der Seele brought Feuchtersleben instant and lasting fame. The book went through fifty editions during the nineteenth century, and it served in translation as a textbook in medical schools in France and England.

In an age of positivism and rapidly growing specialization, the success of Feuchtersleben's book among scientists as well as the general public was surprising. His approach is staunchly holistic: for him, the human being is a whole composed of Geist (mind) and Leib (body). Although he speaks of mutual interaction of body and mind, for Feuchtersleben health is primarily a function of the mind.

Feuchtersleben makes many references to the ancient Greek ideal of *Kalokagathia* (humanity as the synthesis of the good and the beautiful), a concept that was renewed by Goethe, Herder, and Kant. Feuchtersleben sees some merit in physiognomics, the theory that physical features reveal the personality. Beauty, Feuchtersleben maintains, indicates health.

Among the faculties of the mind Feuchtersleben ascribes a special place to the imagination, although he warns that unbridled fantasy can degenerate into illness. It is, however, willpower that assumes the central place in his design. Willpower is the true energy of a person; passions, if not checked by willpower, will control the individual. The goal is Vernunft (reason), and the path to that goal, from sensual drives to the formation of a rounded, harmonious personality, Feuchtersleben – following Herder – calls Bildung. The centerpiece of Bildung is Selbsterkenntnis (self-knowledge). Knowledge of self means understanding the potential and limits of one's mind and comprehending one's place in the world.

There are many impediments to Bildung: contemporary society is artificial and is especially hostile to the development of willpower and a rounded personality. The *mal du siècle,* hypochondria, is caused by a fundamental imbalance between the individual and the social environment, as well as by contradictions within the person. There is a movement toward balance and harmony in history and life, an oscillation that sees to it that extremes are corrected by opposite extremes. Less hopeful than Herder, to whom such ideas are indebted, Feuchtersleben sees few positive models in society. It is through the study of nature that humanity reaches the truth. Health depends on rejecting the customary lies of conventional society and being open to the truth. The study and enjoyment of nature, together with the enjoyment of beauty in the arts, can contribute to the cure of diseases of mind and body.

Feuchtersleben practiced what he preached: he was known for his firmness, his honesty, the clarity of his thought, and his balanced personality. Such demands challenged the mores of most European societies during the Victorian Age – not least in Vienna, where, several decades later, another psychiatrist, Sigmund Freud, would mount another attack on bourgeois conventions.

While in his writings the author's persona is typically that of the lonely man alienated from society, Feuchtersleben's actual career was singularly successful: his medical practice grew, and his writings were well received. In 1840 he was elected a member of the Viennese medical society, and he soon became secretary of the society and editor of its annual proceedings.

Feuchtersleben's second collection of essays, *Lebensblätter* (Pages from My Life, 1841), has a more coherent structure than the *Beiträge* due to the addition of a narrative element. Feuchtersleben is moving here in the direction of Ludwig Tieck's *Phantasus* (1812–1816; translated as *Tales from the Phantasus,* 1845) and similar collections that were then popular. A philosopher, Theodor, is the central figure of Feuchtersleben's book: he is seeking solace in nature and undertakes with his friend Julius a mountain hike that gives the opportunity for descriptions of scenery and meditations on nature, time, and human relationships. Book reviews are incorporated into conversations with both male and female participants, including Feuchtersleben's wife.

Much of *Lebensblätter* is taken up by a collection of aphorisms titled "Blätter aus dem Tagebuch eines Einsamen" (Pages from the Diary of a Lonely Man). They are divided into three sections, reflecting Feuchtersleben's preoccupations: "Wissen" (Knowledge), "Kunst" (Art), and "Leben" (Life). Most are terse statements designed to provoke; for example, in the "Wissen" section he says: "Es gibt keine alte und moderne Literatur, sondern nur eine ewige und eine vergängliche" (There is no old and modern literature, only an eternal and a transitory one). This comment was designed to counteract the attacks on Goethe and the enthusiasm for modernity among the younger generation, especially the writers of the Junges Deutschland (Young Germany) movement. Feuchtersleben's opposition to German Idealism, beginning with Johann Gottlieb Fichte, is expressed in this aphorism: "Kants Philosophie war eine *Arbeit* des Geistes; die Philosophien der Spätern sind geistige *Schwelgereien.* Dort galt es Zwecke, hier Spiele des Denkens" (Kant's philosophy was a *work* of the mind; the philosophies of later thinkers are intellectual *revelries.* In the first case real purposes were the motivation, in the second case mere games of thinking). Feuchtersleben doubted the intellectual honesty of Fichte, Friedrich Wilhelm Joseph von Schelling, and Georg Wilhelm Friedrich Hegel. One of his key criticisms of the age is contained in a few words: "Das Halbwahre ist verderblicher als das Falsche" (The half truth is more pernicious than the falsehood). It was distortion, mannerism, and caricature – expressions of a lukewarm attitude toward life and art – that he feared most.

His fundamental principle of aesthetic criticism, in the "Kunst" section, is: "*Jedes* Kunstwerk enthält das Gesetz in sich, dessen lebendiger Ausdruck es ist. Dieses Gesetz zu finden und in Worte zu bringen, ist die Aufgabe der ächten Kunstkritik" (*Each* work of art contains in itself the law whose living expression it is. To find this law and to express it in words is the task of true art criticism). Criticism has first to understand the work of art, then to explain it to the public, and then, perhaps to pass value judgments on it.

A typical saying in "Leben" is: "Die Blüten des lebendigen Gesprächs, die Früchte des Lebens selbst, schmücken und nähren ein Buch ganz anders als Leichensteine der Gelehrsamkeit" (The flowers of living conversation, the fruits of life itself, decorate and nourish a book in a very different way than the gravestones of mere learning). A book should be informed by life's experiences, not just by other books. There are maxims of behavior: "Nur die Sache ist verloren, die man aufgibt" (Only that cause is lost that one gives up). The aphorism was a favorite mode of expression at that time; for Feuchtersleben, it was a way of life. Not only did he formulate his own thoughts in this form but he also assembled a collection of such sayings from the German classics that was published after his death under the title *Geist deutscher Klassiker* (Spirit of German Classics, 1851).

Feuchtersleben's three-volume edition of Wilhelm Friedrich von Meyern's *Hinterlassene kleine Schriften* (Posthumous Short Writings) appeared in 1842. Meyern is best known for his long, enigmatic novel *Dya-Na-Sore* (1787–1791); his shorter writings were mostly essays and aphorisms. Feuchtersleben was attracted to Meyern, who served in the Austrian artillery and proposed important technical and military innovations, by the latter's devotion to duty and lack of desire for personal glory. Meyern, according to Feuchtersleben's introduction, was a "Selbstdenker" (independent thinker) not swayed by intellectual fashions or opportunism.

In 1844 Feuchtersleben was appointed a professor at the University of Vienna; his lectures had such a large following among the students that other professors had to change the hours of their classes so as not to coincide with his. His lectures were published in 1845 under the title *Lehrbuch der ärztlichen Seelenkunde* (Textbook of Medical Psychology).

Feuchtersleben's literary career was cut short by the involvement in administration and politics that characterized his last years. In 1845 he was elected dean of the medical faculty of the University of Vienna. When he demanded the relaxation of censorship and a more autonomous educational system, he was identified with the anti-Metternich political faction.

In 1847 the medical college celebrated its fiftieth anniversary. In his address Feuchtersleben, in the presence of Metternich himself, called for far-reaching reforms of the educational system. That year, to Metternich's displeasure, Feuchtersleben was appointed vice-director for medical studies. Also in 1847 the founding members of the new Academy of Sciences in Vienna were named; although Feuchtersleben was one of the scholars who had urged the establishment of the academy and had drafted the plans for it, he was excluded from the list. He was nominated a year later, when the government was in a much weakened position.

It was inevitable that Feuchtersleben would be drawn into the revolutionary movement of 1848. He was considered a leading voice of the liberal opposition, and he had demonstrated his organizational and administrative abilities. He felt, moreover, duty-bound to serve the cause of freedom and progress. Feeling unfit for the responsibilities of minister of public education, in July he accepted the position of undersecretary in the Ministry of Public Instruction and directed the effort to reform the public schools. After a popular uprising was crushed by the army in October, Feuchtersleben resigned and left Vienna. After spending some time with his brother in Aussee to try to regain his health, he resumed his duties at the medical college; the hostility of his colleagues, however, forced him to resign his deanship. His professorship was to be suspended as well, but the issue became moot when Feuchtersleben began to suffer from a serious stomach ailment. He died on 3 September 1849.

His anthology *Geist deutscher Klassiker* appeared in 1851; its ten parts, of about 150 pages each, are devoted to Goethe, Jean Paul, Herder, Christoph Martin Wieland, Schiller, Ernst Christian Graf von Benzel-Sternau, Friedrich Maximilian von Klinger, Gotthold Ephraim Lessing, Theodor Gottlieb von Hippel, and Georg Christoph Lichtenberg, respectively. The sequence of authors indicates Feuchtersleben's ranking of them.

Helene Feuchtersleben persuaded the dramatist Friedrich Hebbel, who lived in Vienna but had not been a friend of Feuchtersleben's, to edit his *Sämtliche Werke* (Collected Works, 1851–1853). It includes the sketch of his life that Feuchtersleben had written when he was elected a member of the Academy of Sciences. Although Hebbel undertook the task reluctantly – he was not convinced that Feuchtersleben's writings were first-rate – his edition has remained the most reliable and complete edition of Feuchtersleben's works.

Feuchtersleben's ideas for the reform of public education were applied after 1850. The emperor granted a full pension to his widow in spite of the short time he had served in office; she died in 1882. Feuchtersleben's ideas survived, although his personal fame faded quickly; this fate is exactly that for which he had wished.

Letters:

"Briefe Feuchterslebens an Zauper," edited by Franz Ilwof, *Jahrbuch der Grillparzer-Gesellschaft,* 15 (1905): 290–313;

Aus Briefen Feuchterslebens, 1826–1832, edited by A. T. Seligmann (Vienna: Heller, 1907);

"Unveröffentlichte Briefe Ernst von Feuchterslebens," edited by Egon Schramm, *Euphorion,* 46, no. 3-4 (1952): 421–439.

Bibliography:

Hubert Lengauer, Emma Lesky, Ulrich Schöndorfer, and Herbert Seidler, "Ernst Freiherr von Feuchtersleben: Verzeichnis seiner Schriften," *Anzeiger der phil.-hist. Klasse der Österreichischen Akademie der Wissenschaften,* 112 (1975): 339–351.

Biographies:

Friedrich Hebbel, "Ernst Freiherr von Feuchtersleben. Umrisse zu seiner Biographie und Charakteristik," in Feuchtersleben's *Sämtliche Werke,* edited by Hebbel, volume 7 (Vienna: Gerold, 1853), pp. 221–402;

Richard Guttmann, "Biographisch-literarische Einleitung," in Feuchtersleben's *Ausgewählte Werke,* edited by Guttmann (Leipzig: Hesse, 1907), pp. 11–61.

References:

Wilhelm Bietak, "Grillparzer – Stifter – Feuchtersleben – die Unzeitgemäßen des Jahres 1848," *Deutsche Vierteljahrsschrift für Literaturwissenschaft und Geistesgeschichte,* 24, no. 2 (1950): 243–268;

Paul Gorceix, *Ernst von Feuchtersleben: Moraliste et Pédagogue (1806–1849)* (Paris: Presses Universitaires de France, 1976);

Franz Ilwof, "Feuchterslebens Goethestudien," *Chronik des Wiener Goethevereins,* 17 (1903): 3–7;

Richard Meister, "Feuchterslebens Anteil an der Unterrichtsreform 1848 und an der Akademie der Wissenschaften," *Anzeiger der phil.-hist. Klasse der Österreichischen Akademie der Wissenschaften,* no. 11 (1950): 214–237;

Moriz Necker, "Feuchtersleben, der Freund Grillparzers," *Jahrbuch der Grillparzer-Gesellschaft,* 3 (1893): 61–93;

Hans Ruprich, "Ernst Freiherr von Feuchtersleben: Zur 100. Wiederkehr seines Todestages," *Anzeiger der phil.-hist. Klasse der Österreichischen Akademie der Wissenschaften,* no. 11 (1950): 194–203;

Herbert Seidler, "Ernst Freiherr von Feuchtersleben: Seine geistes- und literaturgeschichtliche Stellung in der österreichischen Restaurationszeit," *Anzeiger der phil.-hist. Klasse der Österreichischen Akademie der Wissenschaften,* 106 (1969): 235–249;

Seidler, *Österreichischer Vormärz und Goethezeit: Geschichte einer literarischen Auseinandersetzung* (Vienna: Verlag der Österreichischen Akademie der Wissenschaften, 1982), pp. 364–381;

Gustav Wilhelm, "Herder, Feuchtersleben und Stifter," *Euphorion,* 16 (1923): 120–134.

Papers:

The largest collection of Ernst Freiherr von Feuchtersleben's papers is at the Stadt-Bibliothek (Municipal Library), Vienna; some papers are at the National-Bibliothek, Vienna. Documents pertaining to Feuchtersleben's official duties in 1848 are in the archives of the Austrian Bundesministerium für Unterricht (Federal Ministry of Education), Vienna.

Ludwig Feuerbach

(28 July 1804 - 13 September 1872)

Glenn A. Guidry

BOOKS: *De ratione, una, universali, infinita* (Nuremberg: Stein, 1828);

Gedanken über Tod und Unsterblichkeit, aus den Papieren eines Denkers, nebst einem Anhang theologisch-satyrischer Xenien, herausgegeben von einem seiner Freunde, anonymous (Nuremberg: Stein, 1830); translated by James A. Massey as *Thoughts on Death and Immortality: From the Papers of a Thinker, along with an Appendix of Theological-Satirical Epigrams, Edited by One of His Friends* (Berkeley: University of California Press, 1980);

Geschichte der neueren Philosophie von Bacon von Verulam bis Benedict Spinoza (Ansbach: Brügel, 1833);

Abälard und Heloise oder Der Schriftsteller und der Mensch: Eine Reihe humoristischer Aphorismen (Ansbach: Brügel, 1834);

Darstellung, Entwicklung und Kritik der Leibnitz'schen Philosophie (Ansbach: Brügel, 1837);

Pierre Bayle, nach seinen für die Geschichte der Philosophie und Menschheit interessantesten Momenten, dargestellt und gewürdigt (Ansbach: Brügel, 1838); revised and enlarged as *Pierre Bayle: Ein Beitrag zur Geschichte der Philosophie und Menschheit* (Leipzig: Wigand, 1848);

Über Philosophie und Christenthum, in Beziehung auf den der Hegel'schen Philosophie gemachten Vorwurf der Unchristlichkeit (Mannheim: Hoff & Heuser, 1839);

Das Wesen des Christenthums (Leipzig: Wigand, 1841); translated by Marian Evans as *The Essence of Christianity* (London: Chapman, 1854; New York: Blanchard, 1855);

Grundsätze der Philosophie der Zukunft (Zurich: Literarisches Comptoir, 1843); translated by Manfred H. Vogel as *Principles of the Philosophy of the Future* (Indianapolis: Bobbs-Merrill, 1966);

Vorläufige Thesen zur Reform der Philosophie (Zurich: Winterthur, 1843);

Das Wesen des Glaubens im Sinne Luther's: Ein Beitrag zum "Wesen des Christenthums" (Leipzig: Wigand, 1844); translated by Melvin Cherno as *The Essence of Faith according to Luther* (New York: Harper & Row, 1967);

Ludwig Feuerbach

Kritik des Anti-Hegels: Zur Einleitung in das Studium der Philosophie (Leipzig: Wigand, 1844);

Das Wesen der Religion (Leipzig: Wigand, 1846); translated by Alexander Loos as *The Essence of Religion; God the Image of Man; Man's Dependence upon Nature the Last and Only Source of Religion* (New York: Butts, 1873; London: Progressive Publishing, 1890);

Erläuterungen und Ergänzungen zum Wesen des Christenthums (Leipzig: Wigand, 1846);

Vorlesungen über das Wesen der Religion: Nebst Zusätzen und Anmerkungen (Leipzig: Wigand, 1851); translated by Ralph Manheim as *Lectures on the Essence of Religion* (New York: Harper & Row, 1967);

Theogonie nach den Quellen des classischen, hebräischen und christlichen Alterthums (Leipzig: Wigand, 1857); republished as *Der Ursprung der Götter nach den Quellen des classischen, hebräischen und christlichen Alterthums* (Leipzig: Wigand, 1866);

Gottheit, Freiheit und Unsterblichkeit vom Standpunkte der Anthropologie (Leipzig: Wigand, 1866);

Aussprüche aus seinen Werken, edited by Leonore Feuerbach (Leipzig: Wigand, 1879);

Sämtliche Werke, 13 volumes, edited by Wilhelm Bolin and Friedrich Jodl (Stuttgart: Frommann, 1903-1911);

Gesammelte Werke, 16 volumes, edited by Werner Schuffenhauer (Berlin: Academie, 1967-1975);

Schriften aus dem Nachlaß, 3 volumes, edited by Carlo Ascheri and Erich Thies (Darmstadt: Wissenschaftliche Buchgesellschaft, 1974-1976).

Edition in English: *The Fiery Brook: Selected Writing of Ludwig Feuerbach,* translated by Zawar Hanfi (New York: Anchor, 1972).

OTHER: Paul Johann Anselm von Feuerbach, *Leben und Wirken aus seinen ungedruckten Briefen und Tagebüchern, Vorträgen und Denkschriften,* 2 volumes, edited by Feuerbach (Leipzig: Wigand, 1852).

SELECTED PERIODICAL PUBLICATIONS – UNCOLLECTED: "Rezension über *Die Idee der Freiheit und der Begriff des Gedankens* von K. Bayer," *Hallische Jahrbücher für deutsche Wissenschaft und Kunst,* 1, no. 6 (1838): 46-56;

"Zur Kritik der Hegelschen Philosophie," *Hallische Jahrbücher für deutsche Wissenschaft und Kunst,* 2 (1839): 1657-1702;

"Rezension über *Grundzüge der paulinischen Glaubenslehre* und *Die kirchliche Tradition über den Apostel Johannes und seine Schriften* von E. C. J. Lützelberger, *Hallische Jahrbücher für deutsche Wissenschaft und Kunst,* 3, no. 23 (1840): 1841-1846;

"Rezension über *Kritik der christlichen Medizin* von J. N. Ringseis," *Hallische Jahrbücher für deutsche Wissenschaft und Kunst,* 4, no. 13 (1841): 521-535;

"Über den Mariencultus," *Deutsche Jahrbücher für Wissenschaft und Kunst,* 5, no. 10 (1842): 37-54;

"Über *Das Wesen der Religion* in Beziehung auf 'Feuerbach und seine Philosophie': Ein Beitrag zur Kritik von R. Haym," *Die Epigonen,* 5, no. 1 (1848): 165-177.

To his own age, Ludwig Feuerbach seemed a Prometheus, a revolutionary who robbed Christianity of its superhuman aura and pointed to the anthropological origin of all religions. In the eyes of the Young Hegelians, among them Karl Marx, he appeared to have prepared the way for humanity's recovery of its rightful heritage and "alienated essence." Feuerbach seemed to show the way to many liberals in the struggle for human self-understanding, authentic existence, and social freedom. The book that contributed most to this reputation and that is still generally considered his most important work is *Das Wesen des Christenthums* (1841; translated as *The Essence of Christianity,* 1854). Less than a decade after its publication, however, Feuerbach's fame had ebbed. Decried by theologians and conservative Idealist philosophers, Feuerbach refused to participate in the Revolution of 1848 and thereby alienated himself from Marx, Friedrich Engels, and the "scientific socialists." Skeptical of the political capacities of his countrymen and therefore of the success of any German political revolution during his lifetime, Feuerbach chose the instruments of reflection to heal what he saw as a fundamental human problem: the propensity of people to remain blind to their material relationship to their environment and to each other and thus fail to realize their full potential. He considered his political action as consisting in the attempt to transform the German people's awareness of themselves.

To leftist thinkers of the time, this stance was too abstract and impractical; the self-confirmation of the human being in his sensuality as the end result of the history of religion and philosophy appeared too general, if not banal. Feuerbach's teachings, however, left their mark on writers who played decisive roles in shaping modern thought, leading some today to deem him an unsung prophet of the twentieth century. Those who have felt his impact include Søren Kierkegaard, Friedrich Nietzsche, Ernst Troeltsch, Sigmund Freud, Nicolay Berdyayev, Martin Heidegger, and Jean-Paul Sartre. To him, as much as to any other, are owed the notions of alienation and the "I-Thou" relationship: Erich Fromm and Martin Buber are inconceivable without Feuerbach.

Even thinkers who rejected Feuerbach developed dialectical continuations of his thought. On the one hand, Marx carried his former mentor's critical reflection on philosophy into a critical reflection on society; moreover, by revealing the extent to which religion and philosophy mask and distort human needs and purposes, Feuerbach also provided the basis for the more general critique of ideology that Marx is credited with starting and that has continued to this day. On the other hand, Karl Barth takes Feuerbach's dissolution of religion into its source in feelings as the occasion to reinterpret God as "der ganz Andere" (the completely Other).

From the perspective of contemporary philosophy, Feuerbach may be considered the first practitioner of deconstruction, a philosophical method most closely associated with Paul de Man and Richard Rorty. Feuerbach delivered a devastating historical critique of professional philosophy that is thorough and systematic, not merely rhetorical and aphoristic like Arthur Schopenhauer's or Nietzsche's. In his development of this critique Feuerbach transformed his early Hegelianism into an empirical realism and materialist humanism that he himself saw as the negation of speculative German Idealism and indeed as the end of philosophy in the old sense.

Ludwig Andreas Feuerbach was born on 28 July 1804 in Landshut, Bavaria, the fourth son of Paul Johann Anselm and Wilhelmina Feuerbach, née Tröster. His father was a distinguished jurist and criminologist who ranks at least as high in the history of legal thinking and criminological studies as his son Ludwig does in the history of philosophy. A champion of liberalism, his greatest monument in German legal history was the path-breaking Bavarian Penal Code of 1813, and his writings on the famous case of Kaspar Hauser provide some of the most important speculations on Hauser's origins and remain classics of early criminology. Shortly before Ludwig's birth he had accepted a chair in law at the University of Landshut. Ludwig's eldest brother, Joseph Anselm, became an archaeologist, professor of classical philology at Freiburg, and author of a well-known study of the Apollo Belvedere; the next eldest, Karl Wilhelm, became a professor of mathematics at Erlangen, and his ingenious alternative proof of a proposition in geometry is still familiar to mathematicians as Feuerbach's theorem; the third eldest, Eduard August, became professor of jurisprudence at Erlangen; and Ludwig's younger brother, Friedrich, abandoned theological studies and turned to philology and the study of Oriental literature. Joseph Anselm's son was the painter Anselm Feuerbach.

For all his liberalism, academic seriousness, and concern with dignity, Paul Johann Anselm Feuerbach was a man of fiery and impulsive temperament, known in the family as "Vesuvius." In 1813 he formed a liaison with a woman named Nannette Brunner; he formally separated from his wife in 1816 to live with her in Bamberg and Ansbach but returned to Wilhelmina a few months after Brunner's death in 1822. Nevertheless, he was a domestic tyrant who closely supervised his children's education even during the separation from his family. Ludwig attended primary school in Munich, where the family had moved in 1805 after Paul Feuerbach lost his temper at the public defense of a doctoral dissertation, stormed from the room, vowed to give no more lectures at Landshut, and took a position in the Ministry of Justice in Munich. In 1817 Ludwig Feuerbach entered the Ansbach Gymnasium, where he could be under the eye of his father. By his sixteenth year he showed a clear religious tendency. He took lessons from the son of a local rabbi, completed his secondary education in 1822, and remained in his reunited parents' home for a year before proceeding to study theology at Heidelberg University. There he attended lectures in speculative theology by Karl Daub, who was strongly influenced by the philosophy of Georg Wilhelm Friedrich Hegel, and on church history by H. E. G. Paulus, who leaned toward the Kantian rationalism of the Enlightenment. Feuerbach was as strongly attracted to Daub's Hegelian idealism as he was repulsed by Paulus's rational biblicism, and he became distrustful of the scholarly exegesis that prevailed at the time. Within a year he decided to transfer to the University of Berlin to study under Hegel and the theologian Friedrich Schleiermacher.

Feuerbach arrived in Berlin in 1824 and, due to police persecution, spent half of the year trying to gain official acceptance into the university: a secret commission had been set up by the Prussian government to investigate a report that the Feuerbach brothers were members of a secret revolutionary organization. On his twentieth birthday Feuerbach was finally admitted to the faculty of theology. Attending Hegel's lectures, he soon felt that he could no longer reconcile his studies in theology with his interest in philosophy. He found himself unable to complete Schleiermacher's course because "the theological mishmash of reason and faith" was repellant to his sensibilities, which demanded "truth, i.e., unity and absoluteness." Feuerbach's distancing of himself from theology was, however, at the same time a step away from Hegel, who believed that the content of dogma could be restated in philosophical terms without being destroyed.

Daub helped to gain Feuerbach's father's grudging permission for him to transfer to the philosophical faculty in 1825. In the same year the Bavarian government refused to renew the stipend that had been granted the Feuerbach children as sons of a civil servant. In the middle of 1826

Feuerbach moved to the University of Erlangen, where expenses were lower, to study the natural sciences. Apparently he had a proclivity toward empiricism and a strong interest in humans' connection with nature even at this early stage. Again, lack of funds made continued study impossible. Returning home to Ansbach, he composed his dissertation, *De ratione, una, universali, infinita* (Reason: Its Unity, Universality, and Infinity, 1828). The work was accepted and praised by the philosophical faculty at Erlangen, and Feuerbach was not only given his doctorate but also offered a position as a lecturer on the history of modern philosophy.

The dissertation takes up a Hegelian, Idealistic theme in a Hegelian, Idealistic way: reason is the activity of the universal, that which comprises nature, gives it significance, and unites thinking and being. Kantian rationalism, by viewing reason as a capability of the individual, creates the very situation that reason, according to the Kantian view, cannot transcend. Not only do rationalist philosophers have no way to measure the limits they posit, but they cut off from reason the comprehension of particulars. Such an understanding of reason falsifies what, according to Hegel, is most true about the individual: its universal substance. Hegel thus inspires Feuerbach with a vision of a philosophy that is able to liberate reason from limits and from the particular. Such a vision reaffirms the classical notion that philosophy seeks out the universal and essential in phenomena.

Feuerbach's aim in his dissertation is to show that thinking is a universalizing act that allows humans to escape the solipsism of individual sense experience and to communicate with one another. In this fashion Feuerbach takes on the task of liberating philosophy from the ego and of releasing the ego from its isolation. Feuerbach is far from empiricism here, since he sees the senses as inadequate and incomplete; but he does deviate significantly from Hegelian Idealism in using the Hegelian conception of reason to criticize Christianity. Reason, he argues, enables the person to break through the borders of individuality and to unite with other people, while Christianity is the religion of subjectivity and egoism. Feuerbach closes his dissertation with an elegant rejection of the limits of reason, cleverly using – as he will often do – his opponent's argument to prove his own case: the Kantian view of the limits of reason presupposes an unlimited standard of measure, for without such a standard we would not even know how to characterize reason. And if the standard were not single, there would be no communication, no common understanding. But we do communicate, and we do understand each other. Therefore, there is one infinite reason.

The subjectivity and egoism of Christianity are explained more clearly in Feuerbach's *Gedanken über Tod und Unsterblichkeit, aus den Papieren eines Denkers, nebst einem Anhang theologish-satyrischer Xenien, herausgegeben von einem seiner Freunde* (1830, translated as *Thoughts on Death and Immortality: From the Papers of a Thinker, along with an Appendix of Theological-Satirical Epigrams, Edited by One of His Friends,* 1980). This book assured the end of his career as a lecturer at Erlangen as well as Feuerbach's exclusion from academe for the rest of his life. A straightforward denial of the Christian belief in personal immortality, the work is also a criticism of the popular movement of Pietism and a satirical assault on the posturings and hypocrisies of the professional theologians of nineteenth-century Germany. It is Feuerbach's first attempt to apply philosophy to concrete reality and his opening attack on modern Christianity, whose emphasis on the individual self ignores the continuity between humans and their terrestrial environment and therefore blinds Christians to the value of life. The work thus presages the full-blown critique of Christianity in Feuerbach's later works.

In contrast to the dissertation, *Gedanken über Tod und Unsterblichkeit* focuses not on subjectivized philosophy but on subjectivized religion. Religion parallels Kantian rationalism as another form of aggrandizement of the ego, extending its commitment to the ego into the doctrine of personal immortality. This doctrine implies that the self is divine and infinite. Such an implication is an affront to the divinity of God: those who enshrine human selfhood dethrone God, who is the beginning and end of all reality. They are atheists; even if they continue to believe in and speak of God, they do so only to enlarge themselves. In this view only the naked self has value; life in the material world is discredited – even the body is nonessential. Sheer selfhood excludes other humans and precludes the possibility of defining the human through relationships such as love. Sheer selves require no time or space to flourish; consequently, they need neither history nor cosmology. The doctrine teaches people to turn away from any realm that thwarts the self; to protect the ego from the threats of the world, the doctrine posits other realms and beings that are purely spiritual. The chief lesson of the doctrine is that life ought to be dedicated to living for the sake of the hereafter; theology thus becomes removed from lived life. Theologians work with an abstract anthropology that attempts to speak of the person apart from sensual elements of concrete life. They do not take the real human into account, only an excerpt – the soul – that lives on forever in the hereafter. Theology is an armchair discipline that misses the holistic and mortal character of existence. It should turn to nature to learn about life.

According to Feuerbach, the view of the individual as the sole source of meaning and fulfillment is the result of modernity's break with the belief that the identity of humans is given by the community within which one lives. In opposition to this modern view, Feuerbach argues that the universal reality at the source of human individuality is more real than the individual; humans are limited expressions of humanity itself, the perfect ideal of humanity that is realized but never exhausted in individuals. The need to love expresses the need of distinct beings for unity; the basis of love is not the attraction of one uniqueness to another uniqueness but the attractiveness of what is shared. Our love for one another expresses our desire for unity with the infinite human reality of which we partake.

The major theme of the life story is growth in the capacity to love; our lives are much more a story of sharing our consciousness than of gaining our own. As we approach the twilight of life, the shared consciousness, in our memory and the memory of others, gains ground against the consciousness of our selves. Death is the ultimate act of sharing, for in it the boundary between ourself and the selves of others is totally obliterated and our self is totally surrendered to others' consciousness of us. The love that is the fulfillment of human life is most completely expressed in death.

Feuerbach ends the portion of the work devoted to philosophical argument – as opposed to the satirical poetic epigrams that follow – by attempting to return the self to the real limits it has violated by its imaginative invention of the afterlife. Individual existence is limited by the infinity of the Creator, by its subjection to the laws of time and space, by its intrinsic connection to an organic body, and by its finite capacity to exercise the infinite powers that characterize it as human – self-consciousness, reason, and will. While this recognition of limitation enjoins resignation to the finality of death, Feuerbach argues that the quality of the limited time we have is superior to that of a life of eternal duration. The life we lead before death is the experience of infinity within the conditions of finitude; for example, through love the finite individual realizes its unity with humanity itself, which is infinite. Here the living human being already experiences death – the annihilation of individual selfhood – but also comes to a knowledge of his or her capacity to stretch to infinity. Thus is finitude conquered within finitude.

The major crisis in a human life is not the point of death itself but the realization that one will die. Feuerbach here anticipates the questions and answers that would become fundamental in the thought of Kierkegaard, Nietzsche, and twentieth-century existentialists. The choice of what to do about death becomes the choice of what to do about life, of what kind of life to live. One can make death the constant theme of one's life by hoping for life after this life – Feuerbach calls this alternative living as if one were dead – or one can decide to live now with the intensity and love that allow the self to be consumed. For Feuerbach, to choose the second alternative is to conquer death within life.

Feuerbach's work was taken as a dangerous and revolutionary document, for it includes an open attack on theology in the service of the police states formed in 1815 in the wake of the Wars of Liberation. The postwar years saw the spread of Pietism throughout the German states; the movement's conservative tone strengthened the authority of the established religious leaders and the German rulers. An attack on Christianity was thus a political act. Although Feuerbach's work was published anonymously, his authorship was soon recognized. Denied promotion at Erlangen, Feuerbach ceased lecturing in 1832 and toyed with the idea of immigrating to Paris. His friend Christian Kapp, professor of philosophy at Erlangen and later at Heidelberg, recommended Feuerbach for various academic posts, but in vain.

Feuerbach attempted to further his professional prospects by producing a series of three academic works on the history of philosophy: *Geschichte der neueren Philosophie von Bacon von Verulam bis Benedict Spinoza* (History of Modern Philosophy from Bacon of Verulam to Benedict Spinoza, 1833), which was based on his lectures at Erlangen and well received in the professional journals; *Darstellung, Entwicklung und Kritik der Leibnitz'schen Philosophie* (Exposition, Development, and Critique of Leibnizian Philosophy, 1837); and *Pierre Bayle, nach seinen für die Geschichte der Philosophie und Menschheit interessantesten Momenten* (Pierre Bayle, as Regards His Most Interesting Moments for the History of Philosophy and Humanity, 1838). Except for a semester in 1835–1836 when his friends persuaded him to give a series of lectures at Erlangen for students who wanted to hear him, Feuerbach remained firm in his resolve that he would not teach as long as he was left in the lowly position of docent.

In 1834 Feuerbach had met Berta Löw; a year older than he, she had inherited a share in a porcelain factory in Bruckberg. A correspondence ensued, and soon the couple regarded themselves as engaged. Attempts at gaining Feuerbach a promotion at Erlangen or an appointment to vacant professorships at the Universities of Marburg, Heidelberg, and Freiburg foundered on objections to his irreligiousness. In 1836 a third attempt to have him promoted at Erlangen came to nothing. In 1837 he threw himself into the study of anatomy and physiology as conscious compensation for the philosopher's one-sided concentration on mind and spirit. On 12 November 1837 he and Löw were married at Bruckberg, Feuerbach's joblessness notwithstanding. For the next twenty-three years they were to live modestly but comfortably in rural seclusion in Berta's family's castle near Bruckberg, supported by the profits of the porcelain factory and the proceeds of Feuerbach's writings. Free of the narrow professionalism and stultifying division of the disciplines imposed by university organization, Feuerbach claimed to be discovering greater insight and native intelligence in peasants and artisans than he had in the works of academic philosophers. He wrote paeans of praise to nature and the natural life.

In his three works on the history of modern philosophy Feuerbach devotes more and more attention to criticizing Idealist approaches, which he regards as philosophical equivalents of Christian theological views, and to positively evaluating non-Idealist views; the third volume champions the empiricist Bayle. Feuerbach emerges with two conclusions that demand a new beginning in philosophy: Christian theology masked the human origin and nature of religious beliefs; and Hegel's philosophy, the culmination of the Idealist tradition, deified thought at the expense of humanity.

Feuerbach elaborated on the second of these conclusions in *Über Philosophie und Christenthum, in Beziehung auf den der Hegel'schen Philosophie gemachten Vorwurf der Unchristlichkeit* (On Philosophy and Christianity, in Reference to the Reproach of Un-Christianness Made against the Hegelian Philosophy, 1839), a devastating critique of what Feuerbach sees as the principal error of Hegel's philosophy: that it reduces existence to thought. The critique of Hegel was followed by Feuerbach's critique of religion in *Das Wesen des Christenthums,* his best-known work. According to Feuerbach, both Christian theology and Idealist philosophy were bound to a manner of thought that betrayed the humanity they should have served: the hypostatization of abstract entities, whether God or Being, that are projections of human qualities and that indirectly express human needs and interests.

Feuerbach characterizes philosophy as the process of human self-understanding. Conceived in this way, philosophy is demystified and recognized for what it is: anthropology. Religion and philosophy are stages of a single process by which humans come to understand their own nature. But this self-understanding becomes possible only after that nature has been projected and objectified as something other than human – in religion, as God. Philosophy in its rigorous abstraction strips away the still personal and sensuously conceived aspects of the divine image of humanity until only the most severe logical and metaphysical attributes remain, and these attributes are reconceived as attributes of an abstract Being. Feuerbach sees his task as that of reversing this process, of bringing the human being to a direct knowledge of what it means to be human by translating the doctrines of theology and philosophy into truths about human nature.

The first ten years in Bruckberg marked the high point of Feuerbach's philosophical career and were probably the happiest years of his life. *Das Wesen des Christenthums* made him the most talked-about philosopher in Germany. In *Grundsätze der Philosophie der Zukunft* (1843; translated as *Principles of the Philosophy of the Future,* 1966), published in Switzerland to evade German censorship, he forges the criteria of a way of thinking that penetrates and remains close to the empirical world. The specific criteria he developed are less important than the attempt to articulate a humanistic empiricism.

While in *Das Wesen des Christenthums* Feuerbach had still elevated reason above the senses as the path to the truth, he rejects this standpoint in *Grundsätze der Philosophie der Zukunft* and emphasizes that only what is perceived by the senses – what Feuerbach calls "die Natur" (nature) – is real. Nature is always individual and cannot be captured by universal concepts, which provide only an illusory image. In contrast to traditional philosophy, which starts from the thesis that the human is purely a thinking being whose body does not belong to its essence, the philosophy of the future is based on the axiom that the body *is* the human essence. Feuerbach goes on to point out that it is only in dialogue with others that the individual can fathom the truth: the other confirms, corrects, or modifies what the isolated individual perceives. Ideas do not arise from the individual, as Idealism holds, but from communication among the members of a community.

Even during the height of the controversy aroused by his writings, Feuerbach remained sequestered in his rural retreat. Although he had

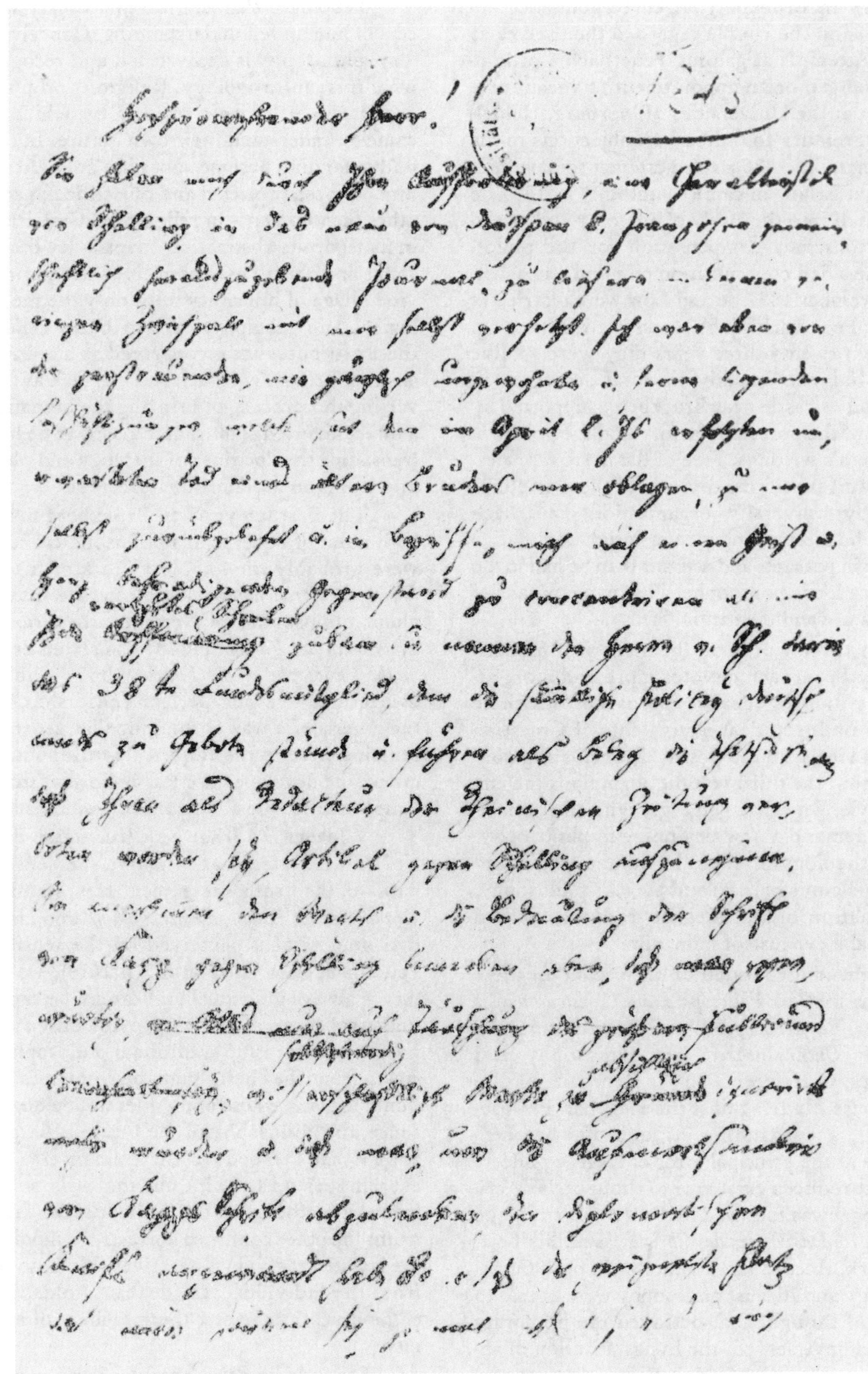

First page of a letter from Feuerbach to Karl Marx (Universitätsbibliothek München)

given some articles to the Young Hegelian Arnold Ruge for his radical journals, he held himself somewhat aloof from the activities of Ruge, Marx, and others who were anxious to flourish the weapon of philosophical criticism in the periodical press. Feuerbach devoted himself increasingly to his studies of religion, revising *Das Wesen des Christenthums,* defending it against critics and writing articles on theological matters. In 1846 appeared his *Das Wesen der Religion* (translated as *The Essence of Religion; God the Image of Man; Man's Dependence upon Nature the Last and Only Source of Religion,* 1873), in which the approach earlier applied to Christianity is extended to other religions. A slight difference in viewpoint is evident in Feuerbach's increasing emphasis on nature, which includes the human being, rather than on humans alone. In *Das Wesen der Religion* the characteristics normally attributed to God are seen as projections of the best not just in human beings but in nature as a whole. Human dependence on nature is the source of religion, and God is nothing but nature itself. This emphasis on nature distinguishes Feuerbach from Marx, who made history rather than nature the basis of his analysis of the human condition.

Despite his aloofness from politics, Feuerbach openly stated that the real content of religion could be best expressed through the establishment of democracy. Consequently, he was often the target of censorship and police investigations. In 1842 the police searched the Feuerbach residence during a visit by Hermann Kriese, a socialist journalist. Nevertheless, throughout the period from 1843 to 1848 Feuerbach was extremely skeptical about the possibility of political revolution in Germany. He had many acquaintances among German radicals, and his thought was widely recognized to have had great influence upon them. On a visit to Heidelberg, for example, he met the poet Georg Herwegh, whose poetry shows strong signs of Feuerbach's influence. Several of the men involved in the 1848 Revolution were friends of his. When the revolution came, he welcomed it, but with caution about its prospects. A newspaper announced that Breslau University was considering calling Feuerbach and Ruge to chairs, and it was widely predicted that Feuerbach would become an academic luminary in a democratic Germany. In Ansbach, the popular assembly proposed Feuerbach as a delegate for the Frankfurt National Assembly; the Frankfurt newspaper published a flowery appeal to Feuerbach to leave his rural retreat and come forth as a delegate.

Feuerbach did not become a delegate, but he did travel to Frankfurt. There he held discussions with Ruge and Carl Vogt, who were members of the National Assembly, and attended the Democratic Congress organized by the radical, free-thinking wing of the German democratic movement to protest against their insufficient representation in the assembly. To the congress, however, Feuerbach lent the distinction of his name rather than his active participation; he was almost completely silent throughout the proceedings. Political activism did not interest him; he was anxious to be writing again. Plans by the Baden Ministry of Education to have him called to a chair of philosophy were moving slowly; he expected nothing to come of them.

Feuerbach, of course, was proved right: the revolution failed, and he was not given a university post. Feuerbach's recognition came from students in Heidelberg who invited him to give a series of lectures on the essence of religion. The lectures were given twice a week in the city hall from 1 December 1848 to 2 March 1849 and were attended by students, academics, and townspeople. Among those attending were the physiologist Jacob Moleschott and the Swiss novelist Gottfried Keller. Keller had wrestled with Feuerbach's philosophy since becoming acquainted with it through Ruge, Karl Grün, and others in Zurich in the early 1840s. Keller had been ambivalent toward Feuerbach's doctrines, but at the Heidelberg lectures he was converted. A personal friendship sprang up, and Feuerbach's thought became one of the most important influences on Keller, especially his aesthetics.

Back in Bruckberg, Feuerbach watched the collapse of the Frankfurt parliament and the conservative reaction with some detachment. Moleschott sent Feuerbach his popular textbook on foodstuffs, published in 1850; Feuerbach reviewed it in an essay purporting to prove that "Man ist, was man ißt" (You are what you eat). The Heidelberg lectures were published in 1851. Meanwhile, Feuerbach's brother Eduard died, and the work of bringing out their father's literary remains fell to Feuerbach. He completed editing the work in 1851; the two volumes were published in 1852 and were expected to sell well, but they had limited success.

Feuerbach toyed with the idea of immigrating to America, but he lacked the funds to do so. He spent almost five years on his study of the foundations of Greek mythology, the *Theogonie nach den Quellen des classischen, hebräischen und christlischen Alterthums* (Theogony According to the Sources of Classical, Hebrew and Christian Antiquity, 1857), in which he defends in a lively and witty polemic – Feuerbach belongs alongside Schopenhauer and Nietzsche as one of the three finest stylists in German philosophy – the view that the gods were personified human wishes. Anticipating Freud's psychological analysis of religious experience, the work treats an abundance of material drawn from Greek mythology, but unfortunately it uses this material for polemical rather than for historical-critical purposes. It was regarded by critics as adding nothing new to the philosophical critique of religion.

The porcelain factory went bankrupt in 1859, and in 1860 Feuerbach and his wife moved to a more modest home in Rechenberg, near Munich. A wealthy admirer, Otto Lüning, raised a collection among Feuerbach's followers and obtained a pension for the Feuerbachs from the Schiller Foundation. It was only with great difficulty that Feuerbach was persuaded to accept the money. At Rechenberg, Feuerbach was still occasionally visited by admirers; and Ferdinand Lassalle sent his writings to Feuerbach from Switzerland as a mark of his respect.

In *Gottheit, Freiheit und Unsterblichkeit vom Standpunkte der Anthropologie* (God, Freedom, and Immortality from the Standpoint of Anthropology, 1866) Feuerbach applied his approach to Kant's ethics. Attempting to develop a concept of freedom from a determinisitc standpoint, he identified the human will with the drive for happiness. He intended the work to be a refutation not only of the duty-based morality of Kant but also of the pessimism of Schopenhauer. It fell flat, failing to arouse interest even among Feuerbach's admirers. Feuerbach continued to keep abreast of political affairs, applauding the movement for women's emancipation and the publication of the first volume of Marx's *Das Kapital* (translated as *Capital,* 1887) in 1867. His financial situation was growing precarious again; friends tried to gain him a national pension, but without success.

In 1870 Feuerbach joined the newly founded Social Democratic party. In the same year he suffered a stroke that left him confused and apathetic; a Social Democratic paper in Würzburg published the news under a headline indicating that the great democratic thinker was in desperate material need. Contributions from Germany, Belgium, England, Austria, and the United States made it possible to seek proper medical care for Feuerbach. He became progressively weaker, however, and died in Nuremberg on 13 September 1872. Two days later the Social Democratic party paid tribute to him with a huge procession attending his burial in Nuremberg's Johannesfriedhof (Saint John's Cemetery).

Letters:

Ludwig Feuerbach in seinem Briefwechsel und Nachlaß, sowie in seiner philosophischen Charakterentwicklung, 2 volumes, edited by Karl Grün (Leipzig: Winter, 1874);

Briefwechsel: 1832 bis 1848, edited by August Kapp (Leipzig: Wigand, 1876);

Ausgewählte Briefe von und an Ludwig Feuerbach, 2 volumes, edited by Wilhelm Bolin (Leipzig: Wigand, 1904).

Biographies:

Adolf Kohut, *Ludwig Feuerbach: Sein Leben und seine Werke* (Leipzig: Eckardt, 1909);

Friedrich Jodl, *Ludwig Feuerbach* (Stuttgart: Frommann, 1921);

Friedrich Lombardi, *Ludwig Feuerbach* (Vienna: Koneger, 1932).

References:

Carlo Acheri, *Feuerbachs Bruch mit der Spekulation* (Frankfurt am Main: Europäische Verlagsanstalt, 1969);

Karl Barth, "Ludwig Feuerbach," in *Theology and Church,* edited by Louise Pettibone Smith (New York: Harper & Row, 1962), pp. 41-62;

William J. Brazill, *The Young Hegelians* (New Haven: Yale University Press, 1970);

Martin Buber, "Das Problem des Menschen," in his *Werke,* volume 1 (Munich: Kösel, 1962), pp. 16-29;

Sergei Bulgakov, *Karl Marx as a Religious Type: His Relation to the Religion of Anthropotheism of Ludwig Feuerbach* (Belmont, Mass.: Nordland, 1979);

William Chamberlain, *Heaven Wasn't His Destination* (London: Allen & Unwin, 1941);

Peter Cornehl, "Feuerbach und die Naturphilosophie: Zur Genese der Anthropologie und Religionskritik des jungen Feuerbach," *Neue Zeitschrift für systematische Theologie und Religionsphilosophie,* 11 (1869): 37-93;

Ivan Dubsky, "Ludwig Feuerbach in der Buberschen Sicht," in *Studi in memoria di Carlo Ascheri,* edited by Claudio Cesa, Ivan Dubsky, and Hans-Martin Sass (Urfino: Argalia Editore, 1970), pp. 49-70;

Julius Ebbinghaus, "Ludwig Feuerbach," *Deutsche Vierteljahrsschrift,* 8 (1930): 283-305;

Friedrich Engels, *Ludwig Feuerbach und der Ausgang der klassischen Philosophie* (Stuttgart: Dietz, 1919);

Michael Gagern, *Ludwig Feuerbach und Religionskritik: Die "Neue" Philosophie* (Munich: Pustet, 1970);

John Glasse, "Barth on Feuerbach," *Harvard Theological Review,* 57 (1964): 69-96;

Glasse, "Review of *Lectures on the Essence of Religion* and *The Essence of Faith according to Luther* by

Ludwig Feuerbach," *Journal of the History of Philosophy,* 10 (January 1972): 101–105;

Frederick M. Gordon, "The Contradictory Nature of Feuerbachian Humanism," *Philosophical Forum,* 8, nos. 2-4 (1979): 31–47;

Johannes Hertrampf, "Die materialistische Bestimmung der Kunst durch Feuerbach," *Deutsche Zeitschrift für Philosophie,* 26, no. 8 (1978): 995–1003;

Walter Jaeschke, "Speculative and Anthropological Criticism of Religion: A Theological Orientation to Hegel and Feuerbach," *Journal of the American Academy of Religion,* 48 (1980): 345–364;

J. Christine Janowski, *Der Mensch als Maß: Untersuchungen zum Grundgedanken und zur Struktur von Ludwig Feuerbachs Werk* (Zurich: Benzinger, 1980);

Eugene Kamenka, *The Philosophy of Ludwig Feuerbach* (London: Routledge & Kegan Paul, 1970);

Hermann Lübbe and Hans-Martin Sass, eds., *Atheismus in der Diskussion: Kontroversen um Ludwig Feuerbach* (Munich: Kaiser, 1975);

James A. Massey, "Feuerbach and Religious Individualism," *Journal of Religion,* 56 (October 1976): 366–381;

Peter Preuss, "Feuerbach on Man and God," *Dialogue,* 11 (June 1972): 204–223;

Simon Radwidowicz, *Ludwig Feuerbachs Philosophie* (Berlin: Reuther & Reichard, 1931);

Hans-Martin Sass, "Diskussionsstrategien und Kritikmodelle in der Feuerbachkritik," *Differenze,* 9 (1970): 245–270;

Sass, *Ludwig Feuerbach in Selbstzeugnissen und Bilddokumenten* (Hamburg: Rowohlt, 1978);

Alfred Schmidt, *Emanzipatorische Sinnlichkeit: Ludwig Feuerbachs anthropologischer Materialismus* (Munich: Hanser, 1973);

Erich Schneider, *Die Theologie und Feuerbachs Religionskritik* (Göttingen: Vanderhoeck & Ruprecht, 1972);

Werner Schuffenhauer, *Feuerbach und der junge Marx: Zur Entstehungsgeschichte der marxistischen Weltanschauung* (Berlin: Deutscher Verlag der Wissenschaft, 1965);

Eric Thies, "Die Verwirklichung der Vernunft: Ludwig Feuerbachs Kritik der spekulative-systematischen Philosophie," *Revue internationale de philosophie,* 26, no. 101 (1972): 275–307;

Thies, ed., *Ludwig Feuerbach* (Darmstadt: Wissenschaftliche Buchgesellschaft, 1976);

Marx W. Wartofsky, *Feuerbach* (Cambridge: Cambridge University Press, 1977);

Josef Winiger, *Feuerbachs Weg zum Humanismus: Zur Genesis des anthropologischen Materialismus* (Munich: Fink, 1979).

Papers:

The Ludwig Feuerbach Archive is in the library of Karl Marx University in Leipzig.

Ferdinand Freiligrath

(17 June 1810 – 18 March 1876)

Otto W. Johnston
University of Florida

BOOKS: *Gedichte* (Stuttgart & Tübingen: Cotta, 1838, enlarged, 1839); translated by Käthe Freiligrath-Kroeker as *Poems from the German* (London: Low, Marston / Leipzig: Tauchnitz, 1869);

Das malerische und romantische Westphalen, by Freiligrath and Levin Schücking (Leipzig: Volckmar, 1841);

Karl Immermann: Blätter der Erinnerung an ihn (Stuttgart: Krabbe, 1842);

Ein Glaubensbekenntnis: Zeitgedichte (Mainz: Von Zabern, 1844);

Leipzigs Todten! (Zurich: Rothpelz, 1845);

Ein Lied vom Tode (Berlin: Fähndrich, 1845);

Ça ira! Sechs Gedichte (Herisau: Literarische Institut, 1846);

Berlin: Neues Revolutions-Lied (London: Eggers, 1848);

Februar-Klänge: Gedicht. London, am 25. Februar 1848 (Berlin: Romolini, 1848);

Freie Presse (Berlin: Schlesinger, 1848);

Die neuesten denkwürdigen Ereignisse in Paris, München, Wien und Berlin in den erfolgreichen Monaten Februar und März 1848; nebst dem neuesten Gedichte (Ulm: Ebner, 1848);

Die Revolution: Gedicht (Leipzig: Grunow, 1848);

Die Todten an die Lebenden: Juli 1848. Gedicht (Düsseldorf: Kampmann, 1848);

Schwarz-Roth-Gold: Neues Revolutions-Lied (London: Eggers, 1848);

Blum: 16. November. Gedicht (Düsseldorf: Kampmann, 1849);

Wien: Gedicht. 3. November 1848 (Düsseldorf: Kampmann, 1849);

Zwischen den Garben: Eine Nachlese älterer Gedichte (Stuttgart & Tübingen: Cotta, 1849);

Neuere politische und sociale Gedichte, 2 volumes (Düsseldorf: Scheller, 1849, 1851);

Nach Johanna Kinkels Begräbniss, 20. November 1858 (London: Trübner, 1858);

Sämmtliche Werke: Vollständige Original-Ausgabe, 6 volumes (New York: Gerhard, 1858–1859);

Painting by Ernst Halder (Zentralbibliothek Zürich)

Festlied der Deutschen in Amerika zur Feier von Schillers hundertjährigem Geburtstage, 10. November 1859 (N.p., 1859);

Festlied der Deutschen in London zur Feier von Schillers hundertjährigem Geburtstage 10. November 1859 (London: Petsch, 1859);

Neuere Gedichte und Freiheits-Lieder: Amerikanische Auswahl (Boston: De Bries, Ibarra, 1860);

Gesammelte Dichtungen, 6 volumes (Stuttgart: Göschen, 1870–1871);

Goethe's Gruß zum "Kölner Mummenschanz," Fastnacht 1873: Gedicht (Cologne: DuMont-Schauberg, 1873);

Neue Gedichte, edited by Ida Freiligrath (Stuttgart: Cotta, 1877);

Nachgelassenes: Mazeppa nach Lord Byron; Der Eggesterstein. Erzählung (Stuttgart: Göschen, 1883);

Sämtliche Werke, 10 volumes, edited by Ludwig Schröder (Leipzig: Hesse, 1907);

Werke in sechs Teilen, 6 volumes, edited by Julius Schwering (Berlin & Leipzig: Bong, 1909; reprinted, 2 volumes, Hildesheim & New York: Olms, 1974);

Werke, 2 volumes, edited by Paul Zaunert (Leipzig: Bibliographisches Institut, 1912);

Werke, edited by Werner Ilberg (Weimar: Volksverlag, 1962).

Editions in English: *Schiller's Homage of the Arts: With Miscellaneous Pieces from Rückert, Freiligrath, and Other German Poets,* translated and edited by Charles T. Brooks (New York: Miller, 1846);

Ireland's Calamity: Poem, translated by C. Peter (Detroit, 1880);

"Selected Poems," translated by M. G. and others, in *The German Classics of the Nineteenth and Twentieth Centuries,* volume 7, edited by Kuno Francke and William Guild Howard (New York: German Publishing Society, 1914).

OTHER: Victor Hugo, *Oden und vermischte Gedichte,* translated by Freiligrath (Frankfurt am Main: Sauerländer, 1836);

Rheinisches Odeon, 2 volumes, edited by Freiligrath, Ignaz Hub, and August Schnezler (volume 1, Koblenz: Hölscher, 1836; volume 2, Düsseldorf: Schreiner, 1838);

Hugo, "Dämmerungsgesänge," translated by Freiligrath, in Hugo's *Herbstblätter; Dämmerungsgesänge,* translated by Freiligrath and H. Fournier (Frankfurt am Main: Sauerländer, 1836);

Molière, *Sämmtliche Werke,* 5 volumes, translated by Freiligrath and others, edited by Louis Lax (Aachen: Mayer, 1837–1838);

Rheinisches Jahrbuch für Kunst und Poesie, 2 volumes, edited by Freiligrath, Karl Simrock, and C. J. Matzerath (Cologne: DuMont-Schauberg, 1840–1841);

Rolands-Album: Zum Besten der Ruine, edited by Freiligrath (Cologne: DuMont-Schauberg, 1840);

Hugo, *Lyrische Gedichte,* translated by Freiligrath (Frankfurt am Main: Sauerländer, 1845);

Englische Gedichte aus neuerer Zeit, translated by Freiligrath (Stuttgart & Tübingen: Cotta, 1846);

Neue Rheinische Zeitung, edited by Freiligrath, 11 October 1848–19 May 1849;

William Shakespeare, *Venus und Adonis,* translated by Freiligrath (Düsseldorf: Scheller, 1849);

The Rose, Thistle and Shamrock: A Selection of English Poetry, Chiefly Modern, edited by Freiligrath (Stuttgart: Hallberger, 1853);

Dichtung und Dichter: Eine Anthologie, edited by Freiligrath (Dessau: Katz, 1854);

The Poems of Samuel Taylor Coleridge, biographical memoir by Freiligrath (London: Moxon, 1856);

Henry Wadsworth Longfellow, *Der Sang von Hiawatha,* translated by Freiligrath (Stuttgart: Cotta, 1857);

The Poems of Samuel Taylor Coleridge, edited by Derwent and Sara Coleridge, biographical memoir by Freiligrath (Leipzig: Tauchnitz, 1860);

Hallberger's Illustrated Magazine, 2 volumes, edited by Freiligrath (1875–1876);

Coleridge, *Der alte Matrose: Nach dem Englischen,* translated by Freiligrath (Leipzig: Amelang, 1877).

Toward the middle of the nineteenth century Ferdinand Freiligrath was one of the most widely read poets in Germany. In his poetry one can trace the transition in German literature from exotic Romanticism to social commitment. His early lyrics tell of faraway places, foreign peoples, and strange customs; his later verse calls for resistance and revolution. He touched off the most significant literary controversy of his day, one concerning the role of the poet in society. He was a masterful translator, especially of English-language poets: he introduced the German reading public to the American writers Henry Wadsworth Longfellow and Bret Harte. The commemoration organized in his honor in 1867 was the largest celebration of a living poet ever held in Germany.

Hermann Ferdinand Freiligrath was born on 17 June 1810 in Detmold at the northern edge of the Teutoburg Forest to Johann Wilhelm Freiligrath, a schoolteacher, and Luise Tops Freiligrath. His mother died in 1816. Three years later Johann Wilhelm Freiligrath married Klara Wilhelmine

Schwollmann; they had four children: Karl, Otto, Karoline, and Gisberte.

Freiligrath was an excellent pupil at the primary school where his father taught and later at the gymnasium in Detmold. One of his gymnasium teachers often sent Freiligrath to the library to return books – only to find him hours later standing on a ladder, reading the books he was supposed to shelve. When he was fifteen, financial difficulties forced him to abandon his formal education. Relatives offered assistance, but Johann Wilhelm Freiligrath insisted that his son learn something practical and apprenticed him to his wife's brother, the merchant Moritz Schwollmann in Soest. By this time Freiligrath had already rendered superior translations of Greek and Latin classics and had written essays and sketches. He began his apprenticeship on 2 July 1825.

A year later he became ill with a respiratory infection. The physician prescribed an elixir made from algae and fungus that grew on rocks in Iceland. The dark green, bitter concoction so invigorated the sixteen-year-old that he wrote his first published poem, "Moostee" (Lichen Tea), in which he describes the effects of his medicine and imagines living on the rugged terrain that produced its ingredients. The work contains all the primary characteristics of Freiligrath's early poetry: exotic imagery, emotional frenzy, astute observation, colorful language, and onomatopoeia. During his convalescence he wrote more poems, translated from English, and fell in love with his stepmother's sister, Karoline, who was ten years his senior.

His father became a partner in Schwollmann's firm and moved his family to Soest. To the consternation of his relatives, the eighteen-year-old Freiligrath began to have his lyrics printed in the *Soester Wochenblatt* (Soest Weekly); *Allgemeine Unterhaltungsblätter* (General Literary Magazine), published in Münster and Hamm; and the *Mindener Sonntagsblatt* (Minden Sunday Newspaper). The Minden paper also published his short story, "Die Eggestersteine" (Stones of Eggester Mountain), for which he received first prize in the paper's writing competition, and some of his best ballads: "Die Blumenrache" (The Flowers' Revenge), "Die Bilderbibel" (The Picture-Book Bible), and "Der Mohrenfürst" (The Prince of the Moors).

Freiligrath's father died at age forty-five on 23 November 1829; Freiligrath expressed his sense of loss in the poem "Der Liebe Dauer" (Lasting Love), based on remarks in Washington Irving's *The Sketch Book of Geoffrey Crayon, Gent.* (1819–1820), and the ode "Beim Jahreswechsel" (At Year's Changing). Around this time he translated poems by Sir Walter Scott, William Wordsworth, and Samuel Taylor Coleridge. He read the works of George Gordon, Lord Byron, and was spellbound by Victor Hugo, whose penchant for the exotic matched his own. Completing his apprenticeship, he journeyed to Amsterdam, where on 18 January 1832 the wholesale firm of Jakob Sigrist employed him as a clerk. For the next four and a half years his imagination was fired by the aroma of goods imported from afar, the tales told by sailors and traveling salesmen, and the sea.

When the Cotta firm published his *Gedichte* (Poems) in 1838, they caused a sensation. Nothing so exotic had been seen in Germany before. Sales were second only to the volumes of lyrics of Emanuel Geibel. With his cycle "Die Nordsee" (The North Sea), published in the first two volumes of his *Reisebilder* (1826–1827; translated as *Pictures of Travel,* 1855), Heinrich Heine had introduced the ocean as a major theme and image in German literature. Heine's lyrical persona shouts into the waves, projects his emotions onto the water, and reflects on the feelings that are produced by the pounding of the surf. Freiligrath, by contrast, asks: what is on the other side? How do we get there? Whom shall we meet? He describes the harbor, the wake of transatlantic steamers, the fog on the masts, the watch tower set against the redbrick city wall, the lifting of the anchor before departure for India. His poems are not recountings of subjective struggles but pictures painted in words. His best lyrics are those in which his persona becomes the Bedouin on the opposite coast, as in "Wär' ich im Bann von Mekkas Toren" (If I were under the spell of Mecca's Gates), or hears the roar of the lion as it wakes up Egypt's royal mummies, as in "Der Wecker in der Wüste" (The Arouser in the Desert); the reader witnesses the king of the beasts feasting on a white explorer in "Unter den Palmen" (Under the Palm Trees) or leaping onto the back of a giraffe in "Der Löwenritt" (The Lion's Ride). Freiligrath takes the reader to the Congo in "Am Kongo" (At the Congo) and shows the title character of "Der Mohrenfürst" (The Prince of the Moors) wielding his sword in battle, losing the fray and ending up as a circus attraction. Freiligrath has unparalleled insight into unseen landscapes in exotic places, an intuitive feeling for the thoughts and customs of his figures with strange-sounding names, and a humble respect for the people who inhabit his poetic imagination. His lyrical "I," which is often an inclusive "we," is not a great white father bringing civilization to the savage but an awe-struck observer who is fascinated by the spectacle before him and by the earthiness and power of those he describes. A reworking of an earlier poem, based again on Irving's *Sketch Book,* became the most popular one in the book: "O lieb', solang du lieben kannst!" (O love, love as long as you can) was set to music by Franz Liszt.

In 1837 Freiligrath took a job with the Von Eynern firm in Barmen. The dismissal that year of seven dissident professors, including Jacob and Wilhelm Grimm, from the University of Göttingen by King Ernst August of Hannover shocked and dismayed Freiligrath. In a May 1838 letter to Ludwig Merckel, Freiligrath asks how anyone can write "Mailieder" (songs of May) after such a disgraceful, arbitrary act: " 's ist eine schwüle Zeit; der Poet steht vereinsamt in ihr, ein überflüssiges Gerät!" (These are oppressive times. The poet stands alone in times like these, a superfluous instrument!). He also praises the work of the politically radical Austrian poets Anastasius Grün and Karl Beck. This and other letters from 1838–1839 in which he expresses outrage at the firings suggest that Freiligrath was moving into the political arena even as his "desert and lion poetry" was coming off the press.

In May 1839 Freiligrath quit his job in Barmen to accept a publisher's commission for a book, *Das malerische und romantische Westphalen* (Picturesque and Romantic Westphalia, 1841); he was to extol the "rote Erde" (red soil) of his native province. During his travels around Westphalia he met the aspiring writer Levin Schücking, with whom he established a lasting friendship. In August he returned to Barmen, where he wrote "Freistuhl zu Dortmund" (The Free Cathedral City of Dortmund), his only notable contribution to the book; his native land could not excite his poetic imagination as had African beasts and Arabian nomads, and he asked Schücking to take over the project. Together with the painter Carl Schlickum he retired to Unkel on the Rhine to begin writing again. He was there in December 1839 when the ruins of the fortress at Rolandseck, a few miles away, collapsed. The fortress was dedicated to Roland, Charlemagne's legendary paladin, famous for his prowess and death in the battle of Roncesvalles in 778. Freiligrath hurried to see what had happened.

At that time the fortress at Rolandseck belonged to a princess who was the sister-in-law of King Friedrich Wilhelm III of Prussia. It was up to her to initiate any restoration. In what was technically a breach of etiquette, Freiligrath, in the poem "Rolandseck," published in the *Kölnische Zeitung* (Cologne Newspaper) on 12 January 1840, pleaded

Freiligrath circa 1841, drawing by J. H. Schramm (Gottfried-Keller-Nachlaß Zentralbibliothek Zürich

for the reconstruction of Roland's Arch. He used a play on words – the word *Bogen* means both arch and bow – to make his point: "Gebt ihm den Bogen wieder!" (Give him [Roland] back his bow [arch]). In the last strophe of the second part of the poem Freiligrath wrote: "Noch einmal ruf' ich: Jeder einen Stein! / Ich will des Ritters Seckelmeister sein" (Once again I implore: let each one contribute a stone! / I'll be the knight's treasurer). The response was overwhelming. Contributions poured in from all parts of Germany. Soon there was enough money to begin work; by July the basic restoration was completed. The princess was delighted. She forgave Freiligrath his breach of protocol, and she used the excess funds to found a school in the nearby town of Rolandswerth. Freiligrath had caught the attention of the Prussian government. When Friedrich Wilhelm IV ascended to the Prussian throne later in the year, he did not forget Freiligrath's service to his aunt.

In 1840 Freiligrath met and fell in love with Ida Melos; at the time both of them were engaged to others. After breaking their respective engagements, they were married in May 1841. During this period Freiligrath wrote the poem "Die Kreuzigung" (The Crucifixion), based on a legend Schücking had recounted during one of their many hikes. In the poem the guards who cast lots for Christ's robe at the Crucifixion are not Romans but Germanic tribesmen from the Teutoburg Forest who had been pressed into Roman service before Arminius's defeat of Varus in A.D. 9. The tribesman who wins the Holy Robe pierces the Savior's side and remains alone with him on Golgotha's heights. The concluding line, "In Christi Mantel der Germane!" (In Christ's robe, the Germanic tribesman!), is a symbolic prophecy of Christian Germany's future supremacy: she is the rightful heir to the legacy of the ancients, the conqueror of Rome; the new day belongs to her. Such verse endeared Freiligrath to the court at Berlin.

At this point a friend, Heinrich Künzel, persuaded Freiligrath to join him in the founding and editing of a new weekly magazine, *Britannia,* to acquaint German readers with English literature; Freiligrath was to write survey articles, reviews, and translations. But when the publishing house in Pforzheim withdrew from the project, Freiligrath faced financial ruin. The Prussian chancellor, Friedrich von Müller, came to his aid by arranging for Freiligrath to meet the king. On 16 September 1842 Friedrich Wilhelm IV received the poet during a wine-tasting tour of the Rhine provinces. Freiligrath also was engaged in conversation by Archduke Johann of Austria, who lavished praise on the epic poem *Ahasver* – which he mistakenly attributed to Freiligrath. (He probably had in mind the 1836 version by Julius Mosen.) Later Freiligrath would mark his break with the aristocratic establishment from the date of this meeting, but his letters from the period immediately following his audience are full of praise for the king and optimism that a civil service position was in the offing. But the king authorized a pension of only three hundred talers; Freiligrath had earned five hundred talers as a clerk in Barmen.

On 2 November 1841 the *Preußische Staatszeitung* (Prussian State Newspaper) carried the story of General Diego Leon's execution in Spain. Leon had championed the cause of the queen regent, Maria Christina, who had been deposed in 1840 by General Baldomero Espartero. Leon and Espartero had been comrades in arms in many battles; when Espartero invited Leon, under a flag of truce and assurances of safe conduct, to peace talks, Leon, not expecting treachery by his old friend, accepted. He was immediately taken prisoner and condemned to death. Leon met his fate in Ciceronian fashion: he arranged the firing squad and gave the order to fire. His last words were allegedly "Exoriare aliquis nostris ex ossibus ultor!" – Dido's prayer from Virgil's *Aeneid* that some avenger may rise from her ashes and punish the perfidy of Aeneas and his followers. The incident inspired Freiligrath's poem "Aus Spanien" (Out of Spain), published in the *Morgenblatt für gebildete Leser* (Morning Paper for Cultured Readers) on 20 November. The poet calls for vengeance against such treachery and for a leader ("Matador") who will end Spain's internal strife. The poem is about deception, heroic forbearance, vengeance, retribution, and, finally, the restoration of peace; it is not an expression of reactionary sentiment, as his critics were soon to proclaim. The poet paraphrases a line from Johann Wolfgang von Goethe in what became the most controversial statement in the poem. In "Noten und Abhandlungen zu besserem Verständnis des West-östlichen Divans" (Notes and Discussions toward a Better Understanding of the *West-östlichen Divan,* 1819) Goethe had written: "Der Dichter steht viel zu hoch, als daß er Partei machen sollte" (The poet stands too tall to take sides); in the ninth of the twelve verses of "Aus Spanien" Freiligrath paraphrases Goethe's words: "Der Dichter steht auf einer höheren Warte, / Als auf den Zinnen der Partei" (The poet stands at a higher pinnacle / Than on the battlements of the party). These lines occur in response to the question whether the poet has succeeded in telling the story of Leon in an aesthetically pleasing way. This context was overlooked completely, as the question of where the poet stood on the ideological spectrum took precedence over any other consideration. In the *Rheinische Zeitung* (Rhine Newspaper) for 21 January 1843 the critic Karl Heinzen branded Freiligrath a "Denunziant" (denunciator) and added a third line to the poet's paraphrase of Goethe: " 'Der Dichter steht auf einer höheren Warte / Als auf den Zinnen der Partei!' / Doch greift er ohne Scheu nach der Standarte / der – Polizei!" ("The poet stands at a higher pinnacle / Than on the battlements of the party!" / Still he grabs unabashedly for the banner of the – police!). Theodor Creizenach responded to Freiligrath with the lines: "Es kann der Mensch, wer er auch sei u. was er auch beginne / Auf keiner besseren Warte steh'n als auf der Freiheit Zinne!" (No one, no matter who he is or what he undertakes / Can stand on any higher pinnacle than on the battlements of freedom!). Freiligrath's most formidable critic, Georg Herwegh, demanded in the poem "Die Partei" (The

Party), published in the second volume of his *Gedichte eines Lebendigen* (Poems of a Living Person, 1841, 1843) that the genuine poet jump headlong into the political arena as a champion of those ideas which move the times. Herwegh's poem concludes with the verse: "Selbst Götter steigen von Olymp hernieder / Und kämpfen auf der Zinne der Partei!" (Even gods come down from Olympus / And fight on the battlement of the party!). Freiligrath mounted a spirited defense, but he could not remove the label of reactionary that had been attached to him.

In July 1842 the legislatures of the Prussian provinces on the Rhine resisted the introduction of a new civil code designed to unify the administration of criminal justice throughout Prussia; the legislatures requested that a new civil code, based on the Code Napoléon, be drawn up for the Rhine provinces. The king was furious and resolved to eradicate all resistance; by late autumn freedom of the press had been greatly curtailed. These events convinced Freiligrath to break all ties to the Prussian government, and he began to put his political convictions into his poetry. Despite warnings from friends, he had a collection of political lyrics published under the title *Ein Glaubensbekenntnis* (A Confession of Faith) in August 1844. He also announced that he would no longer accept the king's pension. He knew that Friedrich Wilhelm IV would never tolerate such a public affront, so he fled to Brussels. There he met Karl Marx, who sharpened Freiligrath's political thinking and drove him ever deeper into the radical camp.

The poems in *Ein Glaubensbekenntnis* are a mixture from various periods of Freiligrath's political evolution. He opens with the politically neutral "Aus Spanien"; bids farewell to Romanticism, which has been supplanted by the spirit of progress and technology, in "Ein Flecken am Rheine" (A Little Place on the Rhine); and cries out for freedom and justice in "Die Freiheit! Das Recht!" (Freedom! Law!). He attacks high Prussian officials and speaks out against censorship, Prussian injustice, and the alliance between Russia and Prussia. In "Die weiße Frau" (The Woman in White) he retells the legend of the Countess Agnes of Orlamünde, who committed infanticide; her spirit was condemned to wander the halls of her castles at Bayreuth and Berlin. Freiligrath has her specter cry out against the aristocrats in the castle, who do nothing but sleep. She claims that the princes are as guilty as she is: she killed her children, but they murdered the trust of their subjects. She implores them to awake and do something for the people, lest she put a curse on them. She departs when she realizes that they will do nothing. The poem "Aus dem schlesischen Gebirge" (From the Silesian Mountains), dated March 1844, calls on the mythical giant Rübezahl to come to the aid of the destitute; it contains the motif of the weavers weaving the "Hunger- und Leichentuch" (shroud of hunger and death), which Heine reworked in his immortal poem "Die schlesischen Weber" (The Silesian Weavers), published three years later. The Prussian government suppressed the volume on the grounds of "Majestätsbeleidigung" (lèse-majesté).

ÇA IRA!

Sechs Gedichte

von

Ferdinand Freiligrath.

Herisau.

Druck und Verlag des literarischen Instituts.

1846.

Title page for a collection of six poems in which Freiligrath calls for revolutionary class struggle

In March 1845 Freiligrath moved to Hottingen, near Zurich, a refuge for German exiles and a hotbed of radical political activity. His encounters with his compatriots were sobering: he was offended by Arnold Ruge's fanatical atheism, disheartened by the malice with which the slightest difference of opinion was expressed, and disappointed by the exiles' bragging and self-glorification. Freiligrath avoided the meetings of the radical factions; instead, he wrote powerful political poetry. The pamphlet *Leipzigs Todten!* (To the Dead at Leipzig!, 1845) and the six poems of *Ça ira!* (It Will Work out Fine!, 1846) are masterpieces of radical verse. The latter volume shows Marx's influence with its call for revolutionary class struggle.

Published in the same year as Eduard Mörike's pastoral epic *Idylle vom Bodensee* (Idyll on Lake Constance) and Adalbert Stifter's placid novella "Der beschriebene Tännling" (The Inscribed Fir Tree), the poems of *Ça ira* demand a radical break with idyllic poetry. The poet cannot remain above the fray; he must describe how the revolution will come about, Freiligrath says in "Wie man's macht" (How It Will Be Accomplished). The title of the collection is a quotation attributed to Benjamin Franklin, who uttered the words when asked in Paris how the American Revolution was going. "Ça ira" then became the opening line in one of the best-known songs of the French Revolution: "Ah! ça ira . . . / Les aristocrates á la lanterne" (Ah! It will work out fine . . . / Just hang the aristocrats from the lamppost). Thus, the title immediately identifies the collection as inflammatory, politically extreme verse. The most widely known poem, "Von unten auf" (From the Bottom Up), tells of a trip down the Rhine on a steamer by the Prussian king and his entourage; as the royal party laughs and marvels at the scenery above deck, the stoker on the bottom deck stares into the flames and recounts his misery. He knows that one blow from him would topple the edifice on which the king stands as the pinnacle. The poem is an attempt to raise the political consciousness of the working class; it underscores the potential power of the worker: "Wir hämmern jung das alte morsche Ding den Staat" (We shall hammer the old rotten thing they call the state into something young), says the poet, as soon as all working-class people unite. In the epilogue to the volume Freiligrath recognizes that these poems will assure his permanent exile from Germany; he has become a "Springer" (jumper), always one step ahead of the police. France, England, and "die Ohio Wiesen" (the meadows of Ohio) are the few sanctuaries open to him. At the end of summer 1846 he fled to London, where he took a job as a clerk.

In his new home he wrote half a dozen poems demanding freedom and decrying tyranny and oppression. He hears the outcry from Ireland in "Irland," sees the poor people working themselves to death in "Das Lied vom Hemde" (Song of the Shirt), describes a suicide in "Die Seufzerbrücke" (The Bridge of Sighs), and calls for the founding of a republic in Germany in "Die Republik." The best-known poem from this period, "Im Hochland fiel der erste Schuß" (The First Shot was Fired in the Highlands), describes the revolutionary movement as it spreads from Switzerland to Italy and from France to Germany; the poem concludes with the assertion that the poet and other revolutionaries are ready to die for the Fatherland.

The upheavals in Berlin on 18 and 19 March 1848 brought Freiligrath back to Germany. Taking advantage of a general amnesty, he settled in Düsseldorf; there, in July 1848, he wrote the gruesome poem *Die Todten an die Lebenden* (The Dead to the Living), in which dead revolutionaries beg the living to take up arms again. He took part in the deliberations of the National Assembly in Frankfurt am Main, but his poetry was so radical that he was arrested on 28 August for inciting civil unrest. A jury acquitted him on 3 October, and a week later Marx and Friedrich Engels hired him as an editor for their *Neue Rheinische Zeitung* (New Rhine Newspaper).

The newspaper ceased publication on 19 May 1849. For the final issue Freiligrath wrote "Abschiedswort der Neuen Rheinischen Zeitung" (Farewell to the New Rhine Newspaper), which foresees the day "wenn die letzte Krone wie Glas zerbricht" (when the last crown will break like glass) and the newspaper will be remembered as an ever loyal companion of the people. His *Zwischen den Garben* (Between the Bundles, 1849) is a collection of love poems, poems of the sea, landscapes, and diverse lyrics that had appeared in newspapers and magazines between 1837 and 1845. The first volume of his *Neuere politische und soziale Gedichte* (Newer Political and Social Poems, 1849) includes "Requiescat," written in Zurich in February 1846, in which the poet is depicted as belonging to the proletariat: "Er auch ist ein Proletar!" (He too is a proletarian!). Writers are paid a pittance and cannot feed their families; they fare no better than other workers who fight for "Menschenleben" (human life). The poems sing the song of death, lift high the black, red, and gold colors of the revolution, and glorify the martyrdom of Robert Blum, who was executed in Vienna for preaching sedition. By 1851, when the second volume of *Neuere politische und soziale Gedichte* appeared, the king of Prussia had read *Die Todten an die Lebenden;* he felt so insulted that he issued a second warrant for Freiligrath's arrest, accusing the poet of disturbing the peace and advocating the violent overthrow of the government. Freiligrath fled

Neue Rheinische Zeitung

Organ der Demokratie.

№ 301. Köln, Samstag, den 19. Mai 1849.

Abschiedswort der Neuen Rheinischen Zeitung.

Kein offner Hieb in offner Schlacht –
Es fällen die Nücken und Tücken,
Es fällt mich die schleichende Niedertracht
Der schmutzigen West-Kalmücken!
Aus dem Dunkel flog der tödtende Schaft,
Aus dem Hinterhalt fielen die Streiche –
Und so lieg' ich nun da in meiner Kraft,
Eine stolze Rebellenleiche!

Auf der Lippe den Trotz und den zuckenden Hohn,
In der Hand den blitzenden Degen,
Noch im Sterben rufend: „Die Rebellion!“ –
So bin ich mit Ehren erlegen.
O, gern wohl bestreuten mein Grab mit Salz
Der Preuße zusammt dem Czare –
Doch es schicken die Ungarn, es schickt die Pfalz
Drei Salven mir über die Bahre!

Und der arme Mann im zerriss'nen Gewand,
Er wirft auf mein Haupt die Schollen;
Er wirft sie hinab mit der fleißigen Hand,
Mit der harten, der schwielenvollen.
Einen Kranz auch bringt er aus Blumen und Mai'n,
Zu ruh'n auf meinen Wunden;
Den haben sein Weib und sein Töchterlein
Nach der Arbeit für mich gewunden.

Nun Ade, nun Ade, du kämpfende Welt,
Nun Ade, ihr ringenden Heere!
Nun Ade, du pulvergeschwärztes Feld,
Nun Ade, ihr Schwerter und Speere!
Nun Ade – doch nicht für immer Ade!
Denn sie tödten den Geist nicht, ihr Brüder!
Bald richt' ich mich rasselnd in die Höh',
Bald kehr' ich reisiger wieder!

Wenn die letzte Krone wie Glas zerbricht,
In des Kampfes Wettern und Flammen,
Wenn das Volk sein letztes „Schuldig!“ spricht,
Dann stehn wir wieder zusammen!
Mit dem Wort, mit dem Schwert, an der Donau, am Rhein, –
Eine allzeit treue Gesellin
Wird dem Throne zerschmetternden Volke sein
Die Geächtete, die Rebellin!

F. FREILIGRATH.

An die Arbeiter Kölns.

Wir warnen Euch schließlich vor jedem Putsch in Köln. Nach der militärischen Lage Kölns wäret ihr rettungslos verloren. Ihr habt in Elberfeld gesehen, wie die Bourgeoisie die Arbeiter ins Feuer schickt und sie hinterher aufs Niederträchtigste verräth. Der Belagerungszustand in Köln würde die ganze Rheinprovinz demoralisiren und der Belagerungszustand wäre die nothwendige Folge jeder Erhebung von Eurer Seite in diesem Augenblicke. Die Preußen werden an Eurer Ruhe verzweifeln.

Die Redakteure der Neuen Rheinischen Zeitung danken Euch beim Abschiede für die ihnen bewiesene Theilnahme. Ihr letztes Wort wird überall und immer sein: Emancipation der arbeitenden Klasse!

Die Redaktion der Neuen Rhein. Zeitung.

Deutschland.

Proklamation an die Frauen.

Georg Weerth.

First page of the final issue of Karl Marx and Friedrich Engels's radical newspaper, for which Freiligrath served as an editor

Anonymous etching of Freiligrath, circa 1849

back to London, where he took a bookkeeping job with the merchant John Oxford for a meager two hundred pounds sterling a year.

By this time Freiligrath's family consisted of Katharine, born on 11 September 1845; Luise, born on 18 August 1849; and Otto, born on 10 August 1850. The Freiligraths had their fourth child, Percy, in London on 7 August 1852. To support his family Freiligrath stopped writing radical verse and concentrated on translating and editing. A collection of his translations, *Englische Gedichte aus neuerer Zeit* (Modern English Poems) had been published by the prestigious Cotta firm in 1846; his anthology of modern English poetry in the original language appeared in 1853 under the title *The Rose, Thistle and Shamrock,* followed the next year by his anthology of German poems, *Dichtung und Dichter* (Poetry and Poets). In 1855 he translated Henry Wadsworth Longfellow's *The Song of Hiawatha* (1855); the translation appeared two years later. He did all of this work after ten hours at his bookkeeping job plus a half-hour train ride to and from work.

In June 1856 his financial situation improved when he was offered a managerial position at the London branch of the General Bank of Switzerland. At work and at home he was visited by refugees and political exiles looking for advice. By the end of the year he had edited *The Poems of Samuel Taylor Coleridge,* for which he wrote a biographical introduction. At this time his relationship with Marx began to deteriorate. In 1858 he became a British subject, and a New York firm began publishing his collected works. His reputation among German-Americans was strengthened by the commemorative song he wrote for the Friedrich Schiller centennial in the United States in 1859: Schiller becomes "Dein Bürger auch, Amerika!" (Your citizen too, America!). The song he wrote for the London celebration, *Festlied der Deutschen in London,* (1859) was more elaborate: Schiller descends from the heights to be with his Germans in Great Britain. The work was set to music by Ernst Pauer and was sung in the Crystal Palace at Sydenham on 10 November 1859 by five male choirs.

In 1865 the General Bank of Switzerland closed its London office, and after nine years of relative financial security Freiligrath was suddenly unemployed. But he was not forgotten. From Milwaukee came the offer of a little farm in Wisconsin; his friends in Barmen also rushed to his aid. Among his many visitors had been the poet Emil Rittershaus, who was determined to save the illustrious Freiligrath from ruin and bring him home to Germany. In April 1867 Rittershaus's poem "Auch eine Dotation" (Also an Endowment) was published in the widely circulated bourgeois magazine *Die Gartenlaube* (The Arbor): it mentions the royal pension Freiligrath had refused and appeals for an endowment to be established by the German people rather than by the government. In Germany the nobility ignored the celebration of the poet, who was, technically, a fugitive from justice; the educated middle class remembered only his early exotic poetry; businessmen claimed him as one of their own; working-class people, who were excluded from the official celebrations, lauded Freiligrath's fight for the dignity and improvement of the proletariat.

The response to the appeal for donations was staggering. Contributions were received from London, Vienna, Chicago, and New York. One poor worker in Dresden gave a taler and wrote in the commemorative book, "dem wackeren Streiter für die Rechte des Volkes" (for the brave champion of people's rights). A woman who signed herself "deutsches Mädchen" (German girl) also gave a taler "dem überzeugungstreuen Sänger und Verbannten" (to the singer and exile who remained true to his convictions). A total of 58,444 talers was raised, which would be the equivalent of nearly two million dollars today. In the summer of 1867 Freiligrath and his wife traveled to Germany incognito; on 6 August a celebration was held in his honor at the Rolandseck, which he had helped rebuild. The authorities looked the other way. Thus, in the same year that Cotta printed the twenty-third edition of his early exotic verse and the first volume of Marx's *Das Kapital* (translated as *Capital,* 1887) appeared, Freiligrath was rehabilitated politically and reintegrated into the establishment.

He returned to England for the wedding of his daughter Katherine, who married the merchant Eduard Kroeker in London on 17 December 1867; when he returned permanently to Germany on 24 June 1868 he was met by more than two hundred well-wishers at Gürzenach, near Cologne. Staying out of politics, he translated the poetry of Walt Whitman and excerpts from the works of Bret Harte. In November he moved to Stuttgart, where he composed the poem "Zu Hölderlins hundertjährigem Geburtstage" (For Hölderlin's One Hundredth Birthday); it was read on 20 March 1870 during the commemoration at the Hölderlin house in Lauffen.

In the summer of 1870 France declared war on Prussia, whereupon the other German states came to Prussia's aid. Freiligrath, who had staunchly opposed the war between the German Confederation and Austria in 1866, was moved to write several poems in support of what he saw as Germany's defensive war. The best known of these poems is "Die Trompet von Vionville" (The Trumpet at Vionville), in which the trumpet sounding the rally for the German troops at the battle of Vionville and Mars-la-Tour on 16 August 1870 is pierced by bullets. "Hurra Germania" exalts the unity Germans have shown in the war effort; "So wird es geschehen" (This Is How It Will Happen) predicts the defeat of Napoleon's nephew, who has impertinently attacked "die Ufer des deutschen Stroms" (the banks of the German stream [the Rhine]). Freiligrath appeared to have become an ideologue of the Prussian state; but the poems were written in August 1870, when the feeling that Germany must defend itself ran high and Prussian chancellor Otto von Bismarck's machinations to manipulate France into a declaration of war were not yet public knowledge. Moreover, the poems speak only of defense; the more bellicose "Ein Ritterstückchen für die dritte Armee" (A Knightly Tale for the Third Army), which commands the defenders to jump on their horses and push the French back to Paris, was not published during Freiligrath's lifetime; it first appeared in a collection edited by his widow in 1877.

His enthusiasm for the war is tempered in other poems in which he bemoans the bloodshed. One poem praises his son Wolfgang for choosing to serve as a medic rather than as a soldier: "Verdien dir deine Sporen / Im Dienst der Menschlichkeit" (Earn your spurs / In the service of mankind). "Freiwillige vor" (Volunteers to the Front) describes the death of a volunteer under a fir tree and asks, "Ein Mann aus dem Volk, / Den sein Heim verlor; / Wer hilft, wer lindert?" (A man from the people, / Who is lost to home and hearth; / who will help, who will ease the pain?). These are hardly the words of a warmonger or a Prussian ideologue. In 1874 he wrote to Berthold Auerbach, "Daß ich aber das Reich für das Höchste halten soll . . ., fällt mir nicht ein. . . . Ich bin froh, daß ich keiner Partei mehr angehöre" (It doesn't even occur to me . . . to regard the empire as the highest good. . . . I am happy that I no longer belong to any party). With these words, Freiligrath leaves the political arena behind. His son Wolfgang was so discouraged by

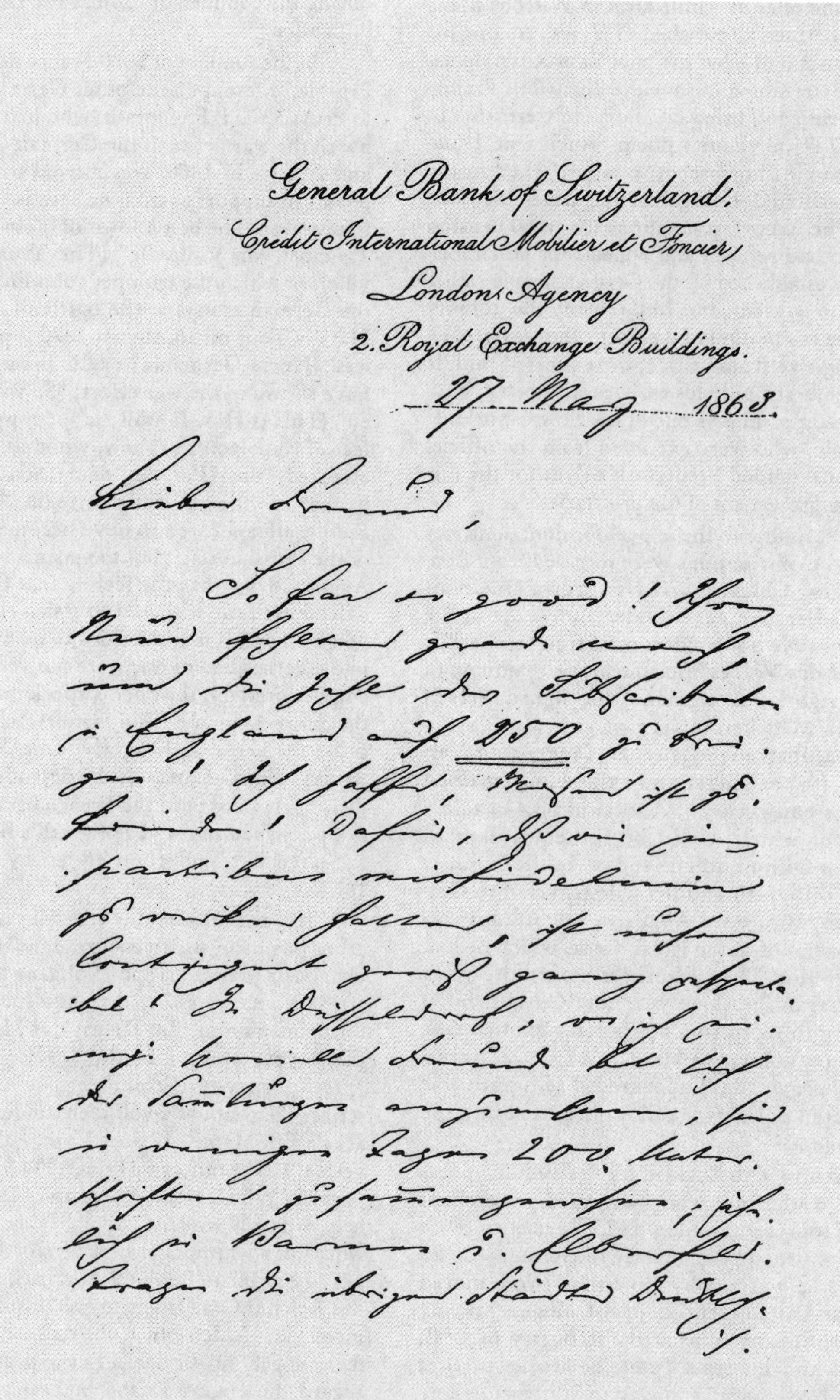

General Bank of Switzerland.
Crédit International Mobilier et Foncier,
London Agency
2. Royal Exchange Buildings.
27 May 1863.

Lieber Freund!

So far so good!

First page of a letter from Freiligrath to the leftist editor Arnold Ruge, written on the stationery of the bank for which Freiligrath worked from 1856 to 1865. The first sentence of the text is in English (from Freiligrath's Werke in sechs Teilen, *edited by Julius Schwering, 1909).*

Prussian militarism and the bloodshed of the Franco-Prussian War that he immigrated to the United States as soon as the fighting ended.

The death of his son Otto on 1 March 1873 left Freiligrath a broken man in failing health. He moved to Cannstatt the following year to accept the editorship of the biweekly *Hallberger's Illustrated English Magazine,* which printed the latest British and American literature. On 18 March 1876 Freiligrath died of an enlarged heart. His funeral brought hundreds of mourners from all over the world to Cannstatt. His widow edited the collection *Neue Gedichte* (New Poems), which Cotta published a year later.

Freiligrath's legacy includes poetry about exotic lands, a politically radical program in verse form, and many translations. The edition of his collected works prepared by Julius Schwering in 1909 contains 711 pages of translations from Italian, French, and English. (Schwering also had access to Freiligrath's translations from the Dutch, which he chose not to include because he felt that they were not up to Freiligrath's exacting standards.) Freiligrath's efforts gave the German reading public its first acquaintance with many British and American lyricists. He was renowned for his mastery of forms, whether he was translating an English sonnet or describing a scene in the tropics. In 1899 the philologist Kurt Albrecht Richter compared Freiligrath's translations from the French and English with later ones by well-known professional translators and concluded that Freiligrath's were superior. The poet also introduced English and American lyricists to the latest poetry from Germany. His influence on contemporary writers was considerable. He even taught those of the preceding generation: Gustav Schwab, Ludwig Uhland, Heine, and Freiligrath's erstwhile enemy Herwegh acknowledged their debt to him. He coined many words, including *Südprofil* (southern profile), *Schweifgeröll* (trail of pebbles), *verlechzen* (languish to death), and *Geloder* (glowing flame) and enriched German literature with exotic images, reflections of the contemporary atmosphere, haunting rhythms, and unusual rhymes.

His poetic genius was not flawless. For example, Freiligrath's poetry lends itself readily to parody. Despite his appreciation of Freiligrath's poetic skill, Heine could not help but parody many of his early poems in *Atta Troll* (1847; translated, 1876), which took for a motto a verse from Freiligrath's "Der Mohrenfürst." In his foreword Heine explains that he read Freiligrath's poetry while he was working on *Atta Troll* and that "Der Mohrenfürst" struck him as so funny that he could not stop laughing. Freiligrath's poetry often lacks any deep philosophical truth; at times the trivial stands next to the truly inspired, or an image is strained to the breaking point.

Freiligrath was not always able to overcome a basic tension in his poetry between objective description and the need for reflection. In too many poems the speaker's persona disappears behind the plot, and there is no reflection at all. Despite the many original elements, there is still an imitation of forms developed earlier to describe other moods and objects. The poetic intention becomes at times so obvious that one cannot appreciate the form. At other times, the mood is abruptly interrupted or only partially created. In a letter to her brother, Clemens Brentano, of 21 April 1839, the writer Bettina von Arnim remarked that Freiligrath's poems, despite their pleasant tone, cannot be sung; they tend to drone on like "das Räd am Dampfschiff" (a paddlewheel on a steamboat).

Nevertheless, Freiligrath's poetry bears witness to a man of integrity and dignity. He followed his poetic muse wherever it took him and forsook the good life when it told him to do so. He was prepared to suffer for his political beliefs and to fight for those who were less fortunate, less free, and less able than he. Few poets match him in strength of conviction and in the ability to turn a political creed into genuine poetry.

Letters:

Ferdinand Freiligrath: Ein Dichterleben in Briefen, edited by Wilhelm Bucher (Lahr: Schauenburg, 1882);

Freiligraths Briefe, edited by Luise Wiens (Stuttgart: Cotta, 1910);

Freiligraths Briefwechsel mit der Familie Clostermeier in Detmold, insbesondere mit Louise Christiane, der späteren Gattin Grabbes, edited by Alfred Bergmann (Detmold: Grabbe-Gesellschaft, 1953);

Freiligraths Briefwechsel mit Marx und Engels, 2 volumes, edited by Manfred Häckel (Berlin: Akademie, 1968);

Kinderbriefe und erste Reimversuche in der Lippischen Landesbibliothek, edited by Annette Hellfaier (Detmold: Selbstverlag der Lippischen Landesbibliothek, 1980).

Biographies:

August Kippenberg, *Ferdinand Freiligrath: Zum Verständnis des Dichters und als Begleitgabe zu seinen Werken* (Leipzig: Mattes, 1868);

Eduard Schmidt-Weissenfels, *Ferdinand Freiligrath: Ein biographisches Denkmal* (Stuttgart: Müller, 1876);

Gisberte Freiligrath, *Beiträge zur Biographie Ferdinand Freiligraths* (Minden: Bruns, 1889);

Lorenz Völlmecke, *Annette von Droste-Hülshoff in ihrem Verhältnis zu Ferdinand Freiligrath* (Bonn: Verein Studentenwohl, 1926);

Gerald W. Spink, *Ferdinand Freiligraths Verbannungsjahre in London* (Berlin: Ebering, 1932);

Herbert Eulenberg, *Ferdinand Freiligrath* (Berlin: Aufbau, 1948);

Ferdinand Freiligrath zum 150. Geburtstag (Dortmund: Stadt- und Landesbibliothek, 1960);

Bruno Kaiser, ed., *Die Akten Ferdinand Freiligrath und Georg Herwegh* (Weimar: Archiv der deutschen Schillerstiftung, 1963);

Gerhard Richter, *Ferdinand Freiligrath: Sein Leben, seine Werke, seine Zeit* (Soest: Staatsarchiv Soest, 1976);

Josef Ruland, ed., *Ferdinand Freiligrath 1876/1976,* translated by Patricia Crampton (Bonn & Bad Godesberg: InterNationes, 1976).

References:

Maria Appelmann, *H. W. Longfellow's Beziehungen zu Ferdinand Freiligrath* (Münster: Westfälische Vereinsdruckerei, 1915);

Ferdinand Freiligrath, ein Dichter des neunzehnten Jahrhunderts: Eine Ausstellung zur Wiederkehr seines 100. Todesjahres (Detmold: Lippische Landesbibliothek, 1976);

Ferdinand Freiligrath: Handschriften und Drucke von Werken und Briefen aus der Freiligrath-Sammlung der Lippischen Landesbibliothek (Detmold: Lippische Landesbibliothek, 1985);

Jörg Christoph von Forster, *Phantasie, Phrasen und Fanatismus im Vormärz: Eine historische Untersuchung von Leben und Werk der Dichter Ferdinand Freiligrath und Georg Herwegh im Spiegel der Literatur* (Nuremberg, 1978);

Oskar Gerschel, ed., *Verzeichnis der von Ferdinand Freiligrath nachgelassenen Bibliothek* (Stuttgart: Kirn, 1878);

Erwin G. Gudde, *Freiligraths Entwicklung als politischer Dichter* (Berlin: Ebering, 1922);

Josef Hallermann, *Freiligraths Einfluß auf die Lyriker der Münchner Dichterschule* (Essen: Fredebeul & Koenen, 1917);

Karl-Alexander Hellfaier, ed., *Die Bibliothek Ferdinand Freiligraths* (Detmold: Lippische Landesbibliothek, 1976);

John F. Kieshauer, *The Reception of Ferdinand Freiligrath's Poetry in England and America (1840–1876)* (New York: Harcourt, 1958);

Marion Dexter Learned, *Ferdinand Freiligrath in America* (Philadelphia: American Germanica, 1897);

Rainer Noltensius, *Dichterfeiern in Deutschland: Rezeptionsgeschichte als Sozialgeschichte am Beispiel der Schiller- und Freiligrath-Feiern* (Munich: Fink, 1984);

Kurt Albrecht Richter, *Ferdinand Freiligrath als Übersetzer* (Munich: Kastner & Lossen, 1899);

Friedrich August Roeschen, *Freiligraths Übersetzungen englischer Dichtungen* (Giessen: Selbstverlag des Englischen Seminars, 1923);

Meno Spann, *Der Exotismus in Ferdinand Freiligraths Gedichten* (Dortmund: Strauch, 1928);

Gerald W. Spink, *Ferdinand Freiligrath als Verdeutscher der englischen Poesie* (Berlin: Ebering, 1925);

Anton Volbert, *Ferdinand Freiligrath als politischer Dichter* (Münster: Schöningh, 1907);

Otto Weddigen, *Lord Byrons Einfluß auf die europäische Literatur der Neuzeit: Ein Beitrag zur allgemeinen Literaturgeschichte, nebst einem Anhang: Ferdinand Freiligrath als Vermittler englischer Dichtung in Deutschland* (Wald im Rheinland, 1901).

Papers:

Ferdinand Freiligrath's papers are in the Lippisches Literaturarchiv (Lippe Literature Archives) at the Lippische Landesbibliothek (Lippe State Library), Detmold; the Heine Institut, Düsseldorf; and the Universitätsbibliothek (University Library), Münster.

Louise von Gall

(19 September 1815 - 16 March 1855)

Hugh Powell
Indiana University

BOOKS: *Frauennovellen,* 2 volumes (Darmstadt: Jonghaus, 1845);

Gegen den Strom: Roman, 2 volumes (Bremen: Schlodtmann, 1851);

Ich hab's gewagt: Lustspiel in zwei Aufzügen (Cologne: Langen, 1851);

Ein schlechtes Gewissen: Lustspiel in einem Aufzuge (Warendorf: Schnell, 1852);

Der neue Kreuzritter: Roman (Berlin: Duncker, 1853);

Familienbilder, 2 volumes, by Gall and Levin Schücking (Prague: Geržabek, 1854);

Familien-Geschichten, 2 volumes, by Gall and Schücking (Prague: Geržabek, 1854);

Frauenleben: Novellen und Erzählungen, edited by Schücking (Leipzig: Brockhaus, 1856).

SELECTED PERIODICAL PUBLICATIONS – UNCOLLECTED: "Drei Wochen in Ungarn im Herbst 1841," *Morgenblatt für gebildete Leser,* 22 August 1842, pp. 797–799; 23 August 1842, pp. 802–804; 24 August 1842, pp. 806–808; 25 August 1842, pp. 809–810; 26 August 1842, pp. 814–815; 27 August 1842, pp. 818–820;

"Korrespondenz Nachrichten," anonymous, *Morgenblatt für gebildete Leser,* 27 February 1843, p. 196;

"Ein Besuch in der Fabrik von Eck und Lefèbvre," *Kölnische Zeitung,* 31 October 1846;

"Aufruf an die rheinischen Frauen und Jungfrauen," *Kölnische Zeitung,* 9 June 1848;

"Ein Menschenherz: Novelle," *Bremer Sonntagsblatt,* 15 May 1853, pp. 155–157; 22 May 1853, pp. 163–166; 29 May 1853, pp. 169–171.

Louise von Gall was one of many authors in the nineteenth century who were judged by the critics to be producers of Trivialliteratur or Unterhaltungsromane (light novels). But some of these authors dealt with matters in need of urgent attention: the arrival of the machine and its impact on society and the economy, the need for political reform and national unity, social injustice and the role of women within and outside the family. Such issues were not given prominence in the "classical" literature of mid-nineteenth-century Germany.

On her father's side Gall came from a long line of aristocrats who for centuries had given military service to their princes. Her grandfather Wilhelm von Gall, commanded a corps of Hessians under Lord William Howe in the American Revolution; her grandson, Walther Schücking, would be a distinguished lawyer and pacifist, a delegate at the treaty negotiations in Versailles in 1919, and later one of the six judges at the International Court of Justice at The Hague. Her father, Ludwig von Gall, distinguished himself as a soldier of the grand duke of Hesse – first on Napoleon's side and then, when his master changed allegiance, against the French. He died in a road accident some weeks before the birth on 19 September 1815 of his only child. Louise, by virtue of her father's rank, was a Freiin (baroness). Her mother, Friederike von Gall, née von Müller, widowed at the age of thirty-one, was a cultured woman who arranged instruction for the child in French, English, and Italian. Gall had an excellent soprano voice; when she was twenty-six she and her mother spent a year in Vienna, where Gall took singing lessons.

In Vienna, she met Marie von Horváth, a young Hungarian whose family invited Gall to Hungary. Her impressions of the Hungarian people and landscape, and in particular of Horváth, were to be recorded in her novel *Gegen den Strom* (Against the Tide, 1851).

On her return from Vienna, where her mother had died, Gall took up residence with her uncle in Darmstadt. She remained in mourning for more than a year, busying herself with reading and with writing feuilletons and novellas. She soon met the gregarious Ferdinand Freiligrath and his wife Ida; in the spring of 1842 she joined a group of literary folk at Sankt Goar that included the Freiligraths, Emanuel Geibel, Karl Simrock, Friedrich Wilhelm Hackländer, Moritz Gottlieb Saphir, and Henry Wadsworth Longfellow. The new social life enabled

Louise von Gall (from Annette von Droste-Hülshoff, Werke, bearbeitet und gedeutet für die Gegenwart, *edited by I. E. Walter, 1954)*

her to accept her bereavement and to look on life more positively, and she was popular with her new friends because of her charm, her intellect, her lively conversation, and her singing. Although her father's rank and fame gave her access to the highest circles, she shunned them in favor of the cultured fellowship of her literary friends. Ferdinand Freiligrath and another member of the group wrote a dozen sonnets in light vein praising her talents and contrasting them with the manner of Ida von Hahn-Hahn, a contemporary writer of autobiographical novels.

One of Freiligrath's friends was Levin Schücking, a protégé of the writer Annette von Droste-Hülshoff, who was eking out a living as a librarian and private tutor. Lonely and ill at ease in these positions, he responded eagerly to Freiligrath's half-serious proposal that he engage in correspondence with Gall, whom he had never met. The nine-month exchange of letters culminated in a betrothal without their ever having seen each other; after a few months of personal acquaintance they were married in October 1843.

Gall's inheritance enabled the young couple to set up a home in Augsburg. Their friends included Gustav Kolb, editor of the distinguished *Allgemeine Augsburger Zeitung* (General Augsburg Newspaper); the playwright and novelist Karl Gutzkow; the poet Nikolaus Lenau; the economist Friedrich List; and the popular playwright Roderich Benedix.

In their correspondence before their marriage, Schücking had minimized the significance of his friendship with Droste-Hülshoff, who, he stressed, was well into her forties and should give Gall no cause for jealousy. When the couple first visited Droste-Hülshoff in May 1844 there was embarrassment and some tension as the young wife learned more about the friendship between the other two. Droste-Hülshoff's letters to her confidante Elise Rüdiger show considerable resentment that Droste-Hülshoff was no longer the anchor in Schücking's life; for her, Gall was an intruder. In the novella

"Erwin," published in her collection *Frauennovellen* (Novellas about Women, 1845), Gall re-creates the triangle; but in the story the younger woman, after witnessing a scene that convinces her that the former relationship between the other two was closer than she had been led to believe, kills herself – both out of resentment and to remove what she believes to be an obstacle to their happiness.

In September 1847 Gall, her husband, and their two children called on Heinrich Heine in Paris. From there they traveled to Marseille, then by ship to Genoa and Leghorn, and finally by train to Pisa and Civitavecchia. The journey is retraced in her novel *Der neue Kreuzritter* (The New Crusader, 1853).

The Schückings returned to Germany in the spring of 1848 and moved to Cologne, where Levin Schücking had an appointment as journalist. There Gall wrote comedies that were performed in that city, in Bremen, and in Berlin. In 1852 they purchased from a relative of Schücking a large house in Sassenberg in Westphalia, and the family – which by this time included four children – moved there.

Deep concern for human suffering and sharp attacks on the causes of social ills and political corruption are at the heart of Gall's two novels. The author does not disguise her contempt for the self-adulation of the "Erbsenprinzen" (pint-pot princes), as she calls the despots ruling over the German principalities. Her friendship with Horváth and her visit to Hungary aroused her sympathy with that country's struggle for independence from Vienna, and *Gegen den Strom* has exciting scenes of the uprising against the Hapsburgs in 1849. Instances of political and social injustice, domestic and international, are woven into the story of the humane, patient, and meek but resolute Agnes von Stein. The eponymous hero of *Der neue Kreuzritter* is a wealthy young aristocrat whose proposals for improving the human condition are unacceptable to the diplomats and statesmen to whom he presents them. When he pleads for the reduction of standing armies and for other economies to provide sanitary homes, free medical care, and cheap food for the population, he is the spokesman of the author. In the story "Zwei Vermächtnisse" (Two Bequests), published in the posthumous collection *Frauenleben* (Women's Lives, 1856), the heroine plans to use her inheritance to build a sanctuary near New York as a shelter for the children of German immigrants until their parents find employment and homes. Gall's compassion was consistent with her lack of class consciousness. When she insisted on preserving her dignity, it was as a woman, not as a scion of an ancient line of blue blood.

The status of women is a recurrent theme in Gall's stories, although she remained aloof from militant feminist campaigns. She concedes the authority of the husband in the home but insists that the woman's dignity remain unassailed. Her works show the idealism and romantic vision of the adolescent girl, the trials of married life experienced by the young wife, the devoted mother, the prima donna renowned in the world of opera but excluded from high society, and the intellectual woman denied access to scientific research. The blight that so often undoes the early promise in marriage is described in her novella "Der Nebenbuhler im Traum" (The Rival in the Dream), published in *Frauenleben,* and in *Gegen den Strom,* where the dreams and hopes of young women are confronted by the unrelenting selfishness of their husbands.

In Gall's writing authorial intrusions are frequent; she is always at the reader's elbow. Her habit of nudging readers to ensure that they do not miss the full import seems tiresome today; but it was by no means peculiar to her among writers of mid-nineteenth-century Germany, to whom Ivan Turgenev gave the advice: "Meidet den Fingerzeig" (Don't point out the obvious). Dialogue plays a prominent part in her narratives, and if some of the sentiments and their mode of expression seem fanciful a century or more later, the conversational passages convey the thrust and parry of debate. The frequent occurrence of repartee suggests the interest in the play of wit that she exhibited among her friends. In contrast to conversation, description – especially of the landscape – is lean when it is not omitted altogether. Irony is a frequently used device.

Gall draws abundantly from her personal life and her throng of acquaintances, indicating a limited inventive power. This deficiency is offset by her rich and varied experience and her keen observation. Prominent contemporary figures, portrayed both with and without disguise, are a conspicuous feature of her work. There is some censure of the manners and values cultivated in England, France, and the United States and of Germans who exiled themselves. She was a patriot who was keenly aware of the maladies in the social and political life of her country. Although unable to prescribe a cure, she insisted that any remedies be nonviolent.

On the whole the contemporary reception of her writings was favorable; the comments on the short stories were more cordial than those on the two novels. Some critics had reservations about the structure of the stories, and exception was taken to the presentation of some of the males as unattractive characters. It was also claimed that the political criticism in the novels was beyond the author's competence, implying that women should not venture into the world of public affairs even in fiction.

The peacefulness of rural Sassenberg was welcome at first, and Gall attacked with enthusiasm the renovation of the eighteenth-century house and the landscaping of the several acres adjoining it. For the Protestant woman accustomed to life in the city, however, residence in the remote, bleak, unfriendly, and rigidly Catholic area proved to be quite difficult. There was no opportunity for intellectual discourse; as the saying went, "In Sassenberg wohnen hundert Schweinehändler, hundert Bettler und hundert Spitzbuben" (In Sassenberg live a hundred hog dealers, a hundred beggars and a hundred rogues). The landed gentry shunned the heretic lady from the south, and her husband was persona non grata because of his novels ridiculing them. The harsh winters affected the family's health: the Schückings' fifth child, born prematurely and the only one baptized in the Lutheran faith, died at the end of 1854 at the age of three months; physically and emotionally exhausted, Gall died on the following 16 March. That life in Sassenberg had embittered her is confirmed by her will: she asked not to be buried in Catholic Sassenberg but in the Protestant churchyard in the neighboring village of Warendorf. This request, and others regarding her children, were not fulfilled by her husband.

Letters:

Briefe von Levin Schücking und Louise von Gall, edited by Reinhold Conrad Muschler, with biographical introduction by Levin Ludwig Schücking (Leipzig: Grunow, 1928).

References:

H. C. Fennenkötter, "Louise von Gall: Zur 125. Wiederkehr ihres Todestages," *Up Sassenbiärg: Mitteilungsblatt des Heimatvereins,* 8 (July 1980): 15–21;

Karin Michaelis, "Zwischen Louise und Annette," in her *Flammende Tage: Gestalten und Fragen zur Gemeinschaft der Geschlechter* (Dresden: Reissner, 1929), pp. 165–171;

Kurt Pinthus, "Levin Schücking und Annette von Droste: Mit ungedruckten Briefen," *Zeitschrift für Bücherfreunde,* new series 6, no. 1 (1914): 160–170;

Hugh Powell, *Louise von Gall: Her World and Work* (Columbia, S.C.: Camden House, 1993);

Elisabeth Wand, *Louise von Gall* (Emsdetten: Lechte, 1935);

Winfried Woesler, "*Lebt wohl:* Die Wiederbegegnung der Droste mit Schücking auf der Meersburg im Mai 1844," *Droste Jahrbuch,* 1 (1986–1987): 53–72.

Papers:

Unpublished manuscripts of Louise von Gall in the Depositum Schücking, Westfälisches Landesmuseum für Kunst und Kulturgeschichte (Westphalian State Museum for Art and Cultural History), Münster, include *Standesehre: Lustspiel in fünf Aufzügen,* a sketchbook, and letters.

Georg Gottfried Gervinus

(20 May 1805 - 18 March 1871)

Brett Wheeler
University of California, Berkeley

BOOKS: *Geschichte der Angelsachsen im Überblick* (Frankfurt am Main: Schmerber, 1830);

Historische Schriften: Geschichte der florentinischen Historiographie bis zum sechzehnten Jahrhundert, nebst einer Charakteristik des Machiavell; Versuch einer inneren Geschichte von Aragonien bis zum Ausgang des barcelonischen Königstamms (Frankfurt am Main: Varrentrapp, 1833);

Zur Geschichte der deutschen Literatur (Heidelberg: Winter, 1834);

Historische Schriften: Geschichte der poetischen National-Literatur der Deutschen, 5 volumes (Leipzig: Engelmann, 1835–1842; revised, 1840–1844; revised, 1846–1852); revised as *Geschichte der deutschen Dichtung*, 5 volumes (Leipzig: Engelmann, 1853; revised by Gervinus and Karl Barsch, 1871–1874);

Über den Göthischen Briefwechsel (Leipzig: Engelmann, 1836);

Grundzüge der Historik (Leipzig: Engelmann, 1837);

Handbuch der poetischen National-Literatur der Deutschen (Leipzig: Engelmann, 1842);

Die Mission der Deutsch-Katholiken (Heidelberg: Winter, 1845); translated anonymously as *The Mission of the German Catholics* (London: Chapman, 1846);

Die preußische Verfassung und das Patent vom 3. Februar 1847 (Mannheim: Basserman, 1847);

Shakespeare, 4 volumes (Leipzig: Engelmann, 1849–1850); translated by Fanny Elizabeth Bunnètt as *Shakespeare Commentaries* (London: Smith, Elder, 1863; New York: Scribner, Welford & Armstrong, 1875);

Einleitung in die Geschichte des neunzehnten Jahrhunderts (Leipzig: Engelmann, 1853); translated anonymously as *Introduction to the History of the Nineteenth Century* (London: Bohn, 1853); excerpts translated by Moritz Sernau and J. M. Stephens as *The Course and Tendency of History, since the Overthrow of the Empire of Napoleon I: Translated from His "Introduction to the History of the Nineteenth Century, to Vindicate Prof. Gervinus from His English Translator in Henry G. Bohn's One Shilling Series* (London: Marlborough, 1853);

Georg Gottfried Gervinus (lithograph by an unknown artist, after an 1841 painting by C. W. F. Oesterley at the Universitätsbibliothek in Heidelberg)

Kritik der Entscheidungsgründe zu dem Urtheile des Mannheimer Hofgerichts in meinem Prozesse (Brunswick: Schwetzke, 1853);

Geschichte des neunzehnten Jahrhunderts seit den Wiener Verträgen, 8 volumes (Leipzig: Engelmann, 1855–1866);

Friedrich Christoph Schlosser: Ein Nekrolog (Leipzig: Engelmann, 1861);

Händel und Shakespeare: Zur Ästhetik der Tonkunst (Leipzig: Engelmann, 1868);

Hinterlassene Schriften, edited by Victoria Gervinus (Vienna: Braumüller, 1872);
G. G. Gervinus Leben: Von ihm selbst. 1860, edited by J. Keller (Leipzig: Engelmann, 1893);
Schriften zur Literatur, edited by Gotthard Erler (Berlin: Aufbau, 1962).
Edition in English: *The Art of Drinking: A Historical Sketch,* translated anonymously (New York: United States Brewers Association, 1890).

OTHER: "Johann Georg Forster," in *Georg Forsters sämtliche Schriften,* volume 7 (Leipzig: Brockhaus, 1843), pp. 1-78;
George Frideric Handel, *Händels Oratorientexte übersetzt,* translated by Gervinus, edited by Victoria Gervinus (Berlin: Duncker, 1874);
Edwin Emerson, *A History of the Nineteenth Century, Year by Year,* introduction by Gervinus (New York: Collier, 1901).

The July 1830 Revolution in Paris, followed by the deaths of the philosopher Georg Wilhelm Friedrich Hegel and Johann Wolfgang von Goethe over the ensuing two years, marked a caesura in German political and cultural history. While the poet Heinrich Heine proclaimed the end of autonomous art and a change in aesthetics from romantic subjectivity to political action, the historian Georg Gottfried Gervinus demanded the end of art in any form. According to his radically functional conception of aesthetics, art had fulfilled and exhausted its historical role; the turn to direct political involvement in Germany had begun. Political involvement meant for him, however, not revolutionary activism but careful study of the historical foundation of contemporary society to reveal the forces and movement of ideas that inform political action. Though the inaccuracy of his predictions in the short term led to charges of false prophecy, in hindsight Gervinus's dire prognostications for Germany lend his clairvoyance tragic credibility. The search for democratic, constitutional traditions in Germany in the 1920s and the 1960s led to the resurrection of Gervinus's work and a reevaluation of what is now seen as his historical insight.

Gervinus was born in Darmstadt on 20 May 1805 to Anna Maria Gervinus, née Schwarz, and Georg Gottfried Gervinus Sr., a craftsman. The year after Gervinus's birth, Napoleon combined Hesse-Darmstadt with fifteen other principalities to form the Rheinbund (Confederation of the Rhine) as a French protectorate. Gervinus's early years were overshadowed politically first by the growth of German nationalism during the Wars of Liberation in 1813-1818 and subsequently by the reactionary politics after the Congress of Vienna. In his posthumously published autobiography Gervinus depicts his gymnasium years as "die Zeit, wo der teutonische Schwindel von der Universität in die Schulen eindrang" (the time when Teutonic giddiness from the university penetrated the schools), referring to conservative mythicizing of the Germanic past for nationalist ends.

In 1819 Gervinus broke off his formal education to pursue commercial training, but he did not give up his academic goals and taught himself English, Spanish, and some French. In 1825 he matriculated at the state university at Gießen, but he transferred to Heidelberg University in the spring of 1826 to study under the historian Friedrich Christoph Schlosser. In 1830 Gervinus submitted his dissertation, *Geschichte der Angelsachsen im Überblick* (Survey of Anglo-Saxon History, 1830). The following year he obtained a position as a private lecturer at Heidelberg University.

From 1830 to 1835 he was preoccupied with the political and historiographic thought of Thucydides and Niccolò Machiavelli; an excursion to the Machiavelli archives in Florence began a lifelong affinity for Italy. Thucydides embodied for Gervinus the purpose of historiographic activity: "Wissenschaft im Dienst der nationalen Politik" (scholarship in the service of national politics).

The Paris uprising in 1830 and the revolutionary Hambacher Fest (Hambach Festival) in 1832 excited Gervinus, though he felt that the radical opposition to the government was unrealistic and incompatible with historical conditions. In the summer of 1831 he offered lectures on the history of constitutional development in Europe "um auf die Schranken der geschichtlichen Gesetze in der Staatenentwicklung zu verweisen, von denen diese brausenden Köpfe keine Ahnung haben" (to point out the limits of historical principles in the development of the state of which these tempestuous heads have no understanding). Gervinus rejected the possibility of transcending the historical conditions of a given period, and he understood political progress to be delineated by historical "ideas" and "movements" identifiable only through careful inquiry.

In 1832 Gervinus began work on what remains his greatest historiographic contribution, the five-volume *Geschichte der poetischen National-Literatur der Deutschen* (History of the Poetic National Literature of the Germans, 1835-1842). He felt that literary history might serve to comfort the German nation and encourage its development, while political history would tend to undermine its spirit by documenting its inadequacy: "Die Geschichte muß, wie die Kunst, zu Ruhe führen, und wir müssen nie von einem geschichtlichen Kunstwerke trostlos weggehen dürfen" (history, like art, must lead to tranquillity, and we must never be able to go away from a historical work of art without consolation). Gervinus's uncharitable review in the *Heidelberger Jahrbücher* (Heidelberg Yearbooks, 1833) of the literary histories of Karl Herzog (1831) and A. Wilhelm Bohtz (1832) points to what he considers their invalid concentration on biographies of individual authors and the aesthetic quality of their work rather than on the construction of historical contexts: "Der ästhetische Beurteiler zeigt uns eines Gedichts Entstehung, sein inneres Wachstum und Vollendung in sich selbst, seinen absoluten Wert dem Ideal gegenüber, sein Verhältnis zu dem künstlerischen Charakter des Dichters überhaupt. Der Historiker zeigt seine Entstehung aus der Zeit, aus deren Ideen, Bestrebungen und Schicksalen, sein inneres Verhältnis – Entsprechen oder Widerspruch – mit diesen, seinen Wert für die Nation, seine Wirkung in Mitwelt und Nachwelt" (The aesthetic critic shows us a poem's genesis, its inner growth and completion in itself, its absolute value in relation to the ideal, its relationship to the artistic character of the poet in general. The historian shows the poem's genesis in the context of its time and from the ideas, trends, and fortunes of the time, its corresponding or contradictory internal relationship to the same, its value for the nation, its contemporary and historical influence).

Beginning before the medieval *Hildebrandslied* (Song of Hildebrand) and ending with the death of Goethe, Gervinus's literary history spans more than a millenium. Analyzing both sociopolitical conditions and their literary representation, Gervinus traces the democratization and individualization of cultural expression. The Reformation and the ensuing Thirty Years' War represent the last gasp of religious domination over culture and politics, but for Gervinus the eighteenth century was the turning point in Germany's history, the time when the spiritual foundation of the nation was laid. Friedrich Gottlob Klopstock and Christoph Martin Wieland developed the German language to its fullest potential, and it was Gotthold Ephraim Lessing who first let himself be carried by the currents of the zeitgeist and the feeling for the needs of the nation. Gervinus portrays these authors as both children and mentors of their time, who both represented the Zeitgeist and also understood how to foster its progress.

In these years artistic genius came to replace political development. What political revolution was for France, cultural revolution was for Germany. Art, science, and literature became inseparable from the nation: "Wir hatten in Deutschland keine Geschichte, keinen Staat, keine Politik, wir hatten nur Literatur, nur Wissenschaft und Kunst. Sie überflügelte Alles, sie siegte allerwege, sie beherrschte daher alle Bestrebungen der Zeit" (In Germany we had no history, no state, no politics; we had only literature, only science and art. They surpassed everything, they were victorious everywhere, they therefore dominated all endeavors of the time). The work contends that the nation must now learn to value action and deeds as highly as feeling and intellect, and it ends with a call to action: "Der Wettkampf der Kunst ist vollendet; jetzt sollten wir uns das andere Ziel stecken, das noch kein Schütze bei uns getroffen hat, ob uns auch Apollon den Ruhm gewährt, den er uns dort nicht versagte" (The contest of art has been completed. Now we must set for ourselves the target which no archer among us has hit, to see whether Apollo, too, will grant us the glory that he did not deny us before).

Contemporary reactions to the literary history were mixed. The poet Georg Herwegh echoed Gervinus's hope that the literary past would help the masses to judge the present better and gather hope for the day when deeds would supplant words; but traditional literary scholars accused him of dilettantism, and his prosaic style was criticized by Heinrich Heine, whose *Zur Geschichte der neueren schönen Literatur in Deutschland* (History of Modern Belletristic Literature in Germany) appeared in 1833: "Gervinus' Literaturgeschichte – die Aufgabe war: was H. Heine in einem kleinen Büchlein voll Geist gegeben, jetzt in einem großen Buche ohne Geist zu geben – die Aufgabe ist gut gelöst" (Gervinus's Literary History – the task was: that which H. Heine had provided in a little booklet full of spirit to provide now in a big book without spirit – the task was well performed).

In 1835 Gervinus received a chair at the University of Göttingen. The following year he married Victoria Schelver.

His stay in Göttingen lasted only two years. In 1837 the new king of Hannover, Ernst August, revoked the liberal constitution of 1833. In response, seven Göttingen professors, among them Gervinus, signed a statement of protest on 18 November; on 22 November it was publicly distributed in Göttingen, and Gervinus directed the pamphlet's circulation to prominent intellectuals in other cities. On 12 December the seven professors were dismissed from the university, and three of them –

Gervinus (middle row, right) and the other members of the "Göttinger Sieben" (Göttingen Seven), seven professors who were dismissed from their positions at Göttingen University after protesting against the abrogation of the constitution of Hannover by King Ernst August in 1837. The others are (top to bottom, left to right) Wilhelm and Jacob Grimm, Wilhelm Eduard Albrecht, Friedrich Christoph Dahlmann, Wilhelm Eduard Weber, and Georg Heinrich August Ewald (lithograph by Carl Rohde).

Gervinus, Friedrich Christoph Dahlmann, and Jacob Grimm – were expelled from the state of Hannover. Though there was widespread support for the professors, Gervinus complained that in Hannover public opposition to the conservative coup was negligible. This experience showed Gervinus the dangers of political activism for scholars.

His turbulent tenure in Göttingen produced the single significant theoretical-methodological work of Gervinus's career, *Grundzüge der Historik* (Fundamentals of History, 1837). In this work the ever-moving realm of "Ideen" (ideas) – an influential concept introduced by Wilhelm von Humboldt – figures both as a philosophy of history and the object of historiography. According to Gervinus, philosophy deals with the world of reason and necessity; poetry and fiction deal with the world of possibility; and history confronts the world of experience and reality, eventually becoming the prerequisite for all other sciences. The historian can achieve objectivity by imaginatively placing himself ("sich hineinversetzen") into the past, thereby bringing the universality of understanding to the particularity of historical events. This aspect of Gervinus's thought was to be a significant influence on the historical hermeneutics of Wilhelm Dilthey a generation later.

Gervinus gave consideration to an offer from the University of Zurich but decided against leaving Germany. After a short stay in Darmstadt and a journey to Italy, he settled in Heidelberg in liberal Baden, a city he knew well from his student years. He received a chair at the University of Heidelberg in 1844.

In 1846–1847, responding to a call from A. L. Reyscher, the first Germanistikversammlung (Meeting of Germanists) met in Frankfurt am Main and Lübeck. At the meetings Gervinus aligned himself with Reyscher, who struggled to avoid reducing the scholarly endeavor to a merely political one. When the historian Leopold von Ranke, under the auspices of the Deutscher Bund, suggested establishing a separate historical society, Gervinus argued unsuccessfully that such an association would endanger the nonpartisan nature of the young discipline.

From these meetings sprang an interest in a journalistic undertaking intended to widen popular support for a unified Germany. After a failed attempt to establish a newspaper in Berlin, Gervinus became the primary player in starting the *Deutsche Zeitung* (German Newspaper) in Baden. The project was laden with controversy: Gervinus's idea of circumventing government censorship through self-censorship alienated many liberals. Despite a misunderstanding with Dahlmann about his overcautious endorsement, which cost the newspaper its funding and nearly cost Gervinus and Dahlmann their friendship, the *Deutsche Zeitung* finally issued its first edition on 1 July 1847. In early 1848, involved heavily in the meetings in Heidelberg to draft a constitution and subsequently as an elected representative to the Nationalversammlung (National Assembly) in Frankfurt am Main, Gervinus let his active leadership of the newspaper lapse.

Gervinus's hope of combining scholarship with journalistic participation in the public sphere met with success. The "Gervinus-Zeitung" (Gervinus Newspaper) as Karl Marx referred to it, reached an impressive subscription rate of five thousand at the height of the revolutions in Germany in 1848. Nonetheless, the proclaimed goal of the paper, "das Gefühl der Gemeinsamkeit und Einheit der deutschen Nation zu unterhalten und zu stärken" (to entertain and strengthen the feeling of commonality and unity of the German nation), went down to defeat as the revolution was suppressed and the proconstitutional, liberally oriented Nationalversammlung was discredited.

During the discussions in Heidelberg, and later in the Nationalversammlung, Gervinus promoted a strong foreign policy and more central military authority. Until late 1848 he supported a unified Germany under Prussian domination. But in the years immediately thereafter he became disillusioned with the evolution of Prussian politics, concluding by 1851 that constitutional reform had failed and revolution had become unavoidable. The years between 1848 and 1851 represent what has become known as the "Linkewende" (turn to the left) in his development.

After an unsuccessful diplomatic mission to England in 1850 attempting to secure an English veto on Russian intervention in Schleswig-Holstein, Gervinus turned to a history of recent constitutional developments in the West that he had been considering since the 1830s. The first stage of the project, *Einleitung in die Geschichte des neunzehnten Jahrhunderts* (Introduction to the History of the Nineteenth Century, 1853), portrays the development of democratization in the West from the Middle Ages to the eighteenth century. While democracy is depicted as the telos of all Western societies, Germany's unique federal arrangement proves especially conducive to individualism, as witnessed by the Reformation and the Enlightenment. There are many parallels to his *Geschichte der poetischen National-Literatur der Deutschen* and *Grundzüge der Historik* in this work; here, however, Gervinus is not only a cultural and historical theorist, but also a political prophet. With Western history moving inevitably toward the expansion of individual freedom and democracy, the constitutions of England and the United States serve as the natural conclusion of the process. "Daß die Bewegungen dieses Jahrhunderts von dem Instinkte der großen Masse getragen werden, daß ihr Ziel ein gemeinsames und gleichartiges ist, daß sie in einem ganz gesetzmäßigen Verlaufe vor sich gehen, dies sind die drei Eigenschaften, die ihre äußere und innere Stärke ausmachen, ihre Naturgemäßheit und ihre Unwiderstehlichkeit verbürgen" (That the movements of this century are carried by the instinct of the great masses, that their goal is a common and similar one, that they are pursuing an entirely prescribed course: these are the three characteristics which form their internal and external strength and which guarantee their accordance with nature and their irresistibility).

Einleitung in die Geschichte des neunzehnten Jahrhunderts attracted the attention of the government of Baden, which perceived an explicit revolutionary potential in its thesis. Between January and May 1853 Gervinus, charged with high treason and endangering peace and order, was forced to prove that his treatise was a scholarly, apolitical work that merely described historical forces and did not prescribe political action. During the court hearings Gervinus strove to show that his views were in agreement with those of the conservative faction, reconfiguring his harsh critique of feudal structures in Europe to apply instead to outdated oriental despotism. It is improbable, however, that Gervinus was unaware of the revolutionary consequences his historical scheme indicates. Though the work was not intended to be a political manifesto, as the prosecution claimed, Gervinus's attempt to assimilate the conservative viewpoint could not have been convincing even to himself.

Gervinus was found innocent of high treason but guilty of endangering peace and order. The local court's decision was appealed to the high court in Mannheim and finally set for jury trial. At this point the state decided against pursuing the charges, and Gervinus was never required to serve the two months' imprisonment to which he had been sentenced.

The controversy surrounding *Einleitung in die Geschichte des neunzehsten Jahrhunderts* augmented Gervinus's fame. In 1853 greatly increased demand for his already popular *Geschichte der poetischen National-Literatur der Deutschen* necessitated a fourth edition, retitled *Geschichte der deutschen Dichtung* (History of German Literature). More copies of the history were sold in the period around the trial than in the almost twenty years since it had first appeared.

In his *Geschichte des neunzehnten Jahrhunderts seit den Wiener Verträgen* (History of the Nineteenth Century since the Vienna Accords, 1855–1866) Gervinus, with the help of several assistants, compiled a chronicle of revolutionary struggles and democratic upheaval in Europe and America. Initially intended to span the years from 1815 to 1850, the project was discontinued after eight volumes reached only to 1830. While Gervinus insists that the scholarly demands of historiography, not partisanship, define his project, he describes the period since 1815 as "die Zeit des Trugs und der Lüge, des Trotzes der Machthaber und der Schlaffheit ihrer Beamten, die Zeit der Congresse und Protocolle, der politischen Verfolgungen und der Verschwörungen, der Hoffnungen und der Täuschungen" (the time of deception and lies, of the obstinacy of rulers and the indolence of their bureaucrats, the time of assemblies and depositions, of political persecutions and conspiracies, of hopes and disappointments).

Gervinus begins with the reactionary measures adopted by European governments from 1815 to 1820, in the wake of the Congress of Vienna. He then recounts the Latin American revolutions and their influence in southern Europe. In volumes five and six he discusses the deterioration of the Ottoman Empire and the Greek Revolution's challenge to the Holy Alliance. In the last two volumes, Gervinus returns to Western Europe and studies the events leading to the July Revolution of 1830 in Paris.

Gervinus interprets the events between 1815 and 1830 less as the traditional struggle between restoration and revolution than as the slow decay of the ancien régime. In these years the "deception and lies" of the European hierarchies became less effective against an increasingly consolidated and educated middle class, resulting in mass movements and popular uprisings.

Gervinus attributes the processes of modernization primarily to the nations of Western Europe. While the Latin-American and southern European opposition to Spanish colonialism and the Holy Alliance was important, the bourgeois revolution of 1830 is seen as the culmination of the secularization and democratization that began with the Reformation. The revolution was a catastrophe for the ancien régime, not merely a military revolt but a popular uprising indicating total disillusionment with and the delegitimization of hegemonic state structures. It marks the end of the restorative-revolutionary struggle and the beginning of the political dominance of the middle classes.

The style of *Geschichte des neunzehnten Jahrhunderts seit den Wiener Verträgen* is far from elegant. Its comparative method, partly borrowed from Schlosser – to whom Gervinus dedicated the work – can be seen as a contribution to historical scholarship. But, lacking analysis of the consequences of the revolution of 1830, the work has no thematic closure.

After 1856 Gervinus's interest in politics was renewed. In 1860 he attempted without success to resurrect the *Deutsche Zeitung* under the editorship of Wilhelm Beseler. Because of his fear of rising Prussian centralism he turned down an invitation to join the Deutscher Nationalverein (German National Union), which had been founded with nationalistic fervor in 1859 on the one hundredth birthday of Friedrich Schiller. He felt that with the accession of Wilhelm I to the Prussian throne in 1861, the Hohenzollern dynasty was destined only to lead Germany to its ruin.

The 1866 Austro-Prussian War turned Gervinus into a virulent opponent of Prussia. He abandoned his *Geschichte des neunzehnten Jahrhunderts seit den Wiener Verträgen,* having reached the conclusion that there were no tangible lessons to be learned from history – a determination in violation of everything Gervinus had represented since the 1830s. After 1866 Gervinus was increasingly politically and personally isolated and separated by death from his compatriots Wilhelm and Jacob Grimm and Dahlmann. Accused of shamelessly using Dahlmann and the Grimms, to whom the fifth edition of his history of German literature was dedicated, for his own political program, Gervinus responded with a sharp polemic asserting Dahlmann's and the Grimms' support for a federal union and their opposition to a centralized and militaristic Germany.

On 18 March 1871, exactly two months after Wilhelm I was crowned emperor of the Second German Empire in Versailles, Gervinus died in Heidelberg at the age of sixty-five. While the conservative scholar Karl Hillebrand described Gervinus as a writer without eloquence, a scholar without method, a thinker without depth, and a politician without foresight, Ranke, though critical of what he considered Gervinus's misconception of the relationship between life and scholarship and of his alleged blindness in the pursuit of democratic rather than military solutions to German problems, saw Gervinus as one who had presented alternative possibilities in politics and history. Nonetheless, Gervinus's oppositional voice could never become dominant either in politics or in the discipline of history; Gervinus was, Ranke said, passed over by events.

Yet hindsight confirms Gervinus's foresight. Foreseeing the consequences of Prussian militarism, in 1867 Gervinus wrote: "Man muß die Dinge der Vorsehung anheim geben, die den ganzen Weltteil (scheint es) einer jener großen Katastrophen entgegen führt" (One must turn over to Providence those things that [it would seem] are leading the whole continent toward one of those great catastrophes).

Letters:

Briefwechsel zwischen den Brüdern Grimm, Dahlmann und Gervinus, edited by Eduard Ippel (Berlin: Dümmler, 1885);

"Jugendbriefe von Gervinus," edited by Alfred Stern, *Preußische Jahrbücher,* 197 (1924): 252–269.

Bibliographies:

Rolf-Peter Carl, *Prinzipien der Literaturbetrachtung bei Georg Gottfried Gervinus* (Bonn: Bouvier, 1969);

Gangolf Hübinger, *Georg Gottfried Gervinus: Historisches Urteil und politische Kritik* (Göttingen: Vandenhoeck & Ruprecht, 1984).

Biographies:

Hermann Baumgarten, *Gervinus und seine politschen Überzeugungen: Ein biographischer Beitrag* (Leipzig: Engelmann, 1853);

Emil Lehmann, *G. G. Gervinus: Eine Charakteristik* (Hamburg: Meissner, 1871);

Karl Esselborn, *Georg Gottfried Gervinus: Schul- und Lehrjahre* (Darmstadt, 1930).

References:

Rolf Böttcher, *Nationales und staatliches Denken im Werke G.G. Gervinus* (Düsseldorf: Nolte, 1935);

Gordon A. Craig, "Georg Gottfried Gervinus: The Historian as Activist," *Pacific Historical Review,* 41 (Feruary 1872): 1–14;

O. Damman, ed., "Klaus Groth und G. G. Gervinus," *Zeitschrift für die Geschichte des Oberrheins,* 97 (1949): 619-628;

Walter Dietze, "Georg Gottfried Gervinus als Historiker der deutschen National-Literatur," *Sinn und Form,* 11 (1959): 445–467;

Alfred Dove, "Nachwort über Gervinus," *Im neuen Reich: Wochenschrift für das Leben des deutschen Volkes in Staat, Wissenschaft und Kunst,* 1, no. 1 (1871): 494–496;

Johannes Dürfel, *Gervinus als historischer Denker* (Gotha: Perthes, 1903);

Wolfgang Ebling, *Georg Gottfried Gervinus und die Musik* (Munich: Katzbichler, 1985);

Gotthard Erler, "Gervinus als Literaturhistoriker," *Weimarer Beiträge,* 8, no. 1 (1962): 34–84;

Karl Esselborn, "G.G. Gervinus' Jugend: Aus dem Nachlaß August Nodnagels mitgeteilt," *Hessische Chronik,* 11 (1922): 2–9;

Karl-Georg Faber, "Gervinus oder: Das Elend einer Geschichtsphilosophie," in *Objektivität und Parteilichkeit in der Geschichtswissenschaft,* volume 1, edited by Reinhart Kosellek and others (Munich: Deutscher Taschenbuch Verlag, 1977), pp. 125–134;

Lothar Gall, "Georg Gottfried Gervinus," in *Deutsche Historiker,* volume 5, edited by H.-U. Wehler (Göttingen: Vandenhoeck & Ruprecht, 1972), pp. 7-26;

Friedrich W. Graf, *Die Politisierung des religiösen Bewußtseins: Die bürgerlichen Religionsparteien im deutschen Vormärz: Das Beispiel des Deutschkatholizismus* (Stuttgart: Frommann-Holzboog, 1978);

Hermann Grimm, "Gervinus," in *Preußische Jahrbücher,* 27 (1871): 475–478;

Jacob Grimm, "Rezension von Gervinus's *Geschichte der poetischen National-Literatur der Deutschen,*" in his *Kleinere Schriften,* volume 5 (Berlin: Dümmler, 1871), pp. 176–187;

Karl Hegel, "Rezension von Gervinus' *Grundzüge der Historik,*" *Jahrbücher für wissenschaftliche Kritik,* 115–117 (December 1839): 913–935;

Knut Hennies, *Fehlgeschlagene Hoffnung und Gleichgültigkeit: Die Literaturgeschichte von G.G. Gervinus im Spannungsfeld zwischen Fundamentalhistorie und Historismus* (Frankfurt am Main: Lang, 1984);

John L. Hibberd, *G.G. Gervinus as Literary Historian* (Oxford: Oxford University Press, 1965);

Karl Hillebrand, "G.G. Gervinus," *Preußische Jahrbücher,* 32 (1873): 379–428;

Charles McClellan, "History in the Service of Politics: A Reassessment of G. G. Gervinus" *Central European History,* 4 (December 1971): 371–389;

Hermann Oncken, "Georg Gottfried Gervinus und das Programm seines Lebens im Jahre 1832," in *Quellen und Darstellungen zur Geschichte der Burschenschaften und der deutschen Einheitsbewegung,* volume 4 (Heidelberg: Winter, 1913), pp. 354–366;

Leopold von Ranke, "Georg Gottfried Gervinus: Eröffnungsrede der 12. Plenarversammlung vor der Historischen Kommission bei der Königlichen Akademie der Wissenschaften zu München vom 27.9.1871," *Historische Zeitschrift,* 27 (1872): 134–146;

Hans Rosenberg, "Gervinus und die deutsche Republik," *Die Gesellschaft,* 6 (1929): 119–136;

Jörn Rüsen, "Gervinus' Kritik an der Reichsgründung: Eine Fallstudie zur Logik des historischen Urteils," in *Vom Staat des Ancien Régime zum modernen Parteienstaat: Festschrift für Theodor Schneider,* edited by H. Berding and others (Munich: Oldenbourg, 1978), pp. 313–329;

Rüsen, "Der Historiker als 'Parteimann des Schicksals,'" in *Objektivität und Parteilichkeit in der Geschichtswissenschaft,* volume 1, edited by Reinhart Kosellek and others (Munich: Deutscher Taschenbuch Verlag, 1977), pp. 77–124;

Max Rychner, *G.G. Gervinus: Ein Kapitel über Literaturgeschichte* (Bern: Seldwyla, 1922);

Vittorio Santoli, "An den Anfängen der 'nationalen Literaturgeschichte': G.G. Gervinus and J. Grimm," in *Festschrift zum 80. Geburtstag von Georg Lukács,* edited by Frank Beseler (Neuwied: Luchterhand, 1956), pp. 357–373;

Gerhard Schilfert and Hans Schleier, "Georg Gottfried Gervinus als Historiker," in *Studien über die deutsche Geschichtswissenschaft,* volume 1, edited by Joachim Streisand (Berlin: Deutsche Akademie der Wissenschaften, 1969), pp. 148–169;

Eduard Schulze, *Gervinus als politischer Journalist: Ein Beitrag zur Publizistik der deutschen Einheitsbewegung* (Leipzig: Vogel, 1930);

Engelbert Strobel, "G.G. Gervinus: Literaturhistoriker, Geschichtsschreiber und Politiker," *Badische Heimat,* 39 (1959): 22–24;

Peter F. Stuhr, *Die Phantasien des Herrn Gervinus und seiner Freunde über die Geschichte und Verfassung Preußens beleuchtet* (Berlin: Hayn, 1847);

R. Hinton Thomas, "Gervinus and the Age of Goethe," *Publications of the English Goethe Society,* 20 (1951): 82–110;

Rudolf Unger, "Gervinus und die Anfänge der politischen Literaturgeschichtsschreibung in Deutschland," in his *Gesammelte Studien,* volume 3 (Darmstadt: Wissenschaftliche Buchgesellschaft, 1966), pp. 298–324;

Jonathan Wagner, *The Political Evolution of Gervinus* (Ann Arbor: University of Michigan Press, 1972);

Erich Wolf, *G.G. Gervinus: Sein geschichtlich-politisches System* (Leipzig: Triltsch, 1931).

Papers:

Georg Gottfried Gervinus's literary remains are in the Heidelberg University Library.

Jeremias Gotthelf
(Albert Bitzius)

(4 October 1797 - 22 October 1854)

Ulrich Scheck
Queen's University, Kingston, Canada

BOOKS: *Der Bauern-Spiegel oder Lebensgeschichte des Jeremias Gotthelf: Von ihm selbst beschrieben,* anonymous (Burgdorf: Langlois, 1837 [i.e., 1836]; revised and enlarged, 1839; enlarged edition, Berlin: Springer, 1851); excerpt translated by Mary Augusta Ward as "The Mirror of Peasants," *Macmillan's,* 48 (1883): 459-461;

Die Wassernot im Emmenthal am 13. August 1837 (Burgdorf: Langlois, 1838);

Leiden und Freuden eines Schulmeisters, 2 volumes (Bern: Wagner, 1838, 1839) revised edition, 1 volume (Berlin: Simion & Springer, 1848); translated anonymously as *The Joys and Sorrows of a Schoolmaster: By One of Themselves* (London: Allan, 1864);

Wie fünf Mädchen im Branntwein jämmerlich umkommen: Eine merkwürdige Geschichte (Bern: Wagner, 1838; enlarged edition, Berlin: Springer, 1851);

Dursli der Branntweinsäufer oder Der Heilige Weihnachtsabend (Burgdorf: Langlois, 1839; revised, 1846);

Die Armennoth (Zurich & Frauenfeld: Beyel, 1840; enlarged edition, Berlin: Springer, 1851);

Wie Uli der Knecht glücklich wird: Eine Gabe für Dienstboten und Meisterleute (Zurich & Frauenfeld: Beyel, 1841); revised as *Uli der Knecht: Ein Volksbuch* (Berlin: Springer, 1846); translated by Julia Firth, revised by John Ruskin as *Ulric the Farm Servant: A Story of the Bernese Lowlands* (Orpington: Allen, 1886; New York: Dutton, 1907);

Eines Schweizers Wort an den schweizerischen Schützenverein (Bern: Rätzer, 1842; revised edition, Solothurn: Jent & Gaßmann, 1844);

Ein Sylvester-Traum (Zurich & Frauenfeld: Beyel, 1842);

Bilder und Sagen aus der Schweiz, 6 volumes (Solothurn: Jent & Gaßmann, 1842-1846); includes in volume 1, "Die schwarze Spinne," translated by H. M. Waidson as *The Black Spider* (London: Calder, 1958; New York: McClelland, 1958); translated by Mary Hottinger as "The Black Spider," in *Nineteenth Century German Tales,* edited by Angel Flores (New York: Doubleday, 1959), pp. 169-249; includes in volumes 2, 4, and 5, "Geld und Geist oder Die Versöhnung," translated anonymously as *Wealth and Welfare,* 2 volumes

Jeremias Gotthelf (lithograph by Irminger after a drawing by J. Barth)

(London & New York: Strahan, 1866); includes as volume 3, *Der letzte Thorberger*;

Wie Anne Bäbi Jowäger haushaltet und wie es ihm mit dem Doktern geht, 2 volumes (Solothurn: Jent & Gaßmann, 1843-1844);

Der Geltstag oder Die Wirtschaft nach der neuen Mode (Solothurn: Jent & Gaßmann, 1846 [i.e., 1845]);

Der Knabe des Tell: Eine Geschichte für die Jugend (Berlin: Springer, 1846);

Jakobs, des Handwerksgesellen, Wanderungen durch die Schweiz, 2 volumes (Zwickau: Verein zur Verbreitung guter und wohlfeiler Volksschriften, 1846-1847);

Käthi die Großmutter oder Der wahre Weg durch jede Noth: Eine Erzählung für das Volk, 2 volumes (Berlin: Allgemeiner deutscher Volksschriftenverein, 1847); translated by L. G. Smith as *The Story of an Alpine Valley; or, Katie the Grandmother* (London: Gibbings, 1896);

Hans Joggeli der Erbvetter; Harzer Hans, auch ein Erbvetter: Zwei Erzählungen für das Volk (Berlin: Simion & Springer, 1848);

Uli der Pächter: Ein Volksbuch (Berlin: Springer, 1849);

Doktor Dorbach der Wühler und die Bürglenherren in der heiligen Weihnachtsnacht anno 1847 (Leipzig: Mayer, 1849);

Erzählungen und Bilder aus dem Volksleben der Schweiz, 5 volumes (Berlin: Springer, 1850-1855); includes in volume 3, "Der Besenbinder von Rychiswyl," translated by Ruskin as "The Broom Merchant," in *The Works of John Ruskin,* edited by E. T. Cook and Alexander Wedderburn (London: Allan, 1907), XXVII: 548-553, 632-635; XXVIII: 55-60, 366-372;

Die Käserei in der Vehfreude: Eine Geschichte aus der Schweiz (Berlin: Springer, 1850);

Hans Jakob und Heiri oder Die beiden Seidenweber (Berlin: Springer, 1851);

Zeitgeist und Berner Geist, 2 volumes (Berlin: Springer, 1852);

Erlebnisse eines Schuldenbauers (Berlin: Springer, 1853);

Die Frau Pfarrerin Ein Lebensbild Berlin: Springer, 1855); excerpt translated by Ward in *Macmillan's,* 48 (1883): 463;

Gesammelte Schriften, 24 volumes (Berlin: Springer, 1856-1858);

Sämtliche Werke, 42 volumes, edited by Rudolf Hunziker, Hans Bloesch, Kurt Guggisberg, and Werner Juker (Erlenbach & Zurich: Rentsch, 1911-1977);

Werke, 20 volumes, edited by Walter Muschg (Basel: Birkhäuser, 1948-1953).

Edition in English: *Tales of Courtship by Jeremias Gotthelf,* translated by Robert Godwin-Jones (New York: Lang, 1984).

OTHER: *Neuer Berner Kalender,* 6 volumes, edited by Gotthelf (volumes 1 and 2, Bern: Rätzer, 1839, 1840; volumes 3-6, Bern: Jenni, 1841-1844).

Some critics have seen the Swiss writer Jeremias Gotthelf as a local scribe who entertained uneducated people with moralistic stories that are unique in their use of dialect and in their realistic depiction of rural life in the canton of Bern. Other critics, who feel that the local aspects of his works are only secondary, place Gotthelf confidently in the realm of world literature. Gotthelf 's compatriot Gottfried Keller was the first to point out that his portrayal of the seemingly closed rural world of Switzerland is really a depiction of human life and human nature in general, and Keller's prediction that Gotthelf would come to be regarded as a world-class writer has certainly come true. During his lifetime Gotthelf was one of the highest-paid authors writing in German; he had a publisher in Berlin and was well known in the northern parts of Germany; and the Prussian court was familiar with his name. Thus, from the beginning his literary fame extended well beyond the borders of Switzerland.

Gotthelf was certainly not the sentimental and naive teller of simplistic peasant tales many of his early readers believed him to be; on the contrary, he crafted his stories carefully. Almost all of his narrative prose is set in the present or the recent past but contains references to historical events such as the French Revolution. Gotthelf tried to reconcile the old agricultural order with the emerging age of industrialization, and his works express the fears and aspirations of people who live at the dawn of a new era. Gotthelf saw himself as a Volksschriftsteller (author who writes for and about people he or she knows and loves).

Gotthelf was born Albert Bitzius on 4 October 1797 in Murten, a village that belonged to both the cantons of Bern and Freiburg. His father, Sigmund Friedrich Bitzius, had been pastor of the reformed parish in Murten since 1786; his mother, Elizabeth Bitzius, née Kohler, was his father's third wife. The family also included Marie, the only child of Sigmund's first marriage, and Friedrich Carl (Fritz), who was born in 1799.

In the spring of 1805 the family moved to Utzensdorf in the canton of Bern. There Albert

Bitzius acquired a firsthand knowledge of peasant life in the Emme River Valley. His father taught him the basics of Greek and Latin until 1812, when he was sent to the gymnasium in Bern. In 1814 he was transferred to the Bern Academy, where he studied old languages, mathematics, philosophy, and theology. During his student years he was an active member of a literary society and familiarized himself with many works of world literature as well as with the theoretical writings of Johann Gottfried Herder, Friedrich Schiller, and Friedrich Schlegel. In 1816 he received the silver medal in a writing contest with an essay on the differences between classical and modern literature. Although in later years he would pretend to be an uneducated village pastor, he was well read and familiar with cultural and literary developments. He was a good student but was subject both to self-doubt and a certain degree of arrogance. He taught school while he was still a student, believing that Christian values could be inculcated much better in school than from the pulpit. Throughout his life he felt that preaching was far less effective than teaching young children the fundamentals of Christian faith.

After he passed his theological examinations in 1820 he became curate to his father in Utzensdorf. In 1821 he went on his only extended journey outside of Switzerland: he spent a year at the University of Göttingen, where he attended lectures in church history, world history, and the history of philosophy and aesthetics; during the fall vacation he traveled for five weeks through northern Germany, visiting Hannover, Lübeck, and Berlin.

After his return to Utzensdorf in the spring of 1822 Bitzius resumed his work as a curate. His father died in 1824, but since Bitzius had served less than five years as curate he was not allowed to follow in his father's footsteps as pastor. His friend Ludwig Fankhauser was appointed to the position, and Bitzius was transferred to Fankhauser's curacy in Herzogenbuchsee.

In Herzogenbuchsee, Bitzius engaged in a prolonged dispute with Rudolf Emanuel von Effinger, the regional representative of the Bern government, over conditions in the schools of his district. In 1826 Bitzius attended a meeting of the Helvetian Society in Langenthal, where he heard the aging educator Heinrich Pestalozzi deliver a speech. Pestalozzi's ideas on educational reform greatly influenced Bitzius's pedagogical opinions. The concept of a national education system that would no longer cater only to the privileged members of society especially appealed to him.

In 1829 Bitzius was transferred to the curacy of the Church of the Holy Spirit in Bern. He did not feel comfortable in the city and almost immediately applied for other positions. After several unsuccessful applications he was given the curacy in Lützelflüh, and on 1 January 1831 he arrived on horseback in the parish that was to be his home for the rest of his life. After twelve years as a curate he was finally promoted to pastor on 9 March 1832.

In January 1833 Bitzius married Henriette Elisabeth Zeender, the granddaughter of the pastor who had been his predecessor in Lützelflüh. The couple had three children: Henriette, born in 1834; Albert, born in 1835; and Cécile, born in 1837. In addition to his duties as pastor, Bitzius tried to reform the schools in his parish. He believed that the situation in the schools contradicted the new Swiss constitution's declaration that all citizens were free individuals. In 1835 he was appointed school commissioner of Lützelflüh and established a boarding school for poor orphans at Trachselwald. From 1834 to 1836 he gave lectures on history during the summers to elementary-school teachers and teaching trainees in Burgdorf. These lectures took place under the supervision of Friedrich Fröbel, the founder of the kindergarten.

The year 1836 marks the beginning of Bitzius's career as a writer. He wanted to reach a larger audience with his pedagogical views. Furthermore, he felt restricted by his work as a pastor; by his peers, who were often critical of his opinions; and by the bureaucracy. Writing became an outlet for him to externalize what he called the "wilde Leben in mir" (intense life within myself). His first novel, *Der Bauern-Spiegel oder Lebensgeschichte des Jeremias Gotthelf: Von ihm selbst beschrieben* (The Peasants' Mirror; or, The Life History of Jeremias Gotthelf: Described by Himself), appeared late in 1836. The novel's protagonist and presumed author, the farmhand Jeremias Gotthelf, tries unsuccessfully to become an independent farmer. He plans to marry the maid Anneli, but she dies in childbirth together with their child. The desperate Jeremias gets into trouble with the law, flees Switzerland, and joins the Swiss Guard in France. Bonjour, a captain who had fought in Russia with Napoleon, becomes Jeremias's mentor and helps him to develop into an able soldier. Jeremias learns to write and eventually becomes a good Christian. During the July 1830 Revolution Jeremias has to do battle with women and children in the streets of Paris, and he begins to wonder whether he is fighting for a just cause. In the end he returns to Switzerland, where he teaches his countrymen about his experiences during the

Der
Bauern-Spiegel
oder
Lebensgeschichte
des
Jeremias Gotthelf.

Dritte durchgesehene und vermehrte Auflage.

Wohlfeile Ausgabe.

Berlin, 1851.
Verlag von Julius Springer.
Zürich: S. Höhr. Bern: Huber u. Comp.

Cover for the third enlarged edition of Gotthelf's first novel, whose protagonist's name was adopted by the author as his pseudonym

revolution. The novel makes it clear that the future belongs to the people, not to the aristocracy. The degradation of the protagonist and the insistence on the value of the individual are reminiscent of Georg Büchner's play *Woyzeck* (translated, 1927), written at about the same time but not discovered and published until 1879. The novel's success led Bitzius to adopt his protagonist's name as his pseudonym.

Gotthelf's second novel, *Leiden und Freuden eines Schulmeisters* (1838, 1839; translated as *The Joys and Sorrows of a Schoolmaster: By One of Themselves,* 1864), is the fictional autobiography of Peter Käser, an impoverished village schoolmaster. Käser recounts his bitter childhood, his work as an underpaid young teacher, and his marriage to the kind and pragmatic Mädeli, the village cobbler's daughter. The unfolding of Käser's life story allows Gotthelf to illustrate and evaluate the sociological and philosophical foundations of the educational system in his canton and to discuss the purpose and benefits of mass education in the emerging industrial age. The theoretical reflections are presented with humor and irony. Gotthelf asserts that there should be no separation of knowledge and belief, of church and school. The novel ends in 1837 with the promise that all teachers will receive higher salaries in the future.

On 13 August 1837 thunderstorms in the Emme Valley caused floods that resulted in the destruction of bridges, homes, and stables and loss of human life. Gotthelf's *Die Wassernot im Emmenthal* (The Flooding of the Emme Valley, 1837) describes the catastrophe as God's judgment on a humanity that has become self-centered and power-hungry. With its metaphorical language saturated with moralistic and prophetic pathos, *Die Wassernot im Emmenthal* is reminiscent of the Old Testament.

Wie fünf Mädchen im Branntwein jämmerlich umkommen: Eine merkwürdige Geschichte (How Five Young Women Die Miserably in Brandy: A Strange Story, 1838) and *Dursli der Branntweinsäufer oder Der Heilige Weihnachtsabend* (Dursli the Brandy Boozer; or, Holy Christmas Eve, 1839) were written to warn of the dangers of alcoholism. *Wie fünf Mädchen im Branntwein jämmerlich umkommen* unfolds within a frame in which the narrator, a traveling salesman, is informed about the previous histories of the five women; he then traces the further unhappy events in their lives. *Dursli der Branntweinsäufer* is not as well constructed as *Wie fünf Mädchen im Branntwein jämmerlich umkommen,* but it has a stronger sociopolitical undertone; the ending promises salvation for the title character, a young alcoholic.

From 1836 to 1838 Gotthelf was president of the administrative commission of the boarding school at Trachselwald. The school inspired *Die Armennoth* (The Plight of the Poor, 1840), his only major essay. Gotthelf does not have much faith in measures taken by the government to solve the problem of poverty; the problem can only be attacked by helping the weakest members of society, the poor and orphaned children, first. It is the responsibility of every Christian as well as the mandate of the church to provide poor children with boarding schools in which education is based on the principles of Christian love. Gotthelf emphasizes that poverty is not decreed by God but is made by humans. Because of some critical comments about King Ludwig I, the book was banned in Bavaria.

From 1839 to 1844 Gotthelf edited the annual *Neuer Berner Kalender* (New Bernese Calendar), which contained humorous and satirical commentaries on contemporary events as well as stories and fairy tales. Gotthelf 's aggressive tone and idiosyncratic views did not meet the expectations of readers who were looking for entertainment.

The publication of *Wie Uli der Knecht glücklich wird: Eine Gabe für Dienstboten und Meisterleute* (How Uli the Farmhand Attains Happiness: A Gift to Servants and Masters, 1841; translated as *Ulric the Farm Servant: A Story of the Bernese Lowlands,* 1886) ushered in the decade during which Gotthelf wrote the novels and stories that established his reputation as one of the great Swiss writers of the nineteenth century. At the outset of the novel the farmhand Uli enjoys drinking and brawling, but with the help of the farmer Johannes he turns into a reliable servant. Johannes recommends him to the elderly farmer Joggeli, who is in need of a trustworthy foreman. After overcoming many obstacles Uli marries Vreneli, a poor relation of Joggeli's wife. When Joggeli retires, the couple leases his farm.

The novel is noted for its use of the Bernese dialect, its many colorful characters, and its vivid depiction of rural events; the hay-making scene and Uli and Vreneli's drive to their wedding are particularly memorable. Intended for a readership of farmhands and maids, the book soon came to be known in Switzerland and abroad as the quintessential peasant novel.

But *Wie Uli der Knecht glücklich wird* has more to offer than the charm of its rural ambience. It addresses a fundamental problem of Gotthelf 's time: that poor people in regions dominated by agriculture had almost no opportunities for social advancement. One of the progressive ideas that was thought to be beneficial to the poor, that of the Sparkasse (savings bank), is supported by Gotthelf in the novel when Johannes advises Uli to take his money to such a bank, which, in addition to offering savings accounts and loans, provides insurance.

The six volumes of Gotthelf 's *Bilder und Sagen aus der Schweiz* (Images and Legends of Switzerland, 1842–1846) contain six stories and a novel. "Die schwarze Spinne" (translated as *The Black Spider,* 1958), Gotthelf 's best-known story, is now considered a classic. The frame narrative of this perfectly constructed novella describes a baptism celebration on a prosperous farm in the Emme Valley. Within this frame, the grandfather's narrative of the black spider describes the horrible events that took place in earlier times. Six hundred years ago the peasants of Sumiswald were ordered to create a beech avenue to their overlord's castle within one month – an impossible task. One day the devil offered his assistance in exchange for a newborn, unbaptized child. Christine, a stranger, agreed to the pact on behalf of the hesitant villagers, and the bargain was sealed by the devil with a kiss on her cheek. After the devil helped the farmers, he was robbed of his reward three times when newborn children were christened before he could claim them. After the third instance he turned Christine into a poisonous spider that killed almost all the villagers. The mother of the third saved child sacrificed her life while imprisoning the beast inside a hollow piece of wood, which subsequently formed part of a window frame. Two centuries later the spider escaped because of a farmhand's evil deed. The owner of the farm sacrificed his life to force the spider back into the window frame, where, according to the grandfather, it still lives.

Gotthelf; pencil drawing by C. von Gonzenbach (Kunstmuseum sankt Gallen)

For almost ninety years this splendidly narrated story was almost completely ignored by critics, who were more interested in Gotthelf 's great peasant novels. In the twentieth century, however, "Die schwarze Spinne" has received well-deserved attention as critics have tried to interpret its symbolism. It is precisely this openness that makes the text so attractive to the modern reader and grants it an exceptional position within Gotthelf 's oeuvre.

The novel *Geld und Geist oder die Versöhnung* (Money and Soul; or, The Reconciliation; translated as *Wealth and Welfare,* 1866) appears in three installments in the second, fourth, and fifth volumes of *Bilder und Sagen aus der Schweiz.* The tension created by the juxtaposition of materialistic attitudes with Christian spirituality is exemplified by two farm families. The patriarch of the Dorngrüt family is an avaricious, self-centered, and power-hungry farmer who is willing to sell his daughter to the highest bidder. He embodies the evil side of human nature. The contrast to this unhappy family is provided by the Liebiwyls, but their idyllic and tranquil life is fragile. The first part of the novel describes how Christen Liebiwyl's illiteracy and ignorance of money matters threaten the unity of the family. Christen's wife, Änneli, is the heroine of *Geld und Geist;* it has often been observed by critics that the women in Gotthelf's oeuvre typically play more important parts and are stronger than the men because of their integrative powers, and Änneli is no exception. She possesses all the qualities that are necessary to achieve peace and happiness: she can admit her own weaknesses, she is not afraid to show love and compassion, and she is capable of forgiveness. She personifies the novel's main concern, the synthesis of earth and heaven within the human heart.

This synthesis is also one of the important themes of Gotthelf's next novel, *Wie Anne Bäbi Jowäger haushaltet und wie es ihm mit dem Doktern geht* (How Anne Bäbi Jowäger Conducts Her Household and What Her Experiences Are with Quackery, 1843–1844). At the time many medical charlatans were active in the canton of Bern, and the Bernese Public Health Commission asked Gotthelf to write a pamphlet against quackery. After doing extensive research, however, he decided to address the problem in a novel that blends medicine with theology by associating the healing of the body with the healing of the soul. The farm wife Anne Bäbi Jowäger is responsible for the partial blindness of her son and the death of her grandchild because she insists on consulting a quack rather than a physician. The narration is frequently interrupted by commentaries on religion, medical ethics, and contemporary politics, and there are many scenes that vividly illustrate life on a Bernese farm during the first half of the nineteenth century. The novel attempts to bridge the gap between religion and science, between the old and the new.

In 1845 Gotthelf was removed from his post as school inspector because of a critical essay he had written on the primary school system in the canton of Bern. His dismissal was a turning point in Gotthelf's life: from that point he became more and more isolated because of his political views.

In the wake of the 1831 ratification of a liberal constitution for the cantons, the political scene in Switzerland had become increasingly divided into liberal and conservative factions. Gotthelf had supported the liberal movement, but he fought against the radical government that revised the constitution in 1846. Critics have often maintained that Gotthelf started out as a liberal, turned into a conservative, and ultimately became a reactionary. This assessment is not entirely accurate. Gotthelf irritated conservatives and liberals alike with his views. For him, the French Revolution had accomplished *liberté* and *egalité* but not *fraternité.* This missing idea of Brüderlichkeit (brotherly love) was of utmost importance to him. Brotherly love meant for Gotthelf compassion and unselfishness and was part of a true Christian's duty. Without Brüderlichkeit there could not be genuine freedom and equality. His address to the participants in a shooting contest in Chur in 1842, *Eines Schweizers Wort an den schweizerischen Schützenverein* (A Swiss's Plea to the Swiss Rifle Club, 1842), depicts America as the embodiment of political extremism and anarchic freedom. At the other end of the spectrum, the Russian monarchy represents the arbitrariness of despotism. His own concept of genuine freedom was based on respect for the rights of the individual and was linked to his conception of Christianity as embracing all aspects of life.

Until 1833 the number of inns in the canton of Bern had been restricted to 431, but a new law permitted anybody who was willing to pay the required registration fee to set one up. The number of inns grew at a tremendous rate, and alcoholism became a topic of heated debate. Gotthelf responded with his novel *Der Geltstag oder Die Wirtschaft nach der neuen Mode* (The Bankruptcy; or, The Inn according to the Latest Fashion, 1845). Most of the novel takes place on the day the widow Eisi has to sell the furniture and equipment of the inn that belonged to her and her alcoholic husband, Steffen. The description of the auction is interspersed with flashbacks that inform the reader about the unhappy marriage of the couple. After the auction Steffen's godfather takes Eisi and her children to live on his farm. Eisi has learned nothing from her bad experiences, and at the end she enters into a new marriage that is unlikely to be more successful than the old one.

In addition to depicting one of the darker sides of rural life, the novel criticizes radical political ideas and misguided liberal policies. In the emerging capitalism, with its emphasis on the generation of profit, Gotthelf saw a new irrational force at work; in *Der Geltstag* he sharply criticizes the practice of lending money at excessive interest rates. The novel exposes the reader to the battle between the old order based on Christian values and the new secular age. *Der Geltstag,* however, does not offer the hope that these two worlds can be reconciled.

Jakobs, des Handwerksgesellen, Wanderungen durch die Schweiz (Jakob the Journeyman's Travels through Switzerland, 1846–1847) is Gotthelf's only novel with a German as the principal character. The idealistic socialist Jakob sets out to hike from Germany through Switzerland to Paris, but he does not reach his destination; while working for a master craftsman in Meiringen, he loses his faith in socialist ideas, and he returns in the end to the grandmother he left behind in the first chapter. The narrative architecture of the novel is perfectly symmetrical: the first fifteen chapters recount Jakob's journey through Switzerland; in the sixteenth chapter he reaches the lowest point in his development, finding himself sick and disappointed in a hospital in Geneva; the last fifteen chapters tell of his healing process, ending with his becoming a master craftsman. In *Jakobs, des Handwerksgesellen, Wanderungen durch die Schweiz* the dichotomy of old and new is present again: Jakob's grandmother is the representative of God's order, and the protagonist is an agent of the modern zeitgeist until he gives up his erroneous political ideas and becomes a Christian.

The tension between tradition and innovation is the central theme of the novel *Käthi die Großmutter oder Der wahre Weg durch jede Noth: Eine Erzählung für das Volk* (Käthi the Grandmother; or, The True Path through All Misery, 1847; translated as *The Story of an Alpine Valley; or, Katie the Grandmother,* 1896). Käthi embodies the old-fashioned way of life of preindustrial times; her motto is *ora et labora* (pray and work), the title of the thirteenth chapter. In contrast to the seemingly emancipated and enlightened citizens of the modern constitutional state who avail themselves of life insurance and government support, she still believes in God as the provider. Käthi supports herself by spinning flax, but new machines in spinning mills threaten her livelihood. Gotthelf's solution is to have Käthi work for customers who prefer handmade linens; thus, he attempts to reconcile the new ways of production and trade with the old order of manual labor.

In a sequel to *Wie Uli der Knecht glücklich wird,* titled *Uli der Pächter: Ein Volksbuch* (Uli the Tenant Farmer: A Book for the People, 1849), Uli is the representative of modern capitalism, a parvenu who listens to the advice of untrustworthy friends. The

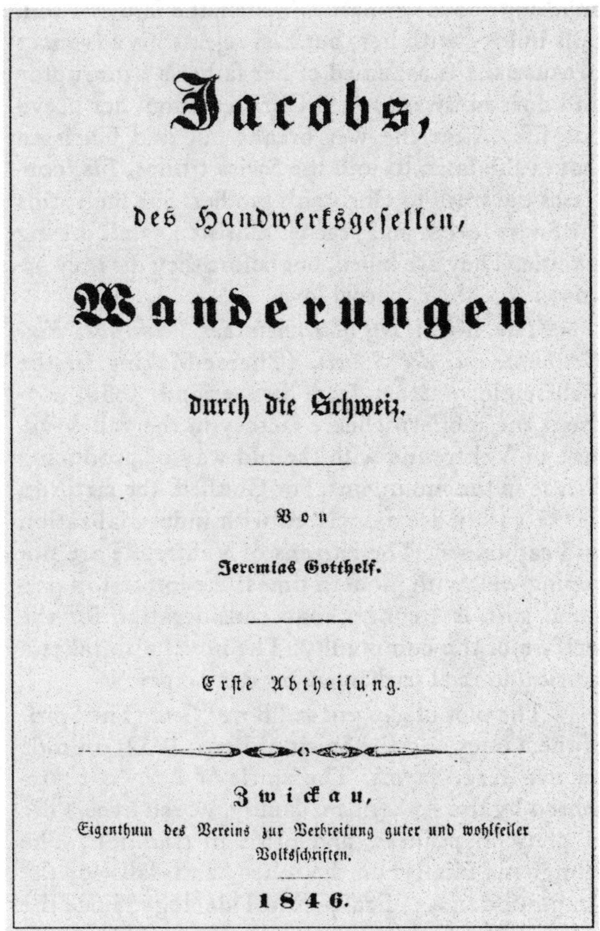
Jacobs,

des Handwerksgesellen,

Wanderungen

durch die Schweiz.

Von

Jeremias Gotthelf.

Erste Abtheilung.

Zwickau,

Eigenthum des Vereins zur Verbreitung guter und wohlfeiler Volksschriften.

1846.

Title page for the first volume of Gotthelf's only novel with a German as the principal character

farm he has leased falls on hard times, and he needs to be reminded by his wife, Vreneli, of the old ethics of prayer and labor and of the necessity to put his trust in God. Hagelhans, Vreneli's father, is the couple's savior: He buys the farm and asks them to stay with him. Hagelhans is one of Gotthelf's most intriguing characters, on the one hand equipped with archaic qualities and reminiscent of a mythological giant – a similar character is the hunter Benedicht Wehrdi in *Leiden und Freuden eines Schulmeisters* – and on the other hand open to progress and innovation.

The five volumes of *Erzählungen und Bilder aus dem Volksleben der Schweiz* (Stories and Images from the Life of the People of Switzerland, 1850–1855) contain several tales of courtship. One of the best-known stories, "Elsi, die seltsame Magd" (1850; translated as "Elsi the Unusual Farm Maid," 1984), is set in 1796 against the historical background of the French invasion of the Swiss cantons. Elsi works as a maid on a farm for a family that does not know anything about her past. Christen, the farmer's son, falls in love with her; but Elsi rejects his advances because she is ashamed of her father's bankruptcy and does not want to tell Christen about her previous life. After the war breaks out and Christen leaves the farm to join the Swiss troops, Elsi confesses the truth to Christen's mother. She then joins the Swiss forces and reaches Christen's unit during a battle. They are killed, but before they die they acknowledge their mutual love.

The novel *Die Käserei in der Vehfreude: Eine Geschichte aus der Schweiz* (Cheese-Making in the Vehfreude: A Story from Switzerland, 1850) contrasts the modern cheese factory in the valley village of Vehfreude with the old way of producing cheese in the mountains. For Gotthelf, the factories in the valley are associated with industrialization and capitalism. The citizens of Vehfreude are not coping well with modern times: the interest in personal gain is stronger than consideration for the welfare of the community. The novel also takes a satirical look at parliamentary democracy.

The plot of *Zeitgeist und Berner Geist* (The Spirit of the Times and the Spirit of Bern, 1852) unfolds on two large farms. The spirit of Bern is represented by the Ankenbenz family, which lives a life of piety, happiness, and pride in tradition. The Hunghans family, on the other hand, falls for the temptation of a radical political ideology. Since the two families had long been friends, in the end the Ankenbenzes come to the rescue of the impoverished Hunghanses. A bitter attack on the Radical government that had been elected by the people of the canton of Bern in 1846, the novel is largely responsible for the image of Gotthelf as a reactionary. It contains many exaggerated claims and false predictions of future political developments: for Gotthelf the Radicals were the Antichrist, and he maintains in *Zeitgeist und Berner Geist* that the constitutional state will be replaced by a state based on Christian values. Although Gotthelf felt that *Zeitgeist und Berner Geist* was his best work, it did not sell well because of its aggressive tone. The novel leaves no doubt that the new and the old, the progressive and conservative forces, the secular and religious ways of life are irreconcilable, and no attempt is made to reach a harmonious solution.

Disappointed by the poor reception of *Zeitgeist und Berner Geist,* Gotthelf 's publisher convinced him to try to win back his audience with another novel. *Erlebnisse eines Schuldenbauers* (Experiences of a Farmer in Debt, 1853), about a simple-minded peasant couple who fall prey to speculators and lose a farm they could not afford in the first place, was supposed to accomplish this task. Gotthelf 's health, however, was deteriorating rapidly: since 1851 he had been plagued by heart pains, coughing attacks, swollen feet, shortness of breath, and dropsy. In the early hours of 22 October 1854 he died of a lung hemorrhage resulting from a severe case of pneumonia.

Many mourners attended his funeral, but some newspapers opposed to his political views notified their readers about his death with brief and in some cases even sarcastic announcements. Gotthelf was buried on the south side of his church in Lützelflüh.

Gotthelf was passionate, hot-tempered, and sometimes unfair. He was certainly not the philistine his early biographers and critics made him out to be. He possessed a great instinct for the zeitgeist and for the innovations and changes that occurred during his lifetime. It sounds strange to the modern reader that schools, hospitals, and banks should have anything to do with Christian beliefs; to Gotthelf, however, the connection was quite apparent.

Bibliographies:

Wolfgang Mieder, "Jeremias Gotthelf Bibliography," *Bulletin of Bibliography and Magazine Notes,* 31 (July-September 1974): 89-95;

Bee Juker and Gisela Martorelli, *Jeremias Gotthelf 1797-1854 (Albert Bitzius): Bibliographie 1830-1975, Gotthelfs Werk – Literatur über Gotthelf* (Bern: Burgerbibliothek, 1983).

Biographies:

Carl Manuel, *Albert Bitzius* (Berlin: Springer, 1858); republished as *Jeremias Gotthelf: Sein Leben und seine Schriften* (Erlenbach & Zurich: Rentsch, 1922);

Gabriel Muret, *Jérémie Gotthelf: Sa vie et ses oeuvres* (Paris: Alcan, 1913);

Rudolf Hunziker, *Jeremias Gotthelf* (Frauenfeld & Leipzig: Huber, 1927);

Friedrich Seebass, *Jeremias Gotthelf: Pfarrer, Volkserzieher und Dichter* (Giessen & Basel: Brunnen, 1954).

References:

Mario Andreotti, *Das Motiv des Fremden im Werke Gotthelfs: Eine Untersuchung anhand ausgewählter Interpretationen* (Thal: Vetter, 1975);

John S. Andrews, "The Reception of Gotthelf in British and American Nineteenth-Century Periodicals," *Modern Language Review,* 51 (October 1956): 543-555;

Winfried Bauer, *Jeremias Gotthelf: Ein Vertreter der geistlichen Restauration der Biedermeierzeit* (Stuttgart: Kohlhammer, 1975);

Hermann Bausinger, "Sitte und Brauch: Zu Jeremias Gotthelfs Erzählung 'Die schwarze Spinne,' " *Deutschunterricht,* 14, no. 2 (1962): 100-114;

Reinhold Buhne, *Jeremias Gotthelf und das Problem der Armut* (Bern: Francke, 1968);

Karl Fehr, *Jeremias Gotthelf (Albert Bitzius),* second enlarged edition (Stuttgart: Metzler, 1985);

Fehr, *Jeremias Gotthelf: Poet und Prophet – Erzähler und Erzieher: Zu Sprache, dichterischer Kunst und Gehalt seiner Schriften* (Bern: Francke, 1986);

J. R. Foster, "Jeremias Gotthelf," in *German Men of Letters,* volume 5, edited by Alex Natan (London: Wolff, 1969), pp. 229-248;

Ernst Gallati, *Jeremias Gotthelfs Gesellschaftskritik* (Bern: Lang, 1970);

Robert Godwin-Jones, *Narrative Strategies in the Novels of Jeremias Gotthelf* (New York: Lang, 1986);

Hans Göttler, *Der Pfarrer im Werk Jeremias Gotthelfs: Ein Beitrag zur Stellung des Geistlichen in der Literatur der Biedermeierzeit* (Bern: Lang, 1979);

Kurt Guggisberg, *Jeremias Gotthelf: Christentum und Leben* (Zurich & Leipzig: Niehans, 1939);

Werner Günther, *Jeremias Gotthelf: Wesen und Werk* (Berlin: Schmidt, 1954);

Steffen Höhne, *Jeremias Gotthelf und Gottfried Keller im Lichte ethnologischer Theorien* (Bern: Francke, 1989);

Hanns Peter Holl, *Gotthelf im Zeitgeflecht: Bauernleben, industrielle Revolution und Liberalismus in seinen Romanen* (Tübingen: Niemeyer, 1985);

Holl, *Jeremias Gotthelf: Leben, Werk, Zeit* (Zurich & Munich: Artemis, 1988);

Ricarda Huch, *Jeremias Gotthelfs Weltanschauung* (Bern: Francke, 1917);

Glyn Tegai Hughes, " 'Die schwarze Spinne' as Fiction," *German Life and Letters,* 9 (1955-1956): 250-260;

Klaus Jarchow, *Bauern und Bürger: Die traditionale Inszenierung einer bäuerlichen Moderne im literarischen Werk Jeremias Gotthelfs* (Frankfurt am Main: Lang, 1989);

Ueli Jaussi, *Der Dichter als Lehrer: Zur parabolisch-didaktischen Struktur von Gotthelfs Erzählen* (Bern: Haupt, 1978);

Bee Juker, *Wörterbuch zu den Werken von Jeremias Gotthelf* (Erlenbach & Zurich: Rentsch, 1972);

R. E. Keller, "Language and Style in Jeremias Gotthelf 's 'Die schwarze Spinne,' " *German Life and Letters,* 10 (1956): 2-13;

Ulrich Knellwolf, *Gleichnis und allgemeines Priestertum: Zum Verhältnis von Predigtamt und erzählendem Werk bei Jeremias Gotthelf* (Zurich: Theologischer Verlag, 1990);

Urs Küffer, *Jeremias Gotthelf: Grundzüge seiner Pädagogik: Untersuchungen über die Fehlformen der Erziehung* (Bern: Haupt, 1982);

Walter Laederach, ed., *Führer zu Gotthelf und Gotthelfstätten* (Bern & Munich: Francke, 1954);

Katherine M. Littell, *Jeremias Gotthelf 's "Die Käserei in der Vehfreude": A Didactic Satire* (Bern: Lang, 1977);

Maclaren Meehl, "Some Features of Authorial Presence in the Prose Narratives of Albert Bitzius," in *Studies in Swiss Literature,* edited by Manfred Jurgensen (Brisbane: University of Queensland Press, 1971), pp. 14-21;

Walter Muschg, *Gotthelf: Die Geheimnisse des Erzählers* (Munich: Beck, 1931);

Muschg, *Jeremias Gotthelf: Eine Einführung in seine Werke* (Bern: Francke, 1960);

Michael H. Parkinson, *The Rural Novel: Jeremias Gotthelf, Thomas Hardy, C. F. Ramuz* (Bern: Lang, 1984);

Roy Pascal, "Jeremias Gotthelf (1797-1854)," in his *The German Novel* (Toronto: University of Toronto Press, 1956), pp. 101-142;

Roger Paulin, "Jeremias Gotthelf," in *Zur Literatur der Restaurationsepoche 1815-1848: Forschungsreferate und Aufsätze,* edited by Jost Hermand and Manfred Windfuhr (Stuttgart: Metzler, 1970), pp. 263-284;

Jamie Rankin, "Spider in a Frame: The Didactic Structure of 'Die schwarze Spinne,' " *German Quarterly,* 61 (Summer 1988): 403-418;

Max Schweingruber, *Die Namen in Gotthelfs Werken* (Burgdorf: Amtsersparniskasse Burgdorf, 1990);

Friedrich Sengle, "Zum Wandel des Gotthelfbildes," *Germanisch-Romanische Monatsschrift,* 7 (1957): 244-253;

Christian Thommen, *Jeremias Gotthelf und die Juden* (Bern: Lang, 1991);

H. M. Waidson, *Jeremias Gotthelf: An Introduction to the Swiss Novelist* (Oxford: Blackwell, 1953);

Waidson, "Jeremias Gotthelf 's Reception in Britain and America," *Modern Language Review,* 43 (April 1948): 223-238.

Waidson, "Jeremias Gotthelf, the Swiss Novelist," *German Life and Letters,* 3 (1949-1950): 92-106;

Papers:

The Gotthelf Archive is at the Bürgerbibliothek (City Library) in Bern, Switzerland.

Christian Dietrich Grabbe

(11 December 1801 - 12 September 1836)

Dwight A. Klett
Rutgers University

BOOKS: *Dramatische Dichtungen: Nebst einer Abhandlung über die Shakspearo-Manie,* 2 volumes (Frankfurt am Main: Hermann, 1827) – includes in volume 2, *Scherz, Satire, Ironie und tiefere Bedeutung: Ein Lustspiel in drei Aufzügen,* translated by Maurice Edwards as *Jest, Satire, Irony and Deeper Significance: A Comedy in Three Acts,* in *From the Modern Repertoire: Series Two,* edited by Eric Bentley (Bloomington: Indiana University Press, 1952), pp. 1–42; translated by Barbara Wright as *Comedy, Satire, Irony and Deeper Meaning: A Play in 3 Acts* (London: Gaberbocchus, 1955);

Don Juan und Faust: Eine Tragödie in vier Akten (Frankfurt am Main: Hermann, 1829); translated by Edwards as *Don Juan and Faust: A Tragedy in Four Acts,* in *The Theater of Don Juan: A Collection of Plays and Views, 1630–1963,* edited by Oscar Mandel (Lincoln: University of Nebraska Press, 1963), pp. 331-397;

Die Hohenstaufen: Ein Cyclus von Tragödien, 2 volumes (Frankfurt am Main: Hermann, 1829–1830);

Napoleon oder Die hundert Tage: Ein Drama in fünf Aufzügen (Frankfurt am Main: Hermann, 1831); excerpts translated by Max Spalter as *Napoleon; or, The Hundred Days,* in his *Brecht's Tradition* (Baltimore: Johns Hopkins Press, 1967), pp. 213–235;

Hannibal: Eine Tragödie (Düsseldorf: Schreiner, 1835);

Aschenbrödel: Dramatisches Mährchen (Düsseldorf: Schreiner, 1835);

Das Theater zu Düsseldorf mit Rückblicken auf die übrige deutsche Schaubühne (Düsseldorf: Schreiner, 1838);

Die Hermannsschlacht: Drama (Düsseldorf: Schreiner, 1838);

Christian Dietrich Grabbe's sämmtliche Werke: Erste Gesammtausgabe, 2 volumes, edited by Rudolf Gottschall (Leipzig: Reclam, 1870);

Christian Dietrich Grabbe's sämmtliche Werke und handschriftlicher Nachlaß: Erste kritische Gesammtausgabe, 4 volumes, edited by Oskar Blumenthal (Detmold: Meyer, 1874);

Christian Dietrich Grabbe; 1836 crayon portrait by Wilhelm Pero (Wallraf-Richartz-Museum, Cologne)

Grabbes Werke, 6 volumes, edited by Spiridion Wukadinowic (Berlin: Bong, 1912);

Werke und Briefe: Historisch-kritische Gesamtausgabe, 6 volumes, edited by Alfred Bergmann (Emsdetten: Lechte, 1960–1973);

Werke, 3 volumes, edited by Roy C. Cowen (Munich: Hanser, 1975).

OTHER: Edward Hartenfels, *Grupello: Historische Novelle,* introduction by Grabbe (Düsseldorf: Forberg, 1840);

Der Cid: Große Oper in zwei bis fünf Akten, music by Norbert Burgmüller, in *Moderne Reliquien,* volume 1, edited by Arthur Mueller (Berlin: Gumbrecht, 1845), pp. 151-182.

From the outset of his brief literary career Christian Dietrich Grabbe believed that he was writing not for his own time but for the future. And indeed, the despair, the often nihilistic attitude toward life, and the radical dissatisfaction with society that pervade his dramatic oeuvre ran counter to the idealistic trend of the day and, not surprisingly, met with little contemporary approval. Consequently, Grabbe was a complete literary and social outsider; plagued by constant trouble and disappointment, he witnessed the staging of only one of his plays, had difficulty in finding publishers for his works, and never found acceptance in any of the leading literary circles. Not until half a century after his death – after Germany had endured an unsuccessful revolution, the rise of industry with its attendant social and political problems, and a subsequent turn away from idealism – was Grabbe "discovered" by a new breed of socially, politically, and artistically disenchanted authors who sought inspiration in his realistic portrayals of the world and all its ills, his explosive expressions of feeling, his natural and unaffected language, and his utter disregard for everything that bourgeois society holds dear. These authors were aligned with such literary movements as naturalism, expressionism, and absurdism, which have at their root the very antitraditionalism and disregard for the Establishment displayed by Grabbe in the bulk of his works. From the standpoint of literary history, then, Grabbe belongs to a line of revolutionary dramatists whose beginning can be traced to the German Storm and Stress movement, which was itself an attack on the bourgeois optimism and rationalism of the Age of Enlightenment.

In the years preceding his rediscovery Grabbe was not forgotten by the literary world, but instead of his works it was his troubled life that usually stood in the forefront. For many, including Heinrich Heine, Grabbe represented the prototypical author of "Zerrissenheit" (confusion, inner strife); his life of drunkenness and debauchery, much of which was consciously played up by Grabbe to conform to his reputation as enfant terrible, reinforced this evaluation. Not least through Grabbe's own doing, as Roy Cowen points out, a Grabbe legend arose that influenced the interpretation of his works – particularly by critics of the positivistic camp, for whom an author's life and works are two sides of the same coin. Only recently did literary scholarship succeed in freeing Grabbe's oeuvre from this legend. Many literary works have been written about him, including Hanns Johst's drama *Der Einsame* (The Solitary Man, 1917); poems by Johannes Bobrowski, Wulf Kirsten, and Volker Braun; and Thomas Valentin's novel *Grabbes letzter Sommer* (Grabbe's Last Summer, 1980).

Born in the provincial town of Detmold in the Duchy of Lippe on 11 December 1801, Grabbe was the only child of Adolf Heinrich and Dorothea Friederike (Grütemeier) Grabbe. The stage for his bizarre life seems to have been set by the circumstances surrounding his early childhood. He grew up within the confines of the Detmold city prison, where his father was warden – an emotionally and intellectually deprived environment that later caused him to remark with characteristic self-irony: "Was soll aus einem Menschen werden, dessen erstes Gedächtnis das ist, einen alten Mörder in freier Luft spazierengeführt zu haben!" (What is to become of a person whose first memory is of taking an old murderer out for a walk in the fresh air!)

Grabbe did receive a solid education, thanks to the constant scrimping and saving of his doting lower-middle-class parents. In 1807 he entered the public school in Detmold; in 1812 he transferred to the local gymnasium. During his school years Grabbe demonstrated a particular interest in history, which was to form the basis of many of his dramas; in literature he read everything he could lay his hands on, especially the works of William Shakespeare. He also began to visit the theater in Detmold and to try his hand at his own dramatic works. The products of this early experimentation – *Theodora* and *Der Erbprinz* (The Successor to the Throne) – have been lost. Their existence is known only through Grabbe's correspondence with the publisher G. S. Göschen, who turned down *Theodora*, as well as through the accounts of his biographer Karl Ziegler.

In 1820 Grabbe enrolled at the University of Leipzig, where he studied law, especially legal history, to prepare himself for the position of archivist for the Duchy of Lippe. In Leipzig he met Georg Ferdinand Kettembeil, who was to become his first publisher. In 1822 Grabbe transferred to the University of Berlin. Berlin held a great attraction for Grabbe because of its famous theater, where he saw the celebrated actor Ludwig Devrient in such roles as that of Shylock in Shakespeare's *The Merchant of Venice*. Also, in 1822 he completed his first two extant works, *Herzog Theodor von Gothland* (Duke Theodore of Gothland, 1827) and *Scherz, Satire, Ironie und tiefere Bedeutung* (1827; translated as *Jest, Satire, Irony and Deeper Significance*, 1952).

Grabbe; engraving by F. X. Stöber after a drawing by Theodor Hildebrandt

Herzog Theodor von Gothland is a tragedy in five acts whose conception dates back to Grabbe's schooldays in Detmold. The product of an untutored and inexperienced talent, it is an uneven work characterized by logical flaws in its plot, unmotivated actions on the part of many characters, and scenes so bombastic as to be unstageable. Yet with its impassioned, often obscene language and its deeply felt emotions, its extreme violence rivaling that of Shakespeare's *Titus Andronicus,* and its penchant for such themes as fratricide and cannibalism, it attacks the meaning and value of human existence in a manner and with an intensity never before witnessed in modern German literature.

Central to the play is a situation that would recur in Grabbe's works: the titanic struggle between two great warlords – the African Berdoa, ruler over the heathen Finns, and Gothland, leader of the Christian Swedes. The bloody war between their armies is at its root an elemental conflict between good and evil in which Gothland's initial idealism, hope, and sense of morality are steadily eroded by the intrigues of Berdoa, a despiser of all humanity. At the end only hate, moral debasement, and a nihilistic attitude toward God and all of existence remain.

The parallels between this play and Johann Wolfgang von Goethe's *Faust* (1808, 1832) cannot be overlooked, except that in Grabbe's work the good succumbs to the Mephistophelean principle. As many critics have pointed out, *Herzog Theodor von Gothland* is a reflection of Grabbe's disillusionment. Like so much of what he was to write later, it is a testament to his lack of idealism and to his belief in an absurd world devoid of divine justice and salvation – a world in which even great men like Gothland must come to recognize and accept their fallibility and their ultimate insignificance.

The reactions of those who read the manuscript for *Herzog Theodor von Gothland* were mixed.

Heine expressed admiration for the dramatic devices employed by Grabbe, calling him "ein betrunkener Shakespeare" (a drunken Shakespeare); but, like Rahel von Varnhagen, the center of a prominent literary salon in Berlin, he objected to the work's cynicism and brutality. Such opinions were repeated by the eminent Romantic poet and theater director Ludwig Tieck, to whom Grabbe had sent a copy of the manuscript in the vain hope of receiving a favorable judgment with which he could impress potential publishers.

Grabbe turned to Tieck not only for patronage but also for literary inspiration, using the latter's successful comedy *Der gestiefelte Kater* (1797; translated as *Puss in Boots,* 1913) as a model for his three-act comedy *Scherz, Satire, Ironie und tiefere Bedeutung.* His best and most frequently translated and performed work, it is, despite being influenced by Tieck, not at all an homage to Romantic literature but a vehement rejection of Romantic values and of idealism in general. It espouses the same weltanschauung as *Herzog Theodor von Gothland* but achieves its goal in a much more subtle manner, replacing graphic violence, blood, and horror with an effective combination of slapstick comedy and black humor. The main characters are the Devil, sent to earth while his young, vivacious grandmother gives hell a thorough spring cleaning; a perpetually drunken schoolmaster and his dim-witted student; and Grabbe himself, who appears at the end of the piece only to be ridiculed as a "zwergigte Krabbe" (diminutive crab) with an "Affengesicht" (monkeylike face) by the characters he created.

The aim of this work, aside from parodying themes of Romantic literature propagated by the untalented epigones of such "real" Romantics as Tieck and August Wilhelm and Friedrich Schlegel, is to show up the world as a second-rate comedy devoid of reason, logic, and significance. Whereas Tieck's comedy satirizes the overly rigid and rationalistic systems of enlightened thought and art and seeks to replace them with an idealistic philosophy based on intuition and creativity, Grabbe's *Scherz, Satire, Ironie und tiefere Bedeutung* negates all schools of thought and leaves the unsettled audience with a philosophical void. Humanity is a minor character trapped in an absurd play: that is the tragicomic "deeper significance" of *Scherz, Satire, Ironie und tiefere Bedeutung* and of most of his ensuing works.

Life in the cultural mecca of Berlin not only inspired Grabbe to continue writing but also to abandon his legal studies in 1823 in favor of an acting career. But despite letters of recommendation from Tieck, he could find no stage work in Leipzig, Dresden, Brunswick, Hannover, or Bremen. Pressed for money, he had no alternative but to return to his dreaded hometown – a place, he once wrote, "wo man einen gebildeten Menschen für einen verschlechterten Mastochsen hält" (where an educated person is considered a kind of inferior fatted ox). In Detmold, Grabbe spent several months in wild debauch before pulling himself together sufficiently to pass the bar examination in 1824. He then opened a small legal practice and was successful in garnering many, albeit mostly petty, cases. He soon replaced his reputation as a drunken carouser with that of a sober and serious, if not teetotaling, worker. In September 1826 he was recommended by Christian Gottlieb Clostermeier, an old family friend, to be the latter's successor as archivist of the Duchy of Lippe – a position for which Grabbe had prepared himself in college but which, for inexplicable reasons, he was never offered. He then received, on the recommendation of Christian von Meien, a government official, the position of assistant to the Auditeur (officer of military justice) in Lippe. After the Auditeur's death a year later, Grabbe was named his successor.

Between 1823 and 1826 Grabbe completed only one work, *Nannette und Maria* (1827), an uninspired three-act tragedy set in Italy. Many of the problems dealt with in *Herzog Theodor von Gothland* resurface here, but in grossly watered-down form as a halfhearted concession to the popular stage.

In 1827 Kettembeil, Grabbe's college friend, inherited the Hermann publishing house in Frankfurt am Main and offered to print his works. For an edition to be titled *Dramatische Dichtungen* (Dramatic Works, 1827), Grabbe submitted *Herzog Theodor von Gothland; Scherz, Satire, Ironie und tiefere Bedeutung; Nannette und Maria;* and *Marius und Sulla,* a tragedy in three acts begun in 1823 but never completed, even though Grabbe had taken up work on it again after Kettembeil's offer.

This fragment reveals a distinct maturation of Grabbe's dramatic technique. In contrast to *Herzog Theodor von Gothland,* the characters are much more rounded and believable, and, most important, the plot is much smoother and more homogeneous and is no longer motivated simply by raw emotions but also by historical fact. The drama portrays the struggle between two great Roman leaders, Marius and Sulla, for control over the remains of a crumbling civilization. The historical conflict is depicted less to bring the past to life than to show the moral, ethical, and psychological development of two heroic figures in a time of crisis – figures who, through their will, influence, and power, just as

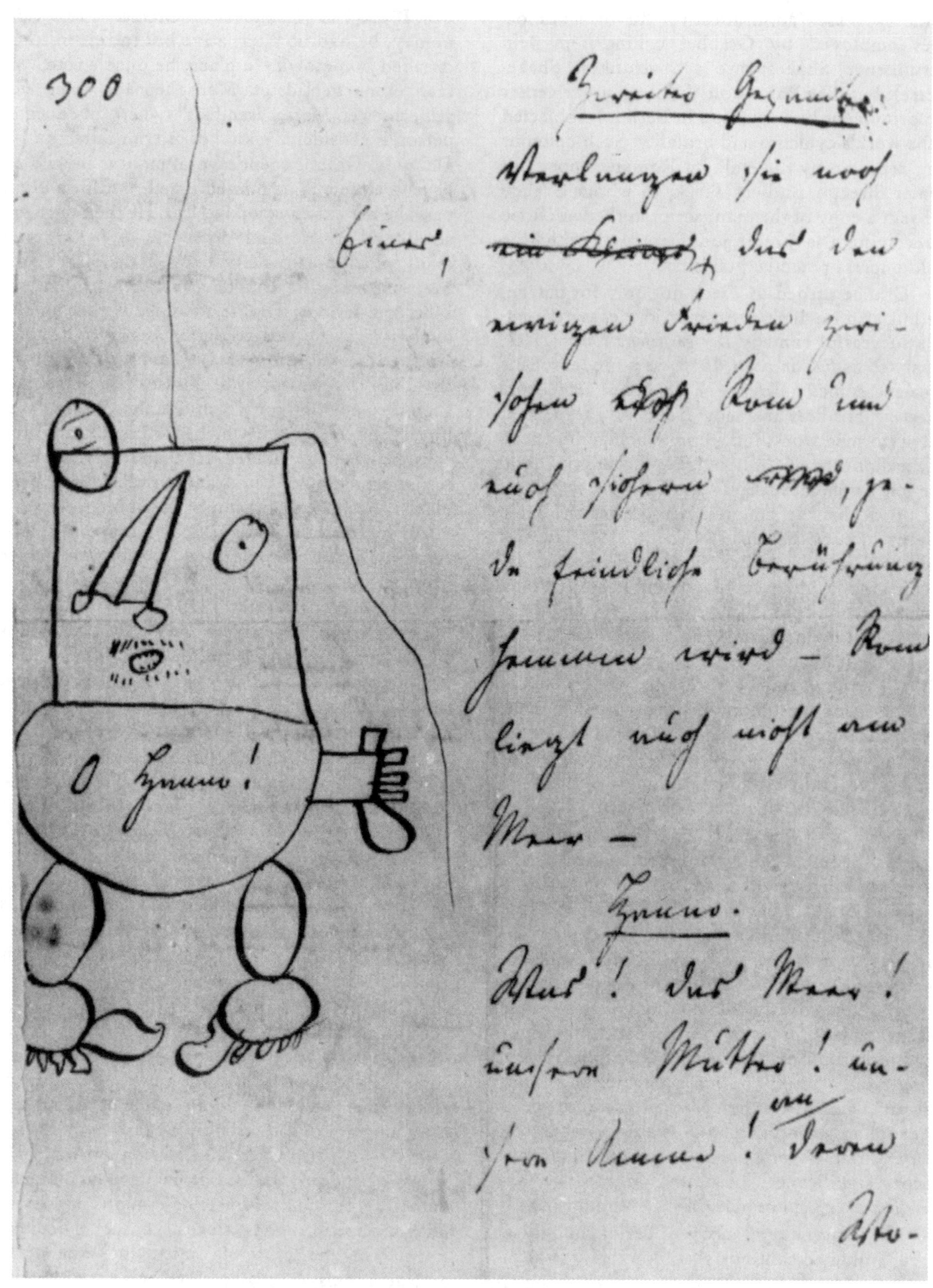

Front and back of a leaf from the manuscript for a draft of Grabbe's tragedy Hannibal *(Lippische Landesbibliothek, Detmold)*

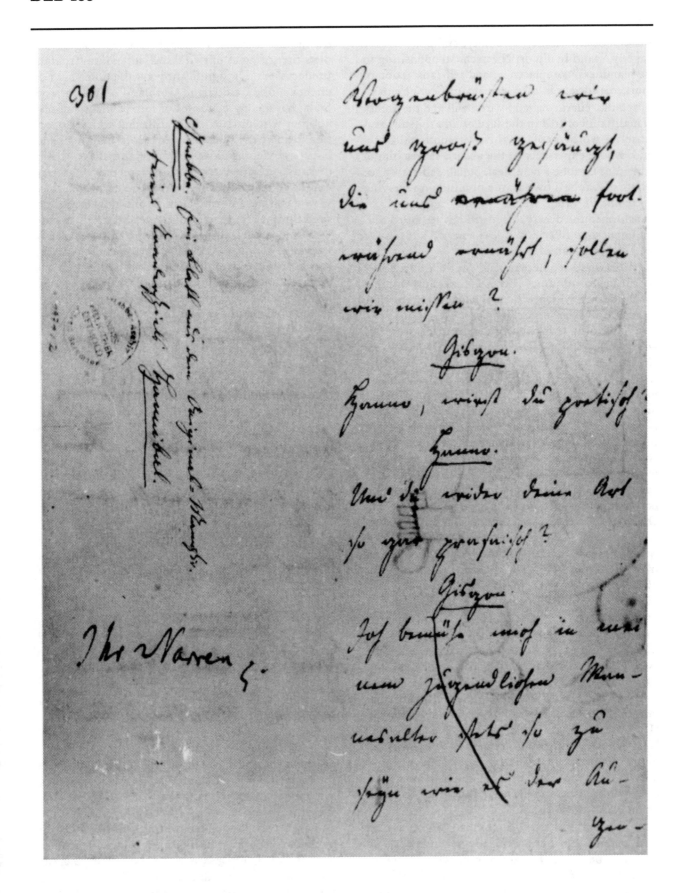

through their humility, fallibility, and potential for tragedy, stand in almost Nietzschean opposition to the blandness, complacency, and self-satisfaction of bourgeois society in the Germany of Grabbe's day.

Sulla, characterized by iron will and the ability to maintain control in the face of an arbitrary and senseless world, replaces the overemotional Gothland, whose experience of the absurd causes him to shatter, as Grabbe's new ideal. Sulla's self-assurance mirrors Grabbe's own frame of mind on receiving Kettembeil's offer, which – if only temporarily – transformed the dreary, disgusted lawyer into a self-confident man filled with ideas, energy, and, above all, a definite plan of literary action.

The first step in that plan was the essay "Über die Shakspearo-Manie" (On the Mania Surrounding Shakespeare), which was completed just in time for inclusion in *Dramatische Dichtungen*. While it is not Grabbe's only critical work – theatrical reviews were collected as *Das Theater zu Düsseldorf mit Rückblicken auf die übrige deutsche Schaubühne* (The Theater in Düsseldorf with Reference to the German Stage at Large, 1835) – it is the one that is most frequently read. Initially a discussion of imperfections in Shakespeare's plays, the essay deteriorates into a diatribe against authors, such as the German Romantics and especially their epigones, who had modeled their works after those of Shakespeare and had thereby stifled their own creative powers just as society thwarts those of its great leaders by enforcing the herd mentality. Grabbe may have written "Über die Shakspearo-Manie" as a warning against his own all-too-frequent borrowing from the Bard. As such, the essay – like the figure of Sulla – would point to the type of strong-willed, inspired, and independent author Grabbe hoped to represent.

Complete independence from literary models was something Grabbe never truly achieved, however. The next three dramas published by Kettembeil, *Don Juan und Faust* (1829; translated as *Don Juan and Faust,* 1963) and – under the collective title *Die Hohenstaufen – and Kaiser Friedrich Barbarossa,* (1829) and *Kaiser Heinrich der Sechste* (Kaiser Heinrich the Sixth, 1830), remain heavily indebted to both Shakespeare and German Romanticism not only in their focus on great figures from medieval history but also in their strict adherence to traditional blank-verse forms.

The best known of these three works is *Don Juan und Faust.* A four-act tragedy begun as early as 1823 and performed to mixed reviews in Detmold on 29 March 1829 with incidental music by Albert Lortzing, it was Grabbe's only drama to be staged during his lifetime. Although this work again depicts the struggles of two titans, it deviates from its predecessors in a significant way: the titans are not enemies, like Berdoa and Gothland or Marius and Sulla, but merely opposites or mirror images of one another who pursue vastly different courses of action to solve the same problem. Both Don Juan and Faust are victims of weltschmerz: they have grown dissatisfied with the goals and interests of society and have rejected everyday existence, which they view as intolerable and absurd, and now must find something to fill the resulting void. Don Juan, the witty and carefree Latin lover, constantly seeks new women to conquer. In Grabbe's portrayal, however, it is not love or even desire that motivates him but the need for the greatest possible variety of earthly pleasures. For him, this variety is the only antidote to boredom and, therefore, the only thing that lends meaning to his life.

The magician Faust, by contrast, eschews the ephemeral as a source of answers to existential questions and, in keeping with his melancholy Germanic demeanor as well as his romantic idealism, looks toward the total transcendence of earthly life in his search for a suitable reason for being. But in the end both the spiritualist Faust and the hedonist Don Juan fall victim to the Devil, who kills Faust after the latter enters into the pact with him and who banishes Don Juan to hell as punishment for his lecherous life-style. In Grabbean terms, this startling conclusion demonstrates that human beings, no matter how powerful, can never define the meaning of existence. There is always a truth higher than anything humanity can conjure up; that truth is Satan in this drama, fate in many of Grabbe's other works. People are constantly pushed back into a state of absurdity from which they cannot escape, regardless of the mode of existence they choose to pursue – a bitter lesson that seems to emerge directly from Grabbe's own disappointing experiences.

Such depressing thoughts are reiterated to a large extent in *Kaiser Friedrich Barbarossa* and *Kaiser Heinrich der Sechste,* whose protagonists pursue paths of honor and unscrupulousness, respectively, in hopes of achieving worldly fame and influence. At the moment when these men believe that their chosen modes of existence have resulted in success, they are struck down by forces greater than they and are thereby reminded of the absurdity inherent in their all-too-human lives. That these tragedies lack the originality and spontaneity of *Don Juan und Faust* may be attributable to their adherence to historical fact. Grabbe planned the works not only as the beginning of a cycle of eight dramas on the Hohenstaufen dynasty but also as the first step toward a new German national theater totally independent of all foreign influences, including Shakespeare.

The other six Hohenstaufen tragedies never materialized, for Grabbe soon shifted his emphasis from medieval history to the contemporary scene, which at that time was characterized by revolutionary fervor throughout Europe. By late 1829 this shift was apparent in Grabbe's work on a drama centering around the second reign of Napoleon and a completed four-act comedy, *Aschenbrödel* (Cinderella, 1835), a parody of the Grimm fairy tale heavily spiked with literary and social satire in the manner of *Scherz, Satire, Ironie und tiefere Bedeutung*. Grabbe submitted the comedy to his friend Kettembeil in 1830, but the latter, much to Grabbe's surprise and dismay, rejected it.

Kettembeil's sudden lack of sympathy for Grabbe marks the end of the author's exuberant and self-confident period of literary creativity that commenced in 1827. While he continued to be productive, Grabbe no longer approached his writing projects with such enormous vigor; for example, a play about the Polish freedom fighter Tadeusz Kosciuszko never made it beyond a fragmentary one and a half acts. But the deteriorating relations with Kettembeil cannot alone be held accountable for this state of affairs, for Grabbe also experienced great and often debilitating personal difficulties during this period.

His attempts to balance an active writing schedule with his heavy work load as Auditeur took their toll in increased alcohol consumption; he was also subject to severe nervous attacks and the persistent spitting of blood. These ills were compounded by frequent bouts of depression, by a fractured arm in 1829 that healed improperly, by gout, and by the bite of a dog. He also had a great deal of misfortune in his relationships with women. In 1829 he became engaged to Luise Clostermeier, ten years older than he and the daughter of the family friend who had unsuccessfully recommended Grabbe for archivist of Lippe. Constant quarreling soon resulted in breaking off the engagement. Heartbroken, Grabbe quickly plunged into a relationship with Henriette Meyer, a simple girl who had no understanding for his writing and who found it difficult to cope with his self-acknowledged mad way of life. She left Grabbe in 1831, and he began wooing Clostermeier anew. She finally agreed to marry him, and the wedding took place in March 1833. The marriage pitted a highly unorthodox and free-thinking artist against a domineering and insensitive representative of bourgeois uniformity in a tragicomic manner reminiscent of Grabbe's own works.

The miserable period from late 1829 to 1834 yielded only one dramatic work, the five-act *Napoleon oder Die hundert Tage* (translated as *Napoleon; or, The Hundred Days,* 1967), which appeared in 1831 as the last effort published by Kettembeil. Napoleon, an independent, charismatic individual, seeks, as Grabbe did himself, to rise above the faceless masses. This great man, a product of specific historical forces who is driven by an extreme will to power, is consumed by the very times that created him; his greatness must ultimately bow before the pettiness and mediocrity of society – the same mediocrity that, in Grabbe's estimation, gave rise to the vilification of his own highly unconventional oeuvre.

What sets this work apart from its predecessors is the modernity of the dramatic devices it employs. It is the first of Grabbe's dramas written entirely in prose – a prose that is revolutionary for the German stage, for it mimics exactly the everyday speech of individuals from a variety of social backgrounds. Characters speak as they would in real life, not in conventional stage German with its stiffness and affectation. This language lends *Napoleon* a measure of realism and directness normally associated with German naturalism. So believable is Grabbe's prose with its expressionistic power, its terseness, and even its occasional choppiness that it makes the history surrounding Napoleon's second ascent to power come to life on the stage, particularly in the mass scenes that are a Grabbe trademark. Every word spoken in the play, whether by proletarians, soldiers, or the great Corsican himself, transmits something of the electrifying spirit of Napoleonic times – a spirit that was quenched in Germany by the political lethargy, complacency, and general mediocrity of the reactionary Biedermeier establishment that reigned from 1815 to 1848.

In 1834 the myriad of problems that had afflicted Grabbe both personally and professionally since 1829 came to a head. Violent quarrels with his wife, erupting into public brawls, prompted suicide threats on his part; his health, already frail, began to decline even further, making him look like a wizened old man although he was only in his early thirties. Together with his poor health, his job as Auditeur, which he often described as being intensely boring, brought Grabbe to the verge of total mental and physical collapse and widened the rift between him and society.

It was in this dejected and disgruntled state that he wrote the five-act tragedy *Hannibal* (1835), which has often been described as the most personal of his works. Hannibal, perhaps the loneliest of all Grabbean heroes, temporarily protects Carthage from foreign domination but is eventually crushed by the Roman war machine, which symbolizes the thoughtlessness and soullessness of the modern world that Grabbe held responsible for his suffering. It is a lonely, brutal world in which Hannibal, like Grabbe and his earlier protagonists, including Napoleon, feels that he has stumbled into a mediocre comedy in which all human efforts are reduced to meaninglessness. This message is underscored by the drama's language, which is devoid of emotion and instead takes the form of the blunt ejaculations typified later by expressionism and absurdism.

Grabbe grew so weary of "das verwünschte Detmold" (that accursed Detmold) that early in 1834 he resigned from his position as Auditeur and, with no means of support and without his wife, embarked on a trip to Frankfurt am Main to begin a new literary career unfettered by the dictates of society. His first stop in Frankfurt was the house of his publisher, Kettembeil, to whom he offered *Hannibal.* But the publisher demanded extensive revisions; unwilling to bow to these requirements, which he viewed as a further extension of society's constant thwarting of personal freedom and individuality, Grabbe broke off all ties to Kettembeil.

Penniless, Grabbe solicited the aid of acquaintances in an attempt to get his career as an independent writer off the ground. Karl Immermann, a dramatist and director of the city theater in Düsseldorf, had met Grabbe several years earlier in Detmold and viewed him as a promising, albeit somewhat disturbed, young author. In December 1834 Immermann invited Grabbe to Düsseldorf, providing him with a small room, work as a copyist, and most important, a new publisher, J. H. C. Schreiner. Although Grabbe's health was in ruins – he needed several glasses of rum to come to life in the morning – Immermann was able to motivate him to revise *Aschenbrödel* and *Hannibal,* both of which were published by Schreiner in 1835. Grabbe even mustered enough energy to write several pieces of literary criticism, as well as an operatic parody centering on the Spanish national hero, El Cid (1845). Additionally, he began planning a comedy on the renowned chapbook character Till Eulenspiegel, tragedies dealing with Alexander the Great and Jesus Christ, and a play about the German patriot Arminius, or Hermann, who defeated the Roman general Varus in the watershed Battle of the Teutoburg Forest in A.D. 9.

Grabbe; lithograph by W. Severin after a lost drawing by Wilhelm Joseph Heine

Of all these dramatic projects, only the one dealing with Arminius came to fruition; it was not published until 1838, after Grabbe's death. *Die Hermannsschlacht* (The Battle of Hermann) is written in prose like *Napoleon* and the revised *Hannibal,* but it lacks their explosive language and, most significantly, their well-defined, realistic, and thoroughly modern characters. Despite shared thematic elements and a similar weltanschauung, of the historical plays written in prose *Die Hermannsschlacht* is by far Grabbe's weakest effort; its poor quality is no doubt attributable to his bad health. But one significant idea does emerge from this work: that Arminius, while he was as great a figure in his time as Napoleon was later, had little impact on the course of world history. His efforts to rally the German tribes into a national force failed because the Germans could not conceive of the concept of unity. Arminius was a man with a good idea who was ahead of his time. He fought alone in the face of an ignorant, selfish mob and was destined to be understood only by future generations who could recognize the importance of his goals and rescue his memory from oblivion. This final play manifests Grabbe's lifelong belief that he himself was ahead of his time: that his dramas, with their emphasis on individuality and on the transcendence of the mundane Biedermeier ethic of his day, could only be appreciated in the future, after society had liberated itself from all normative systems of thought and action.

By 1836 Grabbe had grown disenchanted with Immermann's attempts to introduce order into his existence, and he began to distance himself from his mentor. He sought solace in drink, spending most of his time and money in Düsseldorf's many taverns. After the death of his drinking partner, a minor musician named Norbert Burgmüller who had written the score for his opera about El Cid, Grabbe returned in the spring of 1836 to Detmold and to a wife who shunned him. In his hometown Grabbe took up residence in a tavern to finish *Die Hermannsschlacht,* apparently nourishing himself only with alcohol. When the work was completed in July, his health was so poor that he was forced to return to his wife's home, to which he gained access only with assistance from the police. It was there that he died, not yet thirty-five years of age, on 12 September 1836. No one of importance attended his funeral. In Grabbe's diary an entry seems to summarize his existence in a world with which he was doomed to be at odds: "Wär' ich todt, es wär' mir lieb, lebt' ich nie, es wäre besser" (If I were dead, I would be glad, but it would be better to have never lived at all).

Bibliographies:

Alfred Bergmann, *Grabbe-Bibliographie* (Amsterdam: Rodopi, 1973);

Klaus Nellner, ed., "Grabbe-Bibliographie," *Grabbe-Jahrbuch,* 1- (1982-).

Biographies:

Eduard Duller, "Grabbe's Leben," in Grabbe's *Die Hermannsschlacht: Drama* (Düsseldorf: Schreiner, 1838), pp. 3-91;

Karl Ziegler, *Grabbe's Leben und Charakter* (Hamburg: Hoffmann & Campe, 1855);

Alfred Bergmann, *Christian Dietrich Grabbe 1801–1836: Sein Leben in Bildern* (Leipzig: Bibliographisches Institut, 1936);

Bergmann, *Christian Dietrich Grabbe: Chronik seines Lebens 1801-1836* (Detmold: Tölle, 1954).

References:

Alfred Bergmann, *Die Glaubwürdigkeit der Zeugnisse für den Lebensgang und Charakter Christian Dietrich Grabbes: Eine quellenkundliche Untersuchung* (Berlin: Ebering, 1933);

Bergmann, *Grabbe als Benutzer der öffentlichen Bibliothek in Detmold* (Detmold: Privately printed, 1965);

Bergmann, *Grabbe in Berichten seiner Zeitgenossen* (Stuttgart: Metzler, 1968);

Bergmann, "Grabbeforschung und Grabbeprobleme 1918–1934," *Germanisch-Romanische Monatsschrift,* 22 (1934): 343-357, 437-457;

Oskar Blumenthal, *Nachträge zur Kenntniß Grabbe's: Aus ungedruckten Quellen* (Berlin: Grote, 1875);

Fritz Böttger, *Grabbe: Glanz und Elend eines Dichters* (Berlin: Verlag der Nation, 1963);

Werner Broer and Detlev Kopp, eds., *Christian Dietrich Grabbe (1801–1836): Ein Symposium* (Tübingen: Niemeyer, 1987);

Roy C. Cowen, *Christian Dietrich Grabbe* (New York: Twayne, 1972);

Cowen, "Grabbe's *Don Juan and Faust* and Büchner's *Dantons Tod*: Epicureanism and *Weltschmerz,*" *PMLA,* 82 (October 1967): 342–351;

Cowen, "Grabbe's Napoleon, Büchner's Danton, and the Masses," *Symposium,* 21 (1967): 316–323;

Cowen, "Satan and the Satanic in Grabbe's Dramas," *Germanic Review,* 39 (March 1964): 120–136;

Ernst Diekmann, *Christian Dietrich Grabbe: Der Wesensgehalt seiner Dichtung* (Detmold: Meyer, 1936);

Lothar Ehrlich, *Christian Dietrich Grabbe: Leben, Werk, Wirkung* (Berlin: Akademie-Verlag, 1983);

Winfried Freund, ed., *Grabbes Gegenentwürfe: Neue Deutungen seiner Dramen. Zum 150. Todesjahr Christian Dietrich Grabbes* (Munich: Fink, 1986);

Paul Friedrich and Fritz Ebers, eds., *Das Grabbe-Buch* (Detmold: Meyer, 1923);

Helga-Maleen Gerresheim, "Christian Dietrich Grabbe," in *Deutsche Dichter des 19. Jahrhunderts: Ihr Leben und Werk,* second edition, edited by Benno von Wiese (Berlin: Schmidt, 1979), pp. 229–254;

Martin Greiner, *Zwischen Biedermeier und Bourgeoisie* (Göttingen: Vandenhoeck & Ruprecht, 1953);

Wolfgang Hegele, *Grabbes Dramenform* (Munich: Fink, 1970);

A. W. Hornsey, *Idea and Reality in the Dramas of Christian Dietrich Grabbe* (Oxford: Pergamon Press, 1966);

David Horton, " 'Die Menge ist eine Bestie': The Role of the Masses in Grabbe's Dramas," *German Life and Letters,* new series 35 (October 1981): 14–27;

Horton, " 'Die verselnden Ketten': The Development of Grabbe's Dramatic Language," *Mod-*

ern Language Review, 79 (January 1984): 97–113;

Dwight A. Klett, "The Autobiographical and Critical Function of the 'Schulmeister' in Christian Dietrich Grabbe's *Scherz, Satire, Ironie und tiefere Bedeutung,*" *Essays in Literature,* 16 (Spring 1989): 141–148;

Detlev Kopp, *Geschichte und Gesellschaft in den Dramen Christian Dietrich Grabbes* (Frankfurt am Main & Bern: Lang, 1982);

Richard Kuehnemund, *Arminius or the Rise of the National Symbol: From Hutten to Grabbe* (Chapel Hill: University of North Carolina Press, 1953);

Fritz Martini, "Grabbes niederdeutsches Drama," *Germanisch-Romanische Monatsschrift,* 30 (1942): 87–106, 153–171;

Edward McInnes, "Christian Dietrich Grabbe," in his *Das deutsche Drama des 19. Jahrhunderts* (Berlin: Schmidt, 1983), pp. 63–74;

McInnes, "Grabbe und das Geschichtsdrama," *Grabbe-Jahrbuch,* 1 (1982): 17–24;

McInnes, " 'Die wunderlose Welt der Geschichte': Grabbe and the Development of the Historical Drama in the 19th Century," *German Life and Letters,* 32 (January 1979): 104–114;

Roger A. Nicholls, *The Dramas of Christian Dietrich Grabbe* (The Hague & Paris: Mouton, 1969);

Hans-Werner Nieschmidt, *Brecht und Grabbe: Rezeption eines dramatischen Erbes* (Detmold: Grabbe-Gesellschaft, 1979);

Nieschmidt, *Christian Dietrich Grabbe: Zwei Studien* (Detmold: Schnelle, 1951);

Otto Nieten, *Christian Dietrich Grabbe: Sein Leben und seine Werke* (Dortmund: Ruhfus, 1908);

Carl Anton Piper, *Beiträge zum Studium Grabbes* (Munich: Haushalter, 1898);

Maria Porrmann, *Grabbe, Dichter für das Vaterland: Die Geschichtsdramen auf deutschen Bühnen im 19. Jahrhundert* (Lemgo: Wagener, 1982);

Ferdinand Josef Schneider, *Christian Dietrich Grabbe: Persönlichkeit und Werk* (Munich: Beck, 1934);

Fritz Siefert, *Christian Dietrich Grabbes Geschichtsdramen* (Bad Godesberg: Privately printed, 1957);

Max Spalter, *Brecht's Tradition* (Baltimore: Johns Hopkins Press, 1967);

Margaret Anne Sutherland, *The Reception of Grabbe's Hannibal in the German Theater* (Frankfurt am Main, Bern & New York: Lang, 1984);

Michael Vogt, *Literaturrezeption und historische Krisenerfahrung: Die Rezeption der Dramen Christian Dietrich Grabbes 1827–1945* (Frankfurt am Main & Bern: Lang, 1983);

Benno von Wiese, *Von Lessing bis Grabbe: Studien zur deutschen Klassik und Romantik* (Düsseldorf: Bagel, 1968).

Papers:

The Grabbe Archive is at the Lippische Landesbibliothek (Lippe State Library), Detmold.

Franz Grillparzer

(15 January 1791 --21 January 1872)

Hinrich C. Seeba
University of California, Berkeley

BOOKS: *Die Ahnfrau: Ein Trauerspiel in fünf Aufzügen* (Vienna: Wallishausser, 1817); translated by Letitia Elizabeth Landon as *The Ancestress: A Dramatic Sketch,* in her *The Venetian Bracelet, The Lost Pleiad, A History of the Lyre, and other Poems* (London: Longman, Rees, Orme, Brown & Green, 1828);

Sappho: Trauerspiel in fünf Aufzügen (Vienna: Wallishausser, 1819); translated by John Bramsen as *Sappho: A Tragedy, in Five Acts* (London: Black, 1820);

Das goldene Vließ: Dramatisches Gedicht in drei Abtheilungen (Vienna: Wallishausser, 1822) – comprises *Der Gastfreund*; *Die Argonauten*; *Medea*; *Medea* translated by F. W. Thurstan and Sidney A. Wittmann as *Medea: A Tragedy* (London: Nisbet, 1879); entire work translated by Arthur Burkhard as *The Golden Fleece* (Yarmouth Port, Mass.: Register, 1942) – comprises *The Guest-Friend*; *The Argonauts*; *Medea*;

König Ottokar's Glück und Ende: Trauerspiel in fünf Aufzügen (Vienna: Wallishausser, 1825); translated by Henry H. Stevens as *King Ottocar, His Rise and Fall* (Yarmouth Port, Mass.: Register, 1938);

Ein treuer Diener seines Herrn: Trauerspiel in fünf Aufzügen (Vienna: Wallishausser, 1830); translated by Burkhard as *A Faithful Servant of His Master* (Yarmouth Port, Mass.: Register, 1941);

Melusina: Romantische Oper in drei Aufzügen, music by C. Kreutzer (Vienna: Wallishausser, 1833);

Des Meeres und der Liebe Wellen: Trauerspiel in fünf Aufzügen (Vienna: Wallishausser, 1840); translated by Stevens as *Hero and Leander* (Yarmouth Port, Mass.: Register, 1938);

Der Traum ein Leben: Dramatisches Mährchen in vier Aufzügen (Vienna: Wallishausser, 1840); translated by Stevens as *A Dream Is Life* (Yarmouth Port, Mass.: Register, 1946);

Franz Grillparzer; painting by Heinrich Hollpein, 1836 (Österreichische Nationalbibliothek)

Weh' dem, der lügt!: Lustspiel in fünf Aufzügen (Vienna: Wallishausser, 1840); translated by Stevens as *Thou Shalt Not Lie* (Yarmouth Port, Mass.: Register, 1939);

Sämmtliche Werke, 10 volumes, edited by Heinrich Laube and Josef Weil (Stuttgart: Cotta, 1872) – includes in volume 6, *Esther: Dramatisches Bruchstück,* translated by Burkhard as *Esther,* in *The Jewess of Toledo; Esther* (Yarmouth Port, Mass.: Register,

1953); *Libussa: Trauerspiel in fünf Aufzügen* translated by Stevens as *Libussa* (Yarmouth Port, Mass.: Register, 1941); in volume 7, *Ein Bruderzwist in Habsburg: Trauerspiel in fünf Aufzügen,* translated by Burkhard as *Family Strife in Hapsburg* (Yarmouth Port, Mass.: Register, 1940); *Die Jüdin von Toledo: Historisches Trauerspiel in fünf Aufzügen,* translated by George Henry Danton and Annina P. Danton as *The Jewess of Toledo,* in *The German Classics of the Nineteenth and Twentieth Centuries,* volume 6, edited by Kuno Francke and William Guild Howard (New York: German Publication Society, 1913), pp. 337–408; in volume 8, "Der arme Spielmann," translated by A. Remy as "The Poor Musician," in *The German Classics of the Nineteenth and Twentieth Centuries,* volume 6, pp. 409–454; in volume 10, "Selbstbiographie (1791–1836)," excerpt translated by Remy as "My Journey to Weimar," in *The German Classics of the Nineteenth and Twentieth Centuries,* volume 6, pp. 455–463;

Sämmtliche Werke, 16 volumes, edited by August Sauer (Stuttgart: Cotta, 1887);

Sämtliche Werke: Historisch-kritische Ausgabe, 42 volumes, edited by Sauer and Reinhold Backmann (Vienna: Gerlach & Wiedling, 1909–1916; Vienna: Schroll, 1916–1948);

Sämmliche Werke: Ausgewählte Briefe, Gespräche, Berichte, 4 volumes, edited by Peter Frank and Karl Pörnbacher (Munich: Hanser, 1960–1965);

Dichter über ihre Dichtungen: Franz Grillparzer, edited by Pörnbacher (Munich: Heimeran, 1970);

Tagebücher und Reiseberichte, edited by Klaus Geißler (Berlin: Verlag der Nation, 1980);

Sämtliche Werke: Text und Kommentar, 6 volumes, edited by Helmut Bachmaier (Frankfurt am Main: Deutscher Klassiker Verlag, 1986–1993).

Neither Romantic nor purely realist, Franz Grillparzer has been difficult to place in the established periods of literary historiography. The foremost Austrian writer in the nineteenth century, a time when Austrian literature was trying to define its own identity separate from the rest of literature written in German, Grillparzer soon came to serve as the Austrian classic, comparable only to Johann Wolfgang von Goethe and Friedrich Schiller, the twin heralds of German classicism. He himself unabashedly says in his "Selbstbiographie" (Autobiography, 1872; excerpt translated as "My Journey to Weimar," 1913), written in 1853, that "ich mich nämlich denn doch, trotz allem Anstande, für den Besten halte, der nach ihm [Goethe] und Schiller gekommen ist" (I consider myself, in all due respect, the best who has come after him [Goethe] and Schiller). To many anxious observers who had witnessed the collapse of European Enlightenment into Viennese gemütlichkeit, Grillparzer, who dealt with topics from Greek mythology in classical form, represented the literary counterpart to the musical classicism of Joseph Haydn and Ludwig van Beethoven. Grillparzer would eventually command the unqualified respect of critics within and outside Austria for combining the musicality of Viennese folklore, the tragedic genre of classical antiquity, and the quest for a distinctly Austrian history. He endowed the form of classical drama with a psychological depth that anticipates the discovery of the unconscious by Sigmund Freud two generations later. He has been credited by Claudio Magris with creating the "Hapsburg myth," the myth of an idealized imperial dynasty that helped integrate the multiethnic Austro-Hungarian Empire in the face of growing nationalism. The disintegration of the Soviet Empire has given new political significance to the Hapsburg myth, which is believed by some to have inspired the Eastern European countries' drive for independence, and has drawn new attention to Grillparzer, the major literary advocate of the myth.

In his 1837 essay "Worin unterscheiden sich die österreichischen Dichter von den übrigen?" (In Which Way Are Austrian Writers Different from Others?) Grillparzer defined an Austrian brand of German literature based on what he perceived as virtues of the Austrian character: "Bescheidenheit, gesunder Menschenverstand, und wahres Gefühl" (modesty, common sense, and true feeling). Always contrasting German and Austrian attitudes, Grillparzer saw as underlying art not so much the strain of philosophical reflection he found and detested in the German followers of Friedrich von Schlegel and Georg Wilhelm Friedrich Hegel as the images that enlivened his imagination ever since a maid introduced him as a boy to the wonders of Wolfgang Amadeus Mozart's opera *Die Zauberflöte* (The Magic Flute, 1791). Trying to define a specifically Austrian identity without giving in to the excesses of nationalism that increasingly threatened the survival of the Austrian empire, Grillparzer performed a balancing act that secured his reputation as an Austrian classic. In literary histories Grillparzer is usually classified as a "Biedermeier" writer. The Biedermeier period extended from the Congress of Vienna in 1815 to the March Revolutions of 1848 and is characterized by the idyllic por-

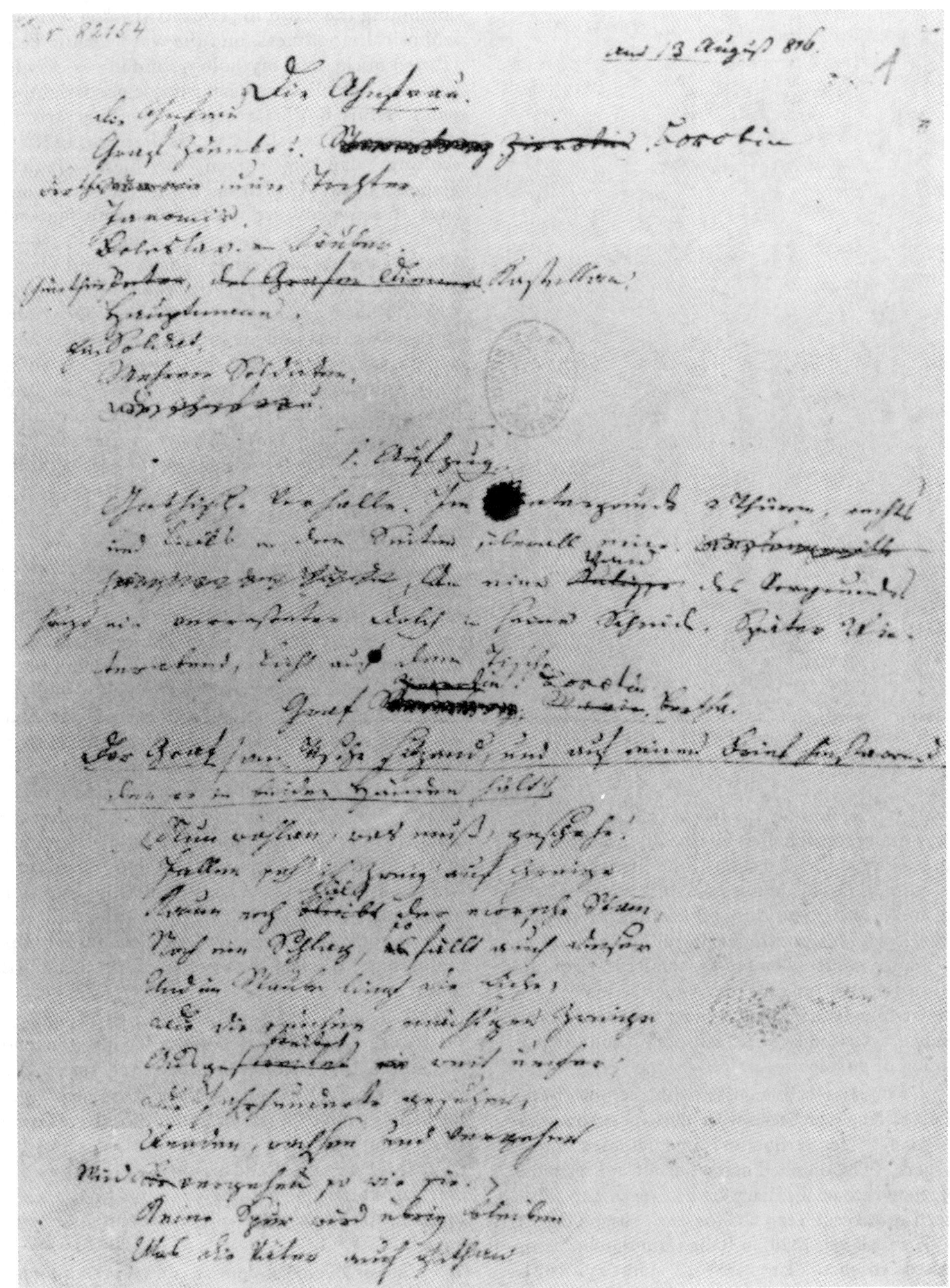

First page of the manuscript for Grillparzer's play Die Ahnfrau *(Österreichische Nationalbibliothek)*

Grillparzer's "eternal bride," Katharina Fröhlich, in 1838; watercolor by Anton Hähnisch (from Grillparzer's Tagebücher und Reiseberichte, *edited by Klaus Geißler, 1981)*

trayal of the private sphere of salons, waltzes, happy bourgeois families, and neatly framed landscapes. The political reality of the time, however, was quite different. In the wake of Napoleon's defeat at Waterloo the Austrian chancellor, Prince Wenzel von Metternich, fearing all political or social change modeled on the French Revolution, established at the Congress of Vienna the thirty-nine-state German Confederation and a system of repression characterized by strict censorship and the persecution of dissidents.

Grillparzer's fascination with the power and pitfalls of language began with uneasiness about his own name: "Der verfluchte Name hat mich immer geärgert" (The damned name has always irritated me), he wrote in his diary on 21 December 1831. After Lord Byron read Grillparzer's drama *Sappho* (1819; translated, 1820) in Italian translation, he remarked in his diary for 12 January 1821: "Grillparzer – a devil of a name, to be sure, for posterity, but they *must* learn to pronounce it." For a long time the name was believed to be a pseudonym combining the word for crickets (*Grillen*), evoking whimsical moodiness, and the word for the Fates (*Parzen*) of classical mythology, and it was easy for critics to ridicule the aspiring tragic playwright. Johann Heinrich Voss reacted to Grillparzer's *Die Ahnfrau* (1817; translated as *The Ancestress,* 1828) by scoffing "daß die Parzen, die diese Tragödie gesponnen, eitel Grillen sind" (that the Fates which spun this tragedy are nothing but vain fantasy). After *Die Ahnfrau* was successfully staged at Goethe's theater in Weimar to mark the birthday of Duchess Luise in February 1819, Karl Ludwig von Knebel remarked in a letter to Goethe: "Der Name ist etwas ominös und die Musen scheinen ihn eben nicht eingesegnet zu haben" (The name is somewhat ominous and the Muses do not seem to have blessed it). The plays on Grillparzer's "devilish" name were not limited to his own time: in John Irving's novel *The World according to Garp* (1978) the name sounds so amusing to Garp that he uses it to signify a dance as well as having sex ("to Grillparzer").

The latter use of his name is rather ironic in that Grillparzer's own relationships with women were generally unhappy. He was in love with his cousin's wife, Charlotte von Paumgartten; with Marie von Smolenitz, who married the painter Moritz Michael Daffinger; and, most notably, with his "ewige Braut" (eternal bride) Katharina Fröhlich, to whom he became engaged in 1821 but never married. Fröhlich eventually became his housekeeper, his nurse, and, finally, his sole heiress and literary executor. The dominant image of Grillparzer the man is that of a grumbling recluse, a gloomy loner – a "Raunzer" in untranslatable Viennese – whose outlook on life was as grim as his face in a photograph taken shortly before his death. It is a faithful portrait of a man whose potential for happiness was stifled by the severe restrictions of his time.

Grillparzer was born in Vienna on 15 January 1791 to the court lawyer Wenzel Grillparzer and Anna Franziska Grillparzer, née Sonnleithner. Following a family tradition, Grillparzer studied law at the University of Vienna from 1807 to 1811. In 1814, after brief assignments as a private tutor for an aristocratic family and an unpaid probationer in the court library, he became an administrator at the Imperial Archives; he would be appointed director in 1832.

The problem of identity is a recurring theme in Grillparzer's works. First performed on 31 January 1817 at the Theater an der Wien, *Die Ahnfrau* combines motifs of the Gothic tale, the fate tragedy, and robber and ghost stories to present a psychological study of the protagonist, Jaromir. It is Jaromir's "fate" to return unknowingly to the Bohemian castle of his ancestors as a robber; ignorant of his origin, he falls in love with his sister, Bertha, and kills their father, Count Borotin; only then does he learn who he really is. Grillparzer shows that one's identity can be established only by accepting one's history, even if it is a bloody family history that becomes visible as the image in a mirror of the vengeful ancestress, the ghostly "Ahnfrau," whose name was also Bertha.

The search for identity of an artist who is forced to relinquish her needs as a woman is the theme of *Sappho.* The poet takes the infatuation of the adolescent Phaon with Sappho the artist to be love for Sappho the woman. When she realizes that her jealousy has driven Phaon to a young girl, Melitta, she commits suicide by jumping from a high rock into the sea, thus creating the classical image of the artist who shuns life in favor of eternal fame: "Dort oben war mein Platz, dort an den Wolken, / Hier ist kein Ort für mich, als nur das Grab" (Up there is my place, there in the clouds. Here is no place for me but the grave). Grillparzer's play is ranked alongside Goethe's tragedy of an artist, *Torquato Tasso* (1790; translated, 1861), and Thomas Mann's depiction of the dichotomy of life and art in "Tonio Kröger" (1903; translated, 1914). The success of the first performance, at the Burgtheater on 21 April 1818, led to an audience with Chancellor Metternich and to Grillparzer's appointment as court playwright at an annual salary of two thousand gulden. His writing would often bring him into conflict with his role as a civil servant, with ever watchful censors probing the propriety of the views he expressed in literary form. Josef Schreyvogel, who had succeeded Grillparzer's uncle Josef von Sonnleithner as secretary of the Burgtheater in 1814, became his mentor and protector and would put several more of Grillparzer's plays on the Burgtheater stage.

Grillparzer's next attempt to deal with Greek antiquity was the trilogy *Das goldene Vließ* (1822; translated as *The Golden Fleece,* 1942), consisting of *Der Gastfreund* (translated as *The Guest-Friend*), *Die Argonauten* (translated as *The Argonauts*), and *Medea* (translated, 1879). Grillparzer juxtaposes two cultures, Greek and barbarian, and dismisses the very classicism whose images are invoked. Medea fails to suppress her wild instincts when she finds herself betrayed by her Greek husband, Jason. Unlike Sappho, Medea does not sacrifice her emotions to an idealized spirituality. In an excessive act of revenge she reaffirms her identity as a barbarian woman who will not allow herself to be "colonized" by a Greek man. The ideal of balanced harmony so much promoted in classical aesthetics is exploded. The trilogy is dedicated to Paumgartten, Grillparzer's cousin's wife, with whom Grillparzer was desperately in love at the time. The first two plays were first performed at the Burgtheater on 26 March 1821 and *Medea* the following night; later, *Medea* was usually performed without the other two plays.

Grillparzer's group of historical dramas begins with *König Ottokar's Glück und Ende* (1825; translated as *King Ottocar, His Rise and Fall,* 1938), a rather patriotic depiction of the beginning of the Hapsburg dynasty as it was recorded in the *Österreichische Reimchronik* (Austrian Rhyming Chronicle, 1318), by Ottokar von Steiermark and in the *Österreichischer Plutarch* (Austrian Plutarch, 1807–1814), by Josef von Hormayr. But as the ascent of Rudolf von Hapsburg to the throne in 1273 was bound to the decline of the Bohemian king Ottokar II, the censors were concerned about the nationalist sensitivities of the Slavic minority. Another concern was the obvious similarity between Ottokar, who divorces his wife, Margarethe, to marry the granddaughter of the just-defeated Hungarian king, Kunigunde, and Napoleon, who had celebrated his victory over Austria by replacing his wife, Josephine, with Marie-Louise, the daughter of Emperor Franz I of Austria; such a reminder of Austria's humiliation did not seem opportune only two years after Napoleon's death. The censors therefore refused the permit for the performance. Only the emperor himself could clear the way to the stage, and the play premiered at the Burgtheater on 19 February 1825. Grillparzer endorses Rudolf's pride in the eternal grandeur of his office: "Was sterblich war, ich hab es ausgezogen, / Und bin der Kaiser nur, der niemals stirbt" (What was mortal I have abandoned, / And am nothing but the emperor who never dies). Yet this emperor is lovingly portrayed as a human being who can be addressed as "Herr Kaiser," as if the title were a bourgeois name, and he gracefully asks a bourgeois woman not to bend her knee before him. Such folksy popularity joins with the claim to immortality to create the utopian Hapsburg myth that was to withstand the destructive forces of growing nationalism in the course of the nineteenth century..

Grillparzer was arrested in 1826 as a member of the writers' and artists' club Ludlamshöhle (Ludlam's Cave), which was falsely suspected of secretly promoting subversive ideas. Even though the

Program for the premiere at the Vienna Burgtheater of Grillparzer's play about the founding of the Hapsburg dynasty

charges were dropped, the incident proved to Grillparzer the arbitrariness of the repressive system. He escaped from this degrading experience by traveling to Germany to visit Ludwig Tieck in Dresden, Hegel in Berlin, and Goethe in Weimar.

The title of his next historical drama, *Ein treuer Diener seines Herrn* (1830; translated as *A Faithful Servant of His Master,* 1941), seems to invoke an idealized attitude that had outlived its social value. The subordination of a loyal servant to his master was the moral message the play was expected to convey at the coronation of the empress Karoline Auguste as queen of Hungary in Preßburg in September 1825. But Grillparzer refused such loyal service to the court and instead used his research in Ignaz Aurel Feßler's *Geschichte der Ungarn* (History of Hungary, 1812–1825) and Hormayr's *Österreichischer Plutarch* to write a psychological portrayal of the suffering victim of a political power game. Bancbanus, counselor to the Hungarian king Andreas II in the thirteenth century, proves himself a "Hüter der Ruhe" (guardian of calm), as if he were a civil servant in the Biedermeier period. While looking after the state's affairs during the absence of the king, he preserves an almost unreal sense of moral duty under extreme and most cruel pressure from the queen's brother, the unscrupulous Otto von Meran, who requires complete self-denial from Bancbanus and then exploits it. Gone mad from unrequited love, yet calculating the conquest with psychological acuity, Otto tries to seduce and humiliate Bancbanus's wife, Erny, who can remain faithful to her husband only by killing herself. Offering, as Grillparzer emphasized in his autobiography, not "eine Apologie der knechtischen Unterwürfigkeit" (a defense of servility) but "den Heroismus der Pflichttreue" (the heroism of responsibility), the play can be read as an indictment of the misuse of political power. The performance at the Burgtheater on 28 February 1828 was a great success – possibly too great a success for such a delicate subject. The emperor, who attended the first three performances, claimed to be so enthralled by the drama of loyalty that he wanted to be "alleiniger Besitzer desselben" (its sole owner) for a price to be determined by Grillparzer. But Grillparzer resisted the attempt at censorship through bribery by claiming that copies of the play were already circulating outside of Austria and were thus beyond his control. It is ironic that in writing and defending this drama of extreme loyalty, Grillparzer twice successfully withstood the pressure of becoming himself "der treue Diener seines Herrn."

Grillparzer had outlined his fifth Greek drama, *Des Meeres und der Liebe Wellen* (Waves of the Sea and of Love, 1840; translated as *Hero and Lean-*

Grillparzer (far right) at a meeting of the Ludlamshöhle, a Vienna writers' and artists' society that was shut down in 1826 by the police. Standing is the composer Carl Maria von Weber.

der, 1938), when he was revising *Das goldene Vließ* in the summer of 1820, but he completed his first two historical dramas before he took it up again in 1826. Grillparzer chose the peculiar title for his drama, which is based on the classical myth of Hero and Leander, to suggest the natural power of love and its deadly potential for those who are swept up by it. The romantic fairy tale of two lovers separated by the sea is presented mainly as a psychological profile of the young priestess, Hero, who awakens from the dreams of her childhood and begins a tragic search for an adult identity. Rather than devoting her life to the service of the goddess of love she becomes a loving woman, only to be severely punished for betraying her holy office: while she is asleep her lover, Leander, drowns when her uncle, the priest, puts out the lamp that was to guide Leander on his swim through the stormy seas of the Hellespont to join her. Due to the death of the actress who was to play Hero, *Des Meeres und der Liebe Wellen* did not premiere at the Burgtheater until 5 April 1831; it was not successful.

In *Der Traum ein Leben* (1840; translated as *A Dream Is Life,* 1946) the Biedermeier notion of "Ruhe" (calm) as the utmost virtue of a good citizen is the background for Rustan's escape into an exotic dream of action that turns so violent that he gladly returns to the reality of his unexciting, idyllic life of conformity: "Eines nur ist Glück hienieden, / Eins, des Innern stiller Frieden / Und die schuldbefreite Brust!" (Only one thing is happiness down here, / Only one: quiet peace inside / And a heart free of guilt!). After tasting the dangerous glamour of usurped power in the dream, he will never again stray from the proper path to private happiness. Based on Voltaire's story *Le Blanc et noir* (1764; translated into German in 1790) and adopting its title from Pedro Calderón de la Barca's *La vida es sueño* (1635), the play presents any attempt at political involvement as a nightmare. A dramatized psychoanalysis of a dream that acts out suppressed desires, the play also effectively reflects its own time of political suppression, censorship, torture, and murder: in the central scene a deaf-mute is so outraged about the system of lies and deceit that he miraculously regains the power of speech to identify Rustan as a murderer. But the fairy tale of Samarkand seemed too far removed in time and

Grillparzer in a photograph taken shortly before his death

space, and its moral too close to the dominant ideology, to arouse the suspicion of the authorities. It was successfully performed at the Burgtheater on 4 October 1834 and long remained a favorite on many stages.

In 1836 Grillparzer escaped from an unhappy love affair by taking a trip to Paris – where he met Alexandre Dumas, Ludwig Börne, and Heinrich Heine – and to London. During his stay in London he was introduced to Edward Bulwer-Lytton, but the author of *The Last Days of Pompeii* (1834) failed to recognize his colleague from Germany. Grillparzer bitterly remarked in his autobiography almost two decades later: "Wenn ein Deutscher nicht Goethe oder Schiller heißt, geht er unbekannt durch die ganze Welt" (If a German's name is not Goethe or Schiller, he wanders through the world unknown).

The last of Grillparzer's completed dramas to be performed during his lifetime was *Weh' dem, der lügt!* (1840; translated as *Thou Shalt Not Lie*, 1939). The performance of his sole comedy at the Burgtheater on 6 March 1838 was a devastating failure due to a mostly aristocratic audience that was offended by the character of the idiotic nobleman, Galomir, and the misalliance between a count's daughter and Leon, a mere cook. Leon's creative playfulness in mixing truth, white lies, and deceit is always well-intentioned and directed at the moral good. His employer, Bishop Gregor, asks Leon to free the bishop's nephew Attalus from imprisonment by Kattwald, an enemy count; but he makes Leon promise not to tell any lies in carrying out the task. While the man of the church has a dogmatic notion of truthfulness that does not allow for any linguistic ambivalence, the man of the palate enjoys the taste of his verbal concoctions and believes that the end justifies the means. He brings to his task an understanding of the cultural difference between the educated French, who know how to enjoy a good meal, and the barbaric Germans, who, like Count Kattwald, long to be educated in Western culture. In their quest for the art of cooking these savages let themselves be tricked into becoming servants to the irreverent foreigner, who, with his culinary and verbal charades, not only frees the bishop's nephew but also rescues Kattwald's daughter Edrita from an arranged marriage with Galomir. Based on the French translation of the sixth-century *Historia Francorum* of Gregory of Tours and set in the Middle Ages, this comedy is also a polemical pronouncement of Grillparzer's aesthetics directed against German critics of the Hegelian persuasion. In contrasting the principle of absolute truth with the reality of ambivalent language and perspectival truths, Grillparzer is implicitly arguing for the superiority of pragmatic, visual, and sensual perception, which he values as characteristically Austrian, over abstract ideas. But his inability to get his philosophical point across in the dramatic imagery of his comedy led him to withdraw completely from the stage: if he could not solve the problem of representing concepts through strong visual images, he would put his plans and sketches for new dramas aside.

Therefore, three major dramas that were outlined early but completed only after the failure of *Weh' dem, der lügt!* never reached the stage during Grillparzer's lifetime "weil ihnen jenes Lebensprinzip fehlt, das nur die Anschauung gibt und der Gedanke nie ersetzen kann" (because they lack the principle of life that lies only in visual perception and can never be replaced with thought), as he said in his diary in 1849. He had begun *Libussa* (1872; translated, 1872) in 1822 and *Ein Bruderzwist in Habsburg* (1872; translated as *Family Strife in Hapsburg*, 1940) in 1827; in his will of 1848 Grillparzer

Grillparzer in his coffin; charcoal drawing by Carl von Stur (Österreichische Nationalbibliothek)

ordered that both manuscripts be destroyed because he felt that they were nothing but conceptual debates in need of visual execution. The dramas undertake the enormous task of representing a historic shift of paradigm, from the mythical to the historical age symbolized in the founding of Prague in *Libussa,* and from medieval authority to the challenge of diversity on the eve of the Thirty Years' War in *Ein Bruderzwist in Habsburg.* The contrast between Libussa and Primislaus in the first drama and the fraternal quarrel between Emperor Rudolf II and Mathias in the second seem to be rationally constructed contests of ideas rather than visually imagined theatrical agons. The first drama is a nostalgic look at the waning power of poetic imagination in matriarchy, the second a warning against the advancing power of vulgar calculation that threatens the order of the world. In Rudolf's prophetic vision the future is ruled by the masses, who like a monster, destroy everything in their path: "Aus eignem Schoß ringt los sich der Barbar, / Der, wenn erst ohne Zügel, alles Große, / Die Kunst, die Wissenschaft, den Staat, die Kirche / Herabstürzt von der Höhe, die sie schützt, / Zur Oberfläche eigener Gemeinheit, / Bis alles gleich, ei ja, weil alles niedrig" (From its own womb breaks away the barbarian, / Who, when no longer reined, / Pulls everything that is great – art, science, state, church – From the protective height down to the surface of its own vulgarity, / Until everything is equal, yes, because everything is base). In these dramas a growing concern Grillparzer nurtured about himself is projected onto changes in history. In 1826 he noted in his diary: "Mein Gemüt verhärtet sich, meine Phantasie erkaltet" (My mind hardens, my imagination cools down). The passing on of power in these historical dramas symbolizes the loss of power, both personal and political, creative and authoritative. *Ein Bruderzwist in Habsburg* successfully premiered in two separate productions, at the Vienna Stadttheater under the direction of Heinrich Laube on 24 September 1872 and at the Burgtheater on 28 September 1872; *Libussa,* whose first act was performed in 1840, had its first complete and little-noticed performance at the Burgtheater on 21 January 1874.

The third drama Grillparzer withheld from the public was *Die Jüdin von Toledo* (1872; translated as *The Jewess of Toledo,* 1913). Based on Lope de Vega's drama *La Judia de Toledo* (1616), this tragedy of illicit love shows how the lure of sensuality undermines political power. The beautiful, spirited Jewess Rahel enters the forbidden royal garden to play the role of the queen in carnival costume and to draw the inexperienced King Alphons of Castile into a game of erotic obsession involving the exchange of pictures. But while Alphons eventually comes to his senses, reaffirming his identity as king and man, Rahel is murdered by the queen and her followers. It seems that Grillparzer is subjecting to moral judgment the very magic of poetic imagery that he tried to uphold in his aesthetic pronouncements. The violent ending of the play also marked Grillparzer's end as a writer: *Die Jüdin von Toledo* was the last drama he completed. It was first performed in Prague on 21 November 1872.

A playwright who can no longer rely on his dramatic imagination and therefore frantically searches for new material in real life is the narrator of Grillparzer's story "Der arme Spielmann" (1848; translated as "The Poor Musician," 1913), which is considered one of the masterpieces of German realism. The narrator's "anthropologischer Heißhunger" (insatiable anthropological curiosity) discovers Jakob, a poor, yet highly educated street fiddler, who is committed to his private religion of music. Like Grillparzer, Jakob is a loner on the margin of society who failed to bring order to his unhappy life. While telling the narrator about his life, he succeeds in imposing order on it. The fiddler's sentimental story becomes a portrayal of alienation in the Biedermeier era on the eve of the revolution of March 1848. The fiddler dies in one of the frequent Danube floods which, in the opening frame of the narrative, is associated with a possible revolution.

Escapism was a trademark of the Biedermeier era, with its exotic travels abroad and its musical soirées at home; Grillparzer escaped into the fantasies of his asocial mind as his creative powers increasingly failed him. The constant battles against suspicion and mediocrity and the lack of support and recognition from his superiors at the archives eventually rendered him an embittered and unproductive hypochondriac. Not only did he never submit any of his later plays to the theater but he only agreed to have his earlier plays performed again after Laube became director of the Burgtheater in 1849. As he confessed in his autobiography, Grillparzer fell into a lifelong depression when he realized "daß unter diesen Umständen in dem damaligen Österreich für einen Dichter kein Platz sei" (that under the circumstances of Austria at the time there was no place for a writer). But unlike Heinrich von Kleist, who had found himself in a similar predicament in Prussia, Grillparzer – whose mother and youngest brother had committed suicide – did not give in to the temptation to take his own life. He lived to receive, with characteristic skepticism, the honors bestowed on him. He was appointed a member of the newly founded Austrian Academy of Science by Metternich in 1847, was named Hofrat (privy councillor) on his retirement from the archives in 1856, received honorary doctorates from the Universities of Vienna and Leipzig in 1859, was appointed a member of the Upper House by Emperor Franz Joseph in 1861, and became an honorary citizen of Vienna in 1864; his eightieth birthday was celebrated as a grand state event with congratulations coming from Versailles, where the German princes were gathering to found the German Empire – Austria's future partner in defeat.

Without ever again inventing a story or play to express the concerns of his life or to re-create his country's history, Grillparzer died on 21 January 1872 at the age of eighty-one. Tens of thousands of people lined the streets of Vienna as his body was carried to the cemetery of Hietzing, which borders on the imperial park of Schönbrunn.

Bibliographies:

Kurt Vancsa, "Grillparzer-Bibliographie: 1905–1937," *Jahrbuch der Grillparzer-Gesellschaft,* 34 (1937): 102–166;

O. Paul Straubinger, "Grillparzer-Bibliographie: 1938–1952," *Jahrbuch der Grillparzer-Gesellschaft,* 1 (1953): 33–80;

Joachim Müller, *Franz Grillparzer* (Stuttgart: Metzler, 1963);

Herbert Seidler, "Grillparzer-Bibliographie," *Grillparzer Forum Forchtenstein* (1965): 95–98; (1966): 114–116; (1968): 131–134; (1969): 100–103; (1970): 97–99; (1971): 123–124; (1972): 162–168; (1973): 196–198; (1974): 153–155; (1975): 137–138; (1976): 236–241; (1978): 113–115;

Heinz Kindermann, ed., *Das Grillparzer-Bild des 20. Jahrhunderts. Festschrift der österreichischen Akademie der Wissenschaften zum 100. Todestag von Franz Grillparzer* (Vienna: Böhlau, 1972), pp. 109–121, 263–284.

Biographies:

August Sauer, *Franz Grillparzer* (Stuttgart: Metzler, 1941);

Douglas Yates, *Franz Grillparzer: A Critical Biography* (Oxford: Blackwell, 1946);

Raoul Auernheimer, *Franz Grillparzer: Der Dichter Österreichs* (Vienna: Ullstein, 1948);

Josef Nadler, *Franz Grillparzer* (Vaduz: Liechtenstein, 1948);

Gerhard Scheit, *Franz Grillparzer* (Reinbek: Rowohlt, 1989);

Humbert Fink, *Franz Grillparzer* (Innsbruck: Pinquin / Frankfurt am Main: Umschau, 1990).

References:

Helmut Bachmaier, *Franz Grillparzer* (Salzburg: Andreas & Andreas, 1980);

Bachmaier, ed., *Franz Grillparzer* (Frankfurt am Main: Suhrkamp, 1990);

Clifford Albrecht Bernd, ed., *Grillparzer's Der arme Spielmann: New Directions in Criticism* (Columbia, S.C.: Camden House, 1987);

Wilhelm Bietak, *Das Lebensgefühl des "Biedermeier" in der österreichischen Dichtung* (Vienna & Leipzig: Braumüller, 1931);

Arthur Burkhard, *Franz Grillparzer in England und Amerika* (Vienna: Bergland, 1961);

Burkhard, *Grillparzer im Ausland* (Cambridge, Mass.: Published by the author, 1969);

Ernst Fischer, "Franz Grillparzer," in his *Von Grillparzer zu Kafka: Sechs Essays* (Frankfurt am Main: Suhrkamp, 1975), pp. 9–65;

Elke Frederiksen, *Grillparzers Tagebücher als Suche nach Selbstverständnis* (Frankfurt am Main: Peter Lang / Bern: Herbert Lang, 1977);

Ulrich Fülleborn, *Das dramatische Geschehen im Werk Franz Grillparzers: Ein Beitrag zur Epochenbestimmung der deutschen Literatur im 19. Jahrhundert* (Munich: Fink, 1966);

Norbert Fürst, *Grillparzer auf der Bühne* (Vienna & Munich: Manutiuspresse, 1958);

Joachim Kaiser, *Grillparzers dramatischer Stil* (Munich: Hanser, 1961);

Claudio Magris, *Der habsburgische Mythos in der österreichischen Literatur* (Salzburg: Müller, 1966);

Walter Naumann, *Franz Grillparzer: Das dichterische Werk* (Stuttgart: Kohlhammer, 1967);

Elfriede Neubuhr, ed., *Begriffsbestimmung des literarischen Biedermeier* (Darmstadt: Wissenschaftliche Buchgesellschaft, 1974);

Heinz Politzer, *Grillparzer oder Das abgründige Biedermeier* (Vienna, Munich & Zurich: Molden, 1972);

Hinrich C. Seeba, "Franz Grillparzer: *Der arme Spielmann* (1847)," in *Romane und Erzählungen zwischen Romantik und Realismus: Neue Interpretationen,* edited by Paul Michael Lützeler (Stuttgart: Reclam, 1983), pp. 386–422;

Seeba, "Franz Grillparzer: *Der arme Spielmann.* 'Wie es sich fügte –': Mythos und Geschichte in Grillparzers Erzählung," in *Interpretationen: Erzählungen und Novellen des 19. Jahrhunderts,* volume 2 (Stuttgart: Reclam, 1990), pp. 99–131;

Seeba, "Das Schicksal der Grillen und Parzen: Zu Grillparzers 'Ahnfrau,' " *Euphorion,* 65 (June 1971): 132–161;

Seeba "Vormärz: Zwischen Revolution und Restauration," *Geschichte der deutschen Literatur,* volume 2: *Von der Aufklärung bis zum Vormärz,* edited by Ehrhard Bahr (Tübingen: Francke, 1988), pp. 411–501;

Herbert Seidler, *Studien zu Grillparzer und Stifter* (Vienna, Cologne & Graz: Böhlau, 1970);

Friedrich Sengle, *Biedermeierzeit: Deutsche Literatur im Spannungsfeld zwischen Restauration und Revolution 1815–1848,* 3 volumes (Stuttgart: Metzler, 1971–1980);

J. P. Stern, "Beyond the Common Indication: Grillparzer," in his *Re-interpretations: Seven Studies in Nineteenth-Century German Literature* (New York: Basic Books, 1964), pp. 42–77;

Bruce Thompson, *Franz Grillparzer* (Boston: Twayne, 1981);

Thompson and Mark G. Ward, eds., *Essays on Grillparzer* (Hull, U.K.: German Department, Hull University, 1981);

Claus Träger, "'Geschichte', 'Geist' und Grillparzer: Ein klassischer Nationalautor und seine Deutungen," *Weimarer Beiträge,* 7 (1961): 449–519;

Annalisa Viviani, *Grillparzer-Kommentar,* 2 volumes (Munich: Winkler, 1972–1973);

George A. Wells, *The Plays of Grillparzer* (London & New York: Pergamon, 1969);

W. E. Yates, *Grillparzer: A Critical Introduction* (Cambridge: Cambridge University Press, 1972).

Papers:

Franz Grillparzer's papers are in the Stadtbibliothek (City Library), Vienna.

Karl Gutzkow

(17 March 1811 - 16 December 1878)

Katherine Roper
Saint Mary's College of California

BOOKS: *Briefe eines Narren an eine Närrin,* anonymous (Hamburg: Hoffmann & Campe, 1832);

Die Divination auf den nächsten Württembergischen Landtag, anonymous (Hanau: König, 1832; reprinted, Frankfurt am Main: Athenäum, 1973);

Maha Guru: Geschichte eines Gottes, 2 volumes (Stuttgart & Tübingen: Cotta, 1833);

Novellen, 2 volumes (Hamburg: Hoffmann & Campe, 1834);

Nero: Tragödie (Stuttgart & Tübingen: Cotta, 1835);

Appellation an den gesunden Menschenverstand: Letztes Wort in einer literarischen Streitfrage (Frankfurt am Main: Streng, 1835);

Oeffentliche Charaktere: Erster Theil (Hamburg: Hoffmann & Campe, 1835);

Soireen, 2 volumes (Frankfurt am Main: Sauerländer, 1835);

Wally, die Zweiflerin: Roman (Mannheim: Löwenthal, 1835); translated by Ruth-Ellen Boetcher-Joeres as *Wally the Skeptic* (Bern & Frankfurt am Main: Lang, 1974);

Vertheidigung gegen Menzel und Berichtigung einiger Urtheile im Publikum (Mannheim: Löwenthal, 1835);

Zur Philosophie der Geschichte (Hamburg: Hoffmann & Campe, 1836; reprinted, Frankfurt am Main: Athenäum, 1973);

Ueber Goethe im Wendepunkte zweier Jahrhunderte (Berlin: Plahn, 1836; reprinted, Frankfurt am Main: Athenäum, 1973);

Beiträge zur Geschichte der neuesten Literatur, 2 volumes (Stuttgart: Balz, 1836);

Seraphine: Roman (Hamburg: Hoffmann & Campe, 1837);

Die Zeitgenossen: Ihre Schicksale, ihre Tendenzen, ihre großen Charaktere: Aus dem Englischen des E. L. Bulwer, 2 volumes (Stuttgart: Verlag der Classiker, 1838);

Blasedow und seine Söhne: Komischer Roman, 3 volumes (Stuttgart: Verlag der Classiker, 1838);

Karl Gutzkow, circa 1860

Götter, Helden, Don-Quixote: Abstimmungen zur Beurtheilung der literarischen Epoche (Hamburg: Hoffmann & Campe, 1838);

Die rothe Mütze und die Kapuze: Zum Verständnis des Görres'schen Athanasius (Hamburg: Hoffmann & Campe, 1838);

Skizzenbuch (Kassel & Leipzig: Krieger, 1839);

König Saul: Trauerspiel in fünf Aufzügen (Hamburg: Hoffmann & Campe, 1839);

Börne's Leben (Hamburg: Hoffmann & Campe, 1840);

Schiller und Goethe: Ein psychologisches Fragment (Hamburg: Hoffmann & Campe, 1841);

Vermischte Schriften, 3 volumes (Leipzig: Weber, 1842) – comprises volume 1, *Oeffentliches Leben in Deutschland: 1838–42;* volume 2, *Vermittelungen: Kritiken und Charakteristiken;* volume 3, *Mosaik: Novellen und Skizzen*;

Richard Savage oder Der Sohn einer Mutter: Trauerspiel in fünf Aufzügen (Leipzig: Weber, 1842);

Die Schule der Reichen: Schauspiel in fünf Aufzügen (Leipzig: Weber, 1842);

Werner, oder Herz und Welt: Schauspiel in fünf Aufzügen (Leipzig: Weber, 1842);

Briefe aus Paris, 2 volumes (Leipzig: Brockhaus, 1842);

Ein weißes Blatt: Schauspiel in fünf Aufzügen (Leipzig: Weber, 1844);

Aus der Zeit und dem Leben (Leipzig: Brockhaus, 1844);

Zopf und Schwert: Historisshes Lustspiel in fünf Aufzügen (Leipzig: Weber, 1844); translated by Grace Isabel Colbron as *Sword and Queue,* in *The German Classics of the Nineteenth and Twentieth Centuries,* volume 7, edited by Kuno Francke and William Guild Howard (New York: German Publication Society, 1914), pp. 252–350;

Gesammelte Werke: Vollständig umgearbeitete Ausgabe, 13 volumes (Frankfurt am Main: Literarische Anstalt, 1845–1852);

Pugatscheff: Trauerspiel in fünf Aufzügen (Leipzig: Lorick, 1846);

Der dreizehnte November: Dramatisches Seelengemälde in drei Aufzügen (Leipzig: Lorick, 1846);

Das Urbild des Tartüffe: Lustspiel in fünf Aufzügen (Leipzig: Weber, 1846; New York: Deutsche Vereins-Buchhandlung, 1851);

Uriel Acosta: Trauerspiel in fünf Aufzügen (Leipzig: Weber, 1847); translated by M. M. as *Uriel Acosta: Tragedy in Five Acts* (New York: Ellinger, 1860);

Ansprache an das deutsche Volk, anonymous (Berlin: Springer, 1848);

Deutschland am Vorabend seines Falles oder seiner Größe (Frankfurt am Main: Literarische Anstalt, 1848; edited by Walter Boehlich, Frankfurt am Main: Insel, 1969);

Wullenweber: Geschichtliches Trauerspiel in fünf Aufzügen (Leipzig: Lorick, 1848);

Imagina Unruh: Novelle (Leipzig: Brockhaus, 1849);

Vor- und Nachmärzliches, volume 4 of *Vermischte Schriften* (Leipzig: Brockhaus, 1850);

Liesli: Ein Volkstrauerspiel in drei Aufzügen (Leipzig: Brockhaus, 1850);

Die Ritter vom Geiste: Roman in neun Büchern, 9 volumes (Leipzig: Brockhaus, 1850–1851);

Aus der Knabenzeit (Frankfurt am Main: Literarische Anstalt, 1852);

Der Königsleutenant: Lustspiel in vier Aufzügen (Leipzig: Brockhaus, 1852);

Philipp und Perez: Historische Tragödie in fünf Aufzügen (Dresden: Teubner, 1853);

Ottfried: Schauspiel in fünf Aufzügen; Fremdes Glück: Vorspielscherz in einem Aufzuge (Leipzig: Brockhaus, 1854);

Die Diakonissin: Ein Lebensbild (Frankfurt am Main: Literarische Anstalt, 1855);

Lenz und Söhne oder Die Kömodie der Besserungen: Lustspiel in fünf Aufzügen (Leipzig: Brockhaus, 1855);

Ein Mädchen aus dem Volke: Bilder der Wirklichkeit (Prague: Grzabek / Leipzig: Hübner, 1855);

Die kleine Narrenwelt, 3 volumes (Frankfurt am Main: Literarische Anstalt, 1856–1857);

Lorber und Myrte: Historisches Charakterbild in drei Aufzügen (Leipzig: Brockhaus, 1857);

Der Zauberer von Rom: Roman in neun Büchern, 9 volumes (Leipzig: Brockhaus, 1858–1861);

Dramatische Werke: Vollständig neu umgearbeitete Ausgabe, 20 volumes (Leipzig: Brockhause, 1862–1863);

Eine Shakespearefeier an der Ilm (Leipzig: Brockhaus, 1864);

Die Curstauben: Novelle (Leipzig: Brockhaus, 1864);

Hohenschwangau: Roman und Geschichte, 1536–1537, 5 volumes (Leipzig: Brockhaus, 1867–1868); revised as *Die Paumgärtner von Hohenschwangau: Historischer Roman,* 3 volumes (Breslau: Schottlaender, 1879);

Vom Baum der Erkenntniß: Denksprüche (Stuttgart: Cotta, 1868);

Die schöneren Stunden: Rückblicke (Stuttgart: Hallberger, 1869);

Lebensbilder, 3 volumes (Stuttgart: Hallberger, 1870–1871);

Die Söhne Pestalozzi's: Roman, 3 volumes (Berlin: Janke, 1870);

Das Duell wegen Ems: Gedanken über den Frieden (Berlin: Puttkammer & Mühlbrecht, 1870);

Der Wärwolf: Historische Erzählung (Vienna: Dittmarsch, 1871);

Dramatische Werke, 20 volumes (Jena: Costenoble, 1871–1872);

Ein Hollandgang: Novelle (Jena: Costenoble, 1872);

Fritz Ellrodt: Roman, 3 volumes (Jena: Costenoble, 1872);

Gesammelte Werke: Erste vollständige Gesammt-Ausgabe, 12 volumes (Jena: Costenoble, 1873–1876);

Rückblicke auf mein Leben, 1829-1849 (Berlin: Hofmann, 1875);

Dschingiskhan: Lustspiel in einem Aufzuge (Vienna: Wallishauser, 1876);

In bunter Reihe: Briefe, Skizzen und Novellen (Breslau: Schottländer, 1877);

Die neuen Serapionsbrüder: Roman, 3 volumes (Breslau: Schottländer, 1877);

Zwei Studenten der Zukunft (Leipzig: Eckstein, 1877);

Dionysius Longinus oder: Ueber den aesthetischen Schwulst in der neuern deutschen Literatur (Stuttgart: Gutzkow, 1878);

Gesammelte Werke, 20 volumes (Jena: Costenoble, 1880-1907);

Ausgewählte Werke, 12 volumes, edited by Heinrich Hubert Houben (Leipzig: Hesse, 1908);

Gutzkows Werke: Kritisch durchgesehene und erläuterte Ausgabe, edited by Peter Müller (Leipzig & Vienna: Bibliographisches Institut, 1911);

Gutzkows Werke, 12 volumes, edited by Reinhold Gensel (Berlin: Bong, 1912);

Unter dem schwarzen Bären: Erlebtes 1811-1848, edited by Fritz Bottger (Berlin: Verlag der Nation, 1971);

Liberale Energie: Eine Sammlung kritischer Schriften, edited by Peter Demetz (Frankfurt am Main: Ullstein, 1974).

OTHER: *Forum der Journal-Literatur: Eine antikritische Quartalschrift,* 3 issues, edited by Gutzkow (Berlin: Logier, 1831);

William Hogarth, *Sammlung Hogarth'scher Kupfer-Stiche,* foreword by Gutzkow (Göttingen: Dieterich, 1834);

Friedrich Schleiermacher, *Vertraute Brief über Schlegel's Lucinde,* edited by Gutzkow (Hamburg: Hoffmann & Campe, 1835);

Deutsche Blätter für Leben, Kunst und Wissenschaft, edited by Gutzkow (Frankfurt am Main: Varrentrapp, 1835);

Literatur-Blatt zum Phönix, edited by Gutzkow (Frankfurt am Main: Sauerländer, 1835);

Frankfurter Börsenzeitung, edited by Gutzkow (Frankfurt am Main: Wilmanns, 1836);

Der Telegraph für Deutschland: Eine Zeitschrift, 6 volumes, edited by Gutzkow (Hamburg: Hoffmann & Campe, 1838-1843);

Unterhaltungen am häuslichen Herd, 10 volumes, edited by Gutzkow (Leipzig: Brockhaus, 1852-1862);

Die Deutsche Revue, edited by Gutzkow and Ludolf Wienbarg, edited by Emile F. J. Dresch (Berlin: Behr, 1904);

Deutsche Revue: Deutsche Blätter, edited by Gutzkow and Wienbarg (Frankfurt am Main: Athenäum, 1971).

"Freiheit! Freiheit! Freiheit!" (Freedom! Freedom! Freedom!) chants the crowd to a newly elected pope. This last line from Karl Gutzkow's novel *Der Zauberer von Rom* (The Magician of Rome, 1858-1861) epitomizes his ideal over almost a half century of activity extending to every realm of literary culture. Called to action by the news of the overthrow of Charles X in Paris in 1830, Gutzkow took up his pen to bring freedom to an enchained German society. From the founding during his student days of his first literary periodical he withstood clashes with German censors, the most sensational of which involved a prison sentence and the condemnation of his works along with those of other members of the Junges Deutschland (Young Germany) movement. Despite such struggles Gutzkow established himself as a prolific literary journalist and preeminent dramatist before achieving his greatest renown with the novel *Die Ritter vom Geiste* (Knights of the Spirit, 1850-1851), whose panoramic portrayal of Prussian society became a literary milestone. Gutzkow built on these achievements with a profusion of essays, critiques, short stories, dramas, and multivolume novels – all the while quarreling with opponents of his various cultural causes.

Gutzkow's rancor, heightened in later life by delusions of persecution, has weighed heavily in the criticism of him, as has the undeniable aesthetic cost of his incessantly hurried production. Such failings, however, do not outweigh his importance in German cultural history in laying the foundations for German realism, in establishing writing as a profession, in introducing literary criticism into popular periodicals, and in building a legacy of democratic literary engagement.

Gutzkow was born in Berlin on 17 March 1811. His memoirs of his childhood recall a rich but bewildering array of experiences in post-Napoleonic Berlin. The profuse details suggest that his inquisitiveness and intelligence were manifest from his earliest years. His account of utterly conflicting childhood influences may also afford a key to the pathological anxieties he suffered as an adult, and it certainly reveals the competing values that would permeate his works.

His father, Karl August Gutzkow, a veteran of the Napoleonic Wars and a trainer in the royal stables, engaged in revelry with his military cronies until his closest comrade committed suicide over a supposed lapse of duty. Austere piety then replaced

Letter from Gutzkow to Georg Büchner, whose play Danton's Tod *Gutzkow serialized in the Frankfurt periodical* Phönix *(Nationale Forschungs- und Gedenkstätten, Weimar)*

Gutzkow; lithograph by Gutsch and Rupp after a drawing by Heinemann

his raucousness, and he led his family from one Berlin church to another for sermons, Bible study, and prayer meetings. A zealous uncle, whom Gutzkow was to dub "der Apocalyptiker" (the apocalyptician)," was given to dire biblical prophesying. Gutzkow's mother, Sophia Gutzkow, née Berg, keeper of the meager budget that sustained the family in its cramped quarters, was more down-to-earth; but her position as a housewife and her near illiteracy did not allow for questioning of the religious practices of her husband.

Gutzkow absorbed the bare essentials offered by the nearby elementary school, but his real education began with an exacting tutorial regimen administered by the portrait painter Karl Friedrich Minter, the father of a friend. A passionate heir of the Enlightenment, Minter introduced Gutzkow not only to vast new worlds of the mind but also to the artists, intellectuals, officers, diplomats, and officials who frequented his drawing room. Trips to the theater with the Minters drew Gutzkow further from the puritanical ways of his father and uncle. In 1821 Minter moved his family to Warsaw, but before he left, he persuaded the Gutzkows to enroll their son at the venerated Friedrichwerdersches Gymnasium. By this time the disparate values of the pietist father and the apocalyptic uncle, on the one hand, and of Herr Minter the freethinker, on the other, had been firmly implanted in him.

At the gymnasium, whose school-leaving examinations he passed brilliantly in spring 1829, and at the University of Berlin, where he studied for five semesters, Gutzkow acquired an encyclopedic command of fundamental texts and current debates in philosophy, theology, literature, and history. In addition to reading voraciously, he heard lectures by such luminaries as the theologian Friedrich Schleiermacher, the young historian Leopold von Ranke, and the reigning philosopher, Georg Wilhelm Friedrich Hegel. The swirl of ideas converged in a "Damascus" experience in the Tiergarten west of Berlin in which the young theology student suddenly reconciled rational and humanistic ideals with his understanding of divine purpose. Knowledge of God, Gutzkow resolved, must be sought in the intellectual, natural, and social realms that surround the individual. Gutzkow thus grounded his commitment to secular pursuits in a religious ideal. Recognition of his intellectual prowess in pursuing this ideal came at a university celebration on 3 August 1830 at which Hegel himself bestowed on the young student a gold medal for his essay on the philosophical significance of the ancient gods.

This triumph was immediately superseded by a second "conversion" experience when the overthrow of the monarchy in France was announced to the gathering. Leaving the auditorium in a daze, Gutzkow seized a newspaper at a café. This moment, he asserted later, marked his turn from transcendental ideals to the urgent concerns of the day. Gutzkow's break with idealism was actually less clear-cut, but he did become a passionate follower of political events and in January 1831 founded a periodical in which he first enunciated his call for literature to engage current questions. Thirteen issues of his *Forum der Journal-Literatur* appeared before Prussian censors ended the enterprise.

In late 1831 Wolfgang Menzel, Germany's reigning literary critic, invited Gutzkow to work on the literary section of the *Morgenblatt für gebildete Stände* (Morning Paper for Cultivated Classes) in Stuttgart. Gutzkow had long admired Menzel's advocacy of a literature that would stimulate reformist impulses in Germany, and Menzel hoped to train a successor to take over the paper so that he could move into politics. He thus assigned the newcomer many reviews and introduced him to an array of literary figures and publishers. Although Gutzkow found the work exhilarating, he had no intention of hewing to his mentor's dictates. In 1832 he returned to Berlin in hopes of becoming the northern counterpart to Menzel.

Soon he was celebrating the publication of his first novel, *Briefe eines Narren an eine Närrin* (Letters from a Madman to a Madwoman, 1832). The epistolary genre, already practiced by such writers as Johann Wolfgang von Goethe, suggests a conventional work, and the Romantic imagery and style of the twenty-seven letters attest to the influence of Jean Paul. But conventionality is countered by jarring irony, sarcasm, and absurd wordplay. A jumbled free association of images, ideas, and accusations pours forth from a letter writer who moves through time and space, surveying the movements of Hannibal's legions in one passage and looking over the world from atop Berlin's Brandenburg Gate in another. The addressee is equally capricious: sometimes married, then unmarried, old, young, unworldly, stylish, intellectual, emotional, nearby, distant, dead, and even a Hegelian world spirit.

This chaos represents Gutzkow's view of an age in which intellectual, moral, and spiritual certainties were disintegrating. Repeatedly identifying himself as a child of the times, the letter writer claims to embrace the confusion even as he hungers after an idea for which he would be willing to die. His religious and cultural ruminations frequently give way to political commentary, as when he contrasts the recent Polish uprisings to the political paralysis of the Germans. His putative insanity, the letter writer implies, is the logical response of a freedom lover to the rigidities of the age. A strongly apocalyptic dimension also emerges, culminating in a lengthy prediction of the end of the world in 1836 that surely echoes Gutzkow's memories of his uncle. The letter writer also discerns, however, a future in which monarchical despotism will be destroyed by a multitude of "kleine Umstände" (little events) and replaced by republicanism, which in turn will dissolve into an age of brotherly harmony.

Although it is impossible to equate the madman's views with the author's, Gutzkow clearly uses his letter writer to expound his own perception of the bankruptcy of existing institutions. The letter writer's emphasis on the role of literature in heralding a liberating transformation of German society proclaims another of Gutzkow's tenets. And his acknowledgment that he has little idea of what will replace the existing system points to a dilemma that would beset Gutzkow for the rest of his life.

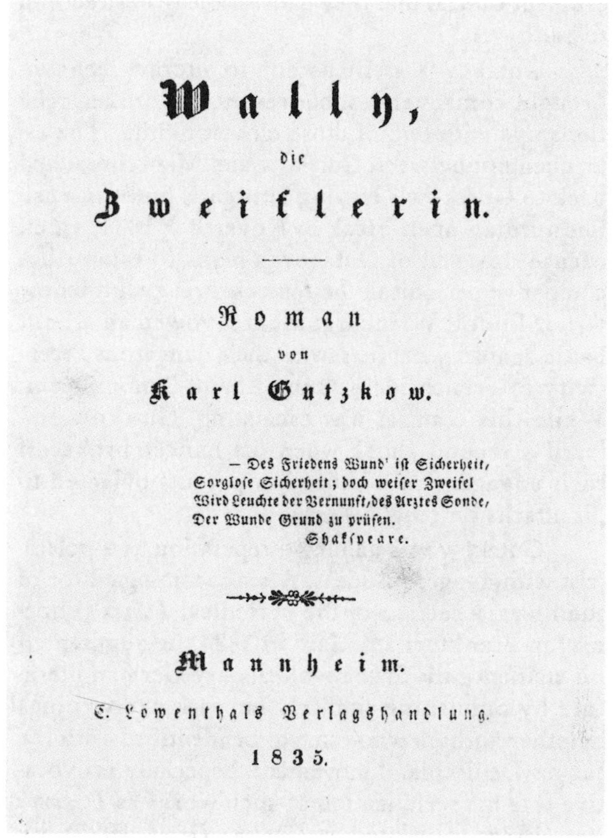

Wally,

die

Zweiflerin.

Roman

von

Karl Gutzkow.

— Des Friedens Wund' ist Sicherheit,
Sorglose Sicherheit; doch weiser Zweifel
Wird Leuchte der Vernunft, des Arztes Sonde,
Der Wunde Grund zu prüfen.
Shakspeare.

Mannheim.

C. Löwenthals Verlagshandlung.

1835.

Title page for Gutzkow's novel about a woman's crisis of religious faith. The book was banned by the authorities in various German states.

Briefe eines Narren an eine Närrin was published anonymously in the wake of the repressive decrees that followed the festival of "German rebirth" in Hambach in 1832. Gutzkow attempted to stave off censorship with a preface claiming that the writings had been seized in a graveyard near the Bedlam insane asylum in London, but the Prussian censors quickly prohibited the book. In later years Gutzkow disparaged his first novel, and most later critics have ignored it; but the work is a striking debut for a writer who aimed to create a new literature to proclaim the revolutionary changes of his era.

Gutzkow secured a doctorate from Jena University in 1832, spent two semesters studying law at Heidelberg and Munich, then abandoned his academic endeavors for a total commitment to writing. A trip to Italy with the author Heinrich Laube in August 1833; the publication that fall of a second novel, *Maha Guru;* and ever-intensifying journalistic activity eclipsed any hopes of Gutzkow's family that he would become the clergyman, scholar, or government official that they had variously desired him to be.

Gutzkow's swift ascent to literary renown brought controversies that resulted in broken relationships with two of those closest to him. The estrangement between Gutzkow and Menzel reached back to Gutzkow's leaving Stuttgart, but it intensified into an open break in November 1834, when Menzel learned of Gutzkow's plans to establish a combative periodical, the *Deutsche Revue,* with fellow writer Ludolf Wienbarg; Menzel vowed an all-out battle against what he saw as their dangerous receptivity to French ideas such as Saint-Simonianism. While this conflict was escalating, Gutzkow suffered a second shock when his fiancée broke off their engagement because her parents objected to his attacks on religious orthodoxy.

Gutzkow was gaining a reputation as a polemicist with dangerous ideas. After becoming editor of the literary section of the periodical *Phönix* (Phoenix) in Frankfurt am Main in 1834, he augmented his strident calls for a revolutionary German literature by publishing similarly impassioned writings by other authors who came to be identified with the Junges Deutschland movement. Especially provocative was his serialization of such works as *Danton's Tod* (1835; translated as *Danton's Death,* 1927), by Georg Büchner, who had just escaped into political exile. Gutzkow also lashed out against the religious orthodoxy that he saw as the cause of his broken engagement. The forum for this attack was his republication in March 1835 of nine letters in which Schleiermacher had defended Friedrich Schlegel's controversial novel *Lucinde* (1799; abridged and translated as "Lucinda," 1913). In his preface Gutzkow imprudently attacked the Berlin religious establishment for omitting these letters from the collected works of the recently deceased Schleiermacher and thereby reinforcing priestly strictures against men and women discovering authentic love. The Prussian authorities quickly prohibited distribution of the book.

This ban proved to be a preliminary skirmish to the warfare that broke loose when Gutzkow's novel *Wally, die Zweiflerin* (translated as *Wally the Skeptic,* 1974) appeared in August 1835. Menzel opened the attack with a series of articles fulminating against the novel's blasphemy and immorality. Not just Gutzkow, he charged, but a whole band of writers known as Junges Deutschland threatened the political stability and moral integrity of the German nation. The Prussian authorities banned the novel in September, those in other German states quickly followed, and Gutzkow was arrested. His cherished project for a new cultural forum, the *Deutsche Revue,* was banned in November 1835 before its first issue could appear. An edict of the German Diet on 10 December banned all of Gutzkow's writings and those of his presumed associates Laube, Wienbarg, Heinrich Heine, and Theodor Mundt. In January 1836 Gutzkow was convicted of having impugned the tenets of Christianity and was sentenced to one month's further imprisonment.

Today's reader of *Wally, die Zweiflerin* is likely to be struck by the novel's frail plot and seemingly chaotic style. An impulsive aristocratic heroine, Wally banters coquettishly with the opinionated freethinker Cäsar about a multitude of fashionable ideas. When she inexplicably decides to marry a Sardinian diplomat, Cäsar convinces her to affirm their own elevated relationship by reenacting the tale of the lady whose knight, before he went out into the world, asked her to show him her total, naked beauty (the fleeting episode of Wally's nakedness severely shocked contemporaries). Wally's marriage soon collapses; Cäsar rescues her, then abandons her to marry a rich Jewish woman. Wally turns to religion and finds only nihilistic doubts. Finally Cäsar gives her his own treatise demythologizing religion, which sends Wally into such despair that she kills herself.

Gutzkow's conjunction of empty-headedness and existential despair in his heroine, his haphazard insertion of Cäsar's religious essay into the text, his awkward use of the diary form, his often careless syntax, and his melodramatic twists all point to artistic failure. The furor caused by the novel, however, gives it historical importance. Despite its abstract treatment of sexuality the novel announces that relations between the sexes must undergo what to contemporaries was a shocking transformation. Despite its ambivalence about women's intellectual capabilities, it condemns society for excluding women from education. Despite its dilution of Wally's religious crisis by making it result from Cäsar's abandonment of her, the novel portrays the urgent need for religion to address the moral and social issues of the modern age. And despite its stylistic haphazardness it mixes Classical, Romantic, and modern elements so as to suggest a literary bridge in an age of transition.

Gutzkow's release from prison brought deportation orders in both Frankfurt and Baden, and his works continued to be prohibited in Prussia until 1843. In July 1836 he married Amalie Klönne, a young Frankfurt woman who had encouraged him throughout his ordeals; they had three sons. Gutzkow cherished her sustaining devotion, even

Gutzkow circa 1840; lithograph by V. Schertle

though his restlessness precluded genuine marital happiness.

Soon after his marriage Gutzkow became editor of the *Frankfurter Telegraph.* Still harassed by deportation threats, he moved with the paper to Hamburg when the Hoffmann und Campe publishing firm took it over and renamed it the *Telegraph für Deutschland* in 1838. His seven-year association with the paper marked his most concerted effort in a lifetime involvement with the periodical press to unite literature and journalism into a new literary form. A collection of literary portraits he wrote for the *Telegraph* was published in 1838 under the title *Götter, Helden, Don-Quixote* (Gods, Heroes, Don Quixote), and some of his liveliest cultural and political critiques were reproduced in the first two volumes of his *Vermischte Schriften* (Mixed Essays, 1842). One of the first German authors to try to make a living from his writings, Gutzkow recognized the dangers of constant pressure to produce. But, conceiving of himself as a literary proletarian, he turned out with a steady stream of works whose social, political, religious, and cultural topics would reverberate one day through his panoramic novels.

The Sisyphean routine of journalistic output and the tensions of ceaseless controversies finally spurred Gutzkow to shift his attention in the early 1840s to the theater. He had begun to write dramas as early as 1833, but the first production came only in 1839, when *Richard Savage* (1842) premiered in Frankfurt to popular and critical acclaim. Of the thirty dramas Gutzkow ultimately wrote, twenty-one were produced – with receptions ranging from shrill hisses to clamorous cheering. Gutzkow responded mercurially to negative criticism, sometimes insisting that a work be pulled from the stage and at other times lashing out defiantly. Both reactions took an emotional toll on him.

At their worst Gutzkow's dramas assailed audiences with convoluted plots impeded by verbose monologues and exchanges between one-dimensional characters. At their best, however, they use

Gutzkow in 1844; pencil drawing by Weinhold (Stadt- und Universitätsbibliothek, Frankfurt am Main)

multidimensional characters to develop a riveting conflict through carefully structured episodes and well-honed dialogue. Although typically placed in historical settings, his dramas invariably depict Gutzkow's relentless current concerns over censorship, religious questioning, political opposition, and relations between the sexes. The pinnacle of his dramatic efforts came in the mid 1840s, when he gravitated to Dresden, where he launched his best dramas to immense popular success.

His finest comedy, *Das Urbild des Tartüffe* (The Prototype for Tartuffe, 1846), is an inventive representation of Molière's struggles to get his *Tartuffe* (1664) past the censors. To critics who challenged the play's historical veracity, Gutzkow replied that he intended to spark awareness of censorship and of hypocrisy in German society of 1844, not to enlighten audiences about an episode in seventeenth-century France.

The play's rapid, pointed dialogue reveals Gutzkow's many satirical targets. Molière is derided for his susceptibility to the dramatist's craving for applause, his rivals for their jealousy of his popularity, and the public for its capricious idolization of playwrights. The Tartuffe character in the play within the play is mocked for his hypocritical gestures of piety; the members of the French Academy are ridiculed for their verbose pretensions and the minutiae of their investigations; professionals – physicians, lawyers, and clerics – are taunted for their petty sensitivities. But censorship provides the main satirical focus: when Louis XIV wavers over whether to prohibit the play, he is tricked into allowing its performance.

Gutzkow's own trick of smuggling his satire onto the stage in the guise of a seventeenth-century French classic allowed his play to slip past suspicious German censors. The successful premiere of *Das Urbild des Tartüffe* in Oldenburg in December 1844 was followed by an even more triumphant opening in Dresden on New Year's Day 1845, and the play was a staple of German repertoires through the 1870s.

Gutzkow's greatest dramatic triumph came in December 1846 with the Dresden premiere of *Uriel Acosta* (1847), whose title character is based on the seventeenth-century Jewish philosopher of that name. Two tragic conflicts develop from Uriel's pursuit of truth: a collision with rabbinical orthodoxy and an even more difficult contest between Uriel's competing allegiances to intellectual integrity and to family and community.

Gutzkow had first treated this subject in "Der Sadduzäer von Amsterdam" (The Sadducee of Amsterdam), published in his *Novellen* (Novellas, 1834). This early version bears the marks of Gutzkow's "Sturm und Drang" period, when he challenged Menzel's authority, confronted his own religious questionings, and had his engagement broken off. Its story of Uriel's persecution, first by the Portuguese Inquisition and later by the Jewish establishment of Amsterdam, devolves into one of passionate struggles for the hand of his beloved, Judith Vanderstraten. At the end a desperate Uriel, having been abandoned by a weak-willed Judith, intends to obtain revenge on his rival suitor. Instead, he shoots Judith by mistake and then turns the gun on himself.

The drama of twelve years later draws a hero who has moved beyond notions of revenge and a heroine who makes a principled decision in the conflict between allegiance to community and to personal belief. The action concerns Uriel's successive decisions, first to flee Judaism's persecution of his philosophical inquiry, then to recant before the elders, and finally to suffer the ban – each responding to his logical assessment of changing circumstances in his quest. Uriel commits suicide not in an act of passion but as an apostle of truth. Judith proceeds through a similar succession of decisions about whether to stand by Uriel or to obey the dictates of her father. Concluding that her father's well-being depends on his acceptance by the community, she marries the hated suitor. After the ceremony she drinks poison so that she can remain true to Uriel and his chosen path. The accidental shooting of a weak-willed daughter in the novella is thus replaced by the deliberately chosen death of a woman who has become the moral helpmate of a philosopher. At the end Judith's physician-uncle pleads for toleration to supplant the persecution that has killed the tragic pair – a plea that prompted comparisons of the play with Gotthold Ephraim Lessing's *Nathan der Weise* (1779; translated as *Nathan the Wise,* 1791).

While it did not attain the stature of Lessing's classic, *Uriel Acosta* ranks as one of Gutzkow's notable artistic achievements. The drama's sequence of episodes systematically reveals the dimensions of the conflict through the interaction of complex characters whose dialogue, in unadorned verse, contains some of Guzkow's most powerful language. In letters Guzkow offered detailed instructions to directors about how *Uriel Acosta* should be produced and performed: how actors should be costumed to convey their characters' respective social positions, how they should deliver their lines to draw the audience into the dramatic situation, why they should avoid using dialect, and how specific scenes should be paced.

In January 1847 Gutzkow accepted the post of production manager of the Dresden Hoftheater (Court Theater), where his productions of plays by a wide range of authors significantly influenced the development of German theater. The job, however, left Gutzkow little time for his own works.

To gain respite from his duties in Dresden, Gutzkow journeyed with his wife in March 1848 to Berlin, where he found a startlingly different atmosphere from the repressed quiet of his youth. Within days he watched with astonishment as revolutionary masses thronged beneath his hotel window. Except for a brief appearance to calm an angry crowd at the palace, Gutzkow took no active part in the events. The immediate reason for this aloofness was his wife's illness; she died of typhus a few weeks after the outbreak of the revolution. But nothing in Gutzkow's earlier or later life suggests that he would have taken to the speaker's platform or the barricades in any case. Nevertheless, a year later, after a last revolutionary outburst erupted in Dresden, Gutzkow lost his post at the Hoftheater.

In September 1849 Gutzkow married Bertha Meidinger, a young cousin of Amalie. She took over the raising of his three sons and gave birth to three daughters as well.

Gutzkow's second wife, the former Bertha Meidinger

The energies the events of 1848–1849 had stirred up in Gutzkow were unleashed not in direct action but in his most important work: *Die Ritter vom Geiste.* This novel began to be serialized in mid 1850 and was published in nine volumes that year and the next, winning immediate popular and critical acclaim for its path-breaking portrayal of German society in the aftermath of the revolution.

In this prototypical Zeitroman (novelistic portrayal of the contemporary era) Gutzkow proposed to abandon what he called "Nacheinander" (one after the other) – the artificially constructed succession of events of conventional novels – in favor of a form that would accord with the actuality of the social world: a simultaneity he called "Nebeneinander" (next to one another). The novel of Nebeneinander was to focus on no single protagonist or group but rather on the era as a whole. The era portrayed in *Die Ritter vom Geiste,* which was characterized by the emergence of a reaction that aimed to quell every vestige of freedom released by the revolution, is depicted through more than one hundred characters linked by a multifaceted plot. The work is a combination of detective mystery, with an intrigue-filled search for a missing portrait and some missing documents of enormous import; city novel (it is the first "Berlin novel"); and social novel, with expansive representation of social, political, economic, cultural, and spiritual forces in post-1848 Prussia.

Gutzkow's strategies for portraying a social totality unfold within a seemingly fragmentary structure that moves back and forth from one scene to another as characters' paths crisscross in unpredictable ways. An omniscient narrator holds the intricate story line together, revealing details that will later become relevant and offering interpretive insights. Characters' social stations and personalities are identified by descriptions of their physical features and clothing, and settings are similarly specified through profuse detail. Letters and excerpts from newspapers document the plot developments. Gutzkow's main technique, however, consists of the many conversations that convey retrospective information, communicate ideas and viewpoints, and provide anticipatory references to new characters.

Although many readers of *Die Ritter vom Geiste* were tempted to match fictional locations and characters with historical counterparts, the novel is far more than a roman à clef. Woven into the dense tapestry of themes and social types is every one of Gutzkow's significant social and intellectual concerns: religion in an age of doubt, old and new forms of political repression, possibilities for democratic transformation, relations between the sexes, social and economic forces constraining the individual, and the emancipatory role of art. Three geographic settings – Berlin, a village on the outskirts of the capital, and a rural estate – are inhabited by characters whose social identities span the social spectrum. Abstract groupings of nobility, middle classes, urban poor, and peasantry quickly break down into complicated variations and interactions in a society reeling from the shock of revolution. Women further complicate the social panorama by sometimes challenging and at other times confirming their conventional roles.

Political themes run throughout the novel, with activity ranging from the oppressive measures of a police state to the underground action of communist agitators. The "Knights of the Spirit" are a secret association of self-proclaimed heirs of the medieval Knights Templar united in a struggle against repressive political authority and a rigid religious establishment. They refuse to enunciate a political program but dedicate themselves to the regeneration of German freedom – an ideal whose abstractness provoked spirited debate over Gutzkow's claims to realism. Defeated by an accelerating political reaction at the end of the novel, the "Knights" disperse to await the destruction that will open an era of freedom.

However demoralizing the reaction of the 1850s was for Gutzkow and his readers, the novel did not fall prey to censorship but underwent three editions in five years. Prefaces to the subsequent editions seem to mute the work's call for completing the German revolution and suggest a moderation of Gutzkow's politics. In his preface to the sixth edition in 1869, for example, Gutzkow denies that he had meant the novel to be a recipe for revolution; rather, he says, he wanted to foster discussion among educated people about the alternatives for liberating German society. Such caution suggests that Gutzkow failed to understand the changes in political institutions that would have been needed to attain the freedom that was his ideal.

The success of the novel and a placid family life contributed to the sense of well-being that emanates from Gutzkow's affectionate portrayals of his childhood in *Aus der Knabenzeit* (From My Boyhood Years, 1852). Another source of satisfaction came in October 1852 with the founding of a new weekly, *Unterhaltungen am häuslichen Herd* (Conversations by the Household Hearth). That Gutzkow's idea of directing cultural discussion to the middle-class household struck a responsive chord is attested by the then-notable five thousand subscriptions, as well as by the quick appearance of the competing *Gartenlaube* (Garden Bower) and *Daheim* (At Home). This venture put Gutzkow at the center of German literary life; during his ten years as editor he published not only his own writings but novellas, essays, and poetry by many other contributors – including quite a few, such as Friedrich Spielhagen, who were making their literary debuts.

Gutzkow created a vast portrayal of Catholicism in a second panoramic novel, *Der Zauberer von Rom*. Although the novel is set in the decade prior to 1848, its concerns are those of the late 1850s, when the forces leading to Italian unification were bringing an end to the temporal powers of the papacy. The novel's depiction of the complexity of the church was intended not only to expose age-old forces of religious repression but also to hold out the possibility of humanity's spiritual and worldly emancipation. The concluding scene, portraying the election of a reformist pope in an indeterminate future time, signifies Gutzkow's ideal of a religious awakening fostered by a universal Christianity that has relinquished its hierarchical rigidities.

Gutzkow's ideas about Catholicism are personified in a multitude of clerical and lay characters, extending from a village parish to the highest levels of the Roman hierarchy. Although some scenes are set in Vienna and Rome, *Der Zauberer von Rom* focuses most expansively on Catholic society in the Rhineland and Westphalia. It treats tensions within the German church both as history, depicting the bitter struggle over mixed marriages in Cologne in 1837–1838, and as prophecy, anticipating conflicts between the Catholic church and the Prussian state such as those that would actually take place in German chancellor Otto von Bismarck's Kulturkampf (struggle for civilization) of the 1870s. Central to the portrayal of internal and external struggles of the church are questions of authority, which the novel develops through characters who variously advocate papal supremacy in a hierarchical church, individual spiritual authority, apostolic community, and the church's leadership in movements for national liberation in Germany and Italy.

A wide range of Catholic piety is also portrayed, with some characters engaged in genuine religious quests while others manipulate their faith hypocritically or proclaim it with zealous fanaticism. Those with whom Gutzkow is most sympathetic develop an ideal of a free inner piety against what they see as the corruptions of the Gospel message by worldly concerns. The major proponent of this ideal is Bonaventura von Asselyn, a priest in an obscure German village who is ultimately elected as the reformist pope of the final scene. Through him the novel represents myriad details of the demanding life of a cleric, from the daily routines of saying mass and hearing confession to profound crises of vocation. It also traces Bonaventura's ascent through the Catholic hierarchy, with its perilous web of religious and secular connections. But most important, Gutzkow uses the novel to propound Bonaventura's vision of a reformed, enlightened, and humanized Catholic church based on a genuine apostolic community. As pope he announces that his first act will be to call a general council, an act that, observers anticipate, will surely result in the abolition of the papacy itself. The crowd's responding chant of "Freiheit!" echoes the call of centuries for what is, the narrator specifies, the God-given heritage of humanity.

As in *Die Ritter vom Geiste,* an omniscient narrator guides the reader through the intricacies and intrigues of the plot while giving detailed descriptions of the setting and its human inhabitants. A chapter

Unterhaltungen am häuslichen Herd

Herausgegeben von Karl Gutzkow.

Neue Folge. Vierter Band. Nr. 1. Wöchentlich ein Bogen. Preis vierteljährlich 20 Ngr.

Inhalt: An unsere Leser. Von Karl Gutzkow. — Winckelmann's Ermordung. I. Von A. von Torn. — Auch zum häuslichen Herd. Von Berthold Sigismund. — Auf dem Gericht. Monolog eines Sachwalters von Edmund Bruno. — Die Schöpfungsplane der Natur. — Stein und Hardenberg. — Die Schönheit der Seele. — Lebensblicke von F. Habicht. — Dem Knäblein eines Freundes. Von Heinrich Zeise.

An unsere Leser.

In unveränderter innerer Richtung begrüßen diese Blätter zum siebenten male die Jahreswende ihres ersten Erscheinens.

Der Kreis unserer Freunde hat sich nicht verringert.

Gleich bei der ersten Ankündigung unserer „Unterhaltungen am häuslichen Herd" lag es nicht in unserer Absicht, in drängender Hast, nur um die Gunst des Publikums werbend, in den Kreis unserer Mittheilungen alles und jedes zu ziehen, dem nur irgend die Neugier der Menge zugewandt ist. Wir suchten die Bildungsvoraussetzungen, die bei unserer so umfassend gewordenen populären Literatur nicht selten von ähnlichen Unternehmungen bis auf das Maß der untersten Volksklassen gegriffen wurden, nur innerhalb der Sphäre, wo sich genugsam Kenntniß der Literatur und ihrer üblichen Hülfsmittel findet, um das Bedürfniß nach Belehrung über das alltäglich Vorkommende an Quellen zu suchen, die in wissenschaftlicher Regelung fließen, nicht in dem Durcheinander von Zeitschriften, die in ihren Mittheilungen das Fremdartigste zu verbinden anfingen, Eingebungen der lyrischen und erzählenden Poesie mit Mitteln gegen die Sommersprossen. Wir haben uns den Erscheinungen der vorzugsweise zur Parole gemachten „Natur" und des materiellen Lebens nicht entzogen, immer aber dabei einen Leserkreis vorausgesetzt, den nicht die Darlegung der rohen Erscheinung fesseln konnte, sondern nur die Anknüpfung derselben an höhere Gesetze entweder der Wissenschaft, was die innere Begründung anlangte, oder des Geschmacks, wo es die Form der Darstellung galt.

Dieser Leserkreis ist uns treu geblieben und ihn auch noch ferner und dauernd zu fesseln, bleibt unsere alleinige Aufgabe.

Dabei leugnen wir unsere nächste Verbindung lediglich mit dem, was man Belletristik zu nennen pflegt, keineswegs. Doch schon lange weiß man, wie sehr das Feld dieser sogenannten schönen Literatur sich erweitert hat. Der Ernst des Lebens ist wie an die Wissenschaft so auch an die Kunst herangetreten. Die Prüfung des Gedankens und der Phantasie an den Anforderungen des Gegebenen hat sich mit einer Nothwendigkeit geltend gemacht, die sogar bis zur Gleichgültigkeit gegen die Theorie,

1858. N. F. IV. 1. 1

First page of an 1858 issue of the cultural journal for the middle class that Gutzkow edited from 1852 to 1862

set in Rome, for example, opens with the narrator commenting in rapid succession on the secret lives led by great prelates within earshot of the bells of Rome's 365 churches, on music resounding from the multitude of organs, on English converts rushing to the catacombs, on German and French tourists swarming through other sacred shrines, and on cloisters throughout the city in which prayers are being raised for the souls of the world's 131 million Catholics. Against such backgrounds the action unfolds through extensive conversations, with insertions of letters and other documents, narrational hints about future events, and explanations of the universal meaning of particular situations.

By 1872 *Der Zauberer von Rom* had sold strongly in four editions, but it failed to achieve the success of *Die Ritter vom Geiste.* In his prefaces to the various editions Gutzkow tried to overcome the apparent indifference of Protestant readers and the suspicions of Catholics toward the Protestant author by emphasizing the centrality of the wider issues of freedom, of aspirations for national unity, of relations between church and state, and of the spiritual needs of modern humanity.

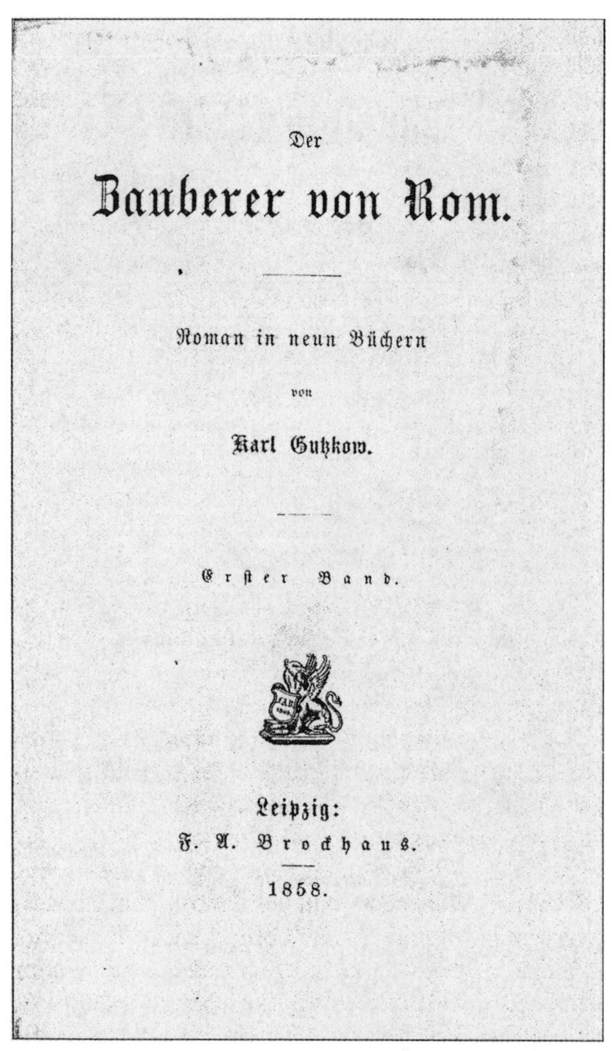

Der

Zauberer von Rom.

Roman in neun Büchern

von

Karl Gutzkow.

Erster Band.

Leipzig:

F. A. Brockhaus.

1858.

Title page for the first volume of Gutzkov's nine-volume novel about Catholicism

Gutzkow's treatment of all these questions makes the novel a valuable historical source.

In the 1860s Gutzkow's acute sensitivity to criticism developed into sinister perceptions of people's wrongdoing toward him, and he engaged in feuds with such prominent figures as Julian Schmidt, Gustav Freytag, Berthold Auerbach, and Heinrich von Treitschke. Financial worries also began to mount; among the strategies by which he tried to ease the pressure, the most unwise was his decision in 1861 to become the general secretary of the new Schillerstiftung (Schiller Foundation) established in Weimar to help needy writers. The annual salary of six hundred talers, although less than the royalties for one of his novels, somehow seemed to him a salvation. Instead, the move to Weimar brought him into a stifling cultural atmosphere in which the ducal court controlled the pervasive Goethe legacy, and he became involved in fierce conflicts over the running of the foundation and the distribution of funds. As worried friends looked on helplessly, signs of his persecution complex mounted. When he finally resigned his post in October 1864, he was on the brink of a complete breakdown. The succeeding months brought worsening psychotic episodes that culminated shortly after New Year's Day in a suicide attempt.

Through most of 1865 Gutzkow was in a sanatorium near Bayreuth; by fall his delirium had eased, and he was released just before Christmas. A collection by friends provided the financial wherewithal to take his family to Vevey on Lake Geneva for five months of recuperation. He soon resumed a feverish pace of work, however, as if to prove that his powers had not diminished. He made extensive travels around Germany doing research for his Reformation novel *Hohenschwangau* (1867–1868). This sprawling work, intended to be the Protestant counterpart to *Der Zauberer von Rom,* received far less notice and, despite its admiring portrait of Martin Luther, alienated many Protestant readers with its denigration of the political involvements of the emergent Evangelical church.

Gutzkow's frenzied activity continued into the 1870s in spite of symptoms of paranoia, eye problems, and chronic insomnia. After a brief attempt to settle in Berlin he fled – convinced that enemies would derail his train – to the home he had established in Kesselstadt bei Hanau, a small town east of Frankfurt. There he poured forth autobiographical writings, stories, novellas, plays, journalistic essays, shortened versions of *Die Ritter vom Geiste* and *Der Zauberer von Rom,* and two more multivolume novels, *Die Söhne Pestalozzi's* (Pestalozzi's Sons, 1870) and *Fritz Ellrodt* (1872). In addition, he undertook the editing of new collections of his dramas and prose works.

That Gutzkow maintained an acute interest in contemporary German affairs is clear from his last novel, *Die neuen Serapionsbrüder* (The New Serapion Brethren, 1877), which portrays Berlin society of the Gründerjahre (Founders' Years), as the turbulent period of speculation following German unification came to be known. In this novel the Nebeneinander of social classes is symbolized through the congestion of the sidewalk, whose narrowness forces urban dwellers into such close contact with one another that it produces a nervous state Gutzkow calls *Trottoirkrankheit* (sidewalk disease). Such pressures of the burgeoning metropolis have been compounded by German unification, which, the novel suggests, has produced a rampant mentality of greed and parvenuism. The crash of 1873 is the inevitable outcome of the frenzy of greed that contaminated every realm of the German nation: economic, social, political, cultural, and, most important, moral. In this atmosphere Gutzkow finds no room for spiritual knights; in the end his heroes retreat into resigned withdrawal.

On 16 December 1878 Gutzkow, drugged by the chloral hydrate he took for his insomnia, knocked over a lamp and suffocated in the resulting fire. His death reinforced the image of a man consumed by mental illness. A more appropriate image, however, would be that of a knight of the spirit, for even in his most pessimistic moods Gutzkow retained his vision of freedom and his commitment to using literature to fight for it. He played a major role in bringing the contemporary world into German literature, and throughout his writing he experimented with new styles, language, and literary forms to represent this world. He also helped to build a modern literary culture that contributed, by its appeal to new social groups, to the democratization of German society.

Letters:

Briefe über Gutzkow's Ritter vom Geiste, edited by Alexander Jung (Leipzig: Brockhaus, 1856);

Gerhard K. Friesen, "Four Previously Unpublished Letters of Karl Gutzkow to Heinrich Albert Opperman," *Modern Language Notes,* 83 (April 1968): 445–454;

Therese von Bacheracht und Karl Gutzkow: Unveröffentlichte Briefe (1842–1849), edited by Werner Vortriede (Munich: Kossel, 1971);

"Karl Gutzkows Briefe an Hermann Costenoble," edited by William H. McClain and Lieselotte E. Kurth-Voigt, *Börsenblatt für den deutschen Buchhandel,* 27 (1971): 2651–2768;

"Karl Gutzkows Briefe an Hermann Costenoble," edited by McClain and Kurth-Voigt, *Archiv für Geschichte des Buchwesens,* 13 (1973): 1–236;

Die Briefe des frühen Gutzkow, 1830–1848: Pathographie einer Epoche, edited by Peter Bürgel (Frankfurt am Main: Lang, 1975);

Friesen, "Es ist schwere Sache mit der Belletristik: Karl Gutzkows Briefwechsel mit Otto Janke, 1864–1878," *Archiv für Geschichte des Buchwesens,* 22 (February 1982): 1–206;

Friesen, "Der Verleger ist des Schriftstellers Beichtvater: Karl Gutzkows Briefwechsel mit dem Verlag F. A. Brockhaus, 1831–1878," *Archiv für Geschichte des Buchwesens,* 28 (1987): 1–213.

Biographies:

Joseph-Emile Dresch, *Gutzkow et la Jeune Allemagne* (Paris: Société nouvelle de librairie et d'edition, 1904);

Heinrich Hubert Houben, "Karl Gutzkows Leben und Schaffen," in Gutzkow's *Ausgewählte Werke,* 12 volumes, edited by Houben (Leipzig: Hesse, 1908), I: 3–156;

Reinhold Gensel, "Lebensbild," in *Gutzkows Werke,* edited by Gensel, volume 1 (Berlin: Bong, 1912), pp. v–lvii;

Magdalene Capelle, "Der junge Gutzkow," Ph.D. dissertation, University of Berlin, 1950;

Eitel Wolf Dobert, *Karl Gutzkow und seine Zeit* (Bern & Munich: Francke, 1968).

References:

Gustav Bacherer, *Die junge Literatur und der Roman Wally: Ein Vademecum für Herrn Carl Gutzkow. Dem deutschen Publikum zugeeignet* (Stuttgart: Hallberger, 1835);

Eliza M. Butler, "Gutzkow and Saint-Simonism," in her *The Saint-Simonian Religion in Germany: A Study of the Young German Movement* (Cambridge: Cambridge University Press, 1926), pp. 257–318;

Peter Demetz, "Karl Gutzkow und Georg Büchner: Szenen aus dem Vormärz," in *Literatur und Kritik,* edited by Walter Jens (Stuttgart: Deutsche Verlags-Anstalt, 1980), pp. 205–218;

Demetz, "Karl Gutzkows *Die Ritter vom Geiste:* Notizen über Struktur und Ideologie," *Monatshefte für deutschen Unterricht, deutsche Sprache und Literatur,* 61 (Fall 1969): 225–231;

Otto Dirr, "Karl Gutzkow und seine großen Zeitromane," Ph.D. dissertation, University of Freiburg, 1970;

Joseph Dresch, *Le roman social en Allemagne (1850–1900): Gutzkow – Freytag – Spielhagen – Fontane* (Paris: Alcan, 1913);

Alo Fell, *Gutzkows Ritter vom Geiste: Psychogenetische Untersuchung zur Frage des Übergangs von Romantik zu Realismus* (Aachen: Aachener Verlags- und Druckerei-Gesellschaft, 1927);

M. Kay Flavell, "Women and Individualism: A Reexamination of Schlegel's 'Lucinde' and Gutzkow's 'Wally die Zweiflerin,' " *Modern Language Review,* 70 (July 1975): 550–566;

Klemens Freiburg-Ruter, *Der literarische Kritiker Karl Gutzkow: Eine Studie über Form, Gehalt und Wirkung seiner Kritik* (Leipzig: Eichblatt, 1930);

Gerhard Friesen, *The German Panoramic Novel of the 19th Century* (Bern: Lang, 1972);

Friesen "Karl Gutzkow und der Buchhandel: Zu seiner Auffassung vom Schriftstellerberuf und seinen Honoraren," *Archiv für Geschichte des Buchwesens,* 19 (December 1978): 1493–1536; 20 (March 1979): 1534–1616;

Friesen, "Politische Dramaturgie: Zur Theorie des Dramas und Theaters zwischen den Revolutionen von 1830 und 1848," in *Deutsche Dramentheorien: Beiträge zu einer historischen Poetik des Dramas in Deutschland,* edited by Horst Denkler and Reinhold Grimm (Wiesbaden: Athenaion, 1980);

Rainer Funke, *Beharrung und Umbruch 1830–1860: Karl Gutzkow auf dem Weg in die literarische Moderne* (Frankfurt am Main: Lang, 1984);

Eberhard Galley, "Heine im literarischen Streit mit Gutzkow: Mit unbekannten Manuskripten aus Heines Nachlaß," *Heine Jahrbuch,* 5 (1966): 3–40;

Frederick C. Graham, "Humanism and Socialism in Gutzkow's 'Ritter vom Geiste,' " Ph.D. dissertation, University of Cincinnati, 1968;

Volkmar Hansen, " 'Freiheit! Freiheit! Freiheit!': Das Bild Karl Gutzkow in der Forschung, mit Ausblicken auf Ludolf Wienbarg," in *Literatur in der sozialen Bewegung: Aufsätze und Forschungsberichte zum 19. Jahrhundert,* edited by Alberto Martino and others (Tübingen: Niemeyer, 1977), pp. 488–542;

Peter Hasubek, "Geschichtsphilosophie und Erzählkunst: Bemerkungen zu Karl Gutzkow und Hermann Broch," *Études germaniques,* 22 (October–December 1967): 517–537;

Hasubek, "Karl Gutzkow," in *Deutsche Dichter des 19. Jahrhunderts: Ihr Leben und Werk,* edited by Benno von Wiese, second edition (Berlin: Schmidt, 1979), pp. 208–228;

Hasubek, "Karl Gutzkow: *Die Ritter vom Geiste* (1850–1851): Gesellschaftsdarstellung im deutschen Roman nach 1848," in *Romane und Erzählungen des Bürgerlichen Realismus: Neue Interpretationen,* edited by Horst Denkler (Stuttgart: Reclam, 1980), pp. 26–39;

Hasubek, "Karl Gutzkows Romane 'Die Ritter vom Geiste' und 'Der Zauberer von Rom': Studien zur Typologie des deutschen Zeitromans im 19. Jahrhundert," Ph.D. dissertation, University of Hamburg, 1964;

Rolf K. Hoegel, "Young German Message Plays," *Monatsheft für deutschen Unterricht, deutsche Sprache und Literatur,* 65 (Winter 1973): 361–369;

Heinrich Hoff, *Karl Gutzkow und die Gutzkowgraphie,* edited by Carl Winter (Heidelberg: Winter, 1977);

Heinrich Hubert Houben, *Gutzkow-Funde: Beiträge zur Litteratur- und Kulturgeschichte des neunzehnten Jahrhunderts* (Berlin: Wolff, 1901; reprinted, Hildesheim: Gerstenberg, 1978);

Houben, *Studien über die Dramen Karl Gutzkows* (Düsseldorf: Tonnes, 1898);

Joachim Jendretzki, *Karl Gutzkow als Pionier des literarischen Journalismus* (Frankfurt am Main: Lang, 1988);

Ruth-Ellen B. Joeres, "The Gutzkow-Menzel Tracts: A Critical Response to a Novel and an Era," *Modern Language Notes,* 88 (October 1978): 988–1010;

Calvin N. Jones, "Authorial Intent and Public Response to 'Uriel Acosta' and 'Freiheit in Krähwinkel,' " *South Atlantic Review,* 47 (November 1982): 17–26;

Herbert Kaiser, "Karl Gutzkow: *Wally die Zweiflerin* (1835)," in *Romane und Erzählungen zwischen Romantik und Realismus: Neue Interpretationen,* edited by Paul Michael Lützeler (Stuttgart: Reclam, 1983), pp. 183–201;

R. J. Kavanagh, "Letters of Intent: Karl Gutzkow's *Briefe eines Narren an eine Närrin,*" *New German Studies,* 7 (1979): 1–15;

Kavanagh, "Portrait of the Artist as a Young German: Karl Gutzkow's Political Attitudes and 1848," in *1848: The Sociology of Literature,* edited by Francis Barker and others (Colchester, U.K.: University of Essex, 1978), pp. 64–78.

Werner Kohlschmidt, "Reformkatholizismus im Biedermeierkleide: Gutzkows Roman 'Der Zauberer von Rom' als religiöse Utopie," *Jahrbuch der Deutschen Schiller gesellschaft,* 10 (1966): 286–296;

Joseph A. Kruse, " 'Wally' und der Verbotsbeschluß," in *Das Junge Deutschland,* edited by Kruse and Bernd Kortlander (Düsseldorf: Hoffmann & Campe, 1987), pp. 39–50;

Ludwig Maenner, *Karl Gutzkow und der demokratische Gedanke* (Munich: Oldenbourg, 1921);

Waltraud Maierhofer, *Wilhelm Meisters Wanderjahre und der Roman des Nebeneinander* (Bielefeld: Aisthesis, 1990), pp. 35–58;

William H. McClain, "From Karl Gutzkow's Letters: The Genesis of the *Gesammelte Werke* as Reflected in the Correspondence with Hermann Costenoble," *Modern Language Notes,* 83 (April 1968): 436–445;

Edward McInnes, "Strategies of Inwardness: Gutzkow's Domestic Plays and the Liberal

Drama of the 1840s," *Maske und Kothurn,* 18, no. 3 (1972): 219–233;

Eduard Metis, *Karl Gutzkow als Dramatiker (mit Benützung unveröffentlichter Stücke)* (Stuttgart: Metzler, 1915);

J. Mitchell Morse, "Karl Gutzkow and the Modern Novel," *Journal of General Education,* 15 (October 1963): 175–189;

Morse, "Karl Gutzkow and the Novel of Simultaneity," *James Joyce Quarterly,* 2 (Fall 1964): 13–17;

Peter Müller, *Beiträge zur Würdigung von Karl Gutzkow als Lustspieldichter, mit einem einleitenden Teil über ein unbekanntes Tagebuch* (Marburg: Elwert, 1910; New York: Johnson, 1968);

Reinhard Nickisch, "Vergeblicher Ruhm: Zur Wirkungsgeschichte von Karl Gutzkows Lustspiel 'Das Urbild des Tartüffe,' " *Études germaniques,* 27 (July–September 1972): 3, 365–378;

Lawrence M. Price, "Karl Gutzkow and Bulwer-Lytton," *Journal of English and Germanic Philology,* 16 (July 1917): 397–425;

J. Proelß, *Das junge Deutschland: Ein Buch deutscher Geistesgeschichte* (Stuttgart: Cotta, 1892);

G. G. Rathje, "Gutzkow's Debt to George Sand," *Journal of English and Germanic Philology,* 41 (1942): 291–302;

Maximilian Runze, *Karl Gutzkow: Ein deutscher Geistesheld* (Berlin: Mecklenburg, 1911);

Jeffrey L. Sammons, "Karl Gutzkow: *Wally die Zweiflerin,*" in his *Six Essays on the Young German Novel* (Chapel Hill: University of North Carolina Press, 1972), pp. 30–51, 156–158;

Otto Paul Schinnerer, *Woman in the Life and Work of Gutzkow* (New York: AMS, 1966);

Arno Schmidt, *Die Ritter vom Geiste: Von vergessenen Kollegen* (Karlsruhe: Stahlberg, 1965);

Franz Schneider, "Gutzkow's Contributions to the 'Kölnische Zeitung,' 1843–1848," *Germanic Review,* 18 (1943): 44–57;

Peter Stein, "Probleme der literarischen Proklamation des Politischen: Karl Gutzkow im Jahre 1835," in *Das Junge Deutschland,* pp. 134–154;

Hartmut Steinecke, "Gutzkow, die Juden und das Judentum," in *Conditio Judaica: Judentum, Antisemitismus und deutschsprachige Literatur vom 18. Jahrhundert bis zum Ersten Weltkrieg,* volume 2, edited by Hans Otto Horch and Horst Denkler (Tübingen: Niemeyer, 1989), pp. 118–129;

Lynn Tatlock, "*Das Haus Dusterweg* und *Wally, die Zweiflerin:* A Note on the Alexis-Gutzkow Connection," *Neophilologus,* 68 (October 1984): 562–570;

Janet Kay Zacha Van Valkenburg, "Karl Gutzkow and *Wally, Die Zweiflerin:* A Biographical Revaluation," Ph.D. dissertation, University of Illinois at Urbana, 1981;

Erwin Wabnegger, *Literaturskandal: Studien zur Reaktion des öffentlichen Systems auf Karl Gutzkows Roman "Wally, die Zweiflerin" (1835–1848)* (Würzburg: Königshausen + Neumann, 1987);

Paul Weiglin, *Gutzkows und Laubes Literaturdramen* (Berlin: Mayer & Müller, 1910; New York: Johnson Reprint, 1970);

Pier Westra, *Karl Gutzkows religiöse Ansichten* (Groningen: Wolters, 1947).

Papers:

Karl Gutzkow's papers, including sketches and preliminary studies, manuscripts, corrected proofs, critiques, and some six thousand letters from and to him, are in the Stadt- und Universitätsbibliothek (City and University Library) in Frankfurt am Main.

Ida Gräfin von Hahn-Hahn

(22 June 1805 - 12 January 1880)

Helga W. Kraft
University of Florida

BOOKS: *Gedichte* (Leipzig: Brockhaus, 1835);

Neue Gedichte (Leipzig: Brockhaus, 1836);

Venezianische Nächte (Leipzig: Brockhaus, 1836);

Lieder und Gedichte (Berlin, Posen & Bromberg: Mittler, 1837);

Aus der Gesellschaft: Novelle (Berlin: Duncker & Humblot, 1838); republished as *Ilda Schönholm* (Berlin: Duncker, 1845); translated anonymously as *Society; or, High Life in Germany* (London: Piper, Stephenson, 1854);

Astralion: Eine Arabeske (Berlin: Duncker, 1839);

Der Rechte (Berlin: Duncker, 1839);

Jenseits der Berge, 2 volumes (Leipzig: Brockhaus, 1840; enlarged, 1845);

Gräfin Faustine (Berlin: Duncker, 1841); translated by H. N. S. as *The Countess Faustina* (London: Clarke, 1844; New York: Winchester, 1845);

Reisebriefe, 2 volumes (Berlin: Duncker, 1841);

Ulrich, 2 volumes (Berlin: Duncker, 1841); translated anonymously as *Ulrich: A Tale* (London: Clarke, 1845);

Erinnerungen aus und an Frankreich, 2 volumes (Berlin: Duncker, 1842);

Ein Reiseversuch im Norden (Berlin: Duncker, 1843); translated by J. B. S. as *Travels in Sweden: Sketches of a Journey to the North* (London: Clarke, 1845; New York: Winchester, 1845);

Sigismund Forster (Berlin: Duncker, 1843);

Die Kinder auf dem Abendberg: Eine Weihnachtsgabe (Berlin: Duncker, 1843);

Cecil, 2 volumes (Berlin: Duncker, 1844);

Orientalische Briefe, 3 volumes (Berlin: Duncker, 1844); translated by Samuel Phillips as *Letters from the Orient; or, Travels in Turkey, the Holy Land, and Egypt* (London: Moore, 1845); translated anonymously as *Letters of a German Countess: Written during Her Travels in Turkey, Egypt, the Holy Land, Syria, Nubia, Etc., in 1843-4,* 3 volumes (London: Colburn, 1845);

Zwei Frauen, 2 volumes (Berlin: Duncker, 1845);

Die Brüder (Berlin: Duncker, 1845);

Ida Gräfin von Hahn-Hahn

Sibylle: Eine Selbstbiographie, 2 volumes (Berlin: Duncker, 1846);

Clelia Conti (Berlin: Duncker, 1846);

Levin, 2 volumes (Berlin: Duncker, 1848);

Von Babylon nach Jerusalem (Mainz: Kirchheim & Schott, 1851); translated by Elizabeth Atcherley as *From Babylon to Jerusalem* (London: Newby, 1851);

Unsrer Lieben Frau: Marienlieder (Mainz: Kirchheim & Schott, 1851);

Aus Jerusalem (Mainz: Kirchheim & Schott, 1851); translated by Atcherley as *From Jerusalem* (London: Newby, 1852);

Gesammelte Schriften, 21 volumes (Berlin: Duncker, 1851);

Die Liebhaber des Kreuzes, 2 volumes (Mainz: Kirchheim & Schott, 1851);

Ein Büchlein Vom Guten Hirten: Eine Weihnachtsgabe (Mainz: Kirchheim, 1853);

Das Jahr der Kirche: In Gedichten (Mainz: Kirchheim, 1854);

Bilder aus der Geschichte der Kirche, 4 volumes (Mainz: Kirchheim, 1856–1866); translated by E. F. B. as *Lives of the Fathers of the Desert* (London: Richardson, 1867);

Maria Regina: Eine Erzählung aus der Gegenwart, 2 volumes (Mainz: Kirchheim, 1860);

Doralice: Ein Familiengemälde aus der Gegenwart, 2 volumes (Mainz: Kirchheim, 1861);

Vier Lebensbilder: Ein Papst, ein Bischof, ein Priester, ein Jesuit (Mainz: Kirchheim, 1861);

Zwei Schwestern: Eine Erzählung aus der Gegenwart, 2 volumes (Mainz: Kirchheim, 1863);

Peregrin: Ein Roman, 2 volumes (Mainz: Kirchheim, 1864);

Ben-David: Ein Phantasiegemälde von Ernest Renan (Mainz: Kirchheim, 1864);

Eudoxia, die Kaiserin: Ein Zeitgemälde aus dem fünften Jahrhundert, 2 volumes (Mainz: Kirchheim, 1866); translated anonymously as *Eudoxia: A Picture of the Fifth Century* (London: Burns, Oates, 1868; Baltimore: Kelly, Piet, 1869);

Die Erbin von Cronenstein, 2 volumes (Mainz: Kirchheim, 1868); adapted by Mary H. Allies as *The Heiress of Cronenstein* (New York & Cincinnati: Benziger, 1900);

Die Geschichte eines armen Fräuleins, 2 volumes (Mainz: Kirchheim, 1869);

Die Glöcknerstochter, 2 volumes (Mainz: Kirchheim, 1871);

Die Erzählung des Hofraths, 2 volumes (Mainz: Kirchheim, 1872);

Vergieb uns unsere Schuld!: Eine Erzählung, 2 volumes (Mainz: Kirchheim, 1874); translated by Maria Elizabeth, Lady Herbert as *Dorothea Waldegrave,* 2 volumes (London: Bentley, 1875);

Nirwana, 2 volumes (Mainz: Kirchheim, 1875);

Eine reiche Frau, 2 volumes (Mainz: Kirchheim, 1877);

Der breite Weg und die enge Straße: Eine Familiengeschichte, 2 volumes (Mainz: Kirchheim, 1877);

Wahl und Führung: Ein Roman, 2 volumes (Mainz: Kirchheim, 1878);

Die heilige Zita: Dienstmagd zu Lucca im dreizehnten Jahrhundert (Mainz: Kirchheim, 1878);

Gesammelte Werke, 45 volumes (Regensburg: Habbel, 1902–1905);

Meine Reise in England, edited by Bernd Goldmann (Mainz: Von Hase & Koehler, 1981).

OTHER: A. Lindau, ed., *Lichtstrahlen aus der Gemüthswelt: Zur Erweckung und Erquickung für Blinde,* foreword by Hahn-Hahn (Dresden & Leipzig: Arnold, 1845);

Legende der Heiligen, volume 3, edited by Hahn-Hahn (Mainz: Kirchheim, 1856);

Leben der heiligen Teresa von Jesus, translated by Hahn-Hahn (Mainz: Kirchheim, 1867);

Das Buch der Klostergründungen nach der reformirten Carmeliter-Regel von der heiligen Teresa von Jesus, translated by Hahn-Hahn (Mainz: Kirchheim, 1868).

Ida Gräfin von Hahn-Hahn was one of the most prolific and widely read novelists of the nineteenth century. She is significant mainly for her early works, which present shockingly unconventional heroines. She rejected the female models prescribed by eighteenth-century writers (especially Johann Wolfgang von Goethe) and left the romantic male fantasies of the "perfect" woman far behind. She dared to fashion a strong and self-directed female figure – usually considered "a monster" – into a heroine. The novels are populated mainly with people from her own aristocratic milieu but do not include actual social and political phenomena of her time. Rather, her novels focus on timeless gender issues, and she attempts a sociopsychological analysis of power relationships between men and women in her society. Her travel accounts are also noteworthy: she attempts to understand people within their own environments and daily experiences, and she was the first writer to describe the achievements of women in her travel writing. The finest of her novels and travel accounts reflect her search for a freer existence as a woman in her society. Her later, popular novels, written after her conversion to Catholicism, are of lesser interest because they present conventional solutions, yet they still display strong women. Her works disappeared from the market and from discussion until the women's movement of the twentieth century rediscovered her.

Ida Marie Luise Friederike Gustave Gräfin (Countess) von Hahn was born on 22 June 1805 in Tressow, Mecklenburg, to Sophie Behr and Count Karl Friedrich von Hahn-Neuhaus. The father's passion for the theater – he was known as "der Theatergraf" (theater count) – led him to maintain his own theater group, which eventually drained the family's wealth. Her mother divorced her husband in 1809 and raised her four children in Rostock, Neubrandenburg, and Greifswald on a tight budget. Although Ida's education was directed by private tutors, it was inadequate to her talents.

In 1826 she married her rich cousin, Friedrich Adolf von Hahn-Basedow, mainly for financial reasons, thus acquiring her double name. A retarded daughter was born in 1829, and the marriage ended in divorce the same year. She entered into a liaison with Baron Adolf Bystram; a son was born from this union in 1831.

At first she wrote poetry; four volumes were published between 1835 and 1837. Although most of the poems are conventional in style, some of them question traditional values and conventions.

Hahn-Hahn lived a restless life until her late forties, living at various times in Berlin, Dresden, Greifswald, and Vienna, and on her estate, Schloß Neuhaus, in Schleswig-Holstein. Although she corresponded with literary figures of her time such as Heinrich Laube, Karl Varnhagen von Ense, and Hermann von Pückler-Muskau, she did not participate in the activities of the fashionable literary salons. She traveled, mostly in the company of Baron Bystram, through Germany and Switzerland in the 1830s; France, England, and Italy in 1839; France in 1839 and 1840; Spain in 1840; and Sweden in 1842. A relationship with Heinrich Simon failed in 1836 because of her unwillingness to marry. In 1838 she found the most suitable medium for her talent when the novel *Aus der Gesellschaft* (Out of Society; translated as *Society; or, High Life in Germany,* 1854) became an instant success. Between 1838 and 1848 she wrote nine additional novels in which women artists and writers are often the central figures. Autobiographical elements are present in most of her works; she even termed her novel *Sibylle* (1846) a "self-biography."

The attempt to place Hahn-Hahn into a literary category seems fruitless. Some literary historians note the influence of the Junges Deutschland (Young Germany) movement and of French literature (she was often called the German George Sand); others place her among the Romantics or the Biedermeier writers. Conventional critics held her disdain for marriage and family against her, never forgetting to mention that she had her own children raised by other people. Most often, a moral danger to society was noted in Hahn-Hahn's novels. Critics did not easily accept her emphasis on women's lives at a time when it was thought that the autonomous human being could only be male. Theodor Mundt criticized her for emphasizing unimportant phenomena from which she attempted in vain to distill something essential. Her novels were viewed at times as "Trivialliteratur" (popular or trivial literature), merely a cut above trashy "Frauenromane" (novels for women). Her focus on strong, emancipated, and productive women was not even applauded by all feminists, some of whom objected to her aristocratic exclusiveness. But by the beginning of the twentieth century Hahn-Hahn's modernity was recognized. It was noted that despite her unwavering aristocratic demeanor, the Countess Hahn-Hahn was, in her own way, a defender of woman's rights: she did not fight for "equal rights" for women because she did not deem the rights of men in her society to be desirable. It was also at the turn of the century that Hahn-Hahn came to be considered one of the two women writers of her time (the other was Bettina von Arnim) who did not imitate the male style but spoke in a woman's voice.

In 1955 Margaret Kober-Merzbach noted that Hahn-Hahn's novels posed a political danger in addition to the moral one. Hahn-Hahn fought not only against the power of men but also against a society in which pure feeling and the positive power of love could not find room. A close reading of her works reveals an attempt to empower women in a men's society. In her first novel the central character, Ilda Schönholm, says, "ich folge dem Beispiel der Männer, die seit sechstausend Jahren lauter Prinzipien zum Vortheil ihres Geschlechts erfunden haben. Warum soll ich nicht für mein Geschlecht sorgen! Wenn man sich emanzipieren will, muß man vor allen Dingen *esprit de corps* haben, fest an einander halten, und da die Männer ihre Hand wider uns aufheben, die unsere drohend wider sie ausstrecken. Wessen Waffen die stärksten sind, muß die Zeit lehren, nicht der Augenschein – denn der ist mit ihnen im Bunde" (I follow the example of men who have been inventing nothing but principles for the advantage of their sex for six thousand years. Why should I not take care of my own sex? If you want to emancipate yourself, above all you must have an *esprit de corps,* you must stand by each other steadfastly, and since men raise their hands against us, we must raise our hands threateningly against them as well. Time must teach whose weapons are the strongest; appearances cannot teach this, because they collaborate with men).

Hahn-Hahn did not believe that democracy, socialism, or communism would offer a better way of life, especially for women. It was her – mistaken – view that the British aristocratic system provided opportunities for people according to their abilities. She did not share the common belief that nature limited women's intellectual capacity: in her novel *Der Rechte* (The Right Man, 1839) the heroine replies to the claim that women are incapable of participating in a scientific discourse: "Unmöglich? – schickt die Mädchen auf die

Universität, und die Knaben in die Nähschule und Küche: nach drei Generationen werdet ihr wissen, ob es unmöglich ist, und was es heißt, die Unterdrückten sein" (Impossible? Send the girls to the university and the boys into the sewing schools and into the kitchen. After three generations you will know if it is impossible and what it means to be suppressed). For Hahn-Hahn it was of utmost urgency that women actualize their greatest strength, their depth of feeling. The men in her novels are rarely a match for the heroines, and only the most excellent men dare to love these extraordinary women.

In most of her novels Hahn-Hahn uses a female or male narrator; but for many pages the characters present themselves in extensive dialogues that lend the works a lively, theatrical flair. This technique also allows for subtle shifts of viewpoint.

The heroine of *Gräfin Faustine* (1841; translated as *The Countess Faustina,* 1844) is a female Faust. But she is not a restless Goethean seeker of pleasure at all costs; she is not staking her soul and the lives of others on a search for experience on all human levels and beyond. She does not digress from the laws of the visible world to plunge into a metaphysical realm to strive for superhuman power and accomplishment. And the female Faust does not need redemption through the sacrifice of a male Gretchen. She mocks the dazzling inventions of male philosophy and aesthetics that are the mark of polarized western man; the dichotomy of Faust's tortured soul is alien to Hahn-Hahn's female Faust.

Countess Faustine's Faustian deed consists in her will to maintain autonomy over her life and to make decisions according to her abilities and feelings, without regard to the expectations of patriarchal society. She is a gifted painter who is able to provide for herself from her inheritance and, significantly, through the sale of her paintings. Another Faustian deed is her rejection of marriage: she openly lives and travels – as Hahn-Hahn did with Baron Bystram – with Count Andover, who respects her independence and accepts her intellectual equality as well as her emotional superiority. Faustine reflects on this arrangement: "Ich war glücklich und fühlte mich durch dies Glück befähigt und stark gemacht, in dieser eigentümlichen Weise es festzuhalten. Dies Glück und diese Weise ließen mich in meiner vollen Selbständigkeit und doch zugleich in der Sphäre des Weibes, welches seine Ausbildung und Befriedigung allein in der Liebe findet" (I was happy and felt empowered through this happiness, to maintain it in this unusual way. This happiness and this way allowed me to live in complete independence but at the same time in the sphere of a woman who finds her development and satisfaction in love alone).

As Faustine develops, her love expands; she becomes fond of another suitor, Mario Mengen. The concept of love becomes an object of revision and reinterpretation for Hahn-Hahn. It no longer signifies the absolute abandonment of a woman to a man in the manner of Gretchen in Goethe's *Faust* (1808, 1832). As her description of the Roman sculpture *Befreite Psyche* (Freed Psyche) indicates, her concern is to provide models for an unbound feminine psyche that is not in the service of men. For Faustine, love means to dedicate oneself to an object of desire; but she asks: does the object always have to remain the same? Love and desire can never find a finite goal but can empower Faustine to find and become her own self through the creative process. She eventually recognizes that her relationships with men are motivated by compassion: "ich bringe es mit dem Mitleid nicht weiter, als mich lieben zu lassen, nicht so weit, um wieder zu lieben" (I do not get further with compassion than to let myself be loved, not so far as to love in return).

Faustine experiences an unquenchable thirst for "etwas anderes" (something different), and nothing material can satisfy her: "Jede vollendete Arbeit war ihr gleichgültig – gleichgültig haben, besitzen, genießen! Streben war ihr alleinziges Glück, und der Moment wo sie das Erstrebte mit der Fingerspitze berührte – ihre Seligkeit. Sollte sie aber festhalten, so ermattete ihre Hand" (Each completed work of art lost interest to her – it did not matter to her to have anything, to own anything, to just enjoy! Striving was her only happiness, and at the moment in which she reached with her fingertips what she had striven for – it was heaven to her. But if she were to hold on, her hand would weaken).

Faustine's pact with the devil, as the critic Gerlinde Maria Geiger sees it, is to stake her soul on marriage. The restrictions of her marriage to Mario Mengen squelch her creative spirit, yet Faustine is able to save her soul because the inner fever driving her cannot be calmed by anything in this world. Her burning insatiability counters the stagnation of marriage and is a sign of an endless capacity for feeling. Recognizing her mistake, the heroine again transgresses societal limits: she leaves her child and husband and enters a convent in the hope that dedication to an absolute being – God – will allow for absolute expansion. Faustine dies shortly thereafter, indicating that a Faustian creative absolute is not a likely option for a woman of her time. The convent was the only oasis where free women could be among themselves, yet it provided a multitude of restrictions as well.

Hahn-Hahn embarked on an extensive trip through the Orient in 1843; she was the first woman to apply for a passport to the region. She traveled to England and Ireland in 1846 and to Italy and Sicily in 1847. Her accounts of her trips were compared in quality to those of Pückler-Muskau, with whom she had a lively correspondence in 1844–1845. These travel books are written in the form of letters and record her immediate impressions. The three-volume *Orientalische Briefe* (1844; translated as *Letters from the Orient,* 1845) reveals her interest in mythology in which women were of prime importance. A whole volume is devoted to Egypt, where she traced the Isis myth in her search for a matriarchal past.

In her autobiographical novel *Sibylle* Hahn-Hahn recreates the years in which she became a writer. While Faustine is the finished, sparkling image of an artist who has found herself, Sibylle is tracing the painful steps that eventually afford a woman the freedom and self-confidence to mature into an artist. Sibylle must find what Faustine has already found. Almost a century before Virginia Woolf, Faustine had insisted: "ich bin eigensinnig! ich will meinen eigenen Platz! sei er so klein wie möglich – ich will meinen eigenen, unantastbaren Platz – oder gar keinen" (I am stubborn! I want my own place, however small it might be – I want my own, inviolate place – or none at all).

The male narrator considers Sibylle cold and unable to love. Even modestly egotistical women who thought of themselves rather than thinking only of their families were denounced as monsters in Hahn-Hahn's time; but she quite daringly makes them into heroines. Geiger maintains that Hahn-Hahn unmasks language as a powerful tool of the patriarchy and tries to destroy it by undermining existing concepts. Thus, not being able to love in the traditional sense means to her to love in the true sense. If love leads to possession and demands, it is evil. Creativity is released by love, desire, and meditation. Love must not be chained to one object, desire must remain open, and meditation must lead to a structuring of the chaos inherent in love and desire before a human being can create a true self. Love and desire in their structureless form are considered feminine by Hahn-Hahn; meditation is for her a masculine trait because it brings scattered elements into order. Yet, these traits are not limited to either sex. Hahn-Hahn shows in *Sibylle* the capability of women to combine all of these traits in an androgynous wholeness. The male artists in the novels never achieve such completeness, although in them, too, the feminine form of creativity – intuition – can surface. For example, the pianist Sedlaczech shows Sibylle how to rely on intuition rather than cling to convention. To become whole, Sibylle realizes at the end, she must renounce any erotic union with a man because it would stymie her creativity. Hahn-Hahn introduces Doppelgänger figures into the text: only after Sibylle's daughter, Benevenuta, representing her traditional side that wants marriage, and her friend Arabella, representing her erotic side, die is she able to dedicate herself totally to art as she invents herself through her writing. The result is the novel *Sibylle* itself. Even though the work reflects Hahn-Hahn's own development, at the end she lets her heroine die, a reflection of her own pessimistic view.

Hahn-Hahn's lack of emphasis on economic structures as the cause of inequality did not endear her to leftist literary criticism; she did not share the Marxist idea that private well-being is achieved when economic hardship is alleviated. Her opposition to the Revolution of 1848 was held against her, although it was based on her fear that it would lead to a worse, more tyrannical rule than the one that already existed.

By 1850 her companion Baron Bystram had died, an eye operation had left her practically blind in one eye, and the reactionary political trends after the failure of the Revolution of 1848 made her want to find a refuge. She was converted to Catholicism in Berlin in 1850 by Wilhelm Emmanuel von Ketteler, who shortly thereafter became bishop of Mainz. She reflects on the drastic step in her book *Von Babylon nach Jerusalem* (1851; translated as *From Babylon to Jerusalem,* 1851). In 1852 she withdrew to a convent of the order "Zum guten Hirten" (At the Good Shepherd) in Angers, and in 1854 she founded her own convent in Mainz; she maintained it with the income from her writings and provided a shelter for unwed mothers, but she never became a nun. Between 1851 and 1860 she wrote mainly poems to the Virgin Mary and historical accounts of Catholic dignitaries. In 1860 she returned to fiction; between then and her death she wrote a series of popular novels in which ethics and religion are closely linked. The time for emancipatory experiments was over; women in Germany were not even allowed to gather in public between the 1850s and the turn of the twentieth century. Hahn-Hahn resigned herself to convention; yet, like her, most of her heroines remained strong women who focused on their own, nonnurturing activities, albeit within the strictures imposed by society. Hahn-Hahn died of heart failure on 12 January 1880.

References:

Heinrich Abeken, *Ein schlichtes Leben in bewegter Zeit,* edited by Hedwig Abeken (Berlin: Mittler, 1904);

Therese von Bacheracht, *Menschen und Gegenden* (Brunswick: Vieweg, 1845);

Sebastian Brunner, *Rom und Babylon: Eine Beleuchtung confessioneller Zustände der Gegenwart* (Regensburg: Manz, 1852);

Gerlinde Maria Geiger, *Die befreite Psyche: Emanzipationsansätze im Frühwerk Ida Hahn-Hahns (1838–1848)* (Frankfurt am Main: Lang, 1986);

Hildegard Gulde, *Studien zum jungdeutschen Frauenroman* (Weilheim: Glenger, 1933);

Lucie Guntli, *Goethezeit und Katholizismus im Werk Ida Hahn-Hahns: Ein Beitrag zur Geistesgeschichte des 19. Jahrhunderts* (Emsdetten: Helios, 1931);

Paul Haffner, *Gräfin Ida Hahn-Hahn: Eine psychologische Studie* (Frankfurt am Main: Foesser, 1880);

Alinda Jacoby, *Ida Gräfin Hahn-Hahn: Novellistisches Lebensbild* (Mainz: Kirchheim, 1894);

Margaret Kober-Merzbach, "Ida Gräfin Hahn-Hahn," *Monatshefte,* 47 (January 1955): 27–37;

Gerd Lüpke, *Ida Gräfin Hahn-Hahn: Ein Lebensbild einer mecklenburgischen Biedermeier-Autorin* (Bremen: Giebel, 1975);

Hans Mayer, *Außenseiter* (Frankfurt am Main: Suhrkamp, 1975), pp. 76-82;

Renate Möhrmann, *Die andere Frau. Emanzipationsansätze deutscher Schriftstellerinnen im Vorfeld der Achtundvierziger-Revolution* (Stuttgart: Metzler, 1977);

Theodor Mundt, *Geschichte der Literatur der Gegenwart* (Leipzig: Simions, 1853);

Katrien van Munster, *Die junge Ida Gräfin Hahn-Hahn* (Graz: Stiasny, 1929);

Gert Oberembt, "Eine Erfolgsautorin der Biedermeierzeit: Studien zur zeitgenössischen Rezeption von Ida Hahn-Hahns frühen Gesellschaftsromanen," in *Kleine Beiträge zur Droste-Forschung,* edited by Wilfried Woesler Dülman (Westphalia: Laumann, 1973);

Oberembt, *Ida Gräfin Hahn-Hahn: Weltschmerz und Ultramontanismus. Studien zum Unterhaltungsroman im 19. Jahrhundert* (Bonn: Bouvier, 1980);

Heidi Sallenbach von Uster, *George Sand und der deutsche Emanzipationsroman* (Zurich: Kommerzdruck und Verlags A.G., 1942);

Otto von Schaching, *Ida Gräfin Hahn-Hahn: Eine biographisch-literarische Skizze* (Regensburg: Habbel, 1904);

Erna Ines Schmid-Jürgens, *Ida Gräfin Hahn-Hahn* (Nendeln, Liechtenstein: Kraus, 1967);

Adolf Töpker, *Beziehungen Ida Hahn-Hahns zum Menschentum der deutschen Romantik* (Bochum: Pöppinghaus, 1937).

Georg Herwegh

(31 May 1817 - 7 April 1875)

Bettina Kluth Cothran
Georgia Institute of Technology

BOOKS: *Gedichte eines Lebendigen,* anonymous, 2 volumes (Zurich & Winterthur: Literarisches Comptoir, 1841, 1843);

Die deutsche Flotte: Eine Mahnung an das deutsche Volk, anonymous (Zurich: Literarisches Comptoir, 1842);

Gedichte und Kritische Aufsätze aus den Jahren 1839 und 1840 (Belle-Vue bei Constanz: Verlags- und Sortimentsbuchhandlung zu Belle-Vue, 1845);

Huldigung: Gedichte (Berlin: Reuter & Stargardt, 1848);

Zwei Preußenlieder (Leipzig: Weller, 1848);

Blum's Tod: Gedicht eines Lebendigen, anonymous (Herisau: Schläfer, 1849);

Die Schillerfeier in Zürich: Prolog für die Fest-Vorstellung im Theater am 10. November 1859 (Zurich: Kiesling, 1860);

Bundeslied für den Allgemeinen Deutschen Arbeiterverein (Zurich: Meyer, 1863);

Neue Gedichte: Herausgegeben nach seinem Tode, edited by Emma Herwegh (Zurich: Verlags-Magazin, 1877);

Herweghs Werke in drei Teilen, edited by Hermann Tardell (Berlin: Bong, 1909);

Aus Herweghs Nachlaß, edited by Victor Fleury (Lausanne: Rouge, 1911);

Herweghs Werke in einem Band, edited by Hans-Georg Werner (Berlin: Aufbau, 1967);

Frühe Publizistik 1837–1841, edited by Bruno Kaiser and others (Glashütten: Auvermann, 1971);

Über Literatur und Gesellschaft (1837–1841), edited by Agnes Ziegengeist (Berlin: Akademie, 1971);

Gedichte und Prosa, edited by Peter Haubek (Stuttgart: Reclam, 1975).

OTHER: Alphonse-Marie-Louis de Prat de Lamartine, *Sämmtliche Werke,* 6 volumes, translated by Herwegh (Stuttgart: Scheible, Rieger & Sattler, 1839–1840);

Einundzwanzig Bogen aus der Schweiz, edited by Herwegh (Zurich & Winterthur: Literarisches Comptoir, 1843);

Georg Herwegh

Lamartine, *Sämmtliche Werke,* 5 volumes, translated by Herwegh (Stuttgart: Scheible, Rieger & Sattler, 1843–1844);

William Shakespeare, *Shakespeare's dramatische Werke nach der Uebersetzung von August Wilhelm Schlegel und Ludwig Tieck, sorgfältig revidiert und theilweise neu bearbeitet, mit Einleitungen und Noten versehen, unter Redaction von H. Ulrici herausgegeben durch die Deutsche Shakespeare-Gesellschaft,* volume 8, translated by Herwegh (Berlin: Reimer, 1870);

Shakespeare, *William Shakespeare's Dramatische Werke,* 7 volumes, translated by Herwegh and others, edited by Friedrich Bodenstedt (Leipzig: Brockhaus, 1870–1871).

Among the German political poets of the Vormärz (Pre-March), the revolutionary years preceding the European March revolutions of 1848, Georg Herwegh probably was the most popular. The two volumes of his *Gedichte eines Lebendigen* (Poems of a Living Person, 1841, 1843) hit the nerve of the time and catapulted him into the front rank of those who advocated freedom and a just social order. A handsome, charismatic appearance, together with a gift for writing rousing poems that appealed to the masses, added to his prominence.

Even before the publication of these successful volumes, Herwegh had been active as a contributor of poems, essays, and critical articles to various literary magazines. In these early writings the poet delineated the topics that were to dominate his entire professional career. Foremost is the call for personal freedom and national unity. Herwegh also defends German classical literature, especially works of Friedrich Schiller and Johann Wolfgang von Goethe, and discusses the function of literature and literary criticism, as well as the position of the poet in society. His idols included the French writers George Sand, whom he venerated as the high priestess of freedom, and Pierre-Jean de Béranger, the advocate of the "Poesie der Hütte" (poetry of the hut). Like them, he saw the poet as the new leader: "Ich schreibe einzig und allein für mein Volk, für mein deutsches Volk! . . . hilft euch das Schwert nicht, hilft euch das Kreuz nicht, so helfen euch am Ende die Musen!" (I write only for my people, my German people! . . . if neither sword nor cross will help you, the muses may do just that!).

Herwegh wanted to spur the people to revolt against existing conditions, which he perceived as ruthlessly exploitative. To him, politics was not just "literaturfähig" (a literary topic) but *the* issue. His contemporary Heinrich Heine warned Herwegh that he might have lost touch with reality: "Herwegh, du eiserne Lerche, / Weil du so himmelhoch dich schwingst, / Hast du die Erde aus dem Gesichte / Verloren – Nur in deinem Gedichte / Lebt jener Lenz, den du besingst" (Herwegh, you iron lark, / While ascending to the heavens, / You have of the earth / Lost sight – Only in your poems / Does the spring you sing about exist). And indeed, Herwegh had the misfortune to see his political dreams unfulfilled and his reputation and personal fortune vanish within his lifetime. The political fervor of his poems and essays binds him to his era, and his emotionalism sounds overwrought to the reader of the late twentieth century – although literary critics in the now-defunct socialist camp held Herwegh's fight against bourgeois values in high esteem.

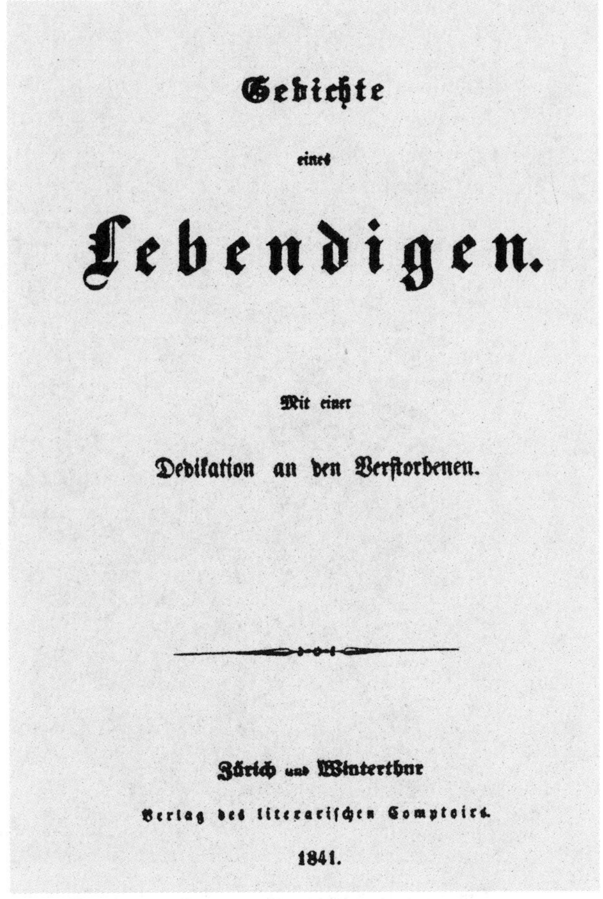
Gedichte

eines

Lebendigen.

Mit einer

Dedikation an den Verstorbenen.

Zürich und Winterthur

Verlag des literarischen Comptoirs.

1841.

Title page for the first volume of Herwegh's collection of radical political poetry

Georg Friedrich Rudolf Theodor Andreas Herwegh was born in Stuttgart on 31 May 1817 to Ludwig Ernst Herwegh and Katharina Herwegh, née Märklin. His father, an innkeeper, never achieved financial stability, and his bad temper made the lives of his wife and son miserable. Herwegh was slender and pale, prone to illness, and impressionable. He loved nature and animals, was never idle, and had a passion for reading.

At age fourteen he passed the lower-school examinations with such high marks that he was admitted to the Maulbronn seminary free of charge. His parents were divorced two years later. During this time Herwegh's poetic ability was admired by his fellow students and his teachers, even though his mathematics professor told him: "Sie dichtet z'viel und denket z'wenig" (You spend too much time on poetry and too little on thinking).

On 23 October 1835 Herwegh enrolled at the Tübingen Stift (Tübingen Theological Seminary); but it soon became clear to him that religious orthodoxy was incompatible with his own ideals, which

Contemporary caricature depicting Herwegh's audience with King Friedrich Wilhelm IV of Prussia on 19 November 1842. In the left panel Herwegh has flung down a gauntlet of defiance before a bust of the king; in the right panel Herwegh grovels in the king's presence while the royal physician holds his nose in disgust (from Heinrich Hubert Houben, Der ewige Zensor, *1978).*

were closer to the liberal attitudes of the poets who made up the group Junges Deutschland (Young Germany) and to the ideas of one of his professors, David Friedrich Strauss, whose historical, secular interpretation of Jesus' life had caused an uproar. A minor incident provoked his dismissal from the Stift, and he was required to repay the money expended on his behalf. (He would repay the four hundred florins from his first major earnings, proceeds from the sale of *Gedichte eines Lebendigen.*) He wanted to abandon his studies and become a contributor to August Lewald's journal *Europa,* but he bowed to his parents' wishes and remained at Tübingen University to study law.

Herwegh's poetic inclinations, however, soon caused a final break with academia, and he moved to Stuttgart in March 1837. Lewald, who gave him a position at *Europa,* prophesied that he would be a new Schiller. Herwegh's first poems were published in the *Lyrisches Album* and the *Album des Boudoirs,* publications associated with *Europa.* Herwegh began to wear extravagant clothing, thus conforming to the appearance expected of a "jugendlicher Schwärmer" (youthful dreamer) or aesthete.

In 1838 Herwegh, believing that as a former member of the Stift he was exempt from military service, ignored several letters calling him to report for induction. On 7 March he was physically taken away and impressed into service, but Lewald procured a temporary reprieve during which Herwegh translated Alphonse-Marie-Louis de Prat de Lamartine's collected works for the Scheible, Rieger and Sattler publishing house in Stuttgart. Within a year Herwegh translated six volumes, which were published in 1839 and 1840. The translation's exact rendering of Lamartine's thoughts is detrimental to the poetic language – a shortcoming of which Herwegh was well aware.

Herwegh's irascible temper changed his life profoundly when it led him to insult an officer: his service reprieve was revoked, and he was called to active duty on 6 July 1839. He fled to Emmishofen,

Switzerland, where he found refuge at the home of a German political emigré. For the following nine months Herwegh wrote essays and poems for *Europa* and for the *Deutsche Volkshalle* (German People's Hall), published by another emigrant, Georg Wirth, in Belle-Vue near Constance. In several articles he defends poets of the Classical and Romantic periods, such as Goethe, Ludwig Tieck, and Jean Paul, against the sentiments voiced by the writers of Junges Deutschland. Although he acknowledges Goethe's seemingly aloof attitude toward politics, he calls Goethe's artistic creations the best Germany has ever produced and maintains that the new generation has much to learn from him. He expresses his conviction that the common people have a "glücklicher Sinn" (happy sense) for truly great poetry; at the same time, they are the "strengste Richter" (most severe judges) and are not to be misled by outdated ideas. About half of Herwegh's contributions to magazines were collected and published without the author's permission in 1845 under the title *Gedichte und Kritische Aufsätze aus den Jahren 1839 und 1840* (Poems and Critical Essays from the Years 1839 and 1840).

Through his host, Herwegh met other members of the German emigré community; one of them, August Follen, had married a wealthy Swiss citizen and lived on a country estate outside Zurich that was a meeting place for political refugees, many of whom attempted to influence German opinion through publications in exile. At Follen's estate Herwegh met Julius Froebel, a professor of mineralogy at Zurich University who was to publish Herwegh's first books, and Professor Lorenz Oken, who had been a friend and promoter of the revolutionary dramatist Georg Büchner, one of Herwegh's idols. A lecturer in anatomy at the University of Zurich who had died of typhoid in 1837 at the age of twenty-four, Büchner had become a symbol of the fight against the oppressive German governments; his outspoken writings had been banned in Germany.

In Zurich, Herwegh wrote most of the poems that were to make him famous. Follen showed Herwegh's manuscripts to his circle of friends, and their enthusiastic response resulted in plans to publish these inspiring calls for a free nation. Froebel founded a publishing house, the Literarisches Comptoir, especially for works that were prohibited in Germany; its inaugural work was the first volume of Herwegh's *Gedichte eines Lebendigen*, published in the summer of 1841. The title refers antithetically to Hermann von Pückler-Muskau's *Briefe eines Verstorbenen* (Letters from a Deceased Person, 1830–1832) because Herwegh despised the irresponsible behavior of the globe-trotting dandy depicted therein. The opening poem of Herwegh's collection, "An den Verstorbenen" (To the Deceased Person), addresses a man of nobility who professes great interest in the fate of faraway empires while squandering his fortune and neglecting issues close to home.

Other short poems repeat many of the topics Herwegh had addressed in his essays. The overriding theme is freedom, which is often linked with spring. The poem "Frühlingslied" (Song of Spring) ends with a cry for revolution: "Ja, o Lenz, sei für die Dichter, / Für die Völker Lenz allein! / Für Tyrannen sollst Du Richter, / Für Tyrannen Rächer sein" (Yes, oh spring, be spring only for the poets, / For the people! / For tyrants be judge, / For tyrants be avenger).

Other poems call for personal freedom; for freedom of speech; and for freedom from the church, which is perceived as having cooperated with the state to rob the people of their rights. The poems' titles give a clear indication of their thrust: "Der Freiheit eine Gasse!" (Clear the Way for Freedom!), "Vive la République!," "Das freie Wort" (The Word in Freedom), "Protest," "Gegen Rom" (Against Rome), "Das Lied vom Hasse" (The Song of Hate). Herwegh's revolutionary fervor is almost boundless, as the final stanza of "Aufruf " (Appeal) illustrates: "Reißt die Kreuze aus der Erden! / Alle sollen Schwerter werden, / Gott im Himmel wird's verzeihn. / Gen Tyrannen und Philister! / Auch das Schwert hat seine Priester, / Und wir wollen Priester sein!" (Tear the crosses from the soil! / All shall be turned into swords, / God in heaven will forgive us. / Let us move against tyrants and philistines! / There are priests of the sword; / Let us be those priests!). This "call to action" combines form, rhythm, language, and imagery to rouse the emotions of the reader. Rhetorically, the poem makes use of the question-and-answer form; exclamations predominate, and direct address is used. Herwegh's poetic language borrows from the repertoire of the folk song: he uses metaphors, repetition – especially of the last lines of verses – inspiring rhythm, and effective rhyme schemes. Repetition of single words, such as *Freiheit* (freedom), and of entire lines hammers the message into the reader's or listener's mind: freedom must be won at all cost. Herwegh appeals to the emotions by evoking symbols of all that was considered German: the oak tree, the colors of the flag, and the Rhine River. The poet is the self-proclaimed leader of the people, their seer and prophet. There is no hidden message here:

Herwegh; lithograph by an unknown artist

Herwegh formulates bluntly what he wants the people to do, following his postulate that the function of the writer is to communicate directly with the people and that poetry should be an incitement to action.

This kind of poetry did not meet with general approval. In Herwegh's time critics spoke out against what they perceived to be politically motivated rhetoric at the expense of aesthetic considerations. In modern criticism Herwegh's poetry is often listed under the heading of "Tendenzdichtung" (tendentious poetry).

For Herwegh, the poem "An den König von Preußen" (To the King of Prussia) proved to be particularly momentous. It called on the newly crowned Friedrich Wilhelm IV, a supposedly liberal-minded romantic, to fulfill the hopes of those who advocated a greater share of political power for the people. Herwegh addresses the king: "Du bist der Stern, auf den man schaut, / Der letzte Fürst, auf den man baut" (You are the star on which one gazes, / The last Prince on whom one depends). Even though many thought it foolhardy to demand political freedom from a monarch, later developments would prove that the king was quite interested in the courageous young poet.

The book made Herwegh instantly famous in Switzerland and Germany; it reached its seventh edition in 1844 and its twelfth edition in 1896. It was also a resounding financial success for Herwegh and his publisher.

Following the success of his publication, Herwegh went to Paris, where he visited the grave of the German emigrant and radical journalist Ludwig Börne and met Heine. Herwegh's appearance was aptly described by another German emigrant, the future director of the Vienna Burgtheater, Franz Dingelstedt: "Von Herwegh willst Du wissen? Fünfundzwanzig Jahre alt, ein echter Fanatiker, ein St. Just, ein Robespierre, nicht ein Mirabeau wie Heine; schwarzes Haar und ein wunderhübsches Auge; schwäbischer Dialekt, bei Männern unbeholfen, bei Weibern wütend. Immer von Bastilletagen in Deutschland träumend. Jetzt noch ein Schwärmer, sogar ein unschädlicher, weil er ins Allgemeine geht und mit Inspirationen statt durch die Ironie wirkt; in zehn Jahren ein gefährlicher Mensch; in zwanzig entweder tot oder – verheiratet. . . . Herwegh hat eine Zukunft, wenn Deutschland eine Revolution erlebt, sonst nicht" (You want to know about Herwegh? Twenty-five years old, a true fanatic, a Saint-Just and Robespierre, no Mirabeau as you might call Heine. Black hair, beautiful eyes; Swabian dialect; clumsy among men and raving with women. He is consumed by dreams of Bastille days in Germany. He is still a visionary and a harmless one at that because he loses himself in generalities and tries to effect things by inspiration instead of irony; he will be dangerous in ten years; in twenty he will be either dead or – married. . . . Herwegh has a future only if we have a revolution in Germany). This observation accurately foreshadowed the poet's ultimate fate.

In February 1842 Herwegh returned to Switzerland and embarked with Froebel on a political newspaper, *Deutscher Bote aus der Schweiz* (German Messenger from Switzerland), that was to contain articles prohibited in Germany. To advertise this venture and gain authors Herwegh undertook a tour through Germany. The beginning of his trip in September 1842 was auspicious. Herwegh was received triumphantly; dinners were given in his honor at all his stops from the Rhineland to Berlin and East Prussia. On 6 November he met Emma Siegmund, the daughter of a Berlin merchant, an admirer of his poetry who shared his excitable nature and keen desire for political change. They were engaged a week later.

Einundzwanzig Bogen

aus

der Schweiz.

Herausgegeben

von

Georg Herwegh.

Erster Theil.

Zürich und Winterthur.

Verlag des Literarischen Comptoirs.

1843.

Title page for a collection of political essays and poems edited by Herwegh. The material was originally gathered for a newspaper that was banned before publication.

The face-to-face meeting with another of the poet's admirers was also fateful, if much less pleasant. Herwegh's audience with Friedrich Wilhelm IV at the king's Berlin castle on 19 November 1842 has been compared to the scene in Schiller's drama *Dom Karlos, Infant von Spanien* (1787; translated as *Don Carlos, Infant of Spain,* 1798) in which the youthful Marquis Posa eloquently demands from the Spanish king freedom for the people. It seems, however, that Herwegh was anything but a Marquis Posa. Accounts of the meeting differ, but it appears to have been an embarrassment to all concerned and caused the gravest consequences for the imprudent poet. The audience, arranged without the knowledge of the king's ministers, was presumably to be kept confidential, but an account of it found its way into the press, possibly through Herwegh's indiscretion. An article in the 27 November 1842 edition of the *Leipziger Allgemeine Zeitung* (Leipzig General Newspaper) quoted the king as having said "Ich liebe eine gesinnungsvolle Opposition" (I appreciate an honest opposition that is true to its principles) and portrayed Herwegh as having been rather shy and quiet during the meeting – a performance that did not earn him the admiration of his liberal followers. On the other hand, the king had compromised his position by meeting with an adversary. He was reported as having dismissed Herwegh with the words: "Ich weiß, wir sind Feinde . . . und wir wollen ehrliche Feinde sein" (I know we are enemies . . . but let us be honest enemies). In the aftermath of the report of the meeting, the king decreed that Herwegh's new journal was to be barred from distribution in Prussia. News of the king's reaction reached Herwegh in Königsberg, East Prussia (today Kaliningrad, Russia), the last station on his trip. Enraged by what he felt to be an unwarranted action belying the king's words, Herwegh hastily wrote a letter intended for the king's eyes only. This letter, however, also found its way into the press: it was published in the *Leipziger Allgemeine Zeitung* on 24 December. In his letter Herwegh expressed indignation over the censorship of a journal that was still in the planning stage. But he went on to point to his own successes as well as to the king's inability to control the circulation of censured books and pamphlets. To the public the letter appeared presumptuous and arrogant. Herwegh's trip, which had started so auspiciously and was expected to enhance his significance as a literary and political figure, ended as a fiasco. Expelled from all Prussian territories, he returned to Switzerland on 29 December 1842.

Herwegh tried to work on the second volume of his poems, which had originally been promised for publication in 1842 and for which he had a sizable number of orders. His mental health, however, had been undermined by the events of the past months. His state caused such concern to his friends that Follen wrote to Herwegh's fiancée, who arrived in Zurich with her father and sister on 18 February 1843. In keeping with the character of both young people, a quick decision was reached to delay marriage no longer. The ceremony was performed on 8 March before an intimate circle of friends.

Herwegh's marriage to the daughter of a wealthy silk merchant was probably his supreme stroke of luck. Not only did he gain an understanding and devoted companion but he also acquired a comfortable allowance from his father-in-law. Although his rise to the upper class raised eyebrows, Herwegh never abandoned the cause of the oppressed. His wife was as strong a republican as he and was determined to stand by his side no matter what their fate might be. At one time she had written to him: "Schatz, wenn Krieg kommt, zieh' ich mit, mein Reiten soll mir zustatten kommen, das soll eine Schlacht werden!" (My dearest, should there be war, I will go with you; my skills in horseback riding will prove helpful then; what a battle that will be!). This comment would prove to be an omen of things to come.

Following their wedding, the young couple set off on a three-month honeymoon that took them to southern France, Italy, and Belgium. In Italy, Herwegh discovered that he had no affinity for a country whose glory was a thing of the past. He had no eye for the beauties of the countryside, the architecture, or the art; he was filled with the desire to be close to the political reality in Germany: "Draußen in Deutschland, Frankreich und England, wo sich's regt, wo noch was geschieht, wenn's auch kaum der Rede wert ist, da ist mein, da ist Dein Posten" (You and I should be out there in Germany, France and England, where things are still stirring and changing, even if only very slightly), he wrote to his fellow poet and political activist Robert Prutz.

No major new works were produced in 1843; the Prussian king's edict had rendered the project of *Deutscher Bote aus der Schweiz* moot, so Follen published the material he and Herwegh had collected for this endeavor as *Einundzwanzig Bogen aus der Schweiz* (Twenty-one Sheets from Switzerland, 1843). The title drew attention to the fact that publications longer than twenty sheets were exempted from censorship; shorter works were thought more likely to be political pamphlets. The contents included essays on the political situation in Germany in general and Prussia in particular as well as political poems, several of them by Herwegh.

Late in 1843 the second volume of *Gedichte eines Lebendigen* was published. In the poem "Auch dies gehört dem König" (This, too, is the King's) Herwegh prophesies the eventual demise of the monarchy. The admissibility of politics as a subject for poetry was hotly debated in the early 1840s; in "Die Partei" (The [Political] Party) Herwegh expressed his conviction that politics can function as a legitimate muse. The poem was conceived as an answer to Ferdinand Freiligrath's "Aus Spanien" (Out of Spain, 1841), which contrasts the politicians with the poet in the last two lines: "Der Dichter steht auf einer höhern Warte / Als auf den Zinnen der Partei" (The poet stands on a higher vantage point / Than on the battlements of the party). Herwegh's spirited answer is: "Ihr müßt das Herz an eine Karte wagen, / Die Ruhe über Wolken ziemt euch nicht; / Ihr müßt euch mit in diesem Kampfe schlagen, / Ein Schwert in eurer Hand ist das Gedicht. / O wählt ein Banner, und ich bin zufrieden, / Ob's auch ein andres als das meine sei; / Ich hab' gewählt, ich habe mich entschieden, / Und meinen Lorbeer flechte die Partei!" (You must attach your heart to a cause; / Peace above the clouds is not your destiny; / You must fight in this battle; / A poem is a sword in your hand. / Just choose your cause, whichever it may be; / I have chosen, I have made up my mind, / And may the party crown my endeavors with a laurel wreath!).

Unpleasant encounters with political factions in Zurich made a further stay in the city undesirable, so the Herweghs moved to Paris in September 1843. The allowance from Herwegh's father-in-law permitted a life of relative luxury, including a fashionable flat with liveried servants. The couple's first son, Horace, was born in 1843; a second son, Camille, was born in 1847 but died a year later. Herwegh made the acquaintance of such well-known French writers as Marie-Catherine-Sophie d'Agoult, George Sand, Béranger, and Victor Hugo. Among the German writers in exile with whom he had contact were Heine and Karl Marx.

To complement his poetic strength, Herwegh decided to study the subject matter most foreign to him: natural science. He enrolled at the University of Paris, where he attended lectures in biology and botany. During the next few years he spent much time and money on the study of organisms such as slugs and sea urchins, which he observed in their natural habitats on the coasts of the Mediterranean and the Atlantic. There is no evidence that these endeavors influenced Herwegh's writings; certainly they did not find their way into the poems written during this time and published posthumously under the title *Neue Gedichte* (New Poems, 1877). An epic that was mentioned from time to time in his correspondence never materialized.

On 24 February 1848 workers of Paris overthrew King Louis Philippe. The revolutionary fervor quickly spread, and the governments of several of the smaller states in southern Germany were toppled. The Germans living in exile in Paris, most of whom were from the working class, felt called upon to rush to the help of their countrymen. They decided to dispatch five thousand men to cross the Rhine and join forces with the radicals in Germany, and they entreated Herwegh to accept the leadership of this "Deutsche demokratische Legion" (German Democratic Legion). Ignoring his friends' pleas to desist from a venture doomed to failure, Herwegh led his troops via Strasbourg to the German border, crossed near Bantzenheim, and met with an ignominious defeat at the hands of the Württemberg regulars. Herwegh and his wife, who had accompanied him on the expedition, escaped through Switzerland to Paris.

The defeat was harmful enough to Herwegh's reputation; the blow that effectively destroyed his name, however, was a malicious story that was first given to the press as the official battle account by a Lieutenant General von Miller: he related that Herwegh and his wife had fled the scene as soon as the troops approached and before the battle had begun. The story was later embellished to portray the cowardly poet hiding under the leather cover of a coach driven by his courageous wife. This version quickly made its way throughout Germany, where great amusement was had at Herwegh's expense. Heine commented on the event in the poem "Simplicissimus I": "Die Sage geht, es habe die Frau / vergebens bekämpft den Kleinmut des Gatten, / als Flintenschüsse seine zarten / Unterleibsnerven erschüttert hatten" (They say that the wife / Tried in vain to overcome the cowardice of her husband, / When the sound of gunshots / Had severely disturbed his sensitive abdominal nerves). The poet Eduard Mörike let it be known that he intended to order coach leather from Strasbourg of which one could fashion fabulous magical hoods that made the wearer invisible.

Herwegh's friends urged him to defend himself, but he never did. A pamphlet attempting to clear his name was written by his wife and published in 1849; it was largely ineffective, and Herwegh's fame steadily declined from this time on. After what appeared to be a shameful personal defeat as well as a defeat of the cause of freedom, Herwegh had lost the respect of his public and his publishers. Even more critical was the loss of support from his father-in-law: the steady income from Berlin ceased, and Herwegh and his family, used to a pleasant life-style, suddenly found themselves in financially straitened circumstances. The family was enlarged by the birth of a daughter, Ada, in 1849.

Herwegh had been under police observation in Paris, and when he was notified of an imminent search of his home at the beginning of July 1849 he left for Geneva. He had to stay away from Paris longer than he had expected, because the French government refused to let him return. This development was not altogether unpleasant for the poet, who in the meantime had made new friends: the Russian revolutionary Aleksandr Herzen and his wife. Herwegh fell passionately in love with the woman and even challenged Herzen to a duel, but the latter refused. Herwegh was able to put this passion behind him, and in August 1850 he rejoined his wife in Nice.

The couple moved back to Zurich, where Herwegh immersed himself once more in the study of science in an attempt to escape the memories of the defeat of his political hopes. During this time Arthur Schopenhauer's *Parerga und Paralipomena* (1851) held a particular fascination for the poet, who probably found a kinship to his own prevailing mood in the pessimistic writings of the philosopher.

In the 1850s Herwegh's home in Zurich was the meeting place for many well-known people, among them the architect Gottfried Semper, the composers Franz Liszt and Richard Wagner, and the socialist Ferdinand Lasalle. Liszt seems to have

Herwegh; painting by Bertha Wehnert-Beckmann (Deutsche Staatsbibliothek, Berlin)

planned to use a text by the poet for a symphony, but the venture presumably never came to fruition. Herwegh's friendship with Wagner began in 1851, when Wagner fled to Zurich after taking part in a demonstration in Dresden. Herwegh considered Wagner both a true revolutionary and a musical genius; Wagner appreciated Herwegh's understanding and friendship and noted: "Für jetzt ist mein Arzt Herwegh; er hat große physikalische und physiologische Kenntnisse und steht mir in jeder Beziehung sympathisch näher als irgendein Arzt" (Right now, Herwegh serves as my physician; his physical and physiological knowledge is considerable and in every respect I feel closer to him than to any medical doctor). Herwegh predicted Wagner's eventual rise to fame and defended him against malevolent voices.

The Herweghs had another son, Marcel, in 1858. In 1861 Herwegh's hope of being employed by the University of Naples as a professor of comparative literature was shattered; it became known later that the French and German governments had objected to a public office being given to a "roter Republikaner" (red republican). It seems that not even the most conducive surroundings and enlightening friends could prod Herwegh to become more productive. One of the great poems of his later years is, however, attributable to his association with the energetic leader of the workers' movement, Lasalle. In 1863 Herwegh became a member of Lasalle's Allgemeiner Arbeiterverein (General Workers' Alliance), for which he composed in 1864 the "Bundeslied für den Allgemeinen Arbeiterverein" (Song for the General Workers' Alliance). These verses illustrate the spirit of the entire poem: "Mann der Arbeit, aufgewacht! / Und erkenne deine Macht! / Alle Räder stehen still, / Wenn dein starker Arm es will" (Awaken, man of manual labor! / And recognize your power! / All wheels will stop turning, / When your strong arm wants it thus). The poem demonstrates Herwegh's unwavering support of the weak and disenfranchised, but it does not show a markedly new development in comparison to Herwegh's earlier work. Neither the poet's erudition, nor any inspiration gained from the intellectual and artistic circle around him, seems to have found expression in a significant new work. Perhaps his silence reflects a feeling of inadequacy as a poet, or of resignation in the face of his dashed hopes for democracy. In the poem "Lied von der Weisheit" (Song of Wisdom) he expresses his resignation: "Ich träumte einstens, überall zu siegen / Und wie ein Wetter durch die Welt zu fliegen; / Da hieß ein Donnerwort mich stille stehen / Und ferner nur im Schneckenschritte gehen" (Once I dreamt of victory on all fronts / And flying like lightning through all creation; / Suddenly a thunderous voice called me to a halt / And made me go at a snail's pace from then on).

Health problems compounded Herwegh's unfortunate situation. In 1861 and 1862 he had undergone treatment for liver problems; he also spent time in the spas of Karlsbad and, in 1865, Wildbad to try to cure the condition. From Karlsbad he went to Vienna, where he met the poets Heinrich Laube and Anastasius Grün and visited his old friend Dingelstedt. Dingelstedt attempted to obtain a position for Herwegh with the royal family, but Herwegh and his wife were enraged at the idea. Herwegh decided to continue to seek his livelihood with his pen, meager as it would be. Among the journals to which he contributed were the *Bieler Handelskurier* (Biel Business Courier) and the *Züricher Intelligenzblatt* (Zurich Advertiser).

After a general amnesty was proclaimed in 1866 the poet and his wife moved back to Germany, settling in Lichtenthal near Baden-Baden. There Herwegh worked as a political correspondent for the French paper *La Republique Française,* translated Shakespeare's *Coriolanus* for the German Shakespeare Society in 1870, and translated, annotated, and introduced Shakespeare's *King Lear, The Two Gentlemen of Verona, The Taming of the Shrew, A Comedy of Errors, All's Well That Ends Well, Troilus and Cressida,* and *As You Like It* for the Brockhaus publishing house in 1870 and 1871.

Herwegh was one of the few political poets who did not share in the general enthusiasm for the new German empire, founded under Prussian leadership after the war with France in 1870 and 1871. In "Epilog zum Krieg" (Epilogue to the War) he writes: "Schwarz, weiß und rot! um ein Panier / Vereinigt stehen Süd und Norden; / Du bist im ruhmgekrönten Morden / Das erste Land der Welt geworden: / Germania, mir graut vor dir!" (Black, white and red! under one flag / Are united South and North; / You have become in glorious murder / First among all the countries: / Germania, you make me shudder!). He went so far as to proclaim Prussia the true enemy: "Die Wacht am Rhein wird nicht genügen, / Der schlimmste Feind steht an der Spree" (The watch on the Rhine will not suffice; / The worst enemy is to be found at the banks of the River Spree). Many chastised Herwegh for what they perceived as his stubborn clinging to obsolete ideas and ideals. His friends and admirers, on the other hand, saw in his position the consistent attitude of an individual gifted with insight and foresight. Future historical developments seem to have proved Herwegh right.

Herwegh never felt quite at home again in Germany. He died on 7 April 1875 and was buried in Liestal, Switzerland. *Neue Gedichte,* published posthumously in 1877 and edited by his wife, did not result in a renaissance of Herwegh's reputation.

Opinions regarding Herwegh's poetry are divided. The main charge against him is that his undeniable talent exhausted itself in his early efforts. On the other hand, the great Swiss poet Conrad Ferdinand Meyer, who praised Herwegh as the inspiration of his youth, judged Herwegh's last works thus: "Die Gedichte von Herwegh haben mir denn doch Eindruck gemacht. Neben den schönen Überbleibseln, die mit der ersten Sammlung rangieren, meist satirische Gedichte à la Heine (letzte Manier), Form schön, witzig, wehmütig, nie unbedeutend. Er hat sein ganzes Talent bis zum letzten Atemzug behalten" (Herwegh's poems were impressive after all. Aside from some nice ones in the manner of the first collection, they are mostly satiric poems in the vein of Heine [in his last stage]. The form was pleasing, they were witty, melancholic, never dull. He was a master to his last breath).

Letters:

Georg Herwegh: Briefwechsel mit seiner Braut, edited by Marcel Herwegh (Paris, 1896);

Briefe von und an Georg Herwegh, edited by Marcel Herwegh (Paris: Langen, 1896);

Briefwechsel mit Marie d'Agoult, edited by Marcel Herwegh (Paris: Gallimard, 1929).

References:

Hans-Peter Bayerdörfer, "Vormärz," in *Geschichte der deutschen Lyrik vom Mittelalter bis zur Gegenwart,* edited by Walter Hinderer (Stuttgart: Reclam, 1983), pp. 308-339;

William J. Brazill, "Georg Herwegh and the Aesthetics of German Unification," *Central European History,* 5, no. 2 (1972): 99-126;

Wolfgang Büttner, "Dann belehren euch die Faust unserer Proletarier?," *Weimarer Beiträge,* 3 (1967): 403-437;

Büttner, *Georg Herwegh – ein Sänger des Proletariats: Der Weg eines bürgerlich-demokratischen Poeten zum*

Streiter für die Arbeiterbewegung (Berlin: Akademie Verlag, 1970);

Horst Denkler, "Zwischen Julirevolution (1830) und Märzrevolution (1848/49)," in *Geschichte der politischen Lyrik in Deutschland,* edited by Hinderer (Stuttgart: Reclam, 1978), pp. 179-209;

Giuseppe Farese, "Georg Herwegh und Ferdinand Freiligrath: Zwischen Vormärz und Revolution," in *Demokratische-revolutionäre Literatur in Deutschland: Vormärz,* edited by Gert Mattenklott and others (Kronberg: Scriptor, 1974), pp. 187-244;

Farese, "Lyrik des Vormärz," in *Vormärz: Biedermier, Junges Deutschland, Demokraten 1815-1848,* volume 6 of *Deutsche Literatur: eine Sozialgeschichte,* edited by Horst Albert Glaser (Reinbek: Rowohlt, 1980), pp. 227-244;

Werner Feudel, "Politische Gedichte und revolutionärer Kampf: Der politische Dichter Georg Herwegh," *Weimarer Beiträge,* 8 (1975): 39-52;

Horst Haase, "Revolutionärer Rufer und Dichter des Proletariats: Georg Herwegh," *Weimarer Beiträge,* 8 (1975): 144-149;

Werner Hahl, "Realitätsverlust im rhetorischen Zeitgedicht des Vormärz: Zu Georg Herweghs Flottengedicht," in *Vom Biedermeier zum bürgerlichen Realismus,* volume 4 of *Gedichte und Interpretationen,* edited by Günter Häntzschel (Stuttgart: Reclam, 1983), pp. 239-249;

Jost Hermand, *Der deutsche Vormärz: Texte und Dokumente* (Stuttgart: Reclam, 1967);

Emma Herwegh, *Zur Geschichte der deutschen demokratischen Legion aus Paris: Von einer Hochverräterin* (Grünberg: Levysohn, 1849);

Heinrich Hubert Houben, *Der weige Zensor* (Kronberg: Athenäum, 1978), pp. 47-48;

Peter Kleiß, *Georg Herweghs Literaturkritik: Demokratisches Programm und repressiver Gestus* (Frankfurt am Main: Lang, 1982);

Ludwig Krapf, "Rezeption und Rezeptionsverweigerung: Einige Überlegungen zur politischen Lyrik Georg Herweghs und Georg Weerths," in *Rezeptionsgeschichte oder Wirkungsästhetik: Konstanzer Beiträge zur Praxis der Literaturgeschichtsschreibung,* edited by Heinz-Dieter Weber (Stuttgart: Klett-Cotta, 1978), pp. 83-100;

Heinrich Leber, *Freiligrath – Herwegh – Weerth* (Leipzig: VEB Bibliographisches Institut, 1973);

Katharina Mommsen, "Georg Herwegh: Dichtung, Sprache und Gesellschaft," in *Dichtung, Sprache, Gesellschaft: Akten des IV. Internationalen Germanisten-Kongresses 1970 in Princeton* (Frankfurt am Main: Athenäum, 1971), pp. 395-402;

Sylvia Peuckert, *Freiheitsträume: Georg Herwegh und die Herweghianer. Politische Gedichte der 1840er Jahre und Metaphern für Freiheit in dieser Zeit* (Frankfurt am Main: Lang, 1985);

Karl Riha, "Georg Herwegh in rezeptionsgeschichtlicher Sicht; Ein Kapitel politischer Ästhetik," in *Antipodische Aufklärungen – Antipodean Enlightenments: Festschrift für Leslie Bodi,* edited by Walter Veit (Frankfurt am Main: Lang, 1978), pp. 389-401;

Robert George Uebel, "The 'Vormärz' and the Poetry of Georg Herwegh: Late Twentieth Century Perspectives and Controversies," Ph.D. dissertation, University of California, Davis, 1991;

Agnes Ziegengeist, "Die Literaturkritik des jungen Georg Herwegh," Ph.D. dissertation, Humboldt University, 1965.

Papers:

Most of Georg Herwegh's papers are in the archives of the Dichtermuseum (Writer Museum) in Liestal, Switzerland, and the Deutsches Literaturarchiv of the Schiller Nationalmuseum in Marbach, Germany.

Karl Immermann

(24 April 1796 - 25 August 1840)

Gunther J. Holst
University of South Carolina

BOOKS: *Ein Wort zur Beherzigung* (Jena, 1817);

Letztes Wort über die Streitigkeiten der Studierenden zu Halle seit dem 4. März 1817: Eine Erwiderung auf C.A.S. Schultze. Der Arzneiwissenschaft Candidat. Nebst drei Beilagen (Leipzig: Klein, 1817);

Die Prinzen von Syrakus: Romantisches Lustspiel (Hamm: Schulz & Wundermann, 1821);

Gedichte (Hamm: Schulz & Wundermann, 1822);

Die Papierfenster eines Eremiten (Hamm: Schulz & Wundermann, 1822);

Ein ganz frisch schön Trauerspiel von Pater Brey, dem falschen Propheten in der zweiten Potenz: Ans Licht gezogen durch Karl Immermann, ictum (Münster: Koerdink, 1822);

Trauerspiele (Hamm & Münster: Schulz & Wundermann, 1822) – comprises *Das Thal von Ronceval, Edwin, Petrarca*;

Brief an einen Freund über die falschen Wanderjahre Wilhelm Meisters und ihre Beilagen (Münster: Koerdink, 1823);

Floia: Cortum versicale de Flois, swartibus illis deiriculis, quae omnes fere Menschos, Mannos, Weibras, Jungfras etc. behuppere et spitzibus suis Snaflis steckere et bitere solent. Auctore Gripholdo Knicknackio ex Flolandia, Editio nova (Hamm: Schulz & Wundermann, 1823);

König Periander und sein Haus: Ein Trauerspiel (Elberfeld: Büschler, 1823);

Das Auge der Liebe: Ein Lustspiel (Hamm: Schulz & Wundermann, 1824);

Der neue Pygmalion: Erzählung (Halle: Hendel, 1825);

Cardenio und Celinde: Trauerspiel in fünf Aufzügen (Berlin: Laue, 1826);

Über den rasenden Ajax des Sophocles: Eine ästhetische Abhandlung (Magdeburg: Heinrichshofen, 1826);

Kaiser Friedrich der Zweite: Trauerspiel in fünf Aufzügen (Hamburg: Hoffman & Campe, 1828);

Die schelmische Gräfin (N.p., 1828);

Das Trauerspiel in Tyrol: Ein dramatisches Gedicht in fünf Aufzügen (Hamburg: Hoffmann & Campe, 1828); revised as *Andreas Hofer: Ein Trauerspiel* (Düsseldorf: Schaub, 1834);

Die Verkleidungen: Lustspiel in drei Aufzügen (Hamburg: Hoffmann & Campe, 1828);

Der im Irrgarten der Metrik umhertaumelnde Cavalier: Eine literarische Tragödie (Hamburg: Hoffmann & Campe, 1829);

Die Schule der Frommen: Lustspiel in drei Aufzügen (Stuttgart & Tübingen: Cotta, 1829);

Gedichte: Neue Folge (Stuttgart & Tübingen: Cotta, 1830);

Miscellen (Stuttgart & Tübingen: Cotta, 1830);

Tulifäntchen: Ein Heldengedicht in drei Gesängen (Hamburg: Hoffmann & Campe, 1830);

Alexis: Eine Trilogie (Düsseldorf: Schaub, 1832);

Merlin: Eine Mythe (Düsseldorf: Schaub, 1832);

Reisejournal (Düsseldorf: Schaub, 1833);
Gedichte (Düsseldorf: Schaub, 1834);
Schriften, 11 volumes (Düsseldorf: Schaub, 1835–1839);
Die Epigonen: Familienmemoiren in neun Büchern, 3 volumes (Düsseldorf: Schaub, 1836);
Das Fest der Freiwilligen zu Köln am Rheine, den 3. Februar 1838: Im Auftrage des festordnenden Comités beschrieben (Cologne: Bachem, 1838);
Münchhausen: Eine Geschichte in Arabesken, 4 volumes (Düsseldorf: Schaub, 1838–1839);
Die Opfer des Schweigens: Ein Trauerspiel (Düsseldorf: Schaub, 1839);
Adolf Schrödter's Bild von der Flasche: Humoristisch zu deuten versucht, by Immermann and W. Cornelius (N.p., 1840);
Memorabilien, 3 volumes (Hamburg: Hoffmann & Campe, 1840–1843);
Tristan und Isolde: Ein Gedicht in Romanzen (Düsseldorf: Schaub, 1841);
Dramen und Dramaturgisches (Düsseldorf: Schaub, 1843);
Fränkische Reise (Hamburg: Hoffmann & Campe, 1843);
Schriften, 10 volumes (Leipzig: Klemm, 1850);
Theaterbriefe, edited by G. zu Putlitz (Berlin: Duncker, 1851);
Schriften, 13 volumes (Berlin: Ehle, 1854);
Der Oberhof: Idyll aus dem Roman Münchhausen (Berlin: Hoffmann, 1863); translated by Paul Bernard Thomas as "The Oberhof," in *The German Classics of the Nineteenth and Twentieth Centuries,* volume 7, edited by Kuno Francke and William Guild Howard (New York: German Publication Society, 1913), pp. 169–240;
Werke, 20 volumes, edited by Robert Boxberger (volumes 2–14, 17–18, Berlin: Hempel; volumes 1, 15–16, 19–20, Berlin: Dümmler, 1883);
Werke: Historisch-kritische Ausgabe, 4 volumes, edited by Max Koch (Berlin & Stuttgart: Spemann, 1887–1888);
Die Nachbarn: Dramatische Idylle in einem Aufzuge, edited by Werner Deetjen (Leipzig: Weicher, 1905);
Werke: Kritisch durchgesehene und erläuterte Ausgabe, 5 volumes, edited by Harry Maync (Leipzig & Vienna: Bibliographisches Institut, 1906);
Werke, 5 volumes, edited by Benno von Wiese, Hans Asbeck and others (Frankfurt am Main: Athenäum, 1971–1977).

OTHER: Sir Walter Scott, *Ivanhoe: Eine Geschichte vom Verfasser des Waverley nach der neuesten Original-Ausgabe übersetzt und mit einem einleitenden Vorwort versehen,* 3 volumes, translated with a preface by Immermann (Hamm: Wundermann, 1826).

In his relatively short life, Karl Immermann was a prolific writer of dramas, fiction, travelogues, memoirs, and poetry. Yet his work suffered from an uneven quality that bore the stamp of his generation, to which he gave the enduring name "Epigonenzeit" (epigonous period). The term designates a mediocre German generation unsuccessfully trying to cope with the overwhelming cultural legacy of the preceding generation, which was marked by the genius of Johann Wolfgang von Goethe and Friedrich Schiller. It comprises the period following the Congress of Vienna in 1815, a period also referred to as the Restoration. It was a time of profound changes, contradictions, and uncertainties. The quality of Immermann's literary production was also affected by his dogged pursuit of a career as a dramatist; he did not realize until a decade before his death that his strength lay in the kind of prose writing that made use of his keen powers of observation and analysis and his natural bent for satire. When he applied these talents to diagnosing his own unsettled time he produced two major novels, *Die Epigonen* (The Epigones, 1836) and *Münchhausen* (1838–1839). These works were the first comprehensive Zeitromane (novels of the mores of the times) in German literature. The "Oberhof" (Farm) segment of *Münchhausen,* as well, was among the first major Dorfgeschichten (stories of rural life) in Germany. While many of his dramas were performed during his lifetime, they did not endure. It is primarily his two major novels that have secured his place in German literature.

Karl Leberecht Immermann was born in Magdeburg on 24 April 1796, to Gottlieb Leberecht Immermann, a Prussian civil servant, and Wilhelmina Immermann, née Wilda. After attending the gymnasium from 1807 to 1813 he was sent to the University of Halle to study law, but in August 1813 Napoleon closed the university. In December Immermann joined the Prussian army but came down with a fever that forced him to spend the next three months in an army hospital. He rejoined his regiment and served until July, when he resumed his studies at the newly reopened University of Halle. On Napoleon's return from Elba, Immermann again volunteered for the army; he participated in the battles of Ligny and Waterloo and entered Paris with the victorious coalition forces. In December 1815 he was discharged at the rank of lieutenant

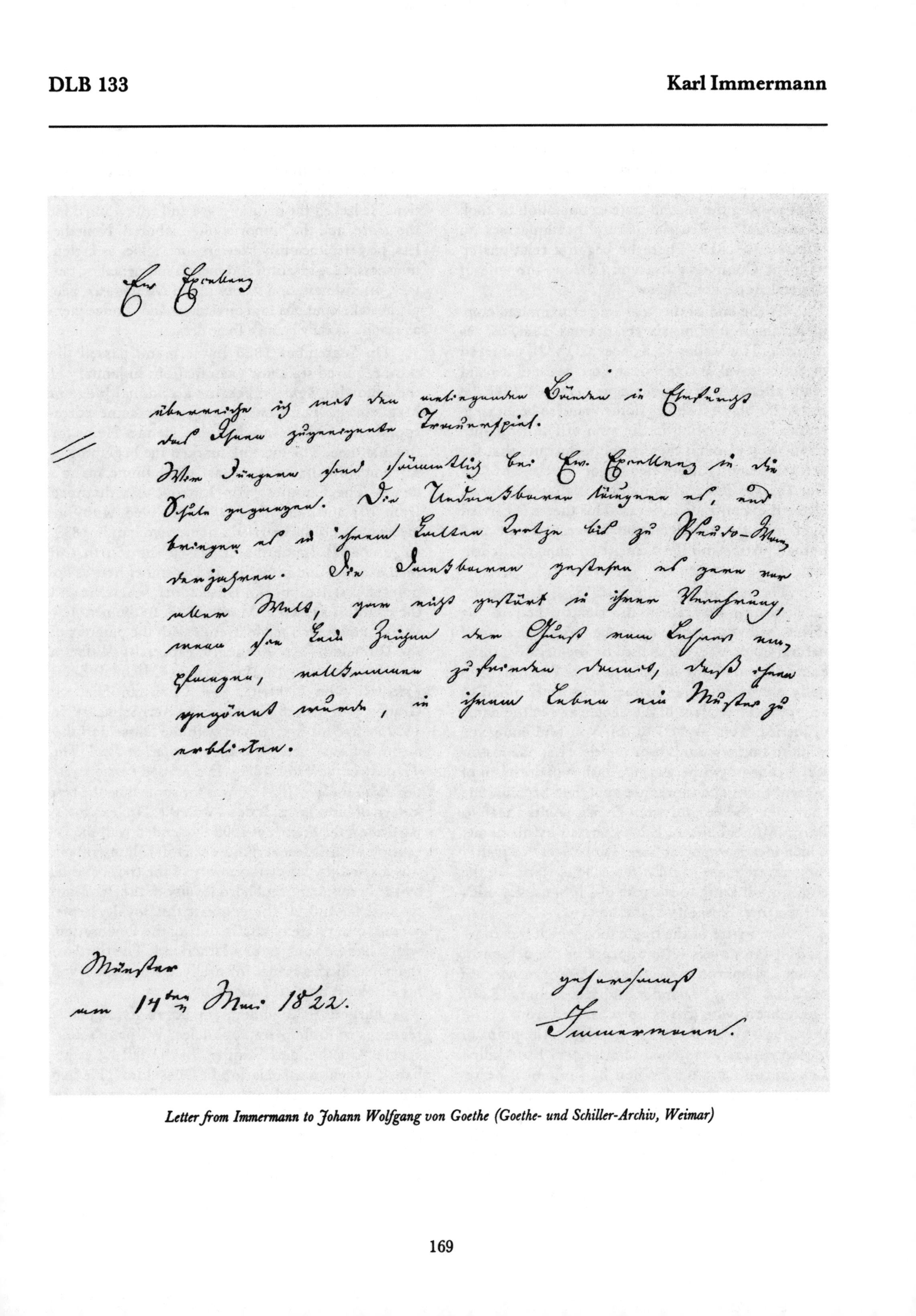

Letter from Immermann to Johann Wolfgang von Goethe (Goethe- und Schiller-Archiv, Weimar)

and again returned to his studies at Halle. In January 1818 he passed his first state examination in law and began practicing in the court in Oschersleben. After passing the second state examination he took a position at Prussian army headquarters in Münster in 1819. There he began a relationship with the Countess Elisa von Lützow, the wife of General Adolf von Lützow.

By the end of the year Immermann had completed the first of his sixteen dramas, *Das Thal von Ronceval* (The Valley of Ronceval, 1822), centered on the betrayal of Ganelon and the death of Roland in the aftermath of Charlemagne's crusade. Like the rest of his plays, it shows Immermann to be an epigonous figure writing in the vein of late Romanticism. Yet it also has themes and techniques that figure prominently in his two major novels. Thus, in *Das Thal von Ronceval* human life is governed by an element of contradictoriness. This theme is carried over into the contradiction between divine and human justice and the ultimate triumph of the former.

The second drama, *Edwin* (1822), is a romantic historical play about the rightful heir to the throne, who has grown up in the forest in a state of natural innocence, untouched by the negative influences of courtly life under a despot. When he is finally elevated to the throne, he is determined to reign for the welfare of the people and in the name of justice. Two aspects of this youthful endeavor point to Immermann's later novels. First, the historical facade notwithstanding, flashes of criticism of present times and mores are apparent. Second, one character, the knightly fool Dunst, points ahead to Baron Münchhausen. Characterized by his name, which means vapor or haze, Dunst seeks to justify the deliberate use of folly in a chaotic world. In the end, his adhering to the role of a fool merely adds to the general insanity of the time.

The figure of the tragic fool, which was to return in the novels, also appears in the person of Prince Lykophron in the tragedy *König Periander und sein Haus* (King Periander and His House, 1823). Lykophron, who grows up separated from his father, Periander, idolizes Periander to the point of idolatry – unaware that Periander had killed Lykophron's mother. When he finds out, he retreats into insanity; life, devoid of all meaning, becomes "Ein klägliches, unsäglich bittres Nichts!" (A pitiful, unspeakably bitter nothingness!). This is the first full-fledged occurrence of the problem of nihilism, where idealism clashes with a reality that lacks all value. This problem was to become one of the central themes in his masterful *Münchhausen.*

In the 1820s Immermann wrote several comedies that, even in the relatively mediocre tradition of that genre in Germany, were accorded little attention. He lacked the natural grace and wit required for the genre, and the humor is often labored. Nonetheless, he perspicaciously skewers such follies as pretentiousness, false idealism and piety, sentimentality, fantasy, prudishness, and vanity. As in *Die Epigonen,* people mistake opinions for convictions and change them as readily as they change their dress.

In September 1823 Immermann passed the third required state law examination; in January of the following year he became a criminal judge in Magdeburg. The same month, after some correspondence with Heinrich Heine, he met Heine for the first time. The meeting marked the beginning of a friendship that was to last until Immermann's death. The Countess von Lützow was divorced from her husband in 1825; she lived with Immermann until he married another woman in 1839. In June 1826 Immermann passed the fourth and final examination in Berlin; in December he was appointed district judge in Düsseldorf, where he and the countess settled in March 1827. In the next few years Immermann made friends with the painters of the Düsseldorf Art Academy, especially Wilhelm von Schadow; with the writers Michael Beer, Friedrich von Üchtritz, and Christian Dietrich Grabbe; and with the art historian Karl Schnaase. In 1829 he had his first contact with the Düsseldorf theater when it staged his *Das Trauerspiel in Tyrol* (The Tragedy in the Tirol, 1828). In a revised version, retitled *Andreas Hofer* (1834), it was for some time the best known of his dramas. It deals with the Tirolean uprising against the French in 1809 that ended with the execution of their leader, Andreas Hofer. Immermann was inspired by his own memory of the tragic events, by the heroism and stubborn loyalty of the Tiroleans to Austria, and by the contrast this loyalty represented to the state of affairs during the Restoration, which had no concept of a fatherland. The third act sharply criticizes Prince Wenzel von Metternich and his absolutist political philosophy.

Early in 1832 Immermann began giving public readings of dramas by Sophocles, William Shakespeare, Goethe, and Schiller. In the fall he established a theater association in Düsseldorf. He had long been interested in the staging of plays and the arts of acting and directing, and he was asked to direct Goethe's *Clavigo* (1774; translated, 1798) with his own epilogue for a performance at the Düsseldorf theater on 24 April 1832. At this time the Düsseldorf theater, like most German theaters, was mediocre, pandering to the superficial taste of the audience. Immermann became the driving force behind an effort to restructure it, and in February 1833 he instituted a series of "Mustervorstellungen" (model productions). Immermann accepted the position of director of the Düsseldorf theater for the 1834–1835 season after securing a leave of absence from the king of Prussia. His philosophy was to give priority to the words and intentions of the author, a practice not common in those days, and to introduce realism to the stage. The works of Goethe, Schiller, Shakespeare, Gotthold Ephraim Lessing, Heinrich von Kleist, and Pedro Calderón de la Barca were performed only after painstaking rehearsals. In time, however, Immermann was forced into more and more concessions to the mediocre taste of the Düsseldorf audiences. He was also faced with increasing financial difficulties as well as petty intrigues. When his application for another leave was denied he had to return to his position as a judge, directing the theater in his spare time. At the end of the 1836–1837 season, which was highly successful artistically, Immermann, unable to continue to carry the twin burdens, resigned from the theater. His efforts to elevate the theater to a high artistic and intellectual level have given Immermann a lofty position in the history of the German theater alongside other great writer-dramaturges such as Lessing, Goethe, Schiller, Ludwig Tieck, and Bertolt Brecht.

Immermann; oil painting by Wilhelm Schadow, 1829 (Städtische Gemäldegalerie, Düsseldorf)

In December 1835 Immermann had completed the last chapter of *Die Epigonen,* finishing a project that he had worked on intermittently for the better part of thirteen years and that had gone through several structural and thematic permutations. The initial plan had envisioned a humorous novel set in the twelfth-century Near East; the idea of a historical setting was probably prompted by the popularity of Sir Walter Scott's novels around 1820. In a fundamental change, Immermann decided to set the novel in Germany in his own time and to forego the comical aspect. By the end of the 1820s his diaries indicate that the novel was to have the title "Hermanns Wanderungen" (Hermann's Travels) and would show the influence of Goethe's *Wilhelm Meisters Wanderjahre* (1821; translated as *Wilhelm Meister's Travels,* 1827) and of Tieck's *Franz Sternbalds Wanderungen* (Franz Sternbald's Travels, 1798). Such a novel, with a single central character, would have been a bildungsroman or Entwicklungsroman (developmental novel). The next intended title, "Die Zeitgenossen" (The Contemporaries), indicates that Hermann was not to be the central figure but that the focus was to be on several characters – indeed, on the character of the time. Furthermore, Hermann does not undergo the substantial changes required of the hero of a bildungsroman or Entwicklungsroman. The concept was thus changed to that of Zeitroman. The final title, *Die Epigonen,* was first used by Immermann in 1830. In his correspondence Immermann says that his intention is to have his novel present the life of the present reflected through the vicissitudes of Hermann and his family.

In the course of the novel Hermann becomes involved in the world of the decaying aristocracy in the persons of a duke and duchess whose claim to nobility is fraudulent. This world is destined for destruction, yet the world of bourgeois culture, as Benno von Wiese points out, amounts to no more than a new kind of barbarism. It is dominated by dilettantism, an epigonism that no longer has a genuine relationship to anything and that cannot distinguish between truth and appearance. In the seventh book Immermann takes issue with the emerging industrialism. These commercial undertakings result merely in a loss of old values without replacing them with positive new ones. The world

Immermann; engraving by Carl Friedrich Lessing, 1837

of Hermann's uncle is dominated by financial gain and run by the clock. It is as artificial as the world of the aristocracy.

The ambiguous character of the Restoration period with its shifting values is most critically dealt with in the episodes set in the glittering Berlin salon of Medon and Johanna. The youthful idealism of the Wars of Liberation that was to create a new and more liberal Prussia has been choked by the political reaction. There are no new ideals, nor is there a new fatherland. While it tries to appear to be more liberal, the Prussian monarchy remains an absolute one. The characters' reactions to the contradictoriness of public and political life ranges from depression to the icy fanaticism of Medon. The most fascinating figure of the novel, he has as his secret goal no less than the overthrow of the state: "Voll von dem ätzenden Gefühle, daß die öffentlichen Einrichtungen Deutschlands im Widerspruche mit einer schönen, freien, großen Entwicklung seien, hielt er dafür, daß der Weg zu einer Erneuerung unsres Lebens durch das Labyrinth einer vollkommenen Anarchie gehe, und daß bis dahin nur eine Zersetzung aller moralischen Bande, welche uns zusammenhalten, die er aber für morsch ansah, führen könne" (Permeated by the corrosive feeling that the public institutions of Germany were in contradiction with a beautiful, free, and sublime development, he was convinced that the path to a renewal of our life had to go through the labyrinth of total anarchy and to get there all our moral ties, which he considered in a state of dry rot, would have to be destroyed).

Medon pretends to be an adherent of the restorative currents, thus acquiring the power to pursue his true goals. Immermann calls him the "Nihilist" of the epigonous era. As Medon changes from a disappointed idealist to a criminal, he is also a victim of his time. As Immermann puts it, "Wir sind, um mit einem Wort das ganze Elend auszusprechen, Epigonen und tragen an der Last, die jeder Erb- und Nachgeborenschaft anzukleben pflegt" (We are, to put the entire misery into a single word, epigones. As such we bear heavily the burden that adheres to each inheritance and to all who have come after).

The characters are victims of the accident of late birth; they are an undistinguished generation following one of brilliance and genius that cannot be equaled. They are condemned to live in an amorphous period when old values can no longer be applied and new ones have not yet been affirmed, where everything is in transition. Hermann is a product of his time: his life appears to have no aim or purpose. Not an exceptional character, he does not represent any of the extremes of his time. "Die Farbe der Zeit konnte er nicht verbergen, aber im Innersten mußte man ihn für unversehrt erklären" (He could not deny having been affected by the times, but in his very core one would have to call him undamaged); as a consequence, he is the suitable person to attempt to mediate between the feuding classes of the industrial bourgeoisie, represented by his uncle, and the aristocracy, in the person of the duke, and ultimately to be heir to both. Hermann accepts his inheritance as a deposit toward a future that is not yet discernible.

Hermann's peregrinations enable Immermann to explore critically the aristocracy and the bourgeoisie, rural and city life, the police state, student life, science, religion, medicine, education, art, philosophy, and the culture of the salons in Berlin. There are lengthy conversations concerning such topics as the institution of the family, the role of women in society, the state, and history. Immermann deals with the various aspects of his time in contrasting fashion, thus reflecting the contradictoriness of an era when the artificial outweighs the genuine, folly takes the place of common sense, and truth, morality, religious faith, originality, and words themselves have become dubious commodities.

The novel does not provide a solution to the problems of the time. As heir to both his uncle and the duke, Hermann decides to close the former's factories and return the latter's landholdings to agriculture. He wants to create a green island for himself and his family that will be impervious to the inevitable development of industrialism. He recognizes that this solution is at best a temporary one, just as everything in the present is merely temporary. The battle between the old and the new has not yet been settled, but from it will originate values as yet unthought of by anyone.

In 1837 Immermann visited Ferdinand Freiligrath in Barmen, traveled to Franconia and Thuringia, visited the philosopher Arthur Schopenhauer in Jena and Goethe's former secretary Johann Peter Eckermann in Weimar, and gave a reading from Freiligrath's poems at the Weimar court. In July 1838 he received an honorary doctorate from the University of Jena. In September he traveled to his hometown of Magdeburg for the baptism of his nephew. At his brother Ferdinand's house he met the nineteen-year-old Marianne Niemeyer, whom he would marry a year later.

Immermann had begun work on *Münchhausen* in 1837; it was published in four volumes in 1838–1839. Wiese calls it one of the few great German novels in existence, yet one that has remained largely undiscovered. One reason for this paradox is the dualistic structure of the novel, which consists of two seemingly independent parts. One is the "Münchhausen" part, revolving around the famous "Lügenbaron" (lying baron) Karl Friedrich Hieronymus, Freiherr von Münchhausen, whose tall tales were first published in a German periodical in 1781 and, in the following five years, in several enlarged editions in English and German. The other is the "Oberhof" part, turning on the larger-than-life figure of the "Hofschulze" (village leader).

Much to the detriment of the novel, the "Oberhof" segment was removed from its context of social criticism and published separately in 1863, becoming one of the works that initiated the popular genre of the Dorfgeschichte (story of rural and village life). In the course of the century this genre became trivialized, and it later formed part of the "Blut und Boden" (Blood and Soil) literature that was later placed in the service of the historical ideology of the National Socialists. As a result of the popularization of the "Oberhof" section as a distinct entity the other part, which is overwhelmingly satiric and parodistic, was neglected. This neglect was also due to the many literary, cultural, and social allusions contained in the "Münchhausen" part, which were not readily understood even by Immermann's contemporaries. Also, the "Münchhausen" section, with its emphasis on social criticism, was a radical departure from the traditional German bildungsroman. Finally, the prevailing opinion was that the two parts, rather than forming an organic whole, constituted opposing entities, one depicting the negative world of the decayed aristocracy, of subjectivism resulting in utter chaos, the other portraying the positive world of the peasants, based on an objective natural foundation. Modern criticism has contradicted this view, holding instead that both parts manifest positive and negative values.

The subtitle of *Münchhausen* is *Eine Geschichte in Arabesken* (A Story in Arabesques). Following Friedrich Schlegel's definition of *arabesque,* which gave the author almost unlimited freedom to use his or her imagination within a loose narrative structure, enables Immermann to bring into play a wide array of perspectives for a comprehensive criticism of his time. The actual plot serves merely as a skeleton: Lisbeth, a foundling of indeterminate origin but endowed with a natural nobility, is a helper at the run-down palace of the silly baron and his equally silly daughter. While collecting taxes from the Westphalian peasants she meets and falls in love with a young man, Oswald, who identifies himself as a forester but is in fact from an aristocratic family. He is trying to track down a mysterious adventurer who slandered his family and finds him in the person of Münchhausen. But much to his chagrin, the elusive Münchhausen turns out to be his beloved Lisbeth's father. After much confusion and the introduction of many comical secondary characters, the lovers are reconciled, illustrating Immermann's claim that love and life are the supremely enduring values in this time of shifting and amorphous mores.

With his acute gift for observation Immermann was able to project his figures onto a many-faceted social and cultural background. He was convinced that the younger generation was being exposed to rapid and contradictory changes: the French Revolution, the Wars of Liberation, the defeat of Napoleon, the Restoration with its deceptive tranquillity, and, finally, the July Revolution of 1830 in Paris. There are fundamental sociological shifts, with the emerging industrial class claiming its rightful place. The generation of epigones is faced with a confusing plethora of intellectual achievements it cannot assimilate: the contradictoriness of the time has rendered all knowledge relative and eliminated generally accepted moral principles. The pervasive ambivalence has rendered individuals incapable of coping with the many challenges facing them; as a consequence, they try to be all things and end up being none. Thus, life becomes self-deception. In the character of Münchhausen, Immermann created an allegorical representation of these phenomena.

But the demented old baron and his daughter are not entirely negative figures, and conversely, the peasant world of the conservative Oberhof, frugal and in harmony with nature, is not entirely positive. The Hofschulze's claim to his authority is based on a fraudulent symbol, and when Oswald interferes in an age-old ritual the Hofschulze goes berserk. Ritual, tradition, and the hierarchical structure have become rigid; they are continued for their own sake rather than in support of an organic way of life. Cracks are clearly visible in this world as well, because Immermann believes in "das große Gesetz der Bewegung und Verwandlung" (the great law of motion and change). Nothing is more negative than a passive persistence in a single state. Society as depicted in *Die Epigonen* and *Münchhausen* is in a chaotic stage. But from it will come new forms and structures that will benefit coming generations.

On 2 October 1839 Immermann married Niemeyer, who was twenty-three years younger than he. After a trip to Dresden and Weimar the couple returned to Düsseldorf. A daughter, Caroline, was born on 12 August 1840. A few days later Immermann fell ill with a lung infection, and he died on 25 August. He had written to his then-fiancée that his life had been split and as a consequence his writings could not be whole and harmonious. Because Immermann felt the elements of dualism and contradiction so acutely within himself, he was perhaps uniquely qualified to depict them as major characteristics of his time.

Letters:

Theater-Briefe, edited by Gustav zu Putlitz (Berlin: Duncker, 1851);

Immermann an Heine: Ein unbekannter Brief Immermanns vom 5. März 1825, edited by Erich Schulz (Dortmund: Ruhfus, 1926);

Briefe: Textkritische und kommentierende Ausgabe, 3 volumes, edited by Peter Hasubek (Munich & Vienna: Hanser, 1978).

Biographies:

Marianne Immermann, *Karl Immermann: Sein Leben und seine Werke, aus Tagebüchern und Briefen an seine Familie zusammengestellt,* edited by Gustav zu Putlitz (Berlin: Hertz, 1870);

Harry Maync, *Immermann: Der Mann und sein Werk im Rahmen der Zeit- und Literaturgeschichte* (Munich: Beck, 1920);

Felix Wolff, ed., *Marianne Wolff, geborene Niemeyer, die Witwe Karl Immermanns: Leben und Briefe* (Hamburg: Ernte, 1925);

Benno von Wiese, *Karl Immermann: Sein Werk und sein Leben* (Bad Homburg: Gehlen, 1969).

References:

C. David, "Über den Begriff des Epigonischen," in *Tradition und Ursprünglichkeit: Akten des III. Internationalen Germanisten-Kongresses 1965,* edited by Werner Kohlschmidt and Herman Meyer (Bern: Franke, 1967);

Werner Deetjen, *Immermanns Jugenddramen* (Leipzig: Dieterich, 1904);

Deetjen, "Zur Beurteilung von Immermanns *Münchhausen,*" *Zeitschrift für den deutschen Unterricht,* 22 (1908): 781–787;

Hanna Fischer-Lamberg, "Immermanns Authoritätsproblem," *Deutsche Vierteljahrsschrift,* 18 (August 1940): 371–386;

Ferdinand Freiligrath, *Karl Immermann: Blätter der Erinnerung an ihn* (Stuttgart: Krabbe, 1842);

Friedrich Gundolf, "Karl Immermann," in his *Romantiker: Neue Folge* (Berlin: Keller, 1931);

Elisabeth Guzinski, *Karl Immermann als Zeitkritiker* (Berlin: Junker und Dünnhaupt, 1937);

Joseph Halm, *Formen der Narrheit in Immermanns Prosa* (Marburg: Elwert, 1972);

Peter Hasubek, "Karl Immermann: Die Epigonen," in *Romane und Erzählungen zwischen Romantik und Realismus: Neue Interpretationen,* edited by Paul Michael Lützeler (Stuttgart: Reclam, 1983), pp. 202–230;

Hasubek, ed., *"Widerspruch, du Herr der Welt!": Neue Studien zu Karl Immermann* (Bielefeld: Aisthesis, 1990);

Gunther Holst, *Das Bild des Menschen in den Romanen Karl Immermanns* (Meisenheim am Glan: Hain, 1976);

Siegfried Kohlhammer, *Resignation und Revolte: Immermanns Münchhausen. Satire und Zeitroman der Restaurationsepoche* (Stuttgart: Metzler, 1973);

Werner Kohlschmidt, "Die Welt des Bauern im Spiegel von Immermanns *Münchhausen* und Gotthelfs *Uli,*" *Dichtung und Volkstum,* 39 (1938): 223–237;

Max Kommerell, "Immermann und das 19. Jahrhundert," in *Max Kommerell: Essays, Notizen, poetische Fragmente,* edited by Inge Jens (Olten & Freiburg: Walter, 1969), pp. 187–222;

Gustav Konrad, "Immermanns *Münchhausen,*" *Acta Germanica,* 3 (1968): 167–185;

Thomas Kreutz, *Immermanns politische Satire* (Münster: 1928);

Wolfgang Kuttenkeuler, "Heinrich Heine and Karl L. Immermann: Produktivität eines wechselseitigen Mißverständnisses," *Zeitschrift für deutsche Philologie,* 91 (1972): 90–110;

Leo Lauschus, *Über Technik und Stil der Romane und Novellen Immermanns* (Berlin: Schriften der literarhistorischen Gesellschaft Bonn, 1913);

Waltraud Maierhofer, *"Wilhelm Meisters Wanderjahre" und der Roman des Nebeneinander* (Bielefeld: Aisthesis, 1990);

Hans Mayer, "Karl Immermanns *Epigonen,*" in his *Studien zur deutschen Literaturgeschichte* (Berlin: Rütten & Loening, 1955), pp. 247–272;

William McClain, "Karl Leberecht Immermann's Portrait of a Folk-Hero in *Münchhausen,*" in *Studies in German Literature of the Nineteenth and Twentieth Centuries: Festschrift for Frederic E. Coenen,* edited by Siegfried Mews (Chapel Hill: University of North Carolina Press, 1970), pp. 55–63;

Herman Meyer, "Karl Immermann: Münchhausen," in *Das Zitat in der Erzählkunst* (Stuttgart: Metzler, 1961), pp. 135–154;

Wolfgang Mieder, "Die Funktion des Sprichwortes in Karl Immermann's *Münchhausen,*" *Zeitschrift für deutsche Philologie,* 90 (1971): 228–241;

Heinz Moenkemeyer, "Das Problem des selbsternannten Erlösers bei Immermann," *Monatshefte,* 52 (March 1960): 121–129;

Beate Mühl, *Romantiktradition und früher Realismus: zum Verhältnis von Gattungspoetik und literarischer Praxis in der Restaurationsepoche (Tieck-Immermann)* (Frankfurt am Main: Lang, 1983);

Allen Wilson Porterfield, *Karl Leberecht Immermann: A Study in German Romanticism* (New York: Columbia University Press, 1911);

Jeffrey L. Sammons, "Karl Immerman," in his *Six Essays on the Young German Novel* (Chapel Hill: 1972), pp. 124–170;

Michael Scherer, "Immermanns Münchhausen-Roman," *German Quarterly,* 36 (May 1963): 236–244;

Werner R. Schweizer, *Münchhausen und Münchhausiaden: Werden und Schicksale einer deutsch-englischen Burleske* (Bern & Munich: Francke, 1969);

Schweizer, *Die Wandlungen Münchhausens in der deutschen Literatur bis zu Immermann* (Leipzig: Dieter, 1921);

Markus Schwering, *Epochenwandel im spätromantischen Roman: Untersuchungen zu Eichendorff, Tieck und Immermann* (Cologne & Vienna: Böhlau, 1985);

Leo Spitzer, "A Note on Immermann's Chiliastische Sonette," *Germanic Review,* 25 (1950): 196–197;

D. Statkov, "Über die dialektische Struktur des Immermann-Romans *Münchhausen:* Zum Problem des Übergangs von der Romantik zum Realismus," *Weimarer Beiträge,* 11 (1965): 200–204;

Benno von Wiese, "Immermann: Münchhausen," in *Der deutsche Roman vom Barock bis zur Gegenwart,* edited by Wiese (Düsseldorf: Bagel, 1963), pp. 353–406;

Manfred Windfuhr, "Der Epigone: Begriff, Phänomen und Bewußtsein," *Archiv für Begriffsgeschichte,* 4 (1959): 182–209.

Papers:

Karl Immermann's papers are at the Stadt- und Landesbibliothek (City and State Library), Dortmund; the Heinrich-Heine-Institut, Düsseldorf; and the Nationalarchiv, Weimar.

Heinrich Laube

(18 September 1806 - 1 August 1884)

Mark J. Webber
York University

BOOKS: *Das neue Jahrhundert,* 2 volumes (Fürth: Korn, 1833) – comprises *Polen, Politische Briefe;* volume 2 also published as *Briefe eines Hofraths oder Bekenntnisse einer jungen bürgerlichen Seele* (Leipzig: Literarisches Museum, 1833);

Die Poeten: Novelle, 2 volumes, part 1 of *Das junge Europa* (Mannheim: Hoff, 1833);

Reisenovellen, 4 volumes (volumes 1-2, Leipzig: Wigand, 1834; volumes 3-4, Mannheim: Hoff, 1836);

Moderne Charakteristiken, 2 volumes (Mannheim: Löwenthal, 1835);

Liebesbriefe: Novelle (Leipzig: Wigand, 1835);

Die Schauspielerin: Novelle (Mannheim: Hoff, 1836);

Die französische Revolution, von 1789 bis 1836, anonymous (Berlin: Duncker & Humblot, 1836);

Das Glück: Novelle (Mannheim: Hoff, 1837);

Die Krieger: Novelle, 2 volumes, part 2 of *Das junge Europa* (Mannheim: Hoff, 1837);

Die Bürger: Novelle, 2 volumes, part 3 of *Das junge Europa* (Mannheim: Hoff, 1837);

Neue Reisenovellen 2 volumes (Mannheim: Hoff, 1837);

Vertraute Briefe über Preußens Hauptstadt (Stuttgart: Rüger, 1837);

Goerres und Athanasius, anonymous (Leipzig: Köhler, 1838);

Geschichte der deutschen Literatur, 4 volumes (Stuttgart: Hallberger, 1839-1840);

Französische Lustschlösser, 3 volumes (Mannheim: Hoff, 1840);

Jagdbrevier (Leipzig: Wigand, 1841; revised edition, Leipzig: Haessel, 1858);

Der Prätendent (Leipzig: Teubner, 1842);

Die Bandomire: Kurische Erzählung (Mitau & Leipzig: Meyer, 1842);

Gräfin Chateaubriant: Roman, 3 volumes (Leipzig: Teubner, 1843);

George Sand's Frauenbilder (Brussels: Haumann, 1845);

Der belgische Graf (Mannheim: Hoff, 1845);

Heinrich Laube

Drei Königsstädte im Norden: Roman, 2 volumes (Leipzig: Weber, 1845);

Dramatische Werke, 13 volumes (Leipzig: Weber, 1845-1875) – comprises as volume 1, *Monaldeschi, oder Die Abenteurer: Tragödie in fünf Acten und einem Vorspiele* (1845); as volume 2, *Rokoko oder Die alten Herren: Lustspiel in fünf Akten* (1846); as volume 3, *Die Bernsteinhexe: Historisches Schauspiel in fünf Akten. Nach Meinhold's Hexenprozesse Marie Schweidler* (1846); as volume 4, *Struensee: Tragödie in fünf Akten* (1847); as volume 5, *Gottsched und Gellert: Charakter-Lustspiel in fünf Akten* (1847); as volume 6, *Die Karlsschüler: Schauspiel in fünf Akten*

(1847); as volume 7, *Prinz Friedrich: Schauspiel in fünf Akten* (1854); as volume 8, *Graf Essex: Trauerspiel in fünf Akten* (1856); as volume 9, *Montrose, der schwarze Markgraf: Trauerspiel in fünf Akten* (1859); as volume 10, *Der Statthalter von Bengalen: Schauspiel in vier Akten* (1868); as volume 12, *Demetrius: Historische Tragödie in fünf Acten. Mit Benutzung des Schiller'schen Fragments bis zur Verwandlung im zweiten Acte* (1872); as volume 13, *Cato von Eisen: Lustspiel in drei Akten (Die Grundidee nach Gorostiza); Nachsicht für Alle: Originalkomödie in fünf Akten, von Manuel Eduardo de Gorostiza, uebersetzt von Hedwig Wolf* (1875);

Briefe über das deutsche Theater, 4 volumes (Leipzig: Hesse, 1846–1847);

Novellen, 10 volumes (Mannheim: Hoff, 1846–1848) – includes *Paris, 1847* (1848);

Reisenovellen, 3 volumes (Mannheim: Hoff, 1847);

Das erste deutsche Parlament, 3 volumes (Leipzig: Weidmann, 1849);

Cato von Eisen: Lustspiel in drei Akten (Die Grundidee nach Gorostiza). (Zum ersten Male aufgeführt im k. k. Hofburgtheater den 9. Februar 1858.) (Vienna: Klopf & Eurich, 1858);

Creszentia, as Gustav von Blittersperg (Leipzig: Haessel, 1859);

Der deutsche Krieg: Historischer Roman in 3 Büchern, 9 volumes (Leipzig: Haessel, 1863–1866) – comprises *Junker Hans: Historischer Roman,* 4 volumes (1863); *Waldstein: Historischer Roman,* 3 volumes (1864); *Herzog Bernhard: Historischer Roman,* 2 volumes (1866);

Das Burgtheater: Ein Beitrag zur deutschen Theater-Geschichte (Leipzig: Weber, 1868);

Böse Zungen (Leipzig: Weber, 1869);

Advocat Hamlet: Schauspiel in 4 Acten (Leipzig: Breitkopf & Härtl, 1870);

Das norddeutsche Theater: Ein neuer Beitrag zur deutschen Theatergeschichte (Leipzig: Weber, 1872);

Das Wiener Stadt-Theater (Leipzig: Weber, 1875);

Erinnerungen, 1810–1840 (Vienna: Braumüller, 1875);

Mitten in der Nacht: Posse in einem Aufzug. Nach dem Französischen (Leipzig: Reclam, 1875);

Gesammelte Schriften, 16 volumes (Vienna: Braumüller, 1875–1882);

Die Böhminger: Roman, 3 volumes (Stuttgart: Hallberger, 1880);

Louison: Novelle (Brunswick: Westermann, 1881);

Entweder – oder: Eine Erzählung (Brunswick: Westermann, 1882);

Erinnerungen, 1841–1881 (Vienna: Braumüller, 1882);

Schauspielerei: Lustspiel in vier Akten, as A. H. Mühlbaum (Vienna: Selbstverlag des Verfassers, 1882);

Die kleine Prinzessin; Blond muß sie sein: Novellen (Breslau: Schottländer, 1883);

Der Schatten Wilhelm: Eine geschichtliche Erzählung (Leipzig: Haessel, 1883);

Franz Grillparzers Lebensgeschichte (Stuttgart: Cotta, 1884);

Ruben: Ein moderner Roman (Leipzig: Haessel, 1885);

Theaterkritiken und dramaturgische Aufsätze: Gesammelt, ausgewählt und mit Einleitung und Anmerkungen versehen, 2 volumes, edited by Alexander von Weilen, Schriften der Gesellschaft für Theatergeschichte, 7–8 (Berlin: Selbstverlag der Gesellschaft für Theatergeschichte, 1906);

Heinrich Laubes ausgewählte Werke, 10 volumes, edited by Heinrich Hubert Houben, (Leipzig: Hesse, 1906);

Heinrich Laubes Meisterdramen: Mit den literarischen Einleitungen und zwei Bildnissen des Verfassers, 2 volumes (Leipzig: Hesse, 1908);

Gesammelte Werke, 50 volumes, edited by Houben and Albert Hänel (Leipzig: Hesse, 1908–1910);

Vermischte Aufsätze (Leipzig: Hesse, 1910?);

Heinrich Laubes dramaturgische Schriften, 4 volumes, edited by Houben (Leipzig: Hesse, 1910);

Kritiken von Heinrich Laube: Ausgewählt und eingeleitet als Beitrag zur Geschichte des "Jungen Deutschland," edited by Samuel Dickinson Stirk (Breslau: Priebatsch, 1934);

Das Theaterbüchlein (Vienna: Gerlach & Wiedling, 1946);

Schriften über Theater, edited by Eva Stahl-Wisten (Berlin: Henschel, 1959).

OTHER: *Aurora: Eine literarische Zeitschrift,* edited by Laube (1829);

Zeitung für die elegante Welt, edited by Laube (1833–1834, 1843–1844);

Mitternachtzeitung für gebildete Stände, edited by Laube (1835–1837);

Victor Hugo, "Bug-Jargal," translated by Laube and Ymbert Galloix, in Hugo's *Sämmtliche Werke,* volume 7 (Frankfurt am Main: Sauerländer, 1836);

Johann Jacob Wilhelm Heinse, *Sämmtliche Schriften,* 10 volumes, edited by Laube (Leipzig: Volckmar, 1837–1838);

"Gans und Immermann," in *Deutsche Pandora: Gedenkbuch zeitgenössischer Zustände und Schriftsteller,* volume 4 (Stuttgart: Literatur-Comptoir, 1841), pp. 3–52;

Pedro Calderón de la Barca, *Das Leben ein Traum,* edited by Laube (Vienna, 1867);

Jules Sandeau, *Das Fräulein von Seiglière: Schauspiel in vier Aufzügen,* edited by Laube (Leipzig: Reclam, 1871);

Franz Grillparzer, *Sämmtliche Werke,* 10 volumes, edited by Laube and Josef Weil (Stuttgart: Cotta, 1872);

Theodor Barriere and P. A. A. Thiboust, *Marmorherzen: Sitten-Schauspiel in fünf Aufzügen,* translated by Laube (Leipzig: Reclam, 1872);

Augustin Eugène Scribe and Gabriel Jean Baptist Ernest Wilfrid Legouvé, *Der Damenkrieg: Lustspiel in drei Aufzügen,* translated by Laube (Leipzig: Reclam, 1874);

Philippe François P. Dumanoir and Ange Bon Marie Le Roy de Karanion, *Die Eine weint, die Andre lacht: Schauspiel in vier Aufzügen,* translated and adapted by Laube (Leipzig: Reclam, 1874);

Octave Feuillet, *Eine vornehme Ehe: Schauspiel in vier Aufzügen und einem Vorspiele,* translated and adapted by Laube (Leipzig: Reclam, 1874);

Victorien Sardou, *Lustspiele,* 5 volumes, edited by Laube (Leipzig: Reclam, 1874);

Guillaume Victor Emile Augier, *Der Pelikan: Schauspiel in fünf Aufzügen,* translated and adapted by Laube (Leipzig: Reclam, 1875);

Der Hauptmann von der Schaarwache: Lustspiel in 2 Aufzügen nach dem Französischen, translated and adapted by Laube (Leipzig: Reclam, 1878);

Delphine Gay de Girardin, *Die Furcht vor der Freude: Schauspiel in einem Aufzug,* translated and adapted by Laube (Leipzig: Reclam, 1879);

Augier, *Eine Demimonde-Heirath: Schauspiel in drei Aufzügen,* translated by Laube (Leipzig: Reclam, 1879);

Sardou, *Daniel Rochat,* translated by Laube (Hamburg: Hoffmann & Campe, 1880);

Gotthold Ephraim Lessing, *Werke: Illustrirte Prachtausgabe,* 5 volumes, edited by Laube (Vienna, Leipzig & Prague: Bensinger, 1882–1883);

Heinrich Heine, *Werke,* 6 volumes, edited by Laube (Vienna: Bensinger, 1884–1886);

Frederick Marryat, *Sigismund Rüstig, der Bremer Steuermann: Ein neuer Robinson, nach Kapitän Marryat, frei für die deutsche Jugend bearbeitet,* adapted by Laube (Leipzig: Teubner, 1887);

"Letzte Erinnerungen," in *Deutsche Schauspieler und Schauspielkunst,* edited by Wolfgang Kirchbach, Deutsche Schriften für Litteratur und Kunst, series 2, number 2 (Kiel & Leipzig: Lipsius & Tischer, 1892), pp. 32–51;

Nicolaus Lenau, *Werke,* 2 volumes, edited by Laube, (Vienna, Leipzig & Prague: Bensinger, n.d.).

Of the young Heinrich Laube a contemporary wrote that he "jumped into literature like an adventure [jumping] in through the window"; but when Laube died, less than two months before his seventy-eighth birthday, his initially radical nature had been tamed. His prolific literary production was accompanied by a distinguished career as director of Vienna's renowned Burgtheater. He was a man of letters whose output encompassed journalism, literary criticism, fiction, and drama. He insisted on situating literature within social, geographic, historical, and political reality. Laube's early attempts to redefine the nature of literature, undertaken in radical-liberal rebellion against the classical aesthetic, earned him fame and notoriety, and his self-stylization as a rebel contributed to his troubles with the police and censorship authorities from the mid 1830s into the 1840s; it also made his name as a "Young German" writer. His works often do not conform to traditional genre classifications. In politics he was too radical for the conservatives, too ready to recant for the leftists.

Laube's career is marked by inconsistencies: though he favors the sharp *pointe,* he is anything but terse; though he began as a literary and political radical, he ended up as a conservative. After approximately ten years devoted primarily to prose, his next decade was dominated by the writing of dramas; the final fifteen years of his career were marked by a lessening of his own original output in favor of producing the dramas of others.

Even in the face of such contradictions and changes, certain basic themes, attitudes, and convictions mark his writing and his life. Laube remained an essentially Protestant, liberal writer with a German national bent. As an agitator, politician, journalist, author of fiction, dramatist, and dramaturge he worked for a culturally and politically unified Germany. A major theme in his work is the adventurer who leaves home, strays from the path of political and social convention, and must pay the price for his greatness. Other themes, which are sometimes presented frivolously, sometimes with great seriousness, are the nature and role of woman and the relationship of men and women.

Heinrich Rudolf Constanz Laube was born in Sprottau, Silesia (today Szprotawa, Poland), on 18 September 1806. As a child he experienced the excitement of the Napoleonic Wars. At fourteen he was sent away to a gymnasium in Glogau (today Glogów, Poland), where he spent five years. After a final year at the gymnasium in Schweidnitz (today Swidnica, Poland) he enrolled at Halle University to study theology. It was not religious fervor that attracted Laube to theology; rather, this field allowed – indeed, demanded – the development of rhetorical skills that were banned from political discourse, and it provided prospects of financial support during and after his studies. During his university years he participated in the activities of the Halle Burschenschaft (liberal student fraternity). The Burschenschaften were outlawed at the time, and Laube's association with the group would cause him considerable trouble later.

Laube transferred to the University of Breslau in the winter of 1827–1828. It was there that his public literary career began with romances published in literary almanacs in 1829 and 1830; he also reviewed theatrical performances for a local paper. In 1829 he founded a short-lived newspaper, *Aurora,* contributing poems and reviews of literary works and theatrical performances. He also had articles published in other papers on other subjects, including politics.

In 1830 Laube became a private tutor with a family in Kottwitz, near the Polish border. The Polish uprising against Russian domination in November 1830 and his meeting with a wounded Polish officer inspired his first book, *Polen* (Poland, 1833). The book is a strange concoction of prose narrative, history, current events, and polemic. As volume one of *Das neue Jahrhundert* (The New Century, 1833), it is an attempt to bring about a new epoch. The new epoch in whose service Laube sees himself, and in whose aid he wishes to move others to enlist, is not solely political; it is marked as well by the passing of the old generation of authoritative voices and authoritarian views with the deaths of the philosopher Georg Wilhelm Friedrich Hegel in 1831 and of Johann Wolfgang von Goethe the following year. The Polish revolution seemed to Laube to suggest a broadening of the struggle against absolutism that had begun with the July Revolution in Paris in 1830.

Growing up in Silesia, on the eastern frontier of Germany, Laube had held many negative stereotypes about the Poles. But the Polish struggle, combined with Laube's encounters with Polish freedom fighters and refugees, changed his mind. In castigating Russia, Prussia's ally, for its subjugation of Poland, Laube was indirectly criticizing Prussia itself in a way he would not have dared to attempt openly. Several years later he was to find out that the Prussian authorities were quite capable of seeing through this ploy and equally capable of taking revenge.

The book runs to 336 pages; since the enactment of the repressive Carlsbad Decrees in 1819, books longer than 320 pages were exempt from censorship before publication. The idea was that any book of this length would be unlikely to be dangerous to the status quo; in the case of the young Laube, the authorities miscalculated.

The second volume of Laube's "New Century," *Politische Briefe* (Political Letters, 1833), begins with a protest against censorship. To evade the Prussian censors, Laube had some copies of the book printed with the misleading title *Briefe eines Hofraths* (Letters of a Privy Councillor, 1833); the spaced dashes that replace "objectionable" passages show that the censors were not completely fooled. The book is couched in the form of letters that comment on contemporary issues in a manner reminiscent of Ludwig Börne's *Briefe aus Paris* (Letters from Paris, 1832–1834). Two correspondents trade opinions on the advantages and disadvantages of constitutional monarchy, liberalism, freedom of the press, republicanism, and literature. Neither of the correspondents is given a name or a distinct personality; as they present their views in minitreatises, the reader sometimes has difficulty remembering whether it is writer A or writer B who is holding forth.

A promised third volume on Saint-Simonianism never materialized, but Saint-Simonian thinking is reflected in several of Laube's works. Based on the ideas of Claude-Henri de Rouvroy, Comte de Saint-Simon, as modified by his two principal disciples, Amand Bazard and Barthélemy-Prosper Enfantin, Saint-Simonianism was a religion, a philosophy of history, and a social movement. It taught that history is a dialectical process that alternates between "organic" epochs of religious and social unanimity and "critical" epochs of dissonance toward a final organic epoch of peace, social harmony, and affluence. Laube's attraction to Saint-Simonianism derived from two of its doctrines. First, the concept of the "critical epoch" explained, and so made more bearable, the condition of fragmentation that prevailed in Germany. Second, in its emphasis on producing a new social, political, and psychological totality, it liberated and elevated that which had been suppressed or repressed. Thus, it preached – though in an ambivalent way – the emancipation of women and the validity of sensuality and free sexual expression.

Laube worked these themes into his first novel, *Die Poeten* (The Poets, 1833), which was the first part of a trilogy titled *Das junge Europa* (Young Europe). The epistolary technique of *Politische Briefe* is repeated in the novel, although the number of correspondents is increased; the characters have names and personalities; the settings, a mixture of fictional and actual, lend flavor to the work; and there is a plot of sorts, involving travel, romance, and political engagement. The work can be considered a cross between a roman à clef, a bildungsroman, and a political tract.

The hero is Valerius, who is loosely modeled on Laube himself; many of the other characters are based on Laube's circle of friends and acquaintances in Breslau and Kottwitz and represent various political and artistic viewpoints. Five male and three female characters – Valerius, Constantin, Hyppolit, William, Leopold, Camilla, Julia, and Alberta – write the bulk of the letters that constitute the novel's two volumes. Most of these characters, and several others who are written about but do not write, are residents of or visitors to Castle Grünschloß, which offers them a convenient venue for their controversial political discussions and equally controversial love affairs.

While the goings and comings at Grünschloß play in the foreground of the novel's plot, the background is represented by such European political events of 1830 as the July Revolution, the Belgian revolt, and the Polish uprising. Leopold, who begins the novel as a romantic dreamer, ends up a physician with the Belgian army. Constantin, a young nobleman disowned by his family for his sensuality and revolutionary views, goes to Paris after the July Revolution and is disabused of his radicalism. William, the proponent of political, religious, and personal overcontrol, murders out of passion. Hippolyt, who can have his pick of women but knows no loyalty, is in the end rejected by a woman. Valerius, on the other hand, is faithful to Camilla, but their love is hindered by jealousy, misunderstandings, and the cause of political freedom. In the novel's penultimate chapter Valerius reports that he is setting out for Warsaw to fight for freedom, even though he is no great lover of the Polish people.

The novel illustrates and advocates the Saint-Simonian notion of the emancipation of the flesh, but this emancipation reveals itself to be a decidedly male enterprise that renders men more free to partake of the pleasures of the flesh and women more free to be partaken of. The limitations of Laube's construction of the female role were to remain with him throughout his life and were shared by most of his fellow liberals. For all the complications of its structure, the abstractness of its argument, and the loss of immediacy inherent in a novel of letters, Laube's first large work of fiction shows an energy and an ability for vivid portrayal that made its publication a promising novelistic debut.

In January 1833 Laube assumed the editorship of the influential *Zeitung für die elegante Welt* (Newspaper for the Elegant World), which was published in Leipzig. His contributions include substantial articles on the interrelationship of literature and history, theater reviews, and discussions of newly published books. Declaring in one article that the present is a "critical epoch," Laube predicts that an unrestrained age of prose will supplant the politically and aesthetically restrictive age of poetry. Laube is here attempting to set the literary and political program for what would come to be called "Junges Deutschland" (Young Germany).

In the summer Laube took a leave of absence and, in the company of a Leipzig friend named Axenfeld and Karl Gutzkow, another young former student of theology, fiction writer, and journalist with whom Laube had been corresponding, undertook a trip to southern Germany, Austria, and Italy. On his return to Leipzig in the fall he resumed his editorial duties and began work on what was to become a lengthy and successful series of prose sketches: the *Reisenovellen* (Travel Novellas). The first two volumes came out in the spring of 1834; volumes three and four were published in 1836; and volumes five and six, titled *Neue Reisenovellen* (New Travel Novellas), appeared the following year. In the travel novellas Laube took up a genre that put him in the company of Börne and of Heinrich Heine, whose *Reisebilder* (1826–1831; translated as *Pictures of Travel,* 1855) was well known.

For liberal writers like Laube, Börne, and Heine, writing about travel offered multiple attractions. Travel entailed a breaking of static patterns of thought and behavior, which was both a precondition and a symbol of progress. Moreover, this mode of writing allowed Laube and his colleagues to reflect indirectly on the situation at home by pointing out contrasting features of the situation abroad. Laube takes advantage of these possibilities, but his novellas also abound with accounts of his erotic near-adventures that gradually become tiresome. At his best, though, Laube succeeds in portraying characteristic figures and events that incorporate the essential quality of a locale and its history through the narration of a pregnant episode that satisfies even the strictest definition of a novella.

In late July 1834 Laube was taken into custody. For the next two weeks he was interrogated about his beliefs, writings, and activities. He put up an effective defense, but in August his activities in the Burschenschaft provided the pretext for further imprisonment; after six weeks he was transferred to a harsher prison, with repeated interrogations on the intent and political thrust of his books, including the *Reisenovellen.*

It was not until January 1835 that he was permitted to write again, albeit in his cell. On 20 March, after eight months of incarceration, he was released. *Moderne Charakteristiken* (Modern Character Sketches), a collection of his most important biographical and literary contributions to the *Zeitung für die elegante Welt,* was published that year. But in November the Prussian government introduced a special censorship order directed against the writers of Junges Deutschland, and on 10 December the German Federal Diet followed suit. The federal decree forbade the publication and dissemination of past, present, and future writings by Laube, Heine, Gutzkow, Theodor Mundt, and Ludolf Wienbarg. Laube's reaction was to dissociate himself from Junges Deutschland and to assert his moderation. He had already begun to moderate his views before the authorities provided him with incentives to do so, but the incentives no doubt had an effect, too.

While in jail Laube had written what Jeffrey L. Sammons has called "in certain respects, the most successful of all Young German prose works": the second part of his *Das junge Europa* trilogy, *Die Krieger* (The Warriors, 1837). Laube's intention was to produce a focused novel of action that would overcome weaknesses of the multivoiced, sedentary, and theoretical approach he had taken in *Die Poeten;* accordingly, he gives up that work's epistolary framework in favor of third-person narration. Once again, Laube deals with the Polish uprising against Russia, which had been his focus in *Das neue Jahrhundert* and which had aroused the ire of the Prussian authorities – a strange choice for an author who had been confined to prison by those authorities. Laube's censor argued against allowing the book and its successor, *Die Bürger* (The Burghers, 1837), to see the light of day, but he was overruled. The warriors of the middle novel's title are Poles of all classes, historical and fictional characters who enter into alliances as well as feuds among themselves and with others: a ghostly old woman who symbolizes the pride and the sufferings of Poland; the smith Florian, whose family has been massacred by the Russians and who is now driven to kill as many Russians as he can; Stanislaus, a young nobleman devoted to ideals of democracy that transcend nationalism; Valerius's love interests, Princess Constantie and Camilla; radicals and conservatives who plot with and against each other for the good cause; and, most strikingly, Valerius's Jewish friend Joel and Joel's father, Manasse. In the final chapter, the dying Manasse reveals that Joel is his son by a Christian noblewoman; Joel and Constantie are half-siblings. Joel's love for the beautiful Hedwig has been in vain because she cannot abide the thought of loving a Jew. Joel's psychological alienation – although he is ready to assimilate to non-Jewish ways, he is rejected by the non-Jewish world – is thus symbolized by his mixed parentage. Joel's struggle for acceptance ends in bitterness and resignation. Valerius, too, is alienated: confronted with the realities of the Polish situation, Valerius finds himself to be incapable of total commitment, which he identifies as a fanaticism.

In the novel's closing paragraphs Valerius reflects on what he has experienced. Talking both to Joel and himself, he recognizes that it is foolish to try to change the course of history. He and his fellow warriors have attempted to do so, and they have been crushed by the historical forces they sought to control. This is also the lesson of Jewish history, which seeks to assert itself against the historical necessity of Christianity. Valerius urges Joel and his coreligionists to give up their faith and become assimilated to the mainstream of society. This advice is typical of nineteenth-century liberal attitudes toward Jewish emancipation.

In the final novel of the trilogy, *Die Bürger,* Valerius is in prison, betrayed by a Pole. Laube abandons the immediacy and incipient realism of *Die Krieger* and returns to the indirect and disjointed style of the epistolary novel. In the end Valerius is released and withdraws to a remote valley, literally to tend his own garden; he is the only one of his circle to have found a semblance of happiness. But even this happiness is muted: he writes Hippolyt that his heart has not grown cold, but it no longer leaps; no vision, no hope can ignite it any longer. He is constructing a new world for himself, he says, and how sad that is! With such a depiction of the outcome of liberalism, it is not difficult to see why the authorities allowed *Die Krieger* and *Die Bürger* to appear.

Laube's moderation seemed to impress the authorities favorably. The Carlsbad Decrees notwithstanding, he was allowed to have his novellas *Liebesbriefe* (Love Letters, 1835) and *Die Schauspielerin* (The Actress, 1836) published and to edit the *Mitternachtzeitung* (Midnight Newspaper), even though his articles in the latter were not allowed to bear his byline. The continuation of the *Reisenovellen* afforded additional income. In 1836 Laube married Iduna Hänel (née Buddeus), the widow of a Leipzig

Laube during his stay in Paris in 1840; drawing by Friedrich Pecht (Museum für Geschichte der Stadt Leipzig)

professor. The authorities suggested that Laube take his honeymoon in France and report back on goings-on there; but in late December he was found guilty of having belonged to the Burschenschaft in Halle and of having insulted the government of Prussia and its allies in his writings and was sentenced to seven years in prison. He decided against an appeal, which he feared might be seen as a provocation; instead, he asked for mercy. In June 1837 the sentence was reduced to one and one-half years. Laube's and his wife's connections achieved yet another amelioration of the sentence, which began in July. Laube's sentence took the form of house arrest at the estate of his friend, Prince Hermann von Pückler-Muskau, in Lausitz. He was accompanied by his wife and his stepson, Albert Hänel; the family was augmented by the birth of another child, Hans, on 8 October 1837.

Laube used his eighteen months in Lausitz to work on several literary projects, most of which he was careful to keep uncontroversial. His four-volume *Geschichte der deutschen Literatur* (History of German Literature, 1839–1840), which begins with the Germanic tribes and works its way up to the late 1830s, is opinionated but keeps within the bounds of what was politically and aesthetically permissible.

Laube did insert himself into a controversy with the anonymous brochure *Görres und Athanasius* (1838), his contribution to a raging debate about Protestant Prussia's treatment of its Roman Catholic subjects in the recently acquired Rhenish provinces. In producing a polemic against the conservative Catholic publicist Joseph Görres's *Athanasius* (1838) Laube was joining forces with other liberal Protestant writers; but he was also on the side of a major German government against those who were questioning its authority.

Laube's first period, marked by major works of prose fiction, was behind him; his enforced presence at Pückler-Muskau's estate coincided with a change in the mode and thrust of his writing. His interest in history remained strong, but it was redirected from the recent to the more distant past; from prose fiction to editing, translation, and drama; and from central and eastern Europe to the West, especially France. Laube was released from imprisonment on 17 January 1839, and he and his wife undertook their postponed trip to France. They arrived in Paris in May.

With Heine as his mentor, Laube immersed himself in a combination of travel; meetings with such literary personalities as Honoré de Balzac, Victor Hugo, and George Sand; and reading French history. A month after his return to Germany in February 1840 he went back to the Pückler-Muskau estate – this time voluntarily – and wrote *Französische Lustschlösser* (French Country Châteaus, 1840). The book recounts Laube's visits to, and the history of, Fontainebleau, Chambord, Eu, Pau, Saint-Germain, Versailles, and, on a side trip to Algiers, the Casbah. There is more travel, and less novella, than in the *Reisenovellen,* but still present are a lively pace and fluid transitions from fiction to historical account, from description to opinion, from a focus on the foreign to reflection about the German. Moreover, the book has a maturity, directness, and vitality that had been lacking in Laube's writing previously.

Laube's experiences in France clearly revitalized him in body and spirit. Embedded in the book are several novellalike tales that captured his imagination to the point that he expanded them into works in their own right. One is the story of Gian Rinaldo Monaldeschi, who was killed in 1657 at Fontainebleau on the orders of Queen Christina of Sweden. In the sixty-five-page introduction to his drama *Monaldeschi, oder Die Abenteurer* (Monaldeschi; or, The Adventurers, 1845), Laube reports that the subject first attracted his attention during his incarceration; in Fontainebleau he rediscovered the story, and only later did he recall his previous interest in it. (Long – sometimes overly long – introductions are typical of Laube, who was fascinated with his own life and assumed that his readers would be, too. His introductions are reminiscent of his travel books, in which biographical writing alternates with description and polemic, and anticipate his multivolume memoirs, in which they sometimes reappear almost verbatim.) Laube composed the drama in 1840 but had difficulty finding a theater willing to produce it because it touched on the interests of France and Sweden, as well as because of religious questions it raised. The premiere in November 1841 in Stuttgart was warmly applauded.

The play constructs a tragic relationship between Christina and Monaldeschi, an adventurer who admires her intellectuality as long as she is willing to rule but who cannot understand her decision to renounce the throne for a life of contemplation. His admiration and loyalty, which stem in part from his desire to exert influence over her and hence over the course of history, turn to doubt about both her strength and her femininity, and ultimately to treachery, when she abdicates. In this drama several of Laube's recurring concerns are treated; his fascination with the ambitious and charismatic personality whose extraordinary appeal and effectiveness are bound up with a willingness to violate legal and social norms; the nature of women; and the possibility of controlling or influencing the course of history.

The introduction to *Monaldeschi* also introduces the first volume of Laube's *Dramatische Werke* (Dramatic Works, 1845–1875) and thus provides insight into his program for the German-speaking stage. Two overriding interests – history and the German nation – inform his agenda, and these interests are linked to the problem of discord between Catholic and Protestant writers as well as to the perversion of the relationship between civil authority and the artist through the imposition of censorship. Laube believes that a nation's history constitutes its unity; Germany's history, however, has been one of political and religious division. Laube exhorts his fellow writers to put aside their differences and create a national literature that incorporates the unifying aspects of German history. In an allusion to Friedrich Schiller, he conjures up the vision of a German national theater as a moral institution that instructs without lecturing. But such a development is not possible as long as governments regard theaters as their private domain and dramatists as their public spokespersons. The prevailing attitude has led to the suppression of plays that might cause embarrassment to the ruling family or its foreign relations and allies. (The insistence on finding a way to bring Catholic and Protestant Germany together may explain why Laube permitted the Vienna Burgtheater to excise the religious references in his play.) Finally, Laube's interest in constructing a German history that both explores and subsumes religious differences illuminates his fascination with historical dramas and novels involving the Thirty Years' War and its aftermath.

Laube in 1848; lithograph by A. Kriehuber

Monaldeschi inaugurated a series of dramas on historical themes. One of the best of these plays, *Struensee* (1847), features a hero who has much in common with Monaldeschi. Johann Friedrich Struensee, a commoner, has risen to prominence and influence at the Copenhagen court of King Christian VII. His position causes all the more resentment among the conservative nobility because he espouses reforms. He also wants to espouse the queen. His strength of character, which does not allow him to compromise on issues of principle, contributes to his undoing as he alienates potential allies.

Also included in Laube's *Dramatische Werke* are the comedy *Gottsched und Gellert* (1847), about the writers Johann Christoph Gottsched and Christian Fürchtegott Gellert, and *Die Karlsschüler* (The Carl's School Cadets, 1847), which depicts Schiller's flight from Württemberg after Duke Karl Eugen forbade him to write and attempted to prevent the production of his first play, *Die Räuber* (1781; translated as

The Robbers, 1792). Laube understood these works as contributions to his project of creating a German history, in this case by recalling well-known writers of the eighteenth century and the principles for which they stood.

During the 1840s Laube continued to write historical novels, such as *Die Bandomire* (The Bandomirs, 1842) and *Gräfin Chateaubriant* (Countess Chateaubriant, 1843), which built on his earlier experiences in Silesia and France as well as on historical research. Interspersed with thoroughly dramatic writing in the form of dialogue are descriptions of landscape that seem to have been copied from travel guides, as well as passages in which the motives of characters are explained by the narrator instead of being made clear from their words and actions. From today's perspective, Laube's account of the downfall of Françoise de Valois, Countess Chateaubriant, who leaves her husband for King Francis I of France, is hopelessly overdrawn. Portions of the three-volume work resemble late-twentieth-century romances, with an abundance of transparently "dramatic" scenes culminating in the trial of the adulteress, the sudden appearance of the king, and her suicide by poison. Laube sensed the problem, for in the remarks appended to the work he summarizes recent historical research on the subject.

George Sand's Frauenbilder (George Sand's Portraits of Women, 1845) offers plot summaries of Sand's novels, focusing on the women characters. The work epitomizes the derivative quality of Laube's writing in the 1840s, for it not only depends for its appeal on the writing of Sand, as opposed to that of Laube, but it also draws on direct and indirect models: a French book by a historian to whom Laube also refers in *Gräfin Chateaubriant* and Heine's *Shakespeares Mädchen und Frauen* (Shakespeare's Girls and Women, 1838).

The most enlightening part of *Paris 1847* (1848) is Laube's account of a conversation he had with Sand and Heine during a visit to Paris. Although the book is not without interesting observations on the political and intellectual life of Paris and on Heine's declining health, on the whole it reads like a tired version of Laube's *Reisenovellen* and is perceptibly less engaged than his book on French country châteaus, which also contains the germ of the Chateaubriant story. Laube's tendency to go to the well more than once too often is also seen in another travel book from this time, *Drei Königsstädte im Norden* (Three Royal Cities in the North, 1845), which recounts a trip he and his wife took to Scandinavia in 1844.

Laube contributed articles to the *Blätter für literarische Unterhaltung* (Papers for Literary Conversation), *Deutsche Allgemeine Zeitung, Deutsche Pandora, Hallische Jahrbücher* (Halle Yearbooks), *Kölnische Zeitung* (Cologne Newspaper), *Leipziger Allgemeine Zeitung, Leipziger Tageblatt, Novellenzeitung,* and the *Zeitung für die Elegante Welt,* to whose editorship he returned in 1843 and 1844. A series of articles collected as *Briefe über das deutsche Theater* (Letters on the German Theater, 1846–1847) both reflected and furthered his growing wish to devote his life to the theater as head of one of its most illustrious institutions, the Vienna Burgtheater.

After the 1848 Revolution Laube accepted a seat in the Frankfurt National Assembly. The former radical and enemy of the state – the censorship restrictions resulting from the ban of 1835 had only been formally lifted in 1842, after Laube had forsworn any intention to insult the state, religion, or morality – had become a Prussian patriot and an advocate of constitutional monarchy. He was quick to see that this kind of politics was not for him – the more so because he was representing not Prussia but an Austrian constituency – and he resigned after less than a year, during which he did not give a single speech. He captured the flavor of the assembly in his book *Das erste deutsche Parlament* (The First German Parliament, 1849).

After complicated negotiations Laube assumed the directorship of the Burgtheater on 31 December 1849. The call to the imperial theater was possible only with the change in the political environment that accompanied the accession of Franz Josef to the Austrian throne in 1848.

Although the artistic, administrative, and political challenges of his position consumed much of his energies, Laube still found time to write. Of his plays, *Graf Essex* (Count Essex, 1856) stands out as vintage Laube. Essex, the favorite of Queen Elizabeth I of England, is an adventurer, a man of political, military, and rhetorical talents. Like Struensee and Monaldeschi, he is undone by a personality that allows him to claim the loyalty of others but prevents him from reciprocating that loyalty. Thus, Lady Nottingham, whose love he has spurned, turns into a political rival, as does the queen when she learns of Essex's secret marriage to Countess Rutland. The two women form a constellation that Essex cannot overcome. Filled with allusions to Shakespeare, the play points to the relationship of language and power as one of its main themes.

Cato von Eisen, which had its debut at the Burgtheater on 9 February 1858 and appeared in book form the same year, is a pleasant comedy in which a "difficult" person is cured of his personality flaw by being subjected to a mix-up in identities. *Montrose, der schwarze Margraf* (Montrose, the Black Margrave, 1859), on the other hand, is a historical tragedy set in seventeenth-century Scotland. James Graham, Marquis of Montrose, is a monarchist who refuses to yield to the Puritans under Oliver Cromwell. In the final act he is offered a chance to retire with honor, but he provokes his accusers by insisting on his loyalty to the crown and is condemned to death.

One of the more delightful of Laube's plays is *Der Statthalter von Bengalen* (The Viceroy of Bengal, 1868). In this satiric comedy of manners, Laube takes on parliamentary politics; the relationship of the aristocracy and the common people; and the role of rhetoric in leading to an overthrow of the ancien régime. The play traces the fates of rivals for an appointment to the Council for Bengal in the 1770s, at the time the "Junius Letters" were appearing in the London *Public Advertiser.* As Laube portrays the matter, the courage of a newspaper publisher, a rebellion by the London city council, and the wisdom of the king combine to ensure that the progressive and eloquent Sir Philip Francis, the author of the letters and defender of liberal causes, receives the appointment. The way in which Laube excoriates the complacency and self-indulgence of the old guard and their practices of censorship and illegal search and seizure is satisfying and amusing. At the same time, however, it suggests the personal and societal costs which can occur when (as in Laube's own case) a tolerant atmosphere does not prevail.

Der Statthalter von Bengalen marked Laube's return to dramatic writing after producing a monumental prose trilogy, *Der deutsche Krieg* (The German War, 1863–1866). The war in question is the Thirty Years' War, to which Laube turned so often as the period of religious and political crisis that explained and exemplified the crisis of German unity in Laube's day and offered a vehicle through which he could suggest approaches for overcoming the crisis. It also gave him an opportunity to work with situations and characters that appealed to his inherently dramatic and flamboyant nature, tempered though it was by his years as a highly respected Viennese official.

Each of the trilogy's constituent novels bears the name of its main character – *Junker Hans* (Squire Hans, 1863), *Waldstein* ([a variant spelling of *Wallenstein*] 1864), and *Herzog Bernhard* (Duke Bernhard, 1866) – in addition to the generic subtitle *Historischer Roman* (Historical Novel). In the trilogy, as he had in *Die Krieger,* Laube creates historical personalities who incorporate the essence of the period in which they live. The protagonists of the three novels embody divergent approaches to the political and religious problems that Laube sees at the heart of the Thirty Years' War.

Laube; engraving by G. Wolf

Laube uses all the techniques at his disposal to bring the characters to life; he does better with fictional characters, such as Squire Hans Starrschädel, than with historical ones, such as Waldstein (Albrecht Eusebius Wenzel von Wallenstein), who offer less opportunity for creative flexibility. The sheer magnitude of the project makes continuity difficult and leads to repetition, but it is Laube's typical strengths and weaknesses that determine the success or failure of the work. His prose style – even in much of his supposed "nonfiction" – is characterized by the juxtaposition of different types of discourse through which he attempts to reveal the character of his subjects while entertaining and persuading his reader. In a short work, such as a travel novella or an essay, this approach works well. But in a large-scale work such as *Der deutsche Krieg,* the coexistence of landscape description, spectacular battle scenes, intrigue, and romance makes it difficult for the modern reader to suspend disbelief. In

Laube in 1870; caricature by Klus

the 1860s and 1870s Laube also brought out adaptations and translations of dramas that had originally appeared in French, German, and Spanish.

In 1867 he resigned from his position at the Burgtheater after clashing with his new superior, Friedrich Halm. He responded with a book, *Das Burgtheater* (1868), and with a play, *Böse Zungen* (Evil Tongues, 1869), which poked fun at the small-mindedness and xenophobia of the Viennese civil service. After an engagement by the Leipzig City Theater ended in another scandal in 1871, Laube responded with his book *Das norddeutsche Theater* (The North German Theater, 1872). Both of these "Beiträge zur deutschen Theatergeschichte" (contributions to the history of the German theater), as Laube designates them, combine analysis, anecdote, programmatic statements, and self-justification.

Laube returned to Vienna and founded the Wiener Stadttheater (Vienna City Theater). He made energetic efforts to establish this theater as an equal to the prestigious Burgtheater but was unsuccessful in maintaining its financial stability. Faced with the prospect of compromising his repertoire to attract a wider audience, he resigned in 1874 and, true to his pattern, brought out a book on the city theater the next year. Asked to take on the theater's directorship again, he struggled until 1879 to keep it going, resigned again, and then resumed the directorship for a few months before stepping down for good in 1880.

The last four years of his life were marked by ill health and the death of his wife. Though he continued to write, the quality of his prose and dramatic works does not measure up to that of his earlier writing. He died in Vienna on 1 August 1884. His memoirs appeared as *Erinnerungen, 1810–1840* (Memoirs, 1810–1840, 1875), *Erinnerungen, 1841–1881* (1882), and "Letzte Erinnerungen" (Last Memoirs, 1892).

Letters:

Heinrich Heine, *Briefe an Heinrich Laube,* edited by Eugen Wolff (Breslau: Schottaender, 1839); also published as *Heinrich Heines Briefe an Heinrich Laube* (Breslau: Schlesische Buchdruckerei / New York: Steckert, 1893);

Charlotte Birch-Pfeiffer und Heinrich Laube im Briefwechsel, auf Grund der Originalhandschriften dargestellt, edited by Alexander von Weilen (Berlin: Gesellschaft für Theatergeschichte, 1917).

Biography:

Walter Lange, *Heinrich Laubes Aufstieg: Ein deutsches Künstlerleben im papiernen Leipzig* (Leipzig: Haessel, 1923).

References:

Wilhelm Johannes Becker, "Zeitgeist und Krisenbewußtsein in Heinrich Laubes Novellen," Ph.D. dissertation, University of Frankfurt am Main, 1960;

Helga Brandes, *Die Zeitschriften des Jungen Deutschland: Eine Untersuchung zur literarisch-publizistischen Öffentlichkeit im 19. Jahrhundert* (Opladen: Westdeutscher Verlag, 1991);

Hannelore Burchardt-Dose, *Das Junge Deutschland und die Familie: Zum literarischen Engagement in der Restaurationsepoche* (Frankfurt am Main: Lang, 1979);

Eliza Marion Butler, *The Saint-Simonian Religion in Germany: A Study of the Young German Movement* (New York: Fertig, 1968);

Walter Dietze, *Junges Deutschland und deutsche Klassik: Zur Ästhetik und Literaturtheorie des Vormärz,* third revised edition (Berlin: Rütten & Loening, 1962);

Alfred Estermann, ed., *Politische Avantgarde 1830–1840: Eine Dokumentation zum "Jungen Deutschland,"* 2 volumes (Frankfurt am Main: Athenäum, 1972);

Reinhold Grimm, "Romanhaftes und Novellistisches in Laubes Reisenovellen," *Germanisch-Romanische Monatsschrift,* new series 18 (1968): 299–303;

Karl Häberle, *Individualität und Zeit in Heinrich Laubes Jungem Europa und K. Gutzkows Ritter vom Geist* (Erlangen: Palm & Enke, 1938);

Heinrich Hubert Houben, *Jungdeutscher Sturm und Drang: Ergebnisse und Studien* (Hildesheim: Olms, 1974);

Ellen von Itter, *Heinrich Laube: Ein jungdeutscher Journalist und Kritiker* (Frankfurt am Main: Lang, 1989);

Helmut Koopmann, *Das Junge Deutschland: Analyse seines Selbstverständnisses* (Stuttgart: Metzler, 1970);

Maria Moormann, *Die Bühnentechnik Heinrich Laubes* (Leipzig: Voss, 1917);

Karl Nolle, *Heinrich Laube als sozialer und politischer Schriftsteller* (Bocholdt: Temming, 1914);

Patricia Margaret Ryan Paulsell, "The Relationship of 'Young Germany' to Questions of Women's Rights," Ph.D. dissertation, University of Michigan, 1976;

Paul Przygodda, *Heinrich Laubes literarische Frühzeit* (Berlin: Ebering, 1910);

Jeffrey L. Sammons, "Heinrich Laube: *Die Krieger,*" in his *Six Essays on the Young German Novel* (Chapel Hill: University of North Carolina Press, 1972), pp. 104–123;

Hartmut Steinecke, *Literaturkritik des Jungen Deutschland: Entwicklungen – Tendenzen – Texte* (Berlin: Schmidt, 1982);

Johannes Ullrich, *Heinrich Laubes politischer Entwicklungsgang bis zum Jahre 1834 (Teildruck)* (Berlin: Ebering, 1934);

Mark J. Webber, "Distanz und Kritik: Das Rußlandbild der Jungdeutschen," in *19. Jahrhundert: Von der Jahrhundertwende bis zur Reichsgründung,* volume 3A of *West-Östliche Spiegelungen, Russen und Rußland aus deutscher Sicht,* edited by Mechthild Keller (Munich: Fink, forthcoming);

Webber, "The Metaphorization of Woman in Young Germany: The Intersection of Rhetoric and *Naturphilosophie,*" in *Geist und Gesellschaft: Zur deutschen Rezeption der Französischen Revolution,* edited by Eitel Timm (Munich: Fink, 1990), pp. 125–138;

Fedor Wehl, *Das junge Deutschland: Ein kleiner Beitrag zur Literaturgeschichte unserer Zeit* (Hamburg: Richter, 1886);

Paul Weiglin, *Gutzkows und Laubes Literaturdramen* (Göttingen: Dietrich, 1910);

Benno von Wiese, "Zeitkrise und Biedermeier in Laubes 'Das junge Europa' und in Immermanns 'Epigonen,'" *Dichtung und Volkstum,* 36 (1935): 163–197;

Wulf Wülfing, *Junges Deutschland: Texte – Kontexte, Abbildungen, Kommentar* (Munich: Hanser, 1978);

Wülfing, "Reiseliteratur," in *Vormärz: Biedermeier, Junges Deutschland, Demokraten 1815–1848,* edited by Bernd Witte, volume 6 of *Deutsche Literatur: Eine Sozialgeschichte,* edited by Horst Albert Glaser (Reinbek: Rowohlt, 1980), pp. 180–194, 339;

Wülfing, *Schlagworte des Jungen Deutschland* (Berlin: Schmidt, 1982).

Eduard Mörike

(8 September 1804 - 4 June 1875)

Jeffrey Adams
University of North Carolina at Greensboro

BOOKS: *Maler Nolten: Novelle in zwei Theilen* (Stuttgart: Schweizerbart, 1832; revised edition, edited by Julius Klaiber, Stuttgart: Göschen, 1877);

Gedichte (Stuttgart & Tübingen: Cotta, 1838; enlarged, 1848; enlarged, 1856; enlarged, 1867); translated by Norah K. Cruickshank and Gilbert F. Cunningham as *Poems* (London: Methuen, 1959);

Iris: Eine Sammlung erzählender und dramatischer Dichtungen (Stuttgart: Schweizerbart, 1839) – comprises "Der Schatz," "Die Regenbrüder," "Der letzte König von Orplid," "Lucie Gelmeroth," "Der Bauer und sein Sohn";

Idylle vom Bodensee oder Fischer Martin und die Glockendiebe: In sieben Gesängen (Stuttgart: Schweizerbart, 1846);

Das Stuttgarter Hutzelmännlein: Märchen (Stuttgart: Schweizerbart, 1853);

Mozart auf der Reise nach Prag: Novelle (Stuttgart & Augsburg: Cotta, 1856); translated by Florence Leonard as *Mozart's Journey from Vienna to Prague: A Romance of His Private Life* (Philadelphia: Presser, 1897); translated by Walter and Catherine Alison Phillips as *Mozart on the Way to Prague* (Oxford: Blackwell, 1934; New York: Pantheon, 1947);

Vier Erzählungen (Stuttgart: Schweizerbart, 1856);

Die Historie von der schönen Lau: Mit sieben Umrissen von Moritz von Schwind (Stuttgart: Göschen, 1873).

Editions and Collections: *Eduard Mörike als Gelegenheitsdichter: Aus seinem alltäglichen Leben,* edited by Rudolf Krauß (Stuttgart: Deutsche Verlags-Anstalt, 1895);

Sämtliche Werke in sechs Bänden, 6 volumes, edited by Krauß (Leipzig: Hesse, 1905);

Werke, 6 volumes, edited by Karl Fischer (Munich: Callwey, 1906–1908);

Miss Jenny Harrower: Eine Skizze, edited by Carl Schüddekopf (Weimar: Gesellschaft der Bibliophilen, 1907);

Eduard Mörike

Werke in vier Teilen, edited by August Leffson (Berlin: Bong, 1908);

Werke, 3 volumes, edited by Harry Maync (Leipzig: Bibliographisches Institut, 1909; revised, 1914);

Ausgewählte Gedichte, edited by Friedrich Seebaß (Vienna: Kirschner, 1948);

Sämtliche Werke, edited by Herbert G. Göpfert (Munich: Hanser, 1954; revised, 1964);

Sämtliche Werke, 3 volumes, edited by Gerhart Baumann and Siegfried Grosse (Stuttgart: Cotta, 1954–1959);

Werke und Briefe, 2 volumes, edited by Hans-Heinrich Reuter (Leipzig: Dieterich, 1957);

Sämtliche Werke: Briefe, 3 volumes, edited by Baumann and Grosse (Stuttgart: Cotta, 1959–1961);

Sämtliche Werke, 2 volumes projected, 3 volumes published, edited by Helga Unger and Jost Perfahl (Munich: Winkler, 1967–1971);

Werke und Briefe: Historisch-kritische Gesamtausgabe, 9 volumes, edited by Hans-Henrik Krummacher, Herbert Meyer, and Bernhard Zeller (Stuttgart: Klett, 1967–);

Werke, edited by Wilhelm Rücker (Berlin: Aufbau, 1969);

Der heitere Mörike: Gedichte und Zeichnungen, edited by Franz Georg Brustgi (Heilbronn: Salzer, 1972);

Jahreszeiten, edited by Peter Lahnstein (Stuttgart: Kohlhammer, 1974);

Eduard Mörike: 1804–1875–1975. Gedenkausstellung zum 100. Todestag im Schiller-Nationalmuseum, edited by Zeller (Munich: Kösel, 1975);

Sämtliche Gedichte; Übersetzungen, edited by Georg Britting (Munich: Deutscher Taschenbuch-Verlag, 1975);

Alte unnennbare Tage . . . , edited by Wolf von Niebelschütz (Frankfurt am Main, 1978);

Maler Nolten: Novelle in zwei Theilen, edited by Wolfgang Vogelmann (Zurich: Juris, 1980);

Du bist Orplid, mein Land: Texte von Eduard Mörike und Ludwig Bauer, edited by Peter Härtling (Darmstadt: Luchterhand, 1982);

Halb ist es Lust, halb ist es Klage: Lyrik und Prosa, edited by Maria Leistner (Leipzig: Reclam, 1983).

Editions in English: *Poems,* translated anonymously, selected and edited by Lionel Thomas (Oxford: Blackwell, 1960);

Friedrich Hölderlin; Eduard Mörike: Selected Poems, translated by Christopher Middleton (Chicago & London: University of Chicago Press, 1972).

OTHER: *Jahrbuch schwäbischer Dichter und Novellisten,* edited by Mörike and W. Zimmermann (Stuttgart: Balz, 1836);

Classische Blumenlese: Eine Auswahl von Hymnen, Oden, Liedern, Elegien, Idyllen, Gnomen und Epigrammen der Griechen und Römer. Nach den besten Verdeutschungen, teilweise neu bearbeitet. Mit Erklärungen für alle gebildeten Leser, translated and edited by Mörike (Stuttgart: Schweizerbart, 1840);

Wilhelm Waiblinger, *Gedichte,* edited by Mörike (Hamburg: Heubel, 1844);

Theocritus, *Buon und Mochus: Deutsch im Versmaße der Urschrift,* translated by Mörike und Friedrich Notter (Stuttgart: Hoffmann, 1855);

Anakreon und die sogenannten Anakreontischen Lieder: Revision und Ergänzung der Johann Fr. Degen'schen Übersetzung mit Erklärungen, translated by Mörike (Stuttgart: Krais & Hoffmann, 1864).

Eduard Mörike is known primarily for his lyric poetry and short prose. He is considered a premier poet of the post-Romantic era; his poems were influenced by Johann Wolfgang von Goethe's, giving him a widespread reputation as "Goethe's spiritual son." His early writings exhibit a struggle with the German Romantics, while later works bear the mark of Greek and Roman models. Though such influences often ring through his verses, he is praised as one of the most original poets of the nineteenth century. Another common image of Mörike is that of a provincial poet; often he is linked with the Biedermeier sensibility, which involves a passive and apolitical acceptance of authority, a contentment within limitations, a withdrawal from social reality, and a nostalgia for a simpler, more idyllic age. Alongside Goethean nature lyrics and Romantic explorations of the depths of human subjectivity stand humorous idylls, fairy tales, and much Gelegenheitsdichtung (occasional poetry). Pointing to his sovereign mastery of literary forms and his aesthetics of beauty mixed with alienation, recent scholarship has attempted to portray him as a precursor of modernism and a relative of Charles-Pierre Baudelaire and the symbolists. Darker aspects of his poetry have been analyzed to create the image of an "existential" poet threatened by demonic forces of Being. While his early poetry flows with his mood swings, registering the stream of his internal experience in diverse rhythms, his later poems eschew subjectivity and assume neoclassical forms. His so-called Dinggedichte (thing poems), for which the Greeks and Goethe were models, are viewed as harbingers of Rainer Maria Rilke's poetry, and his late emphasis on objectivity and realistic detail suggests comparisons to Poetic Realism. After Goethe the most protean poet of the German tradition, he produced multifaceted writings that resist facile categorization. Despite his canonical status in the German tradition, Mörike has remained largely inaccessible to the English-speaking world because his poetry, linguistically nuanced and fixed firmly in the German context, does not lend itself well to translation.

Born in Ludwigsburg, on 8 September 1804, near Stuttgart, Eduard Friedrich Mörike was the seventh of thirteen children. His father, Karl Friedrich Mörike, was a court physician and a man of considerable learning who was completely absorbed in his professional life and had little time for domestic concerns. His mother, Charlotte Dorothea, née Beyer, an intelligent, sympathetic, and artistically talented woman, imparted to Mörike an appreciation of storytelling and the fine arts as well as a moral education. The Mörikes enjoyed the privileges of a middle-class professional family and consorted on occasion with the local aristocracy. Mörike's uncle, Friedrich Eberhard von Georgii, a well-connected attorney, would later open up important doors for him. These early years of domestic security provided ample time for introspection and fantasizing, for which Mörike showed a marked propensity. Traces of this idyllic period can be found in much of his writing, and in some respects his sheltered upbringing left him unprepared for subsequent difficulties in his life. His older sister Luise regarded Mörike with a mothering attitude; after her death in 1827 her maternal role would be assumed by his younger sister Klara, who would live with and keep house for him throughout his life, even after his marriage. He had five brothers, several of whom would burden him with troubles later in life.

In 1811 Mörike began his formal education at the Lateinschule (Latin school) in Ludwigsburg, where he studied classical languages, French, religion, history, and geography. His school record was undistinguished, and he seems not to have had much interest in his studies. Oversensitive and melancholic, he was easily undone by emotional disturbances. In 1815 his father suffered a crippling stroke that left him severely impaired until his death in 1817. During the father's illness the family struggled financially; after the father's death, Georgii took Mörike into his house in Stuttgart and made it possible for him to attend good secondary schools. When Mörike was fourteen Georgii exerted his influence to have the boy admitted to the monastery school in Urach in spite of his mediocre performance in lower schools. Mörike spent the years 1818 to 1822 in Urach preparing for the final stage of his education, a degree in theology from the famed Tübinger Stift (Tübingen Seminary), which boasted among its alumni the poet Friedrich Hölderlin and the philosophers Friedrich Schelling and Georg Wilhelm Friedrich Hegel.

During the Tübingen years Mörike and his friend Ludwig Bauer invented Orplid, an island whose warring factions engage in a tragic conflict that leaves the island culture in disarray and prompts its gods to abandon it. At the center of the tragedy is King Ulmon, who loses his crown to a rival and is cursed to outlive all others on the island in a lonely existence spanning a thousand years. The story of Orplid documents the poet's early subjectivity, his tendency to withdraw from rather than seek the external world. Though he tried to overcome this subjectivity in later writings, his inclination to avoid the demands of reality by escaping into the realm of fantasy continued to dominate his poetry and his fairy tales. Originally not written for publication, the Orplid myth was revised and inserted as a dramatic interlude into Mörike's novel *Maler Nolten* (Nolten the Painter, 1832).

In 1823 Mörike met an itinerant barmaid of rare beauty and exceptional intelligence who was to become for him a symbol of the elemental and demonic power of romantic love. Maria Meyer had been found unconscious on a highway after an epileptic seizure, taken in by a local innkeeper, and then given shelter by the family of Mörike's friend Rudolf Lohbauer. Though brief, their relationship touched Mörike deeply. After hearing rumors of her untoward life-style he rejected her; but first he enshrined her in a cycle of agonizing and highly original poems titled "Peregrina," alluding to her wandering nature. The opening lines of the third poem report concisely on the conclusion of his affair with Maria: "Ein Irrsal kam in die Mondscheingärten / Einer einst heiligen Liebe. / Schaudernd entdeckt' ich verjährten Betrug. / Und mit weinendem Blick, doch grausam, / Hieß ich das schlanke, / Zauberhafte Mädchen / Ferne gehen von mir" (Sin entered the moonlit gardens of a once-holy love. / Shuddering, I discovered a deception long past. / And with tears, but cruelly, / I told the slender, / Magical maiden / To go far from me).

In the poem "An einem Wintermorgen, vor Sonnenaufgang" (On a Winter Morning, before Sunrise), written in 1825, Mörike still under the influence of Goethe and the Romantics, expresses a belief in the restoration of the self and its creative powers through the healing influence of nature. But even here, amid panegyrics to the inspirations of nature, the poet directs his gaze "hinab in lichte Feenreiche" (down into shining fairy realms) where reflections of a "Schwarm von Bildern und Gedanken" (swarm of images and thoughts) crowd out nature's immediacy.

Mörike was ordained by the Lutheran church in 1826; until 1834 he moved from one parsonage to the next, waiting for a permanent position. He referred to this period as his "Vikariatsknechtschaft" (slavery of the curate's life). After the first year doubts about his fitness for the clergy began to plague him as he questioned his religious beliefs and his devotion to the church. On this crucial topic Mörike was equivocal all his life. He was in general as reluctant to write religious poetry as he was to produce sermons. There are, however, a few poems that incorporate orthodox Christian ideas, such as "Wo find' ich Trost?" (Where Do I Find Comfort?), written in 1827; here he invokes the image of Christ as the savior from sin and death but concludes with the unresolved question "Was rettet mich von Tod und Sünde?" (What can save me from death and sin?).

In 1827 he took a long leave of absence, claiming health reasons. Psychosomatic illness is prominent in Mörike's personal history, and it is likely that one cause of his often poor health was his high-strung personality. In letters he speaks of an acute sensitivity to external stimuli and of a paralyzing anxiety in the presence of anyone other than his most intimate associates. Throughout his life he would be subject to ailments of nonspecific origin, and he consistently nursed a notion that his psychic fragility contributed to his physical weaknesses. During his break he rethought his career goals and decided to leave the clergy and go to work for a Stuttgart publisher of a ladies' journal. He quickly discovered, however, that writing stories under deadline pressure gave him even worse stomachaches than writing sermons, and he returned to his rural parsonage convinced that despite its drawbacks the curate's unpressured routine, though dull, was the life best suited for a poet of his sensibility.

In his poem "Besuch in Urach" (Visit in Urach) Mörike records his return in 1827 to the idyllic countryside of his Urach days. The poem's central theme is memory, where "Aus tausend grünen Spiegeln scheint zu gehen / Vergangne Zeit, die lächelnd mich verwirrt" (From a thousand green mirrors seems to move / Bygone time, smiling and bewildering me). Caught in the regressions of memory, the poet seeks identity and self-understanding in a series of recollected images of half-forgotten things and in a Romantic union of self and nature. Unlike those of Goethe and the Romantics, however, Mörike's efforts to transcend time and become a part of nature are thwarted. Nature "bleibt, mehr als der Mensch, verwaist, / Darf nicht aus ihrem eigenen Rätsel steigen!" (remains more than humans, orphaned, / May not rise out of its own enigma!). If there is an identification with nature, it obtains in the poet's sense that both humans and nature are isolated and self-contained. Critics see here a turning point in the history of poetry, for not only does Mörike challenge Goethe's aesthetic law that poetry should stay in touch with present reality and avoid the dangers of subjective remembrance but he also documents a post-Romantic swerve from German Idealism's belief in the possibility of self-transcendence.

Mörike during his student years at the Tübinger Stift; pencil drawing by Johann Georg Schreiner (Schiller-Nationalmuseum, Marbach am Neckar)

Between 1827 and 1832 Mörike wrote some of his best and most-anthologized poetry, much of it nature poetry, including "Septembermorgen" (September Morning) and "Um Mitternacht" (At Midnight), both written in 1827, and "Im Frühling" (In Spring) and "Mein Fluß" (My River), both written in 1828. In these early poems a monologic lyric voice emerges that seeks contact with its external surroundings. Such appeals to nature, however, typically confirm only the primacy of the self. Like "Besuch in Urach," these poems articulate Mörike's questioning of Schelling's nature philosophy and its teaching that there is an absolute identity of human internality and nature's externality. "Im Frühling," for example, presents an intermixing of external images and internal perceptions, an interpenetration of sensual impressions and subjective emotions: "Die Wolke seh' ich wandeln und den Fluß, / Es dringt der Sonne goldner Kuß / Mir tief ins Geblüt hinein; / Die Augen, wunderbar berauschet, / Tun als schliefen sie ein, / Nur noch das Ohr dem Ton der Biene lauschet" (I see the cloud move, and the river, / The golden kiss of the sun penetrates / Deep into my blood; / My eyes, strangely intoxicated, / Act as if they were falling asleep, / Only my ear still listens to the sound of the bees). The power of memory finally crowds out sensory impressions, forcing the poet to descend to submerged levels of consciousness where nature assumes aesthetic qualities. In the final section of the poem the poet asks what this weaving of emotions and perceptions signifies: "Ich denke dies und denke das, / Ich sehne mich und weiß nicht recht, nach was: / Halb ist es Lust, halb ist es Klage; / Mein Herz, o sage, / Was webst du für Erinnerung / In golden grüner Zweige Dämmerung? / – Alte unnennbare Tage!" (I think of this, I think of that. / I long for something, yet do not know really what: / Half of it is pleasure, the other half lament; / My heart, tell me, / What memories are you weaving / In the twilight of golden green branches? / – Old unnameable days!). Themes, images, and lyric forms characteristic of much of Mörike's poetry emerge from these lines: the search for a union of human subject and an increasingly aestheticized nature, twilight as a symbol of the eternal moment – the time of deep memory and creative impulses – and echoes of Goethe's Storm and Stress poetry in rhythms and imagery. The mixed feelings – half pleasure, half pain – occur henceforth in his poems with increasing frequency and refinements as Mörike invents a somatic poetry to record the impulses of the body and their relation to individual identity.

In 1829 Mörike met Luise Rau, who became his fiancée and the inspiration for a series of love sonnets written in the spring of 1830. The bittersweet emotions created by amatory involvements fed Mörike's lyric imagination as no other source could. In "Liebesglück" (Love's Happiness) the poet is concerned with the pain of love and its precariousness: "Auch ich trug einst der Liebe Müh und Lasten, / Verschmähte nicht den herben Kelch zu trinken, / Damit ich seine Lust nun ganz empfinde" (I too once bore the toilsome burden of love, / Did not disdain drinking the bitter chalice, / So that now I experience completely its pleasure). With their strict and regular form, the sonnets mark a change in Mörike's poetry to a tendency to contain rather than release emotions. At this point in his creative development he has realized the necessity of preserving his psychic balance. At the close of the sonnet "Zu viel" (Too Much) the poet retreats to a darkened refuge in the mind: "Lisch aus, o Tag! Laß mich in Nacht genesen! / Indes ihr sanften Sterne göttlich kühlet, / Will ich zum Abgrund der Betrachtung steigen" (Fade out, O day! Let me recover in night! / While you soft stars divinely cool, / I want to descend to the abyss of contemplation).

Following the models of Goethe's *Wilhelm Meisters Lehrjahre* (1795–1796; translated as *Wilhelm Meister's Apprenticeship,* 1824) and the Romantic novels of the previous generation, Mörike interpolated the Luise sonnet cycle as well as the earlier Peregrina cycle and many ballads written between 1824 and 1828 into *Maler Nolten.* As in the poems of this period, in his novel Mörike works through his emotional problems. While *Maler Nolten* is a Künstlerroman (artist's novel) and thus in part a vehicle for Mörike's aesthetic views, the aesthetic problems it raises are overshadowed by the psychological problems of its central characters, whose "elective affinities" and their fateful consequences are of primary concern. Typically, for Mörike representations of the social milieu remain secondary.

The painter Theobald Nolten and his mentor Larkens, an actor, represent different but complementary aspects of their author. Nolten, a sensitive, introverted artist whose style is a blend of the classical and the Romantic – representational yet exotic and experimental – reflects the young Mörike's Romantic influences and his attempts to master them. Nolten's tragic flaw resides in the delusion that art is his salvation and that through it he can transcend the world. This delusion mirrors Mörike's growing awareness that the artist's "abyss of contemplation" is not without its dangers. Nolten's inclination to withdraw into an internalized world of art and to lose himself in nostalgic reverie causes him to avoid or misunderstand interpersonal relationships and, thus, hinders a healthy psychic development.

Larkens also exhibits pathological symptoms. He views himself as an epigone whose life has become a meaningless effort to come to terms with some mysterious past. He is thus incapable of unmediated responses to life, hiding his emptiness behind masks, an actor offstage as well as on. At the same time, Larkens represents Mörike's extroverted side: Mörike had some acting ability and occasionally played parts in public performances. Significantly, Larkens is also a poet, the author of an interpolated shadow play of the Orplid myth as well as of the Luise sonnet cycle and Peregrina cycle, which are, in a somewhat forced fashion, woven into the plot. Identified with King Ulmon of the Orplid myth, Larkens lives out a life of alienation and despair that ends in suicide. While Larkens exerts a positive influence on Nolten by trying to bring the painter out of his delusional inwardness, he also selfishly tries to live vicariously through Nolten by manipulating the artist's relationships with others – an intrusion that initiates a disastrous chain of events ending in tragedy for every main character. As

Aus Gelegenheit der Kirchthurm-Renovation im Juli 1840.

Zu [illegible] im Unterland
Wohl an die hundert Jahr ich stand,
Auf dem Kirchenthurm ein guter Hahn,
Als ein Zierath und Wetterfahn.
In Stürmen und Wind und Regennacht
Hab ich allzeit das Dorf bewacht;
Manch falber Blitz hat mich gestreift,
Der Frost mein rothen Kamm bereift;
Auch manchen lieben Sommertag,
Da man gern Schatten haben mag,
Hat mir die Sonne unverwandt
Auf meinen goldigen Leib gebrannt;

First page of a draft for Mörike's poem "Der alte Turmhahn" (collection of Dr. Fritz Kauffmann, Stuttgart)

critic Jeffrey L. Sammons has written, the novel is "a grim story of quadrangular interaction among three neurotic personalities and a psychopath, unparalleled in . . . German prose in the nineteenth century, although some comparisons with Goethe's *Wahlverwandtschaften* (Elective Affinities) . . . suggest themselves."

There are three female principals, all of them Nolten's love interests: Agnes, an innocent country girl with neurotic tendencies, whom he believes to be unfaithful and rejects; Constanze, an aristocrat; and Elisabeth, a Gypsy who exercises a demonic power over Nolten and those with whom he maintains relationships. After Nolten rejects Agnes, Larkens, hoping to rescue his friend from Constanze, who he imagines can destroy the painter's creative gift, secretly maintains a correspondence with Agnes in Nolten's name. Believing that Nolten still loves her, Agnes encounters Elisabeth, who tells her fortune and predicts that she will not marry Nolten. Devastated when she uncovers Larkens's deception, Agnes falls into a depression and dies mysteriously. Mörike's fiancée, Rau, objected strongly to the Agnes figure, suspecting a reference to herself. Elisabeth is probably the most important female character in the story, though the reader sees little of her. Appearing, muselike, as a mysterious figure in one of Nolten's important paintings and related to him by blood, she exerts an uncanny power over him, working behind the scenes to guide him in his artistic endeavors but also to destroy his relationships with others. The deaths of three main characters are attributable to her.

Many critics have found technical aspects of *Maler Nolten* deficient. The love intrigue that moves the plot forward is said to be derivative, and the prose style imitates Goethe's *Wilhelm Meisters Lehrjahre* and *Die Wahlverwandtschaften* (1809; translated as "Elective Affinities," 1854). At the same time, S. S. Prawer has argued convincingly that *Maler Nolten* is an "anti-Meister," a revisionary response to *Wilhelm Meisters Lehrjahre* and that Elisabeth is an evil reincarnation of Goethe's Mignon, who takes "revenge on that ordered world which received Wilhelm Meister and rejected her." This theme is reflected in a narrative structure that, with its experimental and disruptive flashback narrative technique, reverses the forward movement and coherent development of the Goethean bildungsroman. Mörike does appear to side with the Romantics, who objected to Mignon's demise as symbolic of the decline of poetry in an age of prose. There is general agreement, however, that the novel succeeds as a story about the inner life of its characters, who not only represent aspects of the author's self but can also be generalized to represent universal aspects of the human psyche and its pathologies. The novel is remarkable for its many anticipations of modern psychoanalysis.

In 1833-1834, as a result of the end of his engagement to Rau, Mörike's creativity suffered. He produced only one story, *Miss Jenny Harrower . . .* (1907), later retitled "Lucie Gelmeroth" (1839). It is the story of a young woman who confesses to the murder of her deceased sister's fiancé; actually, she did not kill the fiancé, who was responsible for her sister's death, but encouraged a friend to do so. To atone for her guilt, she claims responsibility for the murder. In this novella, as in *Maler Nolten,* Mörike is concerned primarily with the inner life of the title character. Unlike Nolten, however, Lucie overcomes her mental torment and returns to a healthy psychological state. This positive confrontation with the pathological is indicative of Mörike's attitude as he began to develop an aesthetics of art as therapy.

In 1834 he assumed a permanent position in Cleversulzbach, where he lived with his sister Klara and his mother. With its promise of stability and harmony, life in Cleversulzbach appeared to be his dream come true. In Cleversulzbach he began writing the idyllic poetry for which he is known and that has created the image of him as a naive and withdrawn pastoral poet. What is often not considered in this perception of a happy Mörike is that he suffered increasing health problems during the 1830s, among them serious and chronic abdominal infections that almost cost him his life during his first year in Cleversulzbach. The parsonage, although spacious, was cold and damp – he referred to it as an "Eisgrube" (ice pit) – and it was likely the source of other minor ailments, among them rheumatism. Whether or not some of his poor health was psychosomatic in origin remains an open question, but Mörike himself seems to have thought his health was influenced by his psychological instability. Believing that his mood was affected by the nature of his intellectual and artistic pursuits, he began to study the poets of classical antiquity and the German classics, Goethe and Friedrich Schiller, maintaining that they were healthy influences.

During these years he was often in debt. His modest vicar's income did not suffice to support his family, which included not only his mother and sister but also his brothers, who often relied on him for loans that they were unable to pay back. He was financially dependent on friends, and quarrels with creditors were common. In 1838 Mörike was in debt for sixteen hundred gulden, about two and one-half years' salary. His brothers Karl and Adolf, in particular, caused him considerable anguish. Karl Mörike was in and out of prison during the Cleversulzbach period and eventually died of lung disease contracted during one of his longer stints in jail. Adolf also had trouble with the law and never established himself. A failure at life, he would commit suicide just weeks before Eduard died.

To protect his mental and physical health, Mörike subjected his literary pursuits to strict regulations. The angst-ridden moods of the *Maler Nolten* period were replaced by light-hearted sentiments that found expression in folk songs and fairy tales. This restriction appears to have worked. During the especially productive years 1837–1838 he wrote some of his best folk ballads, as well as the poem "Märchen vom sichern Mann" (Tale of the Trusty Man). Employing humor as a part of his therapy, Mörike combined elements of Germanic and classical mythology to create the tale of "Suckelborst," the "Trusty Man," a Black Forest giant who terrorizes the locals. Lolegrin, the son of Orplid's goddess, Weyla, is sent by the gods to reform the giant, who must reassess his destructive impulses and atone by delivering his revelations to the underworld. During his visit in hell, Satan mocks him. Angered by the devil's disrespect, Suckelborst pulls out his tail, prophesying that the devil will grow a new, slightly shorter tail three times in the history of the world until his power, like his tail, withers away. The poem ends with Suckelborst returning to the Black Forest, while Lolegrin, who had witnessed the scene in Hades, ascends to the gods to report the events. The poem derives its humor from the contrasts between the gods of classical myth and the horned Satan of medieval Christianity, between the classical underworld and the quaint atmosphere of the Black Forest, and between the measured dignity of the poem's classical verse form and the boorishness of its slapstick scenes. In its humor, its folk-tale qualities, and its classical form this poem illustrates Mörike's new direction away from the extravagances of Romantic fantasy.

In 1837 Mörike completed the seventy-two-line poem "Wald-Idylle" (Forest Idyll), begun in 1829. Written in elegiac couplets, the narrative is a fanciful, humorous anecdote portraying the poet as he sits in a secret sylvan glade in Swabia enjoying his favorite book, Grimm's fairy tales. Lost in the tale of Snow White, the obviously autobiographical narrator interweaves bits of the folktale with pieces of his real-life situation to produce a witty meditation on the poetic possibilities of combining fact and fiction. As the narrator contemplates this tale of wish fulfillment a neighbor girl visits him, followed shortly by her older sister, about whom the poet begins to fantasize: together he and the maiden would live in idyllic harmony – he as a hunter, herdsman, and farmer and she as the mother of his children – following the model of a typical happy fairy-tale ending. The poem contains the mixture of Germanic tale and classical verse form typical of this period of Mörike's writing; it also reflects his desire for a permanent relationship.

Mörike circa 1856; engraving after a crayon drawing by Carl von Kurtz

The retreat into the forest portrayed in "Wald-Idylle" typifies Mörike's habitual avoidance of social contact and lax attitude toward his professional duties. Other poems from this time, such as the 1838 "Die Visite" (The Visit), describe his frequent escapes into the countryside, where he sought seclusion and distance from his parishioners: "Philister kommen angezogen: / Man sucht im Garten mich und Haus; / Doch war der Vogel ausgeflogen, / Zu dem geliebten Wald hinaus" (Philistines come marching up: / They seek me in garden and in house; / But the bird had flown, / Out into the beloved woods).

Mörike's collected poems were published in 1838. There were subsequent expanded editions, but the first contained much of his most important lyric work. He finished a fairy-tale opera, *Die Regenbrüder* (The Rain Brothers, 1839), which closed after a short run. Throughout these years Mörike worked on translations of ancient Greek pastoral poetry, which were published in 1840 as *Classische Blumenlese* (Classical Anthology). His short prose works, however, were the most significant product of the mid to late 1830s: "Der Schatz" (The Treasure, 1839) is a literary fairy tale; "Der Bauer und sein Sohn" (The Farmer and His Son, 1839) is a kind of almanac story moralizing against the maltreatment of animals.

"Der Schatz" stands out for several reasons. Although it was criticized by Mörike's contemporaries for perceived genre violations and was never widely recognized by critics, those who have analyzed this tale agree that it displays a sophisticated sense of prose style and that its narrative composition, like that of *Maler Nolten,* is complex and experimental. An intricate frame narrative comprising five interrelated plots, the tale alternates between the misadventures of a journeyman goldsmith and the stories of various characters he encounters; some of the latter are realistically portrayed, others are fairy-tale figures. As the plot develops, these characters and their separate stories are connected with each other and serve in the end as explanations for the outcome of the journeyman's story. Mörike's artful decision not to bring the tale to closure, instead breaking it off and returning to the frame, forces the reader to draw conclusions about the meaning of the events described and emphasizes Mörike's intention to blur the line between fact and fiction.

The late 1830s mark the beginning of a steady production of occasional poetry. Following the lyric drought of 1833–1834 Mörike's productivity returned, with an emphasis on Kleinkunst (miniature art) that foregrounds commonplace objects. In 1835 he wrote his first worthy poem since the separation from Rau: "Auf das Grab von Schillers Mutter" (To the Grave of Schiller's Mother). Composed in classical distichs, these modest verses record Mörike's discovery and rehabilitation of the neglected grave in Cleversulzbach. Apart from the preliminary version of "Wald-Idylle," begun in 1828, Mörike had not previously written in classical forms; but as a result of his renewed study of Greek and Roman antiquity and his reading of the Goethe-Schiller correspondence (to which he attached sacerdotal significance and which, along with *Wilhelm Meisters Lehrjahre,* he read repeatedly), he initiated a new aesthetic program based on classical art. In 1837 he also wrote poems dedicated to the Roman poets Tibullus and Theocritus. There followed a steady stream of poems for birthdays and confirmations, thank-you notes in verse to friends and to his doctor for curing an illness, and a poem detailing a cookie recipe. An ardent animal lover, he even had some lines for his dog, Joli: "Die ganze Welt ist in dich verliebt / Und läßt dir keine Ruh. / Und wenn's im Himmel Hundle gibt, / So sind sie grad wie du" (The whole world is in love with you / And cannot leave you in peace. / And if there are little doggies in heaven, / Then they are just like you).

Of "the whole world" Mörike knew little, except vicariously. Limited by his less than robust physical and financial condition, he was not inclined to go beyond the boundaries of his native Swabia. In 1840, however, he made a trip to Lake Constance with his brother Louis, who had just acquired a farm near Schaffhausen. The impressions Mörike retained from this trip came together six years later to inspire one of his best-known poems, *Idylle vom Bodensee* (Idyll of Lake Constance, 1846). A lengthy epic poem in classical hexameters reminiscent of Goethe's *Hermann und Dorothea* (1798; translated as *Hermann and Dorothea,* 1801) as well as of Homer and Theocritus, Mörike's idyll is the sort of a humorous depiction of the simple country life and peasant folk for which he became famous.

The story revolves around two pranks that Martin, a fisherman, has played on his materialistic neighbors. The first prank, which provides a narrative frame for the second, involves the theft of a church bell. The second practical joke concerns his best friend, Tone, whose girlfriend rejects him to marry a rich but simpleminded rival. In each case Martin sets up a situation in which the foolishness of petty greed is humorously revealed and punished. The poem is of interest not only for its representation of pastoral life but also for Mörike's lighthanded critique of bourgeois values, of the relationship people have to the material objects of everyday life, and of what that relationship can mean in ethical terms. Though Mörike's social commentary is neither obvious nor programmatic, it is integral to the poem and shows that his reputation as a trivializing "idyllic" poet is not entirely deserved. In spite of its underlying critical message, the poem was praised by Mörike's contemporaries as an artfully crafted miniature epic representative of the Biedermeier idyll, an appraisal generally shared by scholars today. On publication of *Idylle vom Bodensee* Mörike was awarded the Tiedge Prize and received cash gifts from the crown prince and princess of Württemberg.

More than any other work, "Der alte Turmhahn" (The Old Weathercock), begun in 1840 and finished in 1852, has contributed to the conception of Mörike as a happy-go-lucky Biedermeier parson. A lengthy poem written in doggerel laced with dialect, "Der alte Turmhahn" seems autobiographical enough; but on closer inspection it is an idealization of the country parson's existence, a life Mörike would perhaps gladly have led but in actuality did not enjoy. The tale is told from the perspective of a weathervane that has been taken from its perch atop the tower and sold to the village blacksmith for scrap. The parson rescues it and has the blacksmith attach it to the top of an old stove in the parsonage. From this vantage point it looks down on and describes the goings-on of the household, in particular the parson's activities. The poem has always been read as a portrayal of the cozy domestic life Mörike enjoyed; but set against the reality of his physical and financial troubles, and given that he finished it well after his vicar's duties had ended, it must be seen as a fantasy of the good life rather than as autobiography.

Mörike (left) with his friend Wilhelm Hartlaub in 1865

After the death of his mother in 1841 Mörike's health again took a turn for the worse. Unable to perform the duties of his office, he requested and was granted an early retirement in 1843. With his retirement began another unsettled period. Mörike and his constant companion and caretaker Klara moved to Wermutshausen, where for six months they resided with Mörike's friend Wilhelm Hartlaub. From this time comes a poem describing a few moments as Mörike sat listening to Hartlaub play the piano. The poem is a testament to the importance of friendship for Mörike (a topic that has been emphasized by scholars), and it is a singular example of the aesthetic heights he achieved in his occasional poetry. "An Wilhelm Hartlaub" (To Wilhelm Hartlaub) is a poem of rare beauty, deeply felt, filled with surprising images and flowing passages attuned to the music it describes. One passage alone could establish Mörike as Goethe's equal in the lyric mode: "Ein jeder Ton ein lang gehaltnes Schweigen. / Da fing das Firmament sich an zu neigen, / Und jäh daran herab der Sterne selig Heer / Glitt rieselnd in ein goldig Nebelmeer, / Bis Tropf' um Tropfen hell darin zerging, / Die alte Nacht den öden Raum umfing" (Each tone a long sustained silence. / Then the firmament began to slope, / And a blessed host of stars slid abruptly down upon it / Rippling into a sea of golden mist, / Till drop on drop they flashed and faded in it, / Ancient night surrounded barren space). Such passages of haunting beauty are punctuated by sudden flashes of joy in the realization of friendship's true value. Mörike's gift for identifying with others is also in evidence: "Zuletzt warst du es selbst, in den ich mich verlor; / Mein Herz durchzückt' mit eins ein Freudenstrahl: / Dein ganzer Wert erschien mir auf einmal" (Finally it was you in whom I lost myself; / Suddenly a ray of joy flashed through my heart: / All at once your complete worth appeared to me).

After a brief stay with Hartlaub, the poet and his sister moved to the rural villages of Schwäbisch Hall and Bad Mergentheim. In retirement Mörike had the leisure to cultivate other interests, especially geology and fossil collecting, an activity documented – again as an occasional poem – in "Der Petrefaktensammler" (The Fossil Collector). Written in 1845, this poem exemplifies not only the rage for collecting and categorizing that characterized the Biedermeier period but also Mörike's retreat from the self-aggrandizing posture of high Romantic poetry. Of his crawling about on all fours in search of fossils the poet, faintly mocking the Romantics' glorified image of the sublime poet-hero, says: "Das ist auch wohl Poesie" (That too can be called poetry).

Between 1842 and 1846 Mörike reached new heights in his development toward neoclassicism in lyric poetry. In the poems of this period he gave renewed life to the neoclassical impulses in the German tradition, extending the "ekphrastic" (visualizing) potential of post-Goethean poetry. In 1842 he wrote "Die schöne Buche" (The Beautiful Beech Tree), a poem in carefully measured distichs that the critic Viktor G. Doerksen thought to be Mörike's most perfect nature poem and that, according to Romano Guardini, is one of the most beautiful of all German poems. The first half of the poem is dominated by an ekphrastic description of the tree, standing in an enchanted grove of numinous tranquillity that is ruled by a genius loci. The poet considers the beech exemplary: "man sieht schöner im Bilde sie nicht" (you cannot see one more beautiful in a picture). The poem's second half attends to the exalted feelings it evokes, equating the tree and the stillness of its surroundings with a creative state of mind informed by profound quietude: "Aber ich stand und rührte mich nicht; dämonischer Stille, / Unergründlicher Ruh lauschte mein innerer Sinn. / Eingeschlossen mit dir in diesem sonnigen Zauber- / Gürtel, o Einsamkeit, fühlt ich und dachte nur dich!" (But I stood and did not move; demonic stillness, / Unfathomable calm my inner sense did hear. / Enclosed with you in this sunny magic circle, / O solitude, I felt and thought only you!). The "demonic" solitude and communion with nature appear Romantic enough, but the distance created by the autonomy of the natural object emphasizes the poet's isolation and self-containment. The beech tree becomes an objective correlative for the writing subject. Considered by the critic Heinrich Henel to be a "Kopernikanische Drehung "(Copernican turn)" in the German lyric tradition, this poem and others like it came to be called *Dinggedichte,* a form and a poetic ethos extended and developed in subsequent poems by Conrad Ferdinand Meyer and Rilke. The Dinggedicht marks the transition in German poetry from a Romantic emphasis on the mystical "experience" of nature to a symbolic objectification of the self in the "second nature" of art.

In 1846 Mörike wrote perhaps his best-known poem: the much-anthologized and often-interpreted "Auf eine Lampe" (On a Lamp) is the apotheosis of the ekphrastic Dinggedicht. An apostrophe to a forgotten artifact, "Auf eine Lampe" evokes a bygone era of finer sensibility: the lamp is "ein Kunstgebild der echten Art" (an aesthetic object of the genuine kind). Its porcelain body, graced with ivy, displays images suggestive of classical themes, its circularity suggests the harmony and symmetry of a well-wrought urn. As a poem that tries to turn verbal art into an aesthetic object with sensuous presence, "Auf eine Lampe" has often been compared to John Keats's iconic "Ode on a Grecian Urn" (1820). Though in its imagery and form (classical trimeters) it appropriates antique traditions, it is essentially a modernist poem. Its movement is beyond the classical-Romantic tradition in German poetry toward "absolute poetry," a kind of symbolist poetry that ascribes to the aesthetic object a meaning without relation to the realm of empirical experience; this aesthetic program is voiced in the final line: "Was aber schön ist, selig scheint es in ihm selbst" (What is beautiful appears [or shines] blessed in itself). Such identification with the self-contained aesthetic object and the intrinsic value of its form seems to justify the poet's withdrawal from the empirical realm so that the fragile self may be protected from the impingements of an increasingly unresponsive reality.

In the early 1950s "Auf eine Lampe" became the focus of a critical controversy between the philosopher Martin Heidegger and the preeminent Swiss Germanist Emil Staiger. Their debate concerned the interpretation of the word *scheint,* Staiger arguing that it means "appears," Heidegger advancing a Hegelian argument for its meaning "shines." While they agree that the mood of the poem is essentially melancholy – the lamp is a neglected relic – they disagree about the source of this melancholy. Staiger attributes it to Mörike's belated arrival on the poetic scene and his sense that a Goethean comprehension of life through art was no longer available to him. Heidegger maintains that the "shining" of the lamp is informed by the Hegelian thesis that Beauty determines itself as the sensory manifestation of the Idea. It would also be possible to analyze this problem with reference to Mörike's increasing desire to avoid hypochondriacal tendencies by projecting the self into the protective form of an aesthetic object.

It has been argued that in the 1840s, with poems such as "Die schöne Buche" and "Auf eine Lampe," Mörike achieved the peak of his potential as a lyric poet. Few poems that follow measure up to the achievements of this decade, which also include "Göttliche Reminiszenz" (Divine Reminiscence) and "Auf eine Christblume" (On a Christmas Rose), poems often cited in discussions of Mörike as a contributor to the development of "absolute poetry." Many critics see the end of the 1840s as the twilight of Mörike's productivity as a

Mörike with his wife, Margarethe

lyric poet; but from the late 1840s until his death he wrote as many as eighty occasional poems, most of which were not included in the various editions of his *Gedichte*. To the extent that Mörike ceased to write for the wider public, it is accurate to say that his lyric creativity showed signs of diminishment.

In 1845, his second year in Bad Mergentheim, Mörike and his sister found permanent lodging in the house of Colonel Valentin von Speeth. On his deathbed the colonel asked Mörike to take care of his daughter, Margarethe ("Gretchen"), a twenty-seven-year-old woman of pleasing physical attributes. While Mörike must have loved her, it is certain that he felt pity for her. After her father's death, Mörike described her in a letter as "ein gejagtes und verletztes Reh" (a hunted and wounded deer). Margarethe's fragility and inclination to depression would find no healing in a life shared with a poet of similar propensities.

In the fall of 1851 Mörike and Margarethe were married and moved to Stuttgart, where he secured a teaching position at the Katherinenstift, a secondary school for girls. His return to Stuttgart from the provinces coincided with his rise to prominence as a literary figure, and in 1852 he was awarded an honorary doctorate of philosophy by the University of Tübingen.

If it is true that Mörike's lyric creativity waned after the 1840s, the same cannot be said of his talent for prose. In 1852 he wrote "Das Stuttgarter Hutzelmännlein" (The Stuttgart Goblin, 1853) a folk fairy tale so authentic-sounding that his friends accused him of cribbing from existing tales and legends. Though he raided the storehouse of German folk-tale motifs and devices, Mörike's appropriation of these elements is certainly original. In the manner of "Der Schatz," "Das Stuttgarter Hutzelmännlein" is a mixture of fairy-tale fantasy and realistic narration populated by creatures of the imagination as well as realistically drawn Swabians. The titular figure, a dwarf with magical powers, appears to Seppe, a naive young cobbler, on the eve of Seppe's departure from Stuttgart, instructing the cobbler to find a certain "Klotzlein Blei" (lump of lead) that contains the "Krachenzahn" (tooth of a magical fish). This charm lends to its owner the power of invisibility. The dwarf benefactor presents the cobbler with a "Hutzelbrot" (special Swabian bread), which always replenishes itself as long as the last bite is not consumed. He also gives Seppe two pairs of

Silhouette of Mörike by Paul Konewka (Schiller-Nationmuseum, Marbach am Neckar)

lucky shoes, one for the cobbler and one for his future bride. Seppe, the fairy-tale fool, mixes up the shoes, a mistake that has humorous consequences.

Seppe's journey leads him to Blaubeuern, where, at the famous wellspring, the "Blautopf" (Blue Bowl), he hears the "Historie von der schönen Lau" (History of the Beautiful Lau). Mörike was accused of stealing this interpolated legend of a water nymph directly from regional folklore; he denied that he had done so. After various twists and turns of plot Seppe finds the magic tooth and returns it to the dwarf, who rewards him by staging an encounter with the girl he is destined to marry. It turns out that she is a neighbor from Stuttgart; thus, the hero finds his fortune not in some faraway realm, as in a fairy tale, but only after he has returned home. This ending suggests a central theme of Mörike's mature writings and of Biedermeier literature in general: true happiness is best found in the circumscribed limits of simple domestic life. The many quaint details and depictions of provincial Swabian life that adorn this skillfully constructed narrative pay tribute to this ethos.

Included in the volume of which "Das Stuttgarter Hutzelmännlein" serves as the title story is another fairy tale, "Die Hand der Jezerte" (The Hand of Jezerte), which the author called "eine Art Märchen im altertümlichen Stil" (a kind of fairy tale in archaic style). By "archaic style" Mörike meant Latin and Oriental elements mixed with medieval Christian beliefs. These influences are evident in the exotic setting and names of the characters, in the allegorical parable form, in specific motifs, and in the tone of expression, which reflects Mörike's interest in the Psalms. Compared to previous tales, "Die Hand der Jezerte" is more stylized and self-conscious, and its derivations are more obvious. In its departure from more familiar traditions it is quite unlike "Das Stuttgarter Hutzelmännlein" or any of Mörike's other fairy tales, a characteristic contributing to the general neglect it has suffered in the critical literature.

Set in exotic and magical gardens perfumed by flowers, the story recounts the legend of a king who mourns his beloved wife Jezerte by worshiping a marble statue of her. His new mistress, Naira, jealous of her dead rival, plots to destroy the king's loving memory of Jezerte by having Jedanja, a young admirer of Naira, steal a hand from the statue. When, as planned, the king discovers the theft and its perpetrator, Jedanja – prompted by Naira – invents the lie that Jezerte had loved him during her engagement to the king, thus convincing the king of her infidelity. During a meditation in his garden shrine the king realizes Jezerte's innocence when the aroma of violets is emitted from the stump where the statue's hand had been attached. This revelation is confirmed when Naira's hand turns to blackened leather, proving her guilt. As punishment she is banished to an isolated island, where, after the spirit of Jezerte visits her to absolve her of guilt, she dies.

The realistic novella *Mozart auf der Reise nach Prag* (1856; translated as "Mozart's Journey from Vienna to Prague," 1913) is Mörike's best-known prose work. In many ways it is a self-portrait and self-analysis. Just as *Maler Nolten* had been a fictionalized version of its author's existence as young artist, so Mozart represents Mörike's mature artistic self.

Set in 1787, the year Wolfgang Amadeus Mozart traveled to Prague to conduct the first performance of his opera *Don Giovanni,* the novella provides a detailed and biographically accurate picture of a fictional day in the life of the composer as he and his wife, Constanze, stop for a rest during their journey. In a key scene early in the narrative Mörike makes the reader privy to Mozart's creative mind as the composer plucks an orange from a tree in the garden of a local aristocrat. As Mozart reaches for the fruit, the sight of it triggers a submerged memory from his boyhood. Picking the orange from the tree, he meditates on the musical theme it inspires, dreamily following its "unbestimmter Spur" (uncertain thread). Instinctively, he takes out a pocketknife and halves the orange; he is apparently admiring its sensual qualities, though "er sieht und sieht es nicht" (he sees it, yet does not see it). The notion of an external object inciting creative reverie was drawn from Mörike's own experience: the inspirational effect sense stimuli had on his creative process is a prominent feature of his poetry and is well documented in his letters. The unconscious aspect of Mozart's play with the orange suggests Mörike's withdrawal from reality into the "Abgrund der Betrachtung" (abyss of contemplation), an almost somnambulant state of Erinnerung (recollection) in which natural objects function as catalysts for the creation of aesthetic constructs.

Mozart is apprehended for his theft of the orange; on discovering the composer's identity the count invites him and his wife to join the wedding celebration of his niece, Eugenie, who is a fan of Mozart's. The composer entertains his hosts with an anecdote about a scene he had witnessed during a boyhood visit to Naples; it was this memory that had been evoked in the scene with the orange. In Naples he had observed a game involving two groups of young people throwing oranges back and forth between fishing boats while Sicilian dance tunes were played in the background. These tunes constituted the musical reminiscence he had experienced at the sight of the orange, and among the melodies he had remembered was a song that gave him an idea for a segment he needed to complete *Don Giovanni.* When Mozart performs this section of the finale for the wedding guests, Eugenie describes it as "eine gemalte Symphonie" (a painted symphony), thus characterizing not only Mozart's synthesis of visual memory and musical expression but also the reconciliation of image and sound in Mörike's mature poems. The story ends on an ominous note with the poem "Denk' es, o Seele!" (Ponder it, O Soul!), which foreshadows Mozart's premature death in symbolic images. The poem can also be read as Mörike's reckoning with his own mortality.

In 1855 Mörike had celebrated the birth of his first child, Fanny. A second daughter, Marie, followed in 1857. Family life agreed with Mörike; in a letter, he writes: "Mein bestes Glück liegt innerhalb des Hauses" (My best happiness lies in the home). The writer Theodor Storm had visited Mörike in 1855; in a reminiscence written in 1877 he describes Mörike's appearance as "ein fast kindlicher Ausdruck, als sei das Innerste dieses Mannes von den Treiben der Welt noch unberührt geblieben" (an almost childlike expression, as if the innermost part of this man had not been touched by the bustle of the world).

In his final years, apart from minor literary projects such as *Anakreon und die sogenannten Anakreontischen Lieder* (Anacreon and the So-Called Anacreontic Songs, 1864) – a modest revision of preexisting translations – and a revision of *Maler Nolten* (1877), Mörike wrote only a handful of published poems. Some of them, however, were important achievements. In 1863 he wrote "Bilder aus Bebenhausen" (Pictures from Bebenhausen) and "Erinna an Sappho" (Erinna to Sappho).

"Bilder aus Bebenhausen," written during a vacation in the village of Bebenhausen, near Tübingen, is a "thing poem" of larger proportions than his earlier ones and is written in classical distichs. It presents a visualizing description of a Cistercian monastery while developing the theme of art's permanence as a hedge against the destructive effects of time. Like its counterparts of the 1840s, "Die schöne Buche" and "Auf eine Lampe," this poem employs a strict verse form to rescue the external object from transitoriness by recording it as a linguistic artifact. More than an attempt to objectify and thus preserve the abbey itself, "Bilder aus Bebenhausen" is an attempt to achieve a union of writing subject and aesthetic object and thereby to save the poet's self from death.

Though it figures in his works from the beginning, the melancholy awareness of death, so apparent in *Mozart auf der Reise nach Prag,* surfaces more frequently in Mörike's later writings and strikingly in "Erinna an Sappho." In an introductory note Mörike explains that Erinna was a poet of Greek antiquity, a student of Sappho who died at the age of nineteen. Displaying the power of empathy that enabled him to project himself into nearly any object, whether human or inanimate, Mörike assumes the identity of Erinna and, through her persona, contemplates the inevitability of death. Staring into a mirror, Erinna relates her premonition of death, a half-smiling demonic spirit who shoots a black-feathered arrow past her brow. Unlike other neoclassical poems by Mörike, "Erinna an Sappho" is written in a free-verse form that conveys Erinna's moods as she meditates on identity and its abrupt dissolution in death. Closer analysis of the form,

Mörike at the age of seventy; pastel by Luise Walther (from Margaret Mare, Eduard Mörike: The Man and the Poet, *1957)*

however, reveals bits of classical meter, partly derived from Sapphic odes. Critics have suggested that this sophisticated and highly self-conscious mixture of forms, with its claims to an "absolute" aesthetic freed from referentiality, points ahead to the symbolist poetry of Paul Verlaine and Arthur Rimbaud. Yet its historical frame and concrete imagery, keep it squarely within the nineteenth-century conception of neoclassicism.

In the twilight of his life Mörike achieved international recognition. In 1862 he was honored by the king of Bavaria with induction into the Kollegium des Maximilliansordens für Kunst and Wissenschaft (Council of the Maximillian Order for Arts and Sciences); in 1864 he was awarded the Ritterkreuz Erster Klasse des Württembergischen Friedrich-Ordens (Knight's Cross First Class of the Württemberg Friedrich Order). He received visits from many fellow writers, among them Friedrich Hebbel, Hermann Grimm, and Ivan Turgenev, who honored and surprised him by reciting "Der alte Turmhahn" from memory. A late-blooming friendship with the Munich painter Moritz von Schwind, who had illustrated some of Mörike's poems, brightened his final days and gave rise in 1868 to the poem "An Moritz von Schwind" (To Moritz von Schwind). For most of his final years the poet remained in Stuttgart, but in typical fashion he sought to escape the admiration of his followers and the public, settling in Lorch from 1867 to 1869 and in Nürtingen in 1870–1871. The ever-faithful Klara remained by his side, caring for him to the end. His marriage, however, had been steadily degenerating, and in 1873 he separated from Margarethe. With Klara and Marie he moved to Fellbach, near Waiblingen. After a few months he returned to Stuttgart, where he died on 6 June 1875.

Letters:

Briefe, 2 volumes, edited by Karl Fischer and Rudolf Krauß (Berlin: Elsner, 1903–1904);

Briefe und Gedichte an Margrete von Speeth, edited by Marie Bauer (Stuttgart: Müller, 1906);

Briefwechsel zwischen Eduard Mörike und Moriz [sic] von Schwind, edited by Hans Wolfgang Rath (Stuttgart: Hoffmann, 1918);

Briefwechsel zwischen Hermann Kurz und Eduard Mörike, edited by Heinz Kindermann (Stuttgart: Hoffmann, 1919);

Briefwechsel zwischen Theodor Storm und Eduard Mörike, edited by Rath (Stuttgart: Hoffmann, 1919);

Luise: Briefe der Liebe, an seine Braut Luise Rau geschrieben, edited by Rath (Ludwigsburg: Schulz, 1921);

Briefwechsel zwischen Eduard Mörike und Friedrich Theodor Vischer, edited by Robert Vischer (Munich: Beck, 1926);

Freundeslieb' und Treu': 250 Briefe Eduard Mörikes an Wilhelm Hartlaub, edited by Gotthilf Renz (Tübingen: Klotz, 1938);

Briefe, edited by Friedrich Seebaß (Tübingen: Wunderlich, 1939);

Unveröffentlichte Briefe, edited by Seebaß (Stuttgart: Cotta, 1941; revised, 1945);

Briefe, edited by Werner Zemp (Zurich: Manesse, 1949);

Briefe an seine Braut Luise Rau, edited by Friedhelm Kemp (Munich: Kösel, 1965).

Biographies:

Hans-Ulrich Simon, *Mörike-Chronik* (Stuttgart: Metzler, 1981);

Peter Lahnstein, *Eduard Mörike: Leben und Milieu eines Dichters* (Munich: List, 1986).

References:

Jeffrey Adams, "The Scene of Instruction: Mörike's Reception of Goethe in 'Besuch in Urach,' "

Deutsche Vierteljahrsschrift, 62 (September 1988): 476-513;

Adams, ed., *Mörike's Muses: Critical Essays on Eduard Mörike* (Columbia, S.C.: Camden House, 1990);

Bernhard Boeschenstein, "Auf eine Christblume," in his *Studien zur Dichtung des Absoluten* (Zurich: Atlantis, 1968), pp. 102-124;

Liselotte Dieckmann, "Mörike's Presentation of the Creative Process," *Journal of English and Germanic Philology,* 53 (1954): 291-305;

Viktor G. Doerksen, *Mörikes Elegien und Epigramme: Eine Interpretation* (Zurich: Juris, 1964);

Doerksen, ed., *Eduard Mörike* (Darmstadt: Wissenschaftliche Buchgesellschaft, 1975);

Susanne Fliegner, *Der Dichter und die Dilettanten: Eduard Mörike und die bürgerliche Geselligkeitskultur des 19. Jahrhunderts* (Stuttgart: Metzler, 1991);

Romano Guardini, *Gegenwart und Geheimnis: Eine Auslegung von fünf Gedichten Eduard Mörikes* (Würzburg: Werkbund, 1957);

Heinrich Henel, "Erlebnisdichtung und Symbolismus," in *Zur Lyrik-Diskussion,* edited by Reinhold Grimm (Darmstadt: Wissenschaftliche Buchgesellschaft, 1974), pp. 218-254;

Renate von Heydebrand, *Eduard Mörikes Gedichtwerk: Beschreibung und Deutung der Formenvielfalt und ihrer Entwicklung* (Stuttgart: Metzler, 1972);

Hans Egon Holthusen, *Mörike in Selbstzeugnissen und Bilddokumenten* (Hamburg: Rowohlt, 1971);

Lee B. Jennings, "Suckelborst, Wispel, and Mörike's Mythopoeia," *Euphorion,* 69, no. 3 (1975): 320-332;

Margaret Mare, *Eduard Mörike: The Man and the Poet* (London: Methuen, 1957);

Birgit Mayer, *Eduard Mörike* (Stuttgart: Metzler, 1987);

Harry Maync, *Eduard Mörike: Sein Leben und Dichten* (Stuttgart: Cotta, 1902);

Herbert Meyer, *Eduard Mörike* (Stuttgart: Steinkopf, 1950);

S. S. Prawer, "Mignon's Revenge: A Study of *Maler Nolten,*" *Publications of the English Goethe Society,* 25 (1956): 63-85;

Prawer, *Mörike und seine Leser: Versuch einer Wirkungsgeschichte* (Stuttgart: Klett, 1960);

Hal H. Rennert, *Eduard Mörike's Reading and the Reconstruction of His Extant Library* (New York: Lang, 1985);

Jeffrey L. Sammons, "Fate and Psychology: Another Look at *Maler Nolten,*" in *Lebendige Form: Festschrift für Heinrich E. K. Henel. Interpretationen zur deutschen Literatur,* edited by Sammons and Ernst Schürer (Munich: Fink, 1970), pp. 211-227;

Friedrich Sengle, "Eduard Mörike," in his *Biedermeierzeit: Deutsche Literatur im Spannungsfeld zwischen Restauration und Revolution 1815-1848,* volume 3 (Stuttgart: Metzler, 1980), pp. 691-751;

Helga Slessarev, *Eduard Mörike* (New York: Twayne, 1970);

Emil Staiger, "Ein Briefwechsel mit Martin Heidegger," in his *Die Kunst der Interpretation: Studien zur deutschen Literaturgeschichte* (Zurich: Atlantis, 1955), pp. 34-49;

Staiger, Martin Heidegger, and Leo Spitzer, "A 1951 Dialogue on Interpretation," translated by Berel Lang and Christine Ebel, *PMLA,* 105 (May 1990): 409-435;

J. P. Stern, "Eduard Mörike: Recollection and Inwardness," in his *Idylls and Realities* (New York: Ungar, 1971), pp. 76-96;

Theodor Storm, "Meine Erinnerungen an Eduard Mörike 1877," *Westermanns Monatshefte,* 41 (1877): 384-392;

Gerhard Storz, *Eduard Mörike* (Stuttgart: Klett, 1967);

Benno von Wiese, *Eduard Mörike* (Tübingen: Wunderlich, 1950);

Theodore Ziolkowski, "Mörike's 'Die schöne Buche': An Arboreal Meditation," *German Quarterly,* 56 (January 1983): 4-13.

Papers:

The majority of manuscripts and other materials by Eduard Mörike are at the Deutsches Literaturarchiv (German Literature Archives) in Marbach, the Nationale Forschungs- und Gedenkstätten der Klassischen Deutschen Literatur (National Research and Memorial Places of Classical German Literature) in Weimar, and the Württembergische Landesbibliothek (Württemberg State Library) in Stuttgart. Smaller collections are at the Universitätsbibliothek (University Library) of the University of Tübingen and at the Bad Mergentheimer Bezirks-Heimatmuseum (Bad Mergentheim District Homeland Museum).

Luise Mühlbach
(Clara Mundt)

(2 January 1814 – 26 September 1873)

Brent O. Peterson
Duquesne University

BOOKS: *Erste und letzte Liebe* (Altona: Hammerich, 1838);

Die Pilger der Elbe (Altona: Hammerich, 1838);

Frauenschicksal (Altona: Hammerich, 1839);

Des Lebens Heiland: Ein Roman (Altona: Hammerich, 1840);

Zugvogel: Novellen und Skizzen, 2 volumes (Altona: Hammerich, 1840);

Bunte Welt: Roman, 2 volumes (Stuttgart: Krabbe, 1841);

Novellettenbuch (Altona: Hammerich, 1841);

Glück und Geld: Roman, 2 volumes(Altona: Hammerich, 1842);

Der Zögling der Natur: Roman (Altona: Hammerich, 1842);

Justin: Roman (Leipzig: Fritzsche & Matthes, 1843); republished as *Welt und Natur: Roman* (Berlin: Herschel, 1862);

Eva: Ein Roman aus Berlins Gegenwart (Berlin: Morin, 1844);

Giesela: Roman (Altona: Hammerich, 1844);

Nach der Hochzeit: Vier Novellen (Leipzig: Fritzsche, 1844);

Novellen und Scenen (Leipzig: Fritzsche, 1845);

Ein Roman in Berlin, 3 volumes (Berlin: Mylius, 1846);

Federzeichnungen auf der Reise: Novellen und Bilder (Berlin: Mylius, 1846); enlarged as *Federzeichnungen auf der Reise nach der Schweiz,* 4 volumes (Berlin: Mylius, 1864–1865;

Hofgeschichten (Berlin: Hirschfeld, 1847);

Die Tochter der Kaiserin: Roman, 2 volumes (Berlin: Simion, 1848); revised as *Prinzessin Tartaroff oder Die Tochter einer Kaiserin: Historischer Roman,* 2 volumes (Berlin: Janke, 1860); translated by Nathaniel Greene as *The Daughter of an Empress: An Historical Novel* (New York: Appleton, 1867 London & New York: Chesterfield Society, 1893);

Aphra Behn: Roman, 3 volumes (Berlin: Simion, 1849);

Der Zögling der Gesellschaft: Roman (Berlin: Simion, 1850); republished as *Der Sohn seiner Zeit: Roman* (Berlin: Janke, 1860);

Johann Gotzkowsky der Kaufmann von Berlin: Roman, 3 volumes (Berlin: Simion, 1850); translated by

Amory Coffin as *The Merchant of Berlin: An Historical Novel* (Akron, Ohio New Werner, 1866; London & New York: Chesterfield Society, 1866);

Katharina Parr: Historischer Roman, 3 volumes (Berlin: Simion, 1851); republished as *König Heinrich VIII. und sein Hof oder Katherina Parr,* 3 volumes (Berlin: Janke, 1858); translated by John Ringwood Atkins as *Katherine Parr; or, The Court of Henry VIII: An Historical Romance,* 3 volumes (London: Newby, 1862); translated by Reverend H. N. Pierce as *Henry VIII and His Court; or, Catharine Parr: A Historical Novel* (Akron, Ohio: Werner, 1864);

Memoiren eines Weltkindes: Roman, 2 volumes (Leipzig: Matthes, 1851);

Friedrich der Große und sein Hof: Historischer Roman, 3 volumes (Berlin: Janke, 1853); translated by Mrs. Chapman Coleman (Ann Mary Butler Crittenden Coleman) and her daughters as *Frederick the Great and His Court: An Historical Romance* (New York: Appleton, 1866; London & New York: Chesterfield Society, 1866);

Berlin und Sanssouci oder Friedrich der Große und seine Freunde: Historischer Roman, 4 volumes (Berlin: Simion, 1854); translated by A. G. Vaughan as *The Romance of a Court; or, Berlin and Sanssouci: A Novel,* 3 volumes (London: Bentley, 1866); translated by Mrs. Coleman and her daughters as *Berlin and Sans-Souci; or, Frederick the Great and His Friends: An Historical Novel* (New York: Appleton, 1867);

Welt und Bühne: A Roman, 2 volumes (Berlin: Janke, 1854);

Friedrich der Große und seine Geschwiester: Historischer Roman, 3 volumes (Berlin: Janke, 1855); translated by Mrs. Coleman and her daughters as *Frederick the Great and His Family: An Historical Romance (New York: Appleton, 1867; London & New York: Chesterfield Society, 1893);*

Historisches Bilderbuch (Berlin: Janke, 1855);

Kaiser Joseph II. und sein Hof, 12 volumes (Berlin: Janke, 1856–1857) – comprises *Kaiser Joseph und Maria Theresia,* 4 volumes; *Kaiser Joseph und Marie Antoinette* 4 volumes; *Kaiser Joseph als Selbstherrscher,* 4 volumes, translated by Adelaide de Vendel Chaudron as *Joseph II and His Court: An Historical Novel,* 4 volumes (Mobile, Ala.: Goetzel, 1864);

Königin Hortense: Ein Napoleonisches Lebensbild, 2 volumes (Berlin: Janke, 1856); translated by Chapman Coleman as *Queen Hortense: A Life Picture of the Napoleonic Era* (New York: Appleton, 1870); translation republished as *Queen Hortense: An Historical Romance* (London & New York: Chesterfield Society, 1870);

Historische Characterbilder, 4 volumes (Berlin: Janke, 1857–1859) – comprises volume 1, *Der Prinz von Wales*; volume 2, *Die Franzosen in Gotha*; volume 3, *Die Gräfin du Cayla; Der Prinz von Lamballe*; volume 4, *Ein Vormittag Friedrichs II. mit Prinzessin Orsini*;

Napoleon in Deutschland, 16 volumes (Berlin: Janke, 1858) – comprises *Rastatt und Jena,* 4 volumes, translated by F. Jordan as *Louisa of Prussia and Her Times: An Historical Novel* (New York: Appleton, 1867); *Napoleon und Königin Louise,* 4 volumes, translated by Jordan as *Napoleon and the Queen of Prussia: An Historical Novel* (New York: Appleton, 1867); *Napoleon und Blücher,* 4 volumes, translated by Jordan as *Napoleon and Blücher: An Historical Novel* (New York: Appleton, 1867 London & New York: Chesterfield Society, 1893); *Napoleon und der Wiener Congress,* 4 volumes;

Karl II. und sein Hof Historischer Roman, 3 volumes (Berlin: Janke, 1859);

Frau Meisterin (Berlin: Janke, 1859);

Die letzten Lebenstage der Katharina II. Historische Novelle (Prague: Kober & Markgraf, 1859);

Erzherzog Johann und seine Zeit, 12 volumes (Berlin: Janke, 1859–1863) – comprises *Andreas Hofer,* 3 volumes (1859), translated by Jordan as *Andreas Hofer: An Historical Novel* (New York: Appleton, 1868; London & New York: Chesterfield Society, 1893); *Erzherzog Johann und Metternich,* 3 volumes (1860); *Erzherzog Johann und der Herzog von Reichstadt,* 3 volumes; *Erzherzog Johann als Reichsverweser,* 3 volumes (1863);

Kleine Romane, 17 volumes (Altona: Hammerich, 1860) – comprises *Zwei Lebenswege,* 3 volumes, translated by Greene as *Two Life-Paths: A Romance* (New York: Appleton, 1869); *Antonio: Eine italienische Geschichte*; *Bonners oder Geschichte eines Millionairs,* 3 volumes, translated by Greene as *The Story of a Millionaire* (New York: Appleton, 1872); *Rebekka,* 2 volumes; *Der Leibeigene; Die Künstlerin: Roman*; *Novellenbuch*; *Die Flüchtlinge in London,* 3 volumes; *Mademoiselle Clairon oder vier Tage aus dem Leben einer Schauspielerin*; *Memoiren eines Kindes*;

Berlin vor fünfzehn Jahren: Roman (Berlin: Janke, 1860);

Kaiser Leopold der Zweite und seine Zeit: Historischer Roman 3 volumes (Prague: Kober & Markgraf, 1860);

Neues Bilderbuch (Berlin: Herschel, 1861);

Kaiserin Josephine: Ein Napoleonisches Lebensbild (Berlin: Janke, 1861); translated by Reverend W. Binet as *The Empress Josephine: An Historical Sketch of the Days of Napoleon* (New York: Appleton, 1867; London & New York: Chesterfield Society, 1867);

Historische Lebensbilder, 2 volumes (Berlin: Janke, 1864);

Prinz Eugen und seine Zeit: Historischer Roman, 8 volumes (Berlin: Janke, 1864) – comprises *Prinz Eugen der kleine Abbé,* 4 volumes; *Prinz Eugen der edle Ritter,* 4 volumes, translated by Chaudron as *Prince Eugene and His Time: An Historical Romance* (Akron, Ohio: New Werner, 1868; London & New York: Chesterfield Society, 1868);

Graf von Benjowsky: Historischer Roman, 4 volumes (Jena: Costenoble, 1865);

Der große Kurfürst und seine Zeit, 11 volumes (Jena: Costenolbe, 1865–1866) – comprises *Der junge Kurfurst,* 3 volumes (1865), translated by Mary Stuart Harrison Smith as *The Youth of the Great Elector: An Historical Romance* (New York: Appleton, 1896); *Der Große Kurfurst und sein Volk,* 4 volumes; *Der große Kurfürst und seine Kinder,* 4 volumes (1866); *Der Große Kurfurst und sein Volk* and *Der große Kurfurst und seine Kinder* translated by Smith as *The Reign of the Great Elector: An Historical Romance* (New York & London: Appleton, 1898);

Marie Antoinette und ihr Sohn: Historischer Roman, 6 volumes (Jena: Costenoble, 1867); translated by William L. Gage as *Marie Antoinette and Her Son: An Historical Novel* (New York: Appleton, 1867 London & New York: Chesterfield Society, 1867);

Kaiserin Claudia, Prinzessin von Tirol: Historischer Roman, 3 volumes (Leipzig: Matthes, 1867);

Deutschland in Sturm und Drang: Historischer Roman, 17 volumes (Jena: Costenoble, 1867–1868) – comprises *Der alte Fritz und seine Zeit,* 4 volumes (1867), translated by Peter Langley as *Old Fritz and the New Era* (New York: Appleton, 1868; New York & London: Chesterfield Society, 1868); *Fürsten und Dichter,* 4 volumes (1867), translated by Chapman Coleman as *Goethe and Schiller: An Historical Romance* (Akron, Ohio: New Werner, 1867; London & New York: Chesterfield Society, 1867); *Deutschland gegen Frankreich,* 4 volumes (1868); *Frankreich gegen Deutschland,* 5 volumes (1868);

Kaiser Alexander und sein Hof: Historischer Roman, 4 volumes (Berlin: Janke, 1868);

Welt des Glanzes: Roman aus der Gegenwart (Berlin: Janke, 1868);

Geschichtsbilder: Historische Novellen, 3 volumes (Jena: Costenoble, 1868);

Kaiser Ferdinand II. und seine Zeit: Historischer Roman, 5 volumes (Prague: Bensinger, 1868–1870);

Kaiser Ferdinand I. und seine Zeit: Historischer Roman, 5 volumes (Prague: Bensinger, 1869);

Von Solferino bis Königgrätz: Historischer Roman, 12 volumes (Berlin: Janke, 1869) – comprises *Kirchenfürsten und Weltfürsten,* 4 volumes; *Solferino,* 4 volumes; *Die beiden Nebenbuhler um Deutschland,* 4 volumes;

Damen-Almanach (Leipzig: Dürr, 1869);

Kaiserburg und Engelsburg; Historischer Roman, 2 volumes (Jena: Costenoble, 1871);

Reisebriefe aus Aegypten, 2 volumes (Jena: Costenoble, 1871);

Mohammed Ali und sein Haus: Historischer Roman, 4 volumes (Jena: Costenoble, 1871); translated by Chapman Coleman as *Mohammed Ali and His House: An Historical Romance* (New York: Appleton, 1872; London & New York: Chesterfield Society, 1893);

Mohammed Ali's Nachfolger: Historischer Roman im Anschluß an "Mohammed Ali und sein Haus," 4 volumes (Jena: Costenoble, 1872);

Der dreißigjährige Krieg: Historischer Roman, 6 volumes (Prague: Bensinger, 1873);

Kaiser Wilhelm und seine Zeitgenossen: Historischer Roman, 4 volumes (Berlin: Große, 1873);

Frauenherzen: Historische Novellen, 2 volumes (Leipzig: Günther, 1873) – comprises volume 1, *Drei Kaiserinnen*; volume 2, *Ein Glas Wasser oder eine Rosenknospe;*

Prostestantische Jesuiten: Historischer Roman, 6 volumes (Leipzig: Günther, 1873–1874);

Von Königgrätz bis Chiselhurst, 6 volumes (Stuttgart: Simon, 1873–1874) – comprises *Um Deutschlands Einheit,* 3 volumes (1873); *Wilhelmshöhe und Chiselhurst,* 3 volumes (1874);

Erinnerungsblätter aus dem Leben Luise Mühlbach's, edited by Thea Ebersberger (Leipzig: Schmidt & Günther, 1902).

In her lifetime Luise Mühlbach was one of Germany's best-loved female authors; whatever the quality of her books, they certainly achieved enormous popularity among the nontraditional readers who patronized private lending libraries. In addition to the historical novels for which she is remembered, Mühlbach also wrote more than a dozen works that can be compared to the social novels of Junges Deutschland (Young Germany) and several volumes of travel literature. Besides shaping the German historical novel and disseminating a personalized and popularized form of historical knowledge, Mühlbach was also an early and forceful advocate of women's emancipation.

Her novels normally appeared in editions of fifteen hundred to five thousand copies, depending on whether the publisher decided to print a small, expensive edition or a popularly priced edition that would appeal to the lending libraries that were the most important purveyors of culture to the growing middle class. By the middle of the nineteenth century these libraries were such important buyers that they could dictate the manner of a book's publication. The three 900-page volumes of *Kaiser Joseph II. und sein Hof* (1856–1857; translated as *Joseph II and His Court,* 1864), for example, were also published in twelve volumes of 250 to 350 pages each; the smaller size allowed for more rapid circulation, and therefore for a higher rate of profit for the libraries. By 1864 the novel was in its eighth printing. Nowadays her work is virtually unavailable in Germany.

Mühlbach was born Clara Müller on 2 January 1814 in Neubrandenburg, where her father was mayor. Clara Müller's early life appears to have been happy, but she was not afforded any of the educational opportunities that were becoming common for boys. Teachers in Neubrandenburg would not even consent to give private lessons to girls, so after having learned as much as she could from the family's governesses Müller was sent to live with her maternal grandmother in Penzlin in order to study with the local pastor. The pastor apparently was uninterested in his charges, but they nevertheless seem to have profited from his well-stocked library; Sir Walter Scott was the author whose works Müller read most diligently.

Unlike many of her female contemporaries, Müller was not forced into a marriage of convenience. Her father's death when she was fourteen meant that she could search out her own husband; enamored of the writings of the Young Germans, she initiated a correspondence with Theodor Mundt, who was generally considered – in spite of his protestations – a member of that liberal movement, and the two were married in 1839. Judging by their letters and the accounts of their acquaintances, the union was a happy one, and the relationship might help explain why Mühlbach's early novels often end by retreating from the criticism of marriage and the social position of women that they initially advance.

In *Der Zögling der Natur* (Nature's Pupil, 1842) Antonio, a handsome young orphan, is brought from an idyllic monastery to the Sicilian court in Palermo – that is, to all the dangers and temptations of the city. Antonio eventually decides to return to nature, the source of his wisdom, and hopes to take a wife along. He proposes to an opera singer, Catharina Gabrieli, who declines even though she loves him: her art is more important to her than any man, and the countryside promises years of boredom in exchange for a few scattered hours of pleasure with a beloved husband. Although she is fully aware of how fleeting her fame might be, this independent woman prefers life alone, and she throws a huge party to celebrate her refusal of Antonio's proposal.

Tonia Lazaro, who eventually does accompany Antonio back to nature, is following her heart but also fleeing from society's unjust treatment of women. Antonio encounters her in the middle of a near riot: Tonia, a member of the lower classes, is being led off to prison for stabbing the new mistress of her former lover, a count who had promised to marry her; the crowd approves of the young woman's act of revenge and attempts to free her from the police. Antonio intercedes with the prince on her behalf; but Tonia has already demonstrated independence and self-sufficiency, and when he leaves Palermo it is with a woman who rescues him from his own self-doubt over the previous rejection rather than one who is grateful for the assistance of a strong male figure.

Antonio's intercession on Tonia's behalf raises another topic typical of Mühlbach's early novels: their often explicit criticism of absolutist governments. Antonio is aware that the law condemns Tonia's deed, but he attempts to justify it by invoking natural law. The prince admits not only that every punishment, however legal, is a form of revenge, but also that princes have no more right to take a life than do their subjects. Princes are, he admits, merely men – certainly no better and perhaps even worse than their fellow human beings.

Even though such writers as Heinrich Heine, Karl Gutzkow, and Mühlbach's husband had seen their work forbidden in the 1830s for their criticism of political institutions and conventional morality, such criticism was common in novels written before the Revolution of 1848. For example, when Alberta Winneburg, the heroine of Mühlbach's novella "Rothe Infusorien (Aus dem Jahre 1848)" (Red Infusorians [From the Year 1848]), in *Historisches Bilderbuch* (Historical Sketchbook, 1855), is forced to choose between a revolutionary poet and a Prussian officer, she initially allies herself with the progressive forces and decides to marry the poet. She even gazes longingly at the barricades, wishing that she were a man and could fight for freedom and democracy. But Alberta really loves the poet's fiery oratory and the uniform of the popular militia that he wears; when he turns out to be a hypocrite and a coward she is quite willing to submit to the Prussian officer, who makes a name for himself while suppressing the revolutionary turmoil in southern Germany. Any emancipatory tendencies that Mühlbach might once have espoused seem to have disappeared; her heroine is utterly dependent on her father and prospective husband. Alberta Winneburg's initial desire to become a man and thus to break out of an inferior social position proves to be as hollow as her belief in democracy and popular sovereignty, and the story contains no positive role models either for women or for the remaining believers in Young Germany.

Similarly, Mühlbach's *Der Zögling der Gesellschaft* (Society's Pupil, 1850) opens with five friends about to escape from the prison in which they had landed after the revolution was suppressed. The narrator explains that the scene is set not in the remote feudal past but in 1849 in an unnamed but average German principality where both sides have learned something from the experience: the prince has learned to despise his subjects, while the subjects have learned to fear their ruler. The novel undermines its critical stance, however, when the reader learns that one of the chief conspirators is a republican not for reasons of principle but as the result of hatred and envy: he is the elder, but illegitimate and therefore disinherited, son of the ruling family. Yet even this tentative criticism was expunged when Mühlbach revised the novel ten years later as *Der Sohn seiner Zeit* (The Son of His Times, 1860). Germany had become far more conservative after the failure of the 1848 revolution; no doubt as a result, Mühlbach increasingly turned her attention to the relative safety of German history.

The historical novel could address two areas that were off limits to the works of professional historians. First, it could provide a glimpse behind the scenes of war and diplomacy that preoccupied political historians, showing great men up close and introducing readers to these men's wives and lovers. Second, historical fiction could show how the political events related by academic historians affected the lives of ordinary human beings – the servants, soldiers, workers, farmers, and clerks with whom most readers could identify. Thus, aside from Friedrich himself, the main characters in one of Mühlbach's most widely read works, *Friedrich der Große und sein Hof* (1853; translated as *Frederick the Great and His Court* (1866), are Friedrich's wife, Elisabeth Christina, and Fritz Wendel, a gardener in the royal household.

It was the unfortunate Elisabeth Christina's fate to be deeply in love with a man who did not reciprocate her feelings, and she spends much of the novel trying to change and then to accept her largely ceremonial role in Friedrich's life. The work shows the difficulties faced by human beings in the roles that a traditional aristocratic society forced on them. For Elisabeth Christina, Friedrich's mother, his two sisters, and their ladies-in-waiting love is an unachievable goal. Nor are the men happy: Friedrich's brother Wilhelm, for example, is forced to abandon a member of the queen's household and marry a princess. Friedrich's sisters, similarly, are forced to marry princes; one of them notes that her social position has turned her into a commodity. Fritz Wendel, the gardener, betrays the unfortunate Prince Wilhelm in an attempt to force Friedrich to approve of Fritz's own engagement to a noblewoman; he ends up in prison. In addition to satisfying readers' interest in gossip about the great and powerful, the effect of the depiction of these intrigues is to make the same sort of critique of absolutist governments that had been made in the early days of the German Enlightenment: in the late eighteenth century it had been the bourgeois norms of love and the family that had held out hope for the writers and intellectuals who were attempting to weaken absolutist rule. If Mühlbach seems dated – or, to use the pejorative term of traditional German literary criticism, "trivial" – it is in part because writers of the next generation made their criticism more expressly and more radically political.

Friedrich is portrayed as a flawed but heroic figure who was willing to sacrifice his own well-being for the common good, defined by Mühlbach as the expansion of Prussia in the cause of German unity. He thus becomes a pan-Germanic figure with whom readers in the process of becoming Germans would be able to identify. In addition, as Mühlbach shows, Friedrich's Prussian Germany could have been far more liberal than the state Otto von Bismarck eventually created. Her Friedrich is a man who not only complains about his own somewhat strained finances as crown prince but also wonders why the people of Berlin should have to beg for bread when the king's granaries are full. Although the reader is led to feel some sympathy for Friedrich's mother, the long-suffering queen, the narrator argues that her crowns, necklaces, earrings, and bracelets are intrinsically useless and that the value they represent could have been put to better use in assuaging human suffering. Moreover, such objects are symbols of a vanishing aristocratic world; Mühlbach has Friedrich tell his mother that in the future Prussia will achieve greatness not because of the battles won by its nobility but because of the riches and power garnered by its industry. *Friedrich der Große und sein Hof* is, therefore, not just personalized history; it is also historiography of a decidedly liberal bent, at least in the context of its times.

A strain of chauvinistic nationalism runs through much of Mühlbach's early work and culminates in the grand historical potboilers for which she is chiefly remembered. Antonio in *Der Zögling der Natur* had a German mother, and one of the priests who takes him in claims to have noticed the foreign blood in Antonio's veins: no son of Italy could be as ambitious or as intellectually curious. The priest's remark probably represents a common prejudice, but it is also clear that Mühlbach came to see it as her calling to glorify the German past. In correspondence with her publisher in 1864 she sketches a plan for a twelve-volume work centered on the Prussian king Friedrich Wilhelm III, who was born in 1770 and died in 1840. Two years later, when Bismarck's unification of Germany was well under way, Mühlbach asked to change her contract because she wanted to write a German rather than a Prussian book: she was understandably worried that readers from southern Germany might not be interested in a novel about the Prussian king. The work appeared in seventeen volumes as *Deutschland in Sturm und Drang* (Germany in Storm and Stress, 1867–1868).

Such works provided a disparate and isolated reading public with a fictionalized common past. Although the idea of a German nation had been a popular topic ever since the Wars of Liberation against Napoleon, the vast majority of prospective Germans more closely identified with their home village or principality than with the still vague notion of Germany. In the 1860s and 1870s most Germans still lived in the countryside and had no reasonable expectation of ever traveling more than a few miles from their birthplaces. If they had ventured further they would in all likelihood not have understood the local dialect, much less have thought themselves to be part of a single community. Moreover, political events such as the Revolution of 1848 mainly took place in Germany's few urban centers, and activists' discussions were of interest primarily to the governing elite and to the tiny minority of well-to-do craftsmen and professionals. If "Germany" were ever to become more than a nebulous geographical category and acquire real emotional and political content for the bulk of the new country's inhabitants, historical novels would have to play an important role in disseminating a "common" past. In the course of her enormous production Mühlbach narrated virtually all of German history from the Thirty Years' War of 1618 to 1648 to German unification under Bismarck and Wilhelm I in 1871.

Mühlbach's husband died in 1861; his income as a writer and professor had never been large, and his illness and Mühlbach's abandonment of writing to care for him left her saddled with debts. She maintained a large, though by no means extravagant household in Berlin, and it was apparently quite expensive to support her two daughters in a style befitting their mother's fame. Except for an occasional visit to the estates of such friends as Prince Hermann von Pückler-Muskau, and two trips to Egypt in 1870 at the invitation and – more important – at the expense of the khedive, Mühlbach was responsible for her own expenses. Hers was a particularly difficult task in patriarchal nineteenth-century Germany, and the result was that she was forever arguing with publishers about her advances, admonishing them to pay for new editions of earlier works, and inquiring about payment for translation rights.

Mühlbach was not only writing in an era when the historical novel enjoyed enormous popularity but also at a time when the academic discipline of history was being shaped by its early theorists and practitioners. Whereas professional historians were constrained both by the positivistic doctrine of scientific history, which limited their sources largely to the material contained in official archives, and by their narrow notion of the kinds of events that constituted real history, writers of historical fiction were free to explore the rest of the past and to present their own versions of history. Historical novelists worked with an alternative epistemology that posited creative authors' ability to feel their way into the minds of their subjects. Utter fabrication was, of course, scarcely possible with figures as well known as Friedrich der Große, and Mühlbach's novels contain footnotes claiming, for example, that a particular passage was taken from the king's own words; these citations seem to be accurate. The rest of the material cannot be verified, but within the confines of the genre of historical fiction the overall effect is one of truth – albeit truth filtered and made palatable for the widest possible audience.

Mühlbach reflects on the problem of historical fiction in the preface to *Der alte Fritz und seine Zeit*

(1867; translated as *Old Fritz and the New Era,* 1868), the first part of *Deutschland in Sturm und Drang.* She claims that while historians are limited to the past's exterior, it is the task of the novelist to inquire into the heart of history. Writers of fiction can shed light on those dark corners of human events that are not recorded in any archive and can make deductions about the thoughts, desires, and motivations of historical personages. It is therefore not important, Mühlbach asserts, that the figures in her novels actually said everything that she attributes to them, only that these utterances are in accord with their characters. Her intent was unabashedly pedagogical, and, within the context of her times and her audience, her interventions were accepted as necessary – even praiseworthy – both by historians and by reviewers in respectable journals.

Mühlbach's novels had considerable success in the United States, where they appeared in pirated German editions and were serialized without her permission in prominent German-American journals and newspapers. At least twenty of her works were also translated into English. Sales of her works and the number of reviews that have been located suggest that Mühlbach was an important author on both sides of the Atlantic, although her prominence in the United States was to a certain degree predicated on the absence until 1891 of international copyright laws. From the beginning of her career in 1838 until her death in Berlin from liver disease on 26 September 1873 Mühlbach produced a steady stream of novels that raised both the important social and political issues of her day and played a significant role in shaping middle-class culture in Germany.

Letters:

"Clara Mundts Briefe an Hermann Costenoble: Zu L. Mühlbachs historischen Romanen," edited by William H. McClain and Lieselotte E. Kurth-Voigt, *Archiv für Geschichte des Buchwesens,* 22 (1981): 917–1250.

References:

Jeannine Blackwell, "Louise Mühlbach," in *Women Writers of Germany, Austria, and Switzerland: An Annotated Bio-Bibliographical Guide,* edited by Elke Fredriksen (New York: Greenwood, 1989), pp. 167–168;

Hartmut Eggert, *Studien zur Wirkungsgeschichte des deutschen historischen Romans 1850–1870* (Frankfurt am Main: Klostermann, 1971);

Lieselotte E. Kurth-Voigt, "Ottilie von Goethe und Clara Mundt: Mit einem unbekannten Brief," *Goethe Yearbook,* 3 (1986): 165–177;

Kurth-Voigt and William H. McClain, "Louise Mühlbach's Historical Novels: The American Reception," *Internationales Archiv für Sozialgeschichte der deutschen Literatur,* 6 (1981): 52–77;

Renate Möhrmann, "Luise Mühlbachs kecke Jahre," in her *Die andere Frau: Emanzipationsansätze deutscher Schriftstellerinnen im Vorfeld der Achtundvierziger-Revolution* (Stuttgart: Metzler, 1977), pp. 60–84;

Möhrmann, ed., *Frauenemanzipation im deutschen Vormärz: Texte und Dokumente* (Stuttgart: Reclam, 1978).

Papers:

Luise Mühlbach's papers are at the Johns Hopkins University Library and the University of Bonn.

Theodor Mundt

(19 September 1808 - 30 November 1861)

Otto W. Johnston
University of Florida

BOOKS: *Das Duett: Ein Roman* (Berlin: Dümmler, 1831);

Die Einheit Deutschlands in politischer und ideeller Entwickelung (Leipzig: Brockhaus, 1832; reprinted, Frankfurt am Main: Athenäum, 1973);

Madelon oder Die Romantiker in Paris: Eine Novelle (Leipzig: Wolbrecht, 1832);

Kritische Wälder: Blätter zur Beurtheilung der Literatur, Kunst und Wissenschaft unserer Zeit (Leipzig: Wolbrecht, 1833);

Der Basilisk oder Gesichterstudien: Eine Novelle (Leipzig: Wolbrecht, 1833);

Moderne Lebenswirren: Briefe und Zeitabenteuer eines Salzschreibers (Leipzig: Reichenbach, 1834);

Charlotte Stieglitz: Ein Denkmal, anonymous (Berlin: Veit, 1835);

Madonna: Unterhaltungen mit einer Heiligen (Leipzig: Reichenbach, 1835; reprinted, Frankfurt am Main: Athenäum, 1973);

Charaktere und Situationen: Vier Bücher. Novellen, Skizzen, Wanderungen aus Reisen und durch die neueste Literatur, 2 volumes (Wismar & Leipzig: Schmidt & Cossel, 1837);

Die Kunst der deutschen Prosa: Aesthetisch, literarisch, gesellschaftlich (Berlin: Veit, 1837);

Spaziergänge und Weltfahrten, 3 volumes (Altona: Hammerich, 1838–1839);

Völkerschau auf Reisen (Stuttgart: Krabbe, 1840);

Thomas Müntzer: Ein deutscher Roman, 3 volumes (Altona: Hammerich, 1841);

Geschichte der Literatur der Gegenwart: Vorlesungen (Berlin: Simion, 1842); revised as *Geschichte der Literatur der Gegenwart: Vorlesungen über deutsche, französische, englische, spanische, italienische, schwedische, dänische, holländische, vlämische, russische, polnische, böhmische und ungarische Literatur. Von dem Jahre 1789 bis zur neuesten Zeit* (Berlin: Simion, 1853);

Gesammelte Schriften, Novellen und Dichtungen, 2 volumes (Leipzig: Berger, 1843, 1844);

Theodor Mundt in 1844; lithograph by Valentin Schertle

Berlin und seine Künste: Ereignisse auf der Berliner Kunstausstellung 1844 (Berlin: Schepeler, 1844);

Zur Universitätsfrage oder Die freie Entwicklung der protestantischen Universität (Berlin: Simion, 1844);

Kleines Skizzenbuch (Berlin: Schepeler, 1844);

Lesebuch der deutschen Prosa: Musterstücke der prosaischen Literatur der Deutschen, nach der Folge der Schriftsteller und der Entwickelung der Sprache (Berlin: Simion, 1844);

Carmela oder Die Wiedertaufe: Ein Roman (Hannover: Kius, 1844);

Geschichte der deutschen Stände nach ihrer gesellschaftlichen Entwickelung und politischen Vertretung (Berlin: Simion, 1844);

Die Geschichte der Gesellschaft in ihren neueren Entwickelungen und Problemen (Berlin: Simion, 1844);

Aesthetik: Die Idee der Schönheit und des Kunstwerks im Lichte unserer Zeit (Berlin: Simion, 1845; re-

printed, with an afterword by Hans Düvel, Göttingen: Vandenhoeck & Ruprecht, 1966);
Der heilige Geist und der Zeitgeist: Zwölf Kapitel (Berlin: Mylius, 1845);
Allgemeine Literaturgeschichte, 3 volumes (Berlin: Simion, 1846);
Die Götterwelt der alten Völker: Nach Dichtungen der Orientalen, Griechen und Römer dargestellt (Berlin: Morin, 1846; revised and enlarged, Berlin: Grobe, 1854);
Mendoza, der Vater der Schelme: Ein Roman, 2 volumes (Berlin: Mylius, 1846, 1847);
Cimaletti: Protestantische Bilder aus Böhmen (Leipzig: Berger, 1847);
Dramaturgie oder Theorie und Geschichte der dramatischen Kunst, 2 volumes (Berlin: Simion, 1847, 1848);
Die Staatsberedtsamkeit der neueren Völker: Nach der Entwickelung ihrer Staatsform (Berlin: Schröter, 1848);
Katechismus der Politik: Darstellung und Erörterung der wichtigsten politischen Fragen und Staats-Verfassungen (Berlin: Simion, 1848);
Die Matadore: Ein Roman aus der Gegenwart, 2 volumes (Leipzig: Brockhaus, 1850);
Machiavelli und der Gang der europäischen Politik (Leipzig: Dyk, 1851); revised as *Niccolò Machiavelli und das System der modernen Politik* (Berlin: Janke, 1861);
Revision oder Vereinbarung?: Eine Ansprache an die preußischen Wähler (Berlin: Schlesinger, 1851);
Geschichte der deutschen Stände nach ihrer gesellschaftlichen Entwickelung und politischen Vertretung (Berlin: Simion, 1854);
Ein französisches Landschloß: Novelle (Prague: Gerzabek / Leipzig: Hübner, 1855);
Krim-Girai, ein Bundesgenosse Friedrichs des Großen: Ein Vorspiel der russisch-türkischen Kämpfe (Berlin: Schindler, 1855); translated by William G. C. Eliot as *Krim-girai, Khan of the Crimea* (London: Murray, 1856);
Der Kampf um das schwarze Meer: Historische Darstellung aus der Geschichte Rußlands (Brunswick: Westermann, 1855);
Ein deutscher Herzog (Leipzig: Voigt & Günther, 1855);
Kleine Romane, 2 volumes (Berlin: Janke, 1857);
Pariser Kaiser-Skizzen (Berlin: Janke, 1857);
Paris und Louis Napoleon: Neue Skizzen aus dem französischen Kaiserreich, 2 volumes (Berlin: Janke, 1858);
Cagliostro in Petersburg: Historische Novelle (Prague & Leipzig: Kober, 1858);
Graf Mirabeau, 4 volumes (Berlin: Janke, 1858); translated by Thérèse J. Radford as *Count Mirabeau: An Historical Novel* (New York: Appleton, 1868);
Robespierre, 3 volumes (Berlin: Janke, 1859);
Italienische Zustände, 4 volumes (Berlin: Janke, 1859–1860);
Czar Paul, 6 volumes (Berlin: Janke, 1861).

OTHER: *Schriften in bunter Reihe zur Anregung und Unterhaltung,* no. 1, edited by Mundt (1834);
Literarischer Zodiacus: Journal für Zeit und Leben, Wissenschaft und Kunst, 1, nos. 1–12; 2, no. 1, edited by Mundt (1835–1836; reprinted, 1 volume, Frankfurt am Main: Athenäum, 1971).
Dioskuren für Wissenschaft und Kunst: Schriften in bunter Reihe, 1–2, edited by Mundt (1836–1837); reprinted, 1 volume, Frankfurt am Main: Athenäum, 1971);
Karl Ludwig von Knebel, *Literarischer Nachlaß und Briefwechsel,* 3 volumes, edited by Mundt and Karl August Varnhagen von Ense (Leipzig: Reichenbach, 1835–1836);
Der Delphin: Ein Almanach, 2 volumes, edited by Mundt (Altona: Hammerich, 1837, 1838);
Der Freihafen: Gallerie von Unterhaltungsbildern, 1–7, edited by Mundt (1838–1844);
Der Pilot: Allgemeine Revue der einheimischen und ausländischen Literatur- und Völkerzustände, 1–3, (1840–1842);
Friedrich von Schlegel, *Geschichte der alten und neuen Literatur: Bis auf die neueste Zeit,* 2 volumes, revised by Mundt (Berlin: Simion, 1841, 1842);
Martin Luther, *Politische Schriften,* 4 volumes, edited by Mundt (Berlin: Simion, 1844);
Johann Jakob Engel, *Mimik,* edited by Mundt (Berlin: Mylius, 1845);
Engel, *Philosoph für die Welt,* edited by Mundt (Berlin: Mylius, 1845);
Ständische Blätter, 2 volumes, edited by Mundt (Berlin: Hirschfeld, 1847).

Despite his protestations Theodor Mundt has gone into German literary history as a preeminent member of the group known as Junges Deutschland (Young Germany). Although he criticized Heinrich Heine and quarreled with Karl Gutzkow, he was named with them, Ludolph Wienbarg, and Heinrich Laube in the Prussian censorship act of 14 November 1835 directed against the Junges Deutschland movement. On 10 December an act of the German Confederation prohibited the publication or distribution of their works. Mundt acknowledged that he would gladly bear upon his shoulders "die gefährlichen Ideen" (the dangerous political ideas) and social visions of the younger generation of German writers, but he denied belonging to any literary group.

Mundt was a prolific writer; there is virtually no aspect of life in his day which escaped his comment either in fiction or in scholarly works. He was a fine, though uneven, stylist, who contributed to the evolution of German prose both as a writer and as an editor. He founded several journals to serve as forums for debate on political, social, and literary topics. He was a scholar whose work bears witness to the progressive democratic tendencies in Germany's intellectual life. He saw himself as expanding Christianity's capacity for development, as mediating between the spiritualists and materialists, and as propagating the higher intellectual development of women. He discovered the city as a literary topic and expressed a faith in civilization and urban life.

On the other hand, he was not particularly original and spent most of his energy clarifying or criticizing the ideas of others. He fought with every major figure in the liberal-progressive camp, including Heine and Ludwig Börne after they left for Paris and parted ways with each other. He overestimated the power of aesthetics and literature to promote political change and never succeeded in systematizing his views into a coherent program of political action. For this reason, he has been branded a "Phantast" (dreamer) rather than a realist in political matters – a liberal in thought but not in deed. As the German states moved closer to the Revolution of 1848, Mundt was overshadowed by the more radical advocates of immediate change.

Mundt was born on 19 September 1808 in Potsdam. His father was a government accountant. Mundt was still quite young when the family moved to Berlin, where received an excellent preparatory education at the prestigious Joachimsthal Gymnasium. He then enrolled at the newly founded University of Berlin. At age sixteen he attended the lectures of the philosopher Georg Wilhelm Friedrich Hegel, which became the primary influence on his life and work. It is assumed that he heard Hegel's lectures on logic, metaphysics, and aesthetics in the summer semester of 1826; it is established that he enrolled in Hegel's courses on logic, the history of philosophy, and philosophy of nature from summer 1827 to summer 1828. Agreements and disagreements with Hegel make up a major portion of Mundt's writing, and his otherwise eloquent style often reverts to Hegel's ponderous language and convoluted sentence structure when he comments on some aspects of the master's philosophy. Hegel taught him the supremacy of reflection over action; the tendency to intellectualize is the major difference between Mundt and the poets of the March 1848 revolution, who demanded action, not pronouncements.

Mundt began to have his writing published at about the time he entered the university. On 24 July 1826 his article "Selbstcharakteristik eines denkenden Müßiggängers" (Self-characterizations of a Thinking Loafer) appeared in the newspaper *Berliner Schnellpost*. Five years later his first novel was published: *Das Duett* (The Duet) analyzes Hegel's system, which is characterized as the philosophy of death. For the modern reader, the most interesting feature of Mundt's novel is the depiction of Heinrich von Kleist's suicide: "So hat der Pistolenschuß des Werthers ihn selbst getroffen, dem Goethe durch diese Dichtung entgangen war" (Thus Werther's pistol shot, which Goethe escaped through his writing, hit him [Kleist] squarely). Unlike Johann Wolfgang von Goethe, Kleist was unable to write away his frustrations; according to Mundt, Kleist's subjective coldness represents a total surrender to Hegelianism. Comments of this kind prompted some critics to insist that Mundt did not understand Hegel at all.

Mundt's second book, *Die Einheit Deutschlands in politischer und ideeller Entwickelung* (The Unity of Germany in Its Political and Philosophical Development, 1832), inaugurates a major theme in his work: the myth of the German nation. An insistence that art, philosophy, and literature are expressions of the uniqueness of a people and a focus on the cultural artifacts that distinguish Germans from other nations run through his fiction and scholarship. For Mundt there would soon be no art but national art, no philosophy but the ideals of the nation.

Mundt's *Kritische Wälder* (Critical Woods, 1833) consists of previously published articles exploring the role of art in modern society. His basic argument is that Goethe's aristocratic era has come to an end; the contemporary world is republican. Therefore artists should promote democratic tendencies. Progress, he argues, can be made gradually, without the need for violent change. In the article "Kampf eines Hegelianers mit den Grazien" (The Struggle of a Hegelian with the Graces) Dr. Fürsich (Dr. For-himself) attempts to incorporate the Graces into Hegel's system. "Entsiehen Sie sich doch nicht länger den Begriff !" (Do not shun conceptualization any longer), he says, as he, like Hegel, postulates the supremacy of philosophical concepts over artistic expression. The Hegelian wins the battle but loses the war: he holds the field with his rigorous thinking but chases away the Graces, thereby implying that divine inspiration flees from Hegel's philosophy. Mundt argues that art provides a direct way of knowing that is superior to systematic thinking.

In the following two years Mundt produced three of his best-known works: the novel *Moderne Lebenswirren* (Modern Life's Entanglements, 1834); a tribute to Charlotte Stieglitz (1835); and a fictional depiction of a modern secular saint, *Madonna: Unterhaltungen mit einer Heiligen* (Madonna: Conversations with a Saint, 1835). The first purports to be the letters and posthumous papers of a salt-mine clerk named Seeliger, who writes to Esperance, a schoolteacher. Seeliger has great aspirations but is overwhelmed by the confusion and difficulties of modern life. He never learned a trade because he was busy writing twenty-three tragedies. The most-quoted line in the novel reflects the impact of the July 1830 revolution in Paris on German intellectual life: "Der Zeitgeist tut weh in mir, Esperance . . . ! Der Zeitgeist zuckt, dröhnt, zieht, wirbelt, und hambachert in mir." (The spirit of the times hurts inside of me, Esperance! . . . The spirit of the times winces, rumbles, drags, whirls, and "hambachs" in me). (The coined word *hambachert* refers to the meeting of liberal student fraternities, democrats, and revolutionaries at a castle in the town of Hambach in May 1832.) The novel soon turns into a satire of social conditions in Germany as Seeliger becomes an ardent supporter of such diametrically opposed movements as liberalism, absolutism, aristocracy, and democracy. He is thus a composite of political thinking in mid-nineteenth-century Germany, which, because of the many movements competing for attention, had become paralyzed. At the end of the novel nothing is decided; it is a sign of the times to hold no firm position at all. The most interesting character in the story is the diplomat Zodiacus, who supports Seeliger in each new position he takes. The name of this modern Mephistopheles appeared again in 1835 when Mundt established his journal *Literarischer Zodiacus.*

It has become commonplace to describe Charlotte Stieglitz as the woman who committed suicide to inspire her husband, Heinrich Stieglitz, a mediocre poet, to greatness. Mundt's private correspondence supports this view, but his *Charlotte Stieglitz: Ein Denkmal* (Charlotte Stieglitz: A Monument) tells a different story. There is no mention of Charlotte's suicide as an impetus to her husband's creativity; on the contrary, Mundt observes that she was "ein seltsames Kind" (a strange child) who was far too "ernsthaft" (serious) and "schwermütig" (depressed) and had been prone to suicide from an early age. At one point she wanted to die like Ottilie in Goethe's *Die Wahlverwandtschaften* (1809; translated as "Elective Affinities," 1854), so she tried to starve herself. Later she desired the death of the child, Otto, from the same novel and tried to drown herself. In brief, Mundt paints the picture of a manic-depressive who was suicidal before she met Heinrich Stieglitz. Her suicide note did not say that her death should serve as a literary theme or as an inspiration but that things would get better for her husband with her gone and that she wanted to set him free from the bonds of married life. Mundt sought to capture what he called "das schmerzende Wachstum der Seele in den begabtesten Naturen" (the painful growth of the soul in the most gifted people).

Mundt's best-known work is *Madonna: Unterhaltungen mit einer Heiligen.* These "Conversations with a Saint" are not meant to assist in the liberation of women from sexual inhibitions in order to make life less frustrating for men, as is often argued. Marie, a secular Madonna, achieves a glimpse of the divine in the fulfillment of her sexuality. A traveling narrator encounters Marie in a Bohemian village and asks her to write down the story of her life in exchange for letters about his travels. She tells of a childhood devoid of parental love and how an aunt took her in and gave her the best things in life, including a good education, fine clothes, and money. To her great humiliation she discovers that these things were provided by a rich count, who wished to prepare her to be his concubine. When the count attempts to seduce her, she is both attracted by his masculine prowess and repelled by his scheme. She almost yields to his advances but then flees to the room of the theology student Mellefont, who confides that he had suspected such a plot for some time. She spends the night with him and finds ultimate pleasure and gratification in lovemaking. He, on the other hand, is seized by overwhelming remorse for what he has "done" to this young woman and commits suicide. Thus he falls victim to a rigid and repressive societal code, while she represents the "violated" woman who enjoys neither internal nor external freedom in a bigoted society. Marie is a secular saint inasmuch as she finds human bonding to be her greatest blessing, giving and receiving love her ultimate fulfillment. Hence she represents the natural, truthful life; Mellefont, with his inhibited religiosity and crippling moral code, symbolizes destruction and demise. The ruling class in the German-speaking world would have none of this: by the end of 1835 both *Charlotte Stieglitz* and *Madonna* were banned throughout the German Confederation along with the other works of Junges Deutschland.

Mundt in the 1830s; lithograph by A. Biow

It was not the first time Mundt had experienced difficulties with censorship. In 1834 he had established a literary magazine, *Schriften in bunter Reihe* (Writings Paired Off), in Leipzig; the Saxon censors had proved troublesome, so the following year he had changed the name to *Literarischer Zodiacus: Journal für Zeit und Leben, Wissenschaft und Kunst* (Literary Zodiacus: Journal for Our Life and Times, Scholarship and Art). Once again, the censors impeded publication and distribution. To stay one step ahead of them he changed the title again the following year, this time to *Dioskuren für Wissenschaft und Kunst: Schriften in bunter Reihe* (Dioscuri for Scholarship and Art: Writings Paired Off). The word *Dioscuren* refers to Castor and Pollux, the twin sons of Zeus and Leda, intended here to represent Science and Art; the twins are also the patrons of those who struggle. This journal was published in Berlin, but it was as short-lived as the others. Mundt published little of his own work in these magazines; for example, he wrote only 69 of the 497 pages of the first issue of *Literarischer Zodiacus,* and 40 of these were an excerpt from his *Madonna.* Instead, he opened the pages to a wide range of topics and opinions.

The outright banning of his works by the German Confederation was much harsher than anything he had come to expect from the Prussian censors; he especially resented being lumped together with Gutzkow. He worked relentlessly to have the ban lifted, and within a few months he was free to publish in Prussia; but he had to submit all his manuscripts to the censor Wilhelm John, whose only credentials for the job appear to have been a few minor essays on the German theater, an antipathy to atheistic writing, and blind obedience to the Prussian authorities.

In the ensuing years Mundt divided his productivity between travelogues and scholarly works. His *Charaktere und Situationen* (Characters and Situations, 1837) and *Spaziergänge und Weltfahrten* (Walks and World Travels, 1838–1839) contain remarks about the people and places he saw on his travels throughout Europe, as well as observations on contemporary literature. He championed the cause of democracy and progressive social thinking; his masterful *Die Kunst der deutschen Prosa* (The Art of German Prose, 1837) analyzes the aesthetic and literary-historical dimensions of German prose in his day without neglecting the social implications. In the article "Heine, Börne und das sogenannte Junge Deutschland" (Heine, Börne and the So-called Young Germany, published in 1840) in his periodical *Die Freihafen* (The Freeport), Mundt distanced himself from the more radical pronouncements of Junges Deutschland, which, according to his account, did not really exist as a group. His most imposing scholarly work to his contemporaries was his *Geschichte der Literatur der Gegenwart* (History of Contemporary Literature, 1842), which summarizes the contributions of writers from thirteen countries. So impressed was the philosopher Friedrich Schelling with this work that he used his influence to secure Mundt a position as a private lecturer in the faculty of philosophy at the University of Berlin in 1842.

In 1839 Mundt married Clara Müller, who in the 1850s would become known for her massive historical novels published under the pseudonym Luise Mühlbach. She worked tirelessly for Mundt's exoneration and liberation from censorship, which he finally attained in 1842. The couple opened one of the more popular salons in Berlin; the literary historian Rudolf Gottschall, who read from his early works at the salon, remembered Mundt as a charming scholar who displayed an elegance and virtuosity lacking in Gutzkow or Laube. Mundt's wife was remembered as "eine Dame, so voluminös wie ihre Romane" (a lady as voluminous as her novels.)

On the eve of the March Revolution in 1848 Mundt was appointed professor of literature and history but transferred to the University of Breslau to keep him away from Berlin, the hotbed of political dissent. In 1850 he returned to the Prussian capital, where he briefly resumed lecturing until his appointment as university librarian.

During the 1840s and 1850s Mundt's literary output was astonishing. His subjects ranged from the evolution of German society to aesthetics and historical personalities. He wrote *Carmela* (1844), a novel about the Baptists; twelve chapters on the Holy Ghost in contemporary society (1845); a description of the gods of antiquity (1846); a catechism of politics (1848); and biographies of Count Alessandrodi Cagliostro (1858), Honoré-Gabriel Riqueti; Comte de Mirabeau (1858), and Maximilien Robespierre (1859). The last of these books contains graphic descriptions of the beheading of Louis XVI and of Robespierre.

From the vantage point of the twentieth century, Mundt's historical novel *Thomas Müntzer* (1841) appears prophetic. It focuses on the sharp differences between the revolutionary pastor Müntzer and Martin Luther and on the plight of the peasants in the sixteenth century; but, according to Mundt, the novel deals with the contemporary political scene as much as with the Reformation because the condition of the peasantry had not changed significantly in three hundred years. Mundt concludes that a violent uprising will fail; he calls for compromise rather than an insurrection that will result in a bloodbath; he shows how quickly revolutionary leaders succumb to hubris. Mundt wanted the genre of the novel to become a forum in which national issues were aired and education took place; for him the novel was a major instrument for producing political change through persuasion instead of force.

Recent attention has focused on Mundt's alleged anti-Semitism: among his otherwise positive remarks about Heine are certain formulations that were ill conceived and influenced by stereotypical thinking. Yet in the October 1835 issue of his *Literarischer Zodiacus* he reports on an incident in a Hamburg coffeehouse that resulted in the forceful expulsion of Jewish patrons; the owners then converted the coffeehouse into a private club and barred all Jews. Mundt speaks out against such discrimination and sympathizes with those who were "gekränkt" (insulted) by the owners. In the December issue he published a lengthy account of the incident by his Jewish friend Gabriel Rießer.

The last years of Mundt's life were filled with disappointment and frustration. What was initially to be a temporary suspension at half pay from his position as university librarian dragged on. Contemporaries found *Thomas Müntzer* disappointing. Under attack by liberals for "intellectualizing" and by reactionaries for his democratic views, by newspaper critics and academics alike, Mundt died in Berlin on 30 November 1861 without receiving the recognition he was due for his copious literary and journalistic production.

References:

Edgar Crowthen Cumings, *Woman in the Life and Work of Theodor Mundt* (Chicago: University of Chicago Press, 1936);

Walter Dietze, "Theodor Mundt und Gustav Kühne," in his *Junges Deutschland und deutsche Klassik* (Berlin: Rütten & Loening, 1957), pp. 91-96;

Otto Draeger, *Theodor Mundt und seine Beziehungen zum Jungen Deutschland* (Marburg: Elwert, 1909);

Annemarie Gethmann-Siefert, "Hegelisches gegen Hegel: Zu Theodor Mundts antihegelschen Entwurf einer Ästhetik," *Hegel-Studien,* 15 (1980): 271-278;

Rudolph Gottschall, "Die Führer des jungen Deutschlands," *Neue Revue,* 1 (1907): 435–436;

Jost Hermand, *Von Mainz nach Weimar* (Stuttgart: Metzler, 1969);

Heinrich Hubert Houben, *Verbotene Literatur von der klassischen Zeit bis zur Gegenwart,* 2 volumes (Berlin: Rowohlt, 1922);

Hans Joachim Kertscher, "Das Bild Thomas Müntzers in den Müntzer-Romanen von Theodor Mundt und Ludwig Köhler," *Wissenschaftliche Zeitschrift der Universität Halle,* 39 (1990): 17–25;

Helmut Kind, *Das Zeitalter der Reformation im historischen Roman der Jungdeutschen* (Göttingen: Vandenhoeck & Ruprecht, 1969);

Hugo von Kleinmayer, *Welt- und Kunstanschauung des jungen Deutschland: Studien zur Geistesgeschichte des XIX. Jahrhunderts* (Vienna & Leipzig: Österreichischer Bundesverlag, 1930);

Hans Knudsen, "Theodor Mundt und Karl Gutzkow," *Euphorion,* 24 (1922): 424–436;

Helmut Koopmann, *Das junge Deutschland* (Stuttgart: Metzler, 1970);

Udo Köster, *Literarischer Radikalismus: Zeitbewußtsein und Geschichtsphilosophie in der Entwicklung vom Jungen Deutschland zur Hegelischen Linken* (Frankfurt am Main: Athenäum, 1972);

Marsha Meyer, "The Depiction of Women in Gutzkow's *Wally die Zweiflerin* and Mundt's *Madonna,*" in *Beyond the Eternal Feminine: Critical Essays on Women in German Literature,* edited by Susan L. Cocalis and Kay Goodman (Stuttgart: Heinz, 1982), pp. 135–138;

Ernst Ulrich Pinkert, " 'Noch Nicht' und 'Doch schon': Theodor Mundts Roman *Thomas Münzer,*" *Der Ginkobaum,* 2 (1983): 59–75;

Hanna Quadfasel, *Theodor Mundts literarische Kritik und die Prinzipien seiner Ästhetik* (Bruchsal: Kruse, 1932);

Jeffrey L. Sammons, "Theodor Mundt: A Revaluation," in his *Six Essays on the Young German Novel* (Chapel Hill: University of North Carolina Press, 1972), pp. 52–80;

Mark Joel Webber, "The Concept of Organic Growth in Young Germany (Laube, Mundt, Wienbarg)," Ph.D. dissertation, Yale University, 1976;

Feodor von Wehl, *Das junge Deutschland* (Hamburg: Richter, 1886);

Hermann F. Weiss, " 'Eine fortwährende Kriegsführung': Zum literarischen Schaffen Theodor Mundts nach 1835," *Jahrbuch des Wiener Goethe Vereins,* 81 (1983): 291–307.

Papers:

A large collection of Theodor Mundt's papers is at the Deutsches Literaturarchiv in Marbach. Twelve letters are in the manuscript collection at the University of Leipzig. Files on Mundt kept by the Prussian Ministry of the Interior are at the Deutsches Zentralarchiv, Merseburg.

Johann Nestroy

(7 December 1801 – 25 May 1862)

Craig Decker
Bates College

Johann Nestroy circa 1860 (photograph by Hermann Klee)

BOOKS: *Der böse Geist Lumpacivagabundus oder Das liederliche Kleeblatt: Zauberposse mit Gesang in drei Aufzügen,* music by Adolf Müller (Vienna: Wallishausser, 1835);

Zu ebener Erde und erster Stock oder Die Launen des Glückes: Lokalposse mit Gesang in drei Aufzügen, music by Müller (Vienna: Wallishausser, 1838);

Eulenspiegel oder Schabernack über Schabernack: Posse mit Gesang in vier Akten, music by Müller (Vienna: Wallishausser, 1841);

Die verhängnißvolle Faschingsnacht: Posse mit Gesang in drei Aufzügen, music by Müller (Vienna: Wallishausser, 1842);

Der Talisman: Posse mit Gesang in drei Akten, music by Müller (Vienna: Wallishausser, 1843); translated by Max Knight and Joseph Fabry as *The Talisman,* in *Johann Nestroy: Three Comedies* (New York: Ungar, 1967);

Einen Jux will er sich machen: Posse mit Gesang in vier Aufzügen, music by Müller (Vienna: Wallishausser, 1844); translated anonymously as *The Matchmaker: A Farce in Four Acts* (New York: French, 1957);

Glück, Mißbrauch und Rückkehr oder Das Geheimniß des grauen Hauses: Posse in fünf Aufzügen, music by Müller (Vienna: Wallishausser, 1845);

Das Mädl aus der Vorstadt oder Ehrlich währt am längsten: Posse in drei Aufzügen, music by Müller (Vienna: Wallishausser, 1845);

Der Zerissene: Posse mit Gesang in drei Akten, music by Müller (Vienna: Wallishausser, 1845); translated by Knight and Fabry as *A Man Full of Nothing,* in *Johann Nestroy: Three Comedies;*

Unverhofft: Posse mit Gesang in drei Acten, music by Müller (Vienna: Wallishausser, 1848);

Freiheit in Krähwinkel: Posse mit Gesang in zwei Abtheilungen und drei Akten, music by Michael Hebenstreit (Vienna: Wallishausser, 1849);

Der Unbedeutende: Posse mit Gesang in drei Akten, music by Müller (Vienna: Wallishausser, 1849);

Mein Freund: Posse mit Gesang in drei Akten, music by J. C. Stenzel (Vienna: Lell, 1851);

Kampl oder Das Mädchen mit den Millionen und die Nähterin: Posse mit Gesang in vier Akten, music by Müller (Vienna: Prix, 1852);

Hinüber – Herüber; Hinüber – Herüber: Intermezzo nach einer Anekdote (Berlin: Kolbe, 1852);

Theaterg'schichten durch Liebe, Intrigue, Geld und Dummheit: Posse mit Gesang in zwei Akten (Vienna: Klopf & Eurich, 1854);

Tannhäuser: Zukunftsposse mit vergangener Musik und gegenwärtigen Gruppierungen in drei Akten, anonymous, music by K. Binder (Vienna: Wallishausser, 1857);

Gesammelte Werke, 12 volumes, edited by Vincenz Chiavacci and Ludwig Ganghofer (Stuttgart: Bonz, 1890–1891);

Der Färber und sein Zwillingsbruder (Berlin & Leipzig: Fried, 1893);

Werke, 2 volumes, edited by Leopold Rosner (Berlin: Knaur, 1903);

Frühere Verhältnisse, edited by Carl Friedrich Wittmann (Leipzig: Reclam, 1905);

Werke, edited by Otto Rommel (Berlin: Bong, 1908);

Zwei unbekannte Manuskripte Nestroys, edited by Fritz Brukner (Vienna: Knepler, 1910) – comprises *Der Zettelträger Papp, Moppels Abenteuer*;

Ausgewählte Werke, edited by Brukner (Leipzig: Hesse & Becker, 1910);

Nur keck, edited by Peter Sturmbusch (Vienna, Berlin & Leipzig: Interterritorialer Verlag "Renaissance," 1923);

Sämtliche Werke: Historisch-kritische Gesamtausgabe, 15 volumes, edited by Brukner and Rommel (Vienna: Schroll, 1924–1930);

Ausgewählte Werke, edited by Franz H. Mautner (Vienna: Lorenz, 1938);

Unbekannter Nestroy, edited by Gustav Pichler (Vienna: Frick, 1953);

Werke, edited by Oskar Maurus Fontana (Munich: Winkler, 1962);

Werke, 2 volumes, edited by Paul Reimann and Hans Böhm (Weimar: Volksverlag Weimar, 1962);

Die schlimmen Buben in der Schule, edited by Pichler (Vienna: Bergland, 1963);

Das Haus der Temperamente, edited by Pichler (Vienna: Bergland, 1965); translated by Robert Harrison and Katharina Wilson as *The House of Humors*, in *Johann Nestroy: Three Viennese Comedies* (Columbia, S.C.: Camden House, 1986);

Die Verbannung aus dem Zauberreich oder Dreißig Jahre aus dem Leben eines Lumpen, edited by Pichler (Vienna: Bergland, 1966);

Sämtliche Werke: Historisch-kritische Gesamtausgabe, 35 volumes projected, 13 volumes published, edited by Jürgen Hein and Johann Hüttner (Vienna & Munich: Jugend und Volk, 1979–).

One frequently encounters the argument that Johann Nestroy's plays do not travel well. Their critical examination of sociopolitical conditions and events in the Hapsburg Empire in the mid nineteenth century, their profuse allusions to theatrical culture in Vienna at the time, and – Nestroy's critics maintain – especially their abundant and ingenious use of a presumably prototypical and highly nuanced Viennese dialect supposedly limit the plays' breadth of appeal and their longevity. Although Nestroy's contemporaries celebrated his acting and writing abilities, elevating his work on and for the stage to legendary proportions, subsequent generations of authors, actors, and audiences allegedly find it increasingly difficult to understand and appreciate his unique talents and accomplishments. To be sure, Nestroy's eighty-three dramas are intricately tied to the political and cultural milieu of mid-nineteenth-century Vienna. Yet despite the unmistakable role that Vienna played in his life and work, Nestroy's career as an actor and author, as well as his continuing impact on the twentieth-century theater, reveal a substantial degree of international success and influence. The extent of that success, and its intriguing mix of indigenous and international ingredients, has been concisely formulated in two epithets: Nestroy has been called the "Viennese Shakespeare" as well as the "Austrian Aristophanes."

Nestroy's theatrical triumphs in Vienna led to repeated and highly acclaimed guest appearances in such cities as Prague, Preßburg, Pest, Ofen, and Graz. His success on these stages, in turn, resulted in invitations and well-received performances far beyond the borders of the Hapsburg Empire. He captivated audiences in many German cities, including Berlin, Hamburg, Hannover, Frankfurt am Main, Mainz, and Munich. Indeed, his reputation within the German-language theater was so great and the audience response so positive that when he was first invited to perform at the Königstädter Theater in Berlin in 1844, one of the theater's principal actors attempted to prevent Nestroy's appearance in the Prussian capital.

Friedrich Beckmann, a Berlin comic actor who had performed with Nestroy at the Theater an der Wien in 1842, knew well Nestroy's effect on an audience. Thus, when he learned that Nestroy had been invited to Berlin, Beckmann wrote anonymously to the king of Prussia, urging the monarch to prohibit Nestroy from performing in the city and to invite Nestroy's Viennese colleague Wenzel Scholz instead. Nestroy's satiric wit, Beckmann wrote, would surely poison the morality of the Prus-

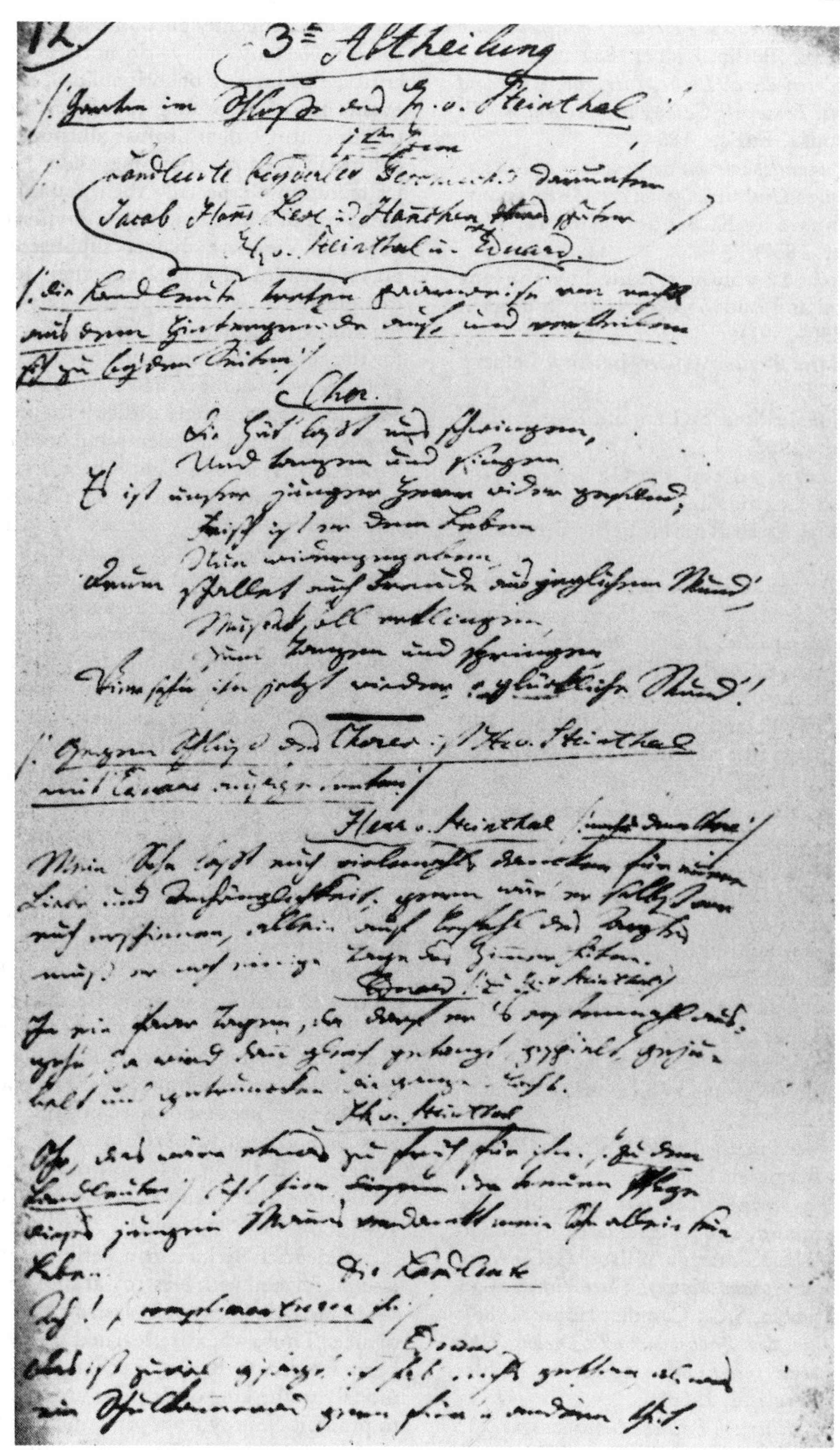

Page from the manuscript for an early play by Nestroy, Die Gleichheit der Jahre, *written in 1833 (Wiener Stadtbibliothek)*

sian audience, while his frequent extemporaneous asides could have dangerous political effects. Beckmann was by no means alone in his reservation about Nestroy's methods and messages: colleagues and critics have called Nestroy the "Napoleon of vulgarity," the "Mephistopheles of popular comedy," and a "messenger from hell." In the end, however, Beckmann could not prevent Nestroy's appearance in Berlin, and in August 1844 Nestroy enjoyed a highly successful month at the Königstädter Theater – the first of his many guest appearances in the Prussian capital.

Despite the seemingly Vienna-bound characteristics of his plays, they, like their author, have traveled extensively. Today Nestroy's dramas form part of the standard repertoire of theaters in Austria, Germany, and German-speaking Switzerland, and they have exerted considerable influence on such major twentieth-century dramatists as Bertolt Brecht, Ödön von Horváth, Friedrich Dürrenmatt, and Peter Turrini. Although few of Nestroy's plays have been translated into English, he has had a direct impact on the English-language theater. His *Einen Jux will er sich machen* (He Wants to Have a Lark, 1844), which premiered in Vienna in March 1842, has been adapted by two prominent playwrights on both sides of the Atlantic. *The Merchant of Yonkers,* which premiered in Boston on 12 December 1938 under the direction of the exiled Viennese director Max Reinhardt, is Thornton Wilder's adaptation of Nestroy's play. Wilder subsequently retitled the drama, which premiered as *The Matchmaker* in Scotland in 1954. *The Matchmaker,* in turn, provided the basis for the stage and film versions of *Hello, Dolly!,* which have been as popular with American audiences as *Einen Jux will er sich machen* was in Nestroy's Vienna. Tom Stoppard's adaptation of the play, *On the Razzle,* appeared in print in 1982.

Johann Nepomuk Eduard Ambrosius Nestroy was born in Vienna on 7 December 1801 to Johann and Magdalena (Constantin) Nestroy, whose first child, Carl Ludwig Corbinian, had been born one year earlier. Magdalena Nestroy bore a total of eight children, three of whom died young. The oldest surviving daughter, Franziska Romana Barbara, born in 1803, also had theatrical aspirations; while she never attained the phenomenal level of success her brother enjoyed, she sang in operas throughout the empire. Her affinity to her brother is perhaps best evidenced in the name she gave her daughter, born in 1823: Johanna Nepomucena Julie Josefa Hoffman. Eventually Johanna Nepomucena would perform with her uncle on the stages of Vienna's popular theaters, most often in parts he wrote especially for her.

Nestroy's father had been born in what is currently part of the Czech Republic, a territory known as Austria-Silesia at the time of his birth. The family name was originally *Nestrui,* a word that in the local dialect has the unfortunate connotation of "good-for-nothing." Perhaps to avoid such a fate the elder Johann Nestroy had moved to Vienna, completed his study of law, became a court attorney, and married Magdalena Constantin, whose family had lived in Vienna for many generations.

From 1811 to 1813 Nestroy attended the Akademisches Gymnasium in Vienna, an institution whose student body consisted of the sons of the aristocracy and the upper middle class. He then transferred to the Gymnasium der Schotten (Scottish Grammar School), where he finished his secondary studies in 1816. His grades were initially excellent; he was considered a particularly disciplined student, and his accomplishments in Latin and Greek were especially noteworthy. Toward the end of his secondary schooling, however, his grades became increasingly less exemplary. Two occurrences may help to explain Nestroy's downward academic trend: Magdalena Nestroy contracted the "Viennese disease," pulmonary tuberculosis, which caused her death on 15 April 1814 at thirty-five years of age. In the same year Nestroy began piano and voice lessons, his devotion to which may have interfered with his academic studies.

In 1817 Nestroy entered the University of Vienna. After completing the required series of three courses in philosophy he matriculated in 1820 as a student of law. In addition to jurisprudence, Nestroy took classes in poetics and rhetoric. His study of law lasted only two semesters; as of 1822 Nestroy's name no longer appears in the university's records. Where those records do refer to Nestroy, they contain such adjectives as "unruhig" (restless), "minder aufmerksam" (inattentive), and "sehr oft abwesend" (very often absent).

During this time Nestroy was actively involved with Viennese musical and theatrical life. He was intent on a career as an opera singer, and his initial appearances on the stage were in singing roles. On 8 December 1818 he debuted at Vienna's Imperial Palace, singing the bass aria from George Frideric Handel's *Alexander's Feast* (1736). The seventeen-year-old's performance was so impressive that he was asked to repeat it the following evening. On 24 August 1822 he sang for the first time in one of Vienna's major theaters, performing the role of Sarastro in Wolfgang Amadeus Mozart's *Die*

Pencil sketch by Franz Gaul of the premiere of Nestroy's Der böse Geist Lumpacivagabundus *in Vienna in 1833. At the far left is Nestroy in the role of Knierem (from Robert Mühler, ed.,* Dichtung aus Österreich, *1969).*

Zauberflöte (The Magic Flute, 1791) at the Theater am Kärntnertor. His theatrical debut received favorable reviews, and on 8 October he signed a two-year contract with the Theater am Kärntnertor. In his first year there he made fifty-six appearances, including roles in Ludwig van Beethoven's opera *Fidelio* (1805) and Gioacchino Rossini's *Otello* (1816).

Although Nestroy was performing professionally, he was also involved with Vienna's amateur stages. There was an abundance of lay theaters in the city, located in private residences. Nestroy became particularly active in the theater in the home of Franz Wilhelm Zwettlinger. There, in 1822, Nestroy met Zwettlinger's stepdaughter, Wilhelmine Philippine Nespiesni. Nespiesni, born on 12 May 1804, had played a variety of roles on the city's amateur stages. She and Nestroy soon decided to marry, but financial concerns caused them to delay their wedding.

Nestroy made his final appearance at the Theater am Kärntnertor on 29 August 1823. He broke his contract with the theater because he had negotiated a more financially advantageous agreement with the Deutsches Theater in Amsterdam. With their financial constraints lessened, Nestroy and Nespiesni were married on 7 September 1823. Two days later they departed for Amsterdam.

On his arrival at the Deutsches Theater, Nestroy's theatrical repertoire consisted of ten operatic roles. By the time of his departure from the city two years later, that number had increased to fifty-two. He debuted at the Deutsches Theater on 18 October 1823 in the role of Kaspar in Carl Maria von Weber's *Der Freischütz* (The Shooting Match, 1821). In Amsterdam, Nestroy also acted in nonmusical theater – nine roles in all – but he considered himself a singer and a pianist. On 9 June 1824, one and one-half months after the birth of his first son, Gustav, Nestroy's contract was renewed with a considerable raise in salary. He remained with the theater until it closed on 15 August 1825, two days after his final performance on its stage.

While under contract to the theater, Nestroy's performances included roles in Rossini's *Tancredi* (1813), *Otello,* and *La cenerentola* (Cinderella, 1817) and Mozart's *La clemenza di Tito* (1791), *Die Entführung aus dem Serail* (The Abduction from the Seraglio, 1782), and *Die Zauberflöte* – this time in the role of Papageno, a part that seemed much more suited to his temperament and talents. In Amsterdam he first appeared as the barber's apprentice

Adam in Johann Schenk's comic opera *Der Dorfbarbier* (The Village Barber, 1796); he would play this part repeatedly throughout his career, doing so for the last time in 1858.

While Nestroy became increasingly involved with comic opera in Amsterdam, it was there that his first professional performance in a popular comedy occurred – a performance that appears, in retrospect, particularly important for his development both as an actor and as a playwright. On 31 December 1823 he appeared in *Die falsche Primadonna* (The False Prima Donna, 1818) by Adolf Bäuerle. Bäuerle was one of the most prolific Viennese authors of the Volksstück, a term literally – and somewhat misleadingly – translated as *folk play*. *Popular drama* seems a much more accurate translation, since it incorporates the notion that the plays address the masses as both subject and audience. Authors such as Bäuerle, Karl Friedrich Hensler, Josef Alois Gleich, Karl Meisl, and Ferdinand Jakob Raimund helped establish the Volksstück as a popular dramatic form in the late eighteenth and early nineteenth centuries. Nestroy would extend and radicalize the genre, transforming the Volksstück into a profoundly democratic – indeed revolutionary – form of theater.

After the closing of the Deutsches Theater, Nestroy signed a contract with the Nationaltheater in Brünn (today Brno, Czech Republic). The initial terms of the contract stipulated four guest appearances, but Nestroy's debut in Brünn proved so successful that the contract was quickly converted into a long-term agreement. While his salary in Brünn did not equal what he had earned in Amsterdam, the stage there was considered an important theatrical springboard to Vienna.

Although Nestroy continued to consider himself first and foremost an opera singer – his roles in Brünn included Figaro in both Mozart's *Le Nozze di Figaro* (The Marriage of Figaro, 1786) and Rossini's *Il barbiere di Siviglia* (The Barber of Seville, 1816) and the title role in Mozart's *Don Giovanni* (1787) – he furthered his transition from singer to actor at this time. His first dramatic role in Brünn was in *Stille Größe* (Quiet Greatness, 1824), by Therese von Artner, followed by performances in Friedrich Schiller's *Wilhelm Tell* (1804; translated as *William Tell*, 1829), August Wilhelm Iffland's *Die Spieler* (The Gamblers, 1798), and Theodor Körner's *Rosamunde* (1815; translated as *Rosamond*, 1830). Perhaps more important, his performances in Brünn included an increasing number of roles in Volksstücke, most often in plays by Bäuerle, Hensler, and Gleich.

Authors and actors in the Austro-Hungarian Empire faced a particularly harsh state censorship.

Nestroy as Knierem in a late performance of Der böse Geist Lumpacivagabundus

The range of theatrical discourses and activities subject to censorship, as well as the punishments accorded to violators, were far more severe in nineteenth-century Austria than in the neighboring German territories. Before a drama could be staged, the censor had to approve of its morality and language. The regulations were so strict and their implementation so mechanical that words such as *Aufklärung* (enlightenment), *Freiheit* (freedom), *Gleichberechtigung* (equality), and *Bruderschaft* (brotherhood) were automatically struck from a text regardless of their context. Accordingly, the line from Mozart's *Don Giovanni*, "Es lebe die Freiheit!" (Long live freedom!), became at the hands of the imperial censor "Es lebe die Fröhlichkeit!" (Long live joyfulness!).

In addition to the regulations concerning written texts, the censors, in concert with the imperial police, oversaw the enforcement of an extensive series of rules regarding theatrical performance. Of major consequence to Nestroy throughout his acting career was the strict prohibition of any form of dramatic extemporization: the performance of a drama could not vary even slightly from the written text approved by the authorities; any deviation could lead to formidable consequences. In Brünn, Nestroy experienced the drastic measures authorities were willing to take if an actor challenged the rules concerning theatrical form and content. On 4 December 1825, following a performance in the role of Adam in *Der Dorfbarbier,* he was summoned before the authorities and reprimanded for his extemporizations. Seven days later he was again charged with violating the laws of theatrical conduct, this time in connection with a performance of Hensler's *Die Teufelsmühle am Wiener Berge* (The Devil's Mill on the Viennese Mountain, 1800). During the performance Nestroy had become so disgusted by hissing from the audience that he purposely played the third act poorly and virtually inaudibly. Although he played the final act audibly and with consummate skill, eliciting hearty applause, he was charged with disdainful behavior toward his audience. The offense resulted in his arrest at nine o'clock the following morning. Subsequent to his incarceration Nestroy's performances were closely monitored by the police, who repeatedly warned him about his extemporizations. He ignored the warnings and insisted that extemporizing was essential to his roles. The tensions between Nestroy and the censors escalated, and on 18 April 1826 he was again called before the police. When he adamantly refused to stop extemporizing, the authorities annulled his contract, even though it had eleven months remaining. On 30 April the police forced Nestroy to leave Brünn.

In the year following his departure from Brünn, during which he was under contract to theaters in Graz and Preßburg, Nestroy's wife left him and their son for an affair with Count Adalbert Batthyány of Graz. While Johann and Wilhelmine Nestroy never reconciled, they were not divorced until 15 February 1845. Although Nestroy's marriage dissolved in Graz, it was also there that, one year later, he met Marie Weiler, a singer whose real name was Marie Lacher. Nestroy and Weiler would become not only stage partners – Nestroy wrote twenty-two roles for her – but long-term lovers as well. They were never able to marry: imperial Austria did not permit civil ceremonies, and the Catholic church refused to marry Nestroy because of his divorce. Despite some particularly stormy periods resulting from Nestroy's affairs with other women, he and Weiler remained together until his death. In addition to rearing Gustav Nestroy, the couple had two children of their own: Carl Anton Johann in 1831 and Maria Cäcilia nine years later.

On his arrival in Graz in 1826 Nestroy's acting repertoire included five Volksstück roles; when he left five years later he had increased that number to eighty-five. These parts included two that would become staples of his stage career: the umbrella maker Chrysostomus Staberl in Bäuerle's *Die Bürger von Wien* (The Burghers of Vienna, 1813) and the one-eyed soldier Sansquartier in Louis Angely's *Sieben Mädchen in Uniform* (Seven Girls in Uniform, 1825). Sansquartier was to become Nestroy's second most frequently played part: he would perform the role 256 times.

Nestroy premiered in the role of Sansquartier on 15 December 1827; preceding the production of *Sieben Mädchen in Uniform* that evening, Nestroy's one-act drama *Der Zettelträger Papp* (The Playbill Carrier Papp, 1910) premiered, marking the first time that Nestroy's name appeared on a theater program as an author. Characteristically for Nestroy, *Der Zettelträger Papp* is a satire; the target is ostensibly the theater. The theater in the play, however, functions as a metaphor for the larger sociopolitical context within which the theater exists. *Der Zettelträger Papp* is also a typical Nestroy product in that it is not an entirely "original" play but is loosely based on another source: virtually all of his eighty-three dramas are localized adaptations of existing texts. Nestroy used French, English, German, Austrian, and Hungarian plays, novels, and short stories as the bases for his Volksstücke. He largely retained the plots but changed dialogues, motives, locales, and the functions of the characters. *Der Zettelträger Papp* has as its source an 1822 work by Nestroy's Volksstück colleague Raimund, who, in turn, had based his text on the farce *Die Heirat durch die Pferdekomödie* (Marriage by Means of the Horse Comedy), by Hermann Herzenkron.

While under contract to the theaters in Graz and Preßburg, Nestroy made guest appearances on stages throughout the Hapsburg Empire. During one such appearance in Vienna from 4 to 22 August 1829 he made his Viennese debut as a dramatist. On 18 August his *Der Tod am Hochzeitstage oder Mann, Frau, Kind* (Death on the Wedding Day; or, Man, Woman, Child) premiered at the Theater in der Josefstadt, with Nestroy playing the role of Herr von Dappschädl. The Theater in der Josefstadt, founded in 1788, was one of the three prominent Viennese Volkstheater (popular theaters [in Ger-

Nestroy (oil painting by an unknown artist; collection of Ingo Nebehay)

man, the singular and plural for *Volkstheater* are the same; they are distinguished by the preceding article of speech]) that emerged in the late eighteenth century. Like the Theater in der Leopoldstadt, established in 1781, and the Theater an der Wien, founded in 1787 as the Theater auf der Wieden and renamed in 1801, the Theater in der Josefstadt was located on the outskirts of the city; hence, the term *Vorstadttheater* (suburban theater) was used along with *Volkstheater* to refer to these institutions.

The Viennese Volkstheater differed from the Hofburgtheater (known as the Burgtheater after 1918) not only in location but also in theatrical fare, cultural function, and spectator response. The Hofburgtheater was in the city center, a location attesting to its status as the institutionalized theater of the feudal aristocracy. The monarchy strictly controlled the selection as well as the performance of Hofburgtheater plays, since such productions were intended to glorify both art and the imperial rulers. Accordingly, plays catering and flattering to the tastes of the upper class formed the vast majority of Hofburgtheater offerings. In contrast to the classical repertoire of the Hofburgtheater, the Volkstheater presented plays with more topical and local appeal. As an independent alternative to the theatrical politics of the Burgtheater, the Volkstheater provided an opportunity for Vienna's nonaristocratic populace to become a meaningful part of the city's cultural life. The Viennese lower classes eagerly attended Volkstheater performances, in large part because such productions presented the concerns of the masses in accessible and uncondescending ways. Whereas the Hofburgtheater primarily served as a holy, imperial temple to high art, the Volkstheater functioned as a lively public forum for the presentation and discussion of pressing sociopolitical questions.

Following Nestroy's second guest appearance at the Theater in der Josefstadt in March 1831 the theater's director, Karl Carl, offered him a contract. Carl, born Karl Andreas Bernbrunn in 1787 in

Nestroy as Titus Feuerfuchs in his play Der Talisman; *oil painting by Gaul (from Robert Mühler, ed.,* Dichtung aus Österreich, *1969)*

Kraków, had begun his career as a comic actor. While he continued to act, he achieved his fame primarily as the most successful – and most notorious – nineteenth-century Volkstheater director. At one point Carl directed both the Theater in der Josefstadt and the Theater an der Wien, using his positions to force actors and authors to submit to particularly harsh working conditions. Carl's contracts with playwrights demanded that they create an inordinate number of dramas per year; contracts with actors provided that if they left his employ they could not work at another Viennese Volkstheater for the next eighteen months. Since no actor could afford to be out of work for so long, he or she was forced to remain Carl's employee. Carl intended to seize control of all three Viennese Volkstheater; but when he attempted to assume the directorship of the Theater in der Leopoldstadt theater fans, fearing his total monopolization of the city's popular theaters, successfully petitioned the government to prohibit Carl from extending his already great power. (In 1838 he would buy the Theater in der Leopoldstadt, which he would tear down and rebuild in 1847 as the Carl-Theater.)

On 23 August 1831 Nestroy signed a contract with Carl. The terms of Nestroy's employment were far better than those affecting most of Carl's personnel, due largely to Weiler's skill as a negotiator and to Nestroy's simultaneous entrance into negotiations with the Theater am Kärntnertor in an attempt to find the most equitable working conditions. His theatrical success to this point afforded him a considerable amount of leverage, and Carl was far too astute to allow the multitalented Nestroy to work for another theater. Nestroy's debut at the Theater an der Wien marked the beginning of a highly profitable and mutually beneficial twenty-three-year collaboration that lasted until Carl's death, at which point Nestroy became director of the theater.

The first new play by Nestroy staged at the Theater an der Wien, a Volksstück titled *Der gefühlvolle Kerkermeister oder Adelheid, der verfolgte Witib* (The Sentimental Jailer; or, Adelheid, the Persecuted Widow, published in volume 10 of Nestroy's *Gesammelte Werke* [collected works], 1890–1891), premiered on 7 February 1832. To underscore the satiric and spectacular dimensions of the drama Nestroy appended an explanation to the play's title: "Gesprochene und gesungene Parodie eines getanzten Dramas mit Verwandlungen, Gruppierungen, Äußerungen, Mutmaßungen, Einsperrungen, Entführungen, Malträtierungen, Rettungen, Dingsda und allem Erdenklichen, was Sie sich selbst wünschen, in drei Akten" (a spoken and sung parody of a danced drama with groupings, transformations, declarations, speculations, arrests, abductions, maltreatment, deliverance, thingamajig, and everything that you can imaginably long for in three acts).

On 11 April 1833 one of Nestroy's most enduringly popular dramas, *Der böse Geist Lumpacivagabundus oder Das liederliche Kleeblatt* (The Evil Spirit Lumpacivagabundus; or, The Slovenly Threesome, 1835), premiered at the Theater an der Wien. The play, which Nestroy designated a *Zauberposse mit Gesang in drei Aufzügen* (a magical farce with music and song in three acts), is loosely based on Karl Weisflog's "Das große Los" (The Big Ticket, 1827), a story that appeared in Weisflog's anthology *Phantasiestücke und Historien* (Imaginary Pieces and Stories, 1824–1829). *Der böse Geist Lumpacivagabundus* (spelled *Lumpazivagabundus* in later editions) chronicles the fortunes and misfortunes of Leim, a joiner (his name means glue in German); Zwirn (the German word for thread), a tailor; and Knieriem (his name means shoemaker's stirrup), a cobbler. The play premiered with Carl in the role of Leim, Nestroy's short and squat friend Scholz as Zwirn, and the long and lean Nestroy starring as Knieriem. Knieriem would become Nestroy's most frequently played part: he assumed the role 258 times.

In a manner typical of the early-nineteenth-century Volksstück, the adventures of Leim, Zwirn, and Knieriem are framed by a supernatural series of events. The play begins in the realm of spirits and fairies who, like their mortal counterparts, are engaged in a struggle between good and evil. The evil spirit Lumpacivagabundus has taken control of certain fairies' children, who consequently only want to drink and make love. The parents beseech Stellaris, king of the fairies, to negate the evil spirit's powers. One of the children, Mystifax's son Hilaris, has fallen in love with Brillantine, the daughter of Fortuna, the mistress of good fortune. To determine whether the forces of good or evil will ultimately have the upper hand, Fortuna proposes a test: she will choose three poor mortals and will shower them with riches; should any of them squander the money, as Lumpacivagabundus predicts they will, Fortuna will allow Hilaris to marry her daughter. Neither the prospective couple nor the majority of supernatural beings believes that the wedding will ever occur; they are convinced that the humans will respond to their good fortune with gratitude and moderation. Fearing the prospect of future privation, Fortuna contends, will cause the lumpen to save their money wisely. While Leim, Zwirn, and Knieriem are asleep, Fortuna appears in their dreams and presents them with the winning lottery number. The journeymen's sudden wealth provides them with the means to enter and attain happiness within bourgeois society, a precept central to the traditional Viennese Besserungsstück (drama of improvement). The subsequent actions of the lumpen, however, serve to criticize the course of events typical of a Besserungstück as well as the sociopolitical ideology underlying the genre. Zwirn and Knieriem, true to Lumpacivagabundus's predictions, squander their money on alcohol and women, gratifying their immediate physical desires and challenging accepted codes of social behavior. A year later the two are as poor and ragged as they were at the beginning of the play. Leim, however, uses his newfound economic resources to integrate himself into the bourgeois social order. He marries his long-desired Peppi and establishes a stable household and a productive joinery. Consequently, Fortuna must admit defeat.

Nestroy in 1839; lithograph by Joseph Kriehuber

Der böse Geist Lumpacivagabundus undermines prevalent conventions of the nineteenth-century Volksstück on several levels. In a traditional Besserungsstück, such as Raimund's *Der Alpenkönig und der Menschenfeind* (The Alpine King and the Misanthrope, 1837; translated as *The King of the Alps,* 1852), the supernatural realm is totally superior to the mortal world. Benevolent fairies and spirits descend to Earth and manipulate the mortals to positive ends. In *Der böse Geist Lumpacivagabundus,* however, the forces of good prove no more effective than those of their adversary. Although Amorosa, the protectress of true love, ultimately experiences a victory, she must share her triumph with Lumpacivagabundus. Furthermore, the human beings in Nestroy's play also take part in the process formerly restricted to supernatural figures. Toward the end of the play Leim offers to provide his friends with the economic resources necessary for the improvement of their social position. They flatly refuse his offer, subverting both the means and the morals of a traditional Besserungsstück. Zwirn's and Knieriem's choice to remain outside the bourgeois social order engendered considerable consternation among Nestroy's contem-

Xylograph depicting Nestroy (left) with his friend and fellow Viennese actor Wenzel Scholz

poraries. Nestroy's critique of the conventional Besserungsstück, however, has endured far more successfully than the model it challenges. In 1901 *Der böse Geist Lumpacivagabundus* became the first Nestroy play to be performed in Vienna's Burgtheater; it has been translated into virtually every European language and continues to engage twentieth-century readers and theatergoers.

While *Der böse Geist Lumpacivagabundus* depicts a decrease in supernatural goodness, Nestroy's subsequent plays feature a complete absence of such fantastic forces. The fanciful and largely benevolent realm of fairies, magicians, and allegorical protectors is replaced by social realities created, as well as potentially changed, solely by human beings. Nestroy's dramas reflect a highly class-conscious society. The rising middle class challenges a socially and economically decaying aristocracy, while at the other end of the social hierarchy the conditions for the formation of a petty bourgeoisie and a proletariat are emerging. The aristocracy in Nestroy's plays strives to maintain its economic and political power by controlling the stringent codes governing appearance, behavior, and language. Such rigid codification, however, paradoxically enables and impels the frequent role changing characteristic of Nestroy's texts: the gaps in the social structure allow for individual mobility for those who are able to recognize and exploit the social and political institutions.

Der Talisman (1843; translated as *The Talisman,* 1967) typifies Nestroy's impulse to portray the mutability of sociopolitical conditions. Adapted from the French comedy *Bonaventure* (1840), by Charles-Désiré Dupeuty and Frédéric de Courcy, the play premiered on 16 December 1840 with Nestroy playing the role of Titus Feuerfuchs, a destitute journeyman barber. Because of his red hair, Titus has been excluded from the dominant social order. Through an accident, however, Titus is able to infiltrate and advance within that society. He stops the runaway wagon of the hairdresser Monsieur Marquis, who gives him a black wig and some wise advice: "die gefällige äußere Form macht viel – beinahe alles" (pleasing outer form does a lot – almost everything). These gifts enable Titus to enter the society that had excluded him. As an outsider Titus was able to observe the dynamics of social convention; now he assumes conventionalized forms of behavior and appearance in order to subvert the system from within. His masterful ruse gives rise to many comic situations while indicting a society blinded to glaring contradictions between appearance and reality.

As a result of his transformed physical appearance and his astounding ability to manipulate language, Titus secures employment at the estate of the wealthy Frau von Cypressenburg, climbing the socio-economic ranks from manual laborer to fashionable personal secretary. Changing both his outer appearance and mode of speech at each stage of his ascent, Titus rises to the top by exploiting the society's uncritical embrace of pleasing outer form. He is well aware that an impressive linguistic formulation, even though its contents may be self-contradictory, redundant, or even nonsensical, will remain unchallenged; similarly, dashing good looks, even if they result largely from cosmetics and clothing, provide an effective means for gaining and maintaining privilege in such a society. In a manner typical of Nestroy's plays, the protagonist advances by outwitting society through a subversive use of its own conventions. *Der Talisman* satirically and systematically censures a society that is incapable of perceiving and acting on significant gaps between appearance and reality – an indictment that informs virtually all of Nestroy's work.

While the humor in *Der Talisman* derives largely from social satire, *Das Mädl aus der Vorstadt oder Ehrlich währt am längsten* (The Girl from the Suburbs; or, Honesty is the Best Policy, 1845) exemplifies Nestroy's gift for literary satire. *Das Mädl aus der*

Vorstadt, which premiered in 1841 with Nestroy in the role of Schnoferl, appears at first glance to replicate the kind of socially affirmative entertainment considered typical of the nineteenth-century Volksstück; this drama of seemingly "eternally human" concerns, however, provides paradigmatic instances of how Nestroy uses prominent conventions from both classical and Volkstheater texts to criticize their sociopolitical implications.

The opening scenes of *Das Mädl aus der Vorstadt* appear to imply a conventional Volksstück plot. The wealthy and widowed Frau von Erbstein plans to marry Herr von Gigl. All the wedding arrangements have been made, and the bride arrives at the appointed time; the prospective husband, however, is nowhere to be found. This situation, especially when staged at a Viennese Volkstheater, gives rise to expectations of a humorous search for the groom, some misunderstandings during the quest, and a happy ending uniting the couple in eternal marital bliss. Nestroy's thematic and structural innovations shatter such expectations, bringing to the fore important issues of social and literary interpretation.

Gigl has decided that he cannot marry Frau von Erbstein, since he does not love her; his heart belongs to the seamstress Thekla, whose name prompts associations with the sublime Princess Thekla of Friedland in Schiller's classical drama of the Thirty Years' War, *Wallenstein* (1800). Throughout the farce Nestroy satirizes classical notions of fate as well as images of the classical protagonist subject to his or her inescapable destiny. Nestroy reworks such lofty classical ideals within the everyday material context of the lower classes, thereby challenging high tragedy's exclusive treatment of historically prominent individuals, undercutting the idealistic connotations associated with classical concepts of destiny, and pointing to the discrepancy between the tragic hero's "fate" and the "lot" of the socially downtrodden. As the sharply contrasting circumstances of Schiller's aristocratic Thekla and Nestroy's dispossessed seamstress make clear, the realm of freedom for the heroic protagonist is far greater than that of his or her disadvantaged counterpart. Nestroy satirically challenges such inequity, dramatizing the need for greater theatrical and social diversity and choice.

In addition to satirizing high tragedy and Volksstück conventions, *Das Mädl aus der Vorstadt* calls into question fundamental characteristics of the Versöhnungsdrama (drama of reconciliation). In a conventional drama of reconciliation, such as Raimund's *Der Bauer als Millionär oder Das Mädchen aus der Feenwelt* (The Peasant as Millionaire; or, The Girl From the Fairy World, 1837), the pure hearts of lovers separated by supernatural evil are reunited as the final curtain falls. In Nestroy's inversion of the paradigm no such reunion occurs: the conclusion of *Das Mädl aus der Vorstadt* does not witness the blissful marriage of Frau von Erbstein and Herr von Gigl. The farce, in typical Nestroy fashion, satirizes

Nestroy; lithograph by an unknown artist

the conventional notion of pure and unselfish hearts: the pursuit of passion reveals a self-serving material basis. The absence of idealistic and idealized representations of love, passion, and fate has resulted in Nestroy's being called the "Schopenhauer of popular comedy." While some of Nestroy's critics attribute his lack of idealism to pessimism, cynicism, or even nihilism, others contend that it signals a healthy and enlightened realism.

Nestroy's realism concerning the course of political events appears, in retrospect, confirmed by *Freiheit in Krähwinkel* (Freedom in Krähwinkel, 1849), his satiric depiction of the events culminating in the Revolution of 1848. Although scholars continue to debate Nestroy's general political tendencies as well as his stance vis-à-vis the revolution, *Freiheit in Krähwinkel* clearly documents his belief in the possibility of and need for revolutionary social change. Moreover, the subsequent failure of the 1848 Revolution corroborates the critique underlying Nestroy's drama. *Freiheit in Krähwinkel* shows that the historical moment demanded the full enfranchisement of the bourgeoisie within a parliamentary form of government; at the same time, however, the play shows that the bourgeoisie was not taking the imperatives of political reorganization seriously enough.

The play premiered in Vienna on 1 July 1848, during the brief period in which Austrian state censorship was lifted. Government troops recaptured the city in October 1848; censorship was reinstituted shortly thereafter, and *Freiheit in Krähwinkel* disappeared from the stages of the Hapsburg Empire. During its three-month run, however, the play was performed thirty-six times, to thunderous applause, with Nestroy in the role of the revolutionary Eberhard Ultra and his friend Scholz appearing as the reactionary beadle Klaus. The public responded with particular enthusiasm to the words and deeds of Ultra. The chronicle and indictment of absolutism in the song he sings in act 1, scene 7, quickly spread throughout the city. The citizens of Vienna not only sang Ultra's song but also added their own topical verses to his witty condemnation of political oppression.

Nestroy situates his representation of subjugation and revolt in a small town whose name signals its backwardness. Krähwinkel has a long history in German and Austrian literature as a symbol of provincial isolation and regression, and *Freiheit in Krähwinkel* continues this tradition. Nestroy's Krähwinkler have been living in peaceful and blind subjugation for years. The city administration has ruthlessly maintained absolute social, economic, and political control. The revolutionary ideals of 1848, however, cannot be stopped from infiltrating even the remote borders of Krähwinkel.

The drama's central conflict involves the demand for a democratic system, advocated most vociferously by Ultra and the night watchman. The Bürgermeister, who heads the city government, insures his tyranny through an elite group of officials. Working closely with the commander of the city's troops and with Krähwinkel's "geheimer Stadtsekretär" (secret city secretary), the Bürgermeister is assured of complete military and bureaucratic support. Equally important to the regime's continued existence is the participation of Pfiffspitz, the editor of Krähwinkel's only newspaper. His submission to censorship allows the administration to control not only the sociopolitical system of the city but also the sole public source for disseminating information – or misinformation – about it.

Like most of Nestroy's plays, *Freiheit in Krähwinkel* reveals language's potential as a means for achieving, maintaining, or subverting social power. Nestroy explores the ways speech can be used to establish and then conceal political inequality. At the same time, he illustrates how language can function to expose the dynamics of oppression and, thus, contribute to its demise. Ultra adopts a variety of roles to undermine and subsequently restructure Krähwinkel's government: a diplomat, a Russian prince, and a Ligorianer (a member of a highly influential and conservative religious order). In a manner analogous to Titus Feuerfuchs, Ultra adopts not only the external characteristics of these social, political, and religious roles but also the various levels of language, formal gestures, and ideologies associated with them. In an illuminating and frequently hysterically funny way, he uses these facades to subvert the political power associated with them, thus transforming traditionally absolutist social roles into vehicles for establishing a new and progressive social order.

Nestroy's work as an actor and author revolutionized the texts and the institutional contexts of the Viennese Volksstück. Toward the end of his life, when operettas began to eclipse popular comedy on the stages of the city's Volkstheater, critics feared that these theatrical institutions had entered a phase of irreversible decline. Nestroy's death in Graz on 25 May 1862, the result of a stroke, compounded the concern regarding the future of the Volkstheater and the distinct dramatic form it enabled to flourish. Nestroy had become such an integral and irreplaceable part of Viennese popular theater that many wondered how, if at all, it could withstand his death.

Letters:

Gesammelte Briefe (1831-1862): Nestroy und seine Bühne im Jahre 1848, edited by Fritz Brukner (Vienna: Wallishausser, 1938);

Briefe, edited by Walter Obermaier (Vienna & Munich: Jugend und Volk, 1977).

Bibliographies:

Karl Gladt, *Die Handschriften Johann Nestroys* (Graz, Vienna & Cologne: Böhlau, 1967);

Jürgen Hein, "Nestroyforschung (1901-1966)," *Wirkendes Wort,* 18 (1968): 232-245;

Hein, "Neuere Nestroyforschung (1967-1973)," *Wirkendes Wort,* 25 (1975): 140-151;

Günter Conrad, *Johann Nepomuk Nestroy 1801-1862: Bibliographie zur Nestroyforschung und -rezeption* (Berlin: Schmidt, 1980).

Biographies:

Otto Basil, *Johann Nestroy: Mit Selbstzeugnissen und Bilddokumenten* (Reinbek: Rowohlt, 1967);

Helmut Ahrens, *Bis zum Lorbeer versteig' ich mich nicht: Johann Nestroy – sein Leben* (Frankfurt am Main: Societäts-Verlag, 1982).

References:

Theodor Adorno, "Reflexion über das Volksstück," in *Noten zur Literatur,* edited by Rolf Tiedemann (Frankfurt am Main: Suhrkamp, 1974), pp. 693-694;

Maria P. Alter, "The Reception of Nestroy in America as Exemplified in Thornton Wilder's Play *The Matchmaker,*" *Modern Austrian Literature,* 20, no. 3/4 (1987): 33-42;

Uwe Baur, "Nestroy und die oppositionelle Literatur seiner Zeit: Zum Verhältnis von 'Volk' und Literatur in der Restaurationsepoche," in *Studien zur Literatur des 19. und 20. Jahrhunderts in Österreich: Festschrift für Alfred Doppler zum 60. Geburtstag,* edited by Johann Holzner, Michael Klein, and Wolfgang Wiesmüller (Innsbruck: University of Innsbruck, 1981), pp. 25-34;

Günter Berghaus, "Rebellion, Reservation, Resignation: Nestroy und die Wiener Gesellschaft 1830-1860," in *Viennese Popular Theatre: A Symposium / Das Wiener Volkstheater: Ein Symposion,* edited by W. E. Yates and John R. P. McKenzie (Exeter, U.K.: University of Exeter, 1985), pp. 109-122;

Dieter Breuer, *Geschichte der literarischen Zensur in Deutschland* (Heidelberg: Quelle & Meyer, 1982), pp. 162-170;

Siegfried Brill, *Die Komödie der Sprache: Untersuchungen zum Werke Johann Nestroys* (Nuremberg: Carl, 1967);

Craig Decker, "Toward a Critical *Volksstück:* Nestroy and the Politics of Language," *Monatshefte,* 79, no. 1 (1987): 42-61;

Alois Eder, " 'Die geistige Kraft der Gemeinheit': Zur Sozialgeschichte der Rezeption Nestroys," in *Theater und Gesellschaft: Das Volksstück im 19. und 20. Jahrhundert,* edited by Jürgen Hein (Düsseldorf: Bertelsmann Universitätsverlag, 1973), pp. 133-153;

Martin Esslin, "Nestroy – Between Hanswurst and Horváth," *Theater,* 12, no. 2 (1981): 62-65;

Ernst Fischer, "Johann Nestroy," in his *Von Grillparzer zu Kafka: Sechs Essays* (Frankfurt am Main: Suhrkamp, 1975), pp. 145-242;

Lawrence V. Harding, *The Dramatic Art of Ferdinand Raimund and Johann Nestroy: A Critical Study* (The Hague: Mouton, 1974);

Jürgen Hein, *Das Wiener Volkstheater: Raimund und Nestroy* (Darmstadt: Wissenschaftliche Buchgesellschaft, 1978);

Helmut Herles, "Nestroy und die Zensur," in *Theater und Gesellschaft: Das Volksstück im 19. und 20. Jahrhundert,* edited by Hein (Düsseldorf: Bertelsmann Universitätsverlag, 1973), pp. 121-132;

Ansgar Hillach, *Die Dramatisierung des komischen Dialogs: Figur und Rolle bei Nestroy* (Munich: Fink, 1967);

Johann Hüttner, "Johann Nestroy und der Theaterbetrieb seiner Zeit," *Maske und Kothurn,* 23 (1977): 233-243;

Kurt Kahl, *Johann Nestroy oder Der wienerische Shakespeare* (Vienna: Molden, 1970);

Heinz Kindermann, "Nestroy: Revolutionär und Bürger," *Maske und Kothurn,* 9 (1963): 132-152;

Karl Kraus, *Nestroy und die Nachwelt* (Frankfurt am Main: Suhrkamp, 1975);

Franz H. Mautner, *Nestroy* (Heidelberg: Stiehm, 1974);

Erich Joachim May, *Wiener Volkskomödie und Vormärz* (Berlin: Henschel, 1975);

John R. P. McKenzie, "Nestroy's Political Plays," in *Viennese Popular Theatre: A Symposium / Das Wiener Volkstheater: Ein Symposion,* pp. 123-138;

Robert Mühler, ed., *Dichtung aus Österreich,* volume 1 (Vienna & Munich: Österreichischer Bundesverlag für Unterricht, Wissenschaft und Kunst, 1969);

Gerd Müller, *Das Volksstück von Raimund bis Kroetz: Die Gattung in Einzelanalysen* (Munich: Oldenbourg, 1979), pp. 26–41;

Wolfgang Neuber, *Nestroys Rhetorik: Wirkungspoetik und Altwiener Volkskomödie im 19. Jahrhundert* (Bonn: Bouvier, 1987);

Gustav Pichler, ed., *Nestroy gehört den Komödianten: Salzburger Nestroy-Gespräche 1977* (Vienna: Bergland, 1978);

Wolfgang Preisendanz, "Nestroys komisches Theater," in *Das deutsche Lustspiel,* volume 2, edited by Hans Steffen (Göttingen: Vandenhoeck & Ruprecht, 1969), pp. 7–24;

Rio Preisner, *Johann Nepomuk Nestroy: Der Schöpfer der tragischen Posse* (Munich: Hanser, 1968);

Otto Rommel, "Johann Nestroy, der Satiriker auf der Alt-Wiener Komödienbühne," in Nestroy's *Gesammelte Werke,* volume 1, edited by Rommel (Vienna: Schroll, 1948), pp. 5–194;

Joel Schechter and Jack Zipes, "Slave Language Comes to Krähwinkel: Notes on Nestroy's Political Satire," *Theater,* 12, no. 2 (1981): 72–75;

Heinrich Schwarz, *Johann Nestroy im Bild: Eine Ikonographie,* edited by Hüttner and Otto G. Schindler (Vienna & Munich: Jugend und Volk, 1977);

Reinhard Urbach, *Die Wiener Komödie und ihr Publikum: Stranitzky und die Folgen* (Vienna & Munich: Jugend und Volk, 1973);

W. E. Yates, *Nestroy: Satire and Parody in Viennese Popular Comedy* (Cambridge: Cambridge University Press, 1972);

Herbert Zeman, "Johann Nestroy – Profile seines Lebens und Schaffens," in *Die österreichische Literatur: Ihr Profil im 19. Jahrhundert (1830–1880),* edited by Zeman (Graz: Akademische Druck- und Verlagsanstalt, 1982), pp. 633–660.

Papers:

Johann Nestroy's manuscripts and letters are in the Wiener Stadtbibliothek (Viennese City Library).

Hermann von Pückler-Muskau

(30 October 1785 – 4 February 1871)

Ellis Shookman
Dartmouth College

BOOKS: *Briefe eines Verstorbenen: Ein fragmentarisches Tagebuch aus England, Wales, Irland und Frankreich, geschrieben in den Jahren 1828 und 1829,* anonymous, 2 volumes (Munich: Franckh, 1830); translated by Sarah Austin as *Tour in England, Ireland, and France, in the Years 1828 and 1829,* 2 volumes (London: Wilson, 1832);

Briefe eines Verstorbenen: Ein fragmentarisches Tagebuch aus Deutschland, Holland und England, anonymous, 2 volumes (Stuttgart: Hallberger, 1832); translated by Austin as *Tour in Germany, Holland and England, in the Years 1826, 1827, and 1828; With Remarks on the Manners and Customs of the Inhabitants, and Anecdotes of Distinguished Public Characters. In a Series of Letters. By a German Prince,* 2 volumes (London: Wilson, 1832);

Andeutungen über Landschaftsgärtnerei, verbunden mit der Beschreibung ihrer praktischen Anwendung in Muskau (Stuttgart: Hallberger, 1834), translated by Bernhard Sickert, edited by Samuel Parsons as *Hints on Landscape Gardening* (Boston & New York: Houghton Mifflin, 1917);

Tutti Frutti: Aus den Papieren des Verstorbenen, anonymous, 5 volumes (Stuttgart: Hallberger, 1834); translated by Edmund Spencer as *Tutti Frutti: By the Author of "The Tour of a German Prince"* (1 volume, New York: Harper, 1834; 2 volumes, London: Bach, 1834);

Jugend-Wanderungen: Aus meinen Tagebüchern; Für mich und Andere, Vom Verfasser der Briefe eines Verstorbenen, anonymous (Stuttgart: Hallberger, 1835);

Vorletzter Weltgang von Semilasso: Traum und Wachen. Aus den Papieren des Verstorbenen, anonymous, 3 volumes (Stuttgart: Hallberger, 1835);

Semilasso in Afrika: Semilassos vorletzter Weltgang. Theil 2. Aus den Papieren des Verstorbenen, anonymous, 5 volumes (Stuttgart: Hallberger, 1836); translated anonymously as *Semilasso in Africa: Adventures in Algiers, and Other Parts of Africa. By Prince Pückler Muskau, Author of "The Tour of a German Prince,"* 3 volumes (London: Bentley, 1837);

Hermann von Pückler-Muskau; drawing by Wilhelm Hensel, circa 1842

Der Vorläufer: Vom Verfasser der Briefe eines Verstorbenen, anonymous (Stuttgart: Hallberger, 1838);

Südöstlicher Bildersaal: Herausgegeben vom Verfasser der Briefe eines Verstorbenen, anonymous, 3 volumes (Stuttgart: Hallberger, 1840–1841) – comprises volume 1, *Der Vergnügling,* volumes 2–3, *Griechische Leiden;*

Aus Mehemed Ali's Reich: Vom Verfasser der Briefe eines Verstorbenen, anonymous, 3 volumes (Stuttgart:

Hallberger, 1844); translated by H. Evans Lloyd as *Egypt under Mehemet Ali: By Prince Puckler Muskau,* 2 volumes (London: Colburn, 1845); translated anonymously as *Egypt and Mehemet Ali,* 3 volumes (London: Newby, 1845);

Die Rückkehr: Vom Verfasser der Briefe eines Verstorbenen, anonymous, 3 volumes (Berlin: Duncker, 1846–1848).

Editions and Collections: *Ironie des Lebens: Aus Schriften und Briefen des Fürsten Hermann von Pückler-Muskau,* 2 volumes, edited by Heinrich Conrad (Munich & Leipzig: Müller, 1910);

Andeutungen über Landschaftsgärtnerei, verbunden mit der Beschreibung ihrer praktischen Anwendung in Muskau, edited by Theodor Lange (Leipzig: Friedrich, 1911);

Semilassos vorletzter Weltgang: Traum und Wachen. Aus den Papieren des Verstorbenen, 2 volumes, edited by Conrad (Munich: Müller, 1913–1914) – comprises volume 1, *In Europa;* volume 2, *In Europa und Afrika;*

Andeutungen über Landschaftsgärtnerei, verbunden mit der Beschreibung ihrer praktischen Anwendung in Muskau, edited by Edwin Redslob (Berlin: Deutscher Kunstverlag, 1933);

Fürst Pückler reist nach England: Aus den "Briefen eines Verstorbenen," edited by Hermann Christian Mettin (Berlin: Von Hugo & Schlotheim, 1938; reprinted, Stuttgart: Deutsche Verlags-Anstalt, 1955);

Fürst Pückler in Athen: Zugleich der Roman einer romantischen Liebe, edited by Alfred Richard Meyer (Berlin: Deutsche Buchvertriebs- und Verlags-Gesellschaft, 1944);

Jugendwanderungen: Aus meinen Tagebüchern. Für mich und andere, edited by Irma Mayring-Gaab (Hamburg: Deutscher Literarischer Verlag, 1947);

Fürst Pücklers orientalische Reisen: Aus den abenteuerlichen Berichten des weltkundigen Fürsten, Pückler-Muskau, edited by Helmut Wiemken (Hamburg: Hoffmann & Campe, 1963);

Briefe eines Verstorbenen, 4 volumes, edited by Jost Hermand (New York & London: Johnson Reprint, 1968);

Südöstlicher Bildersaal: Griechische Leiden, edited by Klaus Günther Just (Stuttgart: Steingrüben, 1968);

Reisebriefe aus Irland, edited by Therese Erler (Berlin: Rütten & Loening, 1969);

Andeutungen über Landschaftsgärtnerei: Verbunden mit der Beschreibung ihrer praktischen Anwendung in Muskau, preface by Graf Lennart Bernadotte, introduction by Albrecht Kruse-Rodenacker (Stuttgart: Deutsche Verlags-Anstalt, 1977);

Südöstlicher Bildersaal, edited by Just (Frankfurt am Main: Societäts-Verlag, 1981);

Fürst Pückler reist in Franken, afterword by Hans Baier (Erlangen: Palm & Enke, 1982);

Ausgewählte Werke, 2 volumes, edited by Heinz Ohff and Ekhard Haack (Frankfurt am Main, Berlin & Vienna: Ullstein, 1985);

Aus Mehemed Alis Reich: Ägypten und der Sudan um 1840, afterword by Günther Jantzen, biographical essay by Otto Flake (Zurich: Manesse, 1985);

Briefe eines Verstorbenen, edited by Heinz Ohff (Berlin: Kupfergraben, 1986);

Andeutungen über Landschaftsgärtnerei: Verbunden mit der Beschreibung ihrer praktischen Anwendung in Muskau, 2 volumes, commentaries by Anne Schäfer and Steffi Wendel (Leipzig: Edition Leipzig, 1986);

Briefe eines Verstorbenen, 2 volumes, edited by Therese Erler, afterword by Konrad Paul (Berlin: Rütten & Loening, 1987);

Andeutungen über Landschaftsgärtnerei: Verbunden mit der Beschreibung ihrer praktischen Anwendung in Muskau, edited by Günter J. Vaupel (Frankfurt am Main: Insel, 1988);

Briefe eines Verstorbenen: Ein fragmentarisches Tagebuch, edited by Vaupel (Frankfurt am Main: Insel, 1990).

Editions in English: *Tour in England, Ireland, and France, in the Years 1826, 1827, 1828, and 1829: With Remarks on the Manners and Customs of the Inhabitants, and Anecdotes of Distinguished Public Characters. In a Series of Letters. By a German Prince,* translated by Sarah Austin (Philadelphia: Carey, Lea & Blanchard, 1833; reprinted, Zurich: Massie, 1940);

A Regency Visitor: The English Tour of Prince Pückler-Muskau, Described in His Letters, 1826–1828, edited by E. M. Butler (London: Collins, 1957; New York: Dutton, 1958);

Pückler's Progress: The Adventures of Prince Pückler-Muskau in England, Wales and Ireland as Told in Letters to His Former Wife, 1826–9, translated by Flora Brennan (London: Collins, 1987).

OTHER: Leopold Schefer, *Gesänge zu dem Pianoforte: Musik vom Dichter,* edited by Pückler-Muskau (Leipzig: Breitkopf & Härtel, 1813).

There is no better barometer of literary life in nineteenth-century Germany than Hermann von Pückler-Muskau. His success as a writer and his far-flung correspondence make him a unique gauge of aesthetic, cultural, and political trends in the years between the empires of Napoleon and Otto von Bismarck. Born a count and later raised to the rank of prince, he hardly seemed destined to write incisively on social revolution, national upheaval, liberal economics, and new technology. In his travel books, however, he observed such changes with a keen narrative eye not only in Europe but also in Africa and the Middle East. Many other writers strongly supported or rejected him, reactions that shed critical light on German literature during his lifetime. His odd mix of progressive views and traditional loyalties often led him to outlandish conclusions, but his spirited accounts of himself and his surroundings earned him a popular reputation and much money. Both those fortunes had declined by the time he died, though his fame as a landscape architect endured, and a frozen dessert – Pückler-Eis (Pückler Ice) – still bears his name. Scholars have found reason to republish much of his work, which remains some of the best travel writing composed at a time when that genre flourished as never before; the facile yet forthright tone of his prose has seldom been matched in German.

Pückler-Muskau, who liked to trace his ancestry to Ruedeger of Bechelaren, a hero of the medieval *Nibelungenlied,* was born on 30 October 1785 on his family's estate in Muskau, on the Neisse River near Cottbus. He was the first child of Count Ludwig Johannes Karl Erdmann von Pückler and the fifteen-year-old Countess Clementine von Pückler, née von Callenberg, whose marriage had united two old and powerful Lusatian families but ended in divorce. His father was ineffective, his mother immature, and both neglected his education, so the strong-willed Hermann soon grew wild. He went through schools in Uhyst, Halle, and Dessau; after a brief show of studying law in Leipzig in 1801 he ran off to join a fashionable regiment in Dresden, where his huge debts and daring pranks soon earned him the name "Mad Pückler." Discharged and destitute by 1804, he fled to Vienna and then traveled in Germany, Switzerland, Italy, and France before returning to Muskau in 1810 just in time for the death of his father, who had tried to disinherit the irresponsible spendthrift. Though his native Saxony sided with Napoleon in 1812, Pückler-Muskau served in the opposing, allied armies of Russia and Weimar, distinguishing himself as the governor of Bruges and visiting Paris and London before returning to Berlin. There he courted Lucie von Pappenheim, the previously married daughter of the Prussian statesman Karl August von Hardenberg, who was nine years older than he.

Lucie von Pappenheim, whom Pückler-Muskau married in 1817

They married in 1817. Her father recompensed him for financial losses suffered when Muskau became part of Prussia in 1815 and helped to have him named prince in 1822.

Anecdotes from each of these stages in his early life attest to Pückler-Muskau's eccentric character. As a boy, he tossed a dummy dressed to look like himself from a tower of the castle in Muskau into the moat, terrifying the adults who had just threatened to punish him. He was thrown out of school in Halle for mocking his superiors, and while a university student he gleefully fleeced his father's secretary by having classmates pose as creditors. He was particularly fond of equestrian escapades, spurring his horse off a crowded bridge over the Elbe in Dresden, thrashing the son of the Austrian chancellor with a riding crop in Vienna, and galloping at breakneck speed from one of the suburbs of Berlin to the Brandenburg Gate. He would also parade down Unter den Linden, the fanciest street in Berlin, in a carriage drawn by a foursome of stags (some say reindeer), then abruptly stop and sit, lost in thought and ostensibly oblivious to the gaping crowd gathered around him. He fought duels; he married Lucie after wooing both of her daughters,

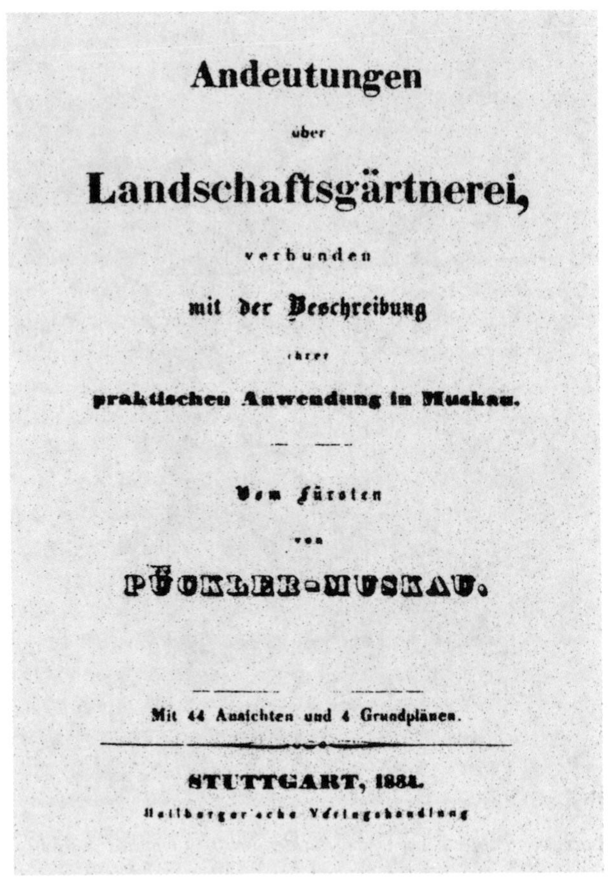

Andeutungen

über

Landschaftsgärtnerei,

verbunden

mit der Beschreibung

ihrer

praktischen Anwendung in Muskau.

Vom Fürsten

von

PÜCKLER-MUSKAU.

Mit 44 Ansichten und 4 Grundplänen.

STUTTGART, 1834.

Hallberger'sche Verlagshandlung

Title page for Pückler-Muskau's book on landscape gardening and park design

one of whom he later tried to enlist in a ménage à trois. Finally, after squandering both his inheritance and her dowry on the large gardens at Muskau, he agreed to Lucie's suggestion that they divorce so that he could find an English heiress who would marry him, make him solvent, and let the two of them carry on as before. In 1827, at the age of forty-two, Pückler-Muskau thus found himself famous for his scandalous stunts but threatened by financial ruin and about to leave for England as a high-class fortune hunter.

He failed to acquire an English bride, but writing came to his rescue when letters he sent to Lucie were reworked and published in four volumes as *Briefe eines Verstorbenen* (Letters of a Deceased, 1830–1832; translated as *Tour in England, Ireland, and France, in the Years 1828 and 1829,* 1832, and *Tour in Germany, Holland, and England,* 1832). The work starts in medias res with his leaving London in 1828 for Wales; the last two volumes contain earlier letters that tell of his meeting Johann Wolfgang von Goethe in Weimar before rushing on to London, where he rubs elbows with the rich while seeing sights high and low: Parliament and Bedlam, country estates and cottages, abbeys and docks, spas and factories. He goes up Mount Snowdon and down into slate mines, rides in a steam engine and a diving bell, visits the dentist, takes boxing lessons, sees dioramas and a tunnel under the Thames, meets Sir Walter Scott, and raves about the banker Nathan Rothschild. He observes a well-dressed dandy's wardrobe, pokes around the British Museum, and tours the great English gardens, thriving on social life in the city but also keen on romantic ruins and picturesque countryside. He reports on English theater (including a Punch and Judy show), explains English eating habits, defines words such as *gentleman* and *temper,* and dabbles in fads such as craniology. His praise of what he sees is mixed with criticism. He enjoys England's material comforts, economic efficiency, and respect for private property, and he decides that modern industry is not all bad even though he feels for underpaid workers. England seems blessed; the English, however, strike him as pretentious, intolerant, cold, and blinded by their class system. He faults the intellectual limits imposed on well-bred daughters and wives; he abhors the English exploitation of Ireland while visiting its political liberator, Daniel O'Connell. He predicts the decline of England and rise of Germany, once the latter wins English political freedom, but he mocks Germans' respect for English money as well as their own slowness to change. Some of his criticism betrays personal motives: his dislike of prying English newspapers, for example, seems to be based on their having gotten wind of him and warning off potential fiancées.

His narrative persona is subjective and complex: he admits to being a nervous hypochondriac ruled by his moods, a lazy yet restless night owl, a danger-loving thrill-seeker, an inconsistent creature of habit, a lighthearted optimist, a would-be capitalist who opts for reading the poetry of George Gordon, Lord Byron. He prefers harmless pleasures to refined curiosities and makes romantic observations on many mundane matters as well as on the sublime and the beautiful; he can build fantastic castles in the sky yet also indulge a down-to-earth love of landscaping. Highly self-conscious, he wishes for a slow death so that he can observe himself dying. "Die Mode ist eine große Tyrannin, und sosehr ich das einsehe, lass ich mich doch auch, wie jeder andere, von ihr regieren" (Fashion is a great tyrant, but as much as I understand that, like everyone else, I still let her rule me), he says, speaking in a narrative voice that sounds capricious yet deeply honest. That tone of voice is deliberately chosen as the style of a well-read travel writer. Pückler-Muskau often comments on his own narration, calling it a mix of fiction and truth meant to give vivid impressions by citing details of everyday life. He admires the French for telling clever stories and is himself a master at finding apt bons mots in English, French, Italian, and Latin. He recounts local legends and amusing anecdotes, and he gives satirical sketches along with accomplished descriptions of landscape. He often cites other authors; Washington Irving is his source of facts about America.

Pückler-Muskau dubbed himself a "Parkomane" (parkomaniac), and his views on parks and gardens are systematically set forth in *Andeutungen über Landschaftsgärtnerei* (1834; translated as *Hints on Landscape Gardening,* 1917). It outlines theoretical principles of landscape architecture and their practical application in Muskau, explaining basic concepts such as size, enclosure, preservation, and the placement of buildings and giving tips on laying out lawns and footpaths, transplanting trees, and using cliffs, earthworks, islands, and bodies of water. Such hints are reinforced by general aesthetic comments: Pückler-Muskau insists that the highest degree of a landscape gardener's art is reached when his work appears to be nature in its noblest guise; his grounds should display an expressive physiognomy, yet their multiplicity, variety, and contrast must be unified, harmonious, and balanced; planning them, therefore, means using few objects to produce many effects, keeping up pleasing appearances so that their novelty never wears off, and leaving much to visitors' imaginations. Such aesthetic concerns are tied to painting, politics, and fiction. Pückler-Muskau notes similarities between landscape architecture and landscape painting: meadows, lawns, and water represent the landscape architect's light, and buildings, forests, and trees his shadow. He also observes that humans strive for the freedom presumably enjoyed by trees, but he argues that such freedom comes from cultivating one's garden – in the sense of Voltaire's *Candide* (1759) – rather than from radical social reform. In politics as in gardens, he thus favors organic evolution. Many of the scenes that he describes had only been planned, so his accounts of Muskau are often pure fiction; and his ideal of naturalness seems to link gardening with his literary work.

Political and literary issues are also mixed in *Tutti Frutti* (1834; translated, 1834) in which Pückler-Muskau regrets that his times are confused and egotistical, litigious and bureaucratic, industrious and industrial, running on steam, money, utility, and sober rationality at the expense of feeling and love. He thinks that this "Nivellierungsperiode" (age of leveling) suffers from merely "chemisches Wissen" (chemical knowledge) that dissolves things into their parts and thus loses sight of the whole; but he concedes that one might be wrong to complain about the new just because it upsets the old with nothing better to put in its place. His politics are accordingly ambivalent, sounding sometimes reactionary yet also often progressive. No apologist for the status quo, he agrees that old traditions should die to make room for new freedom; but such freedom should come gradually, under a constitutional monarch and a reformed aristocracy. Writing on religion, he welcomes the emancipation of the Jews, mocks his school in Uhyst as the "Herrnhutische Heuchelanstalt" (Institute for Moravian Mendacity), and is not surprised that poetic spirits are drawn to the more sensual and aesthetic Catholicism. *Tutti Frutti* is made up of aphorisms, anecdotes, short essays, reviews of current books, excerpts from his diaries and dreams, and an attempted novella. He likens this odd hors d'oeuvre to a conversation with his audience, styling himself a reclusive fantasist and tireless nomad who laughs at human foibles and wants to indulge his own whims. He does so by seeing Berlin from a hot-air balloon and by descending into the family crypt, opening some of its tombs to commune with his forebears, and cutting a lock of hair from his somewhat decayed grandmother's head. He forcefully attacks whatever is foolish, harmful, or evil, wherever he finds it and whoever its perpetrator may be. His style is peppered with playful bons mots, and he admires Heinrich Heine's "Witzfeuerwerke" (pyrotechnic wit). *Tutti Frutti* conveys its shrewd social criticism brilliantly.

Pückler-Muskau tried to exploit his sudden literary fame with *Jugend-Wanderungen* (Hikes in My Youth, 1835), which traces part of his shabby grand tour in Italy and France. The book consists of youthful letters proving their author's panache. Hearing that Mount Vesuvius has started to erupt, he rushes to its rim, barely escaping death. When French and English warships engage off Naples, he compares the battle to a theatrical performance and watches it through opera glasses; he is sad to observe German mercenaries fighting on both sides, however. He sounds prophetic, given the extent of his subsequent travels, when he says: "Wenn ich überdenke, wie viel länger man lebt, wenn man viel erlebt, möchte ich fast wünschen, bis an meinen Tod dieses nomadische Leben zu führen" (When I ponder how much longer one lives by experiencing a great deal, I almost wish to lead this nomadic life until I die).

In 1835 Pückler-Muskau undertook a five-year trip around the Mediterranean, sending back articles to German newspapers such as the *Augsburger Allgemeine Zeitung* under the name "Semilasso." This strange nom de plume connoting lassitude and ennui was also used in the travel book *Vorletzter Weltgang von Semilasso* (Semilasso's Penultimate World Trip, 1835). Setting out across Germany and France, Semilasso believes that Europe has only begun to change and expects that revolution will soon erupt again, but he accepts such change philosophically: "Das *tiers état* bekömmt überall das Uebergewicht, wie billig, denn es ist sein Zeitalter. Das unsere ist vorüber" (The third estate is everywhere gaining the upper hand, as is fitting, for its time has come. Ours is gone). From Muskau to Marseilles fine cuisine is his specialty, and since one never knows what to expect from cooks along the way, he always packs some extra English mustard. Semilasso likes distraction, novelty, and the pleasures of the imagination; he is bored by success but upset if it eludes him; he lives life as a continuous experiment. Pückler-Muskau criticizes such self-absorption, calling Semilasso "ein Kern von Eisen in Eiderdaun gehüllt" (a core of iron wrapped in eiderdown). Pückler-Muskau was feted in Parisian salons and planned to visit Andrew Jackson's America, where his criticism of England had made him popular.

In *Semilasso in Afrika* (1836; translated as *Semilasso in Africa,* 1837) Semilasso gladly escapes the anemic culture of Europe. He is invigorated by African and Arabic customs, which he finds chivalrous and romantic, much like the Middle Ages back home. He enjoys such feudal surroundings, where a man can be pure action and not paralyzed by too much thought. Pückler-Muskau arrived in Algiers only a few years after its subjugation by France in 1830 and was bent on seeing places never before reached by Europeans. His many expeditions in Algeria and Tunisia attest to his insatiable curiosity, and although the number of miles that he covered sometimes seems matched by the number of pages used to describe them, his writing is vigorous. He describes rosy cheeks, sweet breath, supple limbs, and other womanly charms, rejecting timid delicacy so as not to blur readers' images of foreign countries. He calls travel writers soldiers serving their readers, and he reminds his own readers that his stories are hard work and serious business.

Sailing to Malta and on to Greece in November 1835, Pückler-Muskau noted his sojourns in two books. *Der Vorläufer* (The Forerunner, 1838) relates his route from Delphi to Athens, the Aegean, and Crete. Following in Byron's footsteps and dividing his time between diplomats and peasants and between ancient ruins and modern amenities, he sees a Greece still scarred by its war for independence. Ambivalent as always, he welcomes improvement and progress wherever he finds them but thinks European notions of philanthropy wrong and dangerous in revolutionary times and places. He is always on the lookout for haute cuisine and picturesque scenery, but he stresses the iron discipline needed by true travel writers. *Südöstlicher Bildersaal* (Southeast Picture Gallery, 1840–1841) combines further sightseeing with fiction about a rake's progress that is similar to its author's own. Pückler-Muskau differs from many admirers of Greece by stressing its inhabitants' similarities to their former rulers, the Turks. The fictional part of the work is a melodramatic tale of seduction, incest, and ruin. Its dissolute hero bears the name of Pückler-Muskau's father and a damning likeness to Pückler-Muskau himself; it defends the epicurean way of life as more than just sensual enjoyment and warns that such a life must be tempered by true love and faith in God. The same moralism appears in "Acht Frühlings- und Sommertage aus dem Leben Mischlings" (Eight Spring and Summer Days from the Life of Mischling), the novella attempted in *Tutti Frutti.*

He left Crete for Egypt on New Year's Day 1837; he later wrote of the trip in *Aus Mehemed Ali's Reich* (1844; translated as *Egypt under Mehemet Ali,* 1845). Muḥammad 'Alī Pasha was a Turkish soldier who became pasha of Egypt in 1805, founding the dynasty that ruled there until 1952. Pückler-Muskau compares him to Napoleon and Peter the Great for his many public works and economic reforms and calls him the enlightened man whom providence has chosen to clear the way for closer ties between East and West. Not all contemporaries thought so well of Muḥammad 'Alī Pasha, who could be extremely brutal, but Pückler-Muskau criticizes such "hyperliberale Berserker" (hyperliberal berserks). When he exposes bureaucratic corruption to Muḥammad 'Alī Pasha, two guilty officials are duly beheaded. Riding camels in the Sahara and sailing up the Nile, he reaches Nubia and the Sudan, glimpses his first rhinoceros, breaks camp at midnight, and trails a menagerie that includes ibis, stallions, turtles, crocodiles, and an Abyssinian slave named Machbuba, whose silky black body makes her seem a second Venus. (To avoid offending more refined female readers, he prints such lewd details upside down or in Greek letters.)

Pückler-Muskau's tomb in Branitz; he designed the monument and the park in which it is located (wood engraving after a drawing by C. Heyn).

He describes graves, temples, tombs, catacombs, and mausoleums in *Die Rückkehr* (The Return, 1846–1848). This book shows him leaving Egypt and visiting biblical sites in Jerusalem, Bethlehem, Nazareth, Sidon, Beirut, and Damascus. Jews everywhere welcome him as a benefactor, while pashas, beys, emirs, and khans receive him warmly. He dallies with the reclusive and mystical Lady Hester Stanhope. It is a treat for this lover of trees to see the cedars of Lebanon, and his eye for the exotic and erotic continues undimmed. After traveling from Khartoum to Constantinople he returns to Europe, about which he still has mixed feelings: "Wir sprechen immer von unserer Civilisation und der Orientalen Barbarei, ich kann aber nicht lëugnen, daß bei vielen Anlässen sich mir gerade die entgegengesetzte Ansicht aufdrängt" (We always speak of our civilization and the orientals' barbarism, but I cannot deny that on many occasions I am persuaded of just the opposite). Drawn to the "oriental" respect for individuals rather than for abstract ideas, he nonetheless wants Germans to colonize the coast of Asia Minor. He suggests that Christians and Moslems could learn much from each other, calls the Jews a deservedly chosen people, and argues that one should not judge foreign customs too quickly.

By 1839 Pückler-Muskau had converted to Catholicism. His "slave" Machbuba was the toast of Viennese society that season, but she died of tuberculosis shortly after reaching Muskau in 1840. Pückler-Muskau remained as eccentric as ever, retaining a dwarf, a "moor," and a long-distance runner who carried his messages back and forth to Berlin. He sold Muskau in 1845 and retired to his smaller paternal seat in nearby Branitz, where he soon began work on another ambitious park. Declining to serve as a deputy in the Frankfurt Parliament that tried to govern Germany in the revolutionary years 1848–1849, he returned to Paris and London; in the 1850s he began traveling closer to home. His wife, with whom he had continued to live after their divorce, died in 1854. He filled nine volumes of letters and diaries that are as psychologically and culturally revealing as his books. His correspondents included the Prussian royal family, chancellors Otto von Bismarck and Wenzel Lothar von Metternich, Alexander von Humboldt, and Franz Liszt. He took a special liking to literary women, and his letters to and from Bettina von Arnim, Countess Ida von Hahn-Hahn, and Eugenie John (known by her pseudonym E. Marlitt) are remarkable tugs-of-war between an aging cavalier and demonstrative bluestockings. Arnim dedicated her *Goethes Briefwechsel mit einem Kind* (1835; translated as *Goethe's Correspondence with a Child,* 1837–1838) to him, and he included an essay from her in his *Andeutungen über Landschaftsgärtnerei,* but he rejected what he called her rabid "Gehirnsinnlichkeit" (cerebral sensuality). In 1866 the octogenarian Pückler-Muskau volunteered to fight for Prussia against Austria, and in 1870 he offered to serve in the German war against France. He died on 4 February 1871 and was buried in Branitz. Bizarre to the end, he had ordered his own autopsy, cremation, and burial in a tomb built like a pyramid on an island in the middle of a lake.

Pückler-Muskau corresponded with many leading authors of his day. Ludwig Börne, Karl Varnhagen von Ense, Theodor Mundt, Karl Gutzkow, Ludolf Wienbarg, and Heinrich Laube (whose prison sentence for radical politics was reduced, through Pückler-Muskau's influence, to house arrest at Pückler-Muskau's estate in 1838–1839) argued about his style and his social import. A leading guide to writing German railed against "Pücklerei" (Pucklerism) and its heavy use of foreign words; but Goethe praised the prose of *Briefe eines Verstorbenen,* and Heine greeted its author as a kindred spirit in the foreword to his *Lutezia* (1854) after Pückler-Muskau intervened with Heine's stingy relatives and publishers. Pückler-Muskau comes off poorly when he is alluded to in other nineteenth-century literature, from E. T. A. Hoffmann's "Das öde Haus" (The Deserted House, 1817) to Theodor Fontane's *Frau Jenny Treibel* (1893; translated as *Jenny Treibel,* 1976). He was chided in poems by Franz Grillparzer and Georg Herwegh as well as in Charles Dickens's *Pickwick Papers* (1836–1837) and Karl Immermann's novel *Münchhausen* (1838–1839). Fiction based on his life was written as late as the 1950s. He also occasioned many imitations and parodies, including Alexander von Ungern-Sternberg's *Tutu* (1846), in which it is said of Pückler-Muskau that "Er war nicht Dichter, bloß Stoff zu einem Gedicht" (He was no poet, merely the stuff of poetry). His reputation among academic critics has been equally checkered. Moralistic and nationalistic German scholars were hostile to him throughout the nineteenth century, but his personal charm and hagiographic hangers-on helped maintain his stature in Muskau and England. German critics in the early twentieth century treated his self-analysis and cultural criticism more kindly, and his reputation has revived as scholars of travel literature bring greater understanding to his social, psychological, and narrative vagaries. Since 1930 the Fürst Pückler-Gesellschaft has furthered interest in him.

Called by E. M. Butler "too queer to be great in the world of men," Pückler-Muskau never realized his early plans for a diplomatic career. Instead, he led a life of fascinating contradictions and wrote books no less singular than himself. An aristocratic liberal and religious skeptic, an aesthete and a dandy, and a philandering grand seigneur, he was also an astute and talented travel writer. Psychologically, he has been analyzed as traveling so tirelessly to try to outrun his neuroses, as able literally to make the earth move for his beloved parks but unable to change his own notorious ways, as seeking compensation for neglect during his childhood by trying to attract attention for the rest of his life. His semifictional literature recalls Sindbad as well as Scheherazade, the explorer Dr. David Livingstone as well as the essayist Dr. Samuel Johnson. At his best Pückler-Muskau ranks with the most gifted of the angry young men of the "Vormärz" (Pre-March, the month in which the later revolution began), whose personal as well as political causes he often helped advance. With his unique interests, social position, and temperament, however, he remains one of a kind.

Letters:

Briefwechsel und Tagebücher des Fürsten Hermann von Pückler-Muskau: Aus seinem Nachlaß, 9 volumes, edited by Ludmilla Assing-Grimelli (volumes 1–2, Hamburg: Hoffmann & Campe; volumes 3–9, Berlin: Wedekind & Schwieger, 1873–1876; reprinted, Bern: Lang, 1971);

Frauenbriefe von und an Hermann Fürsten Pückler-Muskau, edited by Heinrich Conrad (Munich & Leipzig: Müller, 1912);

Liebesbriefe eines alten Kavaliers: Briefwechsel des Fürsten Pückler mit Ada von Treskow, edited by Werner Deetjen (Berlin: Metzner, 1938);

Briefe aus der Schweiz, edited by Charles Linsmayer (Zurich: Sanssouci, 1981);

Geliebter Pascha! Feurigste Gnomin!: Hermann Fürst von Pückler und Ada von Treskow in ihren Liebesbriefen, edited by Gabriele Seitz (Zurich & Munich: Artemis, 1986).

Bibliographies:

Walter Drangosch, "Versuch einer Pückler-Bibliographie," *Die Bücherstube,* 4, nos. 5–6 (1925): 221–230;

Drangosch, "Hermann Ludwig Heinrich Fürst von Pückler-Muskau: Bibliographie," in Karl Goedeke, *Grundriß zur Geschichte der deutschen Dichtung aus den Quellen,* second edition, volume 14, edited by Herbert Jacob (Berlin: Akademie-Verlag, 1959), pp. 693–730, 1019–1020.

Biographies:

August Jaeger, *Das Leben des Fürsten von Pückler-Muskau* (Stuttgart: Metzler, 1843);

Auguste Erhard, *Le prince de Pückler-Muskau,* 2 volumes (Paris: Petits-fils de Plon et Nourrit,

1927-1928); translated by Friedrich von Oppeln-Bronikowski as *Fürst Pückler: Das abenteuerreiche Leben eines Künstlers und Edelmannes* (Berlin & Zurich: Atlantis, 1935);

E. M. Butler, *The Tempestuous Prince: Hermann Pückler-Muskau* (London, New York & Toronto: Longmans, Green, 1929);

Felix Gross, *Grand Seigneur: The Life and Loves of Prince Hermann Pueckler-Muskau: 1785-1871* (New York: Creative Age, 1943);

Klaus Günther Just, *Fürst Hermann von Pückler-Muskau: Leben und Werk: Mit einer Auswahl aus Pücklers Nachlaß* (Würzburg: Verlag Kulturwerk Schlesien, 1962);

Gerhard Friedrich Hering and Vita Huber, *Ein großer Herr: Das Leben des Fürsten Pückler* (Düsseldorf: Diederichs, 1968);

Heinz Ohff, *Fürst Hermann Pückler* (Berlin: Stapp, 1982);

Ohff, *Der grüne Fürst: Das abenteuerliche Leben des Prinzen Hermann von Pückler-Muskau* (Munich: Piper, 1991).

References:

Hermann Graf von Arnim, *Ein Fürst unter den Gärtnern: Pückler als Landschaftskünstler und der Muskauer Park* (Frankfurt am Main: Ullstein, 1981);

Sophie Gräfin von Arnim, *Goethe und Fürst Pückler* (Dresden: Von Zahn & Jaensch, 1932);

Brigitte Bender, *Ästhetische Strukturen der literarischen Landschaftsbeschreibung in den Reisewerken des Fürsten Pückler-Muskau* (Frankfurt am Main & Bern: Lang, 1982);

Hans Christoph Buch, " 'Sklaverei ist süß! Glaubt es, liebe Liberale!' Außenseiter: Fürst Pückler-Muskau und Ida Pfeiffer," in his *Die Nähe und die Ferne: Bausteine zu einer Poetik des kolonialen Blicks* (Frankfurt am Main: Suhrkamp, 1991), pp. 89-109;

Eva Caskel, *Gärten ruheloser Liebe: Roman um den Fürsten Pückler-Muskau* (Esslingen: Bechtle, 1955);

Lars Clausen, "Fürst Pückler auf dem Höhepunkt der Krise: Eine soziobiographische Erhellung des Landschaftskünstlers," in *Lebenswelt und soziale Probleme: Verhandlungen des 20. Deutschen Soziologentages zu Bremen 1980,* edited by Joachim Matthes (Frankfurt am Main: Campus, 1981), pp. 383-396;

Kasimir Edschmid, "Eine Reise des Fürsten Pückler-Muskau," *Velhagen und Klasings Almanach,* 19 (1927): 101-116;

Eduard Engel, "Die Pücklerei," in his *Deutsche Stilkunst,* thirty-first edition (Leipzig: Freytag, 1931), pp. 198-208;

August Erhard, "Bettina d'Arnim et le prince de Pückler-Muskau: Histoire d'une dédicace," *Revue germanique,* 14 (1923): 1-15;

Erhard, "Le Prince de Pückler-Muskau et la Pückler-Gesellschaft," *Revue germanique,* 25 (1932): 219-220;

Paul Fechter, "Der Schwiegersohn Hardenbergs: Fürst Hermann Pückler-Muskau," *Deutsche Rundschau,* 243 (April-May-June 1935): 205-212;

Otto Flake, "Pückler-Muskau: 1943/1948," in his *Die Verurteilung des Sokrates: Biographische Essays aus sechs Jahrzehnten,* edited by Fredy Gröbli-Schaub and Rolf Hochhuth (Heidelberg: Schneider, 1970), pp. 248-259;

Enid Margarete Gajek, "Die Bedeutung des Fürsten Hermann Pückler für Bettine," in *Herzhaft in die Dornen der Zeit greifen . . . : Bettine von Arnim: 1785-1859,* edited by Christoph Perels (Frankfurt am Main: Freies Deutsches Hochstift – Frankfurter Goethe-Museum, 1985), pp. 253-260;

Gajek, " 'Das gefährliche Spiel meiner Sinne': Gedanken zu Bettine und Pückler," *Internationales Jahrbuch der Bettina von Arnim Gesellschaft,* 3 (1989): 249-261;

"Genialer Erdbändiger," *Der Spiegel,* 41 (15 June 1987): 222-229;

Anna Cecille Grabein, *Der letzte große Kavalier, Hermann Fürst von Pückler-Muskau: Roman* (Berlin: Bernard & Graefe, 1943;

Rainer Gruenter, "Der reisende Fürst: Fürst Hermann Pückler-Muskau in England," in *"Der curieuse Passagier": Deutsche Englandsreisende des achtzehnten Jahrhunderts als Vermittler kultureller und technologischer Anregungen,* edited by Marie-Luise Spieckermann (Heidelberg: Winter, 1983), pp. 119-137;

Karl Hillebrand, "Fürst Pückler-Muskau," in his *Geist und Gesellschaft im alten Europa,* third edition (Stuttgart: Koehler, 1954), pp. 232-250;

Heinrich Hubert Houben, "Der Verstorbene, Semilasso und Kompagnie," in his *Kleine Blumen: Kleine Blätter aus Biedermeier und Vormärz* (Dessau: Rauch, 1925), pp. 60-86;

Eckart Kleßmann, "Hermann Fürst von Pückler-Muskau," in *Genie und Geld: Vom Auskommen deutscher Schriftsteller,* edited by Karl Corino, second edition (Nördlingen: Greno, 1988), pp. 270-279;

Wolfgang Knape and Erich Schutt, *Pücklers Parke* (Leipzig: Brockhaus, 1985);

Carla Sabine Kowohl, *Pückler-Muskau: Letterato e dandy nella Germania dell'Ottocento* (Rome: Edizioni di Storia e Letteratura, 1981);

Heinrich Laube, "Fürst Pückler-Muskau," in his *Gesammelte Werke,* edited by Heinrich Hubert Houben, volume 49 (Leipzig: Hesse, 1909), pp. 354–362;

Fanny Lewald, "Erinnerungen an Fürst Hermann von Pückler-Muskau und Bruchstücke aus seinen Briefen," in her *Zwölf Bilder nach dem Leben* (Berlin: Janke, 1888), pp. 282–330;

Reiner Marx, "Ein liberaler deutscher Adliger sieht Englands Metropole: Die Wahrnehmung Londons in Pückler-Muskaus 'Briefen eines Verstorbenen,' in *Rom-Paris-London: Erfahrung und Selbsterfahrung deutscher Schriftsteller und Künstler in den fremden Metropolen,* edited by Conrad Wiedemann (Stuttgart: Metzler, 1988), pp. 595–610;

Michael Maurer, "Skizzen aus dem sozialen und politischen Leben der Briten: Deutsche Englandsreiseberichte des 19. Jh.," in *Der Reisebericht,* edited by Peter J. Brenner (Frankfurt am Main: Suhrkamp, 1989), pp. 406–433;

Constantia Maxwell, "Hermann Ludwig Heinrich von Pückler-Muskau: A German Prince," in her *The Stranger in Ireland: From the Reign of Elizabeth to the Great Famine* (London: Cape, 1954), pp. 265–277;

Theodor Mundt, "Fürst Pückler: Ein Lebensbild," in *Deutsches Taschenbuch auf das Jahr 1837,* edited by Karl Büchner (Berlin: Duncker & Humblot, 1836), pp. 3–62;

George Paston [Emily Morse Symonds], "Prince Pückler-Muskau in England," in her *Little Memoirs of the Nineteenth Century* (London: Richards / New York: Dutton, 1902), pp. 279–322;

Wolfgang Paul, "Landschaftskünstler und Schriftsteller: Fürst Pückler 200 Jahre (30.10.1985)," *Neue Deutsche Hefte,* 32, no. 4 (1985): 756–768;

E. Petzold, *Fürst Hermann v. Pückler-Muskau in seinem Wirken in Muskau und Branitz sowie in seiner Bedeutung für die bildende Gartenkunst Deutschlands* (Leipzig: Weber, 1874);

Felix Poppenberg, "Mein Fürst," in his *Maskenzüge* (Berlin: Reiss, 1912), pp. 38–76;

Otto Graf Pückler, "Hermann Fürst von Pückler-Muskau: 1785–1871," in *Große Deutsche aus Schlesien,* edited by Herbert Hupka (Munich: Gräfe & Unzer, 1969), pp. 98–108;

Paul Rave, ed., *Fürst Hermann Pückler-Muskau* (Breslau: Korn, 1935);

Julian Schmidt, "Fürst Pückler," in his *Portraits aus dem neunzehnten Jahrhundert* (Berlin: Hertz, 1878), pp. 50–79;

Friedrich Schnapp, "Das 'anmuthige Beispiel' einer Luftfahrt 'geschätzter gräflicher Freunde,' " *Mitteilungen der E. T. A. Hoffmann-Gesellschaft,* 26 (1980): 16–21;

Friedrich Sengle, "Fürst Pückler-Muskau," in his *Biedermeierzeit: Deutsche Literatur im Spannungsfeld zwischen Restauration und Revolution 1815–1848,* volume 3: *Die Dichter* (Stuttgart: Metzler, 1980), pp. 262–265;

Friedrich Thiersch, *Apologie eines Philhellenen wider den Fürsten Hermann L. G. von Pückler Muskau* (Munich: Literarisch-artistische Anstalt, 1846);

Eugen Thurnher, "Jakob Philipp Fallmerayer und Hermann Fürst Pückler-Muskau: Die Reiseschilderung als Akt politischer Willensbildung im XIX. Jahrhundert," in *Sinn und Symbol,* edited by Karl Konrad Polheim (Bern: Lang, 1987), pp. 167–178;

Günter J. Vaupel, "Pückler-Muskau: Eine Betrachtung zur Komposition und Rezeption seiner Werke," *Schlesien,* 31, no. 4 (1986): 236–246;

Wulf Wülfing, "Reiseliteratur und Realitäten im Vormärz: Vorüberlegungen zu Schemata und Wirklichkeitsfindung im frühen 19. Jahrhundert," in *Reise und soziale Realität am Ende des 18. Jahrhunderts,* edited by Wolfgang Griep and Hans-Wolf Jäger (Heidelberg: Winter, 1983), pp. 371–394;

Fritz Zahn and Robert Kalwa, *Fürst Pückler-Muskau als Gartenkünstler und Mensch* (Cottbus: Heine, 1928).

Papers:

Most of Hermann von Pückler-Muskau's papers are in the Jagiellonian University Library in Kraków, Poland. Other materials are in the Goethe-Museum, Frankfurt am Main, and in the Staatsbibliothek Preußischer Kulturbesitz (State Library of Prussian Cultural Property), Berlin.

Levin Schücking

(6 September 1814 - 31 August 1883)

Carroll Hightower
Yale University

BOOKS: *Das malerische und romantische Westfalen,* by Schücking, Ferdinand Freiligrath, and Annette von Droste-Hülshoff (Leipzig: Volckmar, 1841);

Der Dom zu Köln und seine Vollendung, by Schücking and Droste-Hülshoff (Cologne: Boisserée, 1842);

Ein Schloß am Meer: Roman, 2 volumes (Leipzig: Brockhaus, 1843);

Gedichte (Stuttgart: Cotta, 1846);

Novellen, 2 volumes (Leipzig: Wigand, 1846);

Die Ritterbürtigen: Roman, 3 volumes (Leipzig: Brockhaus, 1846);

Eine dunkle Tat: Roman, 2 volumes (Leipzig: Brockhaus, 1846);

Eine Römerfahrt (Koblenz: Hölscher, 1848);

Ein Sohn des Volkes, 2 volumes (Leipzig: Brockhaus, 1849);

Heinrich von Gagern: Ein Lichtbild (Cologne: DuMont-Schauberg, 1849);

Der Bauernfürst, 2 volumes (Leipzig: Brockhaus, 1851);

Die Königin der Nacht: Roman (Leipzig: Brockhaus, 1852);

Familienbilder, 2 volumes, by Schücking and Louise von Gall (Vienna & Leipzig: Günther, 1854);

Familiengeschichten, 2 volumes, by Schücking and Gall (Vienna & Leipzig: Günther, 1854);

Ein Redekampf zu Florenz: Dramatisches Gedicht (Berlin: Schindler, 1854);

Ein Staatsgeheimnis: Roman, 3 volumes (Leipzig: Brockhaus, 1854);

Der Held der Zukunft, 2 volumes (Prague & Hamburg: Richter, 1855);

Geneanomische Briefe (Frankfurt am Main: Brönner, 1855);

Eine Eisenbahnfahrt durch Westfalen (Leipzig: Brockhaus, 1855);

Der Sohn eines berühmten Mannes (Vienna & Leipzig: Günther, 1856);

Die Sphinx (Leipzig: Brockhaus, 1856);

Von Minden nach Köln (Leipzig: Brockhaus, 1856);

Levin Schücking

Günther von Schwarzburg: Historischer Roman (Prague & Vienna: Müller, 1857);

Paul Bronckhorst oder Die neuen Herren, 3 volumes (Leipzig: Brockhaus, 1858);

Aus den Tagen der großen Kaiserin: Historische Novellen, 2 volumes (Prague & Hamburg: Richter, 1858);

Die Rheider Burg, 2 volumes (Vienna & Leipzig: Günther, 1859);

Gesammelte Erzählungen und Novellen, 6 volumes (Hannover: Rümpler, 1859-1866);

Bilder aus Westfalen (Elberfeld: Friderichs, 1860);
Eines Kriegsknechts Abenteuer, 2 volumes (Vienna & Leipzig: Günther, 1861);
Die Geschwornen und ihr Richter, 3 volumes (Hannover: Rümpler, 1861);
Die Marketenderin von Köln: Roman, 3 volumes (Leipzig: Brockhaus, 1861);
Annette von Droste: Ein Lebensbild (Hannover: Rümpler, 1862);
Eine Actiengesellschaft, 3 volumes (Hannover: Rümpler, 1863);
Aus der Franzosenzeit; Landeron: Novellen (Vienna & Leipzig: Günther, 1863);
Ausgewählte Romane, 24 volumes (Leipzig: Brockhaus, 1864–1875);
Aus alter und neuer Zeit, 2 volumes (Vienna & Leipzig: Günther, 1864);
Frauen und Rätsel, 2 volumes (Leipzig: Brockhaus, 1865);
Eine Künstlerleidenschaft: Novelle (Hannover: Rümpler, 1867);
Verschlungene Wege: Roman, 3 volumes (Hannover: Rümpler, 1867; revised edition, Leipzig: Brockhaus, 1874);
Schloß Dornegge oder Der Weg zum Glück: Roman, 4 volumes (Leipzig: Brockhaus, 1868);
Neue Novellen (Berlin: Lesser, 1868);
Die Malerin aus dem Louvre: Roman, 4 volumes (Hannover: Rümpler, 1869);
Luther in Rom, 3 volumes (Hannover: Rümpler, 1870); translated by Mrs. Eudora South as *Luther in Rome; or, Corradina, the Last of the Hohenstaufen: A Religio-Historical Romance* (Boston: Thayer, 1890);
Erinnerungen an Heinrich Heine (Leipzig, 1870);
Jean Jacques Rousseau: Zwei Episoden aus seinem Leben (Leipzig: Günther, 1870);
Filigran, 2 volumes (Hannover: Rümpler, 1870–1872);
Deutsche Kämpfe: Zwei Erzählungen, 2 volumes (Leipzig: Günther, 1871);
Krieg und Frieden: Novellenbuch, 3 volumes (Leipzig: Günther, 1872);
Herrn Didier's Landhaus: Roman, 3 volumes (Hannover: Rümpler, 1872);
Wilderich: In der Löwenapotheke (Berlin: Goldschmidt, 1873);
Die drei Freier (Leipzig: Reclam, 1873);
Die Heiligen und die Ritter, 4 volumes (Hannover: Rümpler, 1873);
Aus heißen Tagen: Geschichten (Stuttgart: Simon, 1874);
Das Capital (Berlin: Goldschmidt, 1875);
Feuer und Flamme: Roman, 3 volumes (Stuttgart: Simon, 1875); translated by Mrs. Evangeline O'Connor as *Fire and Flame* (New York: Appleton, 1876);
Ein Familiendrama (Berlin: Goldschmidt, 1876);
Der Doppelgänger: Roman (Herzberg: Simon, 1876);
Ein Freund in der Not: Novelle (Stuttgart: Kröner, 1877);
Novellenbuch, 2 volumes (Hannover: Rümpler, 1877);
Der Erbe von Hornegg: Roman, 3 volumes (Hannover: Rümpler, 1878);
Die Herberge der Gerechtigkeit: Roman, 2 volumes (Leipzig: Brockhaus, 1879);
Sklaven des Herzens; Viola: Zwei Novellen (Berlin: Goldschmidt, 1879);
Die Mündel des Papstes: Historisches Drama (Leipzig: Reclam, 1879);
Das Recht des Lebenden: Roman, 3 volumes (Leipzig: Brockhaus, 1880);
Seltsame Brüder: Roman, 3 volumes (Leipzig: Brockhaus, 1881);
Wunderliche Menschen: Drei Erzählungen (Berlin: Goldschmidt, 1881);
Etwas auf dem Gewissen (Stuttgart: Spemann, 1882);
Alte Ketten: Roman, 2 volumes (Breslau: Schottländer, 1883);
Heimatlaub: Novellen, 2 volumes (Herzberg: Simon, 1884);
Große Menschen: Roman, 3 volumes (Breslau: Schottländer, 1884);
Ein ehrlicher Mann: Humoristische Erzählung (Berlin: Goldschmidt, 1884);
Zwei Novellen: Virago; In dunkler Nacht (Berlin: Goldschmidt, 1885);
Recht und Liebe (Breslau: Schottländer, 1886);
Lebenserinnerungen, 2 volumes (Breslau: Schottländer, 1886);
Immortellen: Novellen (Breslau: Schottländer Verlags-Anstalt, 1887);
Novellen (Minden: Bruns, 1889);
Der Familienschild, by Schücking and Droste-Hülshoff (N.p., 1898; reprinted, Münster: Aschendorff, 1960).

OTHER: A. Brownell Jameson, *Shakespeare-Frauengestalten: Charakteristiken,* translated by Schücking (Bielefeld: Velhagen & Klasing, 1840);
Rheinisches Jahrbuch für Kunst und Poesie, edited by Schücking (Cologne: Köhnen, 1846);
Helvetia: Natur, Geschichte, Sage im Spiegel deutscher Dichtung, edited by Schücking (Frankfurt am Main: Jügel, 1851);

Italia: Deutsche Dichter als Führer jenseits der Alpen, edited by Schücking (Frankfurt am Main: Jügel, 1851);

Annette von Droste-Hülshoff, *Letzte Gaben: Nachgelassene Blätter,* edited by Schücking (Hannover: Rümpler, 1860);

Alain-René Lesage, *Der hinkende Teufel,* 2 volumes, translated by Schücking (Hildburgshausen: Bibliographisches Institut, 1866);

Jean-Jacques Rousseau, *Bekenntnisse,* 2 volumes, translated by Schücking (Hildburgshausen: Bibliographisches Institut, 1870);

Droste-Hülshoff, *Gesammelte Schriften,* 3 volumes, edited by Schücking (Stuttgart: Cotta, 1878–1879);

Karl Immermann, *Der Oberhof,* introduction by Schücking (Stuttgart: Spemann, 1881).

Schücking, age nineteen; pencil drawing by P. Schilgen (from Annette von Droste-Hülshoff, Werke, *edited by I. E. Walter, 1954)*

Best known in the history of German literature for his friendship with the poet Annette von Droste-Hülshoff, Levin Schücking is a literary figure in his own right. Schücking, who gave up a career in journalism to pursue his literary ambitions full-time, wrote more than thirty novels and many novellas, as well as dramas and lyric poetry. He also wrote travel literature, mostly about his native Westphalia. He was an active and highly esteemed member of the German literary community and had contacts with such major nineteenth-century German authors as Ferdinand Freiligrath, Karl Gutzkow, and Heinrich Heine. For a writer he led a rather placid life; he suffered few privations after his early years, since he was able to earn a more than adequate living by his pen.

The Schücking family can be traced back to the fourteenth century in Westphalia. Schücking was born on 6 September 1814 in Clemenswerth bei Meppen, Westphalia, to Paulus Modestus Schücking, a civil servant, and Katharina Busch Schücking, a poet. When he was sent to the gymnasium in Münster in 1830, he carried with him a letter of introduction from his mother to her friend Droste-Hülshoff, who was living on her mother's small estate, Rüschhaus. Schücking was received there for the first time in the spring of 1831. In the autumn of that year his mother died, and Droste-Hülshoff, who was seventeen years older than Schücking, began to take a motherly interest in the young man.

In 1833 Schücking, like six generations of male Schückings before him, began the study of law, attending in turn the Universities of Munich, Heidelberg, and Göttingen. Unlike his ancestors, however, he had no real interest in jurisprudence, and in 1837 he returned to Münster. In the same year his father, who had remarried, departed for a prolonged visit to America, leaving his son with no means of support. To eke out a living Schücking gave private lessons in modern languages; he also found himself with enough time to devote himself to literary pursuits, which he had begun as a pastime in Göttingen. His own creative efforts brought him no remuneration, but his talent as a critic did: he collaborated with Gutzkow on the latter's journal, *Der Telegraph für Deutschland;* impressed by his critical faculties, Gutzkow offered him the editorship of the journal, but Schücking declined it.

Schücking's association with Droste-Hülshoff was renewed in 1837, when they met at the home of Elise Rüdiger. They found that they had common literary interests, and Droste-Hülshoff took on the task of finding the young man a secure position and salary.

In the summer of 1839 Schücking met Freiligrath, who had come to Münster to do studies for the book *Das malerische und romantische Westfalen* (Picturesque and Romantic Westphalia, 1841). In the course of writing it Freiligrath realized that he was not equal to the task, and Schücking took it over around the end of 1840. Schücking was the perfect person to write the book, given his knowledge of the history of the area, but even he was pushed to complete it on time. Droste-Hülshoff came to the rescue, adding her extensive knowledge of the places and personages of Westphalia to the project, although she was not listed as a collaborator. She also contributed to Schücking's *Der Dom zu Köln und seine Vollendung* (The Cologne Cathedral and Its Completion, 1842) and the novella *Der Familienschild* (The Family Escutcheon, 1898). In the meantime the relationship, which began as that of mentor and protegé, had become a real friendship.

Droste-Hülshoff spent the winter of 1839–1840 at Rüschhaus, where Schücking visited her every week. In September 1841 she moved to the estate of her brother-in-law, Baron Josef von Laßberg, at Meersburg on Lake Constance; a month after her arrival Schücking was offered the job of cataloguing the Provençal manuscripts in the baron's library. The time he spent there was a period of prodigious literary production for Droste-Hülshoff. In his *Lebenserinnerungen* (Memoirs, 1886) Schücking attributes this productivity to a bet he made with the poet that she could not produce a volume of poetry within a few months. Whether or not such a bet existed, it is certain that Schücking's presence was a decisive factor in stimulating her creative powers; for this reason Schücking is often said to have been the most important man in her life.

There has been much speculation as to whether an element of romantic love was present in the relationship between Schücking and his "Mütterchen" (little mother), as he called Droste-Hülshoff. Certainly deep bonds of affection united them, but they were too practical to ignore the differences in age and in class that separated them. Schücking left Meersburg in the spring of 1842 for Ellingen, where he became tutor to the two sons of Prince von Wrede. The position turned out to be unsatisfactory, and by early 1843 Schücking had resolved to leave it.

Around the same time, Schücking was asked by Baron von Cotta to take over the editorship of Cotta's *Allgemeine Zeitung* in Augsburg. Schücking accepted the position eagerly because it would make it possible for him to marry Louise von Gall of Darmstadt. The couple had become acquainted through an increasingly intimate correspondence and had become engaged without ever having seen one another. Gall was also a writer and had had several novellas published in Cotta's *Morgenblatt.* Schücking finally met his fiancée face-to-face in the late spring of 1843, and they were married in October. After an attempt to obtain a professorship at the University of Gießen failed, Schücking took the job in Augsburg that Cotta had offered him. In 1845 he accepted editorship of the *Kölnische Zeitung.*

At Easter 1844 Schücking brought his bride to meet his "Mütterchen." Before his marriage Droste-Hülshoff had counseled prudence, urging him not to commit himself to Gall before he had gotten to know her personally. She accepted the marriage once it was a fait accompli, but naturally the new circumstances introduced an element of distance into their relationship. This distance was increased by the appearance in 1846 of Schücking's *Gedichte* (Poems). Droste-Hülshoff gave the work a cool reception because, although the poems did not actually espouse revolutionary ideals, they embraced the ideas of the liberal "Junges Deutschland" (Young Germany) literary movement too much to suit the loyal member of the Westphalian aristocracy.

Droste-Hülshoff's break with Schücking came when his *Die Ritterbürtigen* (Those of Knightly Birth) was published later that year. The work, a historical novel in the manner of Sir Walter Scott, is characterized mainly by its unsympathetic portrayal of the Westphalian nobility. Many members of that nationality and class blamed Droste-Hülshoff – sometimes rightly – for various revelations contained in the book. The ensuing uproar made Droste-Hülshoff angry enough to refuse to see the Schückings on her next trip to Lake Constance, and she never saw either of them again before her death in May 1848.

In the spring of 1846 Schücking met Heine while on assignment in Paris for the *Kölnische Zeitung.* In the fall of 1847 he went to Rome as the Italian correspondent for the newspaper. The trip resulted in a travel book, *Eine Römerfahrt* (A Trip to Rome, 1848), and an anthology of poems, *Italia* (1851). He returned to Germany in February 1848 and edited the *Kölnische Zeitung* for the next four years. In 1852, desiring more independence, he gave up his job at the newspaper to live from the proceeds of his writing; by this time he was sufficiently well known and prolific that he was able to do so. Later that year he purchased and moved into his family's ancestral estate in Sassenberg, Westphalia.

The Schückings had two sons and two daughters when Luise Schücking died in early 1855. Schücking's grief did not slow his pen: by this time he was writing at least a novel a year, most of them longer than one volume, and was producing novellas and dramas at the same time. His novels from the period following his wife's death include *Paul*

Bronckhorst (1858), *Verschlungene Wege* (Winding Paths, 1867), and *Schloß Dornegge* (Castle Dornegge, 1868). Some of Schücking's novels were translated into English, Dutch, Italian, or Hungarian, and several collected editions of his works appeared.

In addition to his own vast literary production, Schücking worked tirelessly to increase the fame of his late friend Droste-Hülshoff. In 1860 he edited a posthumous edition of her poems, *Letzte Gaben* (Last Gifts), and in 1862 his biography of her, *Annette von Droste: Ein Lebensbild* (Annette von Droste: A Portrait from Life), appeared. He also edited the first edition of her collected works, which was published by Cotta in 1878–1879. He died while visiting his younger son, a physician, in Pyrmont on 31 August 1883.

Critical assessment of Schücking's works is mixed. Some critics recognize in him a true artist, though Johannes Hagemann laments that his reputation is not enhanced by some of the works which he was compelled to write in order to support himself. Hermann Hüffer considers that because of his knowledge of and affection for the area Schücking is at his best when writing about his native Westphalia. All agree that he is overshadowed by Droste-Hülshoff, whose renown he worked so hard to secure.

Levin Schücking

Letters:

Briefe von Annette von Droste-Hülshoff und Levin Schücking, edited by Theo Schücking (Leipzig: Grunow, 1893); enlarged edition, edited by Reinhold Conrad Muschler (Leipzig: Grunow, 1928).

References:

Richard Fritze, *Der Anteil Annettes von Droste-Hülshoff an Levin Schückings Werken* (Greifswald: Adler, 1911);

Johannes Hagemann, *Levin Schücking: Der Dichter und sein Werk* (Emsdetten: Lechte, 1959);

Hagemann, *Levin Schückings literarische Frühzeit* (Münster: Coppenrath, 1911);

Hermann Hüffer, "Levin Schücking," in *Allgemeine Deutsche Biographie,* volume 23, second edition (Berlin: Duncker & Humblot, 1971), pp. 643–647;

Mary E. Morgan, *Annette von Droste-Hülshoff: A Biography* (Bern: Lang, 1984);

Kurt Pinthus, *Die Romane Levin Schückings* (Leipzig: Voigtlander, 1911);

Joseph Raßmann, *Das dramatische Schaffen Levin Schückings* (Ohlau: Eschenhagen, 1937);

Manfred Schier, "Die Droste über Levin Schücking," in *Kleine Beiträge zur Droste-Forschung,* edited by Winfried Woesler (Münster: Stenderhoff, 1970), pp. 7–15;

Schier, "Die Poesie des Schlosses im Werke Levin Schückings," in *Beiträge zur Droste-Forschung* (Dülmen: Laumann, 1977), pp. 129–151;

Levin Ludwig Schücking, "Ferdinand Freiligrath und Levin Schücking" and "Die Lebenserinnerungen Levin Schückings," in his *Essays über Shakespeare, Pepys, Rossetti, Shaw und anderes* (Wiesbaden: Dieterich, 1948), pp. 417–489;

Heinrich Schulte, *Levin Schücking und Wilhelm Junkmann als Lyriker* (Münster: Westfälische Vereinsdruckerei, 1916).

Papers:

Levin Schücking's papers are in the archives of the Schücking family estate in Sassenberg über Warendorf, Westphalia.

Charles Sealsfield
(Carl Postl)
(3 March 1793 – 26 May 1864)

Jeffrey L. Sammons
Yale University

Charles Sealsfield

BOOKS: *Die Vereinigten Staaten von Nordamerika, nach ihren politischen, religiösen und gesellschaftlichen Verhältnissen betrachtet: Mit einer Reise durch den westlichen Theil von Pennsylvanien, Ohio, Kentucky, Indiana, Illinois, Missuri* [sic], *Tennessee, das Gebiet Arkansas, Missisippi* [sic], *und Louisiana,* as C. Sidons, 2 volumes (Stuttgart & Tübingen: Cotta, 1827); volume 1 revised and translated anonymously by Sealsfield as *The United States of North America as They Are in Their Political, Religious, and Social Relations* (London: Simpkin & Marshall, 1828); volume 2 revised and translated anonymously by Sealsfield as *The Americans as They Are: Described in a Tour through the Valley of the Mississippi* (London: Hurst, Chance, 1828);

Austria as It Is: or, Sketches of Continental Courts: By an Eye-Witness, anonymous (London: Hurst, Chance, 1828);

Tokeah; or, The White Rose, anonymous, 2 volumes (Philadelphia: Carey, Lea & Carey, 1829); revised as *The Indian Chief; or, Tokeah and the White Rose: A Tale of the Indians and the Whites,* anonymous, 3 volumes (Philadelphia: Carey, Lea & Carey, 1829; London: Newman, 1829); revised, enlarged, and translated anonymously by Sealsfield as *Der Legitime und die Republikaner: Eine Geschichte aus dem letzten amerikanisch-englischen Kriege,* 3 volumes (Zurich: Orell, Füßli, 1833);

Transatlantische Reiseskizzen und Christophorus Bärenhäuter, anonymous, 2 volumes (Zurich: Orell, Füßli, 1834);

Der Virey und die Aristokraten oder Mexiko im Jahre 1812, anonymous, 3 volumes (Zurich: Orell, Füßli, 1835);

Lebensbilder aus beiden Hemisphären: Die große Tour, anonymous, 2 volumes (Zurich: Orell, Füßli, 1835); revised as *Morton oder Die große Tour,* anonymous, 2 volumes (Stuttgart: Metzler, 1844);

Lebensbilder aus beiden Hemisphären, dritter Theil: Ralph Doughby's Esqu. Brautfahrt oder Der transatlantischen Reiseskizzen dritter Theil, anonymous (Zurich: Orell, Füßli, 1835);

Lebensbilder aus beiden Hemisphären, vierter Theil: Pflanzerleben oder Der transatlantischen Reiseskizzen vierter Theil, anonymous (Zurich: Schultheß, 1836);

Lebensbilder aus beiden Hemisphären, fünfter Theil: Die Farbigen oder Der transatlantischen Reiseskizzen fünfter Theil, anonymous (Zurich: Schultheß, 1836);

Lebensbilder aus beiden Hemisphären, sechster Theil: Nathan der Squatter-Regulator, oder Der erste Amerikaner in Texas. Der transatlantischen Reisekizzen sechster Theil, anonymous (Zurich: Schultheß, 1837);

Neue Land- und Seebilder: Die Deutsch-amerikanischen Wahlverwandtschaften, anonymous, 4 volumes (Zurich: Schultheß, 1839–1840); translated anonymously as *Rambleton: A Romance of Fashionable Life in New York, during the Great Speculation of 1836* (New York: Winchester, 1844);

Das Cajütenbuch oder Nationale Charakteristiken, 2 volumes (Zurich: Schultheß, 1841); translated by C. F. Mersch as *The Cabin Book; or Sketches of Life in Texas* (New York: Winchester, 1844); translated by Sarah Powell as *The Cabin Book; or, National Characteristics* (London: Ingram, Cooke, 1852);

Süden und Norden, anonymous, 3 volumes (Stuttgart: Metzler, 1842–1843); translated by Joel T. Headley as *North and South; or, Scenes and Adventures in Mexico* (New York: Winchester, 1844);

Gesammelte Werke, 18 volumes (Stuttgart: Metzler, 1843–1846);

Die Grabesschuld: Nachgelassene Erzählung, edited by Alfred Meißner (Leipzig: Günther, 1873);

Gesamtausgabe der amerikanischen Romane, edited by Franz Riederer (Meersburg am Bodensee & Leipzig, 1937);

Sämtliche Werke, edited by Karl J. R. Arndt and others, 27 volumes projected (Hildesheim & New York: Olms, 1972–).

Editions in English: *Life in the New World; or Sketches of American Society,* translated by Gustavus C. Hebbe and James A. Mackay (New York: Winchester, 1844);

Scenes and Adventures in Central America, selected and translated by Frederick Hardman (Edinburgh & London: Blackwood, 1852);

Frontier Life; or, Scenes and Adventures in the South West, selected and translated by Hardman (New York: Derby & Miller, 1853);

America: Glorious and Chaotic Land. Charles Sealsfield Discovers the Young United States. An Account of Our Post-Revolutionary Ancestors by a Contemporary, abridged, adapted, and translated by E. L. Jordan (Englewood Cliffs, N.J.: Prentice-Hall, 1969);

The Making of an American, selected, adapted, and translated by Ulrich S. Carrington (Dallas: Southern Methodist University Press, 1974).

SELECTED PERIODICAL PUBLICATIONS – UNCOLLECTED: "A Night on the Banks of Tennessee," *New York Mirror and Ladies' Literary Gazette,* 7 (31 October 1829): 129–130;

"A Sketch from Life," *New York Mirror and Ladies' Literary Gazette,* 7 (7 November 1829): 141–142;

"Early Impressions: A Fragment. By The Author of Tokeah," *Atlantic Souvenir,* 5 (1830): 149–167;

"Scenes in Poland: Nr. I. 1794. Macejovice and Praga," *Englishman's Magazine,* 1 (April 1831): 26–32;

"Scenes in Poland: Nr. II. 1816. Varsovie, Dobravice," *Englishman's Magazine,* 1 (May 1831): 179–190;

"My Little Grey Landlord," *Englishman's Magazine,* 1 (June 1831): 268–280;

"Three Meetings on the King's Highway," *Englishman's Magazine,* 1 (July 1831): 401–410;

"Borelli and Menotti," *Englishman's Magazine,* 1 (August 1831): 608–615.

The writer who called himself Charles Sealsfield was the first important author of fiction about the United States in the German language. German interest in the New World dates virtually from the fifteenth-century voyages of exploration, and it generated a large body of writing – some of it informational, some fanciful – along with motifs and allusions in the works of many writers, among them Johann Wolfgang von Goethe. But Sealsfield was the first to write ambitious novels in German from an American perspective. He became a highly visible and much discussed writer shortly before the middle of the nineteenth century, after which his reputation declined to that of a curiosity on the periphery of literary history; in recent decades interest in him has intensified, and he is once again a topic of lively inquiry and dispute.

Sealsfield lived a mysterious, masked life, and there is much about him that is not known or understood. It is difficult to think with any assurance of any other major German-language writer of the last two centuries about whom less is known unless it were the twentieth-century writer of fiction about America, B. Traven, whose career and disguises bear some resemblances to Sealsfield's. Much of the little Sealsfield had to say about himself is pure invention. Dogged research has unearthed a substantial amount of information, but the remaining puzzles have led to a good deal of sometimes dubiously founded speculation that gets copied from one account to another without examination. Most sources, except for those of the most recent generation of scholars, should be used with caution.

Sealsfield was born Carl Postl on 3 March 1793 in the village of Poppitz in Moravia to Anton Postl, a vintner, and Juliane Postl, née Rabel. After attending a gymnasium in Znaim he became a student at the convent of the Order of the Holy Cross with the Red Star in Prague in 1808. There he encountered the teachings of the liberal, rationalist theologian Bernard Bolzano; much has been written about Bolzano's influence on him. Postl became a monk in the order in 1813, was ordained a priest in 1814, and soon became secretary to the grand master, but he evidently became disaffected. The reactionary regulations of the Metternichian regime, in consequence of which Bolzano was removed from his teaching position and his writings were proscribed in 1819, may have motivated Postl's alienation. In any case, in 1823 he disappeared. The authorities combed Bohemia and Austria but could find no trace of him. For his family, friends, and acquaintances, that was the end of the history of Carl Postl for the next forty years.

It is now known that he turned up later that year in New Orleans; for the next three years he lived variously in Pittsburgh, New York, Philadelphia, and Kittanning, Pennsylvania, spending his winters in Louisiana. He acquired a passport under the name "Charles Sealsfield, Citizen of the United States, clergyman, native of Pennsylvania." Whether he was actually ordained by a Protestant denomination is not known, but for the rest of his life he retained a strong Christian though militantly anti-Catholic allegiance. As is the case with all his sojourns in America, it is unclear what he was doing or how he supported himself. He appears to have had connections with the Freemasons; scholarship on this matter has, however, become contaminated with delusions about international Masonic conspiracies, and the whole question needs to be restudied.

In 1826 he returned to Europe, spending the next year and a half in France, Germany, and England. He opened his literary career with a two-volume expository work on America, published in German in 1827 under the name "C. Sidons, citizen of the United States of North America" as *Die Vereinigten Staaten von Nordamerika* and anonymously in English in 1828 as *The United States of America as They Are* and *The Americans as They Are*, followed in the same year by an assault on the despotism of the Metternichian regime in the guise of an imaginary travel report, *Austria as It Is*. Reportage on America came to be a vast genre in nineteenth-century German letters, particularly as the question of emigration began to preoccupy the minds of millions. Sealsfield is virtually unique among German writers, however, in the intensity with which he associated himself with a particular faction of American politics: the Southern and Western agrarian strand of the Jacksonian movement. His essays on America read like pieces of Jacksonian campaign propaganda. Sealsfield could be rather gullible in political matters; he seems actually to have believed that John Quincy Adams was a Tory bent on establishing a hereditary monarchy in his family.

Sealsfield was a man of violent and inflexible opinions. Although he read and admired the works of Alexis de Tocqueville, he had nothing of Tocqueville's liberality, spirit of inquiry, or sense of the limitations of his own perceptions. He was an evangelist of what he presented as a revolution in the human condition that had taken place on American soil. His new Adam is a free and independent citizen; fanatically patriotic; convinced of the superiority of the American in virtue and sense to all the other servile, priest-ridden peoples of the earth; and committed to the sacredness of private property. The American community is democratic but hostile to and contemptuous of foreigners such as the British, the Mexicans, and the newer Irish and German immigrants. Although Sealsfield traveled all around the United States, his narrative perspective is with few exceptions that of the antebellum, pioneer South; his heroes are yeoman farmers and plantation owners who are virtually a law to themselves under conditions of weak or practically nonexistent government. For the Eastern, urbanizing strand of the Jacksonian movement, which has been regarded as a foundation of modern American democracy, he felt no affinity whatsoever; and when it achieved an apparent ascendancy in the presidency of Martin Van Buren, he lost all respect for American politics.

The Southern perspective raises the sensitive and long-evaded question of Sealsfield's attitude toward slavery. While he judged slavery to be a misfortune and possibly an injustice, he fully internalized the Southern white ideology. He regarded emancipation as impossible, abolitionists as agitators against public order, and slaves as a form of property as inviolable as any other. In addition, he was intensely racist, much more explicitly so than the American Southern writers of his time. His racism is but a facet of an intolerance that is so spectacularly pronounced that it reaches almost comic dimensions, so that one sometimes wonders whether it is meant to be ironic or hyperbolic. It is not, however, an unrealistic depiction of the tone of American life in the 1820s and 1830s. His ferocious anti-

Catholicism exactly reproduces a well-documented strain of public discourse, as does his contempt for Mexicans and his increasingly nativist disdain for Irish and German immigrants. But these attitudes, which can be exasperating and grating for the modern reader, are curiously interconnected with his strengths as a writer, for they are aspects of the tremendous energy of liberty that he saw radiating from the American experience. He reveled in the anarchism, lawlessness, and violence of American life that often worried and repelled other European observers, and he thought Americans were well rid of European culture – the alleged absence of which has been an enduring strand of German anti-American discourse to the present day – for he associated it with a regime of despotic privilege. He was delighted by the boasting and outrageous tall tales that became such a prominent part of American folklore, and he strove, not always with perfect success but more ingeniously than any other writer, to reproduce in German the cadences and locutions of American speech, especially of the frontier.

In 1827 he returned to the United States. He is supposed to have owned and failed with a plantation on the Red River, but no trace of it has ever been found. During this time his sketches and stories began to be published in American and English journals (The bibliography of these ephemera is in an insecure state, and the problem may be insoluble. Many items have been tentatively ascribed to Sealsfield, but only a few are certainly his.)

His first novel, *Tokeah; or, The White Rose* (1829), set at the time of the War of 1812, is a complicated tale of the reintegration into white society of a girl who had been adopted and raised by an Indian tribe. The novel was rather evidently written under the influence of James Fenimore Cooper, three of whose Leatherstocking Tales had appeared by then. Sealsfield came to admire Cooper less as time went on, and the Cooperian influence diminished accordingly. One can see the beginnings of this emancipation in the considerably revised German version, *Der Legitime und die Republikaner* (The Legitimate One and the Republicans, 1833), in which the political significance has been considerably sharpened. Sealsfield is sympathetic with the eventually balked Indian chief Tokeah but is not his partisan. Tokeah is both noble *and* savage, and both the nobility and the savagery are "legitimate" – that is, obsolete, like the absolutist European nobility. The Indians are subject to displacement by the invincible historical wave of the "republicans," the new farmer-aristocracy, which cannot be expected to allow valuable arable land to be roamed by nomadic aboriginal hunters. This view is made explicit by General Andrew Jackson himself in a scene following the Battle of New Orleans.

For some months in 1830 Sealsfield was associated with the *Courrier des Etats-Unis* in New York. This long-lived French-language newspaper was at that time owned by Joseph Bonaparte, the former king of Naples and of Spain, who was then living in exile in New Jersey. Sealsfield apparently became a kind of agent for Bonaparte, running errands for him in Switzerland to the former queen of Holland, Hortense, the mother of the future Emperor Napoleon III. This is another of the tantalizingly unclear episodes in Sealsfield's life.

In 1830 Sealsfield returned to Europe; there is evidence that he then visited Sir Walter Scott, whom he regarded as a model. He traveled in France and England; in 1832 he moved to Switzerland, living in Arenenberg, Aarau, Stein, Baden, and Zurich. He launched the central phase of his literary career with *Transatlantische Reiseskizzen und Christophorus Bärenhäuter* (Transatlantic Travel Sketches and Christopher Loafer, 1834), which contains the first of his stories set in what was then the Southwest of the United States, "George Howard's Esq. Brautfahrt" (translated as "The Courtship of George Howard, Esquire," in *Life in the New World,* 1842). This work was followed by *Der Virey und die Aristokraten oder Mexiko im Jahre 1812* (The Viceroy and the Aristocrats; or, Mexico in the Year 1812, 1835), a novel of the chaotic political struggles in Mexico around 1812. The often opaque narration reproduces the confusion of civil war in a wild, bizarre land; the complexities of class and race; and the intrigues of the British. The point is to demonstrate that Mexicans, unlike Americans, are not mature enough for liberty, and the story ends in compromises by the privileged designed to control the masses. In the same year appeared *Die große Tour* (The Grand Tour), which tells of Morton, a young American who is driven to the brink of suicide by a business failure; he is rescued by a prosperous, elderly German (in Sealsfield's eyes not an immigrant, but a settler from the time of the Revolution), who introduces him to a powerful Philadelphia financier; the latter sends Morton on a mysterious mission to London. The novel is a fragment; there has been some speculation as to why Sealsfield did not continue it. A passage about a miserly moneylender was lifted from Honoré de Balzac's *Gobseck* (1830), and the whole work is colored by the demonization of commerce and finance and is a dark, implausible melodrama of capitalist intrigue and manipulation of world politics.

Sealsfield originally made the two volumes of *Die große Tour* the first two parts of a series, *Lebensbilder aus beiden Hemisphären* (Pictures of Life from Both Hemispheres); but, since it is the only one of these works to take place in the Eastern Hemisphere, for his collected edition beginning in 1843 he made it a separate work and retitled the series *Lebensbilder aus der westlichen Hemisphäre* (Pictures of Life from the Western Hemisphere). For the new first part of that series he took "George Howard's Esq. Brautfahrt" from *Transatlantische Reiseskizzen*; it is the story of a young man who becomes disgusted with the affected, fashionable belles of New York society and wanders to Louisiana in search of a bride. Here can be seen the development of Sealsfield's characteristic structure: interlocking, overlapping stories hooked loosely together in a set of Chinese boxes of first-person narrations, a device that was noted and even parodied in his time. It generates a multiple perspective of opinion and ideology, so that the prejudices and eccentricities of the characters fall at least technically to their account rather than the author's.

The third part of *Lebensbilder aus beiden Hemisphären* is *Ralph Doughby's Esqu. Brautfahrt* (1835; translated as "The Courtship of Ralph Doughby, Esquire," in *Life in the New World*), which concerns a crude, wild Kentuckian who nevertheless is shown to be a positive character, for he is converted from a Federalist to a Jacksonian. The fourth and fifth parts are made up of *Pflanzerleben* (Plantation Life, 1836; translated as "The Life of a Planter," in *Life in the New World*) and *Die Farbigen* (The Colored; translated as "Scenes in the South-West," in *Life in the New World*) and consist of sketches, stories, and conversations about society and politics in Louisiana. The "colored," incidentally, are not the blacks but dark-skinned Creoles suspected of being of mixed race and therefore dangerously sensual and morally suspect. Sealsfield's sexual representations are simultaneously moralistic and lascivious. His American characters are always chaste, a point of which he makes much, but a dangerous sensual magnetism can be generated by women of darker racial composition – a motif that would play an important role in his last novel. His view of the French in Louisiana, as of all non-Anglo-Saxon peoples in America, is condescending; but it is also amusedly tolerant of their childlike frivolity and European social notions. Both Doughby and Howard marry Creoles, thus symbolizing the amalgamation of the two cultures – with the clear understanding that the American culture is superior and must establish the tone of social and political relations.

An assimilated Frenchman is the main narrator of the sixth part of *Lebensbilder aus beiden Hemisphären, Nathan der Squatter-Regulator* (1837; translated as "The Squatter Chief; or, The First American in Texas," in *Life in the New World*), a historical narration that takes the reader back to the time of the Spanish administration of the Louisiana Territory. In Nathan Strong one sees Sealsfield's ideal American leader, now believed to have been modeled after Daniel Boone. He is invincible because he is an agent of the ineluctable spread of freedom. He is a creator of law and discipline, but he can bear no governance outside his own will, and, as the writ of the federal government makes itself increasingly felt after the Louisiana Purchase, he removes to ungoverned Texas (Mexican authority is not regarded seriously) to begin again and become extremely wealthy.

In 1837 Sealsfield made a short visit to the United States for reasons that are unclear; the sea voyage, however, with its alternation of frightening storm and frustrating calm, provided an impressive segment of his next novel, *Die Deutsch-amerikanischen Wahlverwandtschaften* (German-American Elective Affinities, 1839–1840; translated as *Rambleton,* 1844). This work, too, is a fragment, though a bulky one. In large blocks set out of chronological order it recounts the history of a Dutch-American family in New York that splits into two branches, named Ramble and Rambleton, of which one pursues the commercial life and the other remains rural. Much of the novel concerns a comic courtship by a Rambleton boy of a Ramble girl that is characterized by misapprehensions, misunderstandings, and the problems of uncovering sincerity from under a veneer of flirtatious snobbery. In Switzerland, Rambleton makes the acquaintance of a young, liberal Prussian baron who rejoins him in New York. It looks as though the German baron was to marry the American girl while the American was to marry the baron's sister, thus symbolizing, for the only time in Sealsfield's works, a reintegration of European and American cultures. But the novel never gets that far because it founders in an apocalyptic scene of an electoral campaign riot by corrupt plebeians in New York. It has been speculated that it was Sealsfield's despair over the degeneration of American politics that caused him to break off the novel. It is one of his most ingenious works, his only social novel in the common sense of the term.

Sealsfield's next work, *Das Cajütenbuch* (1841; translated as *The Cabin Book,* 1844), consists of three parts: "Die Prärie am Jacinto" (The Prairie on the Jacinto), "Der Fluch Kishogues" (Kishogue's

Curse), and "Der Kapitän" (The Captain). The short story in the middle is an extended Irish joke, and "Der Kapitän," an increasingly sentimental tale of love, courtship and marriage, has been dismissed by critics as the weakest of his works. "Die Prärie am Jacinto," by contrast, became the best known of them; it has been frequently republished, though not usually in its entirety. It is the reminiscence of a colonel of the Texan Republic named Morse, who as a young man foolishly rides out alone into the trackless prairie, becomes hopelessly disoriented, and is dying of thirst when he is rescued by Bob Rock, a hallucinating murderer. Bob is reprieved from execution by the local law official, an American despite his Spanish title of "Alcalde," and this move turns out to have been a wise one, for Bob's violent nature becomes an asset in the subsequent battle for Texan indepedence. The story is justly famous for its panoramic vision of nature and its symbolism. A segment commonly excised consists of a long lecture by the alcalde on the superiority of the "Anglo-Normans" as the only race suited for self-government and, thus, as destined to rule in America.

Sealsfield's last novel, *Süden und Norden* (South and North, 1842–1843; translated as *North and South,* 1844), returns to Mexico and consists of two parts, "Zwei Nächte in Tzapotecan" (Two Nights in Zapotecan) and "Mariquita"; it tells of four Americans and a German who are on some vague statistical mission in what is now the state of Oaxaca but who are actually touring out of curiosity and love of adventure in the midst of the turmoil following Mexican independence in the 1820s. There has been some dispute as to whether Sealsfield ever actually visited Mexico; the consensus of scholars today is that he must have, though it does not matter much here, for this is the most fantastic of all his works. The travelers are caught up in a complex, murky conflict of intrigue among the reactionary Catholic church, the dispossessed aristocracy, and the republican government, a tangle that does not become altogether clear even when it is recapitulated in the third volume. The effect of this exotic environment is to derange the travelers; to bewitch and hypnotize them; and to arouse hallucinations, pathological states, and abrupt personality changes. This effect seems to result in part from the variegated mountainous landscape, which at times appears as a paradise, a Garden of Eden painted in the most gorgeous imaginable colors, at others as a veritable hell in which fever-bearing mosquitoes attain demonic proportions. Two of the travelers are put into a religious ecstasy by the sight of the Southern Cross. But the derangement is also caused by the overwhelming erotic allurement of the Indian girls, who are unrealistically portrayed as though they were houris of the oriental imagination. All the Americans are drawn into this web – the German is too pedantic to be distracted in this way. Three of them free themselves, but one causes an international incident by courting Mariquita, the daughter of a wealthy aristocrat: it is illegal for Mexicans to marry foreigners, and there is a widespread horror of the travelers, who are regarded as infidels and Jews because they are Protestant. In the end, two of the Americans and the German are saved by the United States Marines, while the other two and Mariquita are lost at sea. Much of the novel is driven by Sealsfield's violent anti-Catholicism and his scorn for Mexican immorality, perfidiousness, superstition, and political incompetence. But it is also, as he himself said, the most poetic of his works, and some of its phantasmagorical passages are truly remarkable in their resourcefulness of language and imagery.

This achievement marks the end of his literary career, though he was barely fifty and had another twenty-one years to live. In subsequent years he talked of and negotiated about other books, but nothing further appeared; there may have been some works in manuscript that vanished after his death. There has been much speculation about the reasons for this cessation of production; the most common view is that disappointment in his Jeffersonian-Jacksonian faith in America made it ungratifying for him to continue. Still, it remains puzzling that a writer of such extraordinary and evidently undiminished creative energies would abruptly cease. Sealsfield's inspiration does not seem to have been primarily literary; even his much-noted borrowings from and parallels to other writers, especially contemporary American ones, are not primarily literary in nature but are exploitations of sources. Though uncommonly talented, he was also a remarkably inattentive writer; many of his texts give an appearance of haste in their repetitiousness, their stylistic and even grammatical carelessness, and their passages of dubious English and impossible Spanish. The misprints in the unattractively printed books suggest that he did not waste much time proofreading. In *Süden und Norden* one of the Americans is called "Whitely" in the first two volumes but "Withely" throughout the third. It is conceivable that Sealsfield's lack of commitment to his own art caused his vocation to evanesce.

Curiously, it was just at this time that his reputation suddenly burgeoned in the United States.

This boom was set off by a remark of the prominent literary historian Theodor Mundt in his *Geschichte der Literatur der Gegenwart* (History of Literature of the Present, 1842) that "Seatsfield," as he misread the name, was a major American writer superior to Cooper and Washington Irving. This claim led in 1844 to a flurry of discussion in American newspapers as to the identity of "Seatsfield," the second "Great Unknown" after Scott, and the question of what his nationality might be; some partisans of indigenous literature, among them Edgar Allan Poe, scoffed. An enterprising New York publisher brought with great rapidity several translations of "Seatsfield's" works onto the market. Sealsfield had no benefit from these pirated printings, for there was no copyright protection in the United States for the works of foreign authors; indeed, his bibliography is rife with texts that are not only pirated but excerpted, abridged, and rewritten in both German and English. Thus, though the uproar soon died down, for a long time there continued to be a reading public for unauthorized texts.

Sealsfield, who by 1851 was living in Schaffhausen, Switzerland, seems to have spent the rest of his days tending to his investments, mainly in American railroad stocks. In 1853 he returned to the United States for the fourth time to look after them more closely. He remained until 1858, traveling about in New York, Pennsylvania, and Louisiana. Where the initial capital for his relative prosperity came from is another mystery; certainly it was not from his literary earnings. On his return he settled in Solothurn, Switzerland, where he lived a rather lonely bachelor's existence until his death on 26 May 1864. On his gravestone he had carved "Citizen of the United States of North America," along with the initials of his real name, "C. P." Bequests in his will to family members in Moravia set in motion the inquiry that revealed his true identity. It is not surprising under these circumstances that biographical problems have preoccupied much of the energy of research. There is also much debate about his location in literary history: whether he is to be regarded as an American writer, as he himself claimed, or European (Austrian? Swiss?), and whether he belongs to the Young German movement, to the Biedermeier era, or to early realism. Only in recent years have experts in American studies begun to clarify the details of his social, political, and cultural context in the United States. A body of literary interpretation has been growing, but there is much more to be learned and understood about his complex, centrifugal, verbose, exotic, and sometimes obscure texts.

Letters:

Der große Unbekannte: Das Leben von Charles Sealsfield (Karl Postl). Briefe und Aktenstücke, edited by Eduard Castle (Vienna: Werner, 1955).

Bibliographies:

Otto Heller and Theodore H. Leon, *Charles Sealsfield: Bibliography of his Writings Together with a Classified and Annotated Catalogue of Literature Relating to His Works and His Life* (Saint Louis: Washington University, 1939);

Felix Bornemann and Hans Freising, *Sealsfield-Bibliographie 1945–1965* (Stuttgart: Charles-Sealsfield-Gesellschaft, 1966);

Albert Kresse, *Erläuternder Katalog meiner Sealsfield-Sammlung: Stand am 1. September 1960* (Stuttgart: Charles-Sealsfield-Gesellschaft, 1974);

Alexander Ritter, *Sealsfield-Bibliographie 1966–1975: Mit einem Kommentar von Karl J. R. Arndt zum Publikationsstand der "Sämtlichen Werke."* (Stuttgart: Charles-Sealsfield-Gesellschaft, 1976);

Ritter, "Sealsfield-Bibliographie 1976–1986," in *Schriftenreihe der Charles-Sealsfield-Gesellschaft,* volume 1, edited by Ritter and Günter Schnitzler (Stuttgart: Charles-Sealsfield-Gesellschaft, 1986), pp. 50–65.

Biographies:

Eduard Castle, *Der große Unbekannte: Das Leben von Charles Sealsfield (Karl Postl)* (Vienna & Munich: Manutius Presse, 1952);

Thomas Ostwald, ed., *Charles Sealsfield – Leben und Werk: Biographie aufgrund zeitgenössischer Presseberichte, ergänzt durch Buchauszüge aus Literaturgeschichten* (Brunswick: Graff, 1976).

References:

Nanette M. Ashby, *Charles Sealsfield: "The Greatest American Author." A Study of Literary Piracy and Promotion in the 19th Century* (Stuttgart: Charles-Sealsfield-Gesellschaft, 1980);

Hildegard Emmel, "Vision und Reise bei Charles Sealsfield," *Journal of German-American Studies,* 15 (June 1980): 39–47; republished in her *Kritische Intelligenz als Methode: Alte und neue Aufsätze über sieben Jahrhunderte deutscher Literatur,* edited by Christiane Zehl Romero (Bern & Munich: Francke, 1981), pp. 117–123;

Bernd Fischer, "Baumwolle und Indianer: Zu Charles Sealsfields *Der Legitime und die Republikaner,*" *Journal of German-American Studies,* 19 (1984): 85–96;

Fischer, "Form und Geschichtsphilosophie in Charles Sealsfields *Lebensbildern aus der westlichen Hemisphäre," German Studies Review,* 9 (May 1986): 233–256;

Gerhard Friesen, *The German Panoramic Novel of the 19th Century,* German Studies in America, edited by Heinrich Meyer, no. 8 (Bern & Frankfurt am Main: Lang, 1972);

Hubert Fritz, *Die Erzählweise in den Romanen Charles Sealsfields und Jeremias Gotthelfs: Zur Rhetoriktradition im Biedermeier* (Bern: Herbert Lang / Frankfurt am Main & Munich: Peter Lang, 1974);

Walter Grünzweig, *Charles Sealsfield,* Boise State University Western Writers Series, no. 71 (Boise, Idaho: Boise State University, 1985);

Grünzweig, *Das demokratische Kanaan: Charles Sealsfields Amerika im Kontext amerikanischer Literatur und Ideologie* (Munich: Fink, 1987);

Grünzweig, " 'The Italian Sky in the Republic of Letters': Charles Sealsfield and Timothy Flint as Early Writers of the American West," *Yearbook of German-American Studies,* 17 (1982): 1–20;

Beate Jahnel, *Charles Sealsfield und die Bildende Kunst: Die Landschaftsbilder in den Romanen Charles Sealsfield und ihre Parallelen in der amerikanischen und englischen Malerei des 19. Jahrhunderts* (Stuttgart: Charles-Sealsfield-Gesellschaft, 1985);

Wulf Koepke, "Charles Sealsfield's Place in Literary History," *South Central Review,* 1 (Spring-Summer 1984): 52–66;

Glen E. Lich, "Sealsfield's Texan: Metaphor, Experience, and History," *Yearbook of German-American Studies,* 22 (1987): 71–79;

Claudio Magris, "Der Abenteuerer und der Eigentümer: Charles Sealsfields 'Prärie am Jacinto,' " in *Austriaca: Beiträge zur österreichischen Literatur. Festschrift für Heinz Politzer zum 65. Geburtstag,* edited by Winfried Kudszus and others (Tübingen: Niemeyer, 1975), pp. 151–170;

Juliane Mikoletzky, *Die deutsche Amerika-Auswanderung des 19. Jahrhunderts in der zeitgenössischen fiktionalen Literatur* (Tübingen: Niemeyer, 1988);

Morton Nirenberg, "Review Essay: The Works of Charles Sealsfield," *German Quarterly,* 52 (January 1979): 81–87;

Andreas Peter, *Charles Sealsfields Mexiko-Romane: Zur raum-zeitlichen Strukturierung und Bedeutung der Reisemotivik* (Stuttgart: Charles-Sealsfield-Gesellschaft, 1983);

Rolf Günter Renner, "Transatlantische Landschaften: Zum Bild der neuen Welt bei Charles Sealsfield," in *Schriftenreihe der Charles-Sealsfield-Gesellschaft,* volume 1, edited by Alexander Ritter and Günter Schnitzler (Stuttgart: Charles-Sealsfield-Gesellschaft, 1986), pp. 7–49;

Alexander Ritter, "Charles Sealsfields gesellschaftspolitische Vorstellungen und ihre dichterische Gestaltung als Romanzyklus," *Jahrbuch der deutschen Schillergesellschaft,* 17 (1973): 395–414;

Ritter, "Charles Sealsfields 'Madonnas of(f) the Trails' im Roman *Das Kajütenbuch.* Oder: Zur epischen Zähmung der Frauen als Stereotype in der amerikanischen Südstaatenepik zwischen 1820 und 1850," *Yearbook of German-American Studies,* 18 (1983): 91–112;

Ritter, *Darstellung und Funktion der Landschaft in den Amerika-Romanen von Charles Sealsfield (Karl Postl): Eine Studie zum Prosa-Roman der deutschen und amerikanischen Literatur in der ersten Hälfte des 19. Jahrhunderts* (Stuttgart: Charles-Sealsfield-Gesellschaft, 1970);

Ritter, "Geschichten aus Geschichte – Charles Sealsfields erzählerischer Umgang mit dem Historischen am Beispiel des Romans '*Das Kajütenbuch,*' " *Schriftenreihe der Charles-Sealsfield-Gesellschaft,* 4 (1989): 127–145;

Ritter, "Sealsfields Erzählformel seiner Amerika-Romane: Raum und Zeit als Welt und Geschichte. Anmerkungen zur Erzähltheorie am Beispiel des Romans *Kajütenbuch,*" in *The German Contribution to the Building of the Americas: Studies in Honor of Karl J. R. Arndt,* edited by Gerhard K. Friesen and Walter Schatzberg (Hanover, N.H.: Clark University Press / University Press of New England, 1977), pp. 187–216;

Jeffrey L. Sammons, "Charles Sealsfield: A Case of Non-Canonicity," in *Autoren damals und heute: Literaturgeschichtliche Beispiele veränderter Wirkungshorizonte,* edited by Gerhard P. Knapp (Amsterdam & Atlanta: Rodopi, 1991), pp. 155–172;

Sammons, "Charles Sealsfield: Innovation or Intertextuality?," in *Traditions of Experiment from the Enlightenment to the Present: Essays in Honor of Peter Demetz,* edited by Nancy Kaiser and David E. Wellbery (Ann Arbor: University of Michigan Press, 1992), pp. 127–146;

Sammons, "Charles Sealsfield's 'Deutsch-amerikanische Wahlverwandtschaften': Ein Versuch," in *Exotische Welt in populären Lektüren,* edited by Anselm Maler (Tübingen: Niemeyer, 1990), pp. 49–62;

Sammons, "Land of Limited Possibilities: America in the Nineteenth-Century German Novel," *Yale Review,* 68 (1978–1979): 35–52; republished in his *Imagination and History: Selected Papers on Nineteenth-Century German Literature* (New York, Bern, Frankfurt am Main & Paris: Lang, 1988), pp. 217–236;

Wendelin Schmidt-Dengler, "Charles Sealsfield: Das Kajütenbuch (1841)," in *Romane und Erzählungen zwischen Romantik und Realismus: Neue Interpretationen,* edited by Paul Michael Lützeler (Stuttgart: Reclam, 1983), pp. 314–334;

Günter Schnitzler, *Erfahrung und Bild: Die dichterische Wirklichkeit des Charles Sealsfield (Karl Postl)* (Freiburg: Rombach, 1988);

Jerry Schuchalter, "Charles Sealsfield's 'Fable of the Republic,'" *Yearbook of German-American Studies,* 24 (1989): 11–26;

Schuchalter, *Frontier and Utopia in the Fiction of Charles Sealsfield* (Frankfurt am Main, Bern & New York: Lang, 1986);

Franz Schüppen, "'Der Amerikaner lebt in und durch Stürme': Zur moralisch-didaktischen Dimension von Sealsfields Bild des Nordamerikaners," *Schriftenreihe der Charles-Sealsfield-Gesellschaft,* 4 (1989): 71–126;

Schüppen, *Charles Sealsfield, Karl Postl: Ein österreichischer Erzähler der Biedermeierzeit im Spannungsfeld von Alter und Neuer Welt* (Frankfurt am Main & Bern: Lang, 1981);

Gunter G. Sehm, *Charles Sealsfields Kajütenbuch im Kontext der literarischen Tradition und der revolutionär-restaurativen Epoche des 19. Jahrhunderts* (Stuttgart: Charles-Sealsfield-Gesellschaft, 1981);

Friedrich Sengle, "Karl Postl / Charles Sealsfield," in his *Biedermeierzeit: Deutsche Literatur im Spannungsfeld zwischen Restauration und Revolution 1815–1848,* volume 3: *Die Dichter* (Stuttgart: Metzler, 1980), pp. 752–814;

Reinhard F. Spiess, *Charles Sealsfields Werke im Spiegel der literarischen Kritik: Eine Sammlung zeitgenössischer Rezensionen* (Stuttgart: Charles-Sealsfield-Gesellschaft, 1977);

Hartmut Steinecke, "Literatur als 'Aufklärungsmittel': Zur Neubestimmung der Werke Charles Sealsfields zwischen Österreich, Deutschland und Amerika," in *Die österreichische Literatur: Ihr Profil im 19. Jahrhundert (1830–1880),* edited by Herbert Zeman (Graz: Akademische Druck- und Verlagsanstalt, 1982), pp. 399–422;

Walter Weiss, "Der Zusammenhang zwischen Amerika-Thematik und Erzählkunst bei Charles Sealsfield (Karl Postl): Ein Beitrag zum Verhältnis von Dichtung und Politik im 19. Jahrhundert," *Literaturwissenschaftliches Jahrbuch,* new series 8 (1967): 95–117; republished in *Deutschlands literarisches Amerikabild: Neuere Forschungen zur Amerikarezeption der deutschen Literatur,* edited by Ritter (Hildesheim & New York: Olms, 1977), pp. 272–294.

Papers:

Charles Sealsfield's manuscripts and papers disappeared after his death. An archive of books and materials collected by Albert Kresse is at the Central Library of Solothurn, Switzerland.

Adalbert Stifter

(23 October 1805 - 28 January 1868)

Duncan Smith
Brown University

BOOKS: *Studien,* 6 volumes (Pest & Leipzig: Heckenast, 1844-1850) – comprises in volume 1, "Der Condor," translated anonymously as "The Condor," *Democratic Review,* 27 (1850): 231; "Das Haidedorf," translated by Maria Norman as "The Village on the Heath," in *Rural Life in Austria and Hungary* (London: Bentley, 1850), III: 257-309; "Feldblumen"; in volume 2 (1844), "Der Hochwald," translated by Norman as "The Hochwald," in *Rural Life in Austria and Hungary,* II: 150-307; "Die Narrenburg," translated by Norman as "Crazy Castle," in *Rural Life in Austria and Hungary,* III: 1-159; in volume 3 (1847), "Die Mappe meines Urgroßvaters," translated by Norman as *My Great Grandfather's Notebook,* as volume 1 of *Rural Life in Austria and Hungary*; in volume 4 (1847), "Abdias," translated by Norman as "Abdias the Jew," in *Rural Life in Austria and Hungary,* II: 1-149; "Brigitta," translated by Edward Fitzgerald as *Brigitta* (London: Rodale, 1957); "Das alte Siegel"; in volume 5 (1850), "Der Hagestolz," translated by David Luke as "The Recluse," in *Limestone, and Other Stories* (New York: Harcourt, Brace & World, 1968); "Der Waldsteig"; in volume 6, "Zwei Schwestern," "Der beschriebene Tännling;

Bunte Steine: Ein Festgeschenck, 2 volumes (Pest & Leipzig: Heckenast, 1853); – comprises in volume 1, "Granit," "Kalkstein," translated by Luke as "Limestone; or, The Poor Benefactor," in *Limestone, and Other Stories*; "Turmalin," translated by Luke as "Tourmaline; or The Doorkeeper," in *Limestone, and Other Stories;* in volume 2, "Bergkristall," translated anonymously as *Mount Gars; or, Marie's Christmas-Eve* (Oxford: Parker, 1857); translated by Lee M. Hollander as "Rock Crystal," in *The German Classics of the Nineteenth and Twentieth Centuries,* volume 8, edited by Kuno Francke and William Guild Howard (New York: German Publication Society, 1914), pp. 356-403; "Katzensilber," "Bergmilch";

Adalbert Stifter in 1863

Lesebuch zur Förderung humaner Bildung in Realschulen und in andern zu weiterer Bildung vorbereitenden Mittelschulen, by Stifter and Johannes Aprent (Pest: Heckenast, 1854);

Der Nachsommer: Eine Erzählung, 3 volumes (Pest: Heckenast, 1857); translated by Wendell Frye as *Indian Summer* (New York: Lang, 1985);

Der Weihnachtsabend (Pest: Hackenast, 1864);

Witiko: Eine Erzählung, 3 volumes (Pest: Heckenast, 1865-1867);

Erzählungen, 2 volumes, edited by Aprent (Pest: Heckenast, 1869);

Vermischte Schriften, 2 volumes, edited by Aprent (volume 1, Pest: Hackenast, 1870; volume 2, Leipzig: Amelang, 1870);

Früheste Dichtungen, edited by Heinrich Micko (Prague: Gesellschaft deutscher Bücherfreunde in Böhmen, 1937);

Sämmtliche Werke, 23 volumes, edited by August Sauer, Gustav Wilhelm, and Franz Hüller (Prague: Calve / Reichenberg: Kraus, 1901–1939);

Julius: Eine Erzählung, edited by Hüller (Augsburg: Kraft, 1950);

Erzählungen in der Urfassung, 3 volumes, edited by Max Stefl (Augsburg: Kraft, 1950–1952);

Die Schulakten Adalbert Stifters, edited by Kurt Vancsa (Graz: Stiasny, 1955);

Sämtliche Werke, 3 volumes, edited by Hannsludwig Geiger (Berlin: Tempel, 1959);

Gesammelte Werke, 6 volumes, edited by Stefl (Wiesbaden: Insel, 1959);

Pädagogische Schriften, edited by Theodor Rutt (Paderborn: Schöning, 1960);

Gesammelte Werke, 9 volumes, edited by Stefl (Darmstadt: Wissenschaftliche Buchgesellschaft, 1960–1963);

Documenta Paedagogica Austriaca. Adalbert Stifter, 2 volumes, edited by K. G. Fischer, (Linz: Oberösterreichischer Landesverlag, 1961);

Werke und Briefe: Historisch-kritische Gesamtausgabe, 38 volumes, edited by Hermann Kunisch, Alfred Doppler, and Wolfgang Frühwald (Stuttgart: Kohlhammer, 1978);

Sämtliche Werke, 5 volumes, edited by Fritz Krökel and Karl Pörnbacher (Munich: Winkler, 1978);

Werke, 4 volumes, edited by Joachim Müller (Berlin: Aufbau, 1981).

OTHER: *Wien und die Wiener* in *Bildern aus dem Leben,* edited, with contributions, by Stifter (Pest: Nordmann, 1844).

Adalbert Stifter is the best-known nineteenth-century Austrian prose writer and is among the most highly regarded of all German and Austrian writers of the modern era. His work, along with that of such writers as Christian Dietrich Grabbe, Karl Immermann, Gottfried Keller, Wilhelm Raabe, and Theodor Storm, created the high reputation of the German novel and short story in the nineteenth century. Yet from the time of his earliest publications in the 1840s, Stifter's works have encountered a deeply divided critical response. For some critics and readers, including the great Austrian playwright Franz Grillparzer and the musicians Clara and Robert Schumann, his works combine unsurpassed beauty with a unique ethical sensitivity. Others, led by the German dramatist Friedrich Hebbel, judged his writings as reactionary and boring, mannered in style, and lacking in integrity. Even during his lifetime Stifter's reputation declined steadily from an early popular and critical enthusiasm for his first works to a confused critical silence and the neglect of his later writings. After his death his fame declined still further, and Stifter was relegated by critics to the status of a regional writer who excelled in the descriptions of local natural landscapes. Toward the end of the nineteenth century and in the first decades of the twentieth, his work was rediscovered by such writers as Friedrich Nietzsche, Hugo von Hofmannsthal, Hermann Hesse, and Thomas Mann, who were admirers of the epic novels written in the latter half of his literary career. Attacked by critics Walter Benjamin and György Lukács, Stifter was dubiously rescued by the German nationalists of the 1920s and 1930s who attempted to see in him another glorifier of the German Fatherland and German virtues. Post–World War II reception included ringing endorsements of his modernity, even contemporaneity, as well as continuing disparagement of his literary ability and allegedly reactionary political stance. The debate about his novels and short stories continued into the late twentieth century, typified by the adamant opposition to Stifter by Arno Schmidt and endorsements from Thomas Bernhard and Peter Handke. The enthusiasm of Stifter's admirers is matched by those critics and writers who attack both the admirers and the author as exemplifying the worst kind of reactionary and inaccessible writing. Stifter's works continue to fascinate, puzzle, and challenge critics and readers.

The man around whom such strong reactions still circulate more than a century after his death was born on 23 October 1805 in the small town of Oberplan (today Horné Planà, Czech Republic) in what is still a rural area of Bohemia and was then part of the Hapsburg Empire. His father, Johann Stifter, was a linen weaver who had successfully turned to trading in flax, a principal crop of the region. His mother, Magdalena, née Friepess, was the daughter of an Oberplan butcher. Stifter was the oldest of two brothers and a sister. A stepbrother was born to his mother in a second marriage contracted after Stifter's father was killed in a road accident in 1817.

Page from the manuscript for Stifter's "Die Mappe meines Urgroßvaters," with a marginal notation by his friend Johannes Aprent (Bildarchiv der Adalbert-Stifter-Gesellschaft, Vienna)

Stifter had already been singled out for his accomplishments in school by his first teacher, Josef Jenne, and plans had been made with his parents' encouragement to give the boy additional schooling. His father's death postponed these plans, but his maternal grandfather, Franz Friepess, arranged for Stifter to return to his studies and even to apply for admission to the well-known school at the Kremsmünster Benedictine abbey. Despite discouraging advice from the local priest, who had tutored Stifter in Latin and had judged him incompetent, the school's head teacher, Father Placidus Hall, recognized Stifter's talents and arranged for his immediate enrollment in 1822. He excelled in all his subjects – including Latin – and graduated in 1826 as one of the best pupils in his class. The third of a triumvirate of influential teachers, Georg Rietzlmayr encouraged Stifter's talents in drawing and painting. Stifter had early decided that painting was his vocation in the arts, and he would not devote himself seriously to literature until his mid thirties. He left a variety of mostly landscape paintings and drawings, some of which are still occasionally exhibited; they reveal a high level of skill. Some critics of Stifter's works have suggested that his highly descriptive and detail-conscious literary style is the legacy of this first avocation as a painter, and there are several noteworthy studies of Stifter as a visual artist.

These three teachers had a lasting influence on Stifter's life; of equal importance were his two grandfathers, Friepess and Augustin Stifter, who provided the boy the support from older men that the early death of his father had interrupted. In many of his writings, most notably in "Die Mappe meines Urgroßvaters" (1847; translated as *My Great-Grandfather's Note-book,* 1850), Stifter has set a memorial to the figures of these influential older men of his youth.

In 1826 Stifter enrolled as a student of law at the University of Vienna. He received good grades but left the university without a degree, absenting himself from a mandatory final examination without satisfactory explanation. Willingly or not, therefore – and the evidence points to a deliberate decision – Stifter was spared the fate of becoming a bureaucrat in the Austrian administration, the certain result of a law degree, and devoted himself instead to his art while supporting himself as a private tutor to the wealthy families of Vienna. His familiarity with the world of Viennese aristocrats and patricians is portrayed in many of his works, including the early "Feldblumen" (Wildflowers, 1844), as well as his great novel *Der Nachsommer* (1857; translated as *Indian Summer,* 1985). For most of the 1830s Stifter led what appears to have been a comfortable life, concentrating on his painting; on his relationships with the wealthy families he served, including the family of Count Wenzel von Metternich, prime minister of Austria and architect of post-Napoleonic European order; on his considerable circle of friends; and on walking tours of Austria. On visits back to Oberplan he fell in love with Fanny Greipl, whom he courted assiduously. Stifter, without means and even at times in straitened circumstances, was unacceptable to Greipl's parents unless he improved his situation; once again he escaped from the predicament by intentionally or accidentally failing to appear for an interview on which depended an appointment to an academic post at the University of Prague. He thereby forfeited both the post and Greipl. In 1835 he married the milliner Amalia Mohaupt, who came from a poor family.

Some of Stifter's biographers have dwelt on this strange union between the moody and brilliant young artist and author, who was clearly entering the world of recognized artistic achievement in Vienna and beyond, and a poorly educated young woman who brought her husband neither material nor class advantages. Although the letters Stifter sent to Amalia throughout their marriage reveal affection and devotion, they have been read by some biographers as portrayals of a relationship the writer wished he had rather than the prosaic and unsatisfying marriage he is alleged by some to have had. It is certain that following his marriage Stifter gradually settled into an outwardly bland domestic life from which the literary works that were to make him famous emerged.

He had some poems published in 1830 under the pseudonym Ostade but was otherwise still apparently dedicated to his private lessons, his painting, and the cultivation of his connections among the patrons of arts and letters in the Viennese upper classes. But in 1840 two stories, "Der Condor" (translated as "The Condor," 1850) and "Das Haidedorf" (translated as "The Village on the Heath," 1850), appeared under the name Adalbert Stifter in the literary journal *Iris,* published by Gustave Heckenast in Budapest. They were followed from 1841 to 1843 in *Iris* and other literary journals by "Feldblumen," "Die Mappe meines Urgroßvaters," "Der Hochwald" (translated as "The Hochwald," 1850), "Abdias" (translated as "Abdias the Jew," 1850), "Die Narrenburg" (translated as "Crazy Castle," 1850), the novella "Brigitta" (translated, 1957), and "Das alte Siegel" (The Ancient Seal). Between 1844 and 1850 Heckenast published six volumes of thoroughly revised versions of these stories under the title *Studien* (Studies). The volumes also include "Der Hagestolz" (translated as "The Recluse," 1968), "Der Waldstieg" (The Forest Path), "Zwei Schwestern" (Two Sisters), and "Der beschriebene Tännling" (The Inscribed Fir Tree).

Both the original journal versions and the versions in *Studien* were greeted with critical acclaim. Contemporary critics, however, ignored or missed the odd contradictions between language and object described and the element of looming catastrophe that for many modern readers, beginning with Nietzsche and Mann, are the hallmarks of Stifter's writing. Instead, the young author was praised as an example of the triumph of the aesthetic dimension over the otherwise dominant and shrill voices of the politically engaged writers of the period. Stifter's indebtedness to the German writer Jean Paul was noted, in general favorably, as was his distancing of himself from still-fashionable Romanticism. The oddities of Stifter's literary style were overlooked by most readers, who responded with pleasure to his brilliant descriptions of nature and the ethical dimension of his characterizations and plots. Stifter was established as a promising writer.

Modern criticism of the best known of these stories has tended to address the peculiarities of style and the theme of alienation as well as the ethical and aesthetic dimensions. Stories such as "Der Hagestolz" and "Brigitta" are viewed as examples of Stifter's concern with the inexplicable and the tragic, with accident and accommodation with the results thereof. "Abdias," in which an elderly Jew is deprived of his sight and finally his daughter in a violent natural accident after a life of adventure, greed, and hatred, is a typical example of one of Stifter's leading traits as a writer: the focus on the sudden appearance of an uncompromising natural principle that may or may not be associated with retributive justice or divine guidance. Such terrors are described with an impartiality of style and ethical attitude. Natural phenomena, of which human existence is but one example, are simply what they are, though they may strike an individual as wonderful or terrible.

Another frequent motif in Stifter's early works is that of the father and son, or the older man, related or not, and the younger man or boy. This man-boy motif occurs in some of his finest works, including "Die Mappe meines Urgroßvaters" and "Der Hagestolz," as well as in the critically less regarded novella "Das alte Siegel." In all of these stories the older men play significant roles in the development of the younger men's worldviews, assisting

Title page for the first volume of Stifter's rambling epic novel about a young man's maturation

the younger male figures with the entry into the adult world as if in an initiation rite. In "Der Hagestolz" an isolated and lonely old bachelor is the inspired initiator of his nephew into a bright and broad world, helping the younger man to escape from the narrow if safe world of the bureaucrat to which his life with maternally loving women had led him.

Stifter took part in the discussions and debates that led to the short-lived revolutions throughout Europe in 1848. His position was initially that of a moderate liberal who supported the promulgation of a constitution that would grant a greater measure of political power to the prosperous middle class to which he was himself steadily ascending. But 1848 was also the year of Karl Marx and Friedrich Engels's *Manifest der kommunistischen Partei* (translated as *Manifesto of the Communist Party*, 1888), and the specter of a seizure of power by the proletariat came to haunt Stifter after the ouster of Metternich, the

Stifter at fifty-eight; oil painting by Bartholomäus Szekely (Bildarchiv der Österreichischen Nationalbibliothek)

apparent overthrow of the emperor, and the threat of a "red republic" in Vienna. Stifter's liberalism did not include accommodation with the masses. His doubts increased with the increase in street violence and what he regarded as the rule of the mob. He witnessed the heady moments of apparent triumph by the moderate and loyalist liberals, among whose number he reckoned himself. But he could not tolerate the overthrow of the feebleminded but popular emperor, Ferdinand, who was forced into exile in March 1848 and shortly thereafter was obliged to abdicate in favor of his nephew Franz Josef. Stifter left Vienna, ostensibly for the quiet he needed to pursue his literary work, and retired to the provincial city of Linz, the capital of Upper Austria. There he briefly took on the post of editor of a traditionalist paper, writing in its pages and elsewhere a series of political tracts deploring the growth of mob rule and the accompanying violence and pleading for the restoration of order. These and other essays written in a similar tone have been taken by Stifter's critics as evidence of his essentially conservative, even reactionary political position. In fact, Stifter had become far more conservative during those years of tumult and upheaval. His permanent settlement in Linz, where old traditions still held sway, clearly expressed his antagonism toward the changes that imperiled the old order. Like many liberals who had risen from the rural peasantry or the artisan class, Stifter saw change as welcome only when it did not interrupt the beneficial order of the state and society. Such changes had to happen naturally and organically, and Stifter refused to see in the changes he was witnessing any parallels to the violent interruptions of natural order that his own fictional work so splendidly portrays. The contradictions such deeply held feelings produced in Stifter marked all his work for the rest of his life. It is from this point that Stifter's writing changes to an espousal of moderation, preservation, and loyalist conservatism. Stifter ceased being only an artist and chose to become a preacher of an ethical aesthetics that contains a deep political and social message as well as a deeper artistic contradiction.

Stifter's first post-1848 literary publication was a two-volume collection of stories, most of which were written prior to 1848 in a first version titled *Bunte Steine* (Colored Stones, 1853). This collection has become perhaps the best known of all his works and contains several stories that are regularly anthologized as classics of German literature: "Bergkristall" (Rock Crystal; translated as *Mount Gars; or, Marie's Christmas-Eve,* 1857), "Kalkstein" (translated as "Limestone, or, The Poor Benefactor," 1968), and "Granit" (Granite), all of which appeared in journal versions between 1845 and 1849. The remaining stories are "Bergmilch" (Aragonite), "Turmalin" (translated as "Tourmaline; or The Doorkeeper," 1968), and "Katzensilber" (Mica); the first of these appeared in a journal version in 1843, while "Kalkstein" appeared first in 1848, and "Katzensilber" appeared for the first time in the collection. The themes include infidelity in "Turmalin"; reconciliation and faith in "Bergkristall" and "Granit"; simplicity, justice, self-discipline, and right conduct in "Kalkstein"; disorder, catastrophe, art, and bourgeois values in "Katzensilber"; and war and pacifism in "Bergmilch." The use of a frame narrative in some of the stories serves to suggest universal truths, but the subject matter of the embedded stories is the small details of life, the apparently insignificant events from which true significance is derived. The tone of the stories is sober and instructive, and, since some of them were originally intended for children, they combine edification and rhetorical gentleness. Little violence is portrayed in the stories save for the occasional description of extreme natural phenomena at which Stifter excelled, most notably the snowstorm in "Bergkristall."

"Bergkristall" is the most critically acclaimed story in the collection. Two children from a mountain village are lost overnight in a terrible snowstorm as they attempt to return from a Christmas Eve visit with their grandparents in the village on the other side of the mountain. The search for the lost children by members of both villages forms the basis for reconciliation between the hostile communities. The plot is one of the utmost simplicity; but the descriptions of the children's experience and of the snowstorm itself have fascinated generations of readers and critics, the latter giving the story some of the most fulsome praise Stifter's work was ever to receive.

The somber "Turmalin" is set in Vienna, showing that Stifter was not only the consummate artist of the rural Austrian countryside but possessed equal skill in creating an atmosphere of urban change, which he portrays as part of the natural process. The story relates the changes that overcome the previously comfortable bourgeois lives of the characters: the father dies in the ruins of the house in which he had once lived; and the deformed daughter with whom he had fled after his wife and best friend ran off together is adopted by the narrator and his wife, who intend to counterbalance the strange education the girl had received from her father, but the reader is left with no doubt about the essential darkness of Stifter's vision in the story.

For critics and scholars the "Vorrede" (Introduction) of *Bunte Steine* has been the object of as much attention as the stories. Presumably written as a rebuttal to the already intense criticism of his earlier works by figures such as Hebbel, the "Vorrede" came to be regarded as the essential summation of Stifter's literary and personal philosophy. There are universal laws of justice and morality, Stifter says, but these laws are not to be grasped through any anthropocentric notions of causality. They may, however, be grasped by any reader who simply pays attention to the ways in which nature manifests itself. The "Vorrede" parallels ideas expressed by several contemporary thinkers, but it is an extremely bold statement in a time given over to belief either in God or in the ability of science completely to understand and control the world. It is a quite modern call for a holistic attitude as the best approach to healing a society beset by revolution and change.

But in explicitly stating these principles Stifter forced himself into the difficult task of carrying them out consciously. The style of his writing changed; the lengthy, convoluted sentence structures, the "litanesque" description of objects and events, the apparently straining causal conjunctions have provided challenging material for subsequent generations of critics, especially those interested in the field of narrative theory. Such stylistic phenomena also reduced his popularity with the reading public. Charges of inaccessibility and of readers' boredom with the often astonishing amount of descriptive detail were already current in his lifetime and have plagued his reputation ever since. His later work, including the epics *Der Nachsommer* and *Witiko* (1865–1867) as well as some of the shorter pieces he produced during the remainder of his life are all characterized by this apparent mannerism of literary style.

Stifter; engraving by J. Mahlknecht after a painting by Moritz Michael Daffinger

The years following the publication of *Bunte Steine* were filled with political and military crises in Europe and in Austria. The Crimean War of 1854–1855 between Austria and expansionist Russia; Austria's unsuccessful war in Italy against the nationalists supported by the French in 1859; the growing discord between Prussia under Otto von

Title page for the first volume of Stifter's epic novel set in twelfth-century Bohemia

Bismarck and Austria, culminating in the defeat of Austria by Prussia in 1866; and the growth of capitalism formed the background of much of the literary work of the age. In his fiction Stifter remained aloof from these matters, though his personal dedication to the multinational empire and to the Hapsburg monarchy never wavered. In his career as inspector of primary and secondary schools in Upper Austria, a post he had requested and had received in 1850, he encouraged reforms and improvements. But the newly conservative empire had restored control of the schools to the Catholic church hierarchy, which opposed most of Stifter's suggestions. His textbook, written in collaboration with his Linz colleague Johannes Aprent and published in 1854, was rejected as too radical, and his subsequent career became more and more difficult. Plagued already by the symptoms of increasing ill health that was then more psychological than physiological in origin, he displayed in his reports and letters the considerable ability he possessed as an educator and as a mediator among people. His publisher and friend Heckenast remarked that he was completely at home with the common people, seeking them out in taverns and inns. Stifter received the Ritterkreuz des Franz-Josef Ordens (Knights Cross of Franz Josef) in 1854, honoring his work as one of Austria's foremost prose writers. The growing chorus of critical discontent from the more socially engaged writers was countered by the praise he received from those who valued his ethical and aesthetic stances. His personal life suffered a series of setbacks, beginning with the suicide of his adopted daughter, Juliana Mohaupt, in 1858. Stifter does not appear to have been close to this young woman, whose death may have been the result of a tragic love affair, but it occurred in the same year as the death of his mother, to whom he had remained devoted. The unexpected deaths of two newly discovered young relations, from whose company he had promised himself and his wife compensation for their childless marriage, weighed heavily on him as well. Combined with the increasing difficulties he was experiencing in his career – he was removed as school inspector for the secondary school at Linz in 1856 – Stifter was undergoing difficult times. Yet he remained busy with civic tasks in Linz; visited Vienna on occasion, though with decreasing frequency; and continued to enjoy a growing if disputed national reputation as a writer and artist in German-speaking countries.

Der Nachsommer appeared in three volumes in 1857. Ideas for such epic undertakings had been advanced by Stifter to Heckenast before 1848; a lengthy treatment of Maximilien Robespierre is among the themes mentioned in his correspondence. But when the promised great epic actually appeared, after years of labor in the intervals of his professional work as an educator, it was not devoted to an event or a person of either historical or contemporary importance. In keeping with his profession of belief in the introduction to *Bunte Steine,* Stifter offered his publisher and public a work that is not really a novel at all. It has little actual plot within its hundreds of pages. It is assigned by perhaps desperate Germanists to the genre of the bildungsroman, whose model in German literature has been Johann Wolfgang von Goethe's *Wilhelm Meisters Lehrjahre* (1795–1796; translated as *Wilhelm Meister's Apprenticeship,* 1824). It resembles such novels only in the most general way, however. Instead, it is a mannered mass of didacticism about the good and the beautiful and the right path for a person to take to reach enlightenment and peace and do good in the world. Or it is a most modern work that uses photomontage to the most extraordinary advantage. Critical reactions range from Hebbel's splenetic offer of the crown of Poland to anyone who could say that he or she had, of his or her own free will, read the three volumes from cover to cover, to Nietzsche's, Mann's, and Hofmannsthal's praise of the work. The "story" is slight. Heinrich Drendorf, a young scientist, visits the home of a nobleman, von Risach; hears about von Risach's love affair with Mathilde, who now lives nearby; and falls in love with the nobleman's daughter Natalie, whom he eventually – many hundreds of pages later – marries. Surrounding these bones, however, is a depiction of that constant theme of Stifter's: the gradual and ritualistic maturing of a young man, a process that makes him truly cultured and civilized and, hence, an element of moderate but effective change in society. Each detail – whether dialogue on aesthetics, catalogue of objects in the nobleman's home, the dress of each of the characters, or an apparently endlessly didactic descent of a staircase – is lovingly and carefully recorded by the narrator.

The novel was not a commercial success. Stifter's reputation suffered a setback, and adherents of the Hebbel school of criticism grew in reaction to the work. This was, after all, the time of Charles Dickens and George Eliot in England and Honoré de Balzac in France; in Switzerland, Gottfried Keller was writing novels and novellas with abundant critical social themes combined with the ethical and the aesthetic; Raabe in Germany was narrating, with often biting irony, stories through which today the reader can still discern the social predicaments of the troubled times; Ivan Turgenev's work in Russia included novels and stories of great beauty that also contained direct societal relevance; in Paris, Heinrich Heine had earlier written poems and prose works that combined humor, irony, and beauty with the same topicality. In such a climate *Der Nachsommer* was reserved for the few faithful Stifter admirers who offered him cautious praise but spoke more affectionately and wistfully of his earlier stories. It was in the twentieth century that the novel found its first real critical response. Critics locate in Stifter's alleged mannerism an aesthetic undertaking in which ideology is made prominent by the very attempts of language to obscure it. It also appeals to readers and critics who see in Stifter's determined avoidance of the topical dedication to achieving a state of consciousness in which resistance to the dualistic norms of aesthetic and political discourse is more likely.

While writing *Der Nachsommer* Stifter had proposed to Heckenast the outline of a new epic work with more direct political and social relevance. *Witiko,* perhaps the strangest of all Stifter's writings,

Stifter during his last visit to the spa at Carlsbad; drawing by G. Kordik (Bildarchiv der Adalbert-Stifter-Gesellschaft, Vienna)

is a declaration of the author's views on history, politics, war and pacifism, the right relations of ruler to ruled, and the proper but difficult path to be taken in the achievement of both a just and ordered society and a just and civilized human being. With some retouching of twelfth-century history, Stifter re-creates the period in which Duke Wladyslaw became the ruler of Bohemia, warding off challenges from pretenders to the office whose political principles were permeated by selfishness, greed, and a lack of compassion for the subjects over whom they would rule. Witiko, a famous and just warrior, rallies to the support of the young duke, assisting him throughout the lengthy series of conflicts and providing the reader with a model of self-sacrificing service to a just historical cause. Duke Wladyslaw is victorious, and the novel ends with Witiko in attendance at the Parliament of Nobility held by the fabled Emperor Friedrich Barbarossa – the "King Arthur" of German legends – in 1184.

The epic reveals Stifter's most firmly held convictions about the importance of the maintenance of the Hapsburg Empire as a multinational state ruled by a just emperor to whom men and women should give their utmost loyalty. The work indicates that Stifter remained concerned about contemporary events and issues, though typically he chose not to engage in direct representation of those concerns. Instead, he tried to draw universal parallels. Far from being an expression of reactionary sentiments on the part of an aging writer, the epic may be read as a farsighted work that endorses a vision of state and society not enmeshed in the nationalism that was to lead to the catastrophe of World War I. Stifter's sometimes ridiculed depictions of the virtues of manliness, courage, honor, and bodily strength detract only superficially from the essential themes of the horrors of war and the virtues of diplomacy and compassion. The many battle scenes are rendered in unrealistic fashion, and the greatest emphasis, to the bewilderment of critics and readers alike, is placed on the dialogues between the characters; the importance of the word as deed is stressed throughout.

In Stifter's time the novel was largely rejected, as it has been ever since, though its strangeness – Erik Lunding, one of Stifter's foremost modern interpreters, calls it the strangest prose fiction of the nineteenth century – has also exercised fascination for critics. It has never enjoyed popular success. Early reviews expressed invective or exasperation. Few contemporary readers and critics endorsed the work, which Heckenast nevertheless continued to produce for the steadily diminishing readership. Stifter was satisfied that the work contained a summation of his political and social philosophies and showed the means by which justice – personal and civil – could be approached.

Stifter's illness, a vaguely defined disorder attributed to diet and to job-related stress, worsened after 1863. Although he had concentrated almost exclusively on *Witiko,* he continued to produce such shorter pieces as "Nachkommenschaften" (Descendants), "Der Waldbrunnen" (The Forest Spring), "Der Kuß von Sentze" (The Kiss of Sentze), "Aus dem Bairischen Walde" (From the Bavarian Forest), and the final version of "Der fromme Spruch" (The Pious Saying). All of these stories were published in periodicals and were collected posthumously in 1869 by his friend Aprent in *Erzählungen* (Tales). In 1865 he obtained a provisional retirement from his education post, which became complete retirement with full pay shortly thereafter. He was named Hofrat (court councilor) in 1865 and received from the grand duke of Saxony-Weimar the Order of the White Falcon, First Class.

Contemporary reports of his life in these last years depict a tormented and unhealthy man who moved restlessly from one spa to another, seeking a cure for his still-undiagnosed ailment. He seemed unable to remain in Linz, leaving on any pretext to spend time in village retreats in the mountains or at various health resorts, most notably Kirchschlag and Carlsbad. Biographers have tried to link these flights to marital dissatisfactions, though Stifter's letters to Amalia throughout this period are full of affection and expressions of his sorrow that his illness is making her life so difficult. He disregarded medical advice about his diet, which consisted of rich foods and heavy wines; he also frequently smoked cigars. He continued to write, working on the fourth version of his favorite story: "Die Mappe meines Urgroßvaters." This version was to have been a novel, but he died before completing the work. The final version was published in 1870 in *Vermischte Schriften* (Miscellaneous Writings), edited by Aprent.

"Die Mappe meines Urgroßvaters" is considered by many to be the finest of all of Stifter's works. He devoted more than twenty years to it, suggesting the central significance of its themes within the corpus of his writings. The narrator discovers the notebooks of his great-grandfather Augustinus, who as a young man in the eighteenth century leaves his home in southwestern Bohemia, becomes a doctor, and returns to the village to practice. He encounters a colonel and falls in love with the latter's daughter, Margarita. Through his jealousy, however, he loses her; he is prevented from suicide only by a chance encounter with the colonel, who points out to the despairing Augustinus the beauty of a nearby field, reminding the young man of the totality and the sacredness of all life. To further console him, the colonel tells him the story of his own previously stormy life and loves. Augustinus decides to dedicate himself to his calling as a healer and to write down in his notebooks a record of his experiences. He becomes a person whose identity is established in a near perfect harmony of the ethical individual with the natural world. Order results from acceptance, accommodation, and patient and nonanthropocentric observance of the world. Having become a universally respected man in the region, Augustinus accidentally meets Margarita again; she agrees to resume their engagement.

The four versions of the story record the author's growing shift of interest from descriptions of great events to depictions of ordinary life and the consolations of living life as it is rather than as it could be or ought to be. It is the premier example of the belief in acceptance and accommodation that was articulated in the "Vorrede" to *Bunte Steine*. Augustinus is gradually stripped of all apparent emotional responses to the vagaries of existence. "Die Mappe meines Urgroßvaters" enjoys a considerable following today among Stifter devotees and general readers alike. *Der Nachsommer,* the other work in which such a spiritual quest seems to be portrayed, contains a pedagogic element: it is a novel of instruction in which both Heinrich and the reader are asked to learn and to develop. Neither Augustinus nor the reader of "Die Mappe meines Urgroßvaters" is under such didactic duress. The story meanders from one event to another, with little or no distinction made between anecdotes, and in successive versions such distinctions as did exist are further minimized.

In January 1868 Stifter, in an excess of pain from what now appears to have been the final stages of cirrhosis of the liver, cut his throat with a razor. The doctor arrived in time to prevent him from bleeding to death; but the disease had already taken its toll, and Stifter died, aged sixty-two, on 28 January.

Stifter during the last year of his life; drawing by J. M. Kaiser (Bildarchiv der Adalbert-Stifter-Gesellschaft, Vienna)

Letters:

Briefe, 3 volumes, edited by Johannes Aprent (Pest: Heckenast, 1869);

Ein Dichterleben aus dem alten Österreich: Ausgewählte Briefe, edited by Moriz Enzinger (Innsbruck: Wagnersche Universitäts-Buchdruckerei, 1947);

Briefe, edited by Hans Schumacher (Zurich: Manesse, 1947);

Briefe, edited by Gerhard Fricke (Nuremberg: Carl, 1949);

Adalbert Stifters Jugendbriefe (1822–1839): In ursprünglicher Fassung aus dem Nachlaß, edited by Gustav Wilhelm (Graz: Stiasny, 1954);

Adalbert Stifters Leben und Werk in Briefen und Dokumenten, edited by K. G. Fischer (Wiesbaden: Insel, 1962);

Adalbert Stifter in seinen Briefen, edited by Hanns-Ludwig Bachfeld (Hildesheim: Gerstenberg, 1973).

Bibliographies:

Werner Heck, *Das Werk Adalbert Stifters, 1840–1940: Versuch einer Bibliographie* (Vienna: Kerry, 1954);

"Adalbert Stifter bei den Tschechen in Übersetzungen und wissenschaftlichen Abhandlungen," *Vierteljahrsschrift des Adalbert-Stifter-Institutes des Landes Oberösterreich,* 6 (1957): 46–53;

W. A. Reichart and W. H. Grilk, "Stifters Werk in Amerika und England: Eine Bibliographie," *Vierteljahrsschrift des Adalbert-Stifter-Institutes des Landes Oberösterreich,* 9 (1960): 39–42;

Takashi Yoneda, "Stifters Werk in Japan: Eine Bibliographie," *Vierteljahrsschrift des Adalbert-Stifter-Institutes des Landes Oberösterreich,* 12 (1963): 64–66;

Eduard Eisenmeier, *Adalbert Stifter – Bibliographie* (Linz: Oberösterreichischer Landesverlag, 1964);

"Die Bibliographie der Veröffentlichungen zum 100. Todestag," *Vierteljahrsschrift des Adalbert-Stifter-Institutes des Landes Oberösterreich,* 18 (1969): 52–71;

"Das Adalbert-Stifter-Institut des Landes Oberösterreich," *Jahrbuch für Internationale Germanistik,* 8 (1976): 172–175.

Biographies:

Alois Raimund Hein, *Adalbert Stifter: Sein Leben und seine Werke* (Prague: Calve, 1904);

Urban Roedl [Bruno Adler], *Adalbert Stifter: Geschichte seines Lebens* (Berlin: Rowohlt, 1936; revised, 1948);

Emil Merkur, *Stifter* (Stuttgart: Cotta, 1942);

Karl Privat, *Adalbert Stifter: Sein Leben in Selbstzeugnissen, Briefen und Berichten* (Berlin: Tempelhof, 1946);

Roedl [Bruno Adler], *Adalbert Stifter in Selbstzeugnissen und Bilddokumenten* (Reinbek: Rowohlt, 1965);

Alois Großschopf, *Adalbert Stifter: Leben, Werk, Landschaft* (Linz: Trauner, 1968).

References:

Ruth K. Angress, "Das Ehebruchmotiv in Stifters 'Das alte Siegel': Ein Beitrag zur Literaturgeschichte der bürgerlichen Erotik," *Zeitschrift für Deutsche Philologie,* 103 (1984): 481–502;

H. G. Barnes, "The Function of Conversations and Speeches in *Witiko,*" in *German Studies: Presented to H. G. Fiedler by Pupils, Colleagues and Friends* (Oxford: Clarendon Press, 1938), pp. 1–25;

Ernst Bertram, *Studien zu Adalbert Stifters Novellentechnik,* second edition (Dortmund: Ruhfus, 1966);

Eric A. Blackall, *Adalbert Stifter: A Critical Study* (Cambridge: Cambridge University Press, 1948);

Barton W. Browning, "Cooper's Influence on Stifter: Fact or Scholarly Myth?," *Modern Language Notes,* 89 (October 1974): 821–828;

Walter Horace Bruford, "Adalbert Stifter: *Der Nachsommer,*" in his *The German Tradition of Self-Cultivation. Bildung from Humboldt to Thomas Mann* (London: Cambridge University Press, 1975), pp. 128–146;

Karen J. Campbell, "Toward a Truer Mimesis: Stifter's 'Turmalin,' " *German Quarterly,* 57 (Fall 1984): 576–589;

Robert C. Conrad, "Heinrich Böll's Political Reevaluation of Adalbert Stifter: An Interpretation of Böll's "Epilog zu Stifters 'Nachsommer,' " *Michigan Academician: Papers of the Michigan Academy of Sciences, Arts, and Letters,* 14, no. 1 (1981): 31–39;

Gail Finney, "Garden Paradigms in Nineteenth-Century Fiction," *Comparative Literature,* 36, no. 1 (1984): 20–33;

Kurt Gerhard Fischer, *Die Pädagokik des Meschenmöglichen* (Linz: Landesverlag, 1962);

Gerald Gillespie, "Space and Time Seen through Stifter's Telescope," *German Quarterly,* 37 (March 1964): 120–130;

H. A. Glaser, *Die Restauration des Schönen: Stifters "Nachsommer"* (Stuttgart: Metzler, 1965);

Christian Godden, "Two Quests for Surety. A Comparative Interpretation of Stifter's 'Abdias' and Kafka's 'Der Bau,' " *Journal of European Studies,* 5 (December 1975): 341–361;

Ulrich Greiner, "Der Tod des Nachsommers: Über das Österreichische in der österreichischen Literatur," *Neue Rundschau,* 88, no. 3 (1977): 348-361;

Margaret Gump, *Adalbert Stifter* (New York: Twayne, 1974);

Charles H. Helmetag, "The Gentle Law in Adalbert Stifter's 'Der Hagestolz,' " *Modern Language Studies,* 16 (Summer 1986): 183–188;

Josef Heurkamp, "Das problematische Vorbild: über das schwierige Verhältnis des Schriftstellers Arno Schmidt zu Adalbert Stifter," *Vierteljahrsschrift des Adalbert-Stifter-Institutes des Landes Oberösterreich,* 32 (1983): 163–178;

Hans Höller, "Die kapitalistische Gesellschaft aus der Kirchturmperspektive? Anmerkungen zu Stifters Ästhetik," *Germanica Wratislawiensia,* 32 (1978): 37–51;

Alan Holske, "Stifter and the Biedermeier Crisis," in *Studies in Honor of John Albrecht Walz* (Lancaster: Books for Libraries Press, 1941), pp. 256–290;

Konrad F. Kiensberger, "Mary Howitt und ihre Stifter-Übersetzungen: zur Rezeption des Dichters im viktorianischen England," *Vierteljahrsschrift des Adalbert-Stifter-Institutes des Landes Oberösterreich,* 25 (1976): 13–55;

Rosa Gudrun Klarner, *Pedagogic Design and Literary Form in the Work of Adalbert Stifter* (Bern, Frankfurt am Main & New York: Lang, 1986);

Johann Lachinger, Alexander Stillmark, and Martin Swales, eds., *Adalbert Stifter heute* (Linz: Landesverlag, 1985);

Dominique Lehl, "Realité et Penurie dans l'oeuvre litteraire et picturale de Stifter: A Partir de la Nouvelle Kalkstein et des tableaux de l'Epoque de Bunte Steine," *Etudes Germaniques,* 40, no. 3 (1985): 297–310;

Dagmar Lorenz, "Stifters Frauengestalten," *Vierteljahrsschrift des Adalbert-Stifter-Institutes des Landes Oberösterreich,* 32 (1983): 93–106;

Erik Lunding, *Adalbert Stifter: Mit einem Anhang über Kierkegaard und die existentielle Literaturwissenschaft* (Copenhagen: Nyt nordisk, 1946);

Eve Mason, "Stifter's 'Turmalin': A Reconsideration," *Modern Language Review,* 72 (1977): 348–358;

Joachim Müller, "Die Polemik zwischen Hebbel und Stifter und Stifters Ethos vom 'Sanften Gesetz,' " in *Gedenkschrift für F. J. Schneider*

(1879–1954), edited by Karl Bischoff (Weimar: 1956);

Ursula Naumann, *Adalbert Stifter,* (Stuttgart: Metzler, 1979);

Christine Oertel-Sjörgren, *The Marble Statue as Idea: Collected Essays on Adalbert Stifter's "Der Nachsommer"* (Chapel Hill: University of North Carolina Press, 1972);

Roy Pascal, "Adalbert Stifter: Indian Summer," in his *The German Novel Studies* (Manchester, U.K.: Manchester University Press, 1956), pp. 52–75;

Laurence A. Rickels, "Stifter's 'Nachkommenschaften': The Problem of the Surname, the Problem of Painting," *Modern Language Notes,* 100 (April 1985): 577–598;

D. C. Riechel, "Adalbert Stifter as Landscape Painter: A View from Cézanne's Mont Sainte-Victorie," *Modern Austrian Literature,* 20, no. 1 (1987): 1–20;

Arno Schmidt, ". . . und dann die Herren Leutnants! Betrachtungen zu 'Witiko' und Adalbert Stifter," in his *Adalbert Stifter, die Ritter vom Geist: Von vergessenen Kollegen* (Karlsruhe: Stahlberg, 1965), pp. 282–317;

Herbert Seidler, "Die Adalbert Stifter Forschung der siebziger Jahre," *Vierteljahrsschrift des Adalbert-Stifter-Institutes des Landes Oberösterreich,* 30 (1981): 89–134;

Martin Selge, "Die Utopie im Geschichtsroman: Wie man A. Stifters 'Witiko' lesen kann," *Der Deutschunterricht,* 27 (1975): 86–103;

Lauren Small, "White Frost Configurations on the Window Pane: Adalbert Stifter's 'Der Nachsommer,' " *Colloquia Germanica: Internationale Zeitschrift für Germanische Sprach- und Literaturwissenschaft,* 18, no. 1 (1985): 1–17;

Lothar Stiehm, ed., *Adalbert Stifter: Studien und Interpretationen* (Heidelberg: Stiehm, 1968);

Alexander Stillmark, "Stifter's Early Portraits of the Artist: Stages in the Growth of an Aesthetic," *Forum of Modern Language Studies,* 11 (April 1975): 142–164;

Roman Struc, "The Threat of Chaos: Stifter's 'Bergkristall' and Thomas Mann's 'Schnee,' " *Modern Language Quarterly,* 24 (1963): 323–332;

Martin Swales and Erika Swales, *Adalbert Stifter: A Critical Study* (Cambridge: Cambridge University Press, 1984);

Erika Tunner, "Stifters Faszination auf österreichische Autoren der Gegenwart: Peter Handke, Peter Rosei, Jutta Schutting, Hermann Friedl und Reinhold Aumaier," *Vierteljahrsschrift des Adalbert-Stifter-Institutes des Landes Oberösterreich,* 36 (1987): 57–70;

Walter Weiss, "Antworten österreichischer Gegenwartsliteratur auf Adalbert Stifter," *Vierteljahrsschrift des Adalbert-Stifter-Institutes des Landes Oberösterreich,* 32 (1983): 133–143;

Rudolf Wildbolz, *Adalbert Stifter: Langeweile und Faszination* (Stuttgart: Kohlhammer, 1976);

Philip H. Zoldester, *Adalbert Stifter's Weltanschauung* (Bern: Lang, 1970).

Papers:

Adalbert Stifter's papers are at the Bayerische Staatsbibliothek (Bavarian State Library), Munich; the Stifter Archive, Prague; the Foundation Martin Bodmer, Cologny, Switzerland; the Adalbert-Stifter-Institut, Linz, Austria; and the Oberösterreichisches Landesarchiv (Upper Austrian National Archive), Linz.

David Friedrich Strauß

(27 January 1808 – 8 February 1874)

Edwina Lawler
Drew University

BOOKS: *Das Leben Jesu, kritisch bearbeitet,* 2 volumes (Tübingen: Osiander, 1835–1836; revised, 1837; revised, 1838–1839; revised, 1840); translated anonymously as *The Life of Christ; or, A Critical Examination of His History* (New York: Vale, 1843); translated by George Eliot as *The Life of Jesus, Critically Examined,* 3 volumes (London: Chapman, 1846; New York: Blanchard, 1855);

Streitschriften zur Vertheidigung meiner Schrift über das Leben Jesus, und zur Charakteristik der gegenwärtigen Theologie, 3 volumes (Tübingen: Osiander, 1837); translated by Marilyn Chapin Massey as *In Defense of My Life of Jesus against the Hegelians* (Hamden, Conn.: Archon, 1983);

Sendschreiben an die Herren Bürgermeister Hirzel, Professor Orelli und Professor Hitzig in Zürich: Nebst einer Zuschrift an das Zürchervolk, by Strauss and Johann Caspar von Orelli (Zurich: Orell, Füßli, 1839); translated anonymously as *The Opinions of Professor David F. Strauss, as Embodied in His Letter to the Burgomaster Hirzel, Professor Orelli, and Professor Hitzig, at Zurich: With an Address to the People of Zurich by Professor Orelli* (London: Chapman, 1844);

Charakteristiken und Kritiken: Eine Sammlung zerstreuter Aufsätze aus den Gebieten der Theologie, Anthropologie und Aesthetik (Leipzig: Wigand, 1839);

Zwei Friedliche Blätter: Vermehrter und verbesserter Abdruck der beiden Aufsätze: Über Justinus Kerner, und: Über Vergängliches und Bleibendes im Christenthum (Altona: Hammerich, 1839); "Über Vergängliches und Bleibendes im Christenthum" translated anonymously as *Soliloquies on the Christian Religion: Its Errors and Its Everlasting Truth* (London: Chapman, 1845);

Zwingli vor dem großen Rathe im 1522; Zwingli vor dem großen Rathe im 1839 (Zurich, 1839);

Photograph by Brandseph, Stuttgart

Die christliche Glaubenslehre in ihrer geschichtlichen Entwicklung und im Kampfe mit der modernen Wissenschaft dargestellt, 2 volumes (Tübingen: Osiander / Stuttgart: Köhler, 1840–1841);

Leicht faßliche Bearbeitung des Lebens Jesu, mit besonderer Berücksichtigung schweizerischer Leser (Winterthur: Verlag der Expedition des Landboten, 1842);

Der Romantiker auf dem Throne der Cäsaren, oder Julian der Abtrünnige: Ein Vortrag (Mannheim: Bassermann, 1847);

Sechs theologisch-politische Volksreden (Stuttgart: Cotta, 1848);

Christian Märklin: Ein Lebens- und Charakterbild aus der Gegenwart (Mannheim: Bassermann, 1851);

Leben und Schriften des Dichters und Philologen Nicodemus Frischlin: Ein Beitrag zur deutschen Culturgeschichte in der zweiten Hälfte des sechszehnten Jahrhunderts (Frankfurt am Main: Literarische Anstalt [J. Rütten], 1856);

Ulrich von Hutten, 3 volumes (Leipzig: Brockhaus, 1858–1860); translated by Jane Sturge as *Ulrich von Hutten: His Life and Times* (London: Daldy, Isbister, 1874; London & New York: Routledge, 1874);

Kleine Schriften biographischen, literar- und kunstgeschichtlichen Inhalts (Leipzig: Brockhaus, 1862);

Hermann Samuel Reimarus und seine Schutzschrift für die vernünftigen Verehrer Gottes (Leipzig: Brockhaus, 1862);

Das Leben Jesu für das deutsche Volk bearbeitet (Leipzig: Brockhaus, 1864); translated anonymously as *A New Life of Jesus* (London & Edinburgh: Williams & Norgate, 1865);

Lessing's Nathan der Weise: Ein Vortrag (Berlin: Guttentag, 1864);

Die Halben und die Ganzen: Eine Streitschrift gegen die HH. DD. Schenkel und Hengstenberg (Berlin: Duncker, 1865);

Der Christus des Glaubens und der Jesus der Geschichte: Eine Kritik des Schleiermacher'schen Lebens Jesu (Berlin: Duncker, 1865);

Voltaire: Sechs Vorträge (Leipzig: Hirzel, 1870);

Krieg und Friede: Zwei Briefe an Ernst Renan, nebst dessen Antwort auf den ersten (Leipzig: Hirzel, 1870); excerpt translated anonymously as "To the People of France: Letter to Ernest Renan," in *Letters on the War between Germany and France,* by Strauß, Theodor Mommsen, F. Max Mueller, and Thomas Carlyle (London: Trübner, 1871), pp. 41–57;

Der alte und der neue Glaube: Ein Bekenntniss (Leipzig: Hirzel, 1872); translated by Mathilde Blind as *The Old Faith and the New: A Confession* (London: Asher, 1873; revised edition, New York: Holt, 1873);

Ein Nachwort als Vorwort zu den neuen Auflagen meiner Schrift: Der Alte und der neue Glaube (Bonn: Strauss, 1873);

Poetisches Gedenkbuch: Gedichte aus seinem Nachlasse für die Freunde ausgewählt und als Manuscript ausgegeben von dem Sohne (Bonn: Strauss, 1876);

Literarische Denkwürdigkeiten (Bonn: Strauss, 1876);

Gesammelte Schriften: Nach des Verfassers letztwilligen Bestimmungen zusammengestellt, 12 volumes, edited by Eduard Zeller (Bonn: Strauss, 1876–1878);

Klopstock's Jugendgeschichte und Klopstock und der Markgraf Karl Friedrich von Baden: Bruchstücke einer Klopstockbiographie (Bonn: Strauss, 1878);

Der Papier-Reisende: Ein Gespräch von David Friedrich Strauß, 1856 (Leipzig: Poeschel & Trepte, 1907).

OTHER: *Christian Friedrich Daniel Schubarts Leben in seinen Briefen,* 2 volumes, edited by Strauß (Berlin: Duncker, 1849);

Friedrich Schiller, *Ich habe mich rasieren lassen: Ein dramatischer Scherz. Aus der Originalhandschrift im Einverständnis mit der Familie Schiller's zum erstenmal herausgegeben von Carl Künzel,* edited by Strauß (Leipzig: Payne, 1863);

Friedrich Schleiermacher, *Theologische Enzyklopädie (1831/32),* edited by Walter Sachs, afterword by Strauß (Berlin & New York: De Gruyter, 1987).

In 1835 the first volume of David Friedrich Strauß's *Das Leben Jesu, kritisch bearbeitet* (1835–1836; translated as *The Life of Christ; or, A Critical Examination of His History,* 1843) was published. In this, his most significant work, the twenty-seven-year-old theologian called into question the authenticity of the very foundation for Christian belief and, therewith, its authority.

Strauß was born in Ludwigsburg on 27 January 1808 to Katharina Christiane Strauß, née Beck, and Johann Friedrich Strauß. His birth followed shortly after the death of their eight-year-old son Fritz. A third son, Wilhelm, was born eighteen months later.

In 1821 Strauß entered Blaubeuren, one of the four junior seminaries in Württemberg, a former state in southwest Germany (now part of Baden-Württemberg). One of his schoolmates was Christian Märklin, who would become a theologian and pedagogue. In his 1851 memorial to Märklin, Strauß would recall that life at Blaubeuren was regimented and cloistered but not without its lighter moments. Among his theology teachers at Blaubeuren were Friedrich Heinrich Kern and Ferdinand Christian Baur, both of whom were to join the Protestant theological faculty at the University of

Strauß in 1837 (artist unknown; from Horton Harris, David Friedrich Strauss and His Theology, *1973)*

Tübingen a year after Strauß matriculated there in 1825. With their appointments the rationalized supernaturalism espoused by the faculty began to be replaced by a more scientifically rigorous and influential theology that came to be known as the "Tübingen School."

The theological curriculum at Tübingen consisted of two years of philosophical study, including philology and history, and three years of theology. While the work of the natural philosopher Friedrich Wilhelm Schelling was more palatable to Strauß, who had been raised in Swabia in an atmosphere of romanticism, supernaturalism, and mysticism, than that of the Enlightenment philosopher Immanuel Kant, it was the sixteenth-century mystic Jakob Böhme who awakened in him a belief in the supernatural. Early in his student days Strauß came to treasure the immediacy in Böhme's knowledge of the divine, and he soon desired contact with a contemporary who possessed this same immediacy of intuition. Through a relative in Weinsberg, Strauß was introduced to the physician and poet Justinus Kerner. Kerner arranged for Strauß and some friends to meet Friederike Hauffe, "die Seherin von Prevorst" (the seeress of Prevorst). Strauß made repeated visits to Hauffe but never again experienced the intensity he felt on that first occasion.

Shortly thereafter, the mystical cloud produced by Schelling, Böhme, and Hauffe was lifted. Significant among Strauß's independent readings in theology was Friedrich Schleiermacher's *Der christliche Glaube* (1821–1822; translated as *The Christian Faith,* 1928). The Protestant theologian and preacher Schleiermacher of the University of Berlin was attempting to define the distinctiveness of religious experience, to examine and analyze theological ideas within their historical context, and to demonstrate that if theology and philosophy remained within their respective limits they could coexist in peace. Schleiermacher exercised a liberating influence on Strauß by awakening his critical and historical sense.

Another work of significance for Strauß at this time was Georg Wilhelm Friedrich Hegel's *Die Phänomenologie des Geistes* (1807; translated as *The Phenomenology of Mind,* 1910). Hegel was among the most important representatives of German Idealistic philosophy, but even though he had been teaching in Berlin with great effectiveness since 1818 his work was still virtually unknown in Tübingen. The effect of *Die Phänomenologie des Geistes* on Strauß was unparalleled; he later said in *Christian Märklin* that all his faculties were vitally stimulated by it.

In the fall of 1830 Strauß passed his final examinations with distinction and was appointed pastor of a small church in Klein-Ingersheim. In a letter to Märklin in November Strauß said that he was continuing his study of the works of Schleiermacher and Hegel, particularly of the latter's *Die Logik* (1817; translated as *The Logic of Hegel,* 1874). In 1831 Strauß was appointed a teacher at the monastic school in Maulbronn, but the position lasted only three months. In late October he departed for Berlin, intending to conclude his philosophical education under the personal direction of Hegel and Schleiermacher.

Strauß arrived in Berlin on 3 November and heard Hegel lecture twice; on 14 November Hegel died during the cholera epidemic. At first Strauß intended to return to Tübingen, but he decided to remain in Berlin because, as he wrote to Märklin on 15 November, Hegel was dead but had by no means become extinct there.

This decision to remain in Berlin had determinative consequences for *Das Leben Jesu.* First, Strauß obtained a transcript of Hegel's last lecture on the philosophy of religion from the summer semester of 1831. Strauß's letter to Märklin of 6 February 1832, which describes in detail his plans for the work, is appended to excerpts from this lecture, in which he saw the possibility of arranging his own work into a critical and a philosophical part. Second, Strauß heard Schleiermacher lecture on the New Testament and on his theological encyclopedia and obtained transcripts of Schleiermacher's lectures on the life of Jesus from 1823 and 1829–1830.

Lieber Freund!

D. F. Strauß.

Letter from Strauß to Friedrich Theodor Vischer, dated 26 July 1841 (Schiller-Nationalmuseum, Marbach am Neckar)

Strauß's dissertation, "Die Lehre von der Wiederbringung aller Dinge, in ihrer religionsgeschichtlichen Entwicklung dargestellt" (The Teaching of the Restoration of All Things, Presented in Its Religious-Historical Development), was presented to the Tübingen philosophical faculty in November 1831 and earned him his Ph.D. Strauß traces the doctrine of restoration from its beginning in Indian religion through Schleiermacher's interpretation of it, concluding that Hegelian philosophy offers the correct solution to the problems associated with the doctrine. Strauß's preference for Hegel is obvious; nonetheless, he also marveled at Schleiermacher's critical acumen as revealed in the latter's lectures on the life of Jesus. His appreciation for Schleiermacher, however, did not blind him to a problem he found in the lectures: that Schleiermacher did not offer pure historical criticism but applied dogmatic views to his account. When Strauß returned to Tübingen in May 1832 to teach at the seminary he had worked out his plan for *Das Leben Jesu.*

The work is divided into three parts. The first part, which Strauß calls merely peripheral, is a traditional account of Christian belief. The second part, the historical-critical section, constitutes the main body of the book. Here Strauß attempts to refute all previous rationalistic and supernaturalistic efforts to interpret the Bible. He compares the various accounts of each reported event, points out inconsistencies among them, and attempts to ascertain which features in the reports could be considered historically accurate. He then considers the supernatural view, for him usually represented by Hermann Olshausen, and opposes it with arguments long employed by the rationalists. The rationalistic view is then considered, generally with Heinrich Eberhard Gottlob Paulus as its representative, along with the arguments given against it by the supernaturalists. The absurdities and inconsistencies of these two approaches and the futility of trying to harmonize different versions of the same event are emphasized. Strauß concludes that the mythical view alone is possible: that is, the event, as narrated, is nonhistorical.

As his predecessors in applying the concept of myth in biblical exegesis, Strauß names Christian Gottlob Heyne, Johann Gottfried Eichhorn, Johann Philipp Gabler, Georg Lorenz Bauer, and Wilhelm Martin Leberecht de Wette, faulting them either for not defining the concept adequately or for not applying it comprehensively enough. Further, Schleiermacher's attempts to distinguish historical fact from the varied presentations in the Gospels also influenced Strauß. Discussions with his friend the Hegelian theologian Wilhelm Vatke encouraged Strauß to combine the concept of myth, historical criticism, and speculative hermeneutics in his own fashion.

Strauß was perhaps more radically consistent in applying the concept of myth to the Gospels than were his predecessors, for in his account no incident in the life of Jesus – from his birth through the miracles and speeches to his death, the Resurrection, and the Second Coming – is left untouched. In addition to pointing out the absurdities that result from a literal interpretation, he critically analyzes rationalistic attempts that sought to maintain at least a shred of history. He does not eliminate every historical element, however: Jesus remains a historical person for Strauß, as he was for Schleiermacher; he grew up in Nazareth, was baptized by John, gathered disciples, traveled as a teacher in the Jewish countryside, opposed the Pharisees, preached the kingdom of the Messiah, and was crucified. Strauß did not deny that Jesus was an exemplary man, that the Gospels contain excellent maxims pronounced by him, that Jesus appropriated for himself the messianic role, or that after his death the opinion was formed among Christians that he had arisen from the dead. That Jesus was the incarnate God and that the dogmas espoused by the Church concerning the person of Jesus were based on historical facts, however, Strauß had to deny on the bases of historical criticism and of speculative philosophy.

Strauß foresaw the negative results of his historical criticism, but as he told Märklin in a letter of 6 February 1832 his intention was not to deny or weaken faith but to restore it on a higher level. This restoration was the task of his dogmatic exposition, the final part of *Das Leben Jesu.* In this section, which Strauß considered a mere supplement, he develops his position on the union of the divine and the human.

From the standpoint of the philosophy of religion, Strauß comments, nothing can be determined concerning the authenticity of the biblical narratives. What can be ascertained is whether what is reported had to have happened necessarily because of the truth of certain concepts. On this ground, the necessity of the union of the divine and the human in one person cannot be maintained. To do so is to confuse reality in general with a particular reality: just as it is impossible to derive from the idea of beauty or virtue that one particular person is the sole perfect realization of this idea, so it is impossible to derive from the idea of the union of the human and the divine that it was necessarily real-

An 1842 caricature depicting Strauß (whose name in German means "ostrich") chopping down a cross. He is assisted by fellow radical theologians Bruno Bauer (whose name means "peasant"), pulling on the rope, and Ludwig Feuerbach ("fiery brook"). On the other side is a flock of sheep, representing issues of the conservative Protestant journal Evangelische Kirchenzeitung. *They are being encouraged by the journal's editor, E. W. Hengstenberg (*Heng *means "stallion"). In the tree are the Prussian education minister, Johann Albrecht Eichhorn ("squirrel"), and the orthodox theologian Heinrich Thiele (Bildarchiv Preußischer Kulturbesitz, Berlin).*

ized in Jesus. The realization of this idea, Strauß asserts, is attained in all of humankind. Humanity as a whole is the subject of the predicates that had been assigned to Christ. For Strauß the union of the divine and the human is the essence of religion. On the level of belief this idea is expressed in the narrative or representational form of myth; on the higher level of philosophical speculation it is expressed in conceptual form. If any of the components of biblical history proved to be unhistorical, what was essential in religion would remain and would be raised from the form of representation to that of concept.

Strauß stipulates two sources for the biblical myth: first, the messianic ideas and expectations existing in the minds of the Jewish people prior to Jesus' appearance; second, the impression left by the character, actions, and fate of Jesus. Belief in Jesus' resurrection, itself the product of the Apostles' imagination, gave rise to belief in him as the Messiah. Everything else in the life of Jesus was derived from faith in the Resurrection. While Jesus in no way corresponded to the then-current messianic expectations, the impression he made necessitated recognizing him as the Messiah. Since the impression was not strong enough to sustain the recognition without fulfillment of the expectation, however, the imagination of the first Christians transferred to Jesus what he was lacking.

Up to a point, Strauß was saying the same thing as were advocates of the historical Christian view: belief in the Resurrection was the central Christian belief; the Resurrection was confirmation of the truth of Jesus' divinity. At the same time, he agreed with the critical view that the Resurrection was a product of a myth-forming process.

Despite Strauß's claims to having written a presuppositionless work, his historical-critical investigation of the Gospels was greatly influenced by his philosophical conception of religion and by his implied identification of the mythical with the unhistorical, that is, with the untrue. Despite its faults, *Das Leben Jesu* continues to deserve the consideration of biblical scholars because of its insights into the genesis of the biblical narratives.

As a result of the unfavorable reception the work received, Strauß was relieved of his teaching responsibilities at the Tübingen seminary before the second volume appeared. He was assigned to a gymnasium in Ludwigsburg, where he remained for barely a year. In September 1836 he moved to Stuttgart. For the rest of his life he worked as a private scholar and writer.

A second edition of *Das Leben Jesu,* to which Strauß had added a few remarks to defend or explain his position, appeared in 1837. His *Streitschriften zur Vertheidigung meiner Schrift über das Leben Jesus, und zur Charakteristik der gegenwärtigen Theologie* (Polemical Writings in Defense of My Work on the Life of Jesus, and in Characterizing Contemporary Theology; translated as *In Defense of My Life of Jesus against the Hegelians,* 1983) was published in the same year. Partly in the hope of being called to Zurich as a professor of dogmatics, a position Ferdinand Hitzig and Kaspar Orelli had been trying to secure for him since 1836, Strauß made certain concessions in the third edition of *Das Leben Jesu,* which was published in 1838–1839. These concessions included granting the historical Jesus a more significant role in the founding of Christianity without diminishing the role of myth; questioning his own position on the inauthenticity of the Gospel according to John; and admitting that some of the miracles attributed to Jesus might be true, although he attempted to give naturalistic explanations of them. At the same time, in "Über Vergängliches und Bleibendes im Christenthum" (1838; translated as *Soliloquies on the Christian Religion: Its Errors and Its Everlasting Truth,* 1845) he suggested that Jesus was a religious genius who would never be surpassed. These concessions were to no avail: in Zurich, Strauß's appointment was linked with the radical movement and incited conservative opposition. The government retracted its offer, and Strauß never again tried to become part of the academic world. When the fourth edition of *Das Leben Jesu* appeared in 1840, it was essentially the same as the original 1835–1836 edition. In his *Literarische Denkwürdigkeiten* (Literary Memoirs, 1876), Strauß acknowledged that the concessions made in the third edition were not a true reflection of his position.

In preparation for the hoped-for position in Zurich, Strauß had begun a comprehensive study of the history of dogmatics. From this study emerged *Die christliche Glaubenslehre in ihrer geschichtlichen Entwicklung und im Kampfe mit der modernen Wissenschaft dargestellt* (Christian Doctrine in Its Historical Development and in Its Struggle with Modern Science, 1840–1841). After presenting the development of Christian dogmas from biblical teachings, pointing out contradictions and unresolved difficulties, and tracing the gradual disintegration of dogmas as recognition of these difficulties increased, Strauß denies that the traditional teachings of the Church could continue to exist without an inadmissible reinterpretation of their meaning.

In 1837 Strauß had met the renowned singer Agnes Schebest; they were married in August 1842. For a few months Strauß was truly happy, but the remainder of the four years they spent together failed to provide him with the love, security, and tranquillity he had hoped to find or with an atmosphere in which he could work. In 1846 Strauß and his wife agreed to a separation. In January 1849 he moved to Munich. In the fall of 1851 he was given custody of his son Fritz and his daughter Georgine and moved with them to Weimar and then to Cologne, where his brother resided. In the fall of 1854 Strauß and his children moved to Heidelberg, and in 1860 they moved to Heilbronn. In *Das Leben Jesu für das deutsche Volk bearbeitet* (The Life of Jesus Adapted for the German People, 1864; translated as *A New Life of Jesus,* 1865) the critical results of *Das Leben Jesu* were presented in a more popular style. After his daughter's marriage in 1864 Strauß spent some time in Berlin and Heidelberg, settling in Darmstadt in the fall of 1865. Schleiermacher's lectures on the life of Jesus had been published in 1864; Strauß critiqued them in *Der Christus des Glaubens und der Jesus der Geschichte* (The Christ of Faith and the Jesus of History, 1865). In the same year appeared his *Die Halben und die Ganzen* (The Halves and the Wholes), a polemic directed against Ernst Wilhelm Hengstenberg, a proponent of Lutheranism, and Daniel Schenkel, a theologian close in approach to Schleiermacher.

In a letter to the writer Friedrich Theodor Vischer on 24 February 1849 Strauß had referred to himself as a "künstlerischer Wissenschaftler" (artistic scientist). He explained that the scientific work he had done was born of passion and that without passion he could do nothing; he regarded this passion as the artistic element in his nature. Earlier, however, in a letter to Karl Moritz Rapp on 5 April 1831, Strauß had claimed that he was not a poet because he totally lacked imagination and creativity. Nonetheless, he wrote poetry from his early post-university years to the last year of his life; the poems were published posthumously in 1876 as *Poetisches Gedenkbuch* (Poetic Memorial Book). In him, he says in *Literarische Denkwürdigkeiten,* imagination is a vacuum; at best he has a gift for metaphor and image, but only as something accidental or decorative. And yet, he continues, it was the bit of a poet in him that had provided the foundation on which his intellectual life was built. In this same work Strauß acknowledges that his particular talent lay in the compilation of materials. This talent is evident in *Das Leben Jesu* and in his biographies of Nicodemus Frischlin (1856), Tübingen professor and author of nine school dramas who was killed in 1590 because of his attacks on theologians and the nobility; Ulrich von Hutten (1858–1860), sixteenth-century German poet and reformer; Hermann Samuel Reimarus (1862), eighteenth-century theologian and philosopher; and Voltaire (1870).

Strauß returned to his native city, Ludwigsburg, in the fall of 1872. His last work, *Der alte und der neue Glaube: Ein Bekenntniss* (translated as *The Old Faith and the New: A Confession,* 1873), appeared in 1872, and by 1877 it was in its ninth printing. In a letter to Vischer of 18 July 1863 Strauß had said that he felt an obligation to write a popular ethics to fill the spiritual void left by the loss of belief in traditional Christian teachings; *Der alte und der neue Glaube* may be seen as the fulfillment of this obligation. Strauß tries to show that the ethical system of the "old" faith, the basis for which is present in human nature, can serve as a model for the "new" faith. It is no longer possible to consider oneself a Christian, Strauß maintains, for there is nothing to substantiate the claims made by Christianity about its founder, Strauß points out, and the Christian emphasis on the hereafter and on the Cross is contrary to the modern view of the world. What we know is the here and now; we accomplish our worst and our best in this life. If human institutions and products have nothing of value in themselves, nothing can give them value. What is to be retained from Christianity are the achievements it occasioned as it perpetuated and advanced the culture of Hellenism and ancient Rome.

In agreement with Schleiermacher, Strauß holds that the essential element of religion is dependence. To this concept must be added the need to act against this dependence to regain freedom. We are dependent not on a Supreme Being but on the universe, "das Alles" (the All), the source of the rational and the good. Because among all forms of life we alone intuit within ourselves the disposition to the good and the rational, and because we alone can actualize the good and the rational, we feel not only dependence on but also intimacy with the All. Because the All evokes a feeling of piety, the question as to whether we in the modern age have religion can be answered in the affirmative.

Strauß conceives of the All as an animated material mass in which opposites coexist and complement each other. Human beings arose out of the depths of nature, climbing slowly and gradually from the animal level to ever higher orders. Somehow, and Strauß has been faulted for not explaining how, the instincts of loyalty and sociability enabled higher animals to work toward ethical traits. All moral action, Strauß continues, is self-determination according to the idea of the human species. We should act in such a way that our conduct is a realization of this idea and a recognition and an advancement of it in others of our species. Our struggle for existence is not to be conducted on the raw level of bestiality but with awareness of our higher dispositions and of the oneness of all nature.

Strauß circa 1863

Thus, by combining materialism and natural science with idealism, did Strauß offer his religion of humanity and morality. He found this religion reflected in the works of the Enlightenment dramatist and theoretician Gotthold Ephraim Lessing, the classical writer Johann Wolfgang von Goethe, and the dramatist Friedrich von Schiller, as well as in

Strauß in 1865; engraving by Adolf Neumann

the music of Ludwig van Beethoven, Joseph Haydn, and Wolfgang Amadeus Mozart. His vision, as various critics have noted, was limited, unimaginative, and not without its inconsistencies.

Strauß believed that he had no talent for philosophy and that he remained a dilettante in the field of literature; he felt that he was not a historian because he could not suspend his dogmatic interests; only in theology, he thought, could he accomplish something fundamental. Throughout his life Strauß attempted to reconcile religion with modern consciousness.

After a two-year illness during which he was attended to by a faithful servant and by his son Fritz, a physician in Stuttgart, Strauß died in Ludwigsburg on 4 February 1874. The questions he raised about the relation of history to faith continue to animate contemporary reflection.

Letters:

Ausgewählte Briefe, edited by Eduard Zeller (Bonn: Strauss, 1895);

Briefe David Friedrich Strauß an J. Georgii, edited by Heinrich Maier (Tübingen: Mohr, 1912);

Briefe an seine Tochter: Nebst Briefen seiner Mutter an ihn selbst, edited by F. Heusler and Georgine Strauß Heusler (Heidelberg: Winter, 1921);

Briefwechsel zwischen Strauß und Vischer, 2 volumes, edited by Adolf Rapp (Stuttgart: Klett, 1952–1953);

"Der Briefwechsel zwischen Strauß und Bauer: Ein quellenmäßiger Beitrag zur Strauß-Bauer-Forschung," edited by Ernst Barnikol, *Zeitschrift für Kirchengeschichte,* 73 (1962): 74–125.

Biographies:

Eduard Zeller, *David Friedrich Strauß in seinem Leben und seinen Schriften geschildert* (Bonn: Strauss, 1874); translated as *David Friedrich Strauß in His Life and Writings* (London: Smith, Elder, 1874);

Adolf Hausrath, *David Friedrich Strauß und die Theologie seiner Zeit,* 2 volumes (Heidelberg: Bassermann, 1876–1878);

Theobald Ziegler, *David Friedrich Strauß,* 2 volumes (Strassburg: Trübner, 1908).

References:

Gunther Backhaus, *Kerygma und Mythos bei David Friedrich Strauß und Rudolf Bultmann* (Hamburg: Reich, 1956);

Karl Barth, *David Friedrich Strauß als Theologe 1839–1939* (Zurich: Verlag der Evangelischen Buchhandlung Zollikon, 1939);

Bruno Bauer, *Philo, Strauß und Renan und das Urchristentum* (Berlin: Hempel, 1874; reprinted, Aalen: Scientia, 1972);

Franz Courth, *Das Leben Jesu von David Friedrich Strauß in der Kritik Johann Evangelist Kuhns: Ein Beitrag zur Auseinandersetzung der katholischen Tübinger Schule mit dem deutschen Idealismus* (Göttingen: Vandenhoeck & Ruprecht, 1975);

Richard S. Cromwell, *David Friedrich Strauß and His Place in Modern Thought* (Fair Lawn, N.J.: Burdick, 1974);

Friedrich Wilhelm Graf, *Kritik und Pseudo-Spekulation: David Friedrich Strauß als Dogmatiker im Kontext der positionellen Theologie seiner Zeit* (Munich: Kaiser, 1982);

Horton Harris, *David Friedrich Strauß and His Theology* (Cambridge: Cambridge University Press, 1973);

Christian Hartlich and Walter Sachs, *Der Ursprung des Mythosbegriffes in der modernen Bibelwissenschaft* (Tübingen: Mohr, 1952);

Dietz Lange, *Historischer Jesus oder Mythischer Christus* (Gütersloh: Mohn, 1975);

Edwina G. Lawler, *David Friedrich Strauß and His Critics: The Life of Jesus Debate in Nineteenth Century German Journals* (New York: Lang, 1986);

William Madges, *The Core of Christian Faith: D. F. Strauss and His Catholic Critics* (New York: Lang, 1987);

Marilyn Chapin Massey, *Christ Unmasked: The Meaning of the Life of Jesus in German Politics* (Chapel Hill: University of North Carolina Press, 1983);

Gotthold Müller, *Identität und Immanenz: Zur Genese der Theologie von David Friedrich Strauß* (Zurich: EVZ, 1968);

Friedrich Nietzsche, "David Strauß, der Bekenner und der Schriftsteller," in his *Unzeitgemäße Betrachtungen* (Stuttgart: Kröner, 1964), pp. 1-93;

Georg F. Sandberger, *David Friedrich Strauß als theologischer Hegelianer: Mit unveröffentlichten Briefen* (Göttingen: Vandenhoeck & Ruprecht, 1972);

Albert Schweitzer, *The Quest of the Historical Jesus: A Critical Study of Its Progress from Reimarus to Wrede* (London: Black, 1922).

Papers:

David Friedrich Strauß's manuscripts, letters, and transcriptions of lectures by Hegel, Schleiermacher, and Baur are at the Deutsches Literatur-Archiv and at the Cotta-Archiv, both in Marbach am Neckar. The manuscript for Strauß's dissertation, "Die Lehre von der Wiederbringung aller Dinge in ihrer religionsgeschichtlichen Entwicklung dargestellt," is at the Archiv der Evangelischen Landeskirche, Stuttgart.

Talvj
(Therese Albertine Luise von Jakob Robinson)

(26 January 1797 – 13 April 1870)

Martha Kaarsberg Wallach
Central Connecticut State University

BOOKS: *Psyche: Ein Taschenbuch für das Jahr 1825* (Halle: Ruff, 1825);

Der Mutter Geist: Zwei Balladen von Ludwig Uhland und Talvj, music by Carl Loewe (Berlin: Schlesinger, 1827);

Ihr Spaziergang: Gesänge der Sehnsucht, music by Loewe (Berlin: Laue, 1828);

Versuch einer geschichtlichen Charakteristik der Volkslieder germanischer Nationen, mit einer Uebersicht der Lieder außereuropäischer Völkerschaften (Leipzig: Brockhaus, 1840);

Die Unächtheit der Lieder Ossian's und des Macpherson'schen Ossian's insbesondere (Leipzig: Brockhaus, 1840);

Geschichte der Colonisation von Neu-England: Von den ersten Niederlassungen daselbst im Jahre 1607 bis zur Einführung der Provinzialverfassung von Massachusetts im Jahre 1692. Nach den Quellen bearbeitet. Nebst einer Karte von Neu-England im Jahre 1674 (Leipzig: Brockhaus, 1847); translated and edited by William Hazlitt as *Talvi's* [sic] *History of the Colonization of America,* 2 volumes (London: Newby, 1851);

Historical View of the Languages and Literature of the Slavic Nations: With a Sketch of Their Popular Poetry (New York & London: Putnam, 1850);

Heloise; or, The Unrevealed Secret: A Tale (New York: Appleton, 1850); translated into German by Talvj as *Heloise* (Leipzig: Brockhaus, 1852);

Life's Discipline: A Tale of the Annals of Hungary (New York: Appleton, 1851);

Die Auswanderer: Eine Erzählung, 2 volumes (Leipzig: Brockhaus, 1852); translated by Talvj as *The Exiles: A Tale* (New York: Putnam, 1853); translation republished as *Woodhill; or, The Ways of Providence* (New York: De Witt & Davenport, 1856);

Fünfzehn Jahre: Ein Zeitgemälde aus dem vorigen Jahrhundert, 2 volumes (Leipzig: Brockhaus, 1868); translated by Mary A. Robinson and William C. Bryant as *Fifteen Years: A Picture from the Last Century* (New York: Appleton, 1871);

Gesammelte Novellen: Nebst einer Auswahl bisher ungedruckter Gedichte und einer biographischen Einleitung, 2 volumes, edited by Mary A. Robinson (Leipzig: Brockhaus, 1874).

OTHER: Sir Walter Scott, *Der schwarze Zwerg,* translated by Talvj as Ernst Berthold (Zwickau: Schumann, 1822);

Die Unächtheit
der
Lieder Ossian's
und des
Macpherson'schen Ossian's
insbesondere.

Von
Talvj.

Leipzig:
F. A. Brockhaus.
1840.

Title page for the work in which Talvj argued that the songs supposedly written by the ancient Gaelic bard Ossian were actually the work of their "discoverer," James Macpherson

Scott, *Die Presbyterianer,* translated by Talvj as Berthold (Zwickau: Schumann, 1823);

Volkslieder der Serben: Metrisch übersetzt und historisch eingeleitet, translated and edited by Talvj (Halle & Leipzig: Renger, 1825–1826);

"Der Lauf der Welt," in *Taschenbuch zum gesellschaftlichen Vergnügen auf das Jahr 1829* (Leipzig: Voss, 1829), pp. 96–166;

John Pickering, *Über die indianischen Sprachen Amerikas,* translated and edited by Talvj (Leipzig: Vogel, 1834);

"Aus der Geschichte der ersten Ansiedlungen in den Vereinigten Staaten (Leben des Hauptmanns John Smith 1579/1631)," in *Raumers historisches Taschenbuch,* edited by Friedrich von Raumer (Leipzig: Brockhaus, 1845), pp. 1–192;

Edward Robinson, *Neuere biblische Forschungen in Palestina,* 3 volumes, translated anonymously by Talvj (Berlin: Reimer, 1853–1854);

"Deutschlands Schriftstellerinnen bis vor hundert Jahren," in *Raumers historisches Taschenbuch,* fourth series, no. 2, edited by Raumer (Leipzig: Brockhaus, 1861), pp. 1–142;

Edward Robinson, *Physische Geographie des heiligen Landes,* translated and edited by Talvj (Leipzig: Brockhaus, 1865).

SELECTED PERIODICAL PUBLICATIONS – UNCOLLECTED: "Des Prinzen Mujo Rache," *Über Kunst und Altertum,* 5, no. 2 (1825): 60–62;

"Historical View of the Slavic Languages in its Various Dialects; with Special Reference to Theological Literature," anonymous, *Biblical Repository,* 4 (April 1834): 328–532;

"Popular Poetry of the Teutonic Nations," *North American Review,* 42 (April 1836): 265-339;
"Popular Poetry of the Slavic Nations," *North American Review,* 43 (July 1836): 85-120;
"Spanish Popular Poetry," *North American Review,* 54 (April 1842): 419-446;
"The Loves of Goethe," *Sartain's Union Magazine New Monthly,* 7 (1850): 158-170;
"Early Poetry of France," *Putnam's Monthly Magazine,* 2 (July-December 1853): 361-370;
"The Private Life and Household of Charlemagne," *North American Review,* 81, no. 169 (1855): 112-159;
"On Russian Slavery," *North American Review,* 82, no. 171 (1856): 293-318;
"Ein Ausflug nach dem Gebirge Virginiens im Sommer 1856," *Westermann's Monatshefte,* 1 (January 1857): 373-381; (February 1857): 492-501; (March 1857): 627-637;
"The German Popular Legend of Dr. Faustus," *Atlantic Monthly,* 2 (October 1858): 551-566;
"Anna Louisa Karschin: Ein Lebensbild," *Westermann's Monatshefte,* 4 (August 1858): 451-467; (September 1858): 563-577;
"Die Shaker," *Westermann's Monatshefte,* 8 (1860): 587-591;
"Die Fälle des Ottawa," *Westermann's Monatshefte,* 9 (February 1861): 535-544;
"Die Kosaken und ihre historischen Lieder," *Westermann's Monatshefte,* 26 (August 1869): 467-474;
"Ein Bild aus seiner Zeit," *Westermann's Monatshefte,* 28 (June 1870): 295-306; (July 1870): 394-408; (August 1870): 511-523; (September 1870): 585-605.

Therese Albertine Luise von Jakob Robinson, who wrote under the pen name Talvj, received early recognition as a prose writer, literary critic, and translator of novels and folk songs. She began writing poetry in her teens and had fiction and literary criticism published when she was in her twenties. Her early fame rests on her excellent verse translation of Serbian folk songs (1825-1826), a project she undertook at Johann Wolfgang von Goethe's suggestion. He rightly assumed that since she wrote poetry and knew Latin, English, and Russian, she could easily teach herself Serbian and translate these recently collected songs, which were then exciting the imagination of German literary figures. Her most important achievement as a literary critic is her solution to the controversy over the authenticity of songs attributed to the ancient Scottish bard Ossian: with her experience in folk song, she was able to prove that they were really the creation of the eighteenth-century Scottish writer James Macpherson. Among her prose writings her late novels stand out: written mostly in the United States in the 1850s and 1860s, they were published in English and German versions by prestigious houses and met with both critical and public acclaim.

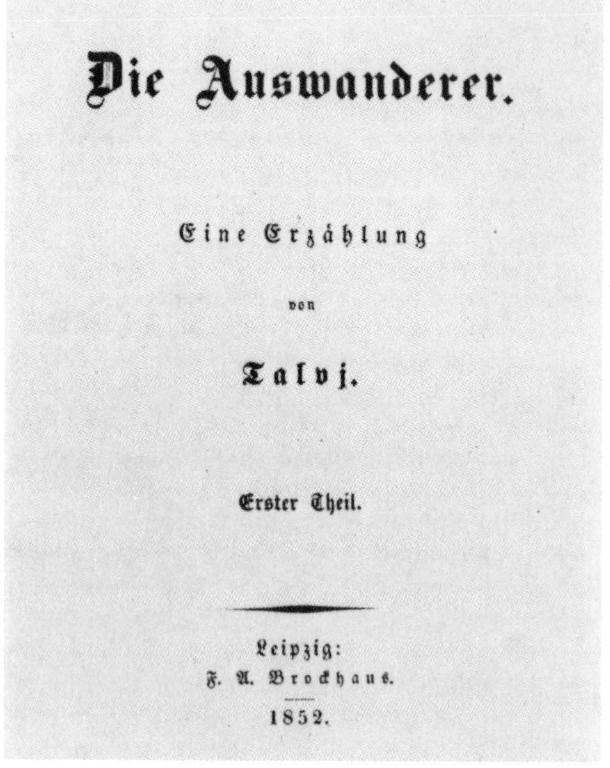
Die Auswanderer.

Eine Erzählung

von

Talvj.

Erster Theil.

Leipzig:
F. A. Brockhaus.
1852.

Title page for Talvj's novel about German emigrants

Born in Halle on 26 January 1797, Therese Jakob was one of four children of Ludwig Heinrich Jakob, a highly regarded professor of government and philosophy, and Auguste Jakob, née Dreissig. She became known as something of a child prodigy among her father's colleagues and students, who called her the "kleines Orakel" (little oracle). She spent a happy and secure early childhood surrounded by an affectionate family that included two sisters and a brother. This idyllic life came to an end when the Napoleonic Wars reached Halle and Napoleon closed the university. Professor Jakob, not wanting to live under French occupation, accepted a position at the newly formed University of Kharkov in southern Russia (today, the Ukraine). On 20 July 1807, the day Prussia conceded defeat to Napoleon's armies, the family set off for Russia in a horse-drawn carriage. Jakob found Kharkov strange and "halb asiatisch" (half Asiatic). She cried over the fate of defeated Germany and expressed her feelings in verses patterned after Friedrich Schiller's poetry. Like her sisters, she at first refused to learn Russian, but she became interested in the language when she heard Russian folk songs at the horse markets in Kharkov. The Jakobs spent four hundred rubles a year for piano and drawing lessons for their daughters – twice as much as their female serf cost them. But Therese Jakob was interested neither in music nor drawing, preferring to read books and write poems. Not having any books but those in the university library, she read a great deal of history and many theoretical works about the fine arts; she even copied some books in their entirety. Teachers were scarce and the children's lessons became sporadic. In 1809 the family moved to Saint Petersburg, where Professor Jakob had become an adviser on state reforms; lessons stopped altogether at that time and were never resumed. The family's financial situation might have had something to do with the cessation of lessons; they had to keep drawing on their savings to make ends meet. Professor Jakob's services to the state were rewarded with an aristocratic title by Czar Alexander I, allowing the Jakobs to add *von* to the family name, but not with an impressive salary. In Saint Petersburg, where many Germans and other West Europeans lived, Therese von Jakob enjoyed a more active social life than had been possible in Kharkov, but she also continued her literary activities. She wrote a great deal of poetry, which she showed to no one, and many letters to an imaginary girlfriend. She also read novels, travel accounts, memoirs, and history books. When German soldiers who had been forced to join Napoleon's army were brought to Saint Petersburg as Russian prisoners of war, she made sacrifices to help make their confinement more comfortable. Her poetry of that time expresses her longing for peace, her patriotic feelings toward Germany, and her desire to return there.

Her wish to return was fulfilled after Napoleon was defeated and the University of Halle reopened. In 1816 she once again saw Germany, a country of which she had developed an idealized notion based on reading the works of such authors as Friedrich de la Motte Fouqué and E. T. A. Hoffmann; she was disappointed by what she saw and came to appreciate Russian qualities she had taken for granted, such as gregariousness and hospitality, which she contrasts with German inhospitality in her letters to Russian friends. In her letters she also complains about the low educational level and the lack of intellectual interests of German women, who allowed their chores and their responsibilities for others to swallow up all their time and considered it their duty not to do anything about their own intellectual development. Jakob, on the other hand, had no responsibilities. She accompanied her father to intellectual gatherings and was encouraged to have her writing published. Her contemporaries considered her appearance impressive: she was of delicate build, blond and blue-eyed, and her pretty face had an air of stubbornness.

Jakob started to write fiction, accepted invitations to write book reviews for literary journals, and translated novels of Sir Walter Scott under the pseudonym Ernst Berthold. It is unclear whether her first poems were published during this time: in a biographical sketch written for an encyclopedia in 1840 she says that she turned down repeated requests to print her poems, but when the sketch was published after her death, her daughter added a footnote insisting that some of the poems were published at this time in the *Abendzeitung* (Evening Newspaper) in Dresden. Biographers list a publication date of 1820 or "around" that year and the pen name Reseda. Subsequent publications appeared under the acronym Talvj, derived from the initials of her full name: Therese Albertine Luise von Jakob. It was long assumed that Talvj was a man.

The fiction she wrote between 1820 and 1828 protests the role of women in society and features heroines of privileged background faced with the difficult decision of whether, when, and whom to marry. It is a decision with which Talvj herself struggled; she did not marry until she was thirty-one. Her early fiction was influenced by her experience in Russia, where she came to love the folk songs and the colorful people living close to nature. One of her tales takes place in Poland; another is set in Hungary, with a Gypsy in costume singing old Slavic folk songs. There are also historical backgrounds that betray the influence of Scott's novels. Talvj's experience of having to leave her homeland during the Napoleonic Wars enabled her to create heroines who are similarly uprooted. Her style is patterned on German classical and Romantic models. In the preface to her first anthology of stories, *Psyche* (1825), she assures her readers that she has not written fiction for mere entertainment and has created not noble characters but human beings with virtues and vices. She asks her readers to apply a natural, not an ideal, standard to her works.

In her first story, "Die Rache" (Revenge), written in 1820, a young woman suddenly finds herself in a position of power through an unexpected inheritance. The conditions attached to the inheritance are that she marry by a certain date and that

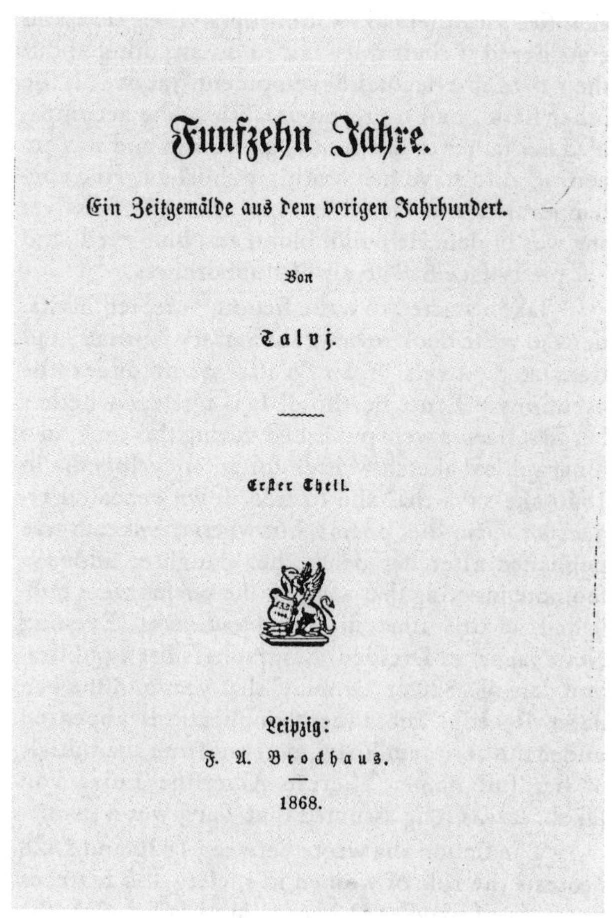
Funfzehn Jahre.

Ein Zeitgemälde aus dem vorigen Jahrhundert.

Von

Talvj.

Erster Theil.

Leipzig:

F. A. Brockhaus.

1868.

Title page for Talvj's final novel

she marry a man willing to take her name. Among the many candidates for her hand is a man who once seduced her cousin. She avenges the cousin by publicly humiliating the seducer, but the seemingly supportive man she eventually marries turns out to be an opportunist. Talvj uses the plot to examine male and female roles: men have too many privileges, women too few. Their privileged position makes men selfish, aggressive, and destructive; they protect each other. Women, on the other hand, are too conscious of their weakness to protect one of their own kind who dares challenge the status quo. The heroine is punished by society for overstepping the boundaries circumscribing women's lives.

In "Verfehlte Bestimmung" (Failed Destiny), also written in 1820, Talvj treats cultural and educational differences that lead to a failed marriage. A learned young woman who is contemptuous of such shallow amusements as fancy dress balls, who even in mixed company is outspoken about her opinions, and who has made a special study of the Age of Chivalry, is wooed and won by a charming Polish count, who is the incarnation of modern-day chivalry. The count, who passes for intelligent and witty because he employs the typical body language and facial expressions with which Polish aristocrats create this impression, is unfaithful even before the wedding. Other Polish characters are equally false: the count's aunt, for example, feigns friendship with her nephew's bride while slowly poisoning her. Polish social conditions are also treated critically: the aunt's castle is surrounded by the miserable huts of poor peasants, and servants in rags greet the German bride on her arrival. Talvj shows that there is an unbridgeable gap between national cultures and levels of education.

A third story included in the anthology, "Menschliche Schwäche" (Human Weakness), written in 1822, takes place during the seventeenth-century Hungarian wars of independence from Austria and reflects the influence of Scott. Talvj later expanded the story into a novel.

In 1823 one of Talvj's sisters died. To overcome her sorrow, she embarked on an arduous project. Goethe had been encouraging her to learn Serbian and translate a collection of Serbian folk songs that had recently been reviewed by Jacob Grimm. She did so, and in 1825 the first volume of the folk songs was published with a dedication to Goethe that says that his interest in these songs guarantees that they embody poetic beauty and human truth. A year later the second volume appeared and was also well received. Only Grimm was somewhat critical: in a letter of 14 August 1825 in which he thanks her for a copy of the book he assures her that he realizes her intentions are good and her knowledge of Serbian is adequate; but he adds that the rooms of German literature are somewhat crowded, that he dislikes most translations, and that so much translation dilutes the German national spirit.

In 1828 Talvj married the theologian Edward Robinson of Southington, Connecticut, who had been studying Oriental languages in Halle. In her letter to Grimm of 8 February 1828 Talvj tells him of her decision to marry and leave the country, adding that Grimm will no longer have to fear her crowding the rooms of German literature: she did not believe that her duties as a housewife would leave her enough time for writing, even though her husband "gehört . . . zu den wenigen Männern, die das lebhafte Interesse für Kunst und Wissenschaft auch von Frauen sehr zu schätzen wissen und würde mich zu literarischen Arbeiten eher aufmuntern, als von ihnen abhalten" (is among the few men who appreciate a lively interest in the arts and the pursuit of knowledge on the part of women and would encourage me in my literary work rather than keep me from it). Ignoring both this comment and her allusion to his earlier remark about the crowded rooms, Grimm suggested in his response that her acquaintance with German literature and history would comfort her in the new world.

In Andover, Massachusetts, where her husband taught at the theological seminary, Talvj studied American Indian languages and annotated and translated into German John Pickering's work on the subject (1834). She also had an article about Slavic languages published in the *Biblical Repository,* which her husband edited. In 1833 the Robinsons had moved to Boston, where the wife of Karl Follen became her first female German acquaintance in America. Karl Follen, a professor of German at Harvard, who had been one of the liberal political refugees to flee Germany in 1830, encouraged Talvj to stimulate American interest in German folk songs; her articles on the subject in the *North American Review* (April 1836) followed. Between 1829 and 1836 Talvj gave birth to four children, of whom only two survived to adulthood. The eldest, Mary Augusta (Marie), became a pianist and composer; the youngest, Edward, became a lawyer, an officer in the Union army during the Civil War, and a United States consul in Strasbourg and Hamburg.

In 1837 Edward Robinson accepted a professorship at the Union Theological Seminary in New York. For the next two years he conducted research in Palestine and Egypt; Talvj did not accompany him, traveling instead to Hamburg, Leipzig, and Dresden. During this period she completed *Versuch einer geschichtlichen Charakteristik der Volkslieder germanischer Nationen* (Essay on a Historical Characterization of the Folk Songs of Germanic Nations, 1840) and her work challenging the authenticity of the Ossian songs. The latter book, also published in 1840, attracted much attention and convinced many people that the songs were not of ancient Gaelic origin, as claimed by Macpherson, but were written by him.

In New York, Talvj overcame her husband's objections to a more active social life and established a salon that became renowned. Among the American intellectuals who frequented Talvj's salon were Washington Irving, who is said to have inspired Talvj to resume work on her poetry, and the feminist Margaret Fuller, who was then literary critic for the *New York Tribune.*

A visit by the German historian Friedrich von Raumer in 1844 reinforced an interest Talvj had developed in American history, and soon she began to write on American historical topics. Her essay on the first settlements in the United States was published in *Raumers historisches Taschenbuch* (Raumer's Historical Pocketbook) in 1845; two years later she brought out a work about the colonization of New England. She also resumed the writing of fiction, with some of her novels appearing in both English and German versions. *Heloise; or, The Unrevealed Secret* (1850), which went through three editions in its first year of publication,was followed by a German version in 1852. In 1851 an expanded English version of her early story "Menschliche Schwäche" was published as *Life's Discipline. Die Auswanderer* (The Emigrants) appeared in Germany in 1852, and its English version, *The Exiles,* in the United States in 1853. The English and German versions contain explanatory notes appropriate for an American or German reading public, respectively. Talvj apparently served as her own translator.

In *Heloise* one can find characterizations, motifs, and quotations from Goethe's plays *Iphigenie auf Tauris* (Iphigenia on Tauris, 1787; translated as *Iphigenia,* 1793) and *Torquato Tasso* (1790; translated, 1861), from his ballad "Die Braut von Korinth" (The Bride of Corinth, 1798), and from Friedrich Schiller's *Wallenstein* trilogy (1800). The heroine, brought up in rural seclusion and privileged circumstances, suddenly finds herself catapulted into the world and confronted with the facts of her socially stigmatized birth. She discovers that Felix, the "brother" with whom she was raised, is not really her brother; that her mother was a princess; and that an "uncle," in Russian exile because he had fallen into disfavor at Court, is really her father. She matures through her association with people who have been purified by their suffering, through her secret love for Felix, through her escape from society, and through her search for her unknown father.

Like Iphigenie, Heloise has to suffer for the sins of her parents, finds herself in an uncivilized wilderness, fights against brutality there, fearlessly makes truth her highest precept, refuses to marry a "noble savage," is saved by her "brother," and returns home. But the distinction between civilized people and barbarians in *Iphigenie auf Tauris* is reversed in *Heloise:* the Europeans are the unprincipled barbarians who conduct war with deceit and without pity; the "noble savages" are motivated by love of homeland: it is their own hearths that they are defending.

Like Iphigenie and like Thekla in the *Wallenstein* trilogy, Heloise is to be sacrificed for her father's war plans. Heloise's father, a general in Russian service, needs allies among the heroic Circassians to bring the Caucasus under Russian rule. While Iphigenie is to be killed on the sacrificial alter, Thekla and Heloise are to be married off favorably – favorably, that is, from the fathers' point of view. In both cases the love of a potential ally is encouraged, and the daughter used as bait. Meanwhile, the real ambitions of the fathers are directed toward crowns for the daughters. In both cases the wishes of the daughters are in conflict with the plans of the fathers, which are destined to fail: Thekla chooses death, while Heloise openly opposes her father's wishes and informs the Circassian prince, Arslan, of her father's double dealings. Heloise's intellectual superiority and her efforts at harmonizing relationships suggest an affinity with the Princess von Este in *Torquato Tasso.* Heloise quotes the princess in dismissing Arslan's comment that female beauty reigns in his homeland: Heloise insists that all women should be honored.

Just as Princess von Este would like to bring about a more harmonious relationship between the young, impatient poet Tasso and the experienced man of the world, Antonio, Heloise would like to see friendship between her father and the young, impatient Arslan. But for her father there is only loyalty to the crown. To achieve his aims he suggests to Arslan the prospect of marriage to Heloise, without any intention of allowing the marriage to take place. A similar deception is found in the *Wallenstein* trilogy, where it is planned and encouraged by Wallenstein's sister; here it is the work of the general himself. Talvj changes the motif by not making the guilty party a stereotypical woman working behind the scenes but a man with absolute power. The general even suggests, using a quotation from "Die Braut von Korinth," that his daughter could tame the other Circassian princes as well.

Like the barbarian king Thoas in *Iphigenie auf Tauris,* Arslan believes that he can induce the stranger to stay and marry him by proposing missionary activity for her: a woman like Heloise, holier and more beautiful than the first Christian missionary to the Circassians, could surely accomplish what the latter had begun. This proposal is made ironically, however, thereby questioning Goethe's text. Heloise, guarded by her father's Cossacks deep in the Caucasus mountains, is abducted by the rejected prince. Felix, her "brother," who has only now discovered the true nature of their family relationship, saves her in deus ex machina style, just as Iphigenie's actual brother Orest arrives on Tauris to rescue her.

In the moment of physical danger Talvj lets her heretofore active and courageous heroine faint; she remains unconscious for days, while her father and Felix watch over her. The author thus imposes at least a superficial adaptation to social expectations on her main character. Heloise has acted quite independently up to this point: she kept the secret of her birth to herself and did not give Felix his mother's written last wishes, in which she expressed the hope that Felix and Heloise would marry each other. Against the advice of a motherly friend and without informing her "brother" or her friends, she sets out for Russia to find her father. Against the advice of her consulate she traveled from Saint Petersburg to her father's camp in the Caucasus. She opposed his wishes and betrayed him to his enemies, but since his game was a false one, she remains morally superior. In the end she marries her true love, Felix, and retreats with him from the evil world into the idyllic country setting of her childhood. Unlike Thekla, she does not have to pay for the conflict with her father with her life: like Iphigenie, she is allowed to return home and enjoy her moral victory.

By changing the function of classical elements in the novel, Talvj is questioning such aspects of European culture as its assumption of superiority, its attempts to convert others to Christianity, and its subordination of women. The vigorous mountain tribe, the Circassians, serve as an idealized mirror of the Europeans.

The Robinsons returned to Palestine in 1851–1852, and Talvj again visited Germany. During a winter in Berlin she spent time with leading intellectuals such as Raumer, Alexander von Humboldt, Jacob and Wilhelm Grimm, and Karl August Varnhagen von Ense. After her return to New York she translated some of her husband's works into German, prepared a new edition of the Serbian folk songs, and wrote essays for the *North American Review* and the *Atlantic Monthly* about the poetry of southern France, the household of Charlemagne, Russian slavery, and Doctor Faustus. She also wrote articles for German periodicals. In her novel *Die Auswanderer* she compares German and American women's roles: although superficially privileged because of the courtesies extended to them, American women have fewer rights to act for themselves than do German women. In portraying female characters in her early stories, Talvj features self-assured, emancipated heroines who challenge the position of women in society; her novels, mostly written when she was in her fifties and sixties, usually show women suffering in more-traditional roles. There is no longer a direct challenge of such roles, only an implied one.

In 1862 the Robinsons traveled to Germany, where Edward Robinson, who was suffering from cataracts, consulted an eye specialist and Talvj met with her publisher Heinrich Brockhaus. The publisher, who had last seen her in 1840, found her to be softer and more pleasant than before. Edward Robinson died a year later and left behind a manuscript for a work about the geography of the Holy Land. Talvj, although suffering from cataracts herself, edited and translated it into German in 1865. She then returned to Europe for good, accompanied by her son and daughter. After visits to Berlin and Italy, Talvj settled in the Strasbourg area. During a winter in Karlsruhe she wrote the novel *Funfzehn Jahre* (1868; translated as *Fifteen Years,* 1871); the following summer, in Baden-Baden, she wrote the story "Ein Bild aus seiner Zeit" (A Picture of his Time, 1870). Her last work was an essay about the Cossacks and their historical songs (1869).

Shortly before her death Talvj moved to Hamburg, where her son was serving as consul. She died on 13 April 1870 and was buried next to Edward Robinson in New York City. Her daughter translated her last novel into English and republished her early stories along with a selection of her poems. Some of the poems are of a highly personal nature; others celebrate impressive natural scenes in North America.

Integrating her understanding of cultural diversity into her fiction is one of the contributions Talvj made to the intellectual life of her time. Having been forced into exile as a child of ten and having chosen to uproot herself again twenty years later to follow her husband to the New World, she became vividly aware of cultural differences. She studied the oral traditions of groups that had little or no contact with modern Western industrial societies, such as the ancient Teutonic, Scandinavian, and Scottish tribes, as well as those of groups forced into contact with the Europeans of her day, such as the mountain tribes of the Caucasus, the Gypsies, and the slaves and Indians of North America. She generally portrays these peoples positively and shows empathy for their struggle to maintain their ethnic identities. The heroines of her novels, however, are Europeans involuntarily transplanted to other areas and awaiting a return home. In Talvj's fiction nobody leaves home for the pure love of adventure, as is frequently the case in eighteenth- and nineteenth-century European novels. Maria Barkoczy in *Life's Discipline* is abducted by a man she later marries; the other main characters follow a father, a husband, or a fiancé. They become isolated, even alienated; they cannot speak the language of their host countries. Only one of these heroines, Heloise, is allowed to return home and find happiness on a country estate in the frequently repeated pattern of nineteenth-century German novels; the heroine of *Die Auswanderer* dies in the attempt to establish such idyllic rural happiness in the United States. Positive characters generally make an effort to maintain their cultural identity, while those who become assimilated to foreign cultures are often negative characters.

Letters:

"Talvjs Briefe an B. Kopitar," *Sammelband der philosophisch-historischen Cl. der Akademie der Wissenschaften, Wien,* 103 (1883): 462–489;

"Briefwechsel zwischen Goethe und Therese von Jakob," edited by E. R. Steig, *Goethe Jahrbuch,* 12 (1891): 33–77;

"Briefwechsel zwischen Jakob Grimm und Therese von Jakob," edited by Steig, *Preußische Jahrbücher,* 76 (1894): 345–366.

References:

Wilhelmine Bardua, *Die Schwestern Bardua: Bilder aus dem Gesellschafts-, Kunst- und Geistesleben der Biedermeierzeit,* edited by Johannes Werner (Leipzig: Koehler & Amelang, 1929);

Friedhilde Krause, "Das Rußlanderlebnis im Schaffen der Therese Albertine Luise von Jakob-Robinson (Talvj)," *Zeitschrift für Slawistik,* 27, no. 4 (1982): 512–522;

Krause, "Talvjs persönliche Kontakte zum Brockhaus-Verlag und ihre Vorbereitung der dritten Ausgabe der Vukschen 'Volkslieder der Serben,'" *Zeitschrift für Slawistik,* 28, no. 4 (1983): 533–540;

Krause, "Talvj und Jovan Ristic," *Wissenschaftliche Zeitschrift der Humboldt-Universität zu Berlin,* 36, no. 2 (1987): 112–117;

Rado L. Lencek, "A Fragment from Jernej Kopitar's Correspondence with Talvj," *Slovene Studies,* 3, no. 1 (1981): 12–19;

Franz Löher, "Talvj, ein deutsches Frauenleben," *Beiträge zur Geschichte und Völkerkunde,* 2 (1866): 451–466;

Miljan Mojaševic, "Eine Leistung Goethe zuliebe," *Goethe-Jahrbuch,* 93 (1976): 164–189;

Elizabeth Pribic, "Sima Milutinovic Sarajlija und Therese Albertine Luise von Jacob (Talvj)," *Südost Forschungen,* 38 (1979): 139–151;

Nikola R. Pribic, "Goethe, Talvj und das südslawische Volkslied," *Balkan Studies,* 10 (1969): 135–144;

Pribic, "Talvj in America," in *Serta Slavic: In Memoriam Aloisii Schmaus. Gedenkschrift,* edited by Wolfgang Gesemann and others (Munich: Trofenik, 1971), pp. 598–606;

Dorothea Diver Stuecher, *Twice Removed: The Experience of German-American Women Writers in the 19th Century,* New German-American Studies, 1 (New York: Lang, 1990);

Irma Elizabeth Voigt, "The Life and Works of Mrs. Therese Robinson (Talvj)," Ph.D. dissertation, University of Illinois, 1913;

Ludwig Wagner, *Talvj, 1797–1870: Biographische Skizze zur Erinnerung an ihren hundertsten Geburtstag* (Preßburg: Wigand, 1897);

Martha Kaarsberg Wallach, "Der Einfluß der Klassik in Talvjs Werken," *Akten des VIII. Internationalen Germanisten-Kongresses Tokyo 1990. Begegnung mit dem "Fremden": Grenzen – Traditionen – Vergleiche,* volume 7, edited by Eijiro Iwasaki, (Munich: Iudicium, 1991), pp. 89–96;

Wallach, "Die Erfahrung der Fremde in Talvjs Leben und Werk," in *Exotische Welt in populären Lektüren,* edited by Anselm Maler (Tübingen: Niemeyer, 1990), pp. 81–92;

Wallach, "Talvj: Lebenserfahrung und Gesellschaftskritik der frühen Erzählungen," in *Autoren damals und heute: Literaturgeschichtliche Beispiele veränderter Wirkungshorizonte,* edited by Gerhard P. Knapp, Amsterdamer Beiträge zur neuern Germanistik 31–33 (Amsterdam & Atlanta: Rodopi, 1991), pp. 211–230;

Wallach, "Women of German-American Fiction: Therese Robinson, Mathilde Anneke, and Fernande Richter," in *America and the Germans: An Assessment of a Three-Hundred-Year History,* volume 1, edited by Frank Trommler and Joseph McVeigh (Philadelphia: University of Pennsylvania Press, 1985), pp. 331–342.

Papers:

Talvj's papers remained with her children. In 1894 her daughter furnished an editor with typewritten copies of Talvj's letters to Jacob Grimm but kept the originals. In 1913 Irma Elizabeth Voigt, who was writing a dissertation on Talvj, was given access to Talvj's remaining papers by her grandson. Their present location is not known. The von Jakob Nachlaß in Halle contains only letters of her early years in Germany.

Friedrich Theodor Vischer

(30 June 1807 - 14 September 1887)

Karl Ludwig Stenger
University of South Carolina – Aiken

BOOKS: *Über das Erhabene und Komische: Ein Beitrag zu der Philosophie des Schönen* (Stuttgart: Innle & Krauß, 1837);

Kritische Gänge, 2 volumes (Tübingen: Fues, 1844);

Akademische Rede zum Antritte des Ordinariats am 21. November 1844 zu Tübingen gehalten (Tübingen: Guttenberg, 1845);

Die Metaphysik des Schönen (Reutlingen & Leipzig: Mäcken, 1846);

Aesthetik oder Wissenschaft des Schönen: Zum Gebrauch für Vorlesungen, 6 volumes (Reutlingen, Leipzig & Stuttgart: Mäcken, 1846–1857; edited by Robert Vischer, Munich: Meyer & Jessen, 1922–1923);

Kritische Bemerkungen über den Ersten Theil von Goethe's Faust (Stuttgart: Meyer, 1857);

Über das Verhältniß von Inhalt und Form in der Kunst (Stuttgart: Meyer, 1858);

Rede zur hundertjährigen Feier der Geburt Schiller's (Zurich: Orell Füßli, 1859);

Kritische Gänge: Neue Folge, 2 volumes (Stuttgart: Cotta, 1860–1873);

Faust: Der Tragödie dritter Theil in drei Acten. Treu im Geiste des zweiten Theils des Götheschen Faust gedichtet, as Deutobold Symbolizetti Allegoriowitsch Mystifizinsky (Tübingen: Laupp, 1862; enlarged, 1886);

Epigramme aus Baden-Baden, anonymous (Stuttgart: Grüninger, 1867);

Der Krieg und die Künste (Stuttgart: Weise, 1872);

Der deutsche Krieg 1870–1871: Ein Heldengedicht, as Philipp Ulrich Schartenmeyer (Nördlingen: Beck, 1873);

Goethes Faust: Neue Beiträge zur Kritik des Gedichts (Stuttgart: Meyer & Zeller, 1875); enlarged edition, including "Zur Verteidigung meiner Schrift *Goethes Faust*" (Stuttgart & Berlin: Cotta, 1920);

Auch Einer: Eine Reisebekanntschaft, 2 volumes (Stuttgart & Leipzig: Hallberger, 1879 [i.e. 1878]; revised edition, Stuttgart: Deutsche Verlags-Anstalt, 1884); excerpt translated by Hans Müller-Casenov as "A Rabid Philosopher," in his *The Humour of Germany* (London: Scott, 1892; New York: Scribners, 1909);

Friedrich Theodor Vischer (photograph by F. Brandseph, Stuttgart)

Mode und Cynismus: Beiträge zur Kenntniß unserer Culturformen und Sittenbegriffe (Stuttgart: Wittwer, 1879);

Altes und Neues, 3 volumes (Stuttgart: Bonz, 1881–1882);

Lyrische Gänge (Stuttgart: Deutsche Verlags-Anstalt, 1882);

Nicht 1a: Schwäbisches Lustspiel (Stuttgart: Bonz, 1884);

Die erste Kunstschöpfung der Enkelin in Sonetten verherrlicht vom Großvater (Stuttgart: Bonz, 1886);

Festspiel zur Uhland-Feier (Stuttgart: Bonz, 1887);

Altes und Neues: Neue Folge, edited by Robert Vischer (Stuttgart: Bonz, 1889);

Allotria, edited by Robert Vischer (Stuttgart: Bonz, 1892);

Das Schöne und die Kunst: Zur Einführung in die Ästhetik. Vorträge, edited by Robert Vischer (Stuttgart: Cotta, 1898);

Shakespeare-Vorträge, 6 volumes, edited by Robert Vischer (Stuttgart & Berlin: Cotta, 1899–1905);

Dichterische Werke, 5 volumes, edited by Robert Vischer (Leipzig: Verlag der Weißen Bücher, 1917);

Ausgewählte Werke, 3 volumes, edited by Gustav Keyssner (Stuttgart & Berlin: Deutsche Verlags-Anstalt, 1918);

Ausgewählte Werke in acht Teilen, 3 volumes, edited by Theodor Kappstein (Leipzig: Hesse & Becker, 1919);

Ein Brevier, edited by Franz Georg Brustgi (Stuttgart: Hohenstaufen, 1941).

Friedrich Theodor Vischer, whom contemporaries called "V-Vischer" to distinguish him from the Heidelberg philosopher Kuno Fischer, was one of the most important and influential aestheticians, cultural critics, and academics in the second half of the nineteenth century. While the Swiss realist writer Gottfried Keller revered him as "der große Repetent deutscher Nation für alles Schöne und Gute, Rechte und Wahre" (the great tutor of the German nation for all that is beautiful and good, right and true), the philosopher Friedrich Nietzsche criticized him as a "Bildungsphilister" (cultural philistine). The Hungarian Marxist literary historian György Lukács regarded him as a key figure in the development of irrationalism and fascism. Vischer's novel *Auch Einer* (Also One, 1878; excerpt translated as "A Rabid Philosopher," 1892) was elevated by some readers to the status of "Gebetbuch" (prayer book), while others were appalled by its lack of structure and its baroque excesses.

This polarized view has given way to a more objective and balanced estimation of the man and his work. Vischer is now seen as a transitional figure between the philosophers Georg Friedrich Wilhelm Hegel and Nietzsche and between the contrasting literary movements of romanticism and naturalism. The profound political, economic, societal, and cultural changes that characterize the nineteenth century are reflected in Vischer's personal and literary development. His aesthetic system progressed from the attempt to regain a supposedly lost unity of the ideal and the real with the help of art in his *Aesthetik oder Wissenschaft des Schönen* (Aesthetics; or, Science of the Beautiful, 1846–1857) to the realization in his later works that such a reconciliation was impossible. Though rooted in the nineteenth century, Vischer sensed some of the dilemmas of the twentieth.

Vischer was born on 30 June 1807 in Ludwigsburg, Württemberg, the youngest of seven children of the deacon Christof Friedrich Benjamin Vischer and Christiane Regine Vischer (née Städlin). Vischer claimed that he inherited imagination, wit, vanity, recklessness, and laziness from his mother and moral anger, sagacity, idiosyncrasies, and the love of animals and nature from his father. Throughout his life Vischer was torn between his artistic desire and his critical acumen, and he traced this dichotomy to his parents' dissimilar temperaments. It was his dearest wish to become a painter, but after his father's death of typhoid fever in 1814 the family's precarious financial situation led Vischer to choose a career as a Protestant clergyman so that he could receive a free education and be assured a secure future. After graduating from the gymnasium in Stuttgart, Vischer entered the seminary at Blaubeuren in 1821. There he became friends with David Friedrich Strauss, who would become a controversial author of theological works. The two were to remain close throughout their lives despite many disagreements. Vischer's first attempts at poetry – witty ballads he wrote under the pseudonym Philipp Ulrich Schartenmayer – date from his stay in Blaubeuren.

After four relatively carefree years, Vischer and the other members of the "Geniepromotion" (graduating class of geniuses) entered the University of Tübingen to continue their theological training. The much more somber and oppressive atmosphere there, along with despair over a failed love relationship, brought Vischer to the brink of suicide. He overcame his depression by immersing himself in Hegel's philosophy and Johann Wolfgang von Goethe's great philosophical play *Faust* (1808). The poems Vischer wrote in this period served a therapeutic purpose, as did his short story "Ein Traum" (A Dream; published in the edition of

Last page of a letter from Vischer to David Friedrich Strauss, dated 23 November 1844 (Schiller-Nationalmuseum, Marbach am Neckar)

Vischer in 1845; lithograph after a drawing by Bonaventura Weiß

Vischer's correspondence with Eduard Mörike, 1926), in which a young man who has committed suicide is treated callously by God. The incipient doubts concerning Christian orthodoxy that form the basis of this story intensified considerably when Vischer served as a curate in the village of Horrheim, near Maulbronn, in 1830-1831. Though an effective and powerful preacher, Vischer soon realized that he had missed his calling and could not remain a clergyman for the rest of his life: he no longer believed in personal immortality, and he rejected the idea that God was a person. He requested a transfer in 1831 and was offered a position tutoring seminarists in Latin, Greek, and Hebrew in Maulbronn.

After his Magister (master) examination and the customary Magister journey, which took him to Berlin, Prague, and Vienna, he returned to the University of Tübingen as a tutor in 1833. His successful lectures on aesthetics and on *Faust* (the second part of Goethe's play had been published in 1832) represented an important step away from theology and toward philosophy. He rejected the offer of a deaconship in the village of Herrenberg in 1834 because he no longer felt any affinity for theology. When the publication of the first volume of Strauss's *Das Leben Jesu* (The Life of Jesus, 1835-1836; translated as *The Life of Christ,* 1843), which questioned the truth of the Gospels, led to Strauss's dismissal from the Tübingen Seminary, Vischer realized the precariousness of his own situation. He proposed to the university the creation of a lectureship in aesthetics and German literature and was offered the position in 1835; a year later he was appointed supernumerary professor. His lectures included the philosophy of Hegel, medieval German literature, the works of William Shakespeare, and the history of painting. In 1837 Arnold Ruge, the editor of the Young Hegelian journal *Hallische Jahrbücher für deutsche Wissenschaft und Kunst* (Halle Yearbooks for German Science and Art), persuaded Vischer to become a contributor. His first article was an impassioned defense of his friend Strauss. A scathing survey of contemporary criticism of *Faust* and an appreciative review of Mörike's novel *Maler Nolten* (Painter Nolten, 1832) followed. Soon, however, the journal became too radical for Vischer, and he turned to the somewhat more moderate *Jahrbücher der Gegenwart* (Yearbooks of the Present). Vischer's writings of this period are characterized by his increasing rejection of Christianity – above all, Pietism – and by his harsh criticism of political fiction. When a collection of these critical essays was published in 1844 he gave it the fitting title *Kritische Gänge* (Critical Lunges). Vischer's outspokenness, which carried over into his lectures, alienated many of his conservative colleagues; when he applied for a full professorship after marrying Thekla Heinz on 7 May 1844, they sought to prevent his appointment. Vischer, however, was successful, and his inaugural address culminated in a blistering condemnation of these enemies in which he promised them "meine volle, ungeteilte Feindschaft, meinen offenen und herzlichen Haß" (my full, undivided enmity and my open, heartfelt hatred). The speech caused a barrage of public denunciations and recriminations in newspaper editorials, pamphlets, and sermons and resulted, despite Vischer's attempt to defuse the situation, in his suspension with pay for two years.

Vischer took advantage of this involuntary sabbatical by immersing himself in his writing. He composed articles on the importance of physical exercise for academic life, the Deutsch-Katholizismus (German Catholicism) religious reform movement, and contemporary painting; and he began work on his monumental *Aesthetik,* which can be considered the last comprehensive system of aesthetics of the nineteenth century.

Although primarily based on the idealistic philosophy of Hegel, Vischer's aesthetic theory differs considerably from that of his predecessor. While Hegel postulated the dialectical development of the Absolute Spirit through the phases of art, religion, and philosophy, Vischer made religion the most primitive member of the triad. He also criticized Hegel's philosophy for not taking into account the crucial role of "Zufall" (chance). The reconciliation of the real and the ideal could be achieved, Vischer thought, with the help of art. As soon as his *Aesthetik* was finished, however, Vischer distanced himself from it; he no longer believed that the alienation of modern humanity, originating in the discrepancy between the real and the ideal, could be overcome. In his later writings the state of alienation is seen as a permanent and unalterable human condition.

Vischer's son Robert was born on 22 February 1847. In March 1848 revolution broke out, and Vischer was elected to the National Assembly in Frankfurt am Main. As a member of the moderate left he strove for the "sanfte Vorbereitung der Republik" (gentle preparation of the republic). His main goal was the unification of Germany on the "Großdeutsch" (Great German) model, meaning the admission of all German states to the federation. He opposed Prussian dominance and abstained from voting when Friedrich Wilhelm IV of Prussia was elected emperor on 28 March 1849. Vischer called 1849 his "Marterjahr" (year of torment) both because he was devastated by the failure of the National Assembly and because he was constantly plagued by ailments. After the dissolution of the Stuttgart rump parliament, Vischer returned home a disillusioned man. Continuing clashes with conservative colleagues and administrators made his life in provincial Tübingen unbearable, and when he was offered a position at the Polytechnic School in Zurich in 1855 he accepted the offer joyfully. When he moved to Zurich, his wife remained in Tübingen.

His new metropolitan surroundings lifted Vischer's spirits, and he became a central figure in the cultural and social life of the city. He was invited to salons and met many celebrities of the time. When the composer Richard Wagner made disparaging remarks about the Germans during a gathering at the home of his patrons, Otto and Mathilde Wesendonk, Vischer severely reprimanded the composer for criticizing his countrymen. Vischer's dislike of the man and his music later formed the basis for the satiric treatment of the archconservative druid Angus and his atrocious music in "Der Besuch: Eine Pfahldorfgeschichte" (The Visit: A Pile Village Story), the central section of Vischer's novel *Auch Einer*.

Vischer at about the age of fifty

Vischer's critical and literary output increased as he produced articles covering such diverse topics as Goethe, the relationship between form and content in art, modern fashion, gambling, and politics. In 1860 a second collection of essays appeared as *Kritische Gänge: Neue Folge* (Critical Lunges: New Series). It included a travelogue of Vischer's most recent journey through Austria and Italy, several essays devoted to Shakespeare, and a critical assessment of Strauss that caused a brief falling-out between the friends.

In the essay "Zum zweiten Teil von Goethes *Faust*" (Concerning the Second Part of Goethe's *Faust*) Vischer suggests a new version of the play in which Faust atones for his misdeeds by entering the political arena and becoming a revolutionary fighter. Vischer's play *Faust: Der Tragödie dritter Theil* (Faust: The Tragedy Part Three) was pub-

Vischer in 1886; photograph by H. Brandseph

lished two years later under the pseudonym Deutobold Symbolizetti Allegoriowitsch Mystifizinsky; using parody and farce, Vischer reduces the allegories and mysticism, which he considered the major weakness of *Faust II,* to absurdity and turns Faust into a "Hasenfuss" (coward) who has to be prodded into action by others and who lacks the sense of guilt and remorse that is the prerequisite for his redemption. By exaggerating Faust's weaknesses, Vischer sought to point out the deficiencies of Goethe's work in a comical manner. When critics attacked Vischer for his irreverence, he replied that his intention had been to defend the young genius Goethe against the old Goethe, whose creative powers had declined. The genuinely harsh criticism that could be found in Vischer's *Faust* was directed not against Goethe but against those interpreters of his work who dug obsessively for the deeper philosophical meaning and those who concentrated on superficial details. The play is of interest to the modern reader primarily as a document of Goethe's reception in the nineteenth century.

In the eleven years Vischer spent in Zurich his health deteriorated, he had problems with his estranged wife and his son, and he was afflicted with a growing sense of alienation. He yearned to return to his native land, and in 1866 he accepted a professorship at Tübingen University. Three years later he moved to Stuttgart, where he spent his remaining years as a respected professor at the Polytechnic School.

Although to the casual observer Vischer may have appeared successful and fulfilled, his personal life was characterized by loneliness, misanthropy, and quiet despair. His last attempt at political involvement was prevented by a triviality: when he wanted to fulfill his patriotic duty in the Franco-Prussian War in 1870, an enormous, painful corn kept him from participating. Many of his friends and relatives died in quick succession – his nephew Karl in 1870, his wife in the summer of 1871, Strauss in 1874, Mörike in 1875, and his nephew Wilhelm in 1876. Several trips to his beloved Italy, which to him represented the home of art's supreme achievements, were failures either because of Vischer's bad health – he was afflicted with catarrh, sciatica, and glaucoma – or because of inclement weather.

Vischer's novel *Auch Einer* can be seen as an expression of the author's pessimism and resignation. A.E., the central figure, is plagued by health problems and despairs over the political situation; torn between two women, he cannot find emotional fulfillment. His attempts to bridge the gap between mind and nature fail, and he is split into an "Ich a" (I a) and an "Ich b" (I b). Few contemporary readers discerned the pessimistic tone of the novel; the majority misread it as an inspirational story of a man who remained steadfast in the face of adversity. A.E.'s remark "Das Moralische versteht sich immer von selbst" (That which is moral is self-evident) became a proverb, and a selection of excerpts from the novel accompanied German soldiers into World War I for moral support. The modern reader, however, will be hard pressed to detect an optimistic view of the world in *Auch Einer.* The interpolated novella "Der Besuch," for example, is replete with cultural criticism and is the expression of a pessimistic view of historical progress. A.E., its author, comes across as the prototypical modern human being – self-alienated, dissonant, and fragmented. The situation of the protagonist is mirrored by the structure of *Auch Einer:* a multitude of narrators – including an omniscient narrator, A.E. as the third-person narrator of the interpolated novella, and A.E. as diarist – results in the absence of a unified narrative perspective, which, together with a lack of chronological order in the plot, points to the fragmentation and chaos of the modern world. The unusual form of the novel, which was criticized by several of Vischer's contemporaries, can now be seen as a daring experiment. *Auch Einer* is an important stepping-stone in the development of the modern German novel.

During the last decade of his life Vischer's publications included a collection of essays, *Altes und Neues* (Old and New, 1881–1882); a collection of poetry, *Lyrische Gänge* (Lyrical Passages, 1882), which included poems representing all periods of his career; and a comedy in Swabian dialect, *Nicht 1a* (Not Top-Notch, 1884). He continued to speak out against wrongs such as environmental pollution, the destruction of historic buildings, cruelty to animals, and anti-Semitism, and he remained one of the leading cultural authorities of his time: his reviews carried great weight, and he was deluged by manuscripts and requests for his critical judgment; Keller called him "Deutschlands Hauptmanuskriptempfänger" (Germany's premier recipient of manuscripts). Vischer continued to be an extremely popular and respected teacher, and on his eightieth birthday he was honored with an enormous torchlight procession. Three months later he set out on his eleventh trip to Venice; stricken ill en route, he died in Gmunden, Austria, on 14 September 1887. He was buried in Gmunden, midway between his Swabian home and his cherished Italy.

Letters:

"Briefwechsel zwischen Gottfried Keller und Fr. Th. Vischer," edited by Karl Emil *Deutsche Dichtung,* 9 (1890): 181–183, 232–235, 306–307; 10 (1891): 27–31, 101–104, 177–179, 225–227;

"Zwei Briefe Friedrich Th. Vischers an Weltrich," edited by Richard Weltrich, *Süddeutsche Monatshefte,* 1 (1904): 751–754;

"Sechs Briefe Friedrich Vischers an Weltrich," edited by Weltrich, *Beilage zur Allgemeinen Zeitung,* 29 June 1907, pp. 46–55;

"Briefe Fr. Th. Vischers aus der Paulskirche," edited by G. Egelhaaf, *Deutsche Rundschau,* 132 (July - September 1907): 203–226;

Briefe aus Italien, edited by Robert Vischer (Munich: Verlag der Süddeutschen Monatshefte, 1907);

"Eleven Unpublished Letters by Friedrich Theodor Vischer," edited by Adolph B. Benson *Philological Quarterly,* 3 (1924): 32-47;

Briefwechsel zwischen Eduard Mörike und Friedrich Theodor Vischer, edited by Robert Vischer (Munich: Beck, 1926);

Briefwechsel zwischen Strauss und Vischer, 2 volumes, edited by Adolf Rapp (Stuttgart: Klett, 1952–1953).

Bibliography:

Oswald Hesnard, *Fr. Th. Vischer: Étude Bibliographique* (Paris: Alcan, 1921).

Biographies:

Oswald Hesnard, *Fr. Th. Vischer* (Paris: Alcan, 1921);

Fritz Schlawe, *Friedrich Theodor Vischer* (Stuttgart: Metzler, 1959).

References:

Kurt Adel, "Friedrich Theodor Vischer und seine Bedeutung für die Geschichte der Faust-Dichtung," in *Ansichten zu Faust: Karl Theens zum 70. Geburtstag,* edited by Günter Mahal (Stuttgart: Kohlhammer, 1973), pp. 169–194;

Berthold Auerbach, "Wissen und Schaffen: Aphorismen zu Friedrich Theodor Vischer's *Auch Einer,*" *Deutsche Rundschau,* 19 (April–June 1879): 269–295;

Otto Borst, "Vischers Leben und Werk," in Vischer's *Auch Einer* (Frankfurt am Main: Insel, 1987), pp. 593–623;

William J. Brazill, *The Young Hegelians* (New Haven & London: Yale University Press, 1970);

W. H. Bruford, "Friedrich Theodor Vischer and His Faust Criticism," *Publications of the English Goethe Society,* new series 37 (1967): 1–30;

Bruford, *The German Tradition of Self-Cultivation: "Bildung" from Humboldt to Thomas Mann* (London & New York: Cambridge University Press, 1975);

Franza Feilbogen, *Fr. Th. Vischers "Auch Einer": Eine Studie* (Zurich: Orell Füßli, 1916);

Ilse Frapan, *Vischer-Erinnerungen: Äusserungen und Worte. Ein Beitrag zur Biographie Fr.Th. Vischers* (Stuttgart: Göschen, 1889);

Hermann Glockner, *Fr. Th. Vischer und das neunzehnte Jahrhundert* (Berlin: Junker & Dünnhaupt, 1931);

Wendelin Göbel, *Friedrich Theodor Vischer: Grundzüge seiner Metaphysik und Ästhetik* (Würzburg: Könighausen & Neumann, 1983);

Reinhold Grimm, "Zur Wirkungsgeschichte von Vischers *Auch Einer,*" in *Gestaltungsgeschichte und Gesellschaftsgeschichte: Literatur-, Kunst- und Musikwissenschaftliche Studien,* edited by Helmut

Kreuzer (Stuttgart: Metzler, 1969), pp. 352–381;

Wendelin Haverkamp, *Aspekte der Modernität: Untersuchungen zur Geschichte des "Auch Einer" von Friedrich Theodor Vischer* (Aachen: Cobra, 1981);

Ruth Heller, "*Auch Einer:* The Epitome of F. Th. Vischer's Philosophy of Life," *German Life and Letters,* 8 (1954–1955): 9–18;

Harvey W. Hewett-Thayer, "The Road to *Auch Einer,*" *PMLA,* 75 (March 1960): 83–96;

Alfred Ibach, *Gottfried Keller und Friedrich Theodor Vischer* (Borna & Leipzig: Noske, 1927);

Gottfried Keller, "Zu Friedrich Theodor Vischer's achtzigstem Geburtstage," *Allgemeine Zeitung,* 30 June 1887, supplement;

Theodor Klaiber, *Fr. Th. Vischer: Eine Darstellung seiner Persönlichkeit und eine Auswahl aus seinen Werken* (Stuttgart: Strecker & Schröder, 1920);

Harry Kürbs, *Studien zur Pfahldorfgeschichte aus Friedrich Theodor Vischers Roman "Auch Einer"* (Borna & Leipzig: Noske, 1914);

M. Lang, "Friedrich Theodor Vischer," *Deutsche Rundschau,* 60 (1889): 29–50, 229–246;

Rätus Luck, *Gottfried Keller als Literaturkritiker* (Bern & Munich: Francke, 1970), pp. 200–259;

György Lukács, "Karl Marx und Friedrich Theodor Vischer," in his *Beiträge zur Geschichte der Ästhetik* (Berlin: Aufbau, 1956), pp. 217–285;

Fritz Mauthner, "*Auch Einer,*" in his *Von Keller zu Zola* (Berlin: Heine, 1887), pp. 41–69;

Laurenz Müllner, "*Auch Einer,*" in his *Literatur- und kunstkritische Studien: Beiträge zur Ästhetik der Dichtkunst und Malerei* (Vienna & Leipzig: Braumüller, 1895), pp. 69–115;

Willi Oelmüller, *Friedrich Theodor Vischer und das Problem der nachhegelschen Ästhetik* (Stuttgart: Kohlhammer, 1959);

Gunter Oesterle, "Die Grablegung des Selbst im Andern und die Rettung des Selbst im Anonymen: Zum Wechselverhältnis von Biographie und Autobiographie in der zweiten Hälfte des 19. Jahrhunderts am Beispiel von Friedrich Theodor Vischers *Auch Einer,*" in *Vom Anderen und vom Selbst: Beiträge zu Fragen der Biographie und Autobiographie,* edited by Reinhold Grimm and Jost Hermand (Königstein: Athenäum, 1982), pp. 45–70;

Ingrid Oesterle, "Verübelte Geschichte: Autobiographische Selbstentblößung, komische Selbstentlastung und bedingte zynische Selbstbehauptung in Friedrich Theodor Vischers Roman *Auch Einer,*" in *Vom Anderen und vom Selbst,* pp. 71–93;

Hilmar Roebling, "Zur Kunsttheorie F. Th. Vischers," in *Beiträge zur Theorie der Künste im 19. Jahrhundert,* volume 1, edited by Helmut Koopmann and J. Adolf Schmoll (Frankfurt am Main: Klostermann, 1970), pp. 97–112;

Friedrich Spielhagen, "Ein 'humoristischer' Roman: Fr. Theodor Vischers *Auch Einer,*" in his *Beiträge zur Theorie und Technik des Romans* (Göttingen: Vandenhoeck & Ruprecht, 1967), pp. 101–128;

Karl Ludwig Stenger, *Die Erzählstruktur von Friedrich Theodor Vischers "Auch Einer": Wesen und Funktion* (New York, Bern & Frankfurt am Main: Lang, 1986);

Ewald Volhard, *Zwischen Hegel und Nietzsche: Der Ästhetiker Fr. Th. Vischer* (Frankfurt am Main: Klostermann, 1932);

Johannes Volkelt, "Die Lebensanschauung Friedrich Theodor Vischers," in his *Zwischen Dichtung und Philosophie: Gesammelte Aufsätze* (Munich: Beck, 1908), pp. 285–329;

Gottfried Willems, *Das Konzept der literarischen Gattung: Untersuchungen zur klassischen deutschen Gattungstheorie, insbesondere zur Ästhetik F. Th. Vischers* (Tübingen: Niemeyer, 1981);

Hans Heinrich Zisseler, *Beiträge zur Entstehungsgeschichte der Dichtung "Auch Einer" von Fr. Th. Vischer* (Göttingen: Kästner, 1913).

Papers:

Friedrich Theodor Vischer's papers are at the Schiller Nationalmuseum, Marbach, Germany, and the library of Tübingen University.

Wilhelm Wackernagel

(23 April 1806 - 21 December 1869)

Kurt R. Jankowsky
Georgetown University

Wilhelm Wackernagel

BOOKS: *Geschichte des deutschen Hexameters und Pentameters, bis auf Klopstock* (Berlin: Fincke, 1831);

Die Verdienste der Schweizer um die deutsche Litteratur: Academische Antrittsrede (Basel: Neukirch, 1833);

Deutsches Lesebuch, 4 volumes (Basel: Schweighauser, 1835–1843; revised and enlarged, 1839–1843);

Die altdeutschen Handschriften der Basler Universitätsbibliothek: Verzeichniss, Beschreibung, Auszüge. Eine academische Gelegenheitsschrift (Basel: Schweighauser, 1836);

Über die dramatische Poesie: Academische Gelegenheitsschrift (Basel: Schweighauser, 1838);

Einige Worte zum Schutz litterarischen Eigenthumes: Beilage zu den Altdeutschen Lesebüchern von Wackernagel und A. Ziemann und Drey Büchern deutscher Prosa von K. Künzel (Basel: Schweighauser, 1838);

Karl Friedrich Drollinger: Academische Festrede (Basel: Schneider, 1841);

Neuere Gedichte, 1832–1841 (Zurich: Beyel, 1842);

Zeitgedichte: Mit Beiträgen von Balthasar Reber. (Basel: Schweighauser, 1843);

Das vierte Säcularfest der Schlacht bei S. Jacob an der Birs: Im Auftrage des Comités mit Beifügung der Festreden und der Festgedichte beschrieben (Basel: Schweighauser, 1844);

Walther von Klingen, Stifter des Klingenthals und Minnesänger: Academisches Programm (Basel: Schweighauser, 1845);

Weinbüchlein (Leipzig: Weidmann, 1845);

Geschichte der deutschen Litteratur: Ein Handbuch, 4 volumes (Basel: Schweighauser, 1848–1855); enlarged as *Geschichte der deutschen Litteratur bis zum dreißigjährigen Kriege: Ein Handbuch,* 1 volume (Basel: Schweighauser, 1872);

Pompeji: Öffentlicher Vortrag, gehalten zu Basel im Namen der antiquarischen Gesellschaft 27. Oct. 1849 (Basel: Schweighauser, 1851);

Gewerbe, Handel und Schiffahrt der Germanen: Öffentlicher Vortrag, gehalten in Basel 1853 (Leipzig, 1853);

Sevilla (Basel: Schweighauser, 1854);

Die deutsche Glasmalerei: Geschichtlicher Entwurf mit Belegen (Leipzig: Hirzel, 1855);

Die goldene Altartafel von Basel: Mit vier lithographierten Blättern (Basel: Bahnmaier, 1857);

Über die mittelalterliche Sammlung zu Basel: Nebst einigen Schriftstücken aus derselben (Basel: Schweighauser, 1857);

Ritter- und Dichterleben Basels im Mittelalter (Basel: Mast, 1858);

ἔπεα πτερόεντα: Ein Beitrag zur vergleichenden Mythologie. Jubelschrift zur 4. Säcularfeier der Universität Basel den 6. September 1860 (Basel: Amberger, 1860);

Die Umdeutschung fremder Wörter (Basel: Schweighauser, 1861; revised edition, Basel: Detloff, 1862);

Die Lebensalter: Ein Beitrag zur vergleichenden Sitten- und Rechtsgeschichte (Basel: Bahnmaier, 1862);

Voces variae animantium (Basel: Schultze, 1867); revised and enlarged as *Voces variae animantium: Ein Beitrag zur Naturkunde und zur Geschichte der Sprache* (Basel: Bahnmaier, 1869);

Johann Fischart von Straßburg und Basels Antheil an ihm (Basel: Schweighauser, 1870);

Über den Ursprung und die Entwickelung der Sprache: Academische Festrede gehalten am 8. November 1866 bei der Jahresfeier der Universität Basel (Basel: Schweighauser, 1872);

Kleinere Schriften, 3 volumes, edited by Moritz Heyne (Leipzig: Hirzel, 1872–1874; reprinted, Osnabrück: Zeller, 1966);

Gedichte: Auswahl, edited by Salomon Voegelin (Basel: Schweighauser, 1873);

Poetik, Rhetorik und Stilistik: Academische Vorlesungen, edited by Ludwig Sieber (Halle: Waisenhause, 1873).

OTHER: *Spiritalia theotisca: Sermonum sex ecclesiasticorum et orationis dominicae rhythmis expositae fragmenta,* edited by Wackernagel (Bratislava: Grassio-Barthianis, 1827);

Das Wessobrunner Gebet und die Wessobrunner Glossen, edited by Wackernagel (Berlin: Schmidt, 1827);

Gedichte eines fahrenden Schülers, edited by Wackernagel (Berlin: Laue, 1828);

Walther von der Vogelweide, *Gedichte,* 2 volumes, translated by Karl Simrock, annotations by Wackernagel (Berlin: Vereinsbuchhandlung, 1833);

Weihnachtsgabe zum Besten der Wassergeschädigten in der Schweiz. Herausgegeben von Freunden der vaterländischen Dichtung, edited by Wackernagel and Karl Rudolf Hagenbach (Basel: Schweighauser, 1835);

Tacitus Germania: Text, Übersetzung, Erläuterung, edited and translated by Wackernagel and Franz D. Gerlach (Basel: Schweighauser, 1835);

Schweizerisches Museum für historische Wissenschaften, volumes 1–3, edited by Wackernagel and others (Frauenfeld: Beyel, 1837–1840);

Der Schwabenspiegel in der ältesten Gestalt: Mit den Abweichungen der gemeinen Texte und den Zusätzen derselben. 1. Theil: Landrecht, edited by Wackernagel (Zurich: Beyel, 1840);

Immanuel Stockmeyer and Balthasar Reber, *Beiträge zur Basler Buchdruckergeschichte,* preface by Wackernagel (Basel: Schweighauser, 1840);

Weihnachtsgabe zum Besten der Brandbeschädigten im Ehrikon Kanton Zürich, edited by K. L. Schuster and Salomon Voegelin, contributions by Wackernagel (Zurich: Meyer & Zeller, 1840);

Weihnachtsgabe für 1842: Zum besten der durch Brand verunglückten Hamburger, edited by Wackernagel and others (Basel: Schneider, 1842);

Die Schlacht bei St. Jacob (1444) in den Berichten der Zeitgenossen: Säcularschrift der Historischen Gesellschaft zu Basel, edited by Wackernagel (Basel: Schweighauser, 1844);

Altfranzösische Lieder und Leiche aus Handschriften zu Bern und Neuenburg: Mit grammatischen und litterarhistorischen Abhandlungen, edited by Wackernagel (Basel: Schweighauser, 1846);

Vocabularius optimus: Zur Begrüßung der in Basel versammelten Philologen und Schulmänner in Auftrage der Universität, edited by Wackernagel (Basel: Schweighauser, 1847);

Meinauer Naturlehre, edited by Wackernagel (Stuttgart: Bibliothek des Literarischen Vereins, 1851);

Das Bischofs- und Dienstmannenrecht von Basel in deutscher Aufzeichnung des XIII. Jahrhunderts, edited by Wackernagel (Basel: Schweighauser, 1852);

Der arme Heinrich Herrn Hartmanns von Aue und zwei jüngere Prosalegenden verwandten Inhalts: Mit Anmerkungen und Abhandlungen, edited by Wackernagel (Basel: Schweighauser, 1855);

Emil O. Weller, *Die Lieder des dreißigjährigen Krieges, nach den Originalen abgedruckt, zum ersten Male gesammelt,* introduction by Wackernagel (Basel: Georg, 1855; reprinted, Hildesheim: Olms, 1968);

Walther von der Vogelweide, nebst Ulrich von Singenberg und Leutold von Seven, edited by Wackernagel and Max Rieger (Giessen: Ricker, 1862);

Sechs Bruchstücke einer Nibelungenhandschrift aus der Mittelalterlichen Sammlung zu Basel, edited by Wackernagel (Basel: Georg, 1864);

Gothische und altsächsische Lesestücke, nebst Wörterbuch, edited by Wackernagel (Basel: Schweighauser, 1871);

Althochdeutsche Lesestücke, edited by Wackernagel (Basel: Schweighauser, 1875);

Altdeutsche Predigten und Gebete aus Handschriften: Mit Abhandlungen, edited by Wackernagel and Rieger (Basel: Schweighauser, 1876; reprinted, Darmstadt: Wissenschaftliche Buchgesellschaft, 1964).

Karl Heinrich Wilhelm Wackernagel was born in Berlin on 23 April 1806. His father, a police officer, died in 1815; three years later his mother died. Wackernagel and his sisters, Friederike and Luise, and their brothers, Philipp and Karl – all older than he – were placed under the guardianship of a former colleague of their father's named Gemmel. Philipp and Karl dropped out of school to support the family; Friederike and Luise helped out by doing artistic embroidery. Wackernagel's brothers and sisters were unanimous in their resolve to make it possible for him to finish high school; they were convinced that he was the most gifted of the siblings.

During his early teens Wackernagel, like many of his friends, became heavily involved in the political upheavals following the defeat of Napoleon. Friedrich Ludwig Jahn, who had gained fame for his efforts to improve national education and to launch far-reaching programs in physical training, captivated the impressionable Wackernagel with his ideas about freedom and unity of the fatherland. Jahn's influence was mediated at first through Philipp, who had been Jahn's favorite pupil in Berlin. When Jahn, charged with demagogy in the aftermath of the murder in 1819 of the dramatist August von Kotzebue by the student Karl Ludwig Sand, was imprisoned in Berlin, Wackernagel visited him. The assassination spurred a flurry of measures to curb any manifestations of liberal thought or democratic aspirations. Philipp Wackernagel, who was working as a clerk in Breslau, had already aroused the suspicions of a government agency, and his mail was being examined by the authorities. Barely thirteen years old, Wilhelm undertook to convey to his brother in a series of letters, beginning on 27 November 1819, his ideas as to how a more democratic arrangement could be achieved in Germany. The country should be divided, he suggested, into fourteen districts, which he elaborately defined. Each district should be administered by councilmen elected by representatives of the nobility and of the common people. Every three years the councilmen would elect from among themselves "Herzöge" (dukes), who, in turn, would elect an emperor for life. The emperor and all other elected officials could be dismissed for cause at any time.

The letters were intercepted, but initially the repercussions were minor. The obligatory interrogation resulted in nothing more than an order not to leave Berlin without permission. But after the letters were published in two Berlin newspapers and Wackernagel, disregarding the travel ban, went to Breslau to visit his brother, he was expelled from high school and sentenced to a flogging. The punishment was reduced to incarceration, and he spent three days in 1821 in Berlin's municipal prison.

A most welcome occurrence at that time was a change in guardianship: the unpleasant Gemmel resigned for reasons of age, and a much more likable and younger man, Eduard Lieber, was appointed as his successor. Wackernagel transferred to a new high school, where he acquired a superb command of Latin, Greek, and French and astonished his teachers with his knowledge of older German literature. In the fall of 1824 he began his university studies in Berlin, concentrating on old German and classical literature with history and philosophy as subsidiary subjects. His teachers included the philologists Friedrich Heinrich von der Hagen, Karl Lachmann, and August Böckh and the philosopher Georg Wilhelm Friedrich Hegel.

Meanwhile, Wackernagel's economic situation was deteriorating. He supported himself mainly by copying manuscripts. On 16 April 1827 he left Berlin for Wielun, Poland, to spend six weeks doing genealogical research for a Polish count. The lucrative fee, however, did not last long, and the following winter he was forced to live, for lack of a cheaper place, in a bowling alley.

Those adverse conditions, however, did not prevent Wackernagel from maturing as a scholar. He started having articles published during his early student days and before reaching the age of twenty-two established himself with his edition of *Das Wessobrunner Gebet und die Wessobrunner Glossen* (The Wessobrunner Prayer and the Wessobrunner Glosses, 1827). This work invalidated positions held by Jacob and Wilhelm Grimm and by Wackernagel's teacher and friend Hans Ferdinand Massmann in that it identified the form and meaning of one of the most important pieces of old German literature and proved its purely Christian origin.

At the end of his formal studies Wackernagel could not afford to pay the fees required for obtaining his degree. He hoped to secure a job that would enable him to pay the fees, but his youthful indiscretion continued to haunt him. His two principal teachers, Lachmann and von der Hagen, had recommended Wackernagel for the position of curator at the royal library, but he got neither that job nor a position as a teacher of German at a vocational school in Berlin. A high official in the Ministry of

Justice, Karl von Kamptz, had not forgotten Wackernagel's 1819 letters to his brother, and he made sure that potential employers were informed of the applicant's "political unreliability." A cabinet order of 12 April 1823 excluded any participant in "demagogic activities" from obtaining employment in government agencies.

In the absence of any immediate prospect of change in his situation, Wackernagel saw no alternative to accepting a long-standing invitation by his friend Hoffmann von Fallersleben (pseudonym of August Heinrich Hoffmann) to come to Breslau and devote himself to his literary and scholarly activities. Hoffmann had sent travel money and promised that free living quarters would be waiting for him in the home of a mutual friend, Friedlieb Ferdinand Runge, a professor of chemistry with strong literary interests. In spite of advice to the contrary from Lachmann and others, who were afraid that the new location would not further Wackernagel's professional ambitions, he left for Breslau on 2 October 1828. There, each Saturday evening, he attended meetings of the Zwecklose Gesellschaft (Purposeless Society), whose members wrote and read poetry, exchanged information about books, and engaged in general conversation. Hoffmann was president of the group, and Wackernagel had been Protokollant (official note taker) since 1827, when he had visited on his way back to Berlin from Poland. The group printed some of its poetic output on various festive occasions.

Wackernagel explored Silesian customs and wrote about them, mostly for Hoffmann's *Monatsschrift.* At the encouragement of Karl Schall, managing editor of the *Breslauer Zeitung,* he reviewed theater performances and wrote articles on literary topics. His scholarly work in Germanic philology also progressed significantly: for a young, untested scholar who had not even graduated, it was a great honor to be asked by two masters in the field, Lachmann and Jacob Grimm, to collaborate with them and to continue projects they had started but would not be able to finish.

Wackernagel's decision to return to Berlin in 1830 was prompted by two factors. The most immediate one was that friction had developed between him and Hoffmann. Hoffmann had been willing to spend part of his salary as custodian of the university library for the support of his friend. He had anticipated, however, that Wackernagel would soon be gainfully employed. But time dragged on with no change other than that Runge likewise came to depend increasingly on Hoffmann's pocketbook. The second factor was Wackernagel's growing determination to find academic employment, and for that his current location held no promise whatsoever.

Back in Berlin, Lachmann was shocked when Wackernagel revealed to him the precariousness of his financial position. While he could not procure permanent employment for Wackernagel because of the events of 1819, he saw to it that copying jobs were supplied to Wackernagel. Lachmann also made it clear that Wackernagel would have his unconditional endorsement for a professorship or librarianship whenever the occasion presented itself.

Wackernagel's friend Karl Simrock asked him to secure the support of the Grimm brothers for Simrock's attempt to obtain his doctorate from Göttingen University on the strength of his published research rather than by submitting to an examination. Wackernagel used the opportunity to plead his own case as well. Jacob Grimm had always addressed him as "Herr Doktor"; he informed Grimm that this title was inappropriate and admitted his inability to pay the fee the university demanded for the degree. Grimm and some friends who were convinced of Wackernagel's excellent qualifications contributed the graduation fee. Wackernagel was found worthy of the degree, but regulations restricted conferral to persons who held academic positions. Finally, Abel Burckhardt, a Swiss friend whom Wackernagel had met in Berlin around 1827, alerted him to the possibility of a professorship at the University of Basel. Although Wackernagel was an unknown foreigner, Burckhardt worked incessantly to turn the odds in his favor. Several Swiss scholars independently studied the files of the five applicants and recommended Wackernagel for the position. In addition, the university contacted two German experts, and their strong endorsements removed any lingering doubts: Jacob Grimm said in his letter of recommendation that he did not know anyone who was better qualified for the position in every respect; Lachmann expressed his belief that Wackernagel could hold his own with the best as far as knowledge of German language and literature was concerned and that in the field of classical philology his knowledge was outstanding. The appointment, effective in the fall of 1833, was initially for two years only and was for the Pädagogicum, not for the university. But from the start the position was advertised as possibly leading to an appointment as full professor at the university.

Basel was willing to remedy Wackernagel's lack of a doctorate by offering him an honorary degree, but on his way to Switzerland he passed through Göttingen, paid the fees with the help of the Grimms, Lachmann, and two other friends, and was finally awarded the degrees of Doctor of Philosophy and Magister of Liberal Arts.

Wackernagel is widely considered the most important Germanist of his time after the death of Jacob Grimm in 1863; he was also a poet of remarkable accomplishment. The two activities cannot be separated, as Wackernagel modeled his poetry on medieval German poetry, especially the Minnesang. He had started writing poetry when he was fifteen, and in 1827 he had misled his teachers and friends by passing off one of his own compositions as two fragments of a Middle High German poem from the twelfth or thirteenth century; even Lachmann had fallen for the hoax. Beginning in 1828 Wackernagel's poems were published with increasing frequency in newspapers and periodicals, and in 1842 the first collection of them appeared. He continued to write verse throughout his life; many of his poems did not survive, as he considered them to be highly personal confessions and destroyed them.

Wackernagel was made full professor at the University of Basel in 1835. It did not take long for German authorities to realize what they had lost by creating conditions that left Wackernagel no choice but to leave. Several German universities, including Berlin and Munich, attempted to win him back, but he declined each time. In 1837 he was awarded honorary citizenship of Basel. In the same year he married Louise Blunchli, the sister of his old friend Johann Kaspar Blunchli. They had five children; the only daughter and the youngest son died before reaching their teens, and Wackernagel's wife died in 1848. He tried to recover from his loss by spending the spring and summer of 1849 traveling in southern France, Spain, and Italy. On his return he married Maria Sarasin, a member of a prestigious old Basel family and the best friend of his deceased wife. They had three sons and a daughter. For several years Wackernagel served as a councilman in the legislative body of his canton. He also participated with great vigor in the church life of the city.

Wackernagel's reputation as a Germanic philologist lags far behind that of Jacob Grimm, even though he is ranked by experts as almost on a par with Grimm. The most obvious reason for this disparity is Wackernagel's location. In comparison with Munich, Berlin, or Vienna, Basel was parochial. The number of students he taught was small, and his work did not lead to the formation of a school of followers as was the case with other great German philologists such as Grimm and Lachmann. Another factor is that Grimm became well known outside the circle of language experts for his and his brother's collections of fairy tales. Finally, while little of Grimm's work was directly connected to his teaching, nearly all of Wackernagel's publications centered around his classroom work. His research was primarily designed not for the benefit of the scientific community at large but for that of his students. His three most important works – *Deutsches Lesebuch* (German Reader, 1835–1843), *Geschichte der deutschen Litteratur bis zum dreißigjährigen Kriege* (History of German Literature to the Beginning of the Thirty Years' War, 1872), and *Poetik, Rhetorik und Stilistik: Academische Vorlesungen* (Poetics, Rhetoric and Stylistics: Academic Lectures, 1873) – illustrate this point. Except for the North Germanic languages, he covered all areas of Germanic philology in his lectures and publications. He investigated the origin of language in his *Über den Ursprung und die Entwickelung der Sprache* (On the Origin and the Development of Language, 1872). In his lectures and published research he also dealt with the comparative grammar of German, Greek, and Latin. The quality and scope of his research hold their own when compared with the publications of Grimm. Even today few of his writings are badly outdated, and all of them make fascinating reading for those with the necessary background.

In the early 1850s Wackernagel's excessive work load began to take a toll on his health. Frequent visits to health resorts could bring only temporary relief, largely because he refused to relax. During the winter of 1868–1869 his health problems became life threatening. He recovered during the ensuing months, but a relapse occurred in November 1869. Wackernagel died in Basel on 21 December 1869.

Standing in the shadow of Jacob Grimm was an unavoidable fate for Wackernagel when it became apparent that he would not, and later on did not want to, be appointed to a German university. The riches buried in the work of Wackernagel wait to be rediscovered by future Germanists.

Letters:

Briefe aus dem Nachlaß Wilhelm Wackernagels, edited by Albert Leitzmann (Leipzig: Teubner, 1916).

Bibliography:

Salomon Voegelin, "Lebensskizze, Characteristik und Schriftenverzeichnis W. Wackernagels," *Zeitschrift für deutsche Philologie,* 2 (1870): 330–342.

Biographies:

Rudolf Wackernagel, *Wilhelm Wackernagels Jugendjahre 1806–1833* (Basel: Detloff, 1885);

Jakob Wackernagel-Stehlin, *Zur Erinnerung an die Baseler Zeit von Wilhelm Wackernagel 19. April 1833–21. Dezember 1869* (Basel: Frobenius, 1933).

References:

Paul Burckhardt, *Geschichte der Stadt Basel von der Zeit der Reformation bis zur Gegenwart* (Basel: Helbig & Lichtenhahn, 1957);

Günter Hess, "Minnesangs Ende: Über dichtende Philologen im 19. Jahrhundert," in *Befund und Deutung: Zum Verhältnis von Empirie und Interpretation in Sprach- und Literaturwissenschaft,* edited by Klaus Grubmüller and others (Tübingen: Max Niemeyer, 1979), pp. 498–525;

Martin Heule, "Wilhelm Wackernagel als Vermittler von Grimmbeiträgen: Ergänzungen und Korrekturen zu Heinz Röllekes Beitrag über die Herkunft der Kinder- und Hausmärchen 165 ('Der Vogel Greif'), 166 ('Der starke Hans') und 167 ('Das Bürle im Himmel')," *Schweizer Archiv für Volkskunde,* 80 (1884): 88–92;

Konrad Kettig, "Wilhelm Wackernagel: Schicksal eines Berliner Demagogen von 1819," *Der Bär von Berlin: Jahrbuch des Vereins für die Geschichte Berlins,* 9 (1960): 7–27;

Heinrich Nidecker, "Wilhelm Wackernagel, Bücher und Freunde: Ein Streifzug durch seine Bibliothek," in *Festschrift Karl Schwarber: Beiträge zur schweizerischen Bibliotheks-, Buch- und Gelehrtengeschichte* (Basel: Schwabe, 1949), pp. 177–191;

Emil Elias Steinmeyer, review of Wackernagel's *Altdeutsche Predigten und Gebete aus Handschriften,* in *Zeitschrift für deutsches Altertum, Anzeiger,* 2 (1876): 215–234;

Eugen Teuscher, "Über den Ursprung der Sprache nach Wilhelm Wackernagel," *Sprachspiegel,* 31 (1975): 65–66;

Carl Weinhold, *Die Sprache in Wilhelm Wackernagels altdeutschen Predigten und Gebeten* (Basel: Schweighauser, 1875);

Jost Winteler, *Naturlaut und Sprache: Ausführungen zu Wilhelm Wackernagels Voces variae animalium* (Aarau: Sauerländer, 1892);

Adolf Ziemann, *Rechtfertigung gegen Herrn Wilhelm Wackernagel* (Quedlinburg: Basse, 1838).

Ludolf Wienbarg

(25 December 1802 - 2 January 1872)

Jeffrey L. Sammons
Yale University

BOOKS: *De primitivo idearum Platonicarum sensu denuo quaesivit Ludolphus Wienbarg* (Itzehoe: Schoenfeldt, 1829);

Holland in den Jahren 1831 und 1832, 2 volumes (Hamburg: Hoffmann & Campe, 1833; reprinted, Frankfurt am Main: Athenäum, 1973);

Aesthetische Feldzüge: Dem jungen Deutschland gewidmet (Hamburg: Hoffmann & Campe, 1834; edited by Walter Dietze, Berlin & Weimar: Aufbau, 1964);

Soll die plattdeutsche Sprache gepflegt oder ausgerottet werden?: Gegen Ersteres und für Letzteres beantwortet (Hamburg: Hoffmann & Campe, 1834);

Wanderungen durch den Thierkreis (Hamburg: Hoffmann & Campe, 1835; reprinted, Frankfurt am Main: Athenäum, 1973);

Menzel und die junge Literatur: Programm zur Deutschen Revue (Mannheim: Löwenthal, 1835);

Zur neuesten Literatur (Mannheim: Löwenthal, 1835; reprinted, Frankfurt am Main: Athenäum, 1973);

Tagebuch von Helgoland (Hamburg: Hoffmann & Campe, 1838; edited by Werner Schendell, Hamburg: Hoffmann & Campe, 1921; reprint of original edition, Frankfurt am Main: Athenäum, 1973);

Geschichtliche Vorträge über altdeutsche Sprache und Litteratur (Hamburg: Hoffmann & Campe, 1838);

Die Dramatiker der Jetztzeit (Altona: Aue, 1839);

Vermischte Schriften: Erster Band. Quadriga (Altona: Aue, 1840);

Hamburg und seine Brandtage: Ein historisch-kritischer Beitrag (Hamburg: Kittler, 1843);

Der dänische Fehdehandschuh (Hamburg: Hoffmann & Campe, 1846);

Die Volks-Versammlung zu Nortorf am 14ten Septbr. 1846 (Hamburg: Hoffmann & Campe, 1846);

Das dänische Königsgesetz oder Das in Dänemark geltende Grundgesetz, in historischer Beleuchtung und zur Inbetrachtnahme für die Frage der Gegenwart (Hamburg: Hoffmann & Campe, 1847);

Ludolf Wienbarg

Krieg und Frieden mit Dänemark: Ein Aufruf an die deutsche Nazionalversammlung (Frankfurt am Main: Oehler, 1848);

Der diesjährige Dänenkrieg und sein Ausgang – bis auf weiter: Dem teuren, unbesiegten, kampfmutigen Nordelbingien gewidmet (Schleswig: Bruhn, 1849);

Darstellungen aus den schleswig-holsteinischen Feldzügen, 2 volumes (Kiel: Schröder, 1850, 1851);

Das Geheimniß des Wortes: Ein Beitrag (Hamburg & Stuttgart: Aue, 1852);

Die plattdeutsche Propaganda und ihre Apostel: Ein Wort zu seiner Zeit, as Freimund (Hamburg: Hoffmann & Campe, 1860);

Geschichte Schleswigs, 2 volumes (Hamburg: Meißner, 1861, 1862);

Der Antheil Dänemark's und der dänischen Behörden an Hamburg's Schicksal im Frühjahr 1813 (Altona: Haendke & Lehmkuhl, 1863).

OTHER: Pindar, *Jason: Episches Gedicht nach Pindar übersetzt, bevorredet und erläutert,* translated by Wienbarg as Ludolf Vineta (Hamburg: Hoffmann & Campe, 1830);

Julius Max Schottky, *Paganinis Leben und Charakter,* abridged by Wienbarg as Vineta (Hamburg: Hoffmann & Campe, 1830);

Rasmus Kristian Rask, *Kurzgefaßte Anleitung zur altnordischen oder altisländischen Sprache,* translated by Wienbarg (Hamburg: Hoffmann & Campe, 1839);

Deutsches Literaturblatt, edited by Wienbarg (1840–1842; reprinted, Frankfurt am Main: Athenäum, 1971);

"Wienbarg über sich selbst," in *Portraits und Silhouetten,* by F. Gustav Kühne, volume 2 (Hannover: Kius, 1843), pp. 179–190;

Armin: Wochenzeitschrift für die reifere männliche Jugend, edited by Wienbarg (1854);

Altonaer Nachrichten, edited by Wienbarg (1864–1867);

Die Deutsche Revue, edited by Wienbarg and Karl Gutzkow, edited by Emile F. J. Dresch (Berlin: Behr, 1904);

Deutsche Revue: Deutsche Blätter, edited by Wienbarg and Gutzkow (Frankfurt am Main: Athenäum, 1971).

Ludolf Wienbarg's conventional place in literary history was defined by a 10 December 1835 decree of the diet of the Deutscher Bund (German Confederation) that banned all his works, along with those of Heinrich Heine, Karl Gutzkow, Heinrich Laube, and Theodor Mundt. The governments of the confederation had invented a conspiracy of writers against everything good and decent, a conspiracy to which they gave the name "Junges Deutschland" (Young Germany) – a term that Wienbarg himself had helped put into circulation. It still survives as a convenient label for the dissident writers of that epoch, though it is now well established that not only was there no conspiracy, there was no real group in the sense of a cohesive movement.

Wienbarg differs from the other Young Germans in two significant ways. For one thing, he was somewhat older; he was closer in generation to Heine, who is more accurately thought of as a precursor than a member of the group. (Wienbarg greatly admired Heine, who, in turn, borrowed motifs from Wienbarg.) In those times, with historical events occurring rapidly, an age difference of even a few years could make a difference in formative experience; for example, Wienbarg was the only Young German old enough to remember the uprising against Napoleon in 1813. Perhaps for this reason he was the most nationalistic of them and the least interested in France, the Paris revolution of 1830, or the Saint-Simonian movement. At the same time he was the most programmatically and systematically democratic of them all – even more so than Heine – demonstrating that in his generation nationalism was not incompatible with a revolutionary commitment to democracy.

The second difference concerns the course of his career. The seriousness and efficacy of the ban of 1835 should not be underestimated, as it sometimes is, but in most cases it did not put the dissident writers permanently out of business. Heine was to become, if he was not already, the major living writer in the German language. Gutzkow, Laube, and Mundt had long careers after the ban, the first as a playwright, novelist, and feared critic; the second as the manager of the prestigious Burgtheater in Vienna; the third as a literary historian and theorist. The ban fell most heavily on Wienbarg. For a time he was a homeless wanderer, virtually an outlaw; he related that when he entered a tavern and gave his name, the other patrons would flee to the safety of their homes. Possibly already an alcoholic, he drifted into obscurity, though other members of the literary world reported encounters with him from time to time. Thus a legend grew up about him as a Germanic freedom fighter – he was of heroic stature in appearance – felled by reactionary governments. Little effort has been made to research Wienbarg's later life, and there is no full record of his journalistic writings. In 1972 a Yale undergraduate, Frank Lehmann, was able to discover more about him than one customarily finds in the published sources.

Wienbarg was born in Altona on Christmas Day 1802 to Wilken Wienbarg, a blacksmith, and Maria Margaretha Wienbarg, née Giese. After he completed elementary school there was some thought of sending him to Baltimore as a commercial apprentice; but in 1815 he entered the Altona gymnasium, a considerable step upward in social status. At the University of Kiel in 1821 he began to study theology, as most impecunious students did, but switched to philosophy. From 1825 to 1828 he served a tedious stint as a tutor in the home of a baron in Lauenburg. He then went to the University of Bonn, receiving his doctorate in 1829 with a dissertation on Plato. He began his literary career with a translation of and commentary on a segment of Pindar's *Jason* and a fifty-page abridgment of Julius Max Schottky's biography of the violinist Niccolò Paganini, both published under the pseudonym Ludolf Vineta in 1830. After working as a tutor for the Danish ambassador to the Netherlands, he produced *Holland in den Jahren 1831 und 1832* (Holland in the Years 1831 and 1832, 1833), a work influenced by Heine's *Reisebilder* (1826–1831; translated as *Pictures of Travel,* 1855).

In 1833 Wienbarg was appointed to teach Danish language and literature at the University of Kiel; instead, he gave a series of lectures on contemporary German literature and theory. Wienbarg's birthplace was a Danish possession, so he was a subject of the Danish crown. Like other German writers in that situation, such as Theodor Storm and Wilhelm Jensen, he was extremely hostile to the Danes. He would oppose Denmark virtually all his life, even taking part in a military campaign against the Danes when he was forty-seven. The struggle against Danish sovereignty was at the core of his German nationalism; at the same time it provided the context for his democratic strivings, for he perceived the Danish system of government as profoundly repressive and reactionary. Thus his refusal to teach Danish at Kiel, a Danish institution, and his insistence on propagating German instead was perceived not only as insubordination but also as sedition, and it led to his dismissal despite vigorous student protests on his behalf.

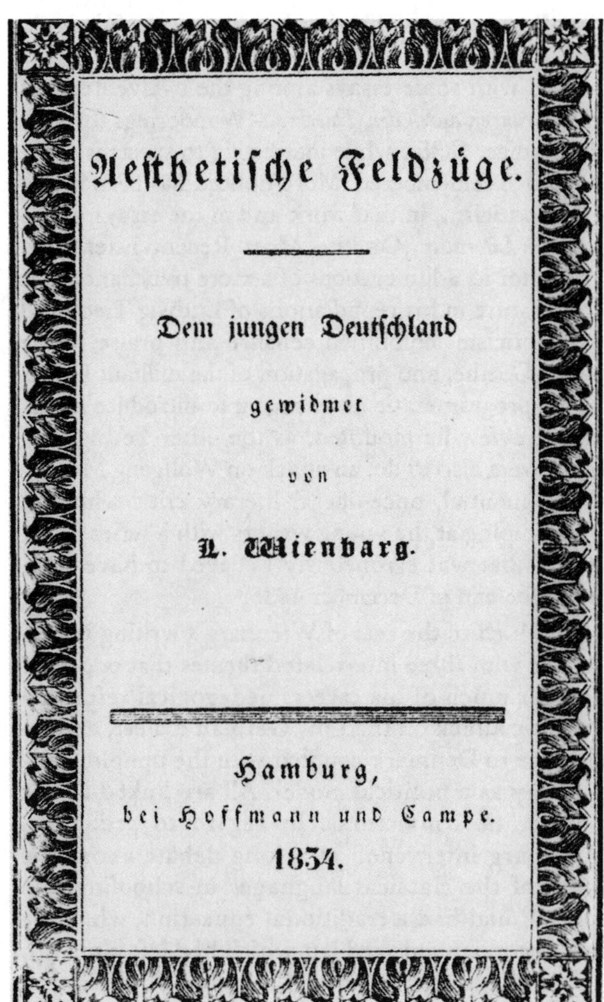
Aesthetische Feldzüge.

Dem jungen Deutschland

gewidmet

von

L. Wienbarg.

Hamburg,

bei Hoffmann und Campe.

1834.

Cover for Heinrich Heine's copy of Wienbarg's controversial lectures on aesthetics (from Heine-Jahrbuch, *1983)*

In 1834 Wienbarg's lectures were published as *Aesthetische Feldzüge: Dem jungen Deutschland gewidmet* (Aesthetic Campaigns: Dedicated to the Young Germany). Undoubtedly it was this work, which was banned immediately on its appearance, that caused him to be included in the comprehensive ban of 1835, though it may be difficult today to see what it contained – apart from its obstreperous, antiacademic, and nationalistic tone – that might frighten governments. At first it looks like a conscientious exposition of contemporary Classical-Romantic aesthetics; rather than seeing aesthetic experience as the medium for the humanization of life and society, however, he sees a social and political renovation as a prerequisite to the development of genuine art. This twist on the aesthetics of Johann Wolfgang von Goethe and Friedrich Schiller, of which the authorities were already suspicious, along with the vitalistic appeal to youth and the praise of George Gordon, Lord Byron, and Heine, was perceived as a coded instigation to revolution. Consequently, Wienbarg became the object of intense police attention. He and Gutzkow attempted in 1835 to found a literary review in Mannheim that would be a forum for all the progressive voices of the time; *Die Deutsche Revue* was banned before the first issue could appear.

Like the other Young Germans, Wienbarg believed in the equal status of imaginative literature and expository prose as vehicles for progressive ideas; also like the others, he was ambitious for literary achievement. But while he had an unusually clear vision of what a modern realism might look like, he never was able to achieve a successful result. His experiments in the novella form, which appeared with some essays among the twelve items of *Wanderungen durch den Thierkreis* (Wanderings through the Zodiac, 1835), while interesting to specialists, are not much remembered. More noticed has been his literary criticism, in that work and in the essays of *Zur neuesten Literatur* (On the Most Recent Literature, 1835), for its adumbrations of a more trenchant mode of literature in his repudiations of Ludwig Tieck and Romanticism, combined censure and praise of the pagan Goethe, and propagation of the militant Heine. In the programmatic essay meant to introduce his literary review he mounted, as the other Young Germans were also to do, an attack on Wolfgang Menzel, the influential, once-liberal literary critic who had been sniping at the young writers with a series of polemics that was erroneously believed to have instigated the ban of December 1835.

Much of the rest of Wienbarg's writing is concerned with three interrelated themes that occupied him for much of his career: pedagogical reform, a quixotic attack on the Low German dialect, and resistance to Denmark coupled with the upholding of Norway as a political model. All are linked by his democratic convictions. In regard to pedagogy, Wienbarg intervened in a long debate about the place of the classical languages in schooling. He himself had had a traditional education, which he had not much enjoyed but which had left him with an excellent command of Latin and Greek and a deep respect for the classical tradition. But he felt that a school system that devoted half its time to the study of the ancient languages was a counterproductive form of hazing children that hindered their development as citizens. In an essay, "Das Studium der Alten" (The Study of the Ancients), which originally appeared in a Hamburg newspaper in 1836 and then in the first and only volume of his *Vermischte Schriften* (Miscellaneous Writings, 1840), subtitled *Quadriga,* he argued that the ancient languages should be electives; that they should be restricted to the upper grades, when pupils are more mature; that instruction should concentrate on the content of texts rather than grammatical drill; and that German should be put at the center of the curriculum. Wienbarg returned to these concerns many times in his writings, propagating, as did many nationalist intellectuals, the study of older Germanic literature.

In one matter Wienbarg deviated from nationalist conventions: he rejected the reverence for dialect as a vehicle of folk culture. He mounted a violent attack on the preservation of the Low German dialect spoken in the northern regions in *Soll die plattdeutsche Sprache gepflegt oder ausgerottet werden?: Gegen Ersteres und für Letzteres beantwortet* (Shall the Low German Language Be Cultivated or Exterminated?: Answered against the Former and for the Latter, 1834) and returned to the topic several times. Wienbarg's concern was that the dialect reinforced class differences, shutting off the lower classes from the modern discourse of enlightenment, progress, and patriotism. He was particularly distressed by the courtroom situation, where Low German speakers were unable to follow procedures conducted in standard German or to express themselves intelligibly to the court. Here one sees his instinctive awareness of the distinction between populism and democracy. The democratic impulse appears everywhere in his writings – for example, in his journalistic account of the great fire that devastated much of Hamburg in May 1842, *Hamburg und seine Brandtage* (Hamburg and Its Days of Conflagration, 1843), in which he contrasts the competence and initiative of the common people to the dithering of the authorities and the aloofness of the privileged.

It was this democratic conviction, and not merely a parochial nationalism, that fired his hostility to Denmark. In one of his many pamphlets in this cause, *Das dänische Königsgesetz oder Das in Dänemark geltende Grundgesetz, in historischer Beleuchtung und zur Inbetrachtnahme für die Frage der Gegenwart* (The Danish Royal Law; or, The Basic Law Valid in Denmark, in the Light of History and in Consideration of the Question of the Present, 1847), he furiously analyzed the Danish *Kongelov* (Royal Law), which served as a constitution. This law, which dated from 1665, was singularly oppressive and reactionary in the nineteenth century, for it lodged all power, without restriction, in the person of the king. In 1814 the Norwegians had rebelled against this despotism, overthrown Danish sovereignty, and formed a more modern constitutional arrangement in union with the crown of Sweden; Wienbarg, though he never visited Norway, portrayed that country as a Germanic utopia in contrast to decadent, downtrodden Denmark.

Among his several representations of this idea is a detailed article-by-article analysis of the Norwegian constitution of 1814, "Geist der Norwegischen Verfassung" (Spirit of the Norwegian Constitution), one of the four essays in *Quadriga.* The essay concentrates on three issues: the restriction of the royal power by the obligation of the monarch to consult with ministers and his right only to a suspensive veto over legislation, the system of indirect election, and – probably most important for a German bourgeois liberal – the abolition of the nobility. The less liberal aspects of the constitution do not trouble him unduly: he passes over the exclusion of Jews and Jesuits from the kingdom with equanimity and positively welcomes an electoral system that explicitly disenfranchises the urban working class. But by German standards of its time the essay was virtually revolutionary. There is, however, no clear evidence that many people read it; its influence may have been restricted by its pedantic, uneconomical style and by Wienbarg's increasing retreat into obscurity.

In 1839 Wienbarg had married Dorothea Marwedel of Altona. They had three sons: Max, born in 1840; Hermann, born in 1841; and Ludolf, born in 1843. Dorothea Wienbarg seems to have died around 1848; two of the sons died young, and the other immigrated to America. After serving as a volunteer in the Schleswig-Holstein campaign against Denmark in 1848–1849 Wienbarg worked as a local journalist, writing for, editing, and co-owning a series of newspapers in Hamburg and Altona well into the 1860s. In 1868 he was confined to a mental institution in Schleswig for acute alcoholism. Some readers of the announcement of his death on 2 January 1872 were surprised to discover that he had still been alive so recently.

A flare-up of interest in the Young German movement, and therefore in Wienbarg, occurred around 1970 but has since diminished considerably. He is the least researched and least understood of the banned writers; the most scholarly and perceptive study of him, Gerhard Burkhardt's Hamburg dissertation of 1956, remains unpublished. He was not a major writer nor always an especially clear thinker, but he has some importance as a champion of the long-inhibited cause of democracy in Germany.

References:

Emil Brenning, "Ludolf Wienbargs Nachlaß," *Euphorion,* 15 (1908): 535–548;

Gerhard Burkhardt, "Ludolf Wienbarg als Ästhetiker und Kritiker: Seine Entwicklung und seine geistesgeschichtliche Stellung," Ph.D. dissertation, University of Hamburg, 1956;

Eliza M. Butler, "Wienbarg and Saint-Simonism," in her *The Saint-Simonian Religion in Germany: A Study of the Young German Movement* (Cambridge: Cambridge University Press, 1926; New York: Fertig, 1968), pp. 398–430;

Walter Dietze, "Ludolf Wienbarg," *Sinn und Form,* 14 (1962): 874–921;

Volkmar Hansen, "'Freiheit! Freiheit! Freiheit!': Das Bild Karl Gutzkows in der Forschung; mit Ausblicken auf Ludolf Wienbarg," in *Literatur in der sozialen Bewegung: Aufsätze und Forschungsberichte zum 19. Jahrhundert,* edited by Alberto Martino and others (Tübingen: Niemeyer, 1977), pp. 488–542;

Walter Hömberg, *Zeitgeist und Ideenschmuggel: Die Kommunikationsstrategie des Jungen Deutschland* (Stuttgart: Metzler, 1975);

Timon Hommes, *Holland im Urteil eines Jungdeutschen* (Amsterdam: Paris, 1926);

Heinrich Hubert Houben, "Ludolf Wienbarg," in his *Jungdeutscher Sturm und Drang: Ergebnisse und Studien* (Leipzig: Brockhaus, 1911), pp. 175–251;

Houben, "Wienbarg, Ludolf," in his *Verbotene Literatur von der klassischen Zeit bis zur Gegenwart,* volume 1 (Berlin: Rowohlt, 1924), pp. 605–617;

Rudolf Kayser, "Ludolf Wienbarg und der Kampf um den Historismus," *German Quarterly,* 29 (1956): 71–74;

Helmut Koopmann, *Das Junge Deutschland: Analyse seines Selbstverständnisses* (Stuttgart: Metzler, 1970);

Frank Lehmann, "Ludolf Wienbarg's Essay 'Das Studium der Alten,'" senior essay, Yale College, 1972;

Hugh Ridley, "Nietzsche and Wienbarg: A Consideration of Parallels between Nietzsche and the Young Germans," *Nietzsche-Studien,* 9 (1980): 338–355;

Jeffrey L. Sammons, "Ludolf Wienbarg and Norway," in his *Imagination and History: Selected Papers on Nineteenth-Century German Literature* (New York, Bern, Frankfurt am Main & Paris: Lang, 1988), pp. 149–175;

Sammons, *Six Essays on the Young German Novel* (Chapel Hill: University of North Carolina Press, 1972);

Viktor Schweizer, *Ludolf Wienbarg: Beiträge zu einer Jungdeutschen Ästhetik* (Leipzig: Wild, 1897);

Hartmut Steinecke, "Ludolf Wienbarg," in his *Literaturkritik des Jungen Deutschland: Entwicklungen – Tendenzen – Texte* (Berlin: Schmidt, 1982), pp. 130–177;

Gert Ueding, "Rhetorik der Tat: Ludolf Wienbarg und seine Ästhetische Feldzüge," in his *Die andern Klassiker: Literarische Porträts aus zwei Jahrhunderten* (Munich: Beck, 1986), pp. 89–109.

Papers:

Ludolf Wienbarg's papers were at one time in the Bremen State Library. During World War II the library's archival materials were sent to Bernburg on the Saale for safekeeping; after the war they disappeared into Eastern Europe.

Ernst Willkomm

(10 February 1810 – 24 May 1886)

Keith Bullivant
University of Florida

BOOKS: *Bernhard, Herzog von Weimar: Trauerspiel in fünf Aufzügen* (Leipzig: Berger, 1833);

Julius Kühn: Eine Novelle (Leipzig: Berger, 1833);

Buch der Küsse: Dreiunddreißig Gedichte (Leipzig: Berger, 1834);

Erich XIV., König von Schweden: Ein dramatisches Gedicht in drei Teilen (Leipzig: Berger, 1834);

Civilisationsnovellen (Leipzig: Wunders Verlags-Magazin, 1837);

Die Europamüden: Modernes Lebensbild, 2 volumes (Leipzig: Wunders Verlags-Magazin, 1838);

Lord Byron: Ein Dichterleben. Novellen, 3 volumes (Leipzig: Engelmann, 1839);

Der Traumdeuter: Ein Roman (Stuttgart: Hoffmann, 1840);

Grenzer, Narren und Lootsen. Eine Sammlung von Novellen, Land- und Seebildern, 3 volumes (Leipzig: Kollmann, 1842);

Denkwürdigkeiten eines österreichischen Kerkermeisters: Nach wahren Begebenheiten erzählt (Leipzig: Reclam, 1843);

Eisen, Gold und Geist: Ein tragikomischer Roman, 3 volumes (Leipzig: Kollmann, 1843);

Sagen und Mährchen aus der Oberlausitz, nacherzählt, 2 volumes (Hannover: Kius, 1843);

Schattenrisse aus dem Volks- und Fürstenleben: Novellen und Wanderskizzen (Leipzig: Kollmann, 1844);

Wallenstein: Historischer Roman, 4 volumes (Leipzig: Kollmann, 1844);

Der deutsche Bauer: Ein Volksbuch auf das Jahr 1844 (Leipzig: Kollmann, 1844);

Weiße Sclaven oder Die Leiden des Volkes: Ein Roman, 5 volumes (Leipzig: Kollmann, 1845);

Blitze: Novellen, Schilderungen und Skizzen, 2 volumes (Leipzig: Kollmann, 1846);

Italienische Nächte: Reiseskizzen und Studien, 2 volumes (Leipzig: Fleischer, 1847);

Die Nachtmahlsbrüder in Rom: Ein Roman, 3 volumes (Leipzig: Kollmann, 1847);

Ein Brautkuß: Irische Novelle (Leipzig: Fleischer, 1848);

Ernst Willkomm (copper engraving by August Weger)

Wanderungen an der Nord- und Ostsee (Leipzig: Haendel, 1850);

Handbuch für Reisende durch das Riesengebirge: Nebst Ausflug nach Prag (Leipzig: Haendel, 1853);

Im Wald und am Gestade: Skizzen und Bilder (Dessau: Katz, 1854);

Die Familie Ammer: Deutscher Sittenroman (Frankfurt am Main: Meidinger, 1855);

Von Berlin nach Hamburg: Nebst Schildereien aus Lübeck und Hamburg (Leipzig: Brockhaus, 1855);

Peter Pommerering: Historischer Roman, 2 volumes (Prague, Vienna & Leipzig: Günther, 1856);

Novellen und Erzählungen, 2 volumes (Hannover: Rümpler, 1856);

Banco: Ein Roman aus dem Hamburger Leben, 2 volumes (Gotha: Scheube, 1857);

Rheder und Matrose: Ein Hamburger Roman (Frankfurt am Main: Meidinger, 1857);

Meteore: Novellen-Cyclus, 2 volumes (Nordhausen: Büchting, 1858);

Neue Novellen, 2 volumes (Nordhausen: Büchting, 1859);

Dichter und Apostel: Roman in vier Büchern, 2 volumes (Frankfurt am Main: Meidinger, 1859);

Am häuslichen Herd: Kriminal- und Strandgeschichten, 2 volumes (Gotha: Opetz, 1859);

Mosaik: Ausgewählte Erzählungen, 2 volumes (Leipzig: Hübner, 1860);

Verirrte Seelen: Ein Roman, 3 volumes (Leipzig: Brockhaus, 1860);

Die Töchter des Vatican, 3 volumes (Leipzig: Thomas, 1860);

Moderne Sünden: Ein Roman, 3 volumes (Nordhausen: Büchting, 1861);

Männer der That: Ein Roman aus der Zeit und dem Leben Arndts, 4 volumes (Leipzig: Thomas, 1861);

Am grünen Tische: Vier Criminalgeschichten, 2 volumes (Leipzig: Luppe, 1862);

Im Bann und Zauber von Leidenschaft und Wahn, von Ernst und Scherz: Licht- und Nebelbilder, 3 volumes (Leipzig: Thomas, 1862);

Aus deutschen Gauen in Nord und Süd: Volks- und Sittenschilderungen (Gotha: Opetz, 1863);

Auf zerborstener Erde: Friesische Geschichten (Frankfurt am Main: Strauß, 1863);

Stalaktiten: Erzählungen in gebrochenem Licht, 2 volumes (Gotha: Opetz, 1863);

Aus alter und neuer Zeit: Vier Erzählungen, 2 volumes (Leipzig: Luppe, 1864);

Frau von Gampenstein: Ein Roman, 3 volumes (Leipzig: Günther, 1865);

Der letzte Trunk: Ein Roman (Berlin: Janke, 1865);

Ein Stiefkind des Glücks: Humoristischer Roman aus dem Leben, 3 volumes (Leipzig: Günther, 1867);

Gesellen des Satan: Roman in zwölf Büchern, 6 volumes (Jena: Costenoble, 1867);

Die Welt des Scheines: Erzählungen, 2 volumes (Gera: Issleib, 1869);

Im Glück verwildert: Roman, 3 volumes (Berlin: Wedekind, 1873);

Wunde Herzen: Roman, 3 volumes (Berlin: Wedekind, 1874);

Das gefährliche Vielliebchen (Stuttgart: Kröner, 1879).

OTHER: *Jahrbuch für Drama, Dramaturgie und Theater,* edited by Willkomm and A. Fischer, 8 issues (1837–1839);

Lübecker Zeitung, edited by Willkomm (1849–1852);

Jahreszeiten: Hamburger Neue Modezeitung, edited by Willkomm (1853–1855);

Staats- und Gelehrte-Zeitung des Hamburgischen unparteiischen Correspondenten, feuilleton edited by Willkomm (1853–1857).

Ernst Willkomm was, until the 1860s, one of Germany's most popular authors. He faded rapidly into obscurity, and it was not until the reemergence of interest in the nineteenth-century social novel during the 1970s that this "schlimmste Vielschreiber seiner Zeit" (most excessively prolific hack of his day) – as Heinrich Schauerte calls him – whose work had been out of print for well over half a century, received new attention. Despite a certain brief scholarly interest, especially in *Eisen, Gold und Geist* (Iron, Gold, and Spirit, 1843) and *Weiße Sclaven oder Die Leiden des Volkes* (White Slavery; or, The Suffering of the People, 1845), no new editions of any of his works were published. None of his writings has been translated into English.

Willkomm's early socially critical writings – *Civilisationsnovellen* (Novellas on the Theme of [European] Civilization, 1837), *Die Europamüden* (Tired of Europe, 1838), and his two social novels written during the stormy 1840s, *Eisen, Gold und Geist* and *Weiße Sclaven* – were widely discussed, and it is on these works that interest in recent years has focused. His popularity in his day was based, however, on his novellas and historical and regional novels. *Rheder and Matrose* (Shipowner and Sailor, 1857), set in the harbor area of Hamburg, was particularly well regarded, as were his travel books, all of which suited the prevailing literary tastes of the middle-class reading public of the time.

Ernst Adolf Willkomm was born on 10 February 1810 in the village of Herwigsdorf, near Zittau; he was the son of the Lutheran pastor Karl Gottlob Willkomm. He studied law and philosophy at the University of Leipzig and, after a year's tour of Italy in 1845–1846 and service as a war correspondent in the Schleswig-Holstein campaign in 1849, became editor of the *Lübecker Zeitung.* In 1852 he became involved in editorial work in Hamburg, where he lived for the next thirty years.

Willkomm's generation of German writers was much influenced by events in France, particularly by the July Revolution of 1830, and by French writers of the day, such as Eugène Sue, Honoré de Balzac, and Alexandre Dumas. His writing of the 1830s is generally allocated by critics to the Junges Deutschland (Young Germany) movement, to which Theodor Mundt and Ludolf Wienbarg also belonged. The writers of this movement essentially rejected existing aesthetic values and demanded a socially engaged literature. The major concern of the *Civilisationsnovellen* is the changing times. Willkomm addresses the impact of the new railways, the consequences of increasing secularization, and, above all, the need for social emancipation, especially of women and the Jews. These concerns are pursued further in *Die Europamüden,* an epistolary novel about a private circle of enlightened men and women reminiscent of the "Gesellschaft vom Turm" (Society of the Tower) in Johann Wolfgang von Goethe's *Wilhelm Meisters Lehrjahre* (1795–1796; translated as *Wilhelm Meister's Apprenticeship,* 1824). The concerns of these noble individuals – freedom of religion and ideas, social justice, and the removal of antiquated constraints that work against the development of the finest human qualities – are essentially social rather than political, but they inevitably have political connotations in the Europe of the day.

In *Eisen, Gold und Geist* Willkomm shifts his attention from the reformist concerns of an educated elite to the problems of the new industrial working class. The new age is, he claims, dominated by the "neue Trinität" (new Trinity) of the title. Iron, symbolizing new industrial production techniques, produces wealth, which leads to an awareness of how to make even more money, so that the modern spirit is made up of slyness and the quick-wittedness necessary for successful speculation. The ruthless capitalist, a familiar figure throughout the nineteenth century, is represented here by Süßlich, who has tricked his former employer out of ownership of a spinning mill. In his lust for ever more profit Süßlich subjects his employees to increasing exploitation, which results in their getting together to discuss their lot, drawing on the experiences of English and French workers. The employees go on strike, pinning their hopes on the intervention of the authorities, but soon they are influenced by agitators and alcohol to follow the example of the machine-wrecking English Luddites. They storm the factory, in which Süßlich has taken cover, and set it on fire. He is seen, in silhouette, plunging into the flames as he tries to escape: "es war als habe sie ihre Bestimmung erfüllt" (it was as if it [the steam engine] had fulfilled its purpose). As a result of the insurrection other local owners immediately increase their employees' wages; the Süßlich factory is taken over by the son of the former owner, who rebuilds it out in the countryside, using waterpower instead of steam. He engages twice as many hands as before and is a mild and considerate employer. The threatened social rebellion of the 1840s, which also haunts the English "Condition of England" novels of the time, is shown as justified but localized, with the one outburst of violence bringing other exploitative owners to their senses.

Between the publication of this novel and the writing of *Weiße Sclaven* occurred the Silesian weavers' revolt of 1844, on which Gerhart Hauptmann's drama *Die Weber* (1892; translated as *The Weavers,* 1899) would be based; the threat of major social upheaval, however, is much greater in Willkomm's 1845 novel. The impetus of the dramatic events in *Weiße Sclaven* is similar to that of *Eisen, Gold und Geist*: increasing exploitation of workers in the interests of more profit produces unrest among the employees of Adrian am Stein. The spokesman for the workers, as they start to resist the deterioration of their working conditions, is Martell, who has lost a son in a mill accident. Adrian arranges to have Martell killed, but the attempted murder only serves to reveal that Martell is Adrian's unjustly disinherited half brother. Martell immediately demands satisfaction from his half brother in a manner appropriate to his new rank: a duel. Determined that Adrian experience the suffering he has inflicted on his workers over the years, Martell selects as his weapon a twelve-hour shift of work at the loom. The untrained Adrian, unable to keep up with the relentless pace of the machine, collapses; he is dragged into the loom by his hair and crushed. The scene is witnessed with some satisfaction by Aurel, Adrian's brother, who has long been repulsed by Adrian's hard-heartedness, and by Vollbrecht, the decent but loyal director of the family business. The initial reaction of the workers is to start to destroy the machinery, but Aurel persuades them that he can reorganize the factory in a way that will turn mechanized labor into "die Quelle unseres gemeinsamen Glückes" (the source of our common happiness).

As in the Condition of England novels, hopes in Willkomm's works are pinned on the emergence of a new generation of decent entrepreneurs who will break with the degrading exploitation that marked the earliest phases of factory work. The similarities between *Eisen, Gold und Geist* and *Weiße Sclaven,* on the one hand, and their English counterparts, on the other, are striking, although none was known in the other country. Like Benjamin Disraeli's *Sybil* (1845), Elizabeth Cleghorn Gaskell's *Mary Barton* (1848), Charles Kingsley's *Alton Locke* (1850), and Charles Dickens's *Hard Times* (1854), Willkomm's novels were motivated by the twin forces of humanitarian concern and fear of social revolution. All of these middle-class writers were appalled by the condition of the workers, but at the same time they were afraid of a socialist uprising. In all instances there is a touchingly naive, perhaps desperate belief in the inevitable triumph of human kindness; the system will not change, but natural justice will ensure that enlightened individuals come to the fore. One manifestation of the organic development of society out of its present "muddle," as Dickens described it, is common to *Sybil, Alton Locke,* and *Weiße Sclaven:* the role of a revitalized aristocracy in helping to bring about a harmonious future.

Comparison of Willkomm's novels of the Vormärz (the period between 1840 and the March 1848 Revolution) with their English counterparts also reveals differences in the novel traditions of the two countries. The Condition of England novels have similar stylistic weaknesses to Willkomm's – black-and-white characterization, a tendency toward melodrama, a heavy reliance on coincidence, and, closely related to the last, a paucity of plot born of the simple message of hope. But they have a recognized place in the history of the English novel, which has always tended to be social in nature; as a result they are still readily available, even in paperback. The traditional aesthetic canon of the German novel, on the other hand, emphasized the inner world of the spirit and decried the outer world of social reality as inferior to it. The consequence is that the novels of Willkomm and others of his day, which enjoyed great popularity outside the confines of the Bildungsbürgertum (educated upper-middle class), are forgotten, condemned to the unread piles of so-called Trivialliteratur (cheap literature) that fall outside the prevailing canon.

With his novels of Hamburg life and his travel books Willkomm remained a popular writer into the 1860s. He continued writing, with a much reduced output, until the mid 1870s, but by then he was already becoming forgotten. Ill health forced him to leave Hamburg in 1880 and return to his native region. He died in Zittau on 24 May 1886.

References:

Hans Adler, "Literatur und Sozialkritik: Versuch einer historischen Spezifikation des sozialen Romans," *Zeitschrift für deutsche Philologie,* 102, no. 4 (1983): 500–521;

Keith Bullivant and Hugh Ridley, *Industrie und deutsche Literatur 1830–1914* (Munich: Deutscher Taschenbuch Verlag, 1976);

Jutta A. Hagedorn, "Der gotische Roman als sozialer Roman des späten achtzehnten Jahrhunderts," Ph.D. dissertation, University of Georgia, 1987;

Ernst Kohn-Bramstedt, *Aristocracy and the Middle-Classes in Germany: Social Types in German Literature 1830–1900,* second edition (Chicago: University of Chicago Press, 1964);

Karl-Heinz Kratz, "Ernst Willkomms *Weiße Sclaven:* Ein sozialer Roman zwischen Jungem Deutschland und Frühnaturalismus," *Colloquia Germanica,* 16, nos. 2–3 (1983): 177–200;

Eda Sagarra, *Tradition and Revolution: German Literature and Society 1830–1890* (London: Weidenfeld & Nicholson, 1971);

Heinrich Schauerte, *Die Fabrik im Roman des Vormärz* (Cologne: Pahl-Rugenstein, 1984);

Peter-Paul Schneider and others, eds., *Literatur im Industriezeitalter,* 2 volumes (Marbach: Deutsche Schillergesellschaft, 1987).

Papers:

The few extant papers of Ernst Willkomm are contained in the Cotta Archive of the Deutsches Literaturarchiv, Marbach.

Checklist of Further Readings

Alker, Ernst. *Die deutsche Literatur im 19. Jahrhundert (1832–1914),* second edition. Stuttgart: Kröner, 1969.

Bark, Joachim. *Biedermeier-Vormärz. Bürgerlicher Realismus,* volume 3 of *Geschichte der deutschen Literatur,* edited by Bark and others. Stuttgart: Klett, 1984.

Behrens, Wolfgang W., and others. *Der literarische Vormärz.* Munich: List, 1973.

Bennett, Edwin K. *A History of the German Novelle,* second edition, revised by H. M. Waidson. Cambridge: Cambridge University Press, 1961.

Bernd, Clifford. *German Poetic Realism.* Boston: Twayne, 1981.

Bock, Helmut, and others. *Streitpunkt Vormärz: Beiträge zur Kritik bürgerlicher und revisionistischer Erbeauffassungen.* Berlin: Akademie-Verlag, 1977.

Boeschenstein, Hermann. *German Literature of the Nineteenth Century.* New York: St. Martin's Press, 1969; London: Arnold, 1969.

Bramstedt, Ernest K. *Aristocracy and the Middle Classes in Germany: Social Types in German Literature, 1830–1900.* Chicago: University of Chicago Press, 1964.

Brenner, Peter J. *Reisen in die neue Welt. Die Erfahrung Nordamerikas in deutschen Reise- und Auswandererberichten des 19. Jahrhunderts.* Tübingen: Niemeyer, 1991.

Hermand, Jost. *Die literarische Formenwelt des Biedermeiers.* Giessen: Schmitz, 1958.

Hermand and Manfred Windfuhr, eds. *Zur Literatur der Restaurationsepoche 1815–1848.* Stuttgart: Metzler, 1970.

Hoemberg, Walter. *Zeitgeist und Ideenschmuggel: Die Kommunikationsstrategie des Jungen Deutschland.* Stuttgart: Metzler, 1975.

Holub, Robert C. "Young Germany," in *A Concise History of German Literature to 1900,* edited by Kim Vivian. Columbia, S.C.: Camden House, 1992, pp. 224–239.

Houben, Heinrich Hubert. *Jungdeutscher Sturm und Drang: Ergebnisse und Studien.* Leipzig: Brockhaus, 1911.

Jansen, Josef, and others. *Restaurationszeit (1815–1848),* volume 1 of *Einführung in die deutsche Literatur des 19. Jahrhunderts,* edited by Jansen and Jürgen Hein. Opladen: Westdeutscher Verlag, 1982.

Jennings, Lee. "Biedermeier," in *A Concise History of German Literature to 1900,* pp. 240–261.

Kircher, Hartmut, ed. *Dorfgeschichten aus dem Vormärz.* Cologne: Informationspresse, C. W. Leske, 1981.

Koopmann, Helmut. *Das junge Deutschland: Analyse seines Selbstverständnisses.* Stuttgart: Metzler, 1970.

Kruse, Josef A., and Bernd Kortländer, eds. *Das junge Deutschland.* Hamburg: Hoffmann & Campe, 1987.

Lützeler, Paul Michael, ed. *Romane und Erzählungen zwischen Romantik und Realismus.* Stuttgart: Reclam, 1983.

Mattenklott, Gert, and Klaus Scherpe, eds. *Demokratisch-revolutionäre Literatur in Deutschland: Vormärz.* Kronberg: Scriptor, 1974.

McInnes, Edward. *Das deutsche Drama des 19. Jahrhunderts.* Berlin: Schmidt, 1983.

Möhrmann, Renate, ed. *Frauenemanzipation im deutschen Vormärz. Texte und Dokumente.* Stuttgart: Reclam, 1978.

Neubuhr, Elfriede. *Begriffsbestimmung des literarischen Biedermeier.* Darmstadt: Wissenschaftliche Buchgesellschaft, 1974.

Prawer, Siegbert Salomon. *German Lyric Poetry: A Critical Analysis of Selected Poems from Klopstock to Rilke.* New York: Barnes & Noble, 1965.

Prawer. *Karl Marx and World Literature.* Oxford: Clarendon Press, 1976.

Rose, Paul Lawrence. *Revolutionary Antisemitism in Germany from Kant to Wagner.* Princeton: Princeton University Press, 1991.

Rosenberg, Rainer. *Literaturverhältnisse im deutschen Vormärz.* Berlin: Akademie-Verlag, 1975.

Sagarra, Eda. *Tradition and Revolution: German Literature and Society 1830–1890.* New York: Basic Books, 1971.

Sammons, Jeffrey L. *Six Essays on the Young German Novel.* Chapel Hill: University of North Carolina Press, 1972.

Schnedl-Bubenicek, Hanna, ed. *Vormärz. Wendepunkt und Herausforderung. Beitrag zur Literaturwissenschaft und Kulturpolitik in Österreich.* Vienna: Geyer, 1983.

Seeba, Hinrich C. "Vormärz: Zwischen Revolution und Restauration," in *Von der Aufklärung bis zum Vormärz,* volume 2 of *Geschichte der deutschen Literatur,* edited by Ehrhard Bahr. Tübingen: Francke, 1988, pp. 411–501.

Sengle, Friedrich. *Biedermeierzeit: Deutsche Literatur im Spannungsfeld zwischen Restauration und Revolution 1815–1848.* Volume 1: *Allgemeine Voraussetzungen, Richtungen, Darstellungsmittel.* Volume 2: *Die Formenwelt.* Volume 3: *Die Dichter.* Stuttgart: Metzler, 1971–1980.

Stein, Peter. *Epochenproblem "Vormärz" (1815–1848).* Stuttgart: Metzler, 1974.

Steinecke, Hartmut. *Literaturkritik des Jungen Deutschland. Entwicklungen, Tendenzen, Texte.* Berlin: Schmidt, 1982.

Swales, Martin W. *The German "Novelle."* Princeton: Princeton University Press, 1977.

Zemann, Herbert. *Die österreichische Literatur. Ihr Profil im 19. Jahrhundert (1830–1880).* Graz: Akademische Druck- und Verlagsanstalt, 1982.

Ziegler, Edda. *Literarische Zensur in Deutschland 1819–1848. Materialien, Kommentare.* Munich: Hanser, 1983.

Contributors

Jeffrey Adams .... *University of North Carolina at Greensboro*
Keith Bullivant .... *University of Florida*
Bettina Kluth Cothran .... *Georgia Institute of Technology*
Craig Decker .... *Bates College*
Glen A. Guidry .... *Nashville, Tennessee*
Carroll Hightower .... *Yale University*
Gunther J. Holst .... *University of South Carolina*
Kurt R. Jankowsky .... *Georgetown University*
Otto W. Johnston .... *University of Florida*
Nancy Kaiser .... *University of Wisconsin – Madison*
Dwight A. Klett .... *Rutgers University*
Wulf Koepke .... *Texas A&M University*
Helga W. Kraft .... *University of Florida*
Edwina Lawler .... *Drew University*
Brent O. Peterson .... *Duquesne University*
Hugh Powell .... *Indiana University*
Katherine Roper .... *Saint Mary's College of California*
Jeffrey L. Sammons .... *Yale University*
Ulrich Scheck .... *Queen's University, Kingston, Canada*
Hinrich C. Seeba .... *University of California, Berkeley*
Monika Shafi .... *University of Delaware*
Ellis Shookman .... *Dartmouth College*
Duncan Smith .... *Brown University*
Karl Ludwig Stenger .... *University of South Carolina – Aiken*
Lawrence S. Stepelevich .... *Villanova University*
Rodney Taylor .... *Northeast Missouri State University*
Martha Kaarsberg Wallach .... *Central Connecticut State University*
Mark J. Webber .... *York University*
Brett Wheeler .... *University of California, Berkeley*
Simon Williams .... *University of California, Santa Barbara*

Cumulative Index

Dictionary of Literary Biography, Volumes 1-133
Dictionary of Literary Biography Yearbook, 1980-1992
Dictionary of Literary Biography Documentary Series, Volumes 1-11

Cumulative Index

DLB before number: *Dictionary of Literary Biography,* Volumes 1-133
Y before number: *Dictionary of Literary Biography Yearbook,* 1980-1992
DS before number: *Dictionary of Literary Biography Documentary Series,* Volumes 1-11

A

B

C

D

Cumulative Index

E

F

G

H

I

J

L

M

N

O

P

Q

R

S

T

U

V

W

Williams, John E. 1922- DLB-6
Williams, Jonathan 1929- DLB-5
Williams, Miller 1930- DLB-105
Williams, Raymond 1921- DLB-14
Williams, Roger circa 1603-1683 ....DLB-24
Williams, Samm-Art 1946- DLB-38
Williams, Sherley Anne 1944- DLB-41
Williams, T. Harry 1909-1979 ....DLB-17
Williams, Tennessee 1911-1983 .... DLB-7; Y-83; DS-4
Williams, Valentine 1883-1946 ....DLB-77
Williams, William Appleman 1921- DLB-17
Williams, William Carlos 1883-1963 .... DLB-4, 16, 54, 86
Williams, Wirt 1921- DLB-6
Williams Brothers DLB-49
Williamson, Jack 1908- DLB-8
Willingham, Calder Baynard, Jr. 1922- DLB-2, 44
Willis, Nathaniel Parker 1806-1867 .... DLB-3, 59, 73, 74
Willkomm, Ernst 1810-1886 ....DLB-133
Wilmer, Clive 1945- DLB-40
Wilson, A. N. 1950- DLB-14
Wilson, Angus 1913-1991 ....DLB-15
Wilson, Arthur 1595-1652 ....DLB-58
Wilson, Augusta Jane Evans 1835-1909 ....DLB-42
Wilson, Colin 1931- DLB-14
Wilson, Edmund 1895-1972 ....DLB-63
Wilson, Ethel 1888-1980 ....DLB-68
Wilson, Harriet E. Adams 1828?-1863? DLB-50
Wilson, Harry Leon 1867-1939 ....DLB-9
Wilson, John 1588-1667 ....DLB-24
Wilson, John 1785-1854 ....DLB-110
Wilson, Lanford 1937- DLB-7
Wilson, Margaret 1882-1973 ....DLB-9
Wilson, Michael 1914-1978 ....DLB-44
Wilson, Thomas 1523 or 1524-1581 ....DLB-132
Wilson, Woodrow 1856-1924 ....DLB-47
Wimsatt, William K., Jr. 1907-1975 ....DLB-63
Winchell, Walter 1897-1972 ....DLB-29
Winchester, J. [publishing house] DLB-49
Winckelmann, Johann Joachim 1717-1768 ....DLB-97
Windham, Donald 1920- DLB-6
Wingate, Allan [publishing house] DLB-112
Winsloe, Christa 1888-1944 ....DLB-124
Winsor, Justin 1831-1897 ....DLB-47
John C. Winston Company DLB-49
Winters, Yvor 1900-1968 ....DLB-48
Winthrop, John 1588-1649 ....DLB-24, 30
Winthrop, John, Jr. 1606-1676 ....DLB-24
Wirt, William 1772-1834 ....DLB-37
Wise, John 1652-1725 ....DLB-24
Wiseman, Adele 1928- DLB-88
Wishart and Company DLB-112
Wisner, George 1812-1849 ....DLB-43
Wister, Owen 1860-1938 ....DLB-9, 78
Wither, George 1588-1667 ....DLB-121
Witherspoon, John 1723-1794 ....DLB-31
Withrow, William Henry 1839-1908 ....DLB-99
Wittig, Monique 1935- DLB-83
Wodehouse, P. G. 1881-1975 ....DLB-34
Wohmann, Gabriele 1932- DLB-75
Woiwode, Larry 1941- DLB-6
Wolcot, John 1738-1819 ....DLB-109
Wolcott, Roger 1679-1767 ....DLB-24
Wolf, Christa 1929- DLB-75
Wolf, Friedrich 1888-1953 ....DLB-124
Wolfe, Gene 1931- DLB-8
Wolfe, Thomas 1900-1938 .... DLB-9, 102; Y-85; DS-2
Wolff, Tobias 1945- DLB-130
Wollstonecraft, Mary 1759-1797 ....DLB-39, 104
Wondratschek, Wolf 1943- DLB-75
Wood, Benjamin 1820-1900 ....DLB-23
Wood, Charles 1932- DLB-13
Wood, Mrs. Henry 1814-1887 ....DLB-18

Y

Z

ISBN 0-8103-5392-X
90000
9 780810 353923

(Continued from front endsheets)

116 *British Romantic Novelists, 1789-1832,* edited by Bradford K. Mudge (1992)

117 *Twentieth-Century Caribbean and Black African Writers,* First Series, edited by Bernth Lindfors and Reinhard Sander (1992)

118 *Twentieth-Century German Dramatists, 1889-1918,* edited by Wolfgang D. Elfe and James Hardin (1992)

119 *Nineteenth-Century French Fiction Writers: Romanticism and Realism, 1800-1860,* edited by Catharine Savage Brosman (1992)

120 *American Poets Since World War II,* Third Series, edited by R. S. Gwynn (1992)

121 *Seventeenth-Century British Nondramatic Poets,* First Series, edited by M. Thomas Hester (1992)

122 *Chicano Writers,* Second Series, edited by Francisco A. Lomelí and Carl R. Shirley (1992)

123 *Nineteenth-Century French Fiction Writers: Naturalism and Beyond, 1860-1900,* edited by Catharine Savage Brosman (1992)

124 *Twentieth-Century German Dramatists, 1919-1992,* edited by Wolfgang D. Elfe and James Hardin (1992)

125 *Twentieth-Century Caribbean and Black African Writers,* Second Series, edited by Bernth Lindfors and Reinhard Sander (1993)

126 *Seventeenth-Century British Nondramatic Poets,* Second Series, edited by M. Thomas Hester (1993)

127 *American Newspaper Publishers, 1950-1990,* edited by Perry J. Ashley (1993)

128 *Twentieth-Century Italian Poets,* Second Series, edited by Giovanna Wedel De Stasio, Glauco Cambon, and Antonio Illiano (1993)

129 *Nineteenth-Century German Writers, 1841-1900,* edited by James Hardin and Siegfried Mews (1993)

130 *American Short-Story Writers Since World War II,* edited by Patrick Meanor (1993)

131 *Seventeenth-Century British Nondramatic Poets,* Third Series, edited by M. Thomas Hester (1993)

132 *Sixteenth-Century British Nondramatic Writers,* First Series, edited by David A. Richardson (1993)

133 *Nineteenth-Century German Writers to 1840,* edited by James Hardin and Siegfried Mews (1993)

Documentary Series

1 *Sherwood Anderson, Willa Cather, John Dos Passos, Theodore Dreiser, F. Scott Fitzgerald, Ernest Hemingway, Sinclair Lewis,* edited by Margaret A. Van Antwerp (1982)

2 *James Gould Cozzens, James T. Farrell, William Faulkner, John O'Hara, John Steinbeck, Thomas Wolfe, Richard Wright,* edited by Margaret A. Van Antwerp (1982)

3 *Saul Bellow, Jack Kerouac, Norman Mailer, Vladimir Nabokov, John Updike, Kurt Vonnegut,* edited by Mary Bruccoli (1983)

4 *Tennessee Williams,* edited by Margaret A. Van Antwerp and Sally Johns (1984)

5 *American Transcendentalists,* edited by Joel Myerson (1988)

6 *Hardboiled Mystery Writers: Raymond Chandler, Dashiell Hammett, Ross Macdonald,* edited by Matthew J. Bruccoli and Richard Layman (1989)

7 *Modern American Poets: James Dickey, Robert Frost, Marianne Moore,* edited by Karen L. Rood (1989)

8 *The Black Aesthetic Movement,* edited by Jeffrey Louis Decker (1991)

9 *American Writers of the Vietnam War: W. D. Ehrhart, Larry Heinemann, Tim O'Brien, Walter McDonald, John M. Del Vecchio,* edited by Ronald Baughman (1991)

10 *The Bloomsbury Group,* edited by Edward L. Bishop (1992)

11 *American Proletarian Culture: The Twenties and The Thirties,* edited by Jon Christian Suggs (1993)

Yearbooks

1980 edited by Karen L. Rood, Jean W. Ross, and Richard Ziegfeld (1981)

1981 edited by Karen L. Rood, Jean W. Ross, and Richard Ziegfeld (1982)

1982 edited by Richard Ziegfeld; associate editors: Jean W. Ross and Lynne C. Zeigler (1983)

1983 edited by Mary Bruccoli and Jean W. Ross; associate editor: Richard Ziegfeld (1984)

1984 edited by Jean W. Ross (1985)

1985 edited by Jean W. Ross (1986)

1986 edited by J. M. Brook (1987)

1987 edited by J. M. Brook (1988)

1988 edited by J. M. Brook (1989)

1989 edited by J. M. Brook (1990)

1990 edited by James W. Hipp (1991)

1991 edited by James W. Hipp (1992)

1992 edited by James W. Hipp (1993)